W9-AEL-797

ECOLOGICAL SANITY

George Claus & Karen Bolander

ECOLOGICAL SANITY

David McKay Company, Inc.
New York

AUTHORS' PREFACE

Twenty years ago, the educated American layman was unfamiliar with the word "ecology." He was probably aware, at least to some degree of the existence of a pollution problem. He knew, too, that a rather remarkable population explosion was taking place during the 20th century on a global scale. He may or may not have reflected on the importance and implications of these phenomena, depending on where he lived, on his profession, and on his personal interests. But the chances are that, even if he thought of pollution and overpopulation as serious problems for which solutions ought to be sought, it never occurred to him to imagine that the very Earth might perish of these social ills.

Since the late 1950s, the collective mentality of the nation has undergone a number of notable changes. One of the most astonishing of these changes is reflected in public attitudes towards environmental problems. The informed layman no longer regards pollution and overpopulation as "neutral" problems which are more or less amenable to rational solutions, if tackled with will and intelligence by appropriate specialists. Participation is the key word these days, and nonscientists are either already involved in environmental and ecological issues, or are being admonished from all quarters to become aware of man's delicate and tenuous relationship with nature and to galvanize themselves into action of one sort or another before indifference leads us over the brink of ecological disaster into the ultimate abyss of self-destruction.

Contrary to the expectations of many, the environmental movement, or the ecology concern, or whatever else one cares to term it, has already outlived the stage of fad and has become a solidly supported activist movement with considerable political muscle. In addition to widespread popular interest and to the sudden growth in the amount of research and space in scientific publications alloted to relevant subjects, important policy decisions relating to the environment are being formulated or enacted within the government at both local and federal levels. It is therefore quite clear that the environmental movement is an important social phenomenon which commands attention and also demands scrutiny.

As scientists, we have observed this burgeoning interest in environmental awareness with mixed feelings. We have been sufficiently involved in ecology, in environmental sciences, and in health-related fields to be thoroughly cognizant that these topics have received all too little attention in the past. We have also long been interested in global problems—in particular those which relate to the provision of adequate food, health care, energy, housing, and education, and thus could aid in raising the standard of living of the peoples of the underdeveloped and developing countries. At first we thought that the growing interest in the quality of life and in reversing the trend that has predominated—during the past one hundred years or so of rapid industrial growth—of simply discarding wastes without much thought of the ill effects on natural systems, would serve to stimulate the formulation of intelligent, workable plans for cleaning up our own domestic pollution, dealing with such problems as the deterioration of cities and inadequate public transport systems; designing new technologies less polluting in their base operations and capable of minimizing the damaging effects of wastes inevitably produced by technological societies. We also hoped that the symbolic emphasis on the "whole Earth" which has been in prominent evidence at least since Earth Day, 1970, would have the effect of intensifying the concern of North

Americans with the day-to-day problems of the less developed countries. Perhaps in the end, the environmental movement will succeed in providing these sorts of stimuli and will prove to have been the first expression of a genuine awakening to global awareness and to concern for tempering economic growth with measures for the preservation of an environment which will be both pleasant to live in and relatively safe from the public-health standpoint.

However, the more we read of the recent environmental literature, both popular and scientific, the more convinced we became that these goals might easily be lost sight of. It seems to us that—as happens with so many mass movements—the ideals which lay behind the interest in ecology have become distorted to such an extent that the concepts which now impel the movement are in many instances caricatures of those original ideals. Even more important is the questionable quality of much of the scientific thinking and scientific work which is being churned out in rather massive quantities in support of certain specific environmental causes. Since a number of the prominent leaders of popular ecology crusades are themselves scientists, and since a good part of the information available to laymen on these matters is scientific in content, it is of central importance that this information should have a solid scientific basis. The main purpose of this book is to examine whether or not this is the case.

When our book was in the planning stages, we had quite another concept of how many topics we could cover and what the final product would be like. From the beginning, we felt that the time had come for scrutiny of the extremist views associated with the environmental movement and for a genuinely critical examination of the scientific literature used in support of extreme points of view on a wide variety of topical issues related to ecology, contamination of the environment or of foods, and pollution clean-up campaigns. Our original intent, however, was to cover this critical material in the first half or so of our book and then go on to discussions of the high-priority problems of severe pollution and of global food and energy needs. We had hoped to be able to describe, in the later chapters, numerous creative approaches to solutions of the most critical problems—some based on existing technologies and others, still futuristic or in the development stages, which seemed to be extremely promising.

We are sorry to say that the critical materials grew and grew, and since it became evident that we had to end somewhere, the best we can do at the present time is to hint at a possible forthcoming second volume and to express the hope that one of the results of our critique might be to increase the readership of the sizable numbers of interesting books already in print which deal with useful "clean" technologies and imaginative planning for the future.

This book is addressed both to general readers and to scientists. We have tried to avoid unnecessary use of technical jargon, and to explain the scientific principles which lie behind controversies among scientists in terms understandable to the layman. However, we have covered some materials which have never been critically reviewed in the scientific literature, and these have inevitably involved occasional excursions into mathematical calculations or the inclusion of technical citations and tables which may be of more interest to scientists than to laymen. In such cases, the general reader should feel quite free simply to skip ahead. We hope that the main line of our arguments, even in those chapters which are rather heavily scientific, can be followed by readers who are not familiar with the technical terminologies. In any event, we wanted to avoid the alternatives of either speaking from authority and rejecting the arguments of certain scientists without demonstrating why they are unsound, or of overpopularizing the scientific materials, since we believe that oversimplification of certain scientific principles is one of the root causes of the spread of misinformation.

Although it is not customary for authors to inform their readers in a preface about the circumstances under which a book has been written, we think that a few words are in order here. One of the most common responses of environmentalists who are under attack on scientific grounds is to state or to imply that their opponents are biased towards industry, government, or other establishment facilities, or even that they have been paid to debate the defenders of the environment by special-interest groups, and that for these reasons their arguments are not credible. We certainly do not want to make any claims for absolute objectivity, but we should like to announce in advance that we have received no support from any industry, government agency, or university to write or produce this book. We wrote it while on leave from our respective posts, on our own time, our own money, and our own impetus.

As for what actually motivated us, it would be dangerous to say for a certainty, since no one can be positive that there are not some hidden unconscious factors involved in the pursuit of any task or goal. But our conscious intent has been to defend the integrity of the scientific process and to bring to attention the possibility that following the advice of some of the leaders of the environmental movement might be a path to social and economic disasters even more serious than the problems of pollution and poverty which are among the central challenges of our times.

Vienna, Austria
December, 1972

A NOTE ON MATHEMATICS
AND UNITS OF MEASUREMENT

Throughout this book, in discussions about the quantities of chemical substances in the environment, or in foods, or in the human body, we shall be dealing in numbers on both an exceeding small and an extremely large scale. To write out such measures in conventional numerical notation is most cumbersome and many pages would be filled with zeros either before or after the decimal place. For instance, in some calculations we will refer to the number of cells in the human body, which is about 140,000,000,000,000 and at the same time to the weight of an average body cell, which is about 0.0000000005 grams. Not only is it very tedious for readers to count zeros in order to try to get an impression of the values represented; but calculating with such conventional notation is difficult. In order to circumvent these problems, mathematicians devised a simple exponential notation system for expressing very large and very small numbers. The expression a^n means that a should be multiplied by itself n times; and as every schoolchild knows, this kind of notation is used for the expressions of the squares and cubes of numbers: $2^2 = 4$, $2^3 = 8$, and so on. Since the exponents of 10 always involve the addition of one more zero, neither tables nor a good memory are needed to carry out exponential calculations to very large numbers, as long as the base (a) is 10. Thus $10^3 = 1000$, $10^5 = 100,000$ and so on. In order to keep the base a 10, the number 140,000,000,000,000 is expressed in this exponential notation as either 14×10^{13} or as 1.4×10^{14}. When the exponent is a negative number, it expresses the reciprocal; thus 10^{-3} means $1/1000$ or 0.001. The cell weight mentioned above is therefore expressed as 5×10^{-10} grams.

When this kind of notation is used, multiplications and divisions become very simple, provided we compare quantities which have the same base. In multiplication the exponents are added, in division they are subtracted. The figures $100 \times 10,000 = 1,000,000$ become $10^2 \times 10^4 = 10^6$. This is most useful in multiplying very large numbers, such as 3 million times 5 billion. This becomes $(3 \times 10^6) \times (5 \times 10^9) = 15 \times 10^{15}$, or 1.5×10^{16}. Expressing the results as 1.5×10^{16} is not only shorter and clearer than writing out all the zeros, but it is also simpler than the verbal designation, which in this case would be 15 quadrillion.

In division, similarly, the subtraction of the exponents when dealing with large numbers greatly facilitates the manipulations. Thus, 9 billion divided by 2,000 can be written as:

$$\frac{9 \times 10^9}{2 \times 10^3} = \frac{9}{2} \times 10^6 = 4.5 \times 10^6$$

Since division is nothing but multiplication by reciprocals, this same calculation can also be written as:

$$(9 \times 10^9) \times (0.5 \times 10^{-3}) = 4.5 \times 10^6$$

Our usual arithmetic has 10 as its base. Only in special cases, such as in some computer languages where Boolean (base 2) arithmetic is employed, do we depart from the decimal system. The metric system of weights and measures has gained acceptance throughout the whole of the world, with the exception of some English speaking countries, since it very conveniently uses 10 as its base. Since this system is unquestionably simpler, easier to work with and more logical than the English system of weights and measures, we shall use metric values throughout this book except where we refer to publications in which measurements are recorded in the English system. Below we present the basic metric units, their multiples and fractions, together with the commonly used abbreviations.

Table 1. *SYSTEM OF MEASURES AND WEIGHTS*

Distance		Weight		Volume	
1 kilometer (km)	$= 10^5$ cm	1 metric ton (T)	$= 10^6$ g	1 kiloliter (kl)	$= 10^6$ ml
1 hectometer (hm)	$= 10^4$ cm	1 kilogram (kg)	$= 10^3$ g	1 hectoliter (hl)	$= 10^5$ ml
1 dekameter (dkm)	$= 10^3$ cm	1 hectogram (hg)	$= 10^2$ g	1 dekaliter (dkl)	$= 10^4$ ml
1 meter (m)	$= 10^2$ cm	1 dekagram (dkg)	$= 10^1$ g	1 liter (l)	$= 10^3$ ml
1 centimeter (cm)	$= 1$ cm	1 gram (g)	$= 1$ g	1 milliliter (ml)	$= 1$ ml
1 millimeter (mm)	$= 10^{-1}$ cm	1 centigram (cg)	$= 10^{-2}$ g		
1 micrometer (μm)		1 milligram (mg)	$= 10^{-3}$ g	1 microliter (μl)	
or 1 micron (μ)	$= 10^{-4}$ cm	1 microgram (μg)		or 1 lambda (λ)	$= 10^{-3}$ ml
1 nanometer (nm)	$= 10^{-7}$ cm	or 1 gamma (γ)	$= 10^{-6}$ g	1 nanoliter (nl)	$= 10^{-6}$ ml
		1 nanogram (ng)	$= 10^{-9}$ g		
		1 picogram (pg)	$= 10^{-12}$ g		
		1 femtogram (fg)	$= 10^{-15}$ g		

Since 1 liter is defined as a volume of water weighing 1 kg (at 4 °C) and this fits into a cube, the edges of which measure 10 cm, volume measurements of water are also customarily expressed as multiples of cm^3 (cubic centimeters). Thus 1 $cm^3 = 1$ ml $= 1$ g; 1 $m^3 = 1$ kl $= 1$ metric ton; and so on.

Surface measurements are the squares of distances. Most commonly used are: 1 square meter (m^2) $= 10^4$ cm^2; 1 are $= 100$ $m^2 = 10^6$ cm^2; 1 hectare (ha) $= 10^4$ m^2 $= 10^8$ cm^2; and 1 square kilometer (km^2) $= 100$ ha $= 10^4$ are $= 10^6$ $m^2 = 10^{10}$ cm^2.

In the English-language scientific literature, it is common to find expressions denoting the quantity of one material in relative terms to another material in which it is dispersed. These are basically expressions of concentration. Thus it is said that 2 parts per million DDT has been identified in adipose tissue of a certain animal, which means that for every kilogram of fat, 2 milligrams of the chemical are dispersed in that quantity of fat. (One milligram is 1/1,000,000 of 1 kilogram.) As long as the chemical is dispersed in water or in living matter, the density of which is close to unity, relative parts can be easily converted into the corresponding metric equivalents (Table 2). However, when this dispersion refers to air, the problem is no longer so simple, since the weight and density of air are only a fraction of those of water. This latter special case will be discussed in Chapter 17. There we shall also try to give some comparisons to facilitate an understanding of how small are the quantities commonly expressed in relative parts.

Table 2. *EXPRESSIONS IN RELATIVE PARTS*

1 part per thousand (ppth)	= 1 g/kg
1 part per million (ppm)	= 1 mg/kg
1 part per billion (ppb)	= 1 μg/kg
1 part per trillion (ppt)	= 1 ng/kg and so on.

Lastly, we have made a concession to American word usage, even when we are dealing with the metric system, since most readers will not be familiar with the differences in expressions between American and European usage. In America, all the multiples of a million are changed in denotation with each addition of three zeros. Thus we call 1,000,000,000 "one billion." In Europe this is called "one thousand million." In America 10^{12}, or 1,000,000,000,000, is designated as "one trillion," whereas in Europe this is "one billion." Throughout the book we shall use the American designations.

We hope that the reader will easily familiarize himself with these expressions and that the quantities and calculations presented in this book will not serve as a deterrent to smooth reading.

N.B. In compiling this note, we made rather free use of a similar prefatory note in the excellent work by Shklovskii and Sagan (1966): *Intelligent Life in the Universe.*

CONTENTS

PART II. THE STAYING POWER OF HALF-TRUTHS

PART III. THE PESTICIDE BUGABOO

Publication of this book, the research for which was completed at the end of 1972, was delayed by reason of production difficulties beyond our control or that of the authors. We regret this delay, but are confident that the continued significance of this book will be apparent to the reader. —*The Publishers*

PART I

A MASS MOVEMENT
FOR THE SEVENTIES

Concern about the environment and the emergence in the United States of a mass movement centered on ecological themes are among the most obvious social phenomena of the past two or three years. And yet, despite the fact that its manifestations could only be missed by a hermit, it is not at all easy to say what this movement is really about. To some, it is an outgrowth of the older conservation movement—somewhat more militant in tone—but centering on the same basic concerns of protection of wildlife and preservation of the wilderness. Some see it as closely allied to the consumer-protection movement, particularly where matters of the purity of foods are at issue. To others, it is an expression of the desire for the Great Cleanup, and

1

really has to do with plain old pollution. Then there are those who see it as a philosophical development which is giving expression to new life attitudes and values based on the principles of the hitherto obscure science of ecology. To still others it is primarily a vehicle of protest against almost everything which can be characterized as "Establishment." And to many, it represents primarily an awakening to awareness of the finite resources and limited carrying capacity in terms of human population of the planet Earth.

But from whatever perspective the individual views this movement, it would seem a fairly safe generalization to state that most Americans have accepted that the environmental movement is a "Good Thing."* This is not to say that environmental alarmists and environmental action groups do not have their critics; nor that anyone accepts in toto all of the assertions, predictions, proposals, tactics, and new legislative decisions which can be associated—directly or indirectly—with this diffuse movement. Nevertheless, it seems that the vast majority of citizens view the environmental movement as a positive social force which is basically idealistic and nonpolitical in its orientation. From this it follows quite naturally that most people will think of the leaders and principal spokesmen of the movement as sincere and honest individuals whose motivations are fundamentally selfless.

We wish to raise the question of whether these unconscious assumptions might not be erroneous in many instances and whether there might not be some excellent reasons for taking a hard look at the implications for society of many of the programs proposed by prominent environmentalist leaders. In these first chapters, we will examine some of the roots of the movement as a whole, and will discuss some aspects of the interactions between science and society.

We ought to make it clear that when we use the word "environmentalist," we are for the most part referring to those laymen and scientists who are leaders of the *extremist* wings of the movement. There are many persons concerned about the environment whose ideas are reasonable and creative, and who are devoting their energies and attention to solutions of the complex technical, economic, and social problems which are related to the broad questions of environmental quality and the dignity of human life. We do not wish in any way to denigrate the efforts of such individuals; nor do we intend to imply that the environmental movement on the whole is a Bad Thing. If we focus on the dangers

---

*We have borrowed this phrase from the satirical pseudohistory of England, *1066 and All That*, by W. C. Sellar and R. J. Yeatman. In their book, the authors describe everything in terms of absolute black and absolute white, labeling historical events as either Good Things or Bad Things and historical personages as Good Men or Bad Men. We think it is not inappropriate to use similar phrases in the context of assessing the environmental movement and its favored issues, since Americans, like their British cousins, have a tendency to want things to be either black or white.

inherent in the uncritical acceptance of extremist views, it is because these are often difficult to perceive, being usually presented under the guise of one or another unimpeachable slogan. Our basic purpose is to examine what lies behind these slogans and to stimulate others to consider whether or not the proposals of the leaders of the environmental movement represent workable solutions to social and environmental problems.

1

EXPOSITION AND VARIATIONS

Oh human race, born to fly upward,
wherefore at a little wind dost thou
so fall?
DANTE ALIGHIERI

_____

To anyone who familiarizes himself with popular books on
ecology, perhaps the most striking of the oft-repeated themes
in this literature is the prediction of the coming end of the world. Among those
concerned with the environment who remain optimists or partially optimistic,
many have accepted René Dubos' explanation that the current proliferation of
doomsday prophecies are an expression of psychic attitudes typical of the closing
period of a millennium. In his book *So Human An Animal,* he wrote: "As the
year 2000 approaches, an epidemic of sinister prediction is spreading all over
the world, as happened among Christians during the period preceding the year
1000" (Dubos, 1968, p. 10).

Dubos may be correct in his suggestion that the most prominent waves of world-ending predictions are expressed in thousand-year periods, for there is historical evidence that similar predictions were also common in the first years of the Christian era. But even if we grant the reality of some kind of broad temporal rhythm in man's collective psyche, Dubos' explanation fails to distinguish the qualitative difference between those world-ending prognostications which center on "the bomb" and those which attribute the causes of our downfall to our everyday, peaceful activities. It also fails to clarify why the occult predictions of imminent world disasters, which center mostly on earthquakes, collision of the Earth with a comet, or other events completely beyond human intervention, have not had the same power to "catch" the emotions of millions as has the notion of "ecocatastrophe."

Since 1948, fictional works dealing with the theme of intentional or accidental nuclear cataclysm have flooded the English-speaking world. Novels and films like *Fail-Safe, On the Beach,* and *Dr. Strangelove* were great successes, and millions who did not read the books saw the films which were based on them. For years, each issue of *The Bulletin of the Atomic Scientists* has carried a picture of a clock set at five minutes to midnight, as a warning that the international powers must reach an agreement on the cessation of nuclear weapons stockpiling. No adult or young person who read or reflected on the fate of mankind could forget the bomb during the tensest years of the Cold War period; the sense of portending doom hung like a sinister cloud over the peoples of the earth. Those who tried actively to influence their governments to work towards a lasting peace seemed destined to a permanent sense of frustration. No one knew precisely, from one "weapons gap" to the next, how real or how imminent was the threat, but for those who perceived that the stalemate approach was a dangerous pseudo-solution, the possibility of a few years of respite was little comfort for their public consciences. It is true that the concern of the broad public waxed and waned during the long postwar years, with plenty of "business as usual" interludes. But at the time of the Cuban missile crisis, the American populace was shocked into the awareness that the possibility of an actual confrontation was *not* fiction. For a few days at least, we felt ourselves to be separated from oblivion by a mere push of the button.

During those postwar years, concern about environmental pollution was largely confined to a few professionals. There was only one area of environmental contamination which became an issue of concern to the broad public: the matter of radioactive fallout.

In the 1950s, wide-scale atmospheric testing of nuclear weapons by both the Soviet Union and the United States resulted in worldwide contamination with radioactive dust. The populace was alerted to the dangers of fallout largely through the efforts of various groups of scientists, and the arousal of public concern probably played some role in the relative ease with which the last stages of the Atmospheric Test Ban Treaty were negotiated. One might suppose, then, that the environmental movement as we know it today really began with the fallout issue in the late 1950s. But in our opinion, it did not; for despite the fact that certain patterns of interactions between scientists and citizens and government officials were laid down at that time, the underlying issue was still the bomb. Unknown or unrecognized contamination of the environment might have been the focal point of the public anxiety and outcry, but it was the "war machine" and international tensions which were seen as the root of the problem.

When did the change come? It is impossible to say precisely, but the first loud tolling of the "chemical fallout" alarm was sounded in the fall of 1962, when Rachel Carson's *Silent Spring* was published.

The Importance of One Small Book

The climate of receptivity for a book about dangerous chemicals was very high in late 1962, for the thalidomide story had broken only a short while earlier. The impact of Miss Carson's book was unprecedented. In it another kind of impending doom was foretold—not a sudden catastrophe visited upon us by our enemies, but a slow and insidious death to all living things. In some respects, her vision of a dying planet was even more frightening than the nuclear threat, for she spoke of a death force already stalking us, wreaking its destruction *now* on plants and animals, but soon to strike the human race as well. All of us will be slowly poisoned on account of the greed of the chemical manufacturers, who are pouring deadly toxins into the environment. The enemy was not abroad, but *among us:* agriculturists; entomologists; lax regulatory agencies failing in their duty to protect us; the heedless "agrichemical complex."

Miss Carson's followers often state that she was not an alarmist, but clearly this is untrue. One reading of *Silent Spring* is enough to throw any psychologically balanced layman into a seesaw syndrome of deep depression and hypochondriacal anxiety. Consider, for example, the terrifying implications of this passage:

> The contamination of our world is not alone a matter of mass spraying. Indeed, for most of us this is of less importance than the innumerable small-scale exposures to which we are subjected day by day, year after year. Like the constant dripping of

water that in turn wears away the hardest stone, this birth-to-death contact with dangerous chemicals may in the end prove disastrous. Each of these recurrent exposures, no matter how slight, contributes to the progressive buildup of chemicals in our bodies and so to cumulative poisoning. Probably no person is immune to contact with this spreading contamination unless he lives in the most isolated situation imaginable. Lulled by the soft sell and the hidden persuader, the average citizen is seldom aware of the deadly materials with which he is surrounding himself; indeed, he may not realize that he is using them at all. (Carson, 1962, p. 157)

What those who claim that Miss Carson was not an alarmist probably mean to say is that she was not a complete pessimist, and in this we would agree. Her book, indeed, rang the alarm signal, but it also suggested a blueprint for action which could involve the individual citizen. The protests of angry and frightened people against the bomb or against the local wars in which our government has embroiled us have been almost without effect on our leaders. On the other hand, the "battle against pollution" was clearly an issue which opened up both the possibility of active participation on the part of citizens and the anticipation of definite results.

Rachel Carson's book and the movement which grew out of it filled a need— a need which stems from the deepest layers of human conscience: the desire to control our own fate.

First Responses

The reviews of *Silent Spring* were mixed. Many of the reviews by nonscientists recommended the book with unequivocal praise. Miss Carson's reputation as one of the finest naturalist writers of the time was well established, and in spite of its grisly subject matter, *Silent Spring* was eloquent and even lyric in style. For literary mastery it is still unmatched by any later books on the environment. Furthermore, that aspect of its message which treated the failure of our public agencies to protect us from hidden dangers was shocking; it was both new—in that it dealt with chemical pesticides—and at the same time it was in part an echo of the radioactive fallout issue. Some reviewers felt that the public should read this book, and they said so in no uncertain terms.

There was nothing wrong in this, for it is the function of good book reviewers to evaluate the worth of a newly released publication and to anticipate whether or not it will have any lasting significance. They were certainly correct in judging it to be an important book, and the lay reviewers could hardly be expected to assess the correctness of its scientific content.

The reviews by scientists were on the whole more cautious, although they varied considerably in point of view. Some emphasized the inaccuracies and rather gross factual distortions in the book. Some flatly dismissed it as "scientific hogwash." Others, however—among them a few prominent biologists—praised the book, even while pointing out weaknesses in some of the material. There were unquestionably excesses in the use of pesticides. Overspraying and unwarranted applications were all too common, and criticisms of these careless practices were well founded. These reviewers undoubtedly hoped that Miss Carson's emphasis on abuses in the application of pesticides would alert regulatory agencies and users to the need for corrective measures. Surely nobody foresaw at that time that the publication of this 400-page volume was the beginning of an avalanche which would eventually precipitate the development of a full-scale environmental action movement, including bitter debates among scientists about issues much wider than their own areas of expertise, and finally, in relation to the particular question of pesticide use, that partial bans on DDT and alarmist demands that its applications be completely forbidden would ensue, not only in the United States, but in other countries as well.

Miss Carson's apologists tend to describe those scientists who were severely critical of *Silent Spring* either as persons with vested interests in the chemical industry or as irresponsible ivory-tower specialists. Journalist Frank Graham, for example, writes in *Since Silent Spring* about the "neutral" scientists: "These 'silent scientists,' as they have been called, spoke only to themselves, and rarely then. They did not choose to make known the facts that vitally concerned the public. They sneered at such techniques as 'popularization,' and recoiled in indignation from the suggestion that they cooperate with the mass media to put across the story that should have been told. For some scientists, Rachel Carson's sin was not only her willingness to tell what she knew, but to tell it in such a way that it was grasped by the public" (Graham, 1970, p. 156).

It is very easy with arguments of this kind to "explain away" any and all objections on the part of working scientists to the scientific content of *Silent Spring*. However, it has to be remembered that the book treated *two* principal themes. The first of these was the abusive or ill-considered application of chemical pesticides. As far as this issue is concerned, it is unlikely that any scientist could find reasonable grounds for objecting to a popular book on the subject. One might claim that in some respects Miss Carson overstated her case, but her followers all admit this anyway. The second theme of the book—which might be summarized as explaining the long-term dangers of man-made chemicals to human health and to the survival of species—is another matter altogether when it comes to "popularization."

Miss Carson was a first-rate naturalist and a skilled library researcher, but she was not a practicing research scientist in the modern sense of the term. In the long chapters which she devotes to discussions of genetics, explanations of the functioning of life at the cellular level, and theories about the causes of cancer, she commits a number of "sins" from the point of view of the scientist, whether or not he believes in the value of popularization of scientific information. To mention only a few points: she consistently misuses the word "mutagen"; she miscites or misinterprets the writings of medical authorities; she gives credence to cancer theories which are either highly speculative or have already been discarded; she describes many chemicals as carcinogenic which are very unlikely to be genuine cancer-causing agents; and, most important of all, she describes chemicals in general as "the sinister and little-recognized partners of radiation in changing the very nature of the world–the very nature of its life" (Carson, 1962, p. 16).

To bring up these matters ten years after the publication of the book might seem to be mere carping criticism of the efforts of a woman who was clearly a gentle, sensitive, and well-meaning person; but, unfortunately, these questionable scientific generalizations have been kept alive both by Miss Carson's followers among laymen and by some of the scientists now leading the environmental battle. We shall return later to discussions of specific problems in scientific practice and we shall devote six chapters to an analysis of the pesticide problem, including its bearings on human health. However, it seemed important at this point, in reviewing the impact of *Silent Spring,* to emphasize that the controversies generated by the book go far beyond the special issue of whether or not we ought to use persistent pesticides as a means of insect control.

Variations on the Contamination Theme

"The most alarming of all man's assaults upon the environment is the contamination of air, earth, rivers, and sea with dangerous and even lethal materials. This pollution is for the most part irrecoverable: the chain of evil it initiates not only in the world that must support life but in living tissues is for the most part irreversible." (Carson, 1962, p. 16)

Thus wrote Rachel Carson. In the contemporary environmental movement, the notion that the pollution of the environment constitutes irreversible and universal contamination persists as a central motif. Most frequently, the emphasis of environmentalists is on the "unseen threats," rather than on visible or obvious environmental deterioration. By now the list of substances described as life-endangering hidden pollutants goes way beyond the chemical pesticides. It includes (just to name a few) mercury, cadmium, and lead; SO_2, CO_2, and nitrous oxides; polychlorinated biphenyls; phosphates, nitrates, and thermal wastes; hidden radiation; asbestos; and phthalate plasticizers.

The degree of danger ascribed to any of these pollutants depends partly on the point of view of the investigator or the "advocate," although most environmentalists are in accord that some represent a more immediate threat than others, either to human health or to planetary survival. Most would also still support Rachel Carson's indictment of the chemical pesticides and herbicides — especially DDT and 2,4,5-T. Nevertheless, the variations on the basic theme are legion, and the list of threatening materials continues to grow. The cry is: "You cannot see these poisonous substances, but they are everywhere — in our food, our water, in the air we breathe. All are destructive to health and even life, and all are insidiously accumulating to dangerous levels."

Now it is true, of course, that man pollutes the water, the air, and the soil of his surroundings. It is also true that the quantities and types of waste products which he releases into the environment have increased rapidly since the advent of industrialization. But is it true that this pollution of the environment represents an *irreversible chain of evil?* We do not believe so, and we shall try, throughout the body of this book, to show that this is not so. There are, on the other hand, two very extreme attitudes which are associated with this basic notion that the effects of environmental contamination are irreversible, both of which represent, in our judgment, very real dangers to the survival of human civilization. The first of these is an unbalanced pessimism which leads to defeatism and despair. The second is a complete rejection of technology, which is often combined with anti-intellectualism and even with the broad claim that Western culture is bankrupt, or was an unfortunate mistake from its very beginnings.

The New Pessimism

Rachel Carson's treatment of the chemical contamination issue included prognostications about the threat to survival represented by our interference with the balance of nature. Nevertheless, despite her sense of urgency, Miss Carson was not a complete pessimist: she was calling for corrective actions. We had to wait until the professional American biologists raised their voices in the public forum before we began to hear the even more depressing prediction: we

may *already* have weighted the scales so heavily, through our polluting practices, that it is only a matter of time before the whole biosphere will "give up,"
and a disastrous tipping of the balance will ensue.

One of the gloomiest expressions of this despairing view is to be found in
a 1968 article by LaMont Cole, an entomologist from Cornell University, entitled "Can the World Be Saved?" In it, Cole suggests that we are altering the
basic biological, geological, and chemical cycles on which life depends, and that
the probabilities are very high that we may tip the carbon-oxygen balance, or
radically alter the climate of the Earth, or interrupt a stage in the nitrogen cycle.
He presents the reader with a bit of very questionable ancient history in which
he implies that the irrigation practices of the Babylonian and the Egyptian
civilizations were the root cause of their ruin and that the Mayan civilization
also collapsed as a result of overexploitation of the land. In his view, we are
apparently well on the road to a similar disaster, although he also emphasizes
that much of the danger to man is summarized in the phrase "We don't know."
He then goes on to talk about the population problem, and in the course of discussion drags out the old Malthusian notion that there will not be enough food.
He ends the article with *one sentence* (containing two "if" clauses), acknowl-
edging that there is an outside possibility that the world might be saved. Nevertheless, the article as a whole leaves the reader with the impression that we
haven't got a chance.

Cole is a distinguished scientist, and since he is described as an ecologist,
a good deal of authority is naturally attributed by the reader to his statements,
despite his agnostic disclaimer regarding our lack of knowledge. This article,
first published in the *New York Times Magazine,* has since been reprinted in
a paperback book; and a number of other American scientists have made similar
predictions of "ecocatastrophe," both in print and in public speeches. It is impossible to estimate how many people have been directly exposed to the dim
prognostications of these professionals, but by now the lay leaders of the environmental movement have picked up the message, and we hear from all
quarters the cry of "terracide." In the meantime, the cautious but measured
counterstatements by meteorologists, climatologists, soil specialists, and other
less glamorous scientists lie buried in professional journals.

From a psychological point of view, we do not feel that such dark prophecies
are healthy, even though it is sometimes argued that, true or untrue, they may
serve to shock us into mending our ways and conducting future human activities
with more respect for natural systems. In the first place, we see no reason why
man's abuses of the environment could not be corrected without scaring people
to death. Secondly, such gloomy prognostications feed the already widespread

feelings of despair and existential anxiety so characteristic of our age. The defeatism to which such doomsday predictions may give rise is especially notable in the very young, and we find it particularly distressing when children come home from school and announce that they have learned that our planet may die before they reach maturity. Having ourselves been children during World War II and still at an impressionable age in the postwar period when fears that nuclear weapons might be deployed were at their height, we are well aware of the psychological damage wrought on our own generation by the terror of annihilation. But at least the last Great War was a reality and the possibility of a nuclear war seemed not improbable at certain stages of the Cold War. Our generation simply had to live with these dark events and possibilities. It seems to us, on the other hand, reprehensible to fill young children with existential fears which are based neither in actuality nor potentiality.

Since environmentalists like to point to human arrogance as a root cause of present difficulties in man's relationship with nature, it is more than a little ironic that the ecocatastrophe predictions are actually expressions of a kind of human arrogance. By this we mean that it is arrogant to assume that human activities—no matter how ill-managed—are capable of disrupting the basic cycles which operate in nature on a global basis. There is no question that man can and does seriously pollute *local* environments—sometimes to the extent where the local system no longer supports certain life forms or is no longer utilizable for specific human activities. But this is a far cry from disrupting the vast cycles of the Earth's biosphere. It has become fashionable of late to describe the biosphere as "delicate," but in fact the natural world is enormously resilient and hardy. Considered from a global viewpoint, man's introduction of pollutants or contaminants into the large reservoirs of the biosphere—the atmosphere, the oceans, the terrain, and the biota—is puny compared with that of nature herself. One has only to consider the huge quantities of sulfurous gases, for instance, which are released during the eruption of a single medium-sized volcano, and compare them with emissions resulting from the sum of man's fossil fuel burning on the whole Earth over a period of ten years to recognize that mankind would have to pollute the environment at a much faster and more intense pace in order really to add significantly to nature's own "contamination" of the large reservoirs. It is true, as the environmentalists have brought to general attention, that certain resources are in finite supply on the planet Earth; but it is still a very large planet and its web of life is not nearly so vulnerable as it has been made out to be. Probably the only way in which human activities could severely disrupt the major geochemical cycles or seriously unbalance the large reservoirs would be through the explosion of nuclear weapons on a vast scale.

Machines as Very Bad Things

A second major theme which rings through the environmental movement, in numerous variations, is that of opposition to technology. Technology and machines in general are everybody's favorite scapegoats, for it is easy enough to claim—and at least partially true as well—that modern industrial operations, the products and by-products of contemporary inventions, and the machines on which we rely so heavily in our daily lives are big polluters. The finger of blame for environmental deterioration is then conveniently pointed at production- and market-oriented industry, the "technocrats" who dominate the applied sciences, and other people who can be said to share what environmentalists usually refer to as "the engineering mentality."

Now let us make it clear from the outset that we have no intention of implying that industrial wastes and the various forms of pollution created by man's use of machines are unrelated to current environmental problems. On the contrary, we are well aware of those respects in which the tremendous and rapid forward strides of modern technology have contributed and continue to contribute very heavily to environmental pollution. We do not believe that our current environmental crisis is so severe that we are in danger of "killing" the biosphere of the planet itself, but we are certainly not so blind as to claim that there are no problems. On the other hand, it is our contention that it is a grave mistake to reject "technological fixes" as solutions. Efficient advanced technologies already exist which can handle both industrial and domestic wastes, although they have not yet been applied on any significant scale. We would further argue that the *deleterious effects* of the contemporary dependence on machines and the rapid development of a highly industrialized and technological society are not the inevitable consequences of man's ingenuity in having invented these machines and developed this supertechnology, but rather the result of his failure, thus far, to be equally inventive and "modern" in his approach to waste management or in the application of his technical skills to reducing those untoward effects on the environment to which his inventions may give rise.

If the environmental movement serves to alert the public and our public officials to the fact that it is high time that we modernized our manner of dealing with all kinds of wastes, then we will hail it as a mass movement which is indeed serving the public good; for it is clear that lack of will and inertia in all quarters has a great deal to do with the fact that we have not focused enough attention on effective and efficient ways of dealing with waste products. Nor have we been willing, to date, to allocate adequate amounts of money towards the solution of these problems. Perhaps a tremendous public outcry is the only thing that can disturb the complacency of those who prefer the tried and true practices of the past, even though it is obvious that many of these practices are no longer viable. And perhaps only a movement which employs the pressure tactics of mass protest can upset the ostrichlike posture which all too often typifies our representatives in Washington. However, we are not convinced that the environmental movement will achieve these desirable ends.

One major reason for our skepticism about the potential effectiveness of this movement to bring about positive change is that all too many of the leading environmentalists are themselves filled with inertia and lack imagination. They long for "the good old days" when the machines were not so numerous and so disturbing to their needs for peace and for beauty. They campaign for "bans" against various products which they regard as destructive or dangerous, but they rarely speak to us about what might replace the banned products if they were to succeed in their campaigns. They prefer to talk about "de-development" rather than to attempt to stir the desire of the public and to stimulate the problem-solving talents of our creative citizens, so that we can move toward a future in which the benefits of modern technology can be enjoyed without undue harm being inflicted upon the natural environment.

Since evidently very few of the environmentalists believe that such a future is possible, they either rail against industry and the machine in general, or they tell us that certain aspects of the technological gains of the recent past must be abandoned. In their most simplistic recommendations, they appear to want to turn off or at least to slow down "the machine." Some are against the use of all agricultural chemicals, or even modern methods of farming in general. Some cry out against plastics, artificial textiles, and other man-made materials which are not easily reassimilated by nature. Some oppose any efforts to construct new sources of power, insisting that there are no legitimate reasons why our national energy needs should grow, and, if they continue to do so, it will only be because of the promotional plot instigated by the power companies and the gadget producers, carried out with the help of the Madison Avenue boys. Others merely announce that we are now an overdeveloped nation and that the time has come to de-develop.

There are a number of basic reasons why the overt expressions of this anti-technology theme are suspect — in addition to the impractical omission of a discussion of workable substitutes for the products whose use is recommended to be limited or altogether suspended. The first refers to the matter of subjective or personal evaluations as to *whose* machines should be turned off. We would not go so far as to call any particular environmentalist a hypocrite on this score, but one cannot but notice that the modern machines which contribute directly to the comfort or pleasure of the environmental speaker are usually not on the list of those which are seen as Very Bad Things. Paul Ehrlich, for example, is fond of speaking about de-development, and he likes to tell people that it is the middle and upper classes who must sacrifice their unnecessary equipment and cut down on consumption, but he himself is said to fly a private airplane. Those who like rock music certainly would not be happy to see limits set on the permissible consumption of power, production of noise, or use of electronic instruments on the part of rock musicians. Yet those very lovers of a form of contemporary music which is absolutely dependent on modern technology have no qualms about announcing that the way to avoid the predicted power shortages of the coming years is not to build new power-generating plants, but to ask suburban housewives to abandon their unnecessary gadgets and to force affluent New Yorkers to give up their air conditioners. And so it goes. Technology and machines are admitted to be bad in general for the environment, but even the purists find it fairly easy to rationalize the use of those inventions which they themselves like or believe to be necessary in their lives.

A much more important difficulty in these antimachine views is that their proponents seem to have lost sight of the irrefutable fact that many of the gains represented by modern technology are directly applicable to the good of everybody. They like to imply that all the benefits of technology go to rich industrialists and to businessmen who must fly across the country several times weekly in order to make a few more dollars. They forget that modern medicine has freed man from the fear of an enormous number of debilitating and deadly diseases, and has extended the average life expectancy in the developed countries from 45 to 71 years in the incredibly short period of a few decades. They forget the extent to which machines have liberated vast numbers of people from the drudgery and misery of dehumanizing kinds of labor. They forget that modern communication systems and the speed with which we can now transport ourselves from one part of the world to another have broadened the horizons of millions of people. Or perhaps they do not really forget these things, but they merely choose to emphasize the negative effects of the machine and to idealize the past, since that is easier than facing the challenge of managing technology with wisdom.

Those "good old days" for which so many seem to be yearning may have been in some respects more tranquil than modern life in a developed country. Still, it is doubtful whether any sizable number of contemporary Westerners would really care to return to live in a past period, if given both the real possibility of doing so and an accurate description of what their life would be like. Furthermore, it is fruitless to speculate about how many people would prefer the past to the present, since we cannot set the clock of history in reverse. A few who voluntarily choose to do so may give up their dependence on technology and may return to work the land according to the practices of their great-grandfathers. Or they may retreat to a simpler life in unsettled wilderness regions or underdeveloped countries. Such choices on the part of individuals or small groups are neither discouraged nor are they impossible to act upon. But for society as a whole, it is quite as impossible to return to times past as it is for an individual to become again a child of 10, when he is in reality a man of 35. Time may be in part a human mental construct, yet it nevertheless refers to some very fundamental reality in the phenomenal world of the cosmos, and as far as we understand time, it can only unfold in a forward direction—except in the realm of memory.

Perhaps the saddest aspect of the prevalence of antitechnology attitudes at the present time is that humanity is at this very moment poised on the threshold of a radical change in the relation between man and his technologies. We have created a technology which is sufficiently advanced so that it could now be applied—given the will—to bring entirely new levels of material well-being to everyone on the planet. At the same time, wise application of our knowledge and imaginative use of our technological tools could solve the problems of environmental deterioration and bring us into a new, more aesthetic, and less exploitative relationship with the Earth which nourishes us. We cannot re-create the past, but it *is* in our power as thinking beings to shape the future.

The psychological roots of the antimachine theme are probably much more complex than its overt expressions, but we shall not delve into them in any depth here. Suffice it to say that there seems to exist in the adult human psyche a general tendency to resist change. Since the pace with which our external experience is altered—at both the social and the individual level—is now irrevocably linked with the speed of technological change, it is perhaps to be expected that some of this internal inertia so common in human beings should find expression in a kind of generalized resentment of technology. But fear of change would appear to be a fruitless avoidance mechanism. Basically, it seems to us that modern men have no realistic choice but to accept that the speed of change will continue to accelerate. If this is true, then the most intelligent response would be to take a stand in favor of *conscious adaptation to change.* From our point of view, it is important that people struggle actively against both personal and collective inertia, for we believe that only if men can learn to move with the currents of their own time will they be able to recognize those in their midst who have the vision and the creativity to direct the new-found technological powers to ends which will benefit all mankind.

The reader will by now perhaps have identified us as "technocrats." If one means by the word people who believe in the positive benefits which can be derived from the tools of modern technology, we would then accept the label as at least partially correct. Unfortunately, however, the pejorative associations to this particular word are very strong, and it tends to evoke an image of the activities of the Corps of Engineers, or of types who believe blindly in "growth at all costs and to hell with the consequences." It should be obvious, if one stops to consider the matter, that there can be many kinds of people and many types of mentality favoring man's inventiveness, some of them heedless, others highly thoughtful. In order to bring home to the reader that even in the latter category, not all those who believe in the positive benefits of man's technical ingenuity are members of a single "camp," we should like to end this section with citations from the writings of three men of very different orientation. The first, Alan Watts, is well-known for his writings on Buddhism and for his evaluations of the many-sided revolution in values taking place in contemporary America. The second, Buckminster Fuller, architect and inventor, is a great favorite of some environmentalists and of young people, even though he is a supertechnocrat (in the good sense of the word), if there ever was one. The third, Nobel laureate Glenn Seaborg, is a "despised technocrat" in many circles, probably largely because he devoted some of his busy years to heading the Atomic Energy Commission. These are then three very different men—but they are all men of vision, who see that "the machine" and man's inventions are at his disposal for creative uses. They are all men who *care* that the Earth should survive and that mankind's future should be one of dignity and peace for all. Here, then, are their words.

In an essay called "Wealth Versus Money," Watts writes: "From this very basic . . . point of view, I see that we have created a marvelous technology for the supply of goods and services with a minimum of human drudgery. Isn't it obvious that the whole purpose of machines is to get rid of work?" (Watts, 1971, pp. 170–171).

Watts is very careful to point out obvious obstacles to a future in which machines free us from work—obstacles deriving from inertia, habit, and attitudes. Also, he does not want to see an expanding technology which results in "Los Angelesizing" the whole Earth. Nevertheless, he is extremely optimistic that technologies which free man can be integrated with aesthetic and creative strivings. He is also clearly aware that one of the principal reasons why we in America are ready for a change in the direction of more aesthetic and/or spiritual values is that we have already experienced the glut of "things" and the emptiness of affluence. Speaking about the year 2000 (which is perhaps a bit too optimistic), he continues:

Mechanical mass production will provide utilities, raw materials, tools and certain foodstuffs, yet will at the same time release us from the necessity for much of the mass-produced trash that we must now buy for lack of time to make anything better—clothes, dishes and other articles of everyday use that were made so much more exquisitely by "primitives" that they now adorn our museums. . . .

The style of life will be colorful and elegant, but it will not, I feel, exhibit the sheer gluttony and greed of certain notorious aristocracies of the past. Speaking perhaps only half-seriously, by A.D. 2000, most of Asia will have followed the lead of Japan and be laced with superhighways and cluttered with hot-dog stands, neon signs, factories, high-rise apartment buildings, huge airports and swarms of Toyotas, with every fellah and coolie running around in a Western business suit. On the other hand, America, having had all this and being fed up with it, will abound with lamaseries and ashrams (but coeducational), expert players of the sitar and the koto, masters of Japanese tea ceremony, schools for Chinese calligraphy and Zen-style gardening— while people stroll around in saris, dhotis, sarongs, kimonos and other forms of comfortable and colorful clothing. Just as now the French are buying sour-dough bread flown by jet from San Francisco, spiritually starved Tibetans and Japanese will be studying Buddhism in Chicago. (*Ibid.*, pp. 176–177)

Although Buckminster Fuller's principal interest is in the potential of the design revolution and of systems technology for changing the very shape of man's physical environment and the nature of his experience, his writings are rich with references to the importance of all of the tools of human invention, from the simplest bowl to the most complex computer. In the poetic and highly popular book, *Operating Manual for Spaceship Earth*, he writes, for example:

. . . we see that, through gradually increasing use of . . . intuition and intellect, man has discovered many of the generalized principles that are operative in the universe and has employed them objectively but separately in extending his internal metabolic regeneration by his invented and detached tool extensions and their remote operation affected by harnassing [sic] inanimate energy. Instead of trying to survive only with his integral set of tool capabilities—his hands—to pour water into his mouth, he invents a more effective wooden, stone, or ceramic vessel so that he not only can drink from it but carry water with him and extend his hunting and berry picking. All tools are externalizations of originally integral functions. But in developing each tool man also extends the limits of its usefulness, since he can make bigger cups hold liquids too hot or chemically destructive for his hands. Tools do not introduce new principles but they greatly extend the range of conditions under which the discovered control principle may be effectively employed by man. There is nothing new in world technology's growth. It is only the vast increase of its effective ranges that are startling man. The computer is an imitation human brain. There is nothing new about it, but its capacity, speed of operation, and tirelessness, as well as its ability to operate under environmental conditions intolerable to the human anatomy, make it far more effective in performing special tasks than is the skull and tissue encased human brain, minus the computer.

What is really unique about man is the magnitude to which he has detached, deployed, amplified, and made more incisive all of his many organic functionings. (Fuller, 1969a, pp. 101–102)

In speaking about the importance of inventions and design in shaping the whole experience of man, Fuller frequently includes numerical calculations informing us about how efficient (or rather inefficient) our technologies are, how much material can be saved through the cleverness of man, and how many people have benefited from modern technology. A characteristic passage is the following, from an essay entitled "The City of the Future": "Inventions alone have raised the number of people enjoying an advanced standard of living, from one percent of all humanity in 1900 to 40 percent in 1966, despite continuously diminishing natural resources. That same advantaged 40 percent are also living three times the number of years that man lived only a century ago. All of this has come about through inventions. Inventions have induced appropriate social reform, but only as accessories after the fact of invention itself.

"Take away all the inventions from humanity and, within six months, half of us would die of starvation and disease" (Fuller, 1971, pp. 222–223).

It is also clear from the whole of Fuller's opus that he recognizes the absolute necessity that we should now think in global terms — that indeed, we cannot afford not to do so. In *Utopia or Oblivion*, for example, we may read: "It is now scientifically clear that we have the ability to make all of humanity physically successful. But it can be done only on the basis of making all of humanity successful. We cannot remain just half successful or with just a minority successful. Industrialization itself relates to the resources of the entire earth, the entire universe, and the entire experience gained by all men in all time. The industrial system is a comprehensive system and if reversingly fractionated will fail" (Fuller, 1969b, p. 242).

Lastly, if we return to the *Operating Manual for Spaceship Earth* we may see that Fuller believes that the survival of humanity depends on whether or not we are able to develop the full capacity of our scientific and inventive imaginations. "But we can scientifically assume that by the twenty-first century either humanity will not be living aboard Spaceship Earth or, if approximately our present numbers as yet remain aboard, that humanity then will have recognized and organized itself to realize effectively that humanity can afford to do anything it needs and wishes to do and that it cannot afford anything else" (Fuller, 1969a, pp. 94–95).

The Seaborg selections are taken from a lecture entitled "Science, Technology, and the Citizen." He too speaks about the creative and humane uses of technology: "Technology can be directed creatively so as to bring human society into close harmony with its natural environment. It can be made to create more wealth with less waste—both waste products and waste of human and natural resources. It can be made to create beauty where we have let it spawn ugliness. It can be made to bring man both greater security and more individual freedom. What it does, however, will be accomplished only when we stop blaming it for our shortcomings, reassert our mastery over it and agree on what we want it to do" (Seaborg, 1971, p. 158).

Although Seaborg expresses his faith in human potential, he clearly recognizes that the difficulty before us is the challenge of extending our knowledge into understanding and learning to apply our great technical tools with compassion, for the benefit of all peoples.

> The real issue before us is not control of science—but control of ourselves. Can we grow? Can we increase both the extent of our knowledge and our capacity to understand it and use it constructively? Can we evolve in social creativity as well as in the technological creativity we have shown over the decades and centuries? Can we become feeling, thinking creatures whose empathy and rationality can encompass a global mankind and a global environment? These are the basic questions with which we are all struggling today— . . . I believe we are witnessing the rise, not the fall, of man. Through my own contacts and dealings with people all around the world—in science, government, education and many other walks of life—I have come to feel that much more is being done that is constructive and for the good of mankind than most people imagine. Perhaps the current emphasis on the problems and evils that abound in the world will serve to drive us to new attainments and therefore will act as a positive force. I hope so.
>
> We must not let the acute awareness of today's problems have a demoralizing and debilitating effect on us. We must not let the search for solutions to these problems divide us when we should be united. We must work against such trends because never before has a unity of will and purpose been as necessary to our survival as it is today. (*Ibid.*, pp. 166, 167)

Lastly, we think it is worthy of attention that Seaborg, the "terrible technocrat," closes his lecture with a citation from the Jesuit scientist-philosopher Teilhard de Chardin: "'Someday, after mastering the winds, the waves, the tides and gravity, we shall harness for God the energies of Love, and then, for the second time in the history of the world, man will discover fire'" (cited in Seaborg, 1971, p. 167).

Man in Nature, or a Retreat to a Local Eden?

The third broad theme which we want to consider is one which is based on what might be called the nature philosophies. It is expressed in variations which include an exceedingly broad spectrum of attitudes, ranging all the way from wise observations to beliefs which are patently ridiculous. It is to be expected that the environmental movement should place considerable emphasis on the philosophical relationship between man and nature, for it is in many respects an outgrowth of the earlier conservation movement. Furthermore, many of the leaders of the movement—including a number of the committed scientists—are firmly allied with one or another school of naturalist thinking. There are, however, rather marked differences in the philosophical orientation of nature lovers, as well as differences in the degree to which naturalists claim that the attitudes they support have universal or absolute value.

Among young people, differences in the content of the beliefs and attitudes about man's relationship to nature are most in evidence; whereas, on the whole, the variations on this theme among older groups tend to differ more in terms of tone and the degree of extremism with which they hold to their beliefs.

In the new nature orientation of the young, there are often found elements of Oriental philosophy which represent a radically different approach to man's understanding of his relations with other animate beings and with inanimate nature than that with which we are familiar in the West. Others among the young have arrived at a naturalist orientation strictly on an experiential basis. They have rediscovered the childlike pleasure of contact between bare soles and earth; they enjoy a kind of "pagan" worship of sun, of trees, of surf. They are more interested in their own bodies than are their elders, and in seeking to establish a more direct connection with the instinctual levels of the human experience they are often led to a new kind of feeling response toward animals.

The older followers of the naturalist movement are much more likely to trace their values to sources in the long Western tradition of literature about nature: they are again reading Rousseau, Thoreau, and the romantics. They are also interested in the popular scientific books on natural history, or, if they are themselves scientists, may feel a strong connection with the early naturalists among zoologists and botanists. This tradition is closely allied to the values expressed by the various conservationist organizations: the importance of wilderness in and for itself; the need that man should act in the interest of the preservation of endangered species; the psychological and spiritual value to man of "communing" with nature; the importance of managing and planning our use of natural resources.

Expression of the values just mentioned are motifs which are heard constantly in the environmental movement. Sometimes they do not seem to be held with the most convincing sincerity. On the other hand, there is evidence that greater numbers of people are attempting now to *live* in accordance with these values in their daily lives, rather than merely promoting them in terms of conservation programs, or getting into part-time personal touch with nature during "wilderness vacations." It would clearly be a philistine stance to denigrate the values of those who are actively seeking to become more closely attuned with the flora and fauna of the planet, and we certainly do not wish to suggest that there is anything wrong with the personal search for a simpler, more natural way of life. On the contrary, those individuals who are really able to live in the wilderness are for the most part gentle and thoughtful people, and they are undoubtedly needed to enrich and balance the social fabric, in the same sense that groups of "meditators" and reflective intellectuals may be seen as balancing factors in our society of active "doers."

Unfortunately, however, not all the followers of naturalist philosophies are living according to their beliefs and permitting others to make their own value choices. The most vocal naturalists in the environmental movement are often either professors or "circuit preachers," and after the fashion of "true believers" they are intolerant of those who do not accept the absolute validity of their views, even though they are clearly an aesthetic minority. We have no quarrel with the attempts to save certain endangered species or to set aside areas as wilderness preserves; in fact, when it comes to affection for wilderness and other matters of personal taste we have to place ourselves within the aesthetic minority. But when it comes to setting priorities for social goals, we cannot accept that a battle to save a single endangered animal species should be permitted to take precedence over pressing human problems such as disease, hunger, and inadequate housing or education. It seems to us that it is a bit too late in human history for men to content themselves with a retreat to local Edens. Contemporary environmentalists like to talk about global pollution, but when they speak about a higher or better "quality of life," they seem all too often to be thinking in insular terms, forgetting that the world is now unavoidably "one world," and that the needs of all the peoples of the planet have to be taken into account.

Another respect in which we find the teachings of many naturalists disturbing is that, in the course of encouraging respect for other species and for the land, they seem to feel it is necessary to denigrate man. They speak to us about man's arrogance towards his fellow creatures, about the brutality of his "conquest of nature"; and they are fond of phrases like "man's war against nature." By way of contrast they talk about the ideal balance in nature, free of man's interventions, and they portray the wilderness in idyllic terms. Some of them go so far as to imply that man is no better than the lowest insect. Consider, for example, this final paragraph from a paper written by an entomologist, which deals with the various "weapons" with which we attack insects and emphasizes the so-called "natural control methods": "It would appear that this philosophy [that of Rachel Carson] has had its effect on those who are trying to develop hormonal controls on insect species. In a summary of recent works in the 1970 Zoecon annual report, Dr. Morton Grosser wrote: 'It is wise to remember that powerful weapons demand great responsibility. Only one-tenth of one percent of the insects do us harm—and they were here first'" (McElheny, 1971, p. 13).

When we read comments of this sort, we cannot but think that it might be useful if their authors were to spend several months camping in the tropics without the benefit of chemical insecticides. We suspect that after a short period of submitting their flesh to the tortures of their insect friends, they might wish to reevaluate their assessment as to which species is making "war" on whom. Furthermore, the temporal primacy of certain insect species in the evolutionary history of the planet has nothing to do with anything when it comes to man's own place on the evolutionary scale. As Polányi put it: "It is the height of intellectual perversion to renounce, in the name of scientific objectivity, our position as the highest form of life on earth, and our own advent by a process of evolution as the most important problem of evolution" (Polànyi, 1966, p. 47).

To the statement that man, as a species, is arrogant, one may reply that the tendency on the part of individuals to behave with arrogance towards their fellow human beings would appear to be a much more significant problem than the collective superiority feelings of *Homo sapiens* towards other species on Earth. In any event, there are correctives for man's inclination to arrogance which are probably much more effective than the rather silly denial of man's uniqueness on this planet. One of the most obvious among these is contemplation of the possibility (now regarded as probable by many scientists) that there may be life forms on other planetary bodies in the universe—perhaps including intelligent beings who are far more advanced in mental evolution than is man. Although we have no particular dislike for most plant and animal species, we find imaginative consideration of beings of higher intelligence than our own to be a more humbling thought than the reminder that some of the insects were here first.

As for the idealization of nature's perfect balances and the idyllic picture of the wilderness, it strikes us that people who write in this vein have not had much extensive and direct contact with the harsher reaches of the wild which may still be found on this planet. Quite aside from the predator-prey relationships among animal species and the violent destructiveness which may be unleashed as a result of natural forces, man's own relationship with his natural surroundings must necessarily be one in which he exercises his mental ingenuity; for if he simply abandons himself to the arms of nature, he will not survive for long.

To summarize: as in so many of the other arguments advanced by environmentalists, there is a kernel of truth in their claim that many modern men are out of touch with their own natural, animal selves, and likewise in the view that in the course of our rapid technological development, we have often ignored the fact that there are limits as to the quantity and the speed with which nature can absorb our wastes. However, we want to bring to attention that even adherence to a mild and apparently harmless philosophy of nature need not be always and in all its forms an unimpeachable stance.

Is Reason Bankrupt?

Closely allied to the antimachine theme and the back-to-nature theme is an undercurrent of anti-intellectualism which is less often clearly articulated than any of the themes discussed earlier, but which is nevertheless an important factor in the environmental movement, since it conditions the climate of receptivity for irrational claims.* As Sir Peter Medawar wrote in 1969: "We are oppressed by a fear of deterioration of the world through technical innovation. We tell ourselves that artificial fertilizers and pesticides are undermining our health; soil and sea are being poisoned by chemical and radioactive wastes . . . there is a sense of doubt about the adequacy of man, amounting in all to what a future historian might describe as a failure of nerve. There is a rootlessness about philosophical thinking as if the discovery or rediscovery of the insufficiency of reason had given paradoxical validity to nonsense" (Medawar, 1969, p. 895).

Now it must be admitted that a general distrust of "impractical" intellectuals has been apparent in American mass culture for a very long time, evidenced by the use of such derogatory terms as "eggheads" to denote those who have spent

---

* Please note the considerable difference between "irrational thinking" and "nonrational thinking." In our definition, the former denotes nonsensical ideas masquerading as reason, whereas the latter refers to mental concepts, paradoxes, intuitions, etc., which cannot be contained within nor expressed through strictly rational language.

a good part of their years on university campuses or buried in libraries. Nevertheless, the pragmatic spirit of the American approach to experience has at the same time led us to admire those whose mastery of rational thinking could be perceived as having practical value. Hence, while a professor of Anglo-Saxon poetry may have been an object of gentle derision in the eyes of the public, scientists, engineers, medical men, designers, inventors, economists, attorneys, and other thinkers whose mental skills could be perceived as being related to the solution of public problems have been valued.

The new currents of antirationalism, however, appear to be quite another matter from the traditional distrust of "eggheads." We can learn from Paul Shepard (1971), for example, that the "project approach" to positive problem solving is one of the *faults* of our culture. In the recent best seller, *The Greening of America,* Charles Reich tells us that those among the young who belong to what he has called "Consciousness III" are definitely suspicious of reason. He writes: "Consciousness III is deeply suspicious of logic, rationality, analysis, and of principles. Nothing so outrages the Consciousness II intellectual as this seeming rejection of reason itself. But Consciousness III has been exposed to some rather bad examples of reason, including the intellectual justifications of the Cold War and the Vietnam War. At any rate, Consciousness III believes it essential to get free of what is now accepted as rational thought. It believes that 'reason' tends to leave out too many factors and values—especially those which cannot readily be put into words and categories" (Reich, 1970, p. 278).

While it is debatable whether Reich's book may be taken as a truly accurate reflection of the new values and life-style of American youth, it is nevertheless clear to anyone who has had wide contact with young people that much of what Reich has written about Consciousness III has some foundation in reality. If, as he states, the suspicion of rationality and logic on the part of Consciousness III types arises from the bad examples they have witnessed of the misuse of logic, then perhaps it is important to assert that among those who value logic, analytical thinking, and rationality as mental tools there are many who abhor rationalization and sophistry as vehemently as do the young.

With respect to the "factors and values which cannot easily be verbalized," it should also be pointed out that the "turned-on Consciousness III's" are not alone in having awakened to the importance of these factors. It is probable that most reflective persons would readily grant that during the last one hundred or more years, Western intellectuals have been inclined to overvalue science, pure rationalism, and technological achievements. It has been said by a number of different people that we mistakenly elevated science and technology to the status of gods, while at the same time other important human functions—such as feeling, the capacity for wonder, intuition, and man's striving toward a trans-cendent fulfillment of the spirit—suffered a certain general neglect. That these neglected aspects of man's potential wholeness should now be receiving more attention can only be regarded as a gain, for clearly we can neither approach nor contain all the multifarious richness of the inner and outer experience of humanness, if we limit our thought processes completely to the tidy ordering system we call logical analysis.

On the other hand, while it may be admitted that during the nineteenth century and the first half of the twentieth there was perhaps a too exclusive emphasis on science and reason, there is a fundamental difference between recognizing the limitations of pure rationalism and rejecting reason as though it had become a worthless tool. The difference is succinctly expressed in the old aphorism: "throwing out the baby with the bath water." Adherence to the view that the development of human reasoning powers represents sui generis a kind of mental prison from which we must escape is most unlikely to lead us in the direction of the transcendent experience; nor will it automatically increase our capacities for compassionate feeling relationships or for intuition. Far from being a guarantee of more humane relations among men, turning our backs on the value of rational thought would seem to constitute a pathway to domains of confusion and nonsense in which even worse kinds of inhumane and insensitive attitudes could prevail than those which are so blithely attributed to the dominance of reason in the technological age.

Throughout much of the rest of this book we shall be using the tools of rationality in a rather traditional reductionist manner and we shall be using such phrases as "truth-value" and "scientific truth" within the framework of rather narrow definitions. If we do so, however, it is not because we are exclusively reductionist materialist thinkers, nor is it because we fail to recognize that truth is elusive and may be approached by many paths. It is rather because this book is primarily about science, and whatever might be the limitations of logic or of analytical thinking in approaching ultimate Truth, these are processes which are fundamental to the practice of Western science as we know it.

2

CITIZENRY AND
SCIENCE

Men with the muckrake are often
indispensable to the well-being of
society, but only if they know when
to stop raking the muck.

THEODORE ROOSEVELT

Since Woodstock, many American students have come to believe
that they are entering a peaceful, brotherhooding Age of Aquarius,
in which the sound of music (rock, of course) shall be heard again in our land. But
within this questing movement, tens of thousands of young people have turned their
own love toward the earth in an effort to repair ravished landscapes, oil-filled harbors
and over-crowded cities, to patch the gaping holes in the quality of modern life. For
them, this is the Age of Ecology. And from Berkeley to Boston, they are demanding an
immediate end to the war against nature. In fact, there is no longer any question that
Environment is *the* major issue on many campuses. "At first," says Edward Thomas,
a Columbia University graduate student who worked in Senator Eugene McCarthy's
presidential campaign, "students worked for civil rights—and got chased out of Mis-

sissippi. Then we tried to change politics and end the war—and got beaten in Chicago. Now a lot of us are turning to the environment. It's right here. It's something we can do something about. And—for a change—we just might win this one." . . . Young people in the U.S. are becoming increasingly concerned—and responsive— for a variety of reasons. Some see the issue as nothing less than the survival of mankind; some see it as a way of attacking the economic and social systems. Others simply wonder where all the flowers went. Michael Rossman, a 30-year-old Berkeley writer and organizer for educational reform, views the environment issue as an extension of the drug culture. "Drugs," says Rossman, "have had profound cultural consequences. One of them is that kids are turned on to colors and to their bodies. Kids are starting to become conscious of their physical selves. The hippie movement is turning toward the care and feeding of the body, to natural childbirth, to a reinvestigation of ourselves as animals on the planet, rather than as a conquering, domineering man, distinct from the rest of the system." Rossman adds that the last five years have been frustrating to young people in this country. "The further we got into the problems of civil rights and Viet Nam," he says, "the more tangled and ugly they seemed. The country today is pretty tense. There's a deep yearning in everybody's heart for one good clean cause. What could be better than erasing pollution?" (Janssen, 1970, pp. 53, 54–55)

This passage from one of the essays in *Ecotactics* gives a fairly good idea of why the environmental movement seems to have such a strong appeal to many young people in America. It would certainly be incorrect, however, to suppose that it is only the young who are involved, for the interest in saving the environment seems to be one of those rare social issues which does not increase the gap between youth and the older generations. Some of the older groups who are active in the movement have been committed for many years to the cause of protecting nature against the ravages of contemporary civilization. These are for the most part people who have supported the Sierra Club, the Audubon Society, and various other organizations devoted to the preservation of wilderness areas and the protection of threatened species. However, in addition to these groups, the environmental movement appears to have a broad appeal to middle-class suburbanites, high-school teachers, and others who are neither very young nor especially oriented towards nature conservancy.

It may be said that these groups share with American youth a certain need for a "good clean cause." As we pointed out earlier when discussing the impact of *Silent Spring*, people do have a need to feel that they have some control over their own fate, and the environmental movement seems to provide ideal forums in which to at least partially fulfill this need. The general tonality in which all of the themes characteristic of the movement are played might be summed up in the phrase: "Something has gone seriously wrong." The participation in citizens' organizations whose purposes are to protest against polluters, to prevent the construction of a power plant in the neighborhood, or, on a larger scale, to establish active lobbies in the nation's capital makes considerable sense if one takes into account the fact that most people feel increasingly dissatisfied with the limited possibilities for direct participation in political life.

Furthermore, many aspects of our current environmental problems are evident as either direct aesthetic affronts, or as irritations affecting our daily activities. For example, it does not require a subtle observing eye to take note of the ugliness of streets and highways littered with junked automobiles; nor is a committee of scientists required to inform the Los Angeles population that smog is different from plain old fog. It would seem fairly natural then, that many people should be responsive to the general outcry against environmental deterioration and become willing followers of those who claim that they are working to "save the environment."

On the organizational front, there exist by now literally thousands of citizens' groups devoted to the ecology cause. The tone, tactics, and specific purposes of local organizations vary widely depending on both the kinds of issues being emphasized and the type of community involved. On the national scale, however, it is fairly clear that the environmental movement has adopted many of the tactics and much of the strategy which characterized the protest movements of the 1960s. There are sit-ins, teach-ins, demonstrations, bumper stickers, protest marches, and all the other overt signs associated with modern American grassroots movements.

The participation of citizens in a large-scale movement and the paraphernalia of the protest movements certainly cannot be said, in itself, to be a Bad Thing. Still, it is important to ask against what are the people protesting? And for what are the organizations lobbying? In some instances, the protests may be perfectly justified. In others, they may represent merely emotional responses to high-sounding slogans.

Among the groups dedicated to one or another aspect of the battle against pollution, there is considerable dissension in the ranks. Nevertheless, in spite of strong areas of disagreement—especially between leaders of environmental action groups—these organizations may be seen to have certain things in common: (1) All are sufficiently alarmed by one or another environmental threat to believe that we are running out of time and can no longer afford the usual slow approaches to problem solving. (2) All believe that if they can generate enough interest in the particular problems on which they are focused, the Earth and its inhabitants may have a chance of survival. The battle is therefore worth waging, despite the apparent hopelessness of the mess we have gotten ourselves into.

(3) The key word for nearly all contemporary environmental organizations is "activism"—and this applies even to those groups formerly associated with highly conservative attitudes, such as the National Audubon Society, for example. (4) All of these organizations promote their cause under the banner of some unimpeachable generality: "Improving the Quality of Life," "Ecological Wisdom," "Saving the Earth for Future Generations," "The Health and Welfare of the Population," "Living in Harmony with Nature," "Restoring the Beauty of the Land," and so forth. (5) Most of them get very good press coverage. This last point is much more important than it may appear at face value, and should be examined in some detail.

The Role of the Press

Science journalism in the daily and weekly press has been a feature of the American printed media for many decades. News coverage of discoveries in science and technology has naturally expanded with the increase in both the number of these developments and the rapidity with which they unfold. Despite a steady increase in newsworthy scientific items, however, until quite recently the number of journalists specializing in "science reporting" has remained rather small. This is perhaps partly accounted for by the fact that science news of national or international import frequently is supplied to local newspapers through the wire services.

The traditional approach to coverage of science news has always been one of objectivity, with the intent of informing the public about interesting facts and developments. When a science news item dealt with a controversy among scientists—either matters of disagreement over the ethical implications of a scientific breakthrough, such as that which has centered on the organ-transplant issue, or matters of differences in interpretive opinions about the phenomenal world, like the "hot-moon, cold-moon" debate— it has been the custom of science journalists to report the existence of the controversy and to give an idea of the main arguments of both parties to the debate, without indicating their own preferences for one or the other point of view.

In the issue of environmental contamination, a peculiar situation has arisen, which is reflected in the style and content of environmental news coverage. Although many aspects of the pollution problem are clearly scientific or technological, others are social and political. Thus, for example, when news about environmental debates such as the controversy over the SST or the location of a new power generating plant clearly involve sociopolitical issues in which both the general public and politicians participate actively, then it is fairly natural that the press should treat these subjects in a polemic rather than an objective manner, although one might still hope that some attempts would be made at fair coverage. On the other hand, when environmental reports center on as yet unresolved scientific problems, such as the doubtful toxicity of DDT residues in food, then one would expect that the opinions of both those scientists who are persuaded of the dangers of these residues and those who deny their significance should be reported at equal length.

Many environmentalists have come out in favor of advocacy journalism on *all* matters pertaining to pollution issues, making no distinction between the social and the scientific sides of these questions. From our observations, it will not be necessary for them to make special efforts to achieve a tactical victory on this front, for most of the new breed of environmental reporters appear already to have established their bias. It is difficult to understand why the tradition of objective and fair coverage seems to have gone by the boards in this broad area of news, even on those sides of the issue which are clearly scientific, and where there are many scientists who strongly oppose the opinions of the environmental alarmists. It may be that the old maxim "No news is good news" ought to be turned around to read "Bad news is interesting news." In other terms, perhaps the continued existence of the special kind of reporting now called environmental news depends to a certain extent on sensational or shocking material. This may very well be the case, just as the renewal of research grants of pollution investigators is, paradoxically, more or less dependent on positive findings (that is, definite bad news). Another possibility is that those who choose to become environmental reporters or to edit pages dealing with environmental problems are themselves alarmists to begin with. Max Ways, an editor of *Fortune,* goes so far as to indict the whole "web of communications" for not "helping to coordinate society's fragmented actions." In his thoughtful essay "How to Think about the Environment," he writes: "Journalism, enslaved to its own outgrown traditions, is eager to report those environmental concerns that are reduced to simple and dramatic 'confrontations,' but journalism is insensitive to the complexities of city planning or of market reform to reduce pollution" (Ways, 1971, p. 186).

But whatever the underlying reasons, in addition to advocacy, three basic tendencies may be perceived in reports pertaining to the environment: sensationalism, unequal coverage, and frequent vagueness with respect to sources of information.*

---

* It is obvious that not every U.S. newspaper or magazine has fallen prey to these tendencies; but here, as in other instances, generalizations are made for the sake of simplifying our analysis. It should also be pointed out that the editorial stance of some newspapers formerly very proenvironmentalist seems now to be changing.

The penchant for sensationalism, which used to be reserved for reports of rape, riot, corruption, and the like, is easily observable in environmental reporting. Let us take, for example, a few headlines from the *New York Times* treating the "heavy metal scare" during the year from the summer of 1970 to the summer of 1971. "Dangerous Levels of Mercury Found in Lakes and Streams in 14 Eastern States by U.S. Investigators" (July 9, 1970). "3 Fish Caught Near Battery Factory on the Hudson Contain Up to 1,000 Times Normal Cadmium" (January 13, 1971). "Senators Hear Mercury Peril to Fish Industry" (May 21, 1971). Headlines similar to these have appeared in the thousands across the nation, while articles dealing with reassurances from public health officials and other scientists to the effect that the reported "dangers" have perhaps been exaggerated are few, and they are often hard to locate in the papers. Also, only a handful of papers carried the puzzling reports, which were later substantiated, of even higher levels of mercury than those described as dangerous on July 9, 1970, in both pristine waters and in 90-year-old preserved fish. Apparently this was not interesting news.

The matter of uneven coverage is difficult to establish without massive statistics. However, readers should be alerted to it because it is the form of bias which is least perceptible to the public. Consider, for instance, the fact that when Sweden decided to outlaw DDT in 1969, this was a major story, printed with large block headlines. On the other hand, when the Swedish parliament rescinded its total ban on DDT only one month following the decision and reintroduced qualified use of the insecticide to protect its vast and economically important forests, the silence from the American press was deafening. It is also known that between 1967 and 1969 the Environmental Defense Fund—a single one of the thousands of conservationist and environmental organizations—received over 19,000 column-inches of press coverage, most of it in connection with the DDT debate. We do not have exact numbers for the space allotted to those who oppose the "ban DDT" movement, but it is definitely only a small fraction of the figure cited above.

Vagueness of sources is another way of distorting the material which the public reads as environmental news. By this we mean the tendency of many journalists to use phrases like: "scientists say . . . ," "ecologists are worried that . . . ," or "it has been found through laboratory analysis that X substance is present in . . ." as prefaces to one or another claim about the state of the environment. This may not seem terribly significant on first thought, but if one considers the matter, it becomes apparent that such generalizations tend to give an impression that there is a consensus of opinion among scientists about the claim involved. That this is very often *not* the case may not come to the attention of the lay public at all; whereas, if the journalists would write instead "a group of scientists claim . . . ," "some ecologists are worried that . . . ," and "the findings of one laboratory suggest the presence of X substance in . . . ," readers might at least imagine that there are other scientific opinions on these matters, even if not directly mentioned.

To be fair to the environmental reporters, it has to be admitted that they sometimes get their news items directly from scientists who are not very careful about the possibility that they may be releasing information prematurely— information which has either not yet been confirmed or is not fully understood, and is therefore not appropriate for distribution to the press. In some instances, too, the journalists may be unwitting dupes of scientists who are deliberately seeking publicity for their own point of view: an approach to scientific debate which is regarded as unethical in scientific circles and is therefore generally not anticipated, although it seems unfortunately to be growing rather common of late.*

On the other hand, environmental reporters are not so naïve as to be un-aware that many of the scientific issues of the environmental debate are matters of controversy. While they may occasionally be caught unawares and innocently report the latest wild speculation as though it were a well-established theory, if they were not to some extent advocates of a cause rather than objective re-porters there would not be so many instances of sensationalism, uneven coverage, and generalizations which attribute minority views to the whole scientific com-munity by implication.

But what is the matter with advocacy, you may ask? Is it not a good thing if our journalists are personally committed to the cause of saving the environ-ment? One may reply that advocacy of a cause is fine for editorials, but where people believe that they are reading *news,* it is not responsible journalism to report on hotly debated issues in accordance with one's own bias. In the words of John Wolfenden, British philosopher and educator:

> The everyday difficulty is to use words "pure and simple," without getting entangled in their emotional lives. At least, it is a difficulty if one is trying to be unemotional. It is no abuse of words to use them for purposes of persuasion. We spend much of our lives trying to convince other people, to persuade them to adopt a course of action, to make them agree with us. That is perfectly legitimate, on two conditions. The first is that in our attempts we should not do violence to the words themselves, for they have their lives and their personalities, to which we must pay proper respect. The second is that we should not confuse *exposition* with *advocacy.* It is one thing to expound a theory, as objectively and as dispassionately as the

* See Chapter 3 for a brief discussion of the ethics of scientic debate.

truth demands; it is another thing to advocate a course of action and to try to convert others to it. To slide from the one to the other is to do violence to language, to *pollute the medium of communication* between one human being and another. (Wolfenden, 1963, p. 21; our emphasis)

Wolfenden wrote these words in 1963, in an essay in which he discussed the advantages of the objective use of language for communication. He clearly was not trying to make a "relevant" point in using the phrase "pollute the medium of communication." However, his passage happens to be both relevant and appropriate to a discussion of how we communicate about matters of environmental pollution, for the confusion between advocacy and exposition is one which is not only propounded by environmental journalists, but has also unfortunately become a central issue in the internal debate which is now going on in the scientific community itself.

The Descent from the Ivory Tower

The contemporary situation of scientists with respect to their involvement or participation in social issues is a complicated one. In the decades since World War II there have been certain fundamental changes in the degree of involvement of the scientific community in social and political problems. Scientists are much more likely now than they were in the past to voice their opinions about social issues and even to attempt to exercise direct political influence. This has been particularly evident on those issues relating to war, defense, and international relations. This development would appear to be more or less inevitable because of the nature of our civilization; and it is in any event clear that in a democratic society scientists have the same rights as other citizens to express their views on political and social questions. Indeed, we are very much in favor of the descent of the intelligentsia from the ivory tower and are in accord with the idea that all thinking persons must reflect on and in some manner participate in the resolution of the major issues of the day.

However, there is an obvious difference between the scientist who takes a public stance on a social or political question as a private person and the one who makes statements, in support of a particular cause, which derive their credibility from his professional authority. This difference is most apparent when a social issue centers around matters which can best be described in scientific terms. The question of environmental contamination is such a socioscientific problem; for while anyone may observe that our streets are littered with garbage and the air over many of our cities is distastefully unclean, only specialists can make judgments about the extent to which particular pollutants represent genuine hazards to human health or to the biotic community.

Among the organizations now devoted to the environmental issue, there are a number of groups consisting principally of scientists. Some of them and their members still adhere to the ideals of objective research, accuracy in reporting, and a balanced assessment of conflicting views—ideals which are absolutely fundamental to the practice of science. If the formation of such professional societies aids scientists in the exchange of ideas and the dissemination of their findings, there is obviously nothing objectionable about this. However, in the environmental movement, there are both individual scientists and several organizations expressing partisan opinions with respect to controversial environmental issues. One result of this partisan commitment is that, in addition to the one-sided treatment of pollution problems by some members of the press, the public has been exposed to statements (and even whole books) by scientists which represent advocacy instead of exposition. This is rather confusing to lay readers, for it is generally assumed that when a scientist makes public statements on scientific matters, he is either expounding a well-demonstrated theory or reporting about known phenomena. If members of the scientific community objecting to the advocacy practices of their colleagues express their disapproval only in professional journals with limited circulation, how is the public to learn about it?

The Use of the Courts

This matter of advocacy on the part of scientists leads us directly into a consideration of one of the most important tactics of the environmental movement: that is, the use of the courts in cases that are now called environmental litigation.

In 1967 the Environmental Defense Fund (EDF) was organized by Victor Yannacone, an attorney from Long Island, New York; Charles Wurster, then assistant professor of biology at the State University of New York at Stony Brook; George Woodwell, a plant physiologist at the Brookhaven National Laboratories on Long Island; and other scientists concerned about environmental problems. The organization now has a sizable number of scientists participating in its Scientists Advisory Committee, of which Dr. Wurster is the chairman. According to their own statement: "The basic aim of the EDF is to create, through litigation, a body of legal interpretations for natural resource conservation and abatement of ecologically perilous situations."

The idea of initiating legal actions in order to protect the public and/or the environment from polluters and pollutants is relatively new. One has to grant that Yannacone and the Environmental Defense Fund pioneered this concept of turning to the courts as a forum for the environmental debate. We wish to discuss the tactics of this particular organization and to distinguish two completely different kinds of litigation relating to pollution. However, we should first give some brief consideration to the background of the American legal system and its relations to the workings of government.

It will be remembered that the Constitution of the United States was designed to create a careful system of checks and balances among the executive, legislative, and judicial branches of government. One of the fundamental purposes of the Constitution is to safeguard the individual against attempts on the part of other persons, legal entities, or even government agencies to infringe upon those freedoms and rights which are the basis of our democracy. Although the Constitution does not speak specifically about the right to a clean environment, it has been tacitly recognized—through the creation of protective agencies and legal regulations—that citizens have a right to an environment which is free from contamination with hazardous substances; or, where the use of dangerous materials (high explosives, for example) is necessary, that adequate safety precautions must be observed in order to protect people from direct exposure to damaging effects. It is further recognized that where the use of certain dangerous products, processes, or activities is justifiable, the benefits obtained through these should outweigh the risks associated with them.

With respect to any process, product, or activity which may represent a threat to human health and welfare, it is the function of the legislative branch of the government to enact laws for regulating the production and subsequent use of dangerous materials, and to set limits on activities which may represent either a direct or an indirect harm to the well-being of citizens. Thus, for example, there are safety rules governing manufacturing processes where workers are exposed to hazardous situations; food items have to meet legislated health standards; and the distribution and use of drugs is similarly highly regulated. With respect to potentially dangerous activities, such as driving a car, legal restrictions are enacted to minimize the harmful effects which might ensue.

The executive branch of the government, through its various agencies, is charged with the responsibility of assuring that not only the letter but also the spirit of the enacted laws should be carried out.

Quite aside from the question of violations of criminal laws, it is probably inevitable in a complex modern state that some of our existing civil laws are at times either ignored (not enforced) or deliberately broken. When an individual (or a group of individuals constituting a "social entity") is adversely affected by the failure of law enforcement, their recourse for remedy is given in the independent judicial system, which hears the complaints of the "individual" and judges them according to their merit. This system of obtaining impartial decisions from a judiciary which is free of vested interests seems to be the best and only known workable form for safeguarding the rights of individuals.

Many laws exist to defend citizens against the potentially harmful effects of applying technologies which might be either willfully misused or negligently abused. Therefore, should cases of misuse or negligence arise, and should the executive arm be unresponsive to the demanded rectification of a legitimate grievance (for instance, by interpreting differently an existing law), turning to a court for judgment is the customary procedure. It would therefore seem only natural that in the issues of environmental deterioration, courts are used more and more frequently by citizens to obtain relief from damage by specific polluters or pollutants. This is basically the most democratic procedure at our disposal, and environmental litigation thus would seem to fall into the main line of our political-social philosophy and should be cherished as a distinct step forward toward the achievement of a truly participatory democracy. We cannot but wholeheartedly agree with this goal. Alas, we would not be human, were we not inclined, at times, to corrupt even the most lofty ideals when we put them into practice.

Overt and "Hidden" Pollutants

From a practical point of view, it is clear that there are two types of environmental problems, and failure to distinguish these from one another, or lumping them together, has resulted in much confusion. One category is overt pollution that does real damage. Discharges of untreated sulfite wastes into rivers or lakes has to be stopped; raw municipal waste effluents entering natural waters cannot be further tolerated; high SO_2 emissions from fossil fuel burning are a disgusting practice that has to cease. These pollutants represent real problems affecting our lives, and if abatement measures are not instituted to combat them — despite the fact that they contravene existing legislation — any person or organization has the right to appeal to a court for relief. Enforcement is then up to the executive branch, which has the whole armamentarium of the legal state at its disposal.

There are, however, other kinds of pollution problems which are not evident as gross threats to the environment or direct hazards to human health, but rather represent the slow accumulation of supposedly harmful effects, the manifestations of which may only become clear in decades or in generations to come. Such "hidden" effects are usually ascribed to persistent pesticides, low-level radiation, and to a lesser degree, to other chemicals and to heavy metals. Whether or not such insidious, slowly developing, but in the long range decidedly poisonous characteristics can indeed be attributed to these pollutants is a hotly debated scientific issue these days. The problems surrounding these contaminants are too complex to admit of any simple conclusion, and the evidence presented on the side of the accusers is usually incomplete, to say the least. These controversial questions are *strictly scientific* in nature, even when they touch on issues with obvious social implications. They cannot be resolved in a court of law through consideration of the testimonies of opposing parties, unless the court is willing to take upon itself the role of pontification.

Debates in science, in contrast to the legal or adversary system, must include *all* the data and facts pertaining to the issue, and no resolution can be arrived at without taking into account *all* the available evidence. In a court case, each party tells only of those points that support his case, and the judge or the jury decides which party sounds more convincing. In issues before courts, the skill of attorneys frequently plays an important role in the decisions which are handed down; but where scientific problems are involved, there is no place for well-trained advocates to utilize their gifts of legal debate, since what really counts is the ultimate truth-value of the scientific statements, rather than the persuasive powers of a brilliant solicitor.

The technical language of science is not easily comprehended by lay people. Even trained scientists not intimately involved in a given discipline frequently fail to note untenable hypotheses, or accept conclusions which are only tenuously supported (if supported at all) by experimental data. The clever construction of graphs or charts and the presentation of calculations in which all but one or two of the basic assumptions are correct can serve as supposedly established scientific evidence in support of a claim, without having anything to do with scientific truth. The propagation of such half-truths and their presentation in court— whereby they acquire the aura of "legalized," that is, legally accepted facts— represents a most dangerous spread of pseudoscience. The eloquence, ardor, sincere passion, and not infrequent showmanship with which some scientists associated with certain pressure groups champion their cause is bound to make a deep impression on a court, whose members, in lack of appropriate scientific training, cannot be expected to see through the tenuousness of argument and the opportunistic use of language that often characterize such proceedings.

This is not to say, of course, that the same one-sided manner of presenting materials involving unresolved scientific problems may not also be employed by the defense in an environmental litigation proceeding. Nor is it to imply that environmental litigation is the only area where the judiciary deals with complex questions not admitting of simple solutions. But the principle point to be taken here is that scientific clarification respecting as yet unresolved scientific problems is most unlikely to be advanced in a court of law, even in cases where there is no question of the sincerity and good intentions of all parties to such suits.

EDF Tactics

Those who follow developments in the environmental movement will undoubtedly by now be aware of the multifarious legal suits which have been instituted by the EDF. It is most instructive to read about the tactics of this group in approaching environmental litigation as they are recounted by one of the great publicists of the movement, journalist Frank Graham, Jr., in his remarkably partisan book, *Since Silent Spring*. Graham describes these maneuverings with unnerving candor in a chapter entitled "Light At the End of the Road."

> . . . the best hope for progress in the struggle against the persistent pesticides might lie after all in responding to his [Yannacone's] battle cry: "Sue the bastards!" . . . Yannacone's method is public exposure, it embarrasses the polluter while educating the public. . . The plaintiff must establish by sound scientific evidence that the offending program will cause "serious, permanent and irreparable damage" to an essential or a unique natural resource belonging to *all* the people of the community. . . . Yannacone lost the battle but won the war. . . . despite the adverse decision in court, Yannacone and the scientists had snatched the victory by convincing the public *through news media* that its case was just [our emphasis]. . . . EDF has followed up its eastern success. In 1967 it filed suit in western Michigan to restrain nine municipalities from using DDT for Dutch elm disease control. Again, *EDF lost in court but attained its objective* [our emphasis]. . . . The widespread publicity given both court actions publicized the strong scientific case against the persistent pesticides and publicly discredited the spray programs. . . . Personalities, however, faded into the background as *headlines* once more told the world what it meant to inject DDT into the open environment [our emphasis]. (Graham, 1970, pp. 224, 226, 227, 228, 230)

These few statements illustrate quite nicely the clever and cynical manner in which the EDF manipulates public sentiments. Although the EDF has lost many of its court battles, they are winning the "war" through the distorted exposure given to them by the news media. Indeed, their purpose would appear to be more one of "educating the public" according to their own views than of settling crucial scientific problems.

The psychological warfare waged by this group does not seem to be in accord with ethical scientific practice. Does not the deliberate manipulation of public fears through a sensation-seeking press seem like a deplorable game—a game far removed from the conservationist's love of nature? And what might be the motivations behind such actions? It seems hard to believe that an altruistic love of nature or a benevolent concern for the public good could lead these fearless champions of the environment to employ such tactics. People who are clever enough to play with deep human emotions, who know the psychological tricks with which entire communities can be brought around to support their cause, and who calculate in advance the impact which their statements will have when quoted by the press, do not seem to belong to the same class as the gentle and sensitive Rachel Carson, who had a genuine, though sometimes misguided, concern for her fellow beings. These "second-generation" environmentalists are "stars," most of whom rose overnight into national prominence. Touring on the environmental bandwagon, there is not much danger of their fading back into obscurity as long as they provide some new variations on their horror tales—unless, of course, the public finally tires of the show.

When the rather questionable results of the Innes study (see detailed discussion in Chapter 14, pp. 350–362) were made public—suggesting that life-long administration of high doses of DDT caused a slight increase in mouse liver tumors over those shown by the control animals—both the Audubon Society and the EDF denounced DDT as a proven carcinogen. EDF made good use of these findings. It was well established that DDT is soluble in fat, that the ingested chemical will tend to accumulate in body fat and will also be secreted by body fluids, such as saliva, tears and mother's milk. Because of its high-fat content, the latter will show somewhat higher concentrations of the pesticide than its levels in the rest of the body. The inference thus was simple: DDT is a carcinogen; mother's milk contains DDT; therefore, mother's milk is carcinogenic and unfit for human consumption. EDF, according to one source, evidently thought such inferences sufficient to justify using them to prop up its apparently faltering finances and, at the same time, gain for it a national reputation as the public defender of the environment. The story is told in the following way in the *Richmond Independent*, a California newspaper:

> The turning point came when [an official of EDF] decided to spend about $5,000 of the organization's total remaining assets of $23,000 on an advertisement

in the New York Times on Sunday, March 29, headlined "Is Mother's Milk Fit for Human Consumption?" It referred to the amounts of DDT in the human body.

The ad appealed for members, starting at $10 for a basic membership. It produced $7,000, a profit, and the EDF turned to a direct mail campaign and now has 10,000 members, a stable financial base and a chance at major foundation support. (*Richmond Independent*, 10, Dec. 17, 1970)

In late 1969, the situation within the innermost circles of EDF apparently went sour. One of the founders, V. Yannacone, appears to have become involved in a serious personal disagreement regarding EDF's tactics about DDT with Charles Wurster, another founding father, and left the organization. That he no longer advocated an unqualified ban on the pesticide is evidenced by his assertion, in September of 1970: "Any law simplistically banning the use, sale, manufacture or distribution of DDT in your state, county, city or even the United States, without at the same time establishing an ecologically sophisticated pesticide regulation program, is a bad law. It won't satisfy anyone very long and will permanently polarize agriculture and conservation to such an extent that common problems can no longer be considered in rational discourse" (Yannacone, 1970, p. 24).

Possible Pitfalls in Environmental Litigation

One of the dangers of environmental litigation lies in the fact that once a court has established a "scientific truth," there cannot be much argument against it, and a severe restriction will have been introduced on the further free application of the results of scientific inquiry. And, as Graham's account of EDF's objectives attests, even should a court fail to hand down a decision favorable to the environmentalists' cause, the press coverage is often enough to propagandize large segments of the population, creating still another obstacle to the later clarification of the issues.

There are other respects in which some types of environmental litigation are disturbing. If such legal actions are initiated without discrimination, they could ultimately lead to a serious disruption of the execution of legislated policies and in this way undermine the fundamental workings of an efficient government. Most of the courts in the United States are already overworked, with a tremendous backlog of pending cases. A new wave of environmental lawsuits (many of them representing the second type of highly complex scientific questions) will tie up courts for years, if not longer. The costs involved are staggering, and the results obtained are usually less than satisfying, prompting appeals and further court actions. In the meanwhile, the orderly process of the execution of legislated laws has to be suspended.

Let us take an example. The environmental radiation standards set by the Atomic Energy Commission have the force of federal law. Congress having invested the AEC with the power to regulate these standards. When the State of Minnesota—under pressure from local environmental action groups—decided to enact much more stringent state standards, the Northern States Power Company was unable to obtain an operating license for its already completed new nuclear power plant at Monticello, since the anticipated levels of radioactivity leaking into the environment would occasionally have been slightly above the new Minnesota standards.* Although in a recent court ruling the federal standards were upheld and the right of the state to set more stringent standards denied, the decision has been appealed to the Supreme Court. During a period of more than a year, this litigation successfully obstructed the starting up of the power plant by preventing the execution of an existing law (application of federal standards). The Minnesota environmentalists also managed to partially paralyze a local industrial giant.

In some instances, too, clogging of the courts, the prevention of the execution of laws, the paralyzing of segments of some industries, and endless tort cases may arise from a desire to control certain practices, technologies, or means of production which the environmentalists consider to be undesirable. Agriculture, in its practice of monoculture, is said to be a Bad Thing. (This will be elaborated upon in a later chapter.) Through the successive banning of certain pesticides and eventually possibly fertilizers, the environmentalists hope to gain control over the use of agricultural chemicals. That this is not speculation may be gleaned from a statement made by Wurster: "Moreover, a battle over control is one of the central issues. Who is going to control pesticides? Historically, complete control has been in the hands of Agriculture. Now that certain pesticides are affecting nonagricultural interests and values, a growing chorus of other voices, including the environmental science community, demand to be

---

*One hundred times more stringent than the federal standards.

heard. If the environmentalists win on DDT, they will achieve, and probably retain in other environmental issues, a level of authority they have never had before. In a sense, then, much more is at stake than DDT" (Wurster, 1969, p. 809).

It is even questionable whether litigation dealing with gross pollution will, in fact, lead to a lessening of our environmental problems. Max Ways voices his doubts about this matter in the following: "If environmental law follows the dismal pattern of automobile tort cases every business and perhaps every individual will be carrying insurance against pollution damage suits. An army of pollution chasers, hot for those contingent fees, will join the present army of ambulance chasers. None of that is going to do the environment any good" (Ways, 1971, p. 185).

And John Ridgeway, criticizing the practice of environmental law from the point of view of the radical left, writes:

> The effects of this attack by lawyers is profound: the court becomes the legislature. Courtroom victories enhance the power and prestige of the trial lawyers within the legal fraternity as well as among the general public. As in so many other fields, litigation has become a principal avenue for correcting corporate abuse. Even members of Congress, despairing of writing laws, sue in court to accomplish their reforms.
>
> Since the court has become the arena where the postindustrial economy is adjusted, every citizen needs a lawyer—not a legislator—to look after his interests . . . . In reality they [the lawyers] are working toward a new definition of a governmental system in which lawyers are a commanding elite. (Ridgeway, 1970, pp. 198–199)

Insofar as environmental litigation is limited to responsible and necessary legal actions, the use of the courts for redress of grievances respecting pollution can be an effective way of protecting citizens. But it is important to be alert to the limitations of what can be effectively accomplished by environmental law, as well as to potential abuses of this kind of legislation. If the courts are used mainly as publicity forums, and if legal actions are initiated and pursued in such a manner as to seriously disrupt the operations of government or vital sectors of our domestic economy, we run the risk of inviting legislative restrictions which would limit, rather than extend, the right of citizens to turn to the courts in their battle for a cleaner and safer environment.

3

O TEMPORA!
O MORES!

People are constantly spoiling a project
when it lacks only a step to completion.

To avoid making a mess of it, be as careful
of the end as you were of the beginning.

LAO TZU

. . . you see, we both committed a crime against the truth. A crime in
good faith, admittedly, honest, simply a mistake. Your mistake, if I may
say so, was even stupider than mine. But there we were; we issued false statements.
Now if false statements are to be allowed, if they are not to be discouraged by every
means we have, science will lose its one virtue, truth. The only ethical principle which
has made science possible is that the truth shall be told all the time. If we do not pe-
nalize false statements in error, we open up the way, don't you see, for false statements by intention. And of course a false statement of fact, made deliberately, is the
most serious crime a scientist can commit. There are such, we both know, but they're
few. As competition gets keener, possibly they will become more common. Unless

45

that is stopped, science will lose a great deal. And so it seems to me that false statements, whatever the circumstances, must be punished as severely as is possible. (Snow, 1934, p. 273)

The above passage is taken from a novel by C. P. Snow, *The Search,* of which the protagonist is a young scientist. It may seem odd to the layman that Snow should have written about the necessity to punish a scientist who makes an innocent mistake. Of course, he meant punishment not in the legal sense, but was rather referring to the corrective pressures which may be exerted by the scientific community on its errant members (such as dismissing them from their posts).

The passage contains a number of important statements, the implications of which are fruitful subjects for reflection. Among them are the idea that the aim of science must be the pursuit of truth; that if errors in scientific publications go uncorrected, they may result in the building up of a whole false structure in the scientific literature; that the failure to censor those who issue false statements resulting from unintentional mistakes may encourage others, who do not feel themselves bound by the ethical principles of scientific practice, to issue statements which are deliberately falsified. *The Search* was first published in 1934, at a time when there were relatively few scientists in comparison to the number today. It is therefore also notable that Snow anticipated the likelihood that far more serious problems in the ethics of scientific debate would develop with a future increase in competitive relations among scientists.

Snow was trained as a scientist and later became a man of letters by choice. He has — probably more effectively than any other single individual — brought home to us the importance and the difficulties inherent in what he has called "the separation of the two cultures," by which phrase he refers to the increasing gap in understanding between those who are trained in science and those who are not. This communication problem is by now fairly well recognized, and considerable attention has been given to it by many other members of the intellectual communities of various nations. There are numerous propositions as to what ought to be done about this communication gap, among them: more science education in basic schooling; more publications about developments in science written specifically for the nonscientist; and so forth. However, what we want to emphasize here is not the relative merits of possible solutions to the "two-culture" gap, but rather the communication difficulties which exist within the scientific community itself.

Nearly everybody knows about the "information explosion" of our times. The scientist, like persons in other occupations, finds it literally impossible to examine *in detail* all of the vast numbers of publications pertinent to his pursuit of knowledge, no matter how thorough his training or how diligent his efforts. There are simply too many of them. Furthermore, the languages and techniques of the various scientific disciplines have now become so specialized that a scientist from one area may have considerable difficulty understanding the publications and professional presentations of scientists from a distant discipline—although he usually will be able to grasp the basic information expressed in their conclusions. Practical considerations may also make it impossible for him to check the experimental procedures which have led other scientists to reach certain conclusions, even should he wish to do so. Let us take a specific example. Suppose that a plant taxonomist, for one reason or another, decides to attend a conference on radio-astronomy. Even assuming that he is able to understand the relatively new language employed by the astronomers to describe their techniques and their results, he would be in no position to check the accuracy of their work by repeating their experiments himself. In the first place, his training and experience would not include knowledge of their special scientific techniques. Secondly, he would simply not be able to gain access to the very expensive and esoteric equipment which they use. The astronomers would not be much better off in evaluating the taxonomist's description of a newly discovered species; for while they might be able to obtain a sample of the species and borrow appropriate microscopes, without a thorough knowledge of botany they could not judge the value or the correctness of his description. It is therefore essential that some kind of checks other than personal verification should operate in modern science, so that we may be fairly confident that other scientists are "telling the truth."

In connection with his considerations of science as a unified body of knowledge, Michael Polányi wrote:

> The acceptance of scientific statements by laymen is based on authority, and this is true to nearly the same extent for scientists using results from branches of science other than their own. Scientists must rely heavily for their facts on the authority of fellow scientists. . . .

> The body of scientific knowledge is what it is by virtue of the fact that referees are constantly engaged in eliminating contributions offered to science which lack an acceptable scientific value, as measured by the compounded coefficients of accuracy, systematic interest, and lay interest of subject matter. (Polányi, 1966, pp. 64, 66)

It may be necessary to explain what is meant, in the world of science, by the word "referee." Journals containing articles that report experiments with significant results today constitute the most important forum for the dissemination of scientific information. It is also through publication that the scientist opens up his work to the scrutiny of others. There are a very large number of scientific journals of all sorts, but most of those generally regarded as respectable outlets for the publications of new discoveries or reports of experiments have some kind of referee policy. This means that the editor(s) of the journal not only reads through the papers submitted for publication himself, but also sends them off for comments to other scientists whose special areas of research and expertise correspond to the particular subject matter of the paper involved. It is the function of a referee to examine whether the investigator is working with a hypothesis that is tenable in terms of established theories, whether the experimental design is meaningful, whether the investigator has familiarized himself thoroughly with earlier work carried out on the same subject, whether the techniques employed in gathering the data and the manner of reporting the results are acceptable and accurate. He must also consider—and this is important—whether the conclusions reached by the investigator are definitely warranted by his findings. Lastly, the referee may make some judgments about the value of the submitted article in terms of interest and of standards that are not exclusively scientific matters, such as whether the paper is written in correct and comprehensible language.

It should be apparent from all of this that if the referees of scientific journals carry out their responsibilities objectively and thoroughly, the possibility of worthless papers being published should be much reduced, although it can never be completely eliminated. Relying on this system of the refereed journal, most scientists tend to feel reasonably confident that the articles which eventually reach publication in respected journals may be read rather quickly. If they are of interest to a particular scientist, he may automatically incorporate their conclusions into his own body of scientific information, without considering that he ought to check carefully the fine points of procedure and reporting, since he assumes that this has already been done by the referees and the journal editor. Indeed, it is not uncommon for scientists perusing papers which treat subjects outside their special areas of interest to read only the abstracts and the conclusions of the articles.

In view of the heavy reliance that scientists place on the referee system, it must also be obvious that should this system break down, all kinds of difficulties may ensue—over and above the simple fact that some worthless papers may find their way into print. The community of scientists who continue their wide reading assuming that referees and editors are carrying out their responsibilities may unwittingly accept erroneous findings. These in turn may be built into a whole structure of untenable theories that are accepted by other scientists because they have not taken note of the earlier mistakes. In the light of these possibilities, perhaps Snow's idea that scientific mistakes should be punished will no longer seem so strange.

There are two basic ways in which the system of refereed journals may fail to operate. The first kind of failure results from laziness or carelessness on the part of referees and editors, who permit the publication of papers in which there are serious mistakes, either of the very obvious kind, or those that become evident only after careful study, but which nevertheless should have been caught before publication. The second kind of failure of this system is much more serious, because it can undermine the very practice of science itself. This will occur if the supposedly unbiased referees are attached to a particular point of view and become anxious to see papers published supporting their point of view, while at the same time "weeding out" those that may contradict their opinions. In such cases —with respect to the "favorable" papers—the referees may fulfull that part of their responsibility which has to do with correcting grammar or minor arithmetical errors, but fail in their duty to eliminate articles which are meaningless or worthless in terms of experimental design, methodology, or unwarranted conclusions. The result may be a scientific disaster, for not only are the checks on the quality of the publications which are then read and absorbed by the scientific community at large lacking, but, in addition, the meaningless or nonsensical papers which find their way into print may be defended against future attacks on the grounds that they appeared in a respected (refereed) journal. This kind of vicious circle of highly unscientific bias appears to have infected the management of some of our best scientific journals, at least in those areas of inquiry which touch on some kinds of environmental matters. One can only hope that this is a temporary situation and will be corrected in time to prevent lasting damage.

Scientists Who Are "Sleeping," but Who Are Not Indifferent

One of the most obvious questions that may come to the reader's mind is: "If the authors allege that a considerable number of the scientific claims of the environmentalists are false and some of the papers which support these claims are worthless or filled with errors, how does it happen that out of the more than 200,000 scientists in the United States, so few have spoken up in a similar vein of protest?" Frankly, this same question occurred to us some time ago, and it must be admitted that it is a sticky one. We have already explained that most scientists who are not directly involved in one or another aspect of environmental science or environmental medicine may have no particular reason to scrutinize carefully the publications in these areas. They may therefore be completely unaware that there are some difficulties with respect to the quality of some of the papers being published in prestigious journals. One cannot really blame them for this, for scientists are generally very busy people who are doing their best to get on with what they regard as their own work. However, we also began to ask ourselves: Are they merely busy and unaware? Or are they also indifferent to what goes on outside their own special branch of science? To satisfy our curiosity on this point, we conducted a small-scale, private sociological experiment, which consisted of the following: We presented four scientists from completely different disciplines with the reprints of three papers of questionable worth, two of which were published in *Science*, the third in the British journal *Nature*.* One paper contained regression line graphs which were all drawn in the opposite direction from that which would result from a standard regression analysis of the data. The second paper was based on a meaningless experimental design, its title was completely misleading, and the conclusions were not warranted even by the data reported. In the third paper, perusal of the fine print in which the experimental results were reported indicated that the authors were either ignorant of or ignored one of the most basic principles of statistical significance.

Three of the scientists to whom we showed these papers were more or less removed from the environmental debate: one was a medical researcher; the second a biochemist; the third an organic chemist. The fourth scientist was a European zoologist who is an ardent conservationist. Of the four, he was the only one who knew all of these papers fairly well, but the others had read through them at the time of their original publication.

The reaction of these four scientists when they realized that the three papers contained gross errors dispelled our doubts about their possible indifference. All were shocked that such sloppy work was being dignified by the name of scientific research, and all were angry that these publications had been permitted to pass the reviewers and editors. (Their anger was of that kind which is called moral indignation, having nothing to do with a fit of temper.) Interestingly, of the four, the conservationist was the most upset. Since he does not permit his interest in species preservation to supersede his respect for good science, he shook his head and announced that he now felt obliged to go home and check carefully all of the many publications which had been the basis of some of his own conclusions about environmental issues.

Possibly not all scientists would react in the same manner as our very small sample of four; nevertheless, this little experiment at least suggests that scientists do care that the standards of practice and of publication in all branches of science should be maintained at as high a level as possible.

---

* Bitman et al., 1969; Heinrichs et al., 1971; and Heath et al., 1969. These three papers will be discussed later on pages 411–416, 367–370, and 405–408, respectively.

Professional Behavior and Tacit Agreements

We have been discussing in this chapter, not *how* scientific work is carried out, but rather those aspects of scientific practice which have to do with the creation of the body of scientific literature. The control of written publications through the referee system plays a very important role in the exchange of information among contemporary scientists. However, there are several other aspects of the manner in which scientific debate is conducted which ought to be brought to attention.

There are certain tacit understandings among scientists which are generally recognized as forming a code of scientific ethics. These are nowhere written down as rules. In the course of his scientific training, however, it is assumed that every young scientist will come to an understanding of the ethics governing the professional behavior of his colleagues and will learn how to carry on his own work in accordance with these ethical standards.

While science deals with the world of objective phenomena, there are always areas of scientific understanding which give rise to debate and controversy. We want to review a few items in the code of scientific ethics which apply specifically to scientific debate or controversy.

1. A scientific debate should be about a scientific subject. This may seem very obvious, but there are areas in the environmental debate where scientific issues become confused with socioeconomic problems. One may conduct a scientific debate about whether a certain amount of thermal enrichment of receiving waters near a power plant will or will not kill fish, but one cannot argue on a scientific basis that people should give up air conditioners because their use leads to a proliferation of power generators. A scientist can calculate the approximate increment in power use represented by the operation of air conditioners, but in his professional role he cannot dictate whether, or how, cuts should be made on energy demand. These are essentially political and social questions.

2. When one scientist debates with another—in print or orally—he may be absolutely devastating in his intellectual arguments, but he is supposed to separate the opus from the person; hence there is no place for innuendo, name-calling, or other methods of blackening the reputation of the opponent which are unrelated to the scientific subject matter of the debate.

3. The work of a scientist must be open to scrutiny. If his hypothesis is unsound on any grounds, he must be ready to be attacked and see his hypothesis refuted. Once refuted, he cannot pursue the point further unless new evidence is amassed. It is also understood that other scientists holding similar views will

refrain from citing his already refuted hypothesis in support of their own arguments.

4. An unproven hypothesis or speculation advanced by someone else should not be quoted in support of one's own views in such a manner as to suggest that it is already an established fact or accepted theory.

5. It is not proper for a scientist to cite evidence or publications in support of his views while ignoring opposing evidence.

6. Where there is serious disagreement about the conclusions to be drawn from available evidence, scientists may battle among themselves for a considerable period; but so long as the disagreement is unsettled, the proponents of one position should not enlist the support of public opinion on their side. Press conferences may be a way of announcing an important discovery to the public, but they are improperly used as a means of publicizing the arguments of only one "camp" in an important scientific controversy.

7. Whenever possible, impartial panels of appropriate experts will be sought to evaluate all the evidence giving rise to controversial interpretations. Appointment to such panels ought to be declined by those who do not feel that they can be impartial—viz., by anyone who has already taken sides in the controversy.

8. In general, a scientist is expected to refrain from misusing the authority of his title.

9. Although personal ambition must be recognized as a natural propensity, it should not supersede the pursuit of scientific truth.

10. The pursuit of scientific understanding should not be subordinated either to an ideology or to a "higher cause."

In the last few years, many speculations having to do with ecology, environmental medicine, and related topics have been circulating. There is no hard and fast rule that a scientist should not speculate: indeed, where he is dealing with certain fascinating but as yet insoluble problems, it is natural that he should do so. It is understood, however, that speculations should be clearly labeled as such, so that there is no danger that anyone else, scientist or nonscientist, should mistake a speculative statement for a factual report.

But in addition to labeling speculations as such, common sense dictates whether or not it is appropriate to air one's speculations to a popular audience. It is one thing, for example, to speculate (without any real evidence) that there *may* be some form of life on Mars. That is exciting and stimulates the imagination, and nobody is likely to mistake the speculation for a factual claim. It is quite another thing to speculate (also without any real evidence) that—let us say— eating chocolate ice cream during pregnancy may result in birth defects. The second speculation may be mistaken by laymen for a fact; it may frighten a sizeable number of women for no good reason; and it has no redeeming value as a stimulus to intellect or imagination.

The lay reader may get the impression that adherence to the rather strict ethics of scientific debate or speculation we enumerated would require an inhuman kind of objectivity, and that it would inhibit the scientist from becoming deeply involved in his own ideas. However, this is not really so, for one may be impassioned about an idea without feeling personally affronted when someone opposes it. It is also possible to be very excited and involved in a hypothesis, and yet to give it up gracefully when it is proved wrong. The scientist has to be willing to risk defeat, but for a person with an inquiring mind, there is usually a new and equally interesting idea just around the corner. There is so much yet to be discovered about the world in which we live that there is no need to fear for any want of excitement in the mental life of a scientist. If the community of scientists insist that the ethics we have discussed are essential to science, it is not because they are traditionalists who regard these "rules of behavior" as they might some arbitrary forms of social etiquette; it is rather because they want to maintain an atmosphere of mental clarity and honor in the world of science, so that the wellspring of truth and understanding should not be muddied by confusion or personal motives.

4

THE PROSTITUTION OF SCIENCE

But of all wrong there is none more
heinous than that of those who when
they deceive us most grossly, so do
it as to seem good men.

CICERO

Scientists are human beings, with the same potential for virtue or for weakness as other members of the race. As individuals, they are no less corruptible than are politicians, or auto mechanics, or persons with any other professional label. They also share with all people the potential for errors in judgment and for making simple mistakes. But while individual scientists are not immune from human error or moral failings, science as such is supposed to represent incorruptible truths—truths which are, to be sure, subject to correction by the progress of our understanding and therefore not immutable, but nonetheless truths which stand apart from the often confused and non-virtuous interactions between individuals or groups in human society.

It is fashionable these days to denigrate science, either because scientists are said to be "amoral," or because too many of them serve the so-called "military-industrial complex."

We do not believe that amorality characterizes the personal attitudes of contemporary scientists, even though the objectivity necessitated by their training may make it appear so. To disabuse oneself of this notion, it is sufficient to read a biography of either Niels Bohr or Albert Einstein. Even though both were involved in the Manhattan Project, if their almost Herculean efforts to influence Allied statesmen had succeeded, the events at Hiroshima and Nagasaki need not have been written into human history, and it is possible that the postwar armaments race could also have been avoided.

There is certainly justification, on the other hand, for saying that science may become corrupted when it serves the needs of a power-seeking group, whether that group is called the military establishment, the barons of industry, or the Nazi "saviors" of the Aryan race. Usually when one talks about this kind of corruption, one means either that the researches of scientists have resulted in some kind of technological breakthrough which can be employed by self-seeking groups for their own ends, and that the scientists who performed the original investigations are ethically indifferent to the final uses of the "pure" discovery; or that the scientist works directly for a group in power and in this way "sells out," abandoning scientific integrity in the interests of money or prestige or even just plain security.

It is generally thought that the disciplines of physics and chemistry are much more vulnerable to these varieties of corruption than are the various branches of biology, since biologists are less likely to make discoveries which can be immediately extended into technological applications serving the purposes of special-interest groups. This is more or less true at the present time, with some exceptions which we need not go into here.

What is all too often forgotten, however, is that any branch of science may be corrupted in an entirely different way: that is, in its most basic levels of theory and practice. This may occur when the practitioners of a branch of science grant greater weight to the tenets of a defined belief system, a political ideology, or any kind of social cause, than they give to the fundamental principles of science itself. There are many historical examples of such subordination of science to belief systems. One of the best documented episodes in recent history is the rise to power of the Lysenkoist "creative biologists" in the Soviet Union to the story of which we will now devote some attention.

The Reformation of Decadent Western Biology

The developments in biology in the Soviet Union during the Stalinist era provide an excellent example of how an entire scientific discipline may become distorted by ideological extremism. The Russian agronomist Trofim D. Lysenko, filled with communist zeal, took it upon himself to reform biology, which was ridden with "dangerous" Western concepts. Although Lysenko was a mediocre researcher, he was undoubtedly possessed of considerable ambition and was a crafty politician. Aided eventually by the personal support of Stalin, he succeeded in altering the whole structure of Russian biological thinking, and he and his followers dominated the field for a period of about thirty years. In accordance with the anti-Western views which Stalin held to so strongly, the Lysenkoists threw out most of the known laws of genetics and embryology and reinterpreted Darwin's teachings to fit the framework of what they called the "new creative biology," which was more consistent with the Stalinist view of reality. Lysenko himself wrote a work which had the marvelously unwieldy subtitle *A New Characterization of the Concept of Biological Species, or the Fight Against the Ideological Basis of the Reactionary Mendel-Morgan Theories, the Falsification of Darwin's Teachings* (1951).

Lysenko and his coworkers accepted and even praised Darwin's teachings on evolution (while rejecting Western neo-Darwinian interpretations), but they had to point out some of the "shortcomings" in his work and "correct" them. There were three important points in Darwin's thesis which were not acceptable from the point of view of Stalinist Marxism. These were:

1. Darwin's denial of evolutionary revolutions (or macromutations, in Goldschmidt's terminology). Darwin believed that evolution takes place at an exceedingly slow pace, through the divergence of almost imperceptible features in subsequent generations.

2. His rejection of Lamarck's hypothesis that acquired characteristics can be inherited.

3. His concept of intraspecific competition.

To understand why these three rather central points in Darwin's teachings were unacceptable to the Lysenkoist biologists, one has to take into account the social ideology of the Stalinist version of Marxism. The idea that slowly accumulating *quantitative* changes are bound to result, at some point, in a change in *quality* served as the very basis of the Theory of Revolution in the writings of Marx, and was also eloquently defended by Engels in his *Anti-Dühring*. To make biology consistent with social theory, this thesis was extended to apply to the whole of the living world. Thus, according to the Lysenkoist interpretation of evolutionary theory, there are times in the speciation process when the slowly accumulating quantitative environmental effects will produce a sudden qualitative change in certain offspring, resulting in a new species.

The debate about whether or not acquired characteristics can be inherited is an old one, but as far as Western biologists are concerned the matter was long ago settled in favor of Darwin's rather than Lamarck's view. To Darwin's followers, including contemporary molecular biologists, the noninheritability of characteristics acquired during the lifetime of an organism is a "central dogma."[*] Weissmann's idea of the immutability of the "germ plasma" to environmental effects is basically still retained: it is, however, now expressed in terms of a newer terminology. We now say that DNA (desoxyribonucleic acid—the molecule in the nucleus of the cell which carries the hereditary information determining all the characteristics of an organism) is self-replicating; that is, it contains all the information necessary to multiply itself and also to define and direct the synthesis of proteins, the basic building blocks of living organisms. It is thought that, since the self-replicating potential of DNA is encoded in the very structure of the molecule itself, external influence[†] cannot alter the process. According to this reasoning, characteristics which were acquired during the lifetime of an organism cannot effect a change in the defined and hereditarily submitted structure of DNA. Clearly, therefore, acquired characteristics cannot become hereditary.

Lysenkoist biologists claimed, on the other hand, that the cytoplasm plays a role of equal importance with that of the nucleus (where the DNA is located) in defining hereditary characteristics. They thought that the cytoplasm could serve as a "plastic material" for the engramming of environmental conditions, and that its protein structure (which they called its "base plasma") would somehow reflect more or less permanently the sum total of environmental influences to which the organism would be exposed during its lifetime. Their reasoning was that if the cytoplasm plays an important role in defining and transmitting hereditary information, and *if* this information could be influenced or changed through the imprinting of environmental factors on the basic structure of the cytoplasm, then, indeed, acquired characteristics would be inheritable.

The extreme importance of this thesis to Lysenko's purposes becomes evident if we examine it on two different levels. On the one hand, there were the practical considerations of the ambitious and hard-pressed agronomist. If ac-

---

[*] This rather curious term has become, since the 1960s, a regular and accepted part of the jargon of molecular biologists.

[†] There are a few known exceptions, notably ionizing radiation. See the discussion in Chapter 12.

quired characteristics can be inherited, many possibilities open up for changing natural species to the advantage of agriculturists. (It should be remembered that one of the biggest problems faced by the Soviet Union in the 1940s was their inability to produce enough food to support the population, after the ruinous policies of Stalin's forced collectivization of the peasants.) The thinking of the Lysenkoists went in something like the following fashion. With extensive training, a man's musculature can be developed in such a way that he becomes a "muscle man," or athlete. Similarly, a cow can be trained to deliver as much as 50 liters of milk per day, given enough attention and conditioning. Now if this productive capacity of the cow (which is an acquired characteristic) is at least theoretically inheritable, then we have only to find a way to *make* the characteristic inheritable, and within a few years, we will revolutionize dairy production, with all Soviet cows happily and naturally delivering 50 liters of milk per day.

The other level at which the theory of imprinting new inheritable characteristics assumed great importance in Stalinist Russia was the level of human social consciousness. The "new Soviet man," as characterized by Stalin, was to be *qualitatively* different from his predecessors. He would work for the common good, but neither out of desire for personal wealth nor because he would be forced to do so. After having proudly and joyfully carried out his work to the best of his abilities and having been rewarded by society according to his needs, the new man would have only one goal: to improve himself, his awareness, his vision of humanity as a whole; to reach an understanding of himself and the world around him through the constant application of the dialectic process of criticism and self-criticism. It was realized that it would take a long time before the whole society would be made up of this new type of man, if one accepted that the evolutionary process is exceedingly slow and gradual. On the other hand, if one were to grant that acquired characteristics can be inherited, then the possibility would be given of developing the new humanity rapidly through education. Makarenko, the educator, became the "Smith of the New Man," and the process of altering the old "oppressed man" through "educational engineering" was begun. The hope was that the communist ethics could be *imprinted* on the present generation and *transmitted by heredity* to the next, who would then already embody a whole society of the new human type. (This "hope" had nothing to do with eugenics, which had become, by the time of Lysenko's elevation to total power, a taboo subject among Soviet biologists.)

The third point on which the Lysenkoist biologists "corrected" Darwin — their outright denial of intraspecific competition — was essential to justify the doctrine of "lasting peace," which was to follow on world acceptance of the communist ideology. If it were true, as Darwin had claimed, that it is an inherent, biologically determined characteristic of a species for its members to compete with each other, then war could never be abolished, even within a world communist system. Stalinist Marxism taught that war as a means of settling conflicts among earlier or even present societies was either a direct result of the exploitation of an oppressed people, or an expression of the desire to expand exploitation. When exploitation ceases to be a factor in social interactions—as would, of course, be the case in a communist world society—then war should automatically become obsolete. Hence it was necessary to "clear" Darwin's teachings of the embarrassing notion of intraspecific competition.*

Lysenkoism in Practice

These, then, are some of the theoretical underpinnings of Lysenkoist biology, seen in the light of their logical relations with the social ideology of Stalinist Marxism. But what of its practical workings? Again there are three main points to be taken into account:

1. The focus of Lysenkoist biology was on production. It was necessary to demonstrate the *practical relevance* of biology to the needs of society. As Bukharin said in 1935: ". . . pure science was a morbid symptom of a class society; under socialism the conception of science pursued for its own sake would disappear, for the interests of scientists would spontaneously turn to problems of the current Five Year Plan" (quoted in Polányi, 1966, p. 3).

2. Amassing of evidence was substituted for causal proof as the means of demonstrating the "correctness" of the underlying hypotheses.

3. Ideological zeal took precedence over pure devotion to science; hence those who failed to conform to the tenets of the new biology could be silenced or suppressed as enemies of the truth. Also, it did not really matter if the Lysenkoist biologists manipulated somewhat their data or their experimental results, since minor falsifications could still support the ideological cause, which represented a higher level of truth than the precise reporting of facts.

During the three decades of the reign of "creative biology" in the Soviet Union, its practitioners never managed to breed a line of cows which would give 50 liters of milk daily, but they did succeed in producing some interesting biologi-

---

* In the Western philosophical tradition, it is generally believed that human consciousness can transcend man's biologically determined nature; therefore the hope that man may cease to war upon his fellow human beings does not necessarily preclude acceptance of the concept of intraspecific competition as a biological phenomenon.

cal curiosities. In the realm of botany, for instance, they rejected Mendelian genetics and concentrated instead on creative grafting techniques. Out of these efforts came a number of weird products like a huge fruit which was a combination of a grapefruit, an orange, and a lemon. Unfortunately, it tasted like the latter, but it was proudly exhibited throughout Russia and the satellite countries. An even greater triumph was the successful crossing of an apple, a rose, and a prune, since this demonstrated that grafting could be accomplished across the subfamily barriers. The resultant product in this case looked like an apple, smelled like a rose, and tasted like a prune!

We have also to look at an example of how the Lysenkoists rested their case on evidence. They insisted that there was no urgency in proceeding to establish a causal, scientific proof of the claims which they based on the amassing of evidence. For example, the claim was made that rye (a species) could develop from wheat (a different species) under certain favorable environmental conditions, such as a colder and drier climate. To provide evidence in support of this claim, huge acreages of wheat were planted in climates favoring the growth of rye. Following the harvest, hundreds of thousands of individual grains were examined. The overwhelming majority of these were wheat, but a certain small proportion of the grains were unquestionably rye. There was the evidence: wheat, under appropriate environmental conditions, had given rise to rye! When these seeds were planted, the offspring were a well-acclimatized rye form. This was undoubtedly the greatest triumph of the Lysenkoists, for unlike the weird fruits which could only be produced by grafting, the transformation of wheat into rye was supposedly hereditary!

A few conservative elements in the scientific community suggested that since the combines used to harvest the wheat fields had been employed in the previous year to harvest rye in the same region, the few rye seeds found among the wheat sample might have been contaminants remaining in the equipment. But the critics were quickly silenced and branded as lackeys of the imperialist, idealist school of Weissman-Morgan Western biology.

In order to produce better evidence for the wheat-rye transformation, some zealous "scientists" went further: they replaced a few of the wheat kernels on spikes of wheat with pasted-in rye grains (Iakubtsiner, 1952). A description of such "miraculous plants" and an account of other interesting ways in which changes of one species into another were "proven" are given in Karapetian's monograph in *Agrobiologiia* (1948).

Another tragic aspect of the dominance of Lysenko's ideas was that in addition to suppressing its critics and retarding Russian biology for a period of 30 years, some of the best minds in Russian science either became infected with this apparent madness, or were forced to get around it in one way or another, if they wanted to continue their real work. Thus Kozo-Polianskii, an eminent geneticist and embryologist, was apparently "converted" and took to writing treatises in the political-ideological tone, such as *The Fight Against Reactionary Idealism in Plant Morphology* (1951). Other scientists, who were skeptical, but were threatened with loss of their working and publishing opportunities if they did not conform to these views, were forced to adjust the direction of their research or to contribute some kind of work which was in accord with the Stalinist ideology. Thus, for example, V. L. Komarow—a botanist of the first rank—delivered lectures with titles like "The Role of the Creative Soviet Biology in the Awakening of the Self-Awareness of the Working Classes" (1952). Only following such acts of "penitence" could he return to work on his monumental and truly important *Flora of the USSR.*

Some who refused to yield to the new ideological dominance in Soviet biology or who were regarded as too dangerous were permanently silenced. Vavilov, for instance, who was recognized as one of the world's greatest geneticists and was at one time the president of the Soviet Agricultural Academy, died in a concentration camp. Finally, there were those who wanted to retain their scientific integrity and were not willing to bow to the new Russian chauvinism (which forbade publication in the "decadent" Western languages), so they published whole books in Latin. This not only got them around the letter of the linguistic regulation, but it also permitted them to evade the censors, who were not altogether fluent in the classical language used by the scholarly scientists.

What Does Lysenkoism Teach Us?

For the most part, scientists and historians in the Western world tend to dismiss the period of Lysenkoist biology in Russia as a kind of temporary aberration in the history of science. But if we merely write it off as a pseudoscience, tossing in a few expressions of admiration for those real scientists who had the courage during the Stalinist era to oppose Lysenko, we may miss some of what Lysenkoism has to teach us.

One thing not usually pointed out is that Lysenkoist biology has a strong internal consistency, and that if one looks at it within the context of the *belief system* which is its point of departure, it is impeccably logical. The Lysenkoist biologists stood with both feet solidly planted in the world of Stalinist Marxism. Since both Marx and Stalin had praised Darwin, they could hardly throw out his whole opus, but they felt no obligation to maintain links—either in terms of language or of concepts—with the traditions of Western biology. On the contrary, they tried consciously to separate themselves from this tradition. Now we hasten to add that internal consistency does not make "creative biology," or Marxism, or any other system of "closed logic" right or acceptable. However, it does have the advantage of making it very much easier for those who stand outside the basic belief system to perceive what is going on and to formulate their criticisms against a clear background.

Lysenkoism was a dogma, but if we describe it as "unscientific" on these grounds, we forget that the neo-Darwinian ideas accepted by most Western biologists are also dogmatic. These ideas are so well established in our thinking that we tend to view any observations from the laboratory or the world of nature which do not "fit" into the neo-Darwinian concepts as phenomena which are not yet completely understood, but which will undoubtedly be integrated eventually into the basic framework. We forget, too, that the very phrase "Theory of Evolution," by which we usually refer in English to Darwin's conceptual contribution to biology, is a misnomer; for in strict usage a theory is a hypothesis which has yielded to what is called proof, whereas Darwin's system is in actuality no more than a working hypothesis. Perhaps, because this is forgotten, there is a tendency either to ignore any individual biologist who dares to question the absolute value of the neo-Darwinian outlook, or even to brand him as a heretic.

It may also be said that Western science, as a whole, represents only one among many possible approaches to the investigation and description of reality. This statement would surely be denied with vehemence by most practicing Western scientists; but those who have given some thought to the history and development of cultures other than our own generally either freely admit that there are other kinds of science, or are forced to "explain away" the scientific efforts of other civilizations by describing them in derogatory terms, such as "superstitious," or "primitive," or "prescientific."

An interesting example of a practice based on an entirely different system of science is that of Chinese acupuncture. Until very recently, this method was dismissed by most Western thinkers with one or another kind of debunking phrase. However, the cautious positive reports lately released by teams of Western physicians who observed the practice in China have piqued the curiosity of scientists, and it is now at least a respectable subject for discussion. Should we conclude that Chinese acupuncture is, indeed, an effective method for treating certain kinds of ailments or for inducing a nonnarcotic anaesthesia, we will be in a most embarrassing position if we try to assimilate it into our medical *theory*, because the body points described as critical in the Chinese method do not appear to correspond to anything we could call anatomical reality. If, on the other hand, we come to the conclusion that the method has pragmatic value (that is to say that it "works" in some way which cannot be satisfactorily explained as due to suggestion), we could, if we so chose, incorporate its *practice* as an adjunct to our applied medicine and still acknowledge that the anatomical principles on which it is based belong to another system of describing reality.

The point we are trying to bring out is that there are aspects of scientific inquiry which clearly cannot be reduced to final proof. These may become most easily apparent when we compare two completely disparate approaches to science, but they are also to be found within our Western scientific tradition in those areas which may be characterized as interpretive stances. Darwin's concept of evolutionary development (as well as the neo-Darwinian position) is an example of a broadly interpretive view of scientific realities which rests at least in part on philosophical preference rather than on final proof. If this statement is accepted, then it follows that we cannot judge Lysenkoist biology as "wrong" solely on the grounds that it denied some of the tenets of neo-Darwinian thought.

But to admit that there are other possible approaches to science and even that some of our scientific interpretations have an element of subjective or cultural preference is not to deny the greatness of Western scientific achievements. Furthermore, we can judge Lysenkoist biology on other grounds than its evolutionary hypotheses. From the point of view of its *accomplishments,* we can say that it does not seem to correspond to reality as well as does Western biology. Surely Borlaug's new strains of wheat are of far greater value to agriculture than were Lysenko's curious fruits. From the point of view of *methodology,* we can criticize the substitution of "evidence" for "proof," because where experimentation rather than broad interpretation is concerned, it may rightly be claimed that proof is essential to support new hypotheses. From the *ethical* point of view, we may judge Lysenkoism harshly on two grounds: (1) that it subordinated the pursuit of scientific truth to a circumscribed social ideology; (2) that it suppressed its critics, either through innuendo or through outright oppression, using all of the destructive machinery of the police state.

Echoes of Lysenkoism in the United States: the Qualitative Jump

Now surely you must be wondering why we have recounted at such length the story of Lysenkoist biology in Stalinist Russia, and why we bother to draw such apparent hairline distinctions with respect to the relative value of differing scientific views. What has this to do with the environmental scientists?

Do we think they are communists? Or secret followers of Lysenko? Hardly, for with a few exceptions, most environmentalists seem to be more conservative than radical in outlook, despite their rather odd appeal to the "romantic" American left. Furthermore, they deplore the abuses of nature in the Soviet materialist state almost as vehemently as they do those which they claim are perpetrated by the American "Establishment." As far as the second suggestion is concerned, that is out too, for probably without exception the American biologists and naturalists involved in the environemtal movement think of themselves as carrying on the mainstream of the Darwinian tradition.

What we mean to bring to the reader's attention is the possibility that, without consciously imitating Lysenko, some aspects of the theories, the methodology, and even the ethics of the environmentalist scientists suggest curious echoes of the Lysenkoist period in Soviet biology. We hasten to add that the scientists in the vanguard of the environmental movement whose concepts or practices are most reminiscent of Lysenkoism have probably never consciously examined either the implications of their thinking or its links with the past. This, however, does not make of them "innocents," for science, like the law, does not recognize ignorance as an exonerating factor. Indeed, the fact that they do not articulate clearly their differences with generally accepted Western biological ideas makes them, in some respects, perhaps more dangerous to the future of biology than was Lysenko, for the very confusion of the thinking of some environmentalists makes it extremely difficult to define in what respects it may be wrong—or at least unacceptable within the system of traditional biology.

Since the unraveling of this confusion at the most basic levels of scientific theory and practice could be the material of another long book, we are again forced to oversimplify. The brief critique which follows should therefore be taken merely as a basis for arriving at a perspective about the scientific claims advanced by some of the prominent environmentalists.

At the theoretical level, there are two basic claims which have been repeatedly put forth and which do not seem to fit into the structure of Western biological thinking. The first is that the presence and continuing release on man's part of poisonous substances into the environment, *in no matter how minute quantities*, is bound eventually to result in disastrous changes in living species. According to some environmentalists certain agents, such as heavy metals and persistent pesticides, are incorporated into all natural produce and are insidiously accumulating in our own bodies (or in organisms high on the food chain). Eventually these small quantitative additions will build up to a point where they will result in a sudden qualitative change in the state of the organism: intoxication, death, or modifications in the genetic material. These changes may not take place during our lifetimes, but we can confidently predict them because we "know" that living organisms are not equipped to handle the impact of all these toxins, especially those which have been made artificially by man.

Now it has to be admitted that some environmentalists are careful to stick to the threshold theory,* and do *not* accept the notion that continuous exposure to even the most minute quantities of persistent toxins will inevitably lead to a qualitative change. However, it is not just the lay writers like Rachel Carson who favor this hypothesis, despite its lack of accord with both classical toxicology and with Western evolutionary thought; one hears this argument expressed in varying degrees of precise articulation by many scientists involved in the movement, especially those who concentrate their attentions on the health dangers of pollution. A few of the environmentalists who argue that there is *no tolerance* for dangerous toxins and that their gradual accumulation will eventually lead to a sudden qualitative change may be aware that they are putting forth a hypothesis which clashes with the established theories of classical Western toxicology; probably most are not. Commoner writes, for example: ". . . many of the new synthetic substances act on basic biochemical processes that occur in some form in all living things; therefore some effect on all forms of life must be anticipated. Since some of these pollutants appear to increase the incidence of cancer and the rate of mutation, it is entirely possible that, like radiation, they act on the cell's system of inheritance. Such changes in inheritance may persist in the offspring of the affected organism. The changes are thereby perpetuated and result in an additive risk of eventual biological harm" (Commoner, 1963, p. 96).

It is almost certain, however, that most environmentalists do not recognize in these ideas an echo of the Stalinist thought of "revolutionary evolution" — that is, the concept that the accumulation of quantitative changes will lead to a sudden qualitative jump (in the speciation process, for instance), which concept is unacceptable to any neo-Darwinian biologist. Either they do not remember much about the history of biology, or they do not notice the parallel because the Lysenkoists were predicting positive leaps in evolution, whereas the environmentalists are anticipating either species extinction or deleterious mutations as the expression of this qualitative change. Nevertheless, the parallel is there.

The Inheritance of Acquired Characteristics

The second theoretical echo of Stalinist biology has to do with the inheritability of acquired characteristics. The argument between Lamarckians and Darwinians went on for a long time in the West but it is generally accepted that the

*See Chapter 11.

notion that acquired characteristics can become inheritable was put to rest around the turn of this century. Apparently not to its final rest, however, for we find it cropping up in the thinking of some environmentalists, although they do not spell it out in precise terms. If we turn, for instance, to Barry Commoner's book *Science and Survival* (1963), we can see that this idea underlies some of his claims about genetics.

In a chapter entitled: "Greater Than the Sum of Its Parts," Commoner argues that molecular biology is not really giving us answers about what life is, because even though the molecular biologists have succeeded in defining the characteristics of the DNA molecule (cracking the genetic code), they have only been able to do so because they are working on dead cells. There are probably some who would agree with his holistic generalization, for the number of biologists in the West who are holists is a fairly sizable minority and there are many who state that—in spite of its dramatic advances in the last fifteen years—molecular biology has still plenty of limitations and a long way to go. However, Commoner is not content with merely pointing out that molecular biology does not hold all the answers about the nature of life. He advances his own hypothesis about the role played by cellular constituents *outside the DNA* in hereditary processes.

> Certainly there is good experimental evidence to support the idea that DNA does influence the hereditary characteristics of living cells in which it occurs, but this is also true of other cellular constituents, such as the enzyme that synthesizes DNA. . . . The "central dogma" involves an admittedly unproven assumption: that while nucleic acids can guide the synthesis of other nucleic acids and of proteins, the reverse effect is impossible—that is, proteins cannot guide the synthesis of nucleic acids. But actual experimental observations deny the second, and crucial, part of this assumption. . . . some proteins—for example, the enzyme that synthesizes DNA— can contribute to the guidance of the synthesis of nucleic acid and help to determine the order in which *its* constituents—nucleotides—appear in the nucleic-acid fiber. (Commoner, 1963, pp. 39–40)

This is not the place to go into the matter of whether the experimental evidence which Commoner speaks about is acceptable or not. Our purpose here is to point out that, whether he realizes it or not, Commoner is implying that acquired characteristics can be inherited. If the DNA molecule itself is only partly responsible for the determination of hereditary patterns, and if the cytoplasmic proteins (i.e., the DNA-synthesizing enzymes) are equally important in the transmission of characteristics, then environmental effects in the form of acquired characteristics could influence the code sequence of DNA and make possible their transmission to the offspring. Commoner admits that he holds a minority view, but it is very unlikely that he would identify his own ideas with Lamarckism or Lysenkoism. Yet once again, if one examines the implications of the ideas expressed, the parallel is there.

Lysenkoist Methods

Now we hasten to point out that, just as we said that one cannot on solely theoretical grounds, dismiss Lysenko's interpretations of evolutionary theory as definitely "wrong," neither can anyone say with certainty that the two respects in which some of the environmentalists diverge from the mainstream of Western neo-Darwinian thinking are "wrong." They are different interpretations, which are unacceptable to most scientists, but since they deal with matters of broad interpretive stances, no one can say with certainty that they might not have some truth in them. Nevertheless, there are two problems involved here, quite aside from the question of rightness or wrongness.

The first is that the resurgence of these ideas, which had long been rejected by Western biologists, is apparently going on unconsciously in the minds of most of those who entertain them. They attempt to work as Western scientists, but fail to inform us that they are operating from basic premises which are not part of Western biological thinking—probably because they themselves do not recognize this. As we mentioned earlier in connection with acupuncture, we feel that knowing and clearly establishing the system in which one is thinking and working is actually much more important than any judgments regarding the absolute superiority of one system over another. Without such clarity, divergence from the mainstream of tradition can only lead to confusion for everybody.

The second difficulty with those who are entertaining these non-Western ideas leads us directly into matters of scientific methods, for like the Lysenkoists, many of the environmentalists seem to feel that the accumulation of evidence is enough to support their speculations, especially since time is pressing, and if we wait around for cause-and-effect proof, it may be already too late to "save the ship."

A succinct expression of this idea was voiced by Michael Belkap, Director of the Mayor's Council on the Environment in New York City: "Although proof of the cause-and-effect of pollution and disease is not established, the evidence is overwhelming" (Belkap, 1971).

At first we thought that this statement was an atypical formulation of environmental non-think. However, having discussed it with some of our environmentalist colleagues, we had to conclude that, on the contrary, the substitution of evidence for causal proof is a typical feature of the movement. But the "overwhelming evidence" implicating environmental pollutants as causing disease is equally meaningless—in lack of rigorous proof—within the framework of our science, as was Lysenko's "evidence" that wheat could be transformed into rye under differing environmental conditions.

Some environmentalists, on the other hand, recognizing the need to establish causal relationships, have made attempts to demonstrate experimentally (and thus prove) at least one of their claims: that is, the ultimately harmful or even fatal effects of slowly accumulating environmental poisons. Many of these investigations center around the persistent pesticide DDT, and a detailed criticism of some of these experiments and their results will be given in Part III.

Although we have not caught any environmentalist pasting rye grains onto ears of wheat, we have noted some more subtle ways in which the experimental method and data evaluation appear to have been manipulated, so that the results would support the preconceived certitude of the investigators. Even though one cannot define a precise ideology permeating the environmental movement, may one not infer that where such "adjustment of data" takes place, it must be an expression of the subordination of scientific truth to a "higher cause"? That the ethics of scientific debate are also frequently abandoned in the service of this "higher cause" is demonstrated by the reaction of many environmentalists to refutations of their work. Instead of either abandoning an unsound hypothesis or defending it against adverse criticism strictly on scientific grounds, they often resort to the use of innuendo or ad hominem attacks to discredit their opponents.

In summary, one could state that if Lysenkoist biology had merely represented concepts about the workings of nature which were different from our own we should have critically evaluated its results, and integrated them into our science or rejected them as unacceptable purely on their merits. Even if the results had had no practical value, we might have cherished "creative biology" for its invigorating novelty. However, because the Lysenkoists not only presented new concepts but also took upon themselves a charismatic mission and claimed to be the sole representatives of truth, and—blessed by the system whose ideology they served—felt no trepidation at stamping out their adversaries through innuendo, intimidation, denunciation, or falsifications, they lost their claim to the title of scientists, pursuers of truth, and furtherers of human understanding. By the same token, if the environmentalists were to content themselves with the presentation of new ideas which, although unacceptable in the terms of our present concepts about the workings of nature, might have in them some kernels of truth, we should cherish their insight and courage in bringing these problems to the attention of an all-too-conservative scientific Establishment. But when, in their ideological fervor, they employ tactics of innuendo, intimidation, and falsification, they are no better than were their Soviet colleagues, for they prostitute science by subjugating it to a zealot's cause.

5

POWER
FOR THE PEOPLE

. . . one of the most immediate dangers . . . is that
too slavish a concern for what is thought to be ecology
will inhibit people from taking prudent
steps to safeguard the future of the human race.

JOHN MADDOX

In the previous chapter we pointed to some of the curious parallels on the theoretical level between Lysenkoist biology and
ideas espoused by certain leaders of the American environmental movement.
In the chapters which form Part III, we shall be bringing out some unfortunate
similarities in the methods by which the environmentalists proselytize their beliefs and "apply" science in support of preconceived ideas. Here we should like
to examine certain components of the social background which permitted the
rise of these pseudoscientific campaigns in both the Soviet Union and the United
States.

From the outset, however, we had best make it clear that these parallels are not intended to be taken literally, nor should they be carried too far. We are hardly suggesting that any American "Establishment scientist" or stubborn classicist would be sent off to Siberia or its equivalent, even were the most extreme scientist spokesmen for environmentalism to achieve real power or win a majority of legislators and government administrators over to their cause. The United States may have its own sociopolitical difficulties, but it is hardly a terrorist police state. Nor do we mean to imply that all American scientists who are involved in environmental activism have abandoned professional ethics or separated themselves from scientific traditions without conscious reflection. Any similarities between the two movements have to be examined from a common-sense point of view and taken with a grain of salt.

It must also be said that one of the underlying factors which conditioned the rise of the American environmental movement is undoubtedly our unparalleled national prosperity, and in this respect conditions in the United States in the 1960s and 1970s could not be more different from those in the Soviet Union during the postrevolutionary period. Nevertheless, in spite of the marked discrepancies in economic growth, and despite tremendous differences in social structure, technological status, and ideology of postrevolutionary Russia and contemporary America, there are some common sociological factors which may serve as partial explanations for the receptivity of the populace to these mass movements.

After the Bolshevik Revolution

The most urgent task faced by the new rulers of Russia after the revolution was the modernization of agriculture. Russian farm production was still at a medieval level. In order to industrialize the country rapidly—a basic tenet of Leninism—the only possibility, since foreign capital was not available, was to extract as much capital from farming as possible. The young Bolshevik State therefore turned with great hopes to the introduction and actualization of advanced agricultural practices. Some of these had already been worked out in experiments by the unquestionably excellent agronomists and plant geneticists of Russia, and for others, the plan was to follow the highly successful pattern of agricultural extension services of the U.S. Department of Agriculture. These professionals had the most enthusiastic support of the Politburo, and they set to work on the tremendous task of aiding the Russian peasant to condense 500 years of progress into a few decades. Some of the experts made rather optimistic forecasts in these early days, clearly underestimating many of the practical obstacles. When it became evident that the more cautious forecasts were correct and that it would be some decades before agricultural productivity could be raised to Western standards, although most of the professionals were prepared to be realistic and reassess their potential rate of progress, both the masses and the party rulers became disillusioned with the scientists. In years of decreasing yields, the climate of impatience and dissatisfaction was high. It was in such an atmosphere that the practical field man Trofim Denisovich Lysenko was "discovered" by a sensational journalist, Fedorovich.

Lysenko had ready remedies for all the ills besetting Russian agriculture and he also had the qualities of a people's hero: conviction, enthusiasm, charisma, and the "right" origins—that is, he was not a member of the intelligentsia. Already, in his first interview, he vehemently attacked the ruling agricultural scientific Establishment, accusing them of dragging their feet in splendid isolation in their ivory towers instead of doing relevant work.

Once public attention was focused on him and he had received some limited support, he always reported fantastic successes from his experiments, and he was ready with simple solutions for all kinds of problems. We select just one, to give the reader some idea of what went on. In southern Russia, potato degeneration is a serious problem. Seed potatoes cannot be grown in the area because of a viral disease which attacks the seed. Agronomists knew the cause of the problem and they had recommended and continued to recommend that seed potatoes should be shipped yearly from the north—over several thousands of miles—for planting in the south. By shipping only certified, virus-free seeds, or by breeding resistant strains, they proposed that within 10 years, they could eliminate the virus. On the other hand, Lysenko claimed that potato degeneration results from hot temperatures and had nothing to do with viruses. (In fact, he later even denied the existence of viruses—with which proclamation he killed Russian virology.) His solution was simple: potatoes should be planted in the summer for late fall harvest; in this way degeneration from heat would be avoided. To the politicians, such a solution seemed cheap, simple, and promising, and several decrees that potatoes must be planted in the summer were made, coupled with tremendous newspaper campaigns to educate the peasants. A few years later, by the time the disastrous failure of the program was evident—in spite of "selective" favorable reports— Lysenko had moved on to "solutions" to other problems.

In retrospect it is clear that all of Lysenko's problem-solving methods were pseudosolutions based on pseudoscience. One can understand how the desperate situation of Russian farm productivity led the urban masses and the party leaders to champion his school. Nevertheless, this does not alter the fact that his were not workable solutions, and Russian agriculture still has not caught up with the West; whereas had the professionals been permitted to do their work, which was more pragmatic in fact but held less promise of immediate results, Soviet farm production might, by now, have reached the level of other developed nations.

Crisis and Concern

There is probably no one who would argue with the plain statement that the United States is today faced with a serious problem respecting environmental degradation. The overt manifestations are seen mainly in gross pollution: accumulations of garbage and junk, mountains of tailings, the deteriorated state of many inland and coastal waters, and filthy air in the cities. Nor are these phenomena uniquely American: similar difficulties are being recognized and discussed in all the highly developed countries, and attempts made to implement solutions with varying timetables, priority issues, and commitments of public funds. It cannot be claimed that severe local pollution is in any sense new or unique to our times; one has only to consider the foul condition of the Thames in eighteenth century London or the status of the air around nineteenth century industrial centers to disabuse oneself quickly of this notion. Nevertheless, there is rather wide agreement that the current situation is an historical first, especially as regards the extensiveness of the pollution of waters.

Attributions of cause are somewhat more difficult to make with precision, but most specialists in Western Europe and also in Japan would agree that many of our common problems of mushrooming gross pollution may be ascribed to the side effects of rapid material advancement, combined with increased population density in major urban and industrial centers. Some of the more noticeable problems stem from the failure to build into systems of production adequate checks on emissions of noxious wastes; some from the widespread habit of using coastal waters as general dumping grounds. Others result from inadequate provisions for municipal waste treatment. In the most prosperous nations there are some pollutional effects which are more or less directly related to the habits of affluence, such as, for example, the unnecessary use of high-powered automobiles in cities. More unique to the United States is the severity of the problem represented by the accumulation of solid wastes—one which in part reflects poor management, but is also seriously compounded by the sectors of our economy which are strictly waste-based—elaborate packaging and "built-in obsolescence," for example. Urban decay, the failure to anticipate mass-transit needs in cities, and land-use problems arising from suburban sprawl are also more marked in the United States than in most European countries, partly on account of differences in tradition, and also because migration in and out of cities has followed a different sociological pattern on the two continents. And there is one important respect in which the United States is more "backward" than any of the countries of Europe—the handling of sewage and domestic wastes—about which we shall elaborate shortly.

Some of the manifestations of environmental degradation are greater in scale and degree than others, and some would seem to call for serious, committed efforts towards cleanup and technological innovations in the near future in order that we avoid sinking ever deeper into the compounded mess of our own wastes. However, there is no true indication that the degradation of natural ecosystems with wastes, junk, and chemical contaminants represents a life-and-death crisis for man or for other life forms on the planet Earth. And yet some variation on the theme of the imminent collapse of the "life support systems" of our "spaceship Earth" is the rallying cry of nearly all the leading American environmentalists. Each has his own manner of describing the steps which led up to this coming disaster, and each has a different prescription for salvation, but the threat to survival theme is the common starting point.

It is an open question how many people really believe the doomsday predictions in a literal sense, but the American environmentalists have at least succeeded in creating a crisis atmosphere. It is in this respect that we see some social parallels with postrevolutionary Russia. Just at the time when considered, long-term planning for a saner and cleaner future has become both possible and probably essential, extremist environmentalists have fanned the feelings of impatience with government and disillusionment with technologists which were already running rather high in the United States. It has been argued—probably with some truth—that nothing gets accomplished in the United States without a crisis atmosphere; but the danger with this present movement is that the public has become receptive to all sorts of false explanations about the nature of the problems as well as to a host of pseudosolutions proclaimed as programs for redemption. Some of these are not too damaging in and by themselves, although they can serve to distract from the implementation of real solutions and do little if anything to improve the quality of the environment. Others are downright disastrous, and if followed, could lead us into a genuinely critical state of affairs. One good example is the suggestion that the use of artificial fertilizers should be cut back in order to abate water pollution.

To illustrate that quite another atmosphere prevails over much of continental Europe, we would like to offer the reader a very brief summary of what is being done there in two essential areas of environmental concern—pollution of inland waters and the production of energy without undue negative environmental effects. We shall focus our discussion on three countries: Switzerland, France, and West Germany.

Hard Rules and Hard Money

Switzerland enacted the first comprehensive federal law covering water use and water-pollution problems in 1955. Between 1955 and 1970, 399 sewage treatment plants were constructed, with the expenditures for building alone amounting to just over 1 billion Swiss francs (now more than $250 million). In 1970, a new law was enacted which granted a 45 percent federal subsidy to municipalities for further construction; an additional 95 plants have been built or are in the planning stage; and 238 million Swiss francs ($65 million) were appropriated to cover the government's share of the cost. When the building program is completed, every village in Switzerland will have sewage treatment. Furthermore, many of the larger plants, such as those on Lake Constance (often cited as one of Europe's most polluted inland lakes) will be built for or updated to the tertiary-treatment stage.* The total expenditures over a fifteen-year period come to about 500 million in U.S. dollars. This may sound like a relatively small figure, but if one recalls that Switzerland is not much larger than New Jersey and that her total population of 6.2 million people is less than that of New York City, the sums are put into a more meaningful perspective.

The 1970 law also incorporated strict regulations for industrial uses of waters. It obliges each industrial establishment to set up its own water-renovating plant and also provides for the establishing of a special police force. on a cantonal basis, to enforce observation of regulations. Like the United States, Switzerland has a strong tradition of local self-government. This particular law, however, supersedes cantonal regulations and treats natural watersheds as districts, more or less ignoring the borders of the cantons (*Neue Züricher Zeitung,* Sept. 4, 1970).

In the energy area, Switzerland is opting for nuclear power, despite the fact that she is one of the few Western countries with large harnessable reserves of hydroelectric power sources. It should not be supposed, either, that this preference represents a decision taken by government technocrats. In September,

---

* Conventional sewage treatment, both that of domestic and of industrial waste, consists of three distinct steps. Primary treatment refers to the simple settling and screening of solids. The effluent contains the nonsettlable solids and all the inorganic and organic nutrients dissolved in the water. Its oxygen demand is high, and it is loaded with both pathogenic and other microorganisms. Its inorganic content is high in terms of fertilizing ability.

Secondary treatment is aimed at reducing the amount of solid matter and at removing approximately 90 percent of the oxygen-demanding substances. Most of the microorganisms are killed through chlorination; and an effluent from a secondary-treatment plant will have only 10 percent organic contents, but it will still contain almost the same amount of nitrates and phosphates in solution as the original sewage.

Tertiary treatment aims at a reduction of another 7 percent of the oxidizable compounds, and concomitantly, the removal of some of the inorganic nutrients.

1972, the Consumer Association conducted a population survey which indicated that an overwhelming majority of the Swiss people believe nuclear power to be the safest and cleanest way of generating electricity (*Neue Züricher Zeitung,* Sept. 23, 1972).

In France, a comprehensive law covering water use, water pollution, and clean-up measures was enacted in 1964, after six years of study, during which period the status of the waters, future national needs, and costs of renovation were carefully assessed. The French law recognizes that in order to secure an adequate, high-quality water supply for the future, present resources will have to be renovated, and it calls for the eventual installation of systems capable of total renewal. The plan authorized the spending of 27.25 billion new francs (about $5.5 billion) over the eight-year period 1964–72. Although France is smaller than Texas in area, she has a population of 55 million; so this eight-year plan amounts to an expenditure of nearly $100 per capita, or about $12 per person per year. These expenditures do not, moreover, include the amounts which private industry is supposed to spend. The law states explicitly that waters must be cleaned up by those who are polluting them; and it prescribes regulatory and criminal sanctions against noncompliant polluters, supported by the creation of a special regulatory police force (Pro Aqua, 1970).

On the energy-production scene, 40 atomic power plants are presently under construction. It is expected that by 1975, 50 percent of the nation's power demand will be met by nuclear power generators. France has also developed the only large-scale working plants for the utilization of solar energy and tidal action in power production; but as these methods are not yet either economical or practical enough to meet the energy needs of the near future, a crash program for intensification of nuclear power production was initiated in 1968.

The West German program for the use and renovation of waters is quite similar to that of France. In the Federal Water Act of July, 1957, regulations were enacted and a long-term financing plan initiated. The act incorporates standardized requirements for sewage treatment plants. It authorized yearly expenditures in the range of $610 million, of which $500 million is designated for the building and updating of sewage-treatment facilities. About one-third of the totals are being spent on the Rhine River alone. In the first regional rehabilitation plan, for instance, which ran from 1950–1959, $650 million were spent on the North Rhine. Later the program was intensified, and $1.5 billion were invested between 1963 and 1967. In the third phase, which extends through 1975, plans call for outlays of an additional $2 billion.

The act also provides that individual states set their own standards for the water quality of industrial effluents and permissible uses of waters for such purposes as cooling. In North-Rhine–Westphalia, ordinances require industries to obtain permits and licenses to release effluents into receving waters, which effluent must be treated before discharge to comply with the standards. In response to punitive taxation for cooling water uses, industrial enterprises in this state have been able to reduce water demand for cooling purposes by 90 percent through installing internal water cycles. Like France and Switzerland, Germany enacted, between 1959 and 1962, a series of federal and state civil and criminal codes for enforcement of use regulations, incorporating the principle that the polluter has to make good for any damage he causes, even if it is inadvertent (Maniak, 1970).

West Germany is a small country in comparison with the United States, having an area not much larger than that of New York State. Like France, on the other hand, her population is almost one-fourth of the U.S. total, being just over 50 million. The stretch of the Rhine into which about $4 billion are being poured just for water-quality improvement — exclusive of industrial installations — is less than 200 kilometers in length, or about the distance from New York City to Philadelphia.

Along this same 200-kilometer stretch of the German Rhine, which is one of the world's most heavily industrialized and most densely populated areas, 15 nuclear power plants are being built or are in the planning stages. The program calls for about 25 percent of the country's electricity demands to be met from these nuclear generators by 1975. It should be remembered that West Germany is sitting on the largest anthracite coal reserves in Western Europe — a supply sufficient under any foreseeable intensification of industrial expansion for a minimum of 250 years. If Germany has opted for nuclear power, it is again not because of lack of alternatives, but rather because it is the considered opinion of scientists and technologists that of all the available, feasible methods of power generation, nuclear power is the cleanest and safest for both man and the environment.

Lest it be objected by American antinuclear activists that these three countries are enthusiastic about atomic power only because of lack of information, it should perhaps be mentioned that there is no shortage of responsible radiation biologists in any of these three countries, and that Germany alone has more professionally trained ecologists than the entire United States.

Now none of this is intended to convey a judgment of European superiority; nor do we mean to imply that these three countries of Western Europe have their environmental problems under control. The summaries of water-pollution abatement measures and energy programs are intended simply as illustrative examples which can later be contrasted with approaches to comparable problems in the United States. It cannot be claimed, either, that there is no environmental activism in Europe. There has been a considerable amount of "fallout" from the American movement, and some countries—especially Sweden, England, and Holland—have generated their own variety of ecological campaigns. However, it ought to be noted that the programs for water renewal which we have just reviewed were all initiated long before there were any signs of popular interest in ecology. And it can be said in general that most Europeans regard pollution as amenable to technological solutions and rational management. In the Western European nations the greatest difficulties associated with programs for improvement of the environment are the obvious ones: Which problems should receive priority? How much money is available? How can it be spent most effectively? There are also some complications relating to international agreements; but existing pacts recognizing the major inland waterways, such as the Danube and the Rhine, as common resources already include discharge standards. Accords dealing with coastal waters and inland seas are somewhat more problematic, particularly in the Mediterranean, but there are signs of progress respecting dumping in the North Sea and the North Atlantic, and the general feeling seems to be that diplomatic patience and equitable planning will eventually lead to more substantial agreements.

Probably for Europeans the most puzzling aspects of the American movement are the doomsday prophecies of prominent environmentalists and the prevalence of antitechnology attitudes. And, even where the voices of extremist Americans have attracted considerable attention, this should not automatically be interpreted as an indication that the content of their message has been accepted. For example, for months *The Limits to Growth*, by Meadows et al. (1972), was on the best-seller list in West Germany. However, its ultimate either/ or prediction—either growth must cease or we are doomed—has not been generally assented to by the German readership. It has been pointed out over and over again in the German press that one of the principal errors in the computer simulations on which the book was based is that the authors failed altogether to take into account the effects of new technologies on future developments. Paradoxically, the book seems to be stimulating growth as well as conversation, for the present and forecasted budgets allotted by German industries for research and development in new technologies has practically doubled in the wake of the book's appearance.

The gloomy tone and the sense of urgency which dominate the American environmental scene simply are not in evidence in Europe, except in very small circles without general influence. Environmental problems are being defined and discussed as important topics; but it is broadly recognized that even where solutions are available, their implementation will take time, money, and energy. In the meantime, expectations are focused neither on a miraculous easy way out nor on a catastrophic collapse of the biosphere.

The rather matter-of-fact approaches and the substantial monetary sacrifices which characterize the Swiss, French, and German programs can be contrasted with what is happening in America in similar areas. Let us begin with water pollution.

A Frightful Price

The deteriorated status of surface waters in the United States has been recognized as serious by water-pollution experts for a long time. Recently, a good deal of attention has been focused on industrial discharges as gross polluters of waters, and nearly everyone seems to be in agreement that measures must be devised—both incentives and punitive laws—to force industrial entrepreneurs to pay for their water use and/or for cleanup of their effluent. However, although the effects of industrial pollution may be severe and highly visible, the contribution of domestic waste and municipal sewage to the degree of water pollution is considerably greater, taken on a national basis. This factor is usually ignored or vastly underestimated by environmentalists, who tend to focus their water-saving campaigns on specific compounds in common use or in dramatic attacks on some local industrial polluter.

Let us consider some unglamorous facts. It will shock some readers to learn that, in our very advanced country in the year 1968, 60 percent of American municipalities had no sewage treatment facilities whatsoever, and only one-third of the communities with some facilities had secondary-treatment plants. Forty-five percent of the U.S. population lives in counties adjacent to the sea. Nine counties, each with populations of over 50,000, empty their sewage with no treatment whatsoever into the ocean. The rest have at least primary treatment, but this does not serve as much of a deterrent to serious pollution of estuaries and shoreline. Into the near-shore areas of the oceans and the Gulf of Mexico, the United States annually dumps 48 million tons of sludge from primary and secondary sewage-treatment plants (Brown and Smith, 1969). In its backwardness with respect to municipal sewage treatment, the United States cannot be compared favorably even to Spain. And, to give the reader some idea of our rapid progress over the years, it may be noted that in 1906, a joint New York–New Jersey commission recommended—among other proposals—the immediate establishment of sewage treatment plants for Lower Manhattan to prevent further pollution of Raritan Bay. At the present time, completely untreated raw sewage is still flowing into the bay from Manhattan!

Another problem which plagues even those communities which do have sewage-treatment facilities is that most of these systems have been designed to channel storm-water runoff as well as domestic wastes through the plant, and the handling capacity of the facility is often overloaded following heavy rainfalls. The remark of Englishman John Maddox (editor of *Nature*) respecting this design problem is interesting, if none too flattering: "It is, of course, a great puzzle that the population of the United States, which made its way in the world in the 1920s on the strength of its reputation in domestic plumbing should still be content with such a rudimentary method of disposing of municipal waste" (Maddox, 1972, p. 132).

By the mid-1960s there were some signs of real concern about the need to rectify this inglorious situation, and even some indications that the federal government would be prepared to foot at least part of the bill. In 1968 the Johnson administration completed a study called "The Cost of Clean Water," which provided politicians with some idea of what the price tag would be. The estimates were based on the still rather backward goal of constructing facilities at the secondary-treatment level for all waste waters in the United States, excluding storm-water or combined sewer overflows, but including industrial operations. In 1968 dollars, the estimate for the achievement of this goal was $26 billion. When this figure is broken down and operating expenses are ignored, the total cost for industrial capital expenditures is $4.6 billion at the highest estimate; whereas building and replacement of municipal treatment works, including sanitary sewer construction, would cost $14.6 billion. This approximately 1 to 4 proportion between industrial and municipal sewage treatment costs is just about the same as the proportionate outlays in West Germany and France, and certainly tends to belie the notion that if industry were forced to clean up, we would not have to worry too much about the contributions of municipal wastes to surface water pollution.

Secondary treatment removes only about 90 percent of organic matter, and none of the inorganic nutrients. In the same study, $100 billion is named as the estimated price for the implementation of tertiary-treatment systems on a national scale. Since experts do not regard secondary treatment as adequate to achieve major improvement in water quality, the politicians who reviewed this study must have finally understood that programs for clean water will be a very costly matter indeed.

Paradoxically, for communities which do not yet have any treatment facilities, it would actually be cheaper to take a quantum leap into the future and install a complete water-renovation technology,* which can achieve an effluent of drinking-water quality (the purists' dream), than it would be to go through the phases of building primary, secondary, and eventually tertiary conventional treatment plants. But nobody seems to be much interested in these new water-treatment technologies. Environmentalists don't like them because they represent the "technological fix" approach to problem solving; politicians don't like them because they don't have enough short-range, high-interest, vote-getting appeal; contractors don't like them because they are less profitable to build; and municipalities don't like them because they are new, and they do cost money, after all.

One might have thought that the participants of the developing environmental movement would have informed themselves about these total water-renovating technologies and embraced them enthusiastically, challenging the inertia of the politicians and municipalities. But exactly when the implementation of a program for a 120-year-old technology with its $26 billion price tag was giving rise to hesitations on Capitol Hill about how much clean water is worth, the environmental movement swung towards a cheap and easy pseudosolution for saving our waters: ban phosphate detergents!

We shall discuss the antiphosphate campaign in a later chapter, but we raise the issue here to illustrate how this grass-roots crusade against a single compound served to deflect attention from the pursuit of real solutions to water pollution. In the end the phosphate issue proved to be one of the notable fiascos of the movement, but in 1969 and 1970 it got tremendous coverage in the media, absorbed all kinds of public energy, and gave people the subjective feeling that by sacrificing "whiter than white" they could help to save our precious waters. In reality, the crusade to eliminate phosphates made no demands on anybody, except a few detergent manufacturers, who were in any event part of the industrial Establishment. But with such a high-interest, no-cost solution at hand, what environmentalist or politician or journalist would have been willing to publicize the unpleasant fact that a goodly proportion of the phosphates in our surface waters originate from our own excrement? Let's face it: there are no quick reputations to be made and not much chance of winning popularity by pressing for more adequate sewage treatment. It is hardly a glamorous subject; and the high-cost, slow-return programs envisaged are much more difficult to promote than a quick and easy ban.

---

* For the reader interested in details about these new water renewal technologies, there are a number of publications describing them. One of the more accessible is a federal document called "Advanced Waste Treatment Research," (U.S. Dept. Interior 1968b).

At the very time of the ban-the-phosphates campaign, the real expenditures at the federal level for water-pollution abatement were as follows: In 1969, $215 million was spent, and although Congress appropriated $800 million for 1970, only $214 million actually went into building. If these figures are translated into total expenditures, to include state and municipal contributions, they come close to $500 million for each of the two years. These quantities should be contrasted with the sums recommended in "The Cost of Clean Water" as the *minimal* amounts needed for improved municipal sewage treatment only: $2.7 and $2.8 billion, respectively. The actual amounts invested come to about $2.50 per capita; whereas in France $12, in Germany $13, and in Switzerland $8 per person were spent annually in the same two-year period.

There are presently some signs that the situation may improve, for in spite of a presidential veto, the ninety-second Congress has approved a solid water-pollution control measure, calling for federal expenditures of about $8 billion annually for the next four years. What will come of this blocked legislation is still an open question, but it might be claimed that the phosphate hullabaloo only retarded by a few years the enacting of meaningful legislation, and did not seriously obstruct it. On the other hand, in spite of all the publicity generated by environmentalists about dying lakes and filthy rivers, there seems to be little if any reason for crediting the movement as the principal stimulus for this long overdue evidence of the political will to clean up our dirty waters.

Backlash Brewing?

To date, the environmentalists have sailed through their fiascos with little damage to the reputation of the movement. Strangely, it is their successes which hold the greatest threat for the immediate social good and are most likely to become eventual obstacles to serious scientific and technological efforts to overcome environmental difficulties. The word "success" has to be defined here as "evidence of real political muscle," for since the demands of activists are primarily negative, acquiescence to them does not imply the solution of problems so much as it does the blocking of programs.

Let us illustrate with reference to a domestic subject which does not seem to elicit any vast public interest except when there is a critical shortage: the matter of fuels and energy supplies.

For years now there have been warnings that power needs cannot be met in a number of heavily populated areas unless the construction of new electric-generating facilities is accelerated. There have also been many predictions from experts that the immediate supplies of oil, diesel fuel, and natural gas are insufficient, and that unless domestic production is intensified and arrangements made for large-scale foreign purchases, we will face such critical shortages that some form of rationing may be necessary. The latter prognostications have been much less publicized than those relating to electric power, but the information on consumption patterns, projected needs, and domestic supply have long been available in easily accessible publications.

No one would claim that the environmentalists are responsible for the existence of such a problem. The United States has never had a coherent national energy policy; and while the demand for energy has been growing at a tremendous pace, until a few years ago not much thought was given to the future, as long as the next two or three years seemed to be taken care of. Recently, however, there has been a general awakening to the necessity of consideration of long-term needs. We still have no defined policy, but a number of decisions have been taken and generalized plans formulated which should at least be capable of heading off any severe crisis in energy supply and of turning us in directions more promising for the future. Central to these plans is an intensification of nuclear energy applications and research. Tapping the offshore oil supplies and piping in the generous flow from the Alaskan fields are expected to increase domestic oil production substantially, but overseas purchases will also have to be increased; and the natural-gas situation seems even more clearly to call for greater imports, at least until such time as price controls are removed on natural gas and domestic companies given more economic incentive to search for further reserves at home.

If such plans could be implemented smoothly, we would probably pass through the next 15 to 20 years regarded by energy experts as critical without experiencing severe shortages of either fuels or delivered power, although undoubtedly the prices would go up. The consensus among experts from abroad as well as the United States is that by the end of the century, advanced technologies that supersede the heavy reliance on fossil fuels will have been developed. And there are signs that long-range planning will be accepted as a necessity by future U.S. administrations.

We do, however, have to face an immediate as well as a distant future; and although the environmentalists have not created the energy supply problem, the record of the extremist wing of the movement with respect to both construction of new power generating facilities and to the delivery of fuel supplies strongly suggests that there may be an antienvironmentalist backlash at the first signs of a real crisis in either area.

The general argument of environmentalists is that we use much more power than we need; that we are a nation of profligate wasters. While there is some truth in the statement, it is not going to cut much ice with city dwellers if one day the lights go out and the elevators cease to function. It seems quite probable that even people who have tacitly assented to campaigns against the construction of new power plants on grounds of ecological damage, or, in the case of nuclear generators, out of fear of minimal radiation leakage or the danger of the improbable, ultimate accident, will think twice about the wisdom of this opposition once their own comfort is severely restricted. It would also not be at all surprising if people shivering in unheated houses and looking around for someone to blame settled on the environmentalists as the proper scapegoats, for their opposition to plans for fuel exploration and delivery has been well publicized.

It is also in the fuels and energy-supply area that environmentalists may be already inviting a "stop these fools" reaction from many members of the federal government, mainly by holding to extreme positions. Consider oil for a moment. Respecting offshore oil drilling, the movement gave tremendous publicity to the Santa Barbara accident, which was an unfortunate event, but hardly a major natural disaster. While exaggerating the ill effects of the man-caused spill on the flora and fauna of the near shore, environmentalists conveniently ignored the long-recognized fact that there are sizable natural leaks in the Santa Barbara field which pour a minimum of 50 barrels of oil per day into the ocean. This natural leakage was first observed and reported by Van Couver in the seventeenth century and has been a constant phenomenon, probably for centuries. According to detailed studies conducted in October, 1969 (Allen et al., 1970), the natural seepage at Coal Oil Point introduces about 50 to 70 barrels of oil per day into the Santa Barbara Channel—quantities at least equivalent to those estimated at the height of the blowout. However, the oil from the largest natural seeps is generally prevented by predominant offshore currents from fouling widely used beaches, whereas the oil from the blowout was unfortunately washed onto heavily frequented beaches.

With Santa Barbara as a high-visibility example, many environmentalists demand a complete moratorium on the issuance of offshore drilling permits, instead of contenting themselves with pressing for a tightening of regulations governing the capping of old drill holes, and similar practical and not unreasonable measures.

The unending arguments over the Alaska pipeline are another example of untenable demands, which give altogether too much support to the "give 'em an inch and they'll take a mile" opinion held about environmentalists by many businessmen. The original objections to a buried pipeline had some point: nobody could be sure what effect the warm oil would have on the frozen ground, and unforeseen technical complications were a possibility. But the purists are not satisfied with proposals to raise the pipe above ground: it turns out that they are dead set against the idea of an oil pipeline across Alaska no matter what design compromises might be made. They argue that the vast stretches of wilderness tundra represent an untouched and as yet unstudied natural ecosystem, which men should not be permitted to disturb, even in the face of pressing human needs. The caribou, which they claim will probably not adapt to *any* changes in the environment introduced by the pipeline, are brought up to add emotional force to the resistance; although similar arguments regarding the reindeer of Lapland and the building of north-south railroad lines proved to be wrong (Klein, 1971). And even if the survival of some caribou were to be definitely threatened, it is questionable whether this possibility should carry any weight against the welfare of the people of Alaska, including the native Eskimo. The huge sums which were invested in the development of the oil fields and the insistence of Alaskan spokesmen that getting the oil flowing is essential to the economy of the state are dismissed as irrelevant to the argument, since these are seen as a reflection of the old exploitative frontier mentality to which environmentalists ascribe a good part of the "mess" in which we presently find ourselves. By this time most continental Americans have become thoroughly bored with the issue, and the patience of officials has been pretty well exhausted. Still, the result is a deadlock, for even though Secretary of Interior Rogers Morton announced his decision in May, 1972, that it is in the national interest to grant the right-of-way permit for the trans-Alaska pipeline, nothing can in fact be done, since the environmentalists still have suits pending to stop the construction.

In even more critical supply at the moment is natural gas, which is admitted by everyone to be one of the least polluting of the fuels derived from fossil deposits. The demand for it is increasing, while known reservoirs in the United States are minimal. Some time ago a contract was negotiated to purchase natural gas from Algeria, for the delivery of which moorings and a terminal have been planned in the Chesapeake Bay vicinity. But construction of the terminal has recently been blocked by initiation of an EDF–Sierra Club class-action suit, on the grounds that the ecology of the bay will be ruined.

In this case one must bear in mind that it is not only national fuel needs which are involved, nor just regional economic interests and those of American-owned oil companies which are pitted against the interests of the environmentalists. All the branches of the federal government involved in international trade agreements are also concerned. And then there is Algeria. Having no lack of alternate markets, the Algerian government announced that it is prepared to cancel the agreement post haste and sell the gas to another customer, unless the delivery and payment arrangements proceed on schedule. It should be obvious that there is nothing to motivate the Algerians to wait with patience and understanding while environmentalists go to court, Congress holds endless subcommittee meetings on the matter, and the final outcome remains a question mark. In this case it is not really the relevance of the claims about ecological damage which are central—or the lack thereof—but the question of whether the right to protest of a few citizens can be allowed to create serious obstacles to meeting the needs of the many.

The antinuclear-power groups are equally recalcitrant in their resistance and their capacity for coming up with a new objection as soon as an earlier one has been either answered or met with concessions. Having won a few points on siting, on environmental-impact statements, and even on allowable radiation releases, they are now concentrating on the dangers of the ultimate, unlikely accident. The latest demand, this time from an organization called the Union of Concerned Scientists, speaking through Ralph Nader, involves a request for a complete moratorium on construction of new and partially built plants (131 in total) and a 50 percent cutback in power production from the 29 operating nuclear plants "until all safety-related issues are resolved." Agreement to such a request could seriously hinder efforts to meet the power needs of the next three or four years and might tip the presently precarious supply/demand balance into a critical shortage, especially in certain heavily populated metropolitan areas such as New York, Chicago, and Miami. So far as we know, there are no legal means by which such a sweeping demand could be brought to the courts. However, it is worth considering what such a blocking program would mean for the country as a whole. The nuclear energy program is central to United States energy planning for the coming decades. Were it to be so seriously curtailed, one has to consider the alternatives and the probable consequences. We cannot substitute gas or oil for the production of power, as these materials are in insufficient supply for other needs, such as transport and heating. We have plenty of coal for the time being, but most of it is "dirty" coal, high in sulfur content. Nobody favors power plants operating on this sort of heavily polluting fuel if it can be avoided. Low-sulfur-containing coal is found mainly in the Western states, and it is extracted primarily by strip mining, to which practice environmentalists also strenuously object. The notion that by simply cutting back on power uses the demand will be radically reduced is for the most part a romantic one which fails to take account of available figures referring to essential demand. It would, of course, be possible to ration power and/or to raise the price of delivered power to the point where individuals and business enterprises would be discouraged from any inessential uses or waste of power, but it is unlikely that either of these measures would be welcomed by the populace at large. Furthermore, even enforced rationing would be insufficient to compensate for the losses which would result from implementation of these proposed cutbacks in operating and planned nuclear generating facilities, and it is highly probable that such a blocking action would at least partially cripple some major cities and crucial industrial sectors.

Now it has to be admitted that discussion of possible accidents in nuclear power plants is a trans-scientific issue, and it is understandable that people who live near such operating or planned facilities are fearful of a major accident, even when they have been told that the probabilities of the occurrence of such an accident are exceedingly low. (It has to be remembered that the secondary coolant system whose proper operation is the focus of concern of these groups of activists is the fourth line of defense against accident in nuclear generating plants and would only be called upon in the event of a series of failures of all other safeguard systems.) On the other hand, it would seem obvious that the availability of power is a concern of broad social significance to any society which, like the United States, has a dense urban population dependent upon power-based technologies. In our view, no discussion of the wisdom of going forward with the nuclear energy program can be meaningful unless it is carried out in the context of essential power needs, consideration of alternatives and application of the risk-benefit equation, evaluation of other means of augmenting the power supply, and determination of the consequences of reducing the supply of de-livered power.

Whatever one's own personal views on any of these specific issues, it does not require a great deal of imagination to perceive that where environmentalists push their protest privileges too far and especially where they are recalcitrant in blocking projects of high national priority, they may be inviting a backlash reaction from a majority of legislators. Certain stances may be so untenable from an economic and realistic point of view as to force even their friends in Congress to side with those who espouse quite unsympathetic attitudes: "Let's get on with business and to hell with nature."

But the real danger of unreasoned opposition, which leads into critical troubles for society or ill-planned programs that fail to solve real problems, is not just a backlash on any particular issue. It can be argued, in fact, that with reference to immediate social needs, a no-nonsense approach to the delivery and implementation of necessary technologies and supplies might be preferable to the current standoff situation. What is more threatening is that the extremist wing of the environmental movement has managed to identify itself in the public mind with the science of ecology and the interest in pollution abatement. If a backlash reaction develops, it could very well include a rejection of science as such—or at least of the biological sciences—as well as a turning away from needed programs for environmental cleanup.

We are going to devote most of the rest of this book to exposing the weaknesses of the scientific thinking and procedures which have characterized many of the high-interest ecology campaigns in America to date. But we would like to make it clear that our purpose is not to discredit the science of ecology per se, nor to dispute the importance of environmental awareness. We feel that it is essential that true science should be more clearly distinguished from pseudo-science, and that genuine concern about the quality of the environment should be separated from emotional, ill-considered crusades to "make the problems go away." If our book is mainly critical, it is because we see a need to make these distinctions now — to clean the slate so that better programs can be written before the interest wanes. We do believe that with patience, will, reflection, planning, and imagination, rational management of the environment is an achievable goal.

6

REVOLUTION, ANYONE?

I'm a radical conservative with
   anarchistic leanings
Who supports the revolution to
   preserve the status quo.
(CABARET SONG from
"What's a Nice Country Like You
Doing in a State Like This?")

Although we have made some references to confused ideologies among environmentalists, we have thus far not discussed the politics of the environmental movement. Before we turn to specific issues, it would seem to be worthwhile to devote a few comments in an attempt at clarifying the differences between the slogans favored by environmentalists and the underlying ideologies which apparently impel them.

Many spokesmen for the environmental movement claim that it has no political orientation, and that it is the only large-scale unifying force in con-

89

temporary America, welcoming any citizen into its ranks, regardless of his political affiliations. And indeed appearances suggest that participation includes strangely mixed groups. On the other hand, people as individuals do subscribe to ideologies; and it is impossible that there should be any "movement" without a framework of commonly accepted ideas to which the majority of the participants adhere. This basic framework will be the ideology of the movement, and it in turn will determine the political stance of the leaders and the kinds of actions recommended by them and followed by the participants.

Playboy editor Geoffrey Norman provides a colorful description of the political spectrum evident at the first big environmental "teach-out," which took place at Northwestern University on January 23, 1970, a few months prior to Earth Day.

> One obvious point that this affair made was that the environmental problem has become a full-blown issue, probably *the* issue. Right now, it's one of the few questions that seem to arouse a response that cuts across political lines, but positions are rapidly becoming politicized. In fact, a person can just about be pinpointed on the left-right spectrum by the label he attaches to the problem. If he says pollution, he's a mainstreamer, right there with the editorial cartoons, radio editorials, citizens' groups and President Nixon. ("This thing's a serious problem and we've got to roll up our sleeves and tackle it before it's too late!") Conservationists are further to the right. They've been talking for years about saving our natural resources. But, like most conservative concerns, the grip on total reality is slight; a part stands for the whole. The slow death of our forests is aesthetically repugnant to these people, but the question of oxygen supply is too remote and too problematic to interest them. If someone talks about ecology, he knows about the support cycle and its breakdown. He can talk about the apocalyptic aspects of the problem with a matter-of-fact smugness: thermal pollution, greenhouse effect, tritium. He's fashionably to the left.
>
> Then there are the jungle lawyers on the hard right. They advocate shackling our impulse to save wretched lives—to control population growth backward; let the weak die off. Environmental fascism or *laissez faire*. Over at the other end are the militant population controllers. They agree with the hard right about the severity of the crisis —a disturbing characteristic of this era. They believe population must be controlled —one way or another—because it's scientifically necessary. We can involuntarily starve, poison or nuke ourselves to death—or take unavoidably stern measures to stem the population explosion and live in a state of reduced material frenzy on a clean planet. Either/or. At the Northwestern teach-out, the hard-liners scored the most points; it was that kind of crowd. (Norman, 1971, pp. 14–15; author's emphasis)

Amusing as it is, this attempt to characterize the political stances of the participants does not correspond to the usually accepted left-right divisions in political ideologies. Norman's acute observation that those he describes as belonging to the far left and the far right are in agreement about the necessity for Draconian controls is correct and we would agree that this is a disturbing characteristic of the era. He falls into the trap, however, of believing that those who declare themselves to be militant radicals must be on the left. To any observer with a grasp of political science, it is very difficult to discern any genuinely leftist ideas in the American environmental movement at all, and least of all among the "population controllers." It is understandable, on the other hand, that many people are deceived when some of the leaders declare themselves to be revolutionaries and repeat slogans with leftist or very liberal colorations.

It is true that the activists in the movement are all firmly antiestablishment, and are fond of preaching the necessity for radical social change. Still, the actual recommendations for change and the conditions envisioned to follow the social upheaval are the antithesis of revolutionary ideas: they are fundamentally reactionary.

In order to substantiate this statement, we should like to bring attention to some of the programs for change offered by two of the movement's most prominent leaders: Paul Ehrlich and Barry Commoner.

Coercion in a Good Cause

Ehrlich was catapulted into the limelight of public fame with *The Population Bomb,* which exploded in 1968. By 1970, it had been reprinted 13 times and had reached more than 2 million readers. It had all the ingredients of an instant best seller. It prophesied universal doom in an easily readable, superficially humorous style; it spoke to the average man as if the prognoses and calculations presented had a firm scientific basis, without forcing him to do any thinking about them; and it proposed a penitent but largely nonactive solution to the problem which we all face—too many mouths to feed in an already crowded world.

Ehrlich's discussion of the problems faced by humanity at large centers on the proliferation of people. It is undeniable that better medical care and public health measures, available for the first time in underdeveloped countries in the early 1930s, have greatly extended the life expectancy of hundreds of millions of people; and the fact that more people are living longer has led to an exponential increase in world population. Most demographers, however, predict a leveling out of the growth curve at the 6 to 10 billion range. In his book, on the other hand, Ehrlich implied that no such leveling off would occur unless drastic steps were taken; and in an impressive scare tactic, he extended the demographic curve all the way up to 500 billion people.

Some of the measures he believed to be justified by the severity of the crisis were the following:

1. Our domestic population has to be brought under control by all possible means. Although he discusses various positive incentive programs, such as favorable tax structures for small families, he seems to feel that coercion will be necessary both to enforce low breeding rates and to design "environmentally sound" programs for the "new society." He therefore recommends the creation of a Department of Population and Environment—to be staffed by systems ecologists—which would have virtually totalitarian powers. This department would be set up with the power to take "whatever steps are necessary" to establish a "reasonable population size" in the United States. It would be charged with developing legislation to stop the wasting of resources, and to establish and regulate energy needs at a level where we no longer will be living "beyond our means."

Recognizing that this department would not be popular. Ehrlich suggests special protection: "It must be carefully insulated against the forces that will quickly be aligned against it. It is going to cost industry money. It is going to cost municipalities money. It is going to hit a lot of us where it hurts." (Ehrlich, 1968, pp. 152-153).

One wonders who would be for this superagency? The systems ecologists running it, perhaps?

2. On the international scene. Ehrlich envisages the application of the "triage system" proposed by the Paddocks (1967) in their book, *Famine—1975!* According to this scheme, areas of the Earth unable to feed their populations would be divided into three categories by the developed countries: (a) Those which are wealthy enough to purchase their food, such as the oil-rich Arab states. To these, crop surpluses would be sold. (b) Those which are beyond hope of rehabilitation, such as India. To these areas neither donations nor sales of food would be recommended. (c) Those in which, with appropriate food shipments and technical aid, the possibility of increase in domestic food production to reach eventual self-sufficiency is given, such as Pakistan. The details are specified thus: "This plan would involve simultaneous population control, agricultural development, and, where resources warrant it, industrialization of selected countries or sections of countries. The bedrock requirement of this program would be population control, necessarily including migration control to prevent swamping of aided areas by the less fortunate. . . . If necessary . . . TV channel[s] could be used to make it clear that the continuance of food supplies depends on

the cooperation of the people in the area." (Ehrlich, 1968, pp. 162, 163).

In practice this program would be tantamount to establishing large concentration camps in the underdeveloped countries to keep the undesirable or unworthy populations out of the areas supplied with food. What is this, if not fascism? It seems clearly to be a travesty of any kind of meaningful political designation to describe the militant population controllers as belonging to the left.

There are also some knotty moral questions respecting the now living human population inherent in Ehrlich's estimates of an "ideal" population size, for not only does he insist that we cannot feed our present population and that it is absolutely out of the question that we could ever feed, much less house, a populations of 8 or 10 billion, but he goes further and states that if we are to live in "ecologically sound" conditions, we must have a *reduction* in population. In *The Population Bomb* he hedges on this question, merely mentioning that 1 or 2 billion people would be preferable to the Earth's present 3.5 billion. But two years later his desire to see the world population shrink had been considerably clarified in terms of numbers: ". . . many scientists think the population of the United States should eventually be reduced to well under 50 million and that of the world to an absolute maximum of 500 million," he said in a *Playboy* interview (Ehrlich, 1971, p. 74). One should read "many scientists" as a euphemism for Ehrlich and a handful of other alarmists. The majority of scientists would be thoroughly horrified at such a statement, for it implies that we must (or should) have mass deaths from multiple causes. The "death rate solution" which Ehrlich forecast from the famines and/or plagues which are inevitably on the way thus begins to look more like a desired solution than a tragic possibility. Ehrlich himself has a bit too much political savvy to say outright that the "coming mass deaths" will be a blessing, but he is not ashamed to quote LaMont Cole, whose views are quite explicit. In reference to the supposed future decrease in the oxygen content of the atmosphere, Cole said: "If this [decrease] occurred gradually, its effect would be approximately the same as moving everyone to higher altitudes, a change that might help to alleviate the population crisis by raising death rates" (cited in Ehrlich, 1968, p. 57).

If read with any attention, Ehrlich comes off in *The Population Bomb* as such an obvious misanthrope that in the end one ceases to be startled when he makes statements like the following: "Our population consists of two groups; a comparatively small one dedicated to the preservation of beauty and wildlife, and a vastly larger one dedicated to the destruction of both (or at least apathetic toward it)" (Ehrlich, 1968, p. 66).

No mention whatsoever is made of the sizable numbers who might happen to be dedicated to the preservation of people.

From the Left

A scathing criticism of the whole environmental movement, and in particular of Ehrlich's population theories, appeared from the core of the American left. Robert Chrisman, editor of *The Black Scholar* and a professor of English at San Francisco State College, published an article called "Ecology, a Racist Shuck" in the August, 1970, issue of the now defunct *Scanlan's* magazine. He wrote: "Ironically, today's ecology enthusiasts do not seem to like living things. Life must be limited, they say, else it will destroy itself. We must have a small population and a lot of space. People corrupt things. They breed, they shit, they eat, they need clothing, they need shelter, they need fuel. We must eliminate people; otherwise they'll *use* the earth" (Chrisman, 1970, p. 47; author's emphasis).

Although admitting that the interest in ecology at first seemed a hopeful sign, Chrisman is unrelenting in his analysis of the basic conservatism of the movement. He describes the followers as an unholy alliance between Birchers and tired liberals, and sees both the science and the social vision as distinctly antiquated. "It is mired in 19th century theories of population and energy, and that in itself represents a willful and reactionary desire to return to the past, deliberately ignoring contemporary knowledge" (*ibid.*, p. 47). About the nature of the efforts for social change and the supposedly revolutionary slogans frequently mouthed by enthusiasts, he writes: "The individual citizen is to be responsible—burn propane, don't burn garbage; save newspapers, don't have kids; write letters to Congress, and sit back, sanctimoniously satisfied. In other words, a Presbyterian revolution" (*ibid.*, p. 48).

He gives considerable attention to the demographic projections favored by the population alarmists and was among the first to point out to the lay public that there is an obvious correlation between prosperity and low population growth. "Prosperity *creates* low population, not vice versa" (*ibid.*, p. 49; author's emphasis). This thesis is widely acknowledged by scholars from many disciplines, including most professional demographers.

Whether Chrisman is correct in his general claim that the ecology movement has developed into a conspiracy of the white American liberal middle class for the further oppression of blacks and third-world peoples is a debatable point. On the other hand, one can easily understand from the general message of *The Population Bomb* why a black leftist intellectual would come to such a conclusion.

In all fairness to Ehrlich, one has to admit that he may have changed his political attitudes quite considerably. Only eight months after his *Playboy* interview—at which time he seemed to hold even more extreme views than those expressed in *The Population Bomb*—he coauthored a book with Richard Harriman called *How to Be a Survivor* (1971). This book seems to point to an almost total political about-face. Although the authors claim that they are not Marxists, a strong influence from current neo-Marxist thinking is evident. But the contrasts with Ehrlich's earlier political recommendations and the 180-degree reversals on many specific issues are, in fact, so sweeping that it is difficult to accept that one is reading Ehrlich at all. For example, on January 23, 1970, he described the Green Revolution as a fraud, and said that improvements in agricultural production could be traced to good weather conditions over the past few years (cited by Norman, 1971, p. 17). In the *Playboy* interview, on April 23, 1970, he stated that "the new high-yield grains . . . produce fragile crops that require large-scale treatment with pesticides that have very serious ecological effects and usually result in pesticide-resistant pests that do even more damage than unsprayed pests because the predators that ordinarily eat them have succumbed to the pesticides. . . . The green revolution wouldn't be ecologically sound even if it could meet the food needs of the world's population, which it can't" (Ehrlich, 1971, p. 87).

In the new book, which appeared in January of 1971 (and must presumably have been completed at least by the early autumn of 1970), the authors write: "The idea behind this Green Revolution is fundamentally sound. Yields will be increased on land already under cultivation, using new strains of crops traditionally grown" (Ehrlich and Harriman, 1971, p. 87).

To support this Green Revolution, they recommend massive foreign aid, in the forms of fertilizer and approved pesticides, and of capital to build fertilizer plants, to construct roads and vehicles to transport both input products and harvested crops, and to build adequate storage facilities. Money is also needed, they state, to hasten development in other economic sectors, to alleviate the severe poverty of the city dwellers in the underdeveloped countries, and thus to create a real market for the increased yields. This is certainly a very different sort of program from the callous, desperation plan represented by the "triage system" of foreign aid which Ehrlich favored earlier.

Throughout the book there are abrupt reversals—or at least apparent reversals—of Ehrlich's positions on other specific issues. And nearly all the socioeconomic blind spots with which Ehrlich's critics charged him are here explicitly redressed: racism, elitism, indifference to the problems of the poor, reliance on Draconian controls, and so on. The authors also come out against any large-scale "return to nature" movement and are strongly in favor of retaining and utilizing our highly developed technologies. In short, though not without its faults, *How to Be a Survivor* is certainly one of the most interesting and thought-provoking of the many books which have been spawned by the recent burgeoning of interest in environmental problems.

One wonders what could have happened to Ehrlich to have produced such a profound change in such a very short period of time. Did he undergo a sort of "conversion experience" during the summer of 1970? Was his fundamental change in personal attitude and understanding of the nature of global environmental problems such that it prompted him to do the massive amount of intellectual work evident in the new book, all in one summer? Or had the book been already more or less written by Harriman, then a graduate student, and did Ehrlich, like a good politican, decide to lend his name to a work which not only answered his critics from the left, but made him appear to be one of them? We cannot answer these questions, but in a practical sense it does not really matter much with respect to the ideology of the environmental movement in America, for one discerns very little in the current mood of the populace and the activities of environmental organizations to indicate any influence from this book. It is the earlier Ehrlich who is parroted by the majority of his followers.

Commoner's New Economics

In contrast with the early Ehrlich, Barry Commoner gives clear expression to a broad social conscience and an awareness that ecological problems cannot be considered separately from social injustices and the developmental problems of the underdeveloped countries. He understands why

> . . . it is often suggested that environmental issues are so innocuous that they serve to divert people from more serious, controversial issues—a kind of ecological "cop-out" from the problems of poverty, racial discrimination, and war. . . . For example, in the ghetto, environmental protection is sometimes regarded as an irrelevant diversion from the plight of the blacks . . . ecological crusaders . . . reason—erroneously, as we have seen—that pollution is caused by the excessive consumption of goods and resources by the United States population. Since the wastes generated by this intense consumption pollute our environment, the eco-activist is advised to "consume less." In the absence of the added statistics that in the United States the per capita consumption by blacks is much less than that of the white population, such observations are not likely to make much sense to blacks or to anyone who is concerned with social justice. (Commoner, 1971, pp. 207–208)

He also perceives that there is a close relationship between environmental issues and poverty. He describes a case where environmental activists blocked the construction of a chemical factory in a South Carolina shoreline area, in spite of protests from poor people in the region who wanted the plant to be constructed because it promised employment. He writes: "For example, if the plant is blocked (which is in fact what happened), this action, in effect, says to the unemployed that their right to a job is less important than the integrity of the environment. The appropriate response may well be that a society that can find the means to save a marsh ought to be equally capable of finding the means to employ these citizens" (*ibid.*, p. 209).

Commoner takes a very strong stance against any coercive programs to control population. Respecting the suggestions of both Garrett Hardin and Paul Ehrlich, he writes:

> . . . some population-minded ecologists hold that "we must have population control at home, hopefully through a system of incentives and penalities, but by compulsion if voluntary methods fail" [Paul Ehrlich]. The outcome would be to constrain, by compulsion, the public choice between the two basic paths toward social progress. More simply stated, this is political repression.
>
> Nor is it possible to disguise this ugly fact by notions such as "mutual coercion, mutually agreed upon" [Garrett Hardin]. If a majority of the United States population voluntarily practiced birth control adequate to population stabilization, there would be no need for coercion. The corollary is that *coercion is necessary only if a majority of the population refuses voluntarily to practice adequate birth control.* This means that the majority would need to be coerced by the minority. This is, indeed, political repression. (*Ibid.*, p. 214; author's emphasis)

These selected comments are typical of Commoner's views on social issues and indicate that he is firmly opposed to "elitist" environmentalism. They are not sufficient to indicate just how far left of center he places himself, however, for at least in principle these are ideals very similar to those held by most American liberals. To gain a clearer picture of his political stance, one must turn to his comments on the capitalist economic system in the light of what he calls "ecological imperatives."

> The total rate of exploitation of the earth's ecosystem has some upper limit, which reflects the intrinsic limit of the ecosystem's turnover rate. If this rate is exceeded, the system is eventually driven to collapse. . . . Hence it follows that there is an upper limit to the rate of exploitation of the biological capital on which any productive system depends. Since the rate of use of this biological capital cannot be exceeded without destroying it, it also follows that the actual rate of use of *total* capital (i.e., biological capital plus conventional capital, or the means of production) is also limited. Thus there must be some limit to the growth of total capital, and the productive system *must* eventually reach a 'no-growth' condition. . . .

In a private enterprise system, the no-growth condition means no further accumulation of capital. If, as seems to be the case, accumulation of capital, through profit, is the basic driving force of this system, it is difficult to see how it can continue to operate under conditions of no growth. (*Ibid.*, pp. 274–275; author's emphasis)

And further: "If . . . it is concluded that the private enterprise system *must* continue to grow, while its ecological base will not tolerate unlimited exploitation, then there is a serious incompatibility between the two" (*ibid.*, p. 277; author's emphasis). Then, after a comparison between socialist and capitalist systems, he comes to the conclusion:

Finally, the socialist system may have an advantage over the private enterprise system with respect to the basic relationship between economic processes and ecological imperatives. While it is true that the Soviet Union and other socialist states, just like capitalist states, have emphasized continued growth of the productive system, the *theory* of socialist economics does not appear to require that growth should continue indefinitely. Moreover, there is no inherent reason in socialist economic theory why it should not be possible to enforce ecologically required differential rates of return from productive activities that are based on different sectors of the ecosystem. (*Ibid.*, pp. 280–281; author's emphasis)

Taken at face value, these statements would seem to indicate that Commoner has a strong preference for socialism and is, indeed, professing to a leftist ideology, emphasizing that, at least theoretically, socialist economics need not be incompatible with ecological imperatives.

When, however, one turns to his practical recommendations for change, the question of where he stands again becomes obscured. The most concise expression of his program is given in the following:

If we are to survive economically as well as biologically, industry, agriculture, and transportation will have to meet the inescapable demands of the ecosystem. This will require the development of major new technologies, including: systems to return sewage and garbage directly to the soil; the replacement of many synthetic materials by natural ones; the reversal of the present trend to retire land from cultivation and to elevate the yield per acre by heavy fertilization; replacement of synthetic pesticides, as rapidly as possible, by biological ones; the discouragement of power-consuming industries; the development of land transport that operates with maximal fuel efficiency at low combustion temperatures and with minimal land use; essentially complete containment and reclamation of wastes from combustion processes, smelting, and chemical operations (smokestacks must become rarities); essentially complete recycling of all reusable metal, glass, and paper products; ecologically sound planning to govern land use including urban areas. (*Ibid.*, pp. 283–284)

One should not be deceived by the phrase "development of major new technologies," for despite the fact that Commoner has a few good ideas about land-use planning, inexpensive land transport, and recommendations to reduce built-in obsolescence, his technological programs are in essence returns to old systems, which have nothing to do with new developments. Nearly all of the post–World War II technologies are, according to Commoner, ecologically unsound—not just because they produce wastes for which we have not yet designed good treatment or disposal systems—but because they are "unnatural" in their foundations. In several later chapters we are going to treat this matter of Commoner's view of the superiority of natural substances in more detail. Here we should like to consider the economic and political implications of his message.

We are not certain whether one should call Commoner's program "radical conservatism" or "reactionary socialism"; but whatever name one gives it, it is clear that his scheme for reorganizing the economy has nothing to do with socialist systems—Western or Communist—as we know them. His is essentially a program for *de-development*; and in its overall implications it is equally negative and regressive as the antitechnology stances of the most conservative of the nature conservancy organizations. Turn the machine down, if not completely off; go back to the use of natural substances; give up detergents, plastics, fertilizers, and pesticides; use as little power as possible. The main difference between Commoner's plan and those of the more obviously conservative and elitist environmentalists is that he thinks a radical change in social structure—and presumably state ownership of the means of production—would be a more equitable way of going about accomplishing this "radical" change in life style than coercive methods. And he does not call for curtailment of consumption, on the grounds that such an approach is unfair to the disadvantaged. The only trouble is that, in Commoner's program, production itself is to be cut back markedly and growth more or less halted; it thus seems fairly obvious that the problem of overconsumption would be solved automatically; we would have returned to a state of "not enough for everyone," while going forward to a "social system of more equitable distribution."

The cost of this program would, he tells us, involve something on the order of $600 billion initially—the price of retooling for de-development. To this would have to be added several hundred billions to restore the environment despoiled by the ecologically unsound technologies to which he ascribes the source of our current environmental problems. Needless to say, all of these economic estimates and recommendations are made following lengthy arguments meant to establish that we really have no choice but to reform in the face of ecological imperatives. Commoner admits that estimates of how much time is left for the survival of the biosphere are subjective, and he always prefers a reasonable to an alarmist tone; but one gathers that he gives us somewhere between 25 and 50 years at the most, provided that we do not blow ourselves up in a nuclear war in the meantime.

We do not intend to draw out all the economic implications of Commoner's proposals for "radical" social change. Anyone with a grain of critical sense can read his book and do so for himself. Nor is it our intention to defend the free-enterprise system, or socialist economics, or to detail the advantages and disadvantages that each has in confronting and resolving environmental difficulties. What we should like to do is examine the main premises underlying Commoner's plan in the light of contemporary Marxist economic philosophy.

Commoner's ideas of how the reformed social and economic structure should be designed in order to be ecologically sound rest on three fundamental premises.

1. The idea of continuing expansion of productivity—whether one calls it growth in gross national product or the fulfillment of the next five-year plan—is fundamentally suicidal from the ecological point of view. Production must be readjusted (downward) to be in harmony with the natural cyclic rates operating in the biosphere. Where increases in production are necessary to meet fundamental human needs, as in agriculture, the gain should be achieved by cultivating more land rather than by attempting to increase yields through fertilizer use and other, similarly "forced" methods.

2. Most contemporary technologies—especially those resting on "unnatural" developments, such as the harnessing of nuclear energy for power and the uses of man-made chemicals—are threatening in two major respects: they endanger human health in often subtle but serious ways, and they are bringing the biosphere to the point of collapse. They have increased production and have made the rich richer, but they have not solved fundamental social problems. The latter argument, with which many would agree, is somehow strangely combined with the "danger to health and biosphere" arguments, which are supported by the by now all-too-familiar environmental scare literature. Commoner gives no consideration to the possibility that the environmental ills spawned by modern technology might be redressed by further developments in that technology. All the "unnatural" approaches to production are *out*.

3. To be fair to Commoner, it has to be admitted that he does not seem to be suggesting a retreat into the very distant past. Presumably he accepts industrialization at about the level of the pre–World War II period. On the other hand, like many of his even more regressive colleagues, he does not see any safe way of producing power. He does not suggest that we should attempt to function without energy production at all, but that power should be used only for those tech-

nologies and products which have high social value. In a remark which is at the least curious from the point of view of socialist goals, he suggests that, wherever possible, human labor should be substituted for processes which are at present heavily reliant on power use.

It would certainly not be right to compare Commoner's opinions about the state of biological and human affairs with those of some hard-nosed engineering type from the socialist bloc. We have therefore chosen as our source for the Marxist view of the socioeconomic aspects of the environmental crisis the most alarmist book which we have come across in the literature of the East-bloc nations. Hailed as a first of its kind, the book is called *The Suicidal Civilization* (1971), and the author, L. Jócsik, seems to have had access to almost all of the recent Western literature on environmental degradation and to have incorporated into his book a good many data typical of the American environmental movement. It should not be supposed, on the other hand, that Jócsik is a dissident or an outsider in East-bloc politics. He is an agricultural economist and lecturer at the Academy of Marxism-Leninism in Budapest; thus one can assume that his views coincide with those of the accepted party ideology.

Jócsik devotes many pages of his book to a discussion of the biological cycles operating in nature:

> . . . with the exception of oxygen, the other biologically essential elements do not stand at our disposal in unlimited quantities; they are in dynamic cycles within the confines of organic life. The cycle stems from the time life took shape on the Earth and proceeds according to given laws. Nature "makes much out of little" by building, degrading and building anew with the bricks of biological existence. In this way the given, limited quantity can secure the state of unlimited plenty. Thus the lower limit of organic life is given by the limited quantity of the biologically essential elements; its upper limit is given by the constant and accelerating—or accelerated—cycle of these elements.
>
> In this cycling, the quantitatively determined elements form ever new combinations, and produce ever new qualitative changes. The laws of the cycling are at the same time the most important laws of the dialectics of nature. If they were not operative, organic life would cease on the Earth. From the other side: the development of humanity poses a categorical imperative for the increase and speeding up of the cycling. (Jócsik, 1971, pp. 14–15; our translation)

He further emphasizes that since man is capable of "bringing the limited resources of the Earth into cycles corresponding to natural ones . . . ," and since these cycles can be speeded up, man can "give the attribute of infinity to the finite, quantitatively limited elements. . . . This statement has the value of a victorious social scientific war of liberation which exorcises for man the specters of famine and want" (*ibid.,* p. 28). Stripped of the bombastic socialist rhetoric, these remarks indicate that while Jócsik recognizes, like Commoner, that there are finite limits to resources and there are natural laws which proceed according to cycles of creation and decay, he would not agree that these limitations are to be taken as "ecological imperatives" which will determine the rates at which resources can be used by man. On the contrary, the "human imperative" forces us to learn how to effectively speed up the cycles operating in nature, create more from less, as Buckminster Fuller would put it, or "lend the attribute of infinity to the finite," as it is here expressed. There are lessons to be learned from the study of ecology and of natural cycles, but in the Marxist view, these are not matters of absolute limits or of categorical "don'ts"; it is rather a matter of learning how to use nature without abusing her.

Technology is severely faulted, but again it is not because there is anything inherently wrong with modern technologies as such, but rather because production has been encouraged to proceed without provisions for combating undesirable side effects.

> The users of technology never gave the slightest thought to damage to the environment and to man. . . . Technology cannot stop at the manufacturing of end products: the goods and profit. It has to be forced to take into account its own consequences [untoward effects]. It also has to work out a technology for these, the goal of which must be the treatment of the effects, the derivatives, the pollutants, the garbage, the noises, in such a way that these should not damage the environment. Technology thus cannot stop at the end product—in the capitalist system at profit. It has to provide a technological solution for the eradication of the damages it causes. Without this, technology is antihuman. It has to be made thoroughly man-centered, even though this may require changes in the social system. (*Ibid.,* pp. 138–139)

It should be clear from these remarks that there is no question here of regressing to earlier technological systems. If technology has failed to take into account untoward effects on the environment and consequently on man (or on the quality of human life), then the solution is that better, or added, technologies must be designed which will eliminate these effects. It is clear from other parts of the book that only a very limited number of contemporary technologies are regarded by Jócsik as fundamentally unsound—all of them replaceable by even more modern, more man-centered systems. Where water supplies are polluted or limited, the author favors the latest techniques of total water renewal and/or of desalination of sea water as solutions, rather than attempts to turn back the clock in the hope that less intense inputs of pollutants will make these systems unnecessary. He claims that modern agricultural practices are fundamentally sound, and would be properly horrified at Commoner's suggestion that food production rate should be limited by the natural rate of soil-nitrogen production, when fertilizers are available to speed up the natural cycle. He regards present industrial technologies as environmentally damaging, but once methods will have been introduced to abate pollution from industrial processes and production costs will include these methods, he will have no further quarrel with these technologies. He emphasizes the recycling of reusable materials, but he does not object to the production of "unnatural" materials in and by themselves. Finally, he recognizes that power is the most essential ingredient of continued growth, which must proceed on three fundamental levels: material, social, and mental.

He states that the burning of fossil fuels is among the worst of the polluting practices of the industrialized nations, and he is anxious to see the transition accomplished to the production of energy by nonpolluting means — in particular the harnessing of the atom. Considering the current opposition of American environmentalists to nuclear generating plants, it is somewhat ironic to read this concerned Marxist's hopes for leadership from the United States in accomplishing this transition: "The United States, which is the biggest consumer of fossil fuels on the Earth, should lead the way in the research efforts and in effecting change to nuclear energy. . . . The peaceful utilization of nuclear energy . . . can absolve humanity from the use of fossil fuels and from the air and environmental pollution originating from their use. In 1966, 15 nuclear plants were operating on a world basis, with a total production of 114 billion megawatts. . . . According to experts, by the year 2000, 70 percent of the electrical energy needs of the world will be supplied by nuclear power" (ibid., p. 167).

If Commoner learned about all of these endorsements of the technologies he has described as threatening to biological life, he might, of course, want to argue that even though Jócsik is sincerely concerned about environmental hazards and even though he reviews a good deal of ecological literature, his views are those of an agricultural economist; he is not, after all, a biologist. This is true; but it is equally true that Commoner is neither a political scientist nor an economist.

Commoner's notion that socialist economic theory does not seem to require continuous growth is the best example of his ignorance in this field. On the contrary, growth is the sine qua non of both the theories of socialism and of communism. A perusal of the classical authors — Engels, Liebknecht, Kautsky, Lenin, Dimitrov — and even cursory readings of contemporary theoreticians ought to be sufficient to make the point clear. Let us quote just one short sentence from Jócsik's environmentalist book: "If there is no room, no possibility for expansion, progress stops" (ibid., p. 133).

One could equally well cite from the works of contemporary socialists writing within the context of Western democratic systems to counter Commoner's notion that Marxist economic theory does not require economic expansion. And, for those who think they recognize in the Chinese brand of Marxism-Leninism a revolution which will be governed by the limits of "ecological imperatives," what is known about Chinese plans for economic and industrial expansion should be sufficient to disabuse them of any romantic notions that China intends to remain an agrarian nation, with human labor elevated to dignity through devotion to the thought of Chairman Mao. In fact, as soon as one goes beyond the little aphorisms about the harmony of the peasant with his land, one can find in the writings of Chairman Mao himself quite clear indications that China is aiming towards a state of material wealth where neither the size of her population nor any limitations on productive capacity should prove to be more than temporary obstacles. As early as 1949 he wrote: "Of all things in the world, people are the most precious. Under the leadership of the Communist Party, as long as there are people, every miracle can be performed. . . . We believe that revolution can change everything, and that before long there will arise a new China with a big population and a great wealth of products, where life will be abundant and culture flourish. All pessimistic views are utterly groundless" (Mao Tse-tung, 1949, in Myrdal and Kessle, 1972, p. 67).

It is not, in our view, necessary to assume that approaches to solutions of real problems of environmental degradation are dependent on adherence to or rejection of either socialist or capitalist systems, any more than it is necessary to assume that one or the other system created these problems in the first place. But to present a program which is essentially reactionary under the cover of revolutionary slogans, as Commoner does, only adds to the ideological confusion which seems to be characteristic of the American environmental movement.

PART II

THE STAYING POWER
OF HALF-TRUTHS

From this point on we shall be dealing in the main with scientific
disciplines and scientific principles relevant to an understanding
of issues concerning pollution of the environment and contamination of foods with
trace chemicals. We shall also describe a number of scientific studies carried out
in recent years and discuss their meaningfulness or lack thereof. Some of the
materials in this section deal with the history of science—Chapter 7, for instance,
in which we try to put the much abused and overused word "ecology" back into
the perspective of its scientific usages in the English-language literature and in
that of Continental Europe. Chapters 8 and 11, which deal respectively with
applied ecology and with toxicology, contain theoretical materials rather con-

105

densed in their presentation and do not make the easiest reading. We felt, however, that it was important to include them because they bear on certain principles of science and interpretations of findings widely misunderstood by laymen and treat matters involving considerable dispute among scientists at the present time.

The three other chapters of this section contain more materials of direct topical interest in current or recent environmental debates: discussions of fertilizer use, the phosphate detergent crisis, the herbicide 2,4,5-T, and general comments on the subject of the threat to health represented by the presence of unseen chemical contaminants. In these chapters we shall also introduce some technical or theoretical materials, but we expect that their immediate relevance to the topical issues will be apparent.

A few words should be said about Chapter 9, which concerns the phosphate detergent crisis. This was the first chapter of this book to be written, and it is the only one which we wrote while in the United States. It treats the detergent issue from the particular time perspective of the summer of 1971, and we did not attempt to revise it in accordance with later developments, nor to rework it stylistically in conformity with the rest of the text.

7

THE SUBJECT OF ECOLOGY

Knowledge is of two kinds. We know
a subject ourselves, or we know where
we can find information upon it.

SAMUEL JOHNSON

As the environmental movement has picked up momentum, not
only has ecology as a biological discipline emerged from its
former obscurity, but a sizable number of people—scientists and laymen alike—
have taken to referring to themselves as ecologists. We have no intention of
attempting to present a short course in ecology, but it seemed worthwhile to
devote a chapter to the general subject, in order to establish a perspective.

Once ecology had become a common household word, there began to appear
in print a number of definitions of the term. One could read, for example, in
New York magazine: "What is ecology?" asked by Elizabeth Barlow; and she gave
the following explanation: "'Eco' comes from the Greek word for house; 'ecology,'

then is the science of efficient housekeeping, and the outcome of the present environmental crisis depends upon the ways in which we put our house in order, both biologically and sociologically" (Barlow, 1970, p. 36).

This definition has since been repeated ad nauseam by many journalists and ecoactivists. However, it is not only lay writers who have provided like explanations. We can also read similar definitions from scientists, such as this one by Garrett Hardin:

> It is interesting that the roots of the words "ecology" and "economics" are similar. The first part of the two words come from the Greek *oikos*, meaning house or home. Both studies have something to do with a house or household. *Logos* means words or discourse and by tradition is used to indicate any field of study. So ecology is the study of households—or perhaps, in modern terminology, we should say of orderly or organized systems. The second part of the word "economics" comes from the Greek *nomos*, which means law or custom. Economics might be defined as the study of the *customary* arrangements of a system. (Hardin, 1970, p. 195; author's emphasis)

These charming etymological lessons are based neither on knowledge of classical Greek (they are the word origins given in ordinary English dictionaries), nor on knowledge of the beginnings of the science of ecology as a discipline. Since so many sweeping generalizations are made about the ecological imperatives of our times which are based on these primitive definitions, we should like to correct them, at the risk of being called pedants.

The common word for house in Greek is *haous* (whence the German word *Haus* and the English *house*); while *oikos* meant a country house, the countryside, and in its broader sense, the terrain or environment. However, it was not the word *oikos* at all from which Haeckel (who first coined the term "ecology") derived the name of this branch of science. He was thinking of *ek*, meaning "out," plus *holos*, meaning "the whole," or *ekolos:* "the total outside." In other terms, his intent was that ecology should refer to the study of everything external to the human body: man's environment, together with all its organisms and functions, considered as a whole.

The Origin of a Discipline

The science of ecology was developed in Germany in the latter part of the nineteenth century. Of course, like any other scientific discipline, it had antecedents in the observations and writings of earlier investigators—natural historians, botanists, zoologists, and amateur naturalists. It is, however, accepted that the first scientific usage of the word ecology originated with the German zoologist Ernst Haeckel in 1866. In 1868, Reiter, a German botanist, coined the same word—apparently quite independently of Haeckel—to designate the study of the relationship of organisms with their environment.

In Haeckel's thinking the meaning and scope of ecology underwent certain changes. Thus, in 1869, he stated that the individual was a product of cooperation between the environment and its own heredity—which relationship he termed oecology. One year later, however, he gave a more precise definition of the subject matter of oecological research, which remained the accepted European usage up until the early 1960s.[*] "By oecology we mean . . . the study of the interrelations of an organism to the sum total of both its inorganic and its organic life conditions; including above all, its active and submissive relations with those animals and plants with which it comes directly or indirectly into contact—in short, oecology is the study of all the complex interrelations referred to by Darwin as the conditions of the struggle for existence" (Haeckel, 1870, p. 358; our translation).

According to this definition, oecology deals with the investigation of the effects of environmental parameters (both climatic and edaphic), such as temperature, light, wind, inclination of ground, composition and structure of soil, and so forth, on individual species *(autoecology)* and on communities *(synoecology)*. The analysis of the dynamic interactions between two individual organisms led to the establishment of the concepts of synergistic relationships (mutually helpful, such as symbiosis), antagonistic relationships (mutually excluding, such as parasitism, antibiosis, and predator-prey relationships), and finally neutral relationships (such as commensualism). When the studies were expanded to investigate the relationships between an organism and the rest of the biotic community, or among groups of organisms within the community, population biology *(demoecology)* was created.

The division of oecological studies into these three subdisciplines — autoecology, synoecology, and demoecology—is apparent in the three massive volumes of Schwerdtfeger's treatise (1963–1971) on the subject, which is a standard European reference work, although it is practically unknown in the United States. In the context of the study of the dynamic interaction of one organism with the rest of the biotic community, man's role in relationship to his

---

[*] In the following, we shall use the spelling "oecology" to designate the discipline as defined by Haeckel and still widely used in Europe. "Ecology" will refer to the concepts treated in the English-language literature as belonging to this branch of science. As we shall see, word usage took a somewhat different trend among English and American investigators than in Continental Europe, leading to considerable confusion and misunderstanding on both sides of the Atlantic.

environment was scrutinized for the first time. This development took place approximately in the second decade of this century.

These investigations of dynamic interactions between species and the environment, and among varying species, formed the basis of the description of food chains, trophic levels, energy-flow calculations, and the partial characterization of some biodynamic spaces. A biodynamic space is any given area—either natural or deliberately circumscribed—in which *all* the oecological parameters are established, together with their secular variations; *all* the species (plants and animals) are identified and *all* their individual numbers are counted; *all* the interactions between the different species, whether synergistic, antagonistic, or neutral are described; and *all* the energy transformations, including rate of photosynthesis and nitrification, anabolic and catabolic balance, heat exchange and kinetic loss, and so on, are accounted for.

Geobotany

In the last part of the nineteenth century, the temporal distribution of organisms in certain locales—both during such short periods as a day, a season, a year, or during the millennia of the geologic past—became a subject of interest. Studies were carried out on diurnal cycles, on seasonal migration, and on the succession of plant and animal life in the different climatic zones during the history of the Earth. These various investigations gave rise to the discipline of *chronology*.

The study of the spatial distribution of plants or animals, the origin of species in certain locales, and the way in which they spread, together with the origin of the individual geoelements in the composition of the local flora and fauna, served as the bases for a third discipline: *chorology*.

Finally, investigations of plant communities led to the recognition that they have elementary units, defined by macro- and micro-climatic as well as edaphic conditions, which units will be comprised of the *same associations* of plants wherever the environmental conditions are the same. This regularity in the pattern of plant communities permitted the systematic analysis of such characteristics of the individual species within the associations as abundance, dominance, constancy, fidelity, and vitality. These studies gave rise to the science which the Swiss botanist Josias Braun-Blanquet called phytosociology in the early part of the twentieth century, but which is now usually called *phytocoenology*.

The American botanist Frederick Clements was one of the most enthusiastic champions of the concept of phytocoenology and a major contributor to its solid theoretical foundations. He went so far as to define "ecology" as the science of the community. However, later American investigators—especially Henry Gleason—tended to deny the objective reality of plant associations as circumscribed entities in nature, the study of which may lead to an understanding of the development of vegetation. Thus, from the early 1930s on, a break occurred in the concepts of the old Continental schools—to which Europe (with the exception of England), the Soviet Union, the North African countries, and Japan belong—and the English-American school.

In the usage of the Continental school, the disciplines of plant chronology, plant chorology, and plant coenology are grouped together and form the science of *phytogeography*. When oecology is also incorporated, one speaks about *oecological plant geography* or *geobotany*.

In the American school the term *ecology* assumed a much broader meaning than oecology. It encompasses the whole of oecology, chronology, and some parts of chorology. However, since the objective reality of coenology was denied, ecology does not deal with this discipline. On the other hand, the term phytogeography, as used by this school, is restricted almost solely to chorology.

Geozoology

Since most terrestrial animals are wanderers, in contrast to the more stationary plants, the study of aggregate interactions among animals and their surroundings is somewhat more difficult than that of plants. It is thus not surprising that zoogeography, which corresponds to phytogeography but deals with animals, developed somewhat later, having its origins basically in this century, in spite of the fact that as early as 1877 Karl Möbius had pointed to the importance of the study of natural communities and the possibility of delineating such assemblages from each other. When investigating oyster beds in the North Sea, he wrote: "Each oyster bed is . . . a community of living beings, a collection of species, and an aggregation of individuals, which find everything essential for their growth and propagation there. . . . Science has, as yet, no single word for such a community, where the sum of species and individuals, being mutually limited and selected under the external conditions of life have . . . continuously possessed a certain defined territory. I propose the word 'biocoenosis' for such a community" (Möbius, 1877, p. 117; our translation).

Still, it was not until 1924 that the first comprehensive zoogeographical text (dealing with chorology, chronology, and some coenology) was published by Hesse in Germany. The author relied heavily on the pioneering work "Animal

Communities in Temperate America" (1913) of Shelford, a towering personality among early American ecologists.

The last discipline to fully develop in the zoological field was zoocoenology. and not until 1958 was a separate treatise published summarizing the results of this science (Balogh). Thus the bases of geozoology were laid about 20 years later than those of geobotany.

Oecological Biogeography

By the early 1950s it became apparent that it is somewhat artificial to keep apart the two major disciplines — botanical and zoological inquiries — and unifying efforts were undertaken. Oecology, if not further specified, meant a science dealing with both animals and plants in their interactions with their environment and with each other. Biogeography aimed at the description of the chronology, chorology, and coenology of both plants and animals. The final synthesis of all these fields has not to date been completed. However, efforts toward synthesis are advancing in the Continental school, and in the new terminology, if the disciplines of geobotany and geozoology are united (i.e., oecology and biogeography), one speaks of *oecological biogeography* or *geobiology*. In 1956, Ökland proposed the word *oecography* for this comprehensive field of investigation, but his term was not generally incorporated into scientific usage, the Continental preference being oecological biogeography.

The vastness of the subject matter of oecological biogeography is demonstrated by the fact that no single work has as yet been published which would deal with its entirety. In English usage, this complex science is called ecology. A nice, simple matter of housekeeping!

Reinventing the Wheel

Geography (as distinct from cartography, which is only one small branch of the former) represents a discipline intermediate between the geological and the social sciences. Biogeography is therefore by definition a science that encompasses the relations among geology, biology, and even the human social sciences. Biogeography has been studied for about 40 years in both Western and Eastern Europe — though admittedly not in its fullest scope, on account of the vast area of inquiry which it comprehends. Nevertheless, it is not new. It was therefore somewhat astonishing to us to read the text of a speech presented at the AAAS Meeting of December, 1969, by Everett M. Hafner. His lecture was entitled: "Toward a New Discipline for the Seventies: Ecography."* What Dr. Hafner was proposing is that we should create a brand new discipline to be called ecography, which will integrate the study of ecology with geography—i.e., the same thing as oecological biogeography. This is an excellent example of the reinvention of the wheel, an activity which occupies a great deal of time and energy on the part of scientists in all disciplines, in spite of the much praised efficiency of our modern methods of communications, computerized bibliographies, and so on. We must, however, excuse Dr. Hafner for this temporary lapse, since he is by training a physicist, and should not therefore be expected to be familiar with the more complex aspects of the biological disciplines, especially when these have been treated principally in books written in French, German, Swedish, and Russian.

The Rift Between Schools

The disparate usage of terminologies between the two major schools pursuing environmental investigations may lie behind the curious recent reviews of works published in translations—from German to English, and vice versa. For instance the English translation of the first edition of Kühnelt's *Grundriss der Ökologie* (1965) elicited mixed but largely unenthusiastic evaluations in the United States. It was thrown up to the author that he treated the subject matter in a narrowly limited manner and that the book was not relevant to present-day problems. The reviewers apparently did not realize that the book dealt solely with oecology, drawing on chronology, chorology, and coenology only when these were essential to developing an understanding of oecological phenomena.† On the other hand, when Odum's *Fundamentals of Ecology* (1959) was evaluated in Europe, some of the reviewers were shocked by its "hodgepodge" of ideas and facts. In their eyes, the author moved across three, if not four, distinct disciplines in a manner which clearly did not differentiate among them. Since the title was translated as *Ökologie* (oecology), Europeans expected that the work would deal

---

* Note that this is the same word as that proposed by Ökland in 1956.

† The new edition of his book (1970) suggests that Kühnelt decided to heed the advice of some of his American critics, for he considerably expanded the scope of the work and also made it more "relevant." In effect, he took over rather uncritically a great deal of recent American material relating to environmental pollution. Apparently the newest trend in certain parts of Europe is to accept the British-American word usage. Since the terminologies and classificatory systems of the Continental schools were originally better defined, this novel tendency among European scientists makes no more sense than if they were to abandon the logical metric system in favor of the chaotic English-American system of weights and measures.

only with this aspect of research, and would not treat problems of species distribution in time or space.

The failure on the part of contemporary U.S. ecologists to comprehend the total scope of ecology in its broadest sense (oecological biogeography) is exemplified by Edward Kormondy's *Concepts of Ecology* (1969). We choose this work from the flood of currently available American texts for two main reasons: (1) It is one of the best of the recent books, being clearly written in a highly literate style, moderate in tone; and the author presents an extremely complex subject matter in the classical reductionist manner—i.e., he deals with important ideas instead of rambling on and losing the reader in details. (2) His name suggests that he is of Middle European origin; and some aspects of the text indicate that he has probably been more directly exposed to research trends typical of the older Continental schools than most other American ecologists.

When Was Coenology Buried?

Indeed, in Kormondy's book, we at least find references to some sages of the European schools of ecological research, and there is even one quotation from a modern Russian work, quite unusual in a contemporary American textbook on this subject. On the other hand, imprecision or simple lack of awareness regarding the extent of the existing literature hampers Kormondy in his attempts to synthesize his concepts into a broad framework. although the bases of this were set down some decades ago.

Following some discussion, he defines ecology thus: ". . . the substance of ecology is found in the myriad of abiotic and biotic mechanisms and interrelations involved in moving energy and nutrients, regulating population and community structure and dynamics. Like many fields of contemporary biology, ecology is multidisciplinary and almost boundless in its concern" (Kormondy, 1969, p. ix).

In the second sentence, lip service is given to the complexity and broad scope of ecology, without precise delineation. The first sentence, however, is nothing but an echo of Haeckel's definition. The "abiotic and biotic mechanisms and interrelations involved in moving energy and nutrients" is tautonymous to Haeckel's "the study of the interrelations of an organism both to the sum total of its inorganic [abiotic] and its organic [biotic] life conditions"; and "regulating population and community structure and dynamics" is the same as "its active and submissive relations with those animals and plants [that is, community] with which it comes directly or indirectly into contact." There is nothing in Kormondy's definition which would broaden the Haeckelian scope of oecology. No mention is made of studies dealing with the distant or more recent past, nor of the understanding gained regarding the mechanisms which operated and are still operating in *bringing about distributions* of individuals and communities in both space and time. The phrase "community structure and dynamics" in Kormondy's definition refers to the given—present situation—but not to the factors which shaped in time the emergence of defined communities where they now are. The fundamental concept of Möbius (completely misunderstood by the present-day U.S. ecologists when they synonymize community with biocoenosis) that there is a possibility of delineating "such a community where the sum of species and individuals . . . continued in possession of a certain territory"—in other terms, that there is an objective basis for coenological investigations—is ignored. In short, Kormondy's definition still would seem to exclude chronology, chorology, and coenology from the scope of ecological inquiry.

Notwithstanding this, he goes ahead and at least partially treats chronology and chorology in his book, in the best tradition of the new U.S. ecologists. But when it comes to coenology, he can only marvel!

> The several diagrams described indicate that the deciduous forest biome is dominated by deciduous trees—a tautology, of course. But this statement does not imply that only a given species is characteristic. Sugar maple, for example, is widely distributed in the eastern half of North America, but it is dominant only in the northern portion, sharing this status with basswood *(Tilia)* to the west and beech *(Fagus)* to the east. Although many of the deciduous tree species of the biome are widely distributed, their area of dominance is restricted and typically shared with one or more other species. This is well illustrated in the forest regions of eastern North America. . . . The map suggests sharp discontinuities between forest types, but how discrete are these boundaries and, within each of these forest regions, how uniform are the communities? What are the regulative factors involved in these patterns? It is obvious that we need to turn from the more generalized vegetative and physiognomic description of structure to a consideration of species composition and to a consideration of the peculiar factors that dispose a particular organization of types to occur in particular regions. *(Ibid.,* pp. 133, 135)

The answers to these obvious questions comprise the subject matter of coenology, a science studied since the early 1900s. The fact that such giants of phytocoenological investigation as Braun-Blanquet, DuRietz, Magdeburg, Tüxen, Komarow, Soo', Gams, or Gaumann—just to name a few—are not mentioned in any ecology textbook written after the mid 1950s in the United States is a sad reflection on the provincialism of current American ecological teachings. It also gives rise to the question: How did it happen that a good third of present knowledge about the biotic environment (coenology) was not incorporated into the American literature, although as Kormondy's words quoted above show, the problems this discipline seeks to solve were raised and are still being raised?

Indeed, the ideas and investigations of coenology as promulgated by Braun-Blanquet fertilized the studies of early American ecologists. Two outstanding representatives of this trend were the botanist Clements in Nebraska, and the zoologist Shelford, in Chicago. These extraordinarily careful, insightful, and visionary researchers had a deep faith that, in spite of the tremendous complexity of the biotic world, there are some smaller units in nature, well-delineated coenoses, the investigation of which could lead to an understanding of the workings (or structure and function, if you like) of the living environment.

To the views of Clements, Gleason—a plant ecologist—took exception. He wrote in 1926: ". . . the vegetation of an area is merely the resultant of two factors, the fluctuating and fortuitous immigration of plants and an equally fluctuating and variable environment. As a result, there is no inherent reason why any two areas of the earth's surface should bear precisely the same vegetation, nor any reason for adhering to our old ideas of the definiteness and distinctness of plant associations" (Gleason, 1926, p. 17).

This seemingly advanced statement actually bespeaks an agnostic philosophy. The debate is highly similar to that waged in the Middle Ages between the nominalists and the universalists about the objective reality of a species. As we all know, the universalists won. If plant associations do not exist as definite and distinct entities in nature (as the nominalists would have asserted), they obviously cannot be studied. If there are no biocoenoses which can be delineated in relation to other such entities, the study of circumscribed communities can lead at most to their description frozen in the immediate moment of observation, which will unfortunately be obsolete in the next moment because of the fluctuation, fortuitousness, and variability of conditions. Furthermore, since there are no two associations identical in space, the study of any particular one will not yield any clues as to the structure and function of any other. The final conclusion is that nature is too complex for our understanding, and thus, it is really not worthwhile to bother with its investigation. (We hasten to add that Gleason never voiced such an extreme opinion, but if his views are carried to their ultimate implications, they lead inevitably to the absurd statement expressed above. This technique of formal logic—*deductio ad absurdum*—will be employed frequently for the reader's amusement throughout the rest of the text.) That there is nothing new in such a philosophical approach to the study of nature can be shown by quoting the motto of the great agnostic nineteenth-century physiologist Emil DuBois-Reymond: "*Ignoramus et ignorabimus.*"

Both Clements and Shelford were great teachers, and they established two strong schools of ecology in the Middle West. These produced such respected scholars as the botanist Paul Sears and the zoologists W. C. Allee, Orlando Park, and Thomas Park. Nevertheless, the beliefs articulated by Gleason, whether consciously or not, had somehow permeated American ecology by the time of World War II. An opportunistic factor undoubtedly had some role here: for the practice of coenology requires a mastery of taxonomy, a difficult and "boring" field. In order to carry out the analysis of biocoenoses efficiently, one should be able to identify rapidly, without the use of keys, the species of flora and fauna of the area. (The use of taxonomic keys slows down the field work to such a degree that it becomes self-defeating.) Without precise identification of all the organisms present in the coenosis, it is impossible to delineate one association from another. Since taxonomy is one of the least popular of the biological sciences—it is difficult, not too stimulating, and very unglamorous—there is a world-wide shortage of expert taxonomists, felt especially in the United States. It is no wonder, therefore, that coenology failed to develop as a viable discipline in this country. Lamentable as it may be, when we recall that the bases for the full flowering of geobotany and geozoology were laid in America by Clements and Shelford respectively, the generation of scientists after the 1950s did not elect to build on these foundations. Some even went so far as to deny the existence of the science of coenology. What is even more disturbing is that the present young generation of ecologists does not seem to know that there exists a tremendous body of knowledge written in European languages—and some of it even translated into English—which represents an integral part of ecology, but which has not yet been incorporated into English-language textbooks. It is astonishing, for example, that the "Saprobic System" of Kolkwitz (1950), which is the work most widely used in Europe for the characterization of water-pollution levels on the basis of biological criteria and is the foundation of the subdiscipline, *saprobiology,* is apparently completely unknown in the United States, although it was first worked out in 1926 and has since been several times updated and vastly refined. There are literally hundreds of books—not simple textbooks, but detailed monographs—written in German, Russian, French, Swedish, and other European tongues treating the various disciplines of ecology; and the initial volumes of comprehensive synthesizing works are now being published. In this context it seems to us obvious nonsense that a trained biologist like Paul Ehrlich (who is not, however, a trained ecologist) can be so simplistic about ecology as to state that the basis of this science will be easy for the lay public to master (see in Ehrlich, 1971).

It is a credit to the ingenuity and self-sufficiency of the American people that by using such aids as books written for the nonspecialist and prefabricated kits, a bookkeeper can almost overnight transform himself into a carpenter, a TV repairman, or a hi-fi specialist. The do-it-yourself trend is a big money saver in an expensive labor market, and it contributes in a meaningful way to the creative use of leisure time. Unfortunately, however, the application of the same principle to science simply does not work. There is no such thing as an "instant ecologist," even though recently a great many people have suddenly assumed the title. It would be well if, once and for all, we dismissed the erroneous notion that ecology is a *simple* discipline.

Is Ecology a Weltanschauung?

Equally nonsensical is the attempt to negate the validity of ecology as a scientific discipline because of its obvious complexity, and to describe it in terms of some ill-defined eclectic philosophy or pseudoreligious ideas. "Ecology deals with organisms in an environment and with the processes that link organism and place. But ecology as such cannot be studied, only organisms, earth, air, and sea can be studied. It is not a discipline: there is no body of thought and technique which frames an ecology of man. It must be therefore a scope or a way of seeing. Such a *perspective* on the human situation is very old and has been part of philosophy and art for thousands of years" (Shepard, 1971, p. 210; author's emphasis).

Such a view is obviously unscientific. It is the same as saying that anatomy per se cannot be studied: only muscles, bones, nerves, and so on can be studied. Accordingly, anatomy must be a *perspective* on the human body, and as such it would belong to philosophy or art, and could not be called a scientific discipline. Ideas like those expressed in Shepard's essay deny, in their ultimate exposition, the possibility of objective, empirical investigations of nature, implying instead that "ecological wisdom" can be achieved through some kind of mysterious "deep sense of engagement with the landscape, with profound connections to surroundings and to natural processes central to all life" (*ibid.*, p. 216).

Notwithstanding the poetic value of this last statement, its irrationality cannot be overlooked. Ecology *is* a science. It is exceedingly complex; nevertheless, it is a discipline, the problems of which have to be attacked by scientific techniques within the framework of our scientific causality. It is not a *Weltanschauung* or a pantheistic religion.

8

FROM THE ARMCHAIR

The main danger of using what is
clearly an inadequate hypothesis is
that it may stand in the way of a
better one. With continued use and
a certain degree of usefulness the
inadequacy of the hypothesis may
gradually be lost sight of, as the
vivid comparison with the original
situation is soon forgotten.

EDWARD DE BONO

Man's quest to understand the rules operating in nature goes
back to the very dawn of civilization. The manner in which
both the questions and the answers have been formulated, however, depends
on many factors: some stemming from the cultural outlook and intellectual
axioms of particular civilizations; others from the accumulation of more information, better observations, and more precise data about the world around
us. Even now it is not always easy to be aware of those cultural factors which
may partially precondition many careful thinkers to expect certain kinds of findings and to reject others which are obvious but "should not be," and thus to lose
sight of the path which represents progress in our understanding of the natural

world. Still, even though modern scientists may suffer from some built-in prejudices which prevent them from perceiving certain aspects of reality, we may legitimately think of the expansion of Western scientific knowledge as a growth process, in which most new developments eventually lead to a clearer understanding of what is going on in the phenomenal world.

In all branches of the natural sciences, the understanding of the governing principles behind phenomena is subject to new interpretations, which although not continuous, seem for the most part to represent closer approaches to reality. Put in another way, the truth value of the explanations given for the behavior of natural phenomena appears to have increased with the unfolding of historical time. Sometimes, of course, there are periods of retrogression in understanding which may last for a very long time, as happened when the heliocentric school of astronomy of the Pythagorean Greek cosmologist Aristarchus of the third century B.C. "lost out" to the Ptolemaic school, and more than 16 centuries passed before the Copernican revolution restored the perspective which forms the basis of modern astronomy. Much more common in the history of science, however, are those relatively brief "dark ages" during which scientists become overly attached to an explanation which is partially adequate or at least psychologically satisfying and permit it to obscure their further observations and the formulation of more comprehensive principles.

It would appear that one of the basic features of the human psyche is man's low frustration tolerance for the unanswered or unanswerable question. While there are vast differences in the kinds of questions which preoccupy varying human societies, it would seem to be a general principle that once a question has been raised and recognized as vital to understanding, speculative or fanciful or mythic-religious answers will be given long before the empirical bases for objective explanations have been established. Let us take as an example the very ancient and common question: "What is fire?"

We know that this question was raised by many early civilizations and that one common denominator of the superstitious formulations of the "law of fire" was that fire is one of the attributes of the divine. The explanation that fire is one of the four fundamental "elements" apparently seemed satisfactory to most questioners in our own civilization until about the seventeenth century. It was thought, according to this view, that the presence of fire represented a manifestation of the divine spark; and as a corollary, that things which did not burn were either made completely of or contained such large fractions of one of the other three fundamental elements—earth, air, and water—that fire was prevented from manifesting itself. This teaching about the distribution of the four "elements" in the cosmos was codified by Aristotle, which might account for its very long staying power.

Sometime during the sixteenth century, a few thinkers began to be interested in the fact that certain materials, such as hard wood, yield comparatively little ash when burnt, whereas others, like peat, produce a great deal of ash. To account for this observation, it was postulated that only a given proportion of any burnable material represented the potential for fire. This proportion was thought to consist of a special substance, which was given the name "phlogiston." The phlogiston hypothesis gave a neat and much more scientific-seeming explanation for the fact that some materials burn more efficiently and leave less ash than others: they simply contained more phlogiston. Thereafter, serious searches were undertaken to identify pure phlogiston in nature. Some thought that they had succeeded when they ignited petroleum, or naphtha; but alas, they could not identify this "essence" in other burnable materials.

We know now that the phlogiston hypothesis was wrong; in fact, it does not seem much more satisfactory to us than the explanation that fire is one of the four cosmic "elements." Nevertheless, the invented law which proclaimed that the uneven distribution of phlogiston in nature accounts for the phenomenal behavior of burnable materials served as the basis for further experimental investigations, which led eventually to a much more tenable explanation. By the end of the eighteenth century the French chemist Lavoisier was able to show experimentally that there is no such thing as phlogiston and to demonstrate that fire is basically a chemical reaction. The fact that Lavoisier could not interpret his findings on the nature of fire in terms of molecular oxidation or reduction reactions does not detract from the importance of his discovery: that burning has nothing to do with a hypothetical essence, but is simply the result of a reaction taking place at elevated temperatures between the material which is burnt and certain components of the air (oxygen). Our present knowledge only adds refinements and describes some apparent exceptions to this fundamental finding.

The observation and study of natural ecosystems has involved similar processes of prescientific explanations, speculations, and the formulation of hypothetical laws to describe the phenomena observed. One of the broadest of these formulations — and the one which is perhaps most frequently cited in support of alarmist cries that man's activities are causing serious disruptions to the biosphere — is that which states that species diversity is a necessary condition of stability. It is this general idea which we wish to examine in the remainder of this chapter.

Attitudes and Speculations

Many centuries before the industrial revolution and long before the founding of the first cities as centers of human civilization, man took the first step in human alteration of the natural environment: he began to cultivate the land. Surely, none of our primitive ancestors worried themselves about any detrimental changes which their first farming practices might have effected in their surroundings. But our more immediate forebears raised the question: "What is the state of nature, and what is man's place therein?"

The first speculations about the stability of ecosystems probably arose from the fundamental observation that there are large systems in nature—such as the continental forests, the prairies and savannas, and the oceans—which had not changed substantially within human memory. When man interfered with the natural state in smaller ecosystems—when he cleared the forests or tilled the grasslands—one of the first signs of change was that the game disappeared from the altered landscape. It was only a step from this observation to the supposition that the stability of the landscape is directly connected to the abundance of life forms, and the converse. In those parts of Europe where clearing and cultivation had proceeded without any constraints or precautions, there were denuded cliffs and eroding, infertile fields which seemed almost as lifeless as deserts. The latter were the ultimate symbol of instability: environments hostile to life, where each small breeze shifted the sand dunes.

Thus when the question was finally seriously posed as to why large ecosystems are stable in nature, the answer was ready at hand: because they harbor a diversity of life forms. In this way, a new law of nature was created from the armchair: the law of ecosystem stability as defined by species diversity. Put in other terms, it was (and is) thought that the more species which live together in a locale, the more stability they provide for the system.

In connection with this concept, all kinds of elaborations of the basic "law" have been offered and are still being offered. By the second half of the nineteenth century, a theoretical consideration of a two-component ecosystem—such as grassland and rabbits—was put forth. This famous rabbit–grass example has been repeated so many times that it is trite, but it is as good a starting point as any.

If there is plenty of grass for the nourishment of rabbits, the latter will multiply rapidly, consuming ever greater quantities of grass. As soon as all the available food has been eaten, the vast majority of the rabbits will starve to death, which will permit a buildup of the grass stand. As grass becomes again abundant, rabbits will start to reproduce in large numbers, until their population collapses again, and the whole cycle starts anew. This simple system is obviously highly unstable. The two species—grass and rabbit—show extreme fluctuations, each being constantly exposed to the danger of extinction.

If foxes are now introduced to the system, the rapid expansion of the rabbit population will be prevented. The foxes will hunt the rabbits and their population will increase, while the grass will develop relatively undisturbed, since the rabbits will be decreasing in numbers because of the presence of the foxes. Ultimately foxes may become overabundant and no longer find the few remaining rabbits in the tall grass. They will start to starve, which will permit a rapid expansion of the rabbit population, with a concurrent removal of large grass stands. The few foxes that were left will then find it again easy to hunt for their food, and their numbers will rapidly increase, starting a new cycle. In this three-member system the oscillations of the populations are lessened in comparison to the one previously discussed, and it can be said that the foxes introduce a "damping effect" which makes the system more stable. The three members comprise a natural food chain, from the grass (the producer) through the rabbit (the consumer) to the fox (the predator or secondary consumer).

If a fourth component were then added to this chain (for instance man, who hunts the foxes under restricted conditions so as to prevent their complete eradication), the complexity and simultaneous stability of the system would be further increased.

The argument of the theorizers then follows: Since in nature not three or four species, but several hundreds are present in any particular ecosystem, these comprising food chains in an intricate web of organismic interactions, it seems obvious that the complexity of these systems, reflected in the diversity of the species, serves as a stabilizing factor which tends to damp the effects of any perturbations to which the systems are subject. It would seem to follow that the agricultural practices of man interfere drastically with the complexity of ecosystems. Planting large areas with single crops—that is, the practice of monoculture—eliminates natural diversity, thus creating highly unstable systems.

It is further argued that, in order to secure some stability for his monoculture, the modern farmer has to invest considerable external energy into his system in the form of work, fertilizers, and pesticides, great portions of which, however, "leak out" by runoffs, evaporation, blowing away, and so on, from his fields. These materials, basically representing energy originating from the man-created unstable systems, will then reach other natural (by definition stable) systems where they will produce a perturbation which, if it becomes large enough, will no longer be damped by the diversity of these natural systems and will bring them into imbalance. In short, when man attempts to stabilize his monocultures, he jeopardizes the stability of the rest of nature. Agriculture is therefore inherently a Bad Thing, especially when it is practiced as monoculture.

This kind of argument may give some background to the statements one can hear and read these days from many sources, differing in formulation and the degree of popularization, but essentially expressing the same theme. Paul Erhlich, for instance, told a *Playboy* interviewer: "I sometimes start my speeches by saying the environmental crisis began on January 2, 8000 B.C. The levity escapes my audiences, more often than not, but the message is there. As soon as man began to farm the land, he began to significantly alter the ecology of the planet. Everything he has done since has made the situation worse" (Ehrlich, 1971, p. 110).

And here are Frank Graham's concise remarks on the horror that is monoculture: "Monoculture is a word which causes the ecologist to shudder . . . The stablest natural community is a complex one" (Graham, 1970, p. 203).

We have a pretty good idea ourselves as to which ecologists Graham must be referring, but it would be nice if he would specify them, so that his readers would realize that not all professionals are so oversensitive, or so worried about modern farming. Already the Romans knew: *"Naturam expelles furca tamen usque recurret."*

The Professionals Speak

The strictly armchair theorizing we have just reviewed is enough to satisfy a lot of the "instant ecologists." There are, however, more serious, professional concepts related to the "law" we are discussing which have been elaborated at some length—some of them based on real work, and others on intellectual gymnastics.

We will have to begin with the idea of succession, as understood by ecologists.

Life has a long history on Earth. Its forms evolved through constant adaptations to their environment. Plant and animal species coevolved with each other, and the ecosystems they comprised with their environment changed gradually throughout the eons. Geomorphologic forces created new habitats, mountains arose and became eroded, and the flora, followed by the fauna, invaded and colonized the new and as yet uninhabited areas. The establishing of vegetation helped to make further changes in the characteristics of the terrain through its interaction with the environment. The plants altered the surroundings in such ways that the new conditions were favorable for subsequent but different complexes. This process in which, through time, different types of communities give way to others, is called *natural succession,* and this basic phenomenon of chronology was first analyzed in depth by the eminent American ecologist Clements.

He found that natural communities are mainly influenced by the prevailing climate of their locale during their development. Under this influence, communities will tend to progress convergently, no matter from what conditions they started, to one typical vegetation characteristic for that area. This he called the *climax* community. The routes of vegetational development, the subsequent changes in communities, represent a "seres," and Clements showed that in the North American temperate forest region four different seres will all ultimately lead to the beech–sugar-maple forest, which is the climax vegetation there. He found that habitats as divergent as sands, clays, flood plains, or ponds filling up during their successional development will all converge in this same climax. Subsequent investigators provided additonal information about the processes of succession and the influences which determine a climax community. It was found that some particular local condition (usually edaphic) may prevent the development of the climax vegetation. For example, exposed steeply inclined slopes will not permit the occurrence of forests. However, in these cases, too, characteristic communities, composed of certain shrubs, will develop and remain stable for hundreds of years. These types of vegetation are called *subclimax*. Communities which had already reached a climax state but were subsequently drastically perturbed and have therefore become highly deteriorated are named *paraclimax*.

In the above description, it has been emphasized that the climax represents the end point of a natural developmental sequence and, as such, is stable because it is in balance with the environmental factors. Up to this point, all investigators seem to agree. But when it comes to a precise description of the phenomena occurring during succession and to conditions prevailing in climax communities, the opinions diverge considerably. It will be necessary for the development of our argument to quote several definitions which are representative of different schools of ecological thought. Margalef, the Spanish limnologist and theoretical ecologist, wrote:

> Succession could be defined as a gradual, irreversible change taking place in the structure of a mixed population, resulting in the replacement of relatively unstructured systems, which have rapid dynamics, are comprised of smaller organisms with a high productivity/biomass relationship, and are adapted to the ready utilization of the resources of their surroundings, by other, more stable communities composed of larger organisms with a greater thermodynamic output, adapted to an efficient utilization of the environmental resources, and having a lower productivity/biomass relationship. (Margalef, 1967, p. 381; our translation)

E. P. Odum, an eminent contemporary American ecologist, summarizes the current theory in the following way: "Stability and diversity increase while productivity decreases during succession" (Odum, 1969, p. 262).

Here is the summary of Woodwell, a plant ecologist and spokesman for EDF:

That is what happens as an ecosystem matures: consumer populations increase substantially, adding to the respiration of the plants [Rs_A] the respiration (Rs_H) of the heterotrophs, the organisms that obtain their energy from the photosynthesizing plants. For an ecosystem . . . NEP equals GP–(Rs_A + Rs_H). [GP = gross production.] NEP is the net ecosystem production, the net increase in energy stored within the system. Rs_A + Rs_H is the total respiration of the ecosystem.

This last equation establishes the important distinction between a "successional," or developmental, ecosystem and a "climax," or mature, one. In the successional system the total respiration is less than the gross production, leaving energy (NEP) that is built into structure and adds to the resources of the site. . . . In a climax system, on the other hand, all the energy fixed is used in the combined respiration of the plants and the heterotrophs. NEP goes to zero: there is no energy left over and no net annual storage. Climax ecosystems probably represent a most efficient way of using the resources of a site to sustain life with minimum impact on other ecosystems. (Woodwell, 1970, p. 69)

Another current American version is given by Kormondy:

It is thus current theory that the stability of the climax community is a function of its species diversity and that the aging phenomenon or succession in an ecosystem is well described as an evolution toward high diversity—a large number of ecological niches and its counterpart of a large number of species. . . . The number of ecological niches in a given ecosystem is a function of the history and evolution of the system and of its productivity; thus one becomes a measure of the other, productivity of diversity, diversity of productivity. (Kormondy, 1969, p. 159)

We next consider the definition of Soó, whose views are representative of the Middle and Eastern European schools of geobotany:

The essence of natural (biotic) succession is that the life activities of a phytocoenosis produce conditions which become more and more limiting for itself while making them gradually more favorable for another plant community to which it eventually has to yield; thus succession tends to achieve, through the temporary beginning and intermediary stages, a permanent closing plant association, the climax. The climax is the plant association showing the highest degree of organic matter production and is composed of the most levels *(facies)* which can develop in the climate of a certain region; it is in a dynamic balance with its environment and with itself. (Soó. 1953, p. 27; our translation)

The definition by Orlando Park, the most prominent follower of the Clements-Shelford school, is the most divergent:

> Succession represents a process of increasing integration between life and environment. It apparently tends to follow the principle of LeChatelier as developed by Bancroff; i.e., heterogenous systems tend progressively toward a condition of minimum disturbance by external forces and internal stresses. . . . succession also tends toward a progressively more efficient use of energy. The climax community is a close-knit and delicately balanced system which stores and uses solar energy . . . it represents the maximum in organic economy, as contrasted with the extreme of energy waste in a bare area.
>
> Like the processes of physiographic change and soil development, biological interaction is convergent in character, leading from initial heterogeneity to ultimate homogeneity. (Park, 1963, pp. 919–920)

It is not essential that the reader follow in detail this rather condensed jargon. However, since it is agreed that natural climax communities are the most stable, we will not even have the basis for an "armchair law" (stability = diversity) unless it is also agreed, at the minimum, that these stable communities are the most diverse.

1. Margalef does not refer to diversity at all. (His description of a stable community, it should be noted, derives from marine algal studies.) In his view, the stable community is one in which larger organisms which make efficient use of the resources and reproduce more slowly have replaced the smaller, less structured populations. Although it is not stated explicitly here, the less structured mixed populations are actually more diverse than the highly structured stable ones which replace them.

2. Odum's opinion does not require any explanation. It is a succinct expression of the current orthodoxy of the dominant American school.

3. Woodwell's view is similar to that of Odum, except that the matter of productivity in different stages of succession is carefully qualified. In a developmental ecosystem, there is "energy left over"—that is, primary producers fix more energy than is "used up" by the community as a whole, and a process of enrichment goes on. On the other hand, in a fully developed climax community all the energy fixed is used and there is no net annual storage. This seems to imply a relatively static situation. Thus, if an organism foreign to the community, such as man, extracts any amount of energy from a natural climax formation (such as removal of trees, for instance), he will be "stealing" from this perfectly balanced budget, so to speak, since there was no extra energy fixed whatsoever.

On a purely theoretical level, this seems to be a basic logical contradiction to the claim that these stable communities can withstand perturbations more efficiently than developing systems; for if there is no excess energy stored, the removal of even small quantities of energy should seriously disturb such systems.

4. Kormondy's view is different in one very important respect: he equates stability not only with diversity, but also with maximal productivity, in contrast to Odum and Woodwell. In fact, he says that these terms are all interchangeable. Thus, the most productive system must be both the most diverse and most stable, the most diverse must be the most productive, and so on.

5. Soó is in agreement with Kormondy with respect to productivity. The climax community will show the highest degree of production of organic matter. He does not say, however, that it is the most diverse, but rather the one composed of the most *levels* of different organisms.

6. Finally, there is the definition of Park, which is the most divergent of the six. He agrees with all the others that the climax community is stable and makes the most efficient use of energy, but he describes the ultimate climax as tending towards *homogeneity* — i.e., reduction in the number of species.

This is, obviously, an exactly opposite view from that of the two current American schools of ecological thought. Although Park belongs to an earlier generation and his ideas are not in fashion at the present time, one cannot, in this instance, assume that the new theoreticians have necessarily come up with better explanations. In fact, it is really quite difficult to fathom how this "stability depends on diversity" postulate could have taken hold, not only among the instant ecologists, but among so many professionals, since only rather slight field knowledge and a bit of reflection should point to the exceptions to this supposed law. Think, for instance, of the species composition of a climax boreal forest, at the primary-producer level. With the exception of the lower life forms, such as soil algae, there are not more than 40 to 50 species making up this level in the whole climax ecosystem. However, if some acres of the forest are clear-cut, herbs and grasses will take over, and in this paraclimax community, easily 250 to 300 species will be found at the primary-producer level, where productivity will also be greater than in the climax forest. As the trees grow back, the species number will decrease.

One might ask whether there would not be more herbivores and carnivores in the climax forest than in the clear-cut area; but this is not the case. It follows from another accepted rule of ecology that the biomass and diversity of the primary producers determines both the numbers of species and of individuals at subsequent trophic levels.

Let us take another example, this time a preclimax community. In the type of high moor which will eventually develop into a coniferous forest, species diversity is immense on the primary producer level, although productivity is relatively low. One can find as many as 300 to 400 species of one single algal group: the desmids. All kinds of mosses and grasses are also characteristic of this preclimax. Once the climax forest develops, only 20 to 30 species of primary producers will remain. In this particular case, the productivity of the climax will be much higher, even though the species diversity is just a fraction of that of the preclimax moor.

There are also paraclimax communities which are stable and highly productive. One of the best examples of such are the alpine pastures of Europe. There, the typical climax community is composed mainly of small coniferous shrubs. For hundreds of years the mountain cowherds and shepherds have piled up the rocks and removed the shrubs. The grasses have taken over, and their luxurious growth is checked only by the grazing herds. These are communities which were seriously perturbed by man, but by now, as paraclimax ecosystems, they have reached stability. Their productivity is orders of magnitude higher than the corresponding climax, and they are admired as natural, balanced environments, giving much aesthetic pleasure to recreation-seeking nature lovers.

What seems to happen in nature during the chronological development of communities—that is, the aging process—is that at first a few pioneering organisms appear, making up a very simple community. With time, the community becomes more and more complex, and a great diversity of species is found. With further development, however, the conditions become less supportive for a large number of highly divergent forms, and a secondary simplification sets in. Since this process takes thousands of years in large ecosystems, it is difficult to study, but there are certain special circumstances where the time scale is condensed. Early stages of succession can be studied when a new volcanic island appears, for example. Or in a microecosystem such as a newly opened hot spring, the succession of the algal communities can be investigated during the ensuing years as the water temperature drops. In our studies of hot-spring communities, we were able to confirm this phenomenon of a developmental progression from simple→complex→secondarily simple (Claus, 1959).

It is also known from phylogenetics that the evolutionary course of all the major groups of plants and animals show the same tendency, starting from relatively simple progenitors, achieving great complexity, and then undergoing a secondary morphological simplification. This principle is operative at the most varied taxonomic levels.

Thus it would seem that there is considerable evidence to support Park's now unpopular view that the true climax community for a given climate, while stable, is much simpler in terms of species composition than are the developing communities which precede it. Nevertheless, both the majority and the minority orthodoxy of the current schools of American ecology deny that this is the case, insisting that stability and diversity are interchangeable.

The majority view, here represented by Odum and Woodwell, claims that (1) stability is derived from diversity, and (2) during succession, productivity decreases. The minority opinion, as expressed by Kormondy, is that (1) stability = diversity = productivity, and (2) during succession, productivity increases. If any of these postulates represents a natural law, it should have predictive value. Let us now see what happens when researchers finally decide to test these laws in nature. In doing so, we shall confine ourselves to three recent papers from North America, so that it will not be supposed that we are further perpetuating the rift between the American and European schools.

Two Fields

We have two ecosystems in close proximity to each other, with the same climate and the same edaphic conditions, but differing in that one is more advanced in the successional process and contains a greater variety of species than the other. One would expect, according to the theorizers, that the older and more complex system would be more stable, and (in the Odum-Woodwell view) less productive than the younger one. An equal perturbation inflicted on both systems should, as predicted by the stability-diversity law, have less effect on the older than on the younger system.

A group of Syracuse University researchers (Hurd et al., 1971) set out to test the postulates we have been discussing by introducing an external disturbance into two systems like those above, and comparing their responses. They defined stability as the ability of the system to maintain or return to its ground state after an external perturbation. The assumption was that the greater variety of species composition in the older system should create a "damping effect" which would reduce the amplitude of the change in comparison with the younger system, if current theory is correct.

They selected two adjacent old hayfields for experimentation. One had not been used agriculturally for 7 years, the other for 16 years. The diversity of flora and fauna at the start of the experiment was higher in the second field (which they designated the "old field") than it was in the first (referred to as the "young field"). They divided the fields into two control and two experimental plots, and to the latter they added a commercial fertilizer at the rate of 560 kilograms per hectare. Their reasoning was that the addition of the fertilizer would serve as an efficient destabilizing agent, perturbing both the old and young field ecosystems. They sampled the fields monthly for producers (grasses), herbivore consumers (arthropods feeding on the grasses), and carnivorous consumers (arthropods which feed on the herbivores). Thus they could compare the changes at three different trophic levels.

Their findings can be summarized in the following points:

1. After fertilization, productivity at the primary-producer level increased significantly in both plots, although species composition did not change.

2. The increase in productivity at this trophic level was less in the old field than in the young field (71 percent versus 97 percent).

3. At the second trophic level, there was an increase in both productivity and species diversity in both fields.

4. This increase was significantly greater in the old field.

5. At the third trophic level, diversity increased in both fields.

6. Productivity of carnivores increased in the old field and decreased in the young field.

With the exception of the first two points, these results do not look good at all as far as the stability derived from diversity postulate is concerned. The perturbation indeed caused a smaller change in primary productivity in the more diverse old field, and one could suppose that the greater variety of plant species had served to damp the effects of the external influence. However, at the second and third trophic levels, the old field showed a greater response than the young field, in spite of the fact that its species diversity was originally greater at these levels also. The authors conclude: "In contrast to current ecological theory, greater diversity at a trophic level was accompanied by lower stability at the next higher level" (Hurd et al., 1971, p. 1134).

These findings also fail to substantiate the broad hypothesis that during succession productivity decreases. This was true only at the primary-producer level, whereas the greater productivity of the old field at higher trophic levels was quite dramatic.

This experiment raises at least three fundamental difficulties in connection with current ecological theory. First, as the authors themselves bring out, greater stability was not dependent on species diversity. Secondly, during successional aging, even if the complexity of a system increases, its stability is decreased. Lastly, the accepted idea that the primary-producer level determines the produc-

tivity and composition of the subsequent levels seems to be thrown in doubt also.
What is left of the majority-view orthodoxy?

More of Everything

In 1972, three Canadian researchers (McAllister, et al.) published a report of their experiments concerning the effect of serious artificial perturbations on a large oligotrophic lake on Vancouver Island. (By oligotrophic is meant that the waters are very low in nutrients and the condition of the lake is essentially pristine.) They investigated the changes in species composition and productivity at three trophic levels (in this case: producers–algae, consumers–grazers, and carnivores), after addition five times weekly, from June to October, of a total of 90 tons of fertilizer. (The lake was 4,850 hectares in area, with an average depth of 200 meters.) They added the fertilizer in quantities which they expected would produce such a high enrichment that the standing stock of phytoplankton (algae) would double every seven days. This represents a very massive perturbation.

According to standard theory, one would predict the following:

1. The perturbation should introduce a serious imbalance, manifesting itself in a drastic reduction in species diversity.

2. A few hardy but not desirable algae should develop into blooms. Productivity at the primary-producer level would be high, but many desirable species would be lost.

3. At higher trophic levels, there should be a decimation of some species, and any percentage increase in productivity should be less than at the primary level.

These are the expectations from theory; none of them was confirmed by the results.

The Canadian team found that, by the end of the experiment, primary productivity was at least doubled, with no change in species diversity. The consumers and the carnivores together increased in productivity by a factor of 8, again with no change in their species composition. The authors concluded: "It has been possible to enrich artificially a large body of water without causing either undesirable eutrophication or the elimination of species. . . . in spite of increased production, trophic stability was maintained in that the diversity of food organisms was substantially the same before and after nutrient enrichment" (McAllister et al., 1972, p. 562).

Both these papers indicate that the hypotheses held to be axioms by most modern American theoretical ecologists do not have predictive value. They there-fore cannot be said to express laws operating in nature.

A Pattern Emerges

The last cherished idea which is intimately connected with the problem of ecosystem stability and diversity is the postulate that net energy production (NEP in Woodwell's formulae) decreases during succession. As we have seen, Woodwell goes so far as to claim that in a climax system, NEP is zero, and "there is no net annual storage." The results of an ambitious investigation of world pat-terns in plant energetics were published recently (Jordan, 1971), raising a serious challenge to Woodwell's thesis.

Jordan calculated ratios between energy bound in long-lived tissues per year and energy stored in short-lived tissues, for all major plant communities of the world. Here is his distinction: "Energy stored as wood in the trunk and large branches of trees is bound in parts which remain intact for most of the life of the plant. Energy stored as leaves and other litter, including fruits, flowers, bark, and twigs, is energy that is quickly available to herbivores and decom-posers" (*ibid.*, p. 425). Among other factors, such as availability of solar energy and precipitation, he investigated the changes in these ratios during succession.

He found that during the normal successional process, the ratio of wood production to litter production increases. When these ratios are expressed in terms of caloric concentrations, one finds that grasses and herbs accumulate fewer calories than bushes and trees. He wrote: "It is evident that, within a given locality, grasses and herbs have lower caloric concentrations than trees. This pattern coincides with the pattern of ratios in that both the ratios and caloric concentrations are lower in herbs and grasses than in trees" (*ibid.*, p. 431).

This means that during succession caloric concentrations in plants increase, reaching their maximum in the climax community. Jordan pointed out that the impression that productivity decreases during succession may derive from mea-surements taken only of the aboveground biomass, whereas more energy is ac-tually being stored in woody underground tissues as the community ages. This was his polite way of correcting some of Odum's reported measurements. If, as Jordan states, a continual gradient towards a greater annual energy accumula-tion and storage occurs during the successional process, then it is clear that Wood-well's formulae need to be rewritten.

Recognizing that patterns do exist from which can be derived formulae with predictive value, Jordan closes: "One objective of science is to seek order in the universe; when we find order, we gain the ability to predict. When we find order in plant production on a worldwide scale, we are able to predict the productive capability of the world. The importance of finding the pattern of plant energetics is that it provides a basis on which the productive capability of the continents can be calculated" (ibid., p. 433).

Does It Matter?

A natural and quite legitimate question from the point ot view of the reader would be: "What do all these in-group professional arguments have to do with the claims of environmental activists?" In effect, the settling of the diversity-stability question should be a matter for strictly professional debate, and we would not bother our readers with it, were it not for the fact that this invented law is constantly being brought up in connection with various environmental issues.

From extremists and complete purists one hears the diversity-stability law used as an argument against *all* the basic ingredients of modern farming methods: agriculture itself is inherently bad, since it reduces natural diversity. One may even hear the extraordinarily illogical assertion that the practices associated with monoculture—by which the productive capacity of acreage under cultivation can be increased manyfold—can become a *cause* of famine. When discussing why the Green Revolution is doomed to fail, Paul Ehrlich illustrates his point by bringing up the famous Irish potato famine of the 1840s:

> A perfect example is the Irish potato famine. That followed a green revolution. There were two million Irishmen living in misery in Ireland. Then they had a green revolution; the potato was introduced. The Irish planted a huge monoculture of potatoes, an ecologically stupid thing to do, since monocultures are simple and, therefore, vulnerable systems. Then, in the middle of the last century, along came the potato blight, which killed the potatoes. By that time, the Irish had bred up to eight million people on this huge supply of potatoes. When the blight hit, about one million Irishmen starved and two million emigrated. Had there been no place for them to go, three million people would have starved because a green revolution was introduced to two million people. (Ehrlich, 1971, p. 88)

Leaving aside some questions about the numbers Ehrlich is using, one must consider whether the disaster following the Irish potato blight has any real relevance to our times, and also whether starvation of large numbers was in fact an

inevitable consequence of the crop failure. The argument lying behind this example is that a monoculture is far more vulnerable to plant diseases and pest
infestations than a more heterogeneous crop. On its face value this statement
is true. However, with the modern armamentarium of plant-protecting chemicals,
even a new plant disease or infestation with an unfamiliar pest can usually be
brought quickly under control. There is no need to fear that widespread famine
would follow from the sudden appearance of a "new" pest where modern farming methods are practiced; unless, of course, environmentalists are sufficiently
successful in their campaigns to limit the use of agricultural chemicals so that
the hands of agriculturists are tied.

Furthermore, Ehrlich leaves out of his account the significant role played
by British politics of the times in relation to the loss of lives which followed the
blight. The desperate conditions of hunger among the Irish populace could have
been alleviated had not the ruling Tory government—embroiled in and committed to a laissez faire policy—prevented the unloading of grain shipments
in Irish ports and continued the export of Irish produce to England. The factor
of man's callousness towards his fellow human beings played a greater role in
the famine itself than did the natural event represented by the blight. Only a
few years ago, a parallel situation arose when the Nigerian army would not permit the distribution of food relief shipments to the starving Biafrans.

When pressed, environmentalists usually admit that even a much smaller
human population would not survive without some form of agriculture. But they
dislike large-scale mechanized farming and appear to be deaf to arguments about
the practicality or necessity of modern argricultural practices. Especially common is their condemnation of the heavy reliance of modern farmers on fertilizers
and pesticides. As we mentioned earlier, their most fundamental objection is
that these artificial substances cannot be confined to the farmer's land, but will
be carried over into natural systems—rivers, lakes, oceans—where they will
seriously perturb existing balances. We are quite ready to admit that there may
be particular circumstances (usually local ones) where it is true that farming
practices have a notable side effect on some natural ecosystem. At the present
time, however, it has become almost impossible to proceed, when claims about
such side effects are raised, with a straightforward, objective investigation of
whether or not there is a real basis for concern. The conviction and righteousness
stemming from supposed ecological axioms adds to the atmosphere of irrationality surrounding such charges, just at the time when we need most to pursue matters bearing on ecological effects with cool heads and solid, accurate collections
of data.

The "stability law" is also used to justify the argument that *any* change in species composition of a particular ecosystem is the beginning of the end. Thus the threatened loss of a "desirable species" is proclaimed to be a symptom of destabilization which signals the collapse of the whole biosphere. Anyone with a grain of common sense realizes that this is not true. In historical time the disappearance of some animal species is known, but their extinction had no lasting effect on the natural ecosystems. It is further acknowledged that many animals would probably have become extinct during the last hundred years as the result of natural aging, and that even though man's activities may eliminate many habitats for wildlife, it is man's intervention on behalf of these endangered species which has kept them alive. It is highly questionable whether the sudden disappearance of all the 800 or so species now on the world list as "endangered" would result in any significant change in natural balances. Such an event might represent a great emotional loss for those interested in wildlife and attached to rare species, but the ecological significance of these animals is practically nil. But facts are beside the point, and the activists will counter such statements with the "scientific law of ecology: diversity is essential to maintain stability." Even the skeptical critic with a good deal of common sense may be at a loss how to respond when all three loaded words — "ecology," "scientific," and "law" — are thrown at him all at once.

Thirdly, and perhaps most important, is the fact that a natural law, if it really describes the dynamics of reality, can be used for predictive purposes. It is not at all rare to find that critics of certain environmental pollutants have no hard data on either the degree of contamination of a natural ecosystem, nor data showing measurable effects on the flora and fauna of that system. This does not disturb them, however, for, relying on the diversity-stability law, they confidently state that the impact of the environmental insult will be felt in the near future. The recognition by the current American school of ecology of this armchair theory as a law thus often absolves researchers from the need to produce real data from the field.

Lastly, if one examines the ultimate implication of formulations of this supposed law — especially as computerized by Odum and Woodwell — it becomes evident that modern man is excluded from the natural system. The provincialism of the new American ecologists and their failure to accept man's activities as an integral part of nature prompted W. H. Drury (himself an Audubon Society officer) to write, in his review of Ehrenfeld's *Biological Conservation:*

> His theoretical basis . . . is that of the American ecological Establishment: complexity and diversity buffer the community against disturbance from the physical environment; the diverse, buffered community is the evolutionary purpose of eco-

logical succession. . . . I think the author errs in ignoring the fact that these assumptions have been repeatedly challenged by other American ecologists. . . . Ecologists in Europe, Australia, and elsewhere have avoided this polarization into extreme theoretical positions and have developed more objective means of describing ecosystems, which provide more rational bases for managing them. . . . American ecologists do not resolve, or even recognize, these underlying theoretical problems. . . .

For the future, practical goals must be defined so that everyday small decisions can help work American society out of the mess into which everyday small decisions have brought it. At an early stage ecologists must present a rational body of community theory freed of the Procrustean concepts of succession and climax about which (as Egler said) ecologists have been mumbling in academese while hiding in their ivory towers. (Drury, 1970, p. 1333)

9

CLEANLINESS IS
NEXT TO GODLINESS

Men, it has been well said, think in
herds; it will be seen that they go mad
in herds, while they only recover
their senses slowly, and one by one.
CHARLES MACKAY

The story of detergent developments in America is a tale that
begins with a soapy problem, takes a nice turn with a clean
solution, and then spirals into a series of scientific disagreements, hasty conclusions, bad advice, and forced adjustments on the part of the cleaning-compound
manufacturers. The present state of affairs does not look good. We may now have
some serious problems on our hands, but if you think the source of the problems
is phosphate and that we are on our way to eliminating the villain of this piece,
you may be in for some unpleasant surprises.

After World War II, new cleaning compounds were developed, most of
which were quaternary ammonium-salt-type detergents. At first these seemed to

138

work efficiently, but by the early fifties, foams riding on the surfaces of a number of the rivers of the United States became noticeable, and even water coming out of wells felt slippery and developed surface suds when it dispersed. These phenomena resulted from the fact that the detergents, by that time in wide use, were bactericidal and were not subject to breakdown by microorganisms. The nonbiodegradable detergents seeped through the soil into underground passages, and in this way entered drinking-water wells as well as rivers. Where there were clothes to be washed, there were foaming waters. Considerable public pressure was placed on the detergent manufacturers, whose response was to substitute biodegradable phosphate compounds for their earlier products. The suds disappeared, and the detergent problem appeared to be solved.

The phosphate compounds got clothes and dishes clean all right, but their use soon gave rise to a great clamor about pollution of our waters. By now the very word "phosphate" has dreadful connotations in the minds of laymen, for we have all been told that the phosphates are terrible contributors to eutrophication, a major cause of algal blooms, and are generally very bad for the environment.

The background of all this sound and fury involved some highly sensitive ecological problems, which are supposedly understood theoretically, but in practice still seem to elude exact understanding. To comprehend the pollution problems said to be related to these detergents, it is necessary to consider some theories dealing with plant nutrition.

What Are the Limits of the Limiting Factors?

While investigating the growth requirements of plants, around 1860 the German chemist Liebig discovered a law which he termed "the law of the minimum," governing the inorganic nutritional needs of plants. He found that plants need phosphorus, nitrogen, and sulfur, and a host of trace elements, such as magnesium, zinc, manganese, boron, iron, etc. If any of these is missing, plant growth will cease, even if all the others are present in abundance. The first of any of these elements to be exhausted by a particular plant species is termed "the limiting factor." Basically, what this means is that the element or nutrient which is in shortest supply in relation to all factors necessary for growth is the one which will limit growth. This is not a particularly easy concept to grasp—even many scientists have difficulties in identifying the limiting factor exactly—but if the reader will bear with us for a few pages we hope that the basic principle will become clearer.

Nitrogen and phosphorus are the elements utilized in the largest quantities by plants, and clearly a shortage of either will act to limit plant growth. That the absence of any of the trace elements may also be a limiting factor, however, can be illustrated by the following example. In certain areas, soil contains relatively small amounts of magnesium. Apple and peach trees apparently have a higher requirement for this element than most other plants, and it has happened in certain areas that in spite of the best care, whole orchards of apple or peach trees died off. The puzzle was solved when it was discovered that the magnesium in the soil had been exhausted. Addition of magnesium salts restored the fertility of the soil.

Nitrogen and phosphorus are accessible for plant uptake in the forms of nitrate and phosphate. These compounds are present in soils and natural waters in an approximate ratio of 10:1 (nitrate to phosphate). During their evolutionary history, plants have adapted to this ratio.

Natural pristine streams contain relatively small quantities of dissolved nitrates and phosphates, since these elements must enter the waters from the surroundings. Such streams therefore support only a very limited plant growth. Pristine lakes, depending on the soil in the surrounding area, may contain much higher quantities of these nutrients, since in closed bodies of water the nutrients will tend to accumulate.

The eutrophication of closed bodies of water — so often associated exclusively with man's activities — is actually a natural process. The literal meaning of the word is "gaining in nutrients" or "rich feeding." This process of enrichment takes place without man's presence, through sedimentation, erosion, and so on. When man adds nutrients to waters, he speeds up this natural aging.

In general, the inland and coastal waters of modern America may be described as eutrophic. One must admit that they reached this state with such rapidity because of man's careless practices of discharging untreated wastes into the waters. This problem is not unique to contemporary civilizations; we know, for instance, that in ancient Rome, the Tiber was so polluted with human wastes that the once famous oyster beds at Ostia died out.

Eutrophic waters do present conditions favorable for algal blooms. The actual mechanism which triggers the appearance of a bloom is still not completely understood by specialists, however, even though one may read all about it in popular books on ecology. The uncomfortable truth is that limnologists (specialists in inland water studies) are unable to say with any certainty exactly why an algal bloom appears in a particular place at a particular time.

From the turn of the century on it was more or less accepted that nitrates were the natural limiting factor for the growth of aquatic plants. Around the mid-1950s, however, when more precise techniques were introduced for measuring phosphate concentrations in waters, scientists began to speculate that phosphate might be the true limiting factor in nature. It was recognized that excreta from both animals and man contained disproportionate amounts of phosphate (20 times more than in nature, shifting the phosphate-nitrate ratio to 2:1 in favor of phosphate). It was a fairly natural jump to the conclusion that it is the continuous addition of phosphates to receiving waters which was encouraging algal growth and thence to the new theory that phosphates are the limiting factor. Unfortunately, even secondary sewage plants do not remove phosphates from human and animal wastes, as we mentioned in Chapter 5. Thus, wherever receiving waters are enriched either with raw sewage or with effluents from primary and secondary sewage treatment facilities, there will be plenty of nutrients available for plant growth, regardless of detergent-use patterns.

The "new theory" that phosphates are the limiting factor underlies the detergent crisis of the late 1960s. The public was taught, or in any event told, that phosphates were providing "rich feeding," and causing algal blooms, which were in turn rather imprecisely indicated to be major symptoms of the generally deteriorated status of our inland and coastal waters.

The true situation is, unhappily, much more complex. No matter how much phosphate there is in a body of water, if nitrates are not present, algae will not grow. It is the *ratio* between the two compounds which is important. Let us suppose, to illustrate simply, that a body of water contains 1 kg of phosphates and 10 kg of nitrates, which will support the growth of 680 kg of algae. In another situation, there are 3 kg of phosphates and 10 kg of nitrates, which will still produce only 680 kg of algae—but 2 kg of phosphates will be left behind. It should be obvious that if another 10 kg of nitrates are then added to the 2 kg of phosphates which were left over, growth of a second 680 kg of algae can be supported. Thus, in the second example, the *nitrates* were the limiting factor. With further nitrate supplies, growth of algae will continue until all the phosphorus has been used up. Then phosphorus once again becomes the limiting factor.

Since there are about 20 elements essential for plant growth, along with several organic compounds (such as vitamins), and, of course, carbon dioxide, *any of which may also serve as the limiting factor,* it may be seen that the whole problem has been seriously oversimplified when phosphorus alone is blamed for algal blooms.

By the time of this writing (August, 1971), it has been established that 56 percent of the coastal waters and many of the inland waters of the United States have a phosphate-to-nitrate ratio of 3:10, and in some places, even of 1:1. Since this means basically that the waters are phosphate-saturated, it should be obvious that substituting nitrate-based compounds for phosphate detergents is ecological suicide, or, as John Ryther, director of the Department of Ecology at the Woods Hole Oceanographic Institute has put it, "only adding fuel to the fire" (Ryther and Dunstan, 1971, p. 1013). And yet that is exactly what was done in one of the first major actions as a result of pressure against the use of phosphate detergents.

But now let us go back—way back—in time, before we examine the latest events in the battle with dirt.

How to Get Clean

In ancient Greece and Rome, dirt was removed from clothes by the "pounding on rocks in the river" method. For personal cleanliness, the ancients smeared olive oil on their bodies, scraped the entire surface of the skin with wooden knives, and then washed off the remaining oil with hot water. It was not until the fifteenth century that potash became a household item in the West, although it had been known to the Chinese for several thousand years. The finest-quality potash was manufactured in the Mediterranean countries by burning algae.

Soap came into general use only at the end of the eighteenth century. Although soap was a great boon for those who desired to keep their own bodies clean, it was not too good for washing clothes, since most of the surface waters of the Earth are hard waters in which soap does not form suds.

Around 1830, sodium carbonate was synthesized and produced industrially, and it has been used ever since as a water softener. Up until the early 1950s it was used universally as washing soda. Caustic soda was also produced during the 1800s, and caustic soda solutions were preferred by many women for a really clean wash. Unfortunately, however, both sodium carbonate and caustic soda (sodium hydroxide) are dangerous substances, and their use led to great numbers of accidental deaths and cases of blindness through splashing into the eyes.

Then came the big cleaning breakthrough, another triumph of modern chemistry. As we have already mentioned, the early detergents were efficient and nontoxic, but they were nonbiodegradable and we had a suds problem. The phosphate detergents, on the other hand, seemed ideal, since they were nontoxic and biodegradable, and they got the clothes very clean indeed.

Where was the problem?

The overt manifestations of the problem were a continuing increase in general enrichment of inland and coastal waters and, in many cases, concomitant growth of undesirable aquatic plants—not just algae—but various other nuisance organisms. Considering our brief discussion of the factors involved in plant nutrition, it may perhaps be understood that there was no certainty at all at the time when the phosphate crisis blew up that phosphates were indeed the limiting factor for plant growth in most of our surface waters. But a pseudoproblem was created by a partial evaluation of the facts. According to those modern theorists whose work was publicized at that time phosphates *were* the limiting factor. There were lots of algae, and everyone knows that is bad. No one bothered to point out that phosphate concentrations in waters are the easiest to determine, and that this might have been a "factor" in making phosphate the "sure" limiting factor. The role of raw domestic sewage and sewage effluents in contributing phosphorus to receiving waters was minimized, and the finger of blame was pointed exclusively at phosphate detergents. The possibility that some bodies of water might be phosphate-saturated to the point where the limiting factor had shifted to nitrates was not aired publically at all.

Industry Warns the Environmental Alarmists

The detergent manufacturers were not as compliant about the pressures against phosphate detergents as they had been with regard to the suds problem. But the reason was not, as has been alleged, the greed motive. It was quite simply a matter of no good substitute being available. Detergent specialists made a plea for time; they were quite frank about the fact that there were no really efficient and safe replacements for the phosphate compounds. But the movement would hear no excuses. The pressure mounted, and the industry responded with a feverish research and development effort. They saw that the bans might come soon, and indeed they were right, for even now we see legal bans against detergents containing more than 3 percent phosphates enacted in Indiana, and a 7 percent phosphate limit proposed in Montana. Some localities, like Suffolk County in New York, instituted total bans on the sale of phosphate-containing detergents some time ago. The first response of the detergent manufacturers was the release of compounds containing NTA (nitrilotriacetate) and the enzyme detergents. By 1969, 125 tons of NTA had been produced and marketed.

NTA is remarkably free of direct toxic effects and is readily decomposed by aerobic bacteria (Jancovic and Mann, 1969). Certain of its effects were not very well understood when it was first brought out, but in the beginning everyone was for it because it was not a phosphate. However, it is unfortunately the case that when nitrates are added to phosphate-saturated water, more algal blooms result. But in addition to that, NTA has certain other characteristics which were not fully explored before it was released. It has recently been claimed

(Epstein, 1970) that under certain environmental conditions, NTA will not decompose readily and will act as a chelating agent for heavy metals, greatly increasing their toxicity. In general, we are not too impressed with the heavy-metal scare, but the possible synergistic actions of NTA with mercury and cadmium under natural conditions, though not thoroughly enough evaluated for any conclusive comments, do argue against its precipitate introduction as a substitute for a known safe compound. In experiments with rats, it was shown that while 4 ppm of cadmium chloride was not acutely toxic to the rodents, the same amount combined with NTA resulted in a 55 percent death rate (U.S. Senate Committee on Public Works, 1970). It is not too surprising that these data were picked up by alarmists, and that one could read statements like the following, when the "dangers" of NTA began to leak to the public: "Take the time to understand what price you are paying for clean clothes and keep informed. Don't leave the environment for someone else to control; it doesn't happen. These terrifying stories will keep unfolding and there is no reason to assume that the horrors will decrease. It is our problem now and it won't go away until we make environmental sanity part of our everyday life" (Anonymous, 1971, p. 7).

Well, we are very much in favor of environmental sanity. But who is to tell us what is a sane course? The members of conservation organizations? A handful of hurried limnologists? The press? Who creates the crises, and who proposes the bans? Is the industry really to be blamed, when they insisted that they needed more time, and that the phosphate detergents perhaps really weren't all that evil?

To give some idea of the kind of pressure which manufacturers experience from the new awareness of environmental effects, we would like to quote a passage from a lecture given by Paul McCloskey, then a Congressman from California.

> I have been fascinated in Congress by testimony of the detergent industry's three major producers, Colgate-Palmolive, Lever Brothers, and Procter and Gamble, who turn out something like 500 million pounds of detergents each year. About 50 percent of those detergents are phosphates, one of the major causes of eutrophication. If the testimony is correct, the 10 million people living in the Lake Erie basin pay about $1 per capita annually for the phosphates that go into those detergents to prevent tattle-tale gray. Our modern standard of cleanliness requires a cleaning level that to date has been obtained only by the phosphates.
>
> We in Congress asked the detergent industry how to handle the problem that developed after those phosphates had transformed about one-third of Lake Erie into a dead lake by the algal growth they stimulate. The industry responded, in effect, with the suggestion that we should build tertiary sewage-treatment plants so that the phosphates could be taken out of the waste water *before* it flows into Lake Erie [author's emphasis]. . . .

Our congressional inquiry disclosed that if such an annual cost should be imposed [that the industry should pay the cost of the sewage treatment plants], the industry then might turn to a substitute for phosphate called NTA, which has been tested for some time and *which does not have an eutrophication effect* [our emphasis]. That would increase the cost of phosphates [sic] perhaps 30 percent, from $1 to $1.30 per year, far less than the additional $2.30 per capita tax that would be required for tertiary sewage plant construction. (McCloskey, 1970, pp. 91–92)

We do not know exactly who were the scientists who testified about eutrophication at these Congressional hearings, but they obviously succeeded in persuading Congressman McCloskey of their expertise and thus quickly educating him about the dangers of phosphates in contrast with the environmentally "safe" NTA. We hope at least that they did not go quite so far as to attribute the "death" of Lake Erie to phosphates alone—or to algae. That is probably the Congressman's own contribution.

The second group of early substitutes introduced by the detergent industry contained enzymes. What this means, in most cases, is that these detergents use as their active ingredient a crude autolysate of *Bacillus subtilis.* Since the enzymes are not separated and purified, many of the compounds of the cells are present in the preparations. These can sensitize individual persons and make them more susceptible to certain diseases. In the amounts employed in detergents, these additional cellular components are not toxic to humans, but the possibilities that they could cause allergic reactions or decrease the natural resistance of the body have not been ruled out (Dubos, 1971). Completely safe enzyme detergents could be produced by using purified enzymes as active ingredients, but this would be rather expensive, probably costlier on a per capita basis than installation of advanced waste-treatment systems.

These two examples—NTA and the enzyme detergents—represent attempts to replace with the greatest haste a compound the effects of which were more or less well understood; and the "danger to the environment" factor it represented was certainly exaggerated if not completely unfounded.

What's New at the Supermarket?

The slightly worn-out saying of the wise Rabbi Akiba ("There is nothing new under the sun") rang familiarly in our ears when we paid a short visit to our local supermarket the other day to sample the new washing aids on the shelf. One product carried the following items on the label:

New formula
SOFT DETERGENT
(biodegradable)
>   Ingredients will decompose in
>   sewage systems and septic tanks
>   and will leave no harmful residue
>   in our nation's water supply.

Caution: Keep out of reach of small children. If taken
internally, administer large amounts of vinegar or
orange, lemon, or grapefruit juice. If splashed in eyes,
flush thoroughly with warm water. In either case,
consult a physician.

What's this, we thought, safe for the environment but not for children? This
sounds like either good old caustic soda or washing soda, though there was
nothing on the label identifying the active compound. Sliding back about 140
years in human civilization and technical development, though admittedly in a
relatively unimportant area of human life: how to keep clean.

We mentioned earlier that caustic soda can cause blindness if splashed in the
eyes, and that it is quite dangerous to people. Of course, the FDA requires that
anything containing caustic materials must carry a label like the one above. But
unfortunately, children crawling on the floor next to the washing machine cannot
read, and contemporary women are not as cautious as their great-grandmothers
were about what the kids get into, having grown accustomed to safe cleaning
compounds. How seriously will people take this warning, especially knowing that
the stuff is "safe" for septic tanks and the nation's water supply?

The swallowing of one good gulp of a 0.1 percent solution of caustic soda can
cause serious erosions in the mouth, the soft palate, the eosophagus, and the
stomach, much as if they had been burned. The pain is intolerable. The victim
writhes and shrieks in agony as long as his vocal cords are not affected; then he
can only moan. The strong base may even perforate the stomach wall, and death
from shock may ensue. Immediate medical help may prevent death, but extensive
burning of the soft parts of the anterior portion of the digestive system will heal
only very slowly, with scars and strictures making each act of swallowing—even
of liquids—excruciatingly painful. Recovery requires the best of hospital care for
some time so that the eosophageal strictures can be dilated. In some cases extensive surgical reconstruction may be necessary. It is no wonder that so much effort
was expended to find safer effective substitutes for the cleaning compounds
based on caustic substances. Now, thanks to our concerned nature lovers, they

are back on the shelf again, with a small print "warning" and the assurance that they are not bad for our precious waters.

We had the feeling that we were back in the 1830s. If further regressions are equally quick—it took less than two years to undo the work of 140 years in this case—then in no time at all we shall be back in the Middle Ages.

Actually the Middle Ages may be what the environmentalists are aiming for, since at that time cleanliness was not yet thought of as next to godliness. On the contrary, bathing was considered sinful, and was permitted only once a week. There is a nice story about Elizabeth of Thuringia (1207–1231) which we should like to tell for the reader's edification. The Queen, out of penitence, made a public vow that she would not bathe for an entire year. As the result of a most unfortunate accident, however, she fell into a latrine long before the year was up. A special courier was sent to Rome to request a dispensation from her vow from the Holy Father. It is chronicled that the courier made the journey in the record time of six weeks, though no mention is made of the Queen's condition during this interval. She eventually became a Saint of the Church, for she was a woman of great virtue, this vow being but a single example of her pure character.

Perhaps soon bathing will be banned, for might it not be regarded as an activity which endangers nature? This time may be fast approaching, as illustrated by the following anecdote. An acquaintance of ours recently returned from a camping trip in the high Sierras, where there is a beautiful mountain lake. He told us about a Boy Scout leader—a member of the Sierra Club—who would not let his troop of fifteen boys swim in the lake because they might pollute it. As far as we know, this is not yet the official policy of the Sierra Club. Nevertheless, with the example of the distant past, it may soon be established that swimming is a sin against nature; and a strong moral value could be placed on remaining unclean, yet pleasing in the sight of God.

That such attitudes might indeed become accepted by some extremists may be gleaned from the following statement by Stephanie Mills, feminist leader of the zero-population-growth movement: "Hippies evidently are ecologically sound. Bathing is wasteful as a compulsion: it uses up too much water. We probably should not bathe unless we smell bad" (Mills, 1971, p. 131).

This statement might seem to many people to be merely a joke, but it has, in effect, some serious implications. In the past few years there has been an astronomical upsurge in reported cases of body lice—not only among hippies— but apparently even among middle-class youths and college students. This unpleasant pest, which was thought to be almost completely eradicated (at least in the developed countries), is a serious disease vector; and public health officials are gravely concerned about the possibility that a typhus epidemic might break out at any time. Soap is not an effective cure for body lice, but cleanliness *does* help to prevent their spreading!

A Soap Opera

Before we go on to discuss what might be some of the other "new" substitutes, we should like to read into the record the words of a scientist, testifying before a hearing of the Federal Trade Commission (April 27, 1971). "'Is it true that scientists now feel that phosphates in detergents are only a minor source of water pollution problems?' 'Definitely not,' stated the Rochester scientist. [He] also *documented* the fact that some non-phosphate detergents now being produced are both effective as cleaning agents and safe from an environmental and public health standpoint" (Anonymous, 1971 b, p. 9; our emphasis).

Unfortunately we do not know which might be those nonphosphate detergents that are both safe, as far as the general public and the environment are concerned, and also effective. There are basically three types of "new" nonphosphate and environmentally safe (i.e., also nitrogen-free) detergents marketed at the moment. One type we have already described: those with caustic materials as active ingredients—direct derivatives of potash. These are the most dangerous. The second group are those which contain hydrocarbonates. These are far less poisonous, but they are also less effective than anything we have become accustomed to. A "safe" example of this type is baking soda, which is fine for brushing teeth in the event of a toothpaste ban, but have you tried doing dishes with it lately?

The third group of detergents which have no phosphates, nitrates, or enzymes are the compounds which contain inorganic or organic moieties of boron. These are not new either. The oldest of them are those containing borax, which has been with us for well over a hundred years. Borax and the different borates (salts of boric acid) show varying degrees of human toxicity. "*Boron:* The element itself has low toxicity, but some boron compounds are moderately or highly toxic. . . . See Boric acid. . . . *Boric Acid:* Death has occurred from less than 5 grams in infants and from 5 to 20 grams in adults. Chronic use may cause borism (dry skin, eruptions, gastric disturbances). Caution: Several cases of fatal poisoning have occurred following its absorbtion from granulating wounds and abraded skin areas" (*The Merck Index,* 8th ed., 1968, pp. 160-161).

Which are the *new, nontoxic* and *efficient* detergents the scientist so factually documented? They cannot be the caustics, nor the boron derivatives, since both are too toxic or dangerous. The hydrocarbonates are not efficient enough and not environmentally sound. We wish we knew what he meant.

In connection with phosphate substitutes, we have to underline the importance of yet another factor in the causation and sustaining of algal blooms. Carbon dioxide (CO_2) is the *most essential* compound for plant growth. Natural waters usually contain enough CO_2 to permit the normal development of aquatic plants, if all of the essential elements and nutrients are also present. Should the available supply be used up, the waters can replenish their CO_2 from the atmosphere. However, at times of exponential growth—when algae are in full bloom—the CO_2 may become exhausted and its diffusion from the air into the water may fail to keep pace with the explosion of the algal population. In such circumstances *CO_2 becomes the limiting factor,* and growth will cease (Kuentzel, 1969). There are, however, other supply routes for CO_2 than the atmosphere. The two most important ones are the inorganic carbonates or hydrocarbonates, and decaying organic matter.

Limestone is an important source of inorganic carbonate, but it is practically insoluble in most natural waters. On the other hand the carbonates of sodium, potassium, and ammonium are highly soluble. These are exactly the substances several of the "new" detergents use.

It is almost impossible to foresee what would be the exact consequences in terms of proliferation of algal blooms of dumping millions of pounds of carbonates into receiving waters. One thing is, however, known for a certainty. CO_2 is not only essential for plant growth, but is a *growth stimulator.* Anybody who has even a cursory knowledge of biology knows that in order to promote algal growth in the laboratory, one bubbles air highly enriched with CO_2 into the water. In this way a fast and luxurious growth of algae can be achieved. In one day, as much as 24 grams dry weight per liter can be produced (Burlew, 1953). The product, before drying, will be a thick green pulp something like creamed spinach.

Is this the safe and "environmentally sound" solution our experts prefer? They say they are ecologists and limnologists, but a freshman biology student should not make such a blunder.

A second, indirect source of CO_2 in water is the decay of organic matter. The major constituents of organic materials are carbon, oxygen, hydrogen, and nitrogen, and during the decomposition process, carbon becomes linked with oxygen to form CO_2 mainly as a result of microbial action. Thus, in waters high in organic matter, there is an additional supply route for CO_2, which in turn provides further stimulus for the development and sustaining of algal blooms. The higher the organic load, the longer lasting the bloom is likely to be, unless it becomes so high that a completely polysaprobic condition develops (to be discussed in Chapter 10). Since our waters already contain in many places the inorganic substances necessary for abundant algal growth, any addition to them of organic-containing wastes will only exacerbate the problem. And yet, although environmentalists are fond of publicizing the half-truth that when algae die they add to the organic load of the aquatic ecosystem, nobody seems to be much interested in the far more substantial enrichment with organic matter represented by untreated sewage and animal wastes.

Madison Avenue Helps to "Educate the Public"

The advertising establishment has caught up with the environmental movement, and is now aiding in the education of the public, although presumably from different motives than those of the conservationist campaigners. On the packages of the "new" washing aids, one can now read lengthy messages which are both "moral" and "scientific" in content.

Obviously the people who make detergents are not yet ready to undermine the love of cleanliness and return to the morality of the Middle Ages. A way out of the bind is expressed in the blurb found on one of the new products.

> This laundry product contains absolutely no phosphates, enzymes, NTA or any non-functional fillers that promote water pollution.
>
> When you use it, you are, in effect, saying "I will not sacrifice clean water for clean clothes."
>
> But neither must you sacrifice clean clothes for clean water.
>
> We, the makers of . . . thank you for deciding to help reduce the serious problem of water pollution, and wish you a happy wash day.
>
> A happy, healthy wash day.

This moral message is mild, though, compared with the ambitious educational program printed on the package of a second product.

> Polluting algae kills fish, stagnates water, and turns lakes into swamps. And phosphates in detergents make polluting algae grow.
>
> But now you can have a clean wash and keep America clean, too [in red print].
>
> The solution is . . . detergent. It's free of water polluting phosphates because it replaces phosphates with an active water softener found in nature itself.
>
> Every time you use it, you'll help save our lakes, rivers, and waters from phosphate pollution, while you enjoy a fresh, clean wash.

From this helpful message, the public learns that *algae are the pollutants,* that they cause fish kills, and are the real villains which make the waters stagnant and turn lakes into swamps. In case anybody is still unaware of it, the point is brought home that it is phosphate-containing detergents which cause these "deadly organisms" to thrive.

Are the environmental alarmists rejoicing in the willing help lent to their cause by the advertising industry? Probably; for although many of them are loud in their criticisms of the wasteful luxury and mindless consumerism encouraged by Madison Avenue, if their campaign can be furthered by the very voice of the enemy, the "ban phosphates" champions will be satisfied, according to their own announced ecotactics. What does it matter that *not a single one* of the statements in the first paragraph of this educational advertisement is true?

We are not happy that the public should be thus educated, for two principal reasons. First, the ad man has written that algae are pollutants. Sometimes they are nuisance organisms, but all scientists—even those who are environmental extremists—recognize that algae are a source of oxygen for the planet, as well as the fundamental base of the aquatic food chain. Second, the campaign has been so rapid and so successful that by now only the illiterate and the completely indifferent remain in ignorance of the "phosphate problem."

What would now happen if, after careful consideration, it were to be concluded that phosphate detergents after all remain among the safest, most efficient and least polluting of the available cleaning compounds. Would we be able to re-educate the public after this mass programming? A well-trained scientist is taught that good science demands a careful evaluation of all the interacting factors involved in any one problem. But the cry of the environmental alarmists is "There is no time! The ship is sinking, and the appointment of research teams to study the matter will not prevent her from going down." Well, we do see some serious pollution problems, but to date we have not seen any evidence that there is so much as a major hole in this ship we call the planet Earth, much less a hold full of water. But on account of the urgency which has replaced the earlier complacency, we are being treated to a series of precipitous irrational action campaigns to "save the environment." The ban-phosphates frenzy is perhaps not so serious in its implications for society as are some of the other crusades which we shall be discussing. Nevertheless, while accomplishing nothing to improve the deteriorated status of our waters, this campaign may do a great deal to discredit science.

Note Added in Proof

On September 15, 1971, both the Office of the Surgeon General and the Environmental Protection Agency issued a statement urging consumers to use phosphate detergents, since all other substitutes introduced are either toxic or highly caustic.

10

FOOD ON EARTH

Where the price of mineral fertilizers
and the farmers' mentality permitted,
the fertilizers could be used with startling effectiveness, doubling average grain
yields on top of the doubling achieved
by the spread of modern crop rotation.
D. A. PRYANISHNIKOV (On conditions of
Russian agriculture in 1913)

Although it has become fashionable of late in environmental
circles to attack agriculture in general and its use of chemicals
in particular, not all ecologists, even in North America, have maintained such
negative attitudes towards farming and the benefits of modern agricultural tools.
It is of interest to note that Paul Sears, who is cultivated as a sort of elder states-
man by environmentalists, expresses views which are almost heretical by present
standards, even in his popular publications on ecological subjects. In his 1969
book *Lands Beyond the Forest* — a moving descriptive treatise on the plains — one
can find such thought-provoking passages as the following:

152

We are likely to forget that we owe what advantages we possess to domestica-
tion. It was this great art that led our race from the life of primitive animal toward
civilization. . . .

The sedentary nature of cereal cultivation not only made possible the establishment of larger communities but, as we have noted, gave leisure to develop organization and arts. The release of even a small minority from food production has been
significant. This figure has ranged from perhaps 5 percent in early times to about 20
percent in the nineteenth century United States where it has risen, thanks to improved technology, to over 85 percent. . . .

Like all plant life rice requires mineral nutrients. . . . But under the pressure of
harvested crops such nutrients are rapidly exhausted. . . . This difficulty, compounded by the attacks of disease and pests, the lack of artificial fertilizers and
scientific controls, keep the world's Rice Bowl, now expanded far beyond its original
limits, from being an Eden of security and plenty. . . . Ancient patterns of land ten-
ure, credit, and lack of equipment persist to complicate the need for crop improvement, sustained fertility, and pest control. (Sears, 1969, pp. 41-42, 45, 150-151)

It is really gratifying to read these passages in a book by an ecologist who has
spent his whole life in the investigation of natural ecosystems and is a hero to the
younger environmentalists, for these assessments of the realities of farming are
very similar to those of pragmatic agriculturalists

Put in somewhat more specific terms, we can review the following factual
data:

At the time of the Middle Ages in Western Europe, agriculture had developed to a point where one farmer could support approximately four people. The
three other persons were thus free to involve themselves in matters which were
not directly related to the production of food—endeavors such as manufacturing,
defense, science, and the fine arts. From 1780 to the present time, we have
available relatively good statistics on a world basis referring to grain production. If one expresses production in terms of the ratio between the amount of
grain needed for seed to the amount in the total harvest, we find that in 1780
the figures were 1:8 for rice, 1:4 for corn, and 1:5 for wheat. By 1970, these
ratios had shifted to 1:360 for rice, 1:400 for corn, and 1:30 for wheat. During
this period of 190 years, the general increase in rice yields may be seen to be
45-fold, that of corn 100-fold and that of wheat 6-fold.

If we look only at the United States, using a slightly different measure it
may be seen that by 1945, one U.S. farmer could raise enough produce to support
12 people in addition to himself. By 1970, the number of people he could support
had more than doubled, being about 26, and by now nearly 50. That the efficiency of the modern American farmer permits 49 out of 50 people to be in-

volved in endeavors unrelated to the production of food has far-reaching implications. It is the basis of our whole social structure; and our cultural as well as our economic achievements largely derive from the ready availability of high-quality and abundant food.

These relatively high efficiency figures for the United States do not represent anything close to maximum potential productivity. In fact, according to a 1954 book by Harrison Brown, the United States has a long way to go before it reaches the per-acre productivity of many Western European countries. In his by now classic book, *The Challenge of Man's Future,* he wrote:

> The increases in crop yield in the United States have been dramatic, but we still have far to go before we attain the agricultural level that prevails in Europe. The production of grain in the United States amounts to 18.6 bushels per acre as compared with yields in Germany and the United Kingdom of about 30 bushels per acre, and yields in Denmark, the Netherlands, and Belgium which approach 40 bushels per acre. The United States produces 110 bushels of potatoes per acre, as compared with 320 bushels per acre in Belgium. In a group of nineteen European countries only one has an average potato yield of less than 150 bushels per acre. However, it will be some time before crop yields such as are obtained in Western Europe become economic necessities for the United States.
>
> When we compare existing average crop yields with the maximum yields that have been achieved under favorable conditions, we can obtain some idea of possible future increases in soil productivity. While the present yield of potatoes in the United States is 110 bushels per acre, yields of 1000 bushels per acre have been reported. Our average corn yield is 35 bushels per acre; yields of 150 bushels have been obtained. (Brown, 1954, p. 137)

If we look at the country where postwar growth has been most spectacular, Japan, we can see the gains made over a short period of time. In 1944, 60 percent of the population was needed for farming. By 1969, only 18 percent were farmers. During this 25-year period 20 percent of the acreage formerly in rice crops was retired, while total production of rice per hectare increased by 45 percent. Contrary to statements by Ehrlich and others that Japan has to import most of her food (one might think so, without looking at statistics, since she is such a small group of islands), by 1970, she had become one of the major rice-exporting countries. She supplied 87 percent of the food consumed by her population, including most luxuries, and had to import mainly fodder, salad oil, raw sugar, and tropical fruits such as bananas (Japanese Ministry of Foreign Affairs, 1971). One should contrast these facts with the unfounded propaganda spread by Ehrlich: "Japan already has to import around half of her food and she has to take from the sea roughly one and a half times the protein she is able to grow on land. She's involved in a race with other countries to get the last protein out of the sea. She is soon going to have very grave feeding problems and, with her present population-doubling rate of about 70 years, she will eventually have to turn aggressively toward the mainland" (Ehrlich, 1971, pp. 78–79). Quite aside from his failure to look up the available data and his nasty innuendo about Japanese imperialism, Ehrlich, as a supposed population expert, certainly ought to have been aware that Japan achieved zero population growth in the 1960s.

Ehrlich and the other Cassandras who focus on population and world food needs are fond of stating that the optimists have been proven wrong in the past, and one may therefore predict that they will be wrong in their hopes for a future of plenty. In this connection, we would like to cite H. Landsberg:

> A few years ago, contemplation of past history led Resources for the Future to project corn yields at 70 bushels per acre. Because yields ranged between 53 and 55 bushels per acre in the three years preceding 1961, the year in which we had to make our projections, we thought our prediction a little daring; some scholars who were asked to review what was then a manuscript thought we were very daring. But by 1965 the yield had climbed to 74 bushels and had outrun the projection. The average yield in Iowa had jumped above 80 and in Indiana and Illinois above 90 bushels per acre. Our projected yield of 100 bushels in the year 2000, a faraway guess when made, had begun to move into clear view. (Landsberg, 1970, p. 112)

Famine in the Underdeveloped Countries?

While discussing some figures which may give the reader an idea of the accomplishments and potential accomplishments of increases in food productivity in the developed nations, one does not want to minimize the present problems of the developing and underdeveloped nations in this respect. There is no arguing with the fact that at least one-third of the world's present population is undernourished or malnourished, and that more hungry mouths are on the way. There are no scientific reasons for accepting the assertions of the population alarmists that the world population will continue to grow indefinitely at an exponential rate; in fact, there are good reasons to think that it will level out some time in the next 50 to 100 years. However, since we do not intend to enter into an argument on this point, we must be realistic and consider that even one or two further doublings of the present world population will present a challenge of serious dimensions in terms of food needs alone. The question of whether this challenge can be met has obvious connections with political disagreements among nations which seriously affect the distribution of food. However, those who start from the premise that defeatism, isolationism, and indifference to the hungry masses in other lands are unacceptable attitudes, and who are willing to examine the potential for increases in food supply for both individual countries and for the planet as a whole, usually maintain some measure of optimism, despite the discouraging obstacles which may arise from such uncontrollable events as poor weather or outbreaks of hostilities in areas where attempts are being made to increase self-sufficiency in food production. From the technological point of view, there is every reason to be optimistic; and very little disagreement is expressed among nutritional experts that a world population considerably in excess of the present one *can* be fed—and even quite well fed—provided that agricultural technology is not set back by reactionary measures and that the politicians of various nations can keep their arguments sufficiently restrained so as not to interfere too drastically with food distribution.

There are a large number of documents and books which deal with the food-productivity potential of specific countries and of the planet as a whole. From most of them one can glean varying but essentially similar information, none of it pessimistic about production capability per se.

In his monograph *The Planetary Food Potential* Walter Schmitt (1965) includes some instructive figures relating to the average crop losses in both developed and underdeveloped countries, independent of per-acre production figures. He states that at least 30 percent of crops are lost between harvest and the consumer's table, the principal causal factors being rodent destruction and spoilage. Both of these are obviously much more serious problems in countries where storage facilities are inadequate and where transportation is primitive. However, it should not be supposed that the factor of loss after harvest has been eliminated even in a country like the United States. Annual losses in grains during storage, mainly to rodents, amount to about $5 billion in the United States. And one interesting piece of information which most people do not know or have forgotten is that only a few years ago, the federal standard for cereals delineated 3 percent as the maximum tolerable quantity of rodent excrement. It seems a bit ironic that while people will fuss about pesticide residues in food in the parts-per-billion range, they ate their "naturally protein-enriched" corn flakes and Wheaties without complaint.

The average crop loss in developed countries *before* harvest—to plant diseases, insects, and so on—is only about 10 to 15 percent, taken over a long range. In less developed countries, where fewer pesticides are used, the average is at least 50 percent, and in some countries the figure may be much higher. Then there is the additional minimal 30 percent loss of the remaining crop *after* harvest. Looking only at loss factors, and leaving aside all questions of increasing production through more intensive farming methods, Schmitt states: "The potential gains through prevention of losses are impressive. Not only would they wipe out the present food deficit, but feed as many people again as there are now" (Schmitt, 1965, p. 681).

He then goes on to enumerate the many factors which are important both in increasing production and protecting crops from loss, the most vital of which are the use of chemical fertilizers, adequate irrigation where natural water supplies are limited, mechanization and general efficiency techniques, good storage and transport facilities, and the use of various methods for chemical pest control. He states that losses after harvest could be halved on a global basis, and that effective control of plant diseases and pests in those areas where agricultural chemicals are not yet in use could double the world harvest. He then concludes: "Among the many possibilities for increasing productivity, fertilization and irrigation (and some other necessary associated cultivation practices) appear to be the most effective, and together could probably treble average yields. The complementary application of these and other connected measures could, we expect, raise present foodstuff production up to 18 times versus an expected tenfold rise in dietary demand" (*ibid.,* p. 653).

By the "expected tenfold rise in dietary demand" Schmitt is referring to a possible global population of 30 billion persons—that is, one which is ten times the present size. His basic claim is that if modern agricultural techniques could be applied in all countries, the foodstuff produced (or rather reaching the table) could be increased 18-fold, without adding significant acreage to the land presently under cultivation, which represents about 7 percent of the land surface of the planet. We would hold that the likelihood of the world population leveling out somewhere between 6 to 9 billion is much greater, but these potential production figures of agricultural experts are important since, contrary to the arguments raised by Ehrlich, Hardin, and others who fear the population explosion in the less developed countries, there is good evidence that the main factors in achieving a stable population are *not* famine, war, and pestilence, but prosperity, freedom from debilitating diseases, and full stomachs. The reader who is interested in an answer to Ehrlich on demographic grounds should read John Maddox' recent book *The Doomsday Syndrome* (1972), in which one chapter is devoted to the specific question of how long the population growth curve will continue on a steep incline.

Returning once more to Schmitt's projections, it ought to be underlined that in calculating an 18-fold potential increase in agricultural production, he was not including the much more dramatic food increases which could be foreseen if we really pushed the application of intensive growing techniques. The new high-yield grains were not used in his figures at all, nor did his projections take into account what could be achieved if we were to develop fully such intensive growing techniques as hydroponics, algae culture, or microbial protein production. With hydroponics, for example (by which is meant growing plants in a liquid nourishing medium rather than in soil), yields of 160 *tons* of potatoes per hectare have been achieved. Some of these methods for vertically intensive production have already been well demonstrated as both workable and economic, but they are not applied on any scale, since food needs are not great enough to provide the incentive to growers to switch over to these techniques. Schmitt's estimates, therefore, reflect the production increments which could be achieved if the agricultural technologies of the less developed countries could be raised to levels comparable to those of the ordinary practices in the developed Western countries in the 1960s.

No one, not even the most unrelenting optimist, would pretend that there are no serious problems involved in feeding the world's poor; nor that the supply of food is the only problem to be met for the world population. There are obviously many other necessities in demand: housing, energy supply, social services such as health care and education, to name only a few other basic human needs. But the point of bringing up the optimistic projections of technologists involved in agriculture and nutrition is that they are able to report with some confidence that the state of the art is such that the food needs of a much larger world population could be met. Whether the socioeconomic and political factors which largely determine both the rate of change and the possibilities of distributing food where it is most needed will permit the nourishing of the poor are other questions altogether; matters which tend to temper the optimism about food increase potentials with sober realism at the least, if not with some pessimism. But what probably was not anticipated even a few years ago by anyone involved in food technologies was the recent rise to prominence of a group of influential environmental activists—including in their midst some scientists—who are challenging the very foundations on which our highly successful Western agriculture has been built: in particular, mechanization of farming and irrigation; the discovery and application of modern herbicides, fungicides, and synthesized organic insecticides; and the somewhat earlier, most vital introduction of chemical fertilizers into widescale use. It is the attack on this last technique—much less publicized than the opposition to some of the pesticides—which we want to discuss next.

Commoner's Account of "Illinois Earth"

While most of the prominent environmentalists have been focusing their attacks on pesticides, power plants, automobiles, fuels, phosphate detergents, heavy metals, plastics, or simply people, Barry Commoner—who among the scientists associated with the movement is probably the best known to the public —has summed up the general case against postwar technologies in his latest book, *The Closing Circle* (1971), adding to the lengthening lists of terrible chemicals the artificial nitrogen fertilizers. That only the really purist health food faddists worried earlier about this group of agricultural chemicals is probably in part due to the fact that they "imitate nature"—i.e., the artificially produced compounds are the same in molecular structure as the natural ones.

There is no "ban nitrates" movement as yet in evidence on the public scene (although there are some indications of attempts to limit applications through legislation). However, Commoner's influence on the movement is a considerable one, and one may assume that the majority of his readers will accept his judgment that the nitrate pollution problem is serious, that it results mainly from use on crops, and even more specifically, that it can be traced to the use of the artificially manufacturerd nitrogen fertilizers. One may also assume that the scientific generalizations of this "professor with a class of millions"—as he is advertised on the book jacket—will be accepted as holy writ by at least those of his followers who are not trained in science. It is therefore of importance to examine what he is teaching. To review all of the ideas he presents would require a close textual analysis of the entire book, since behind most of his broad concepts, his descriptions of contemporary environmental ills, his tracings of cause, and his prescriptions for change, there lie assumptions which need to be examined, as well as detailed problems with his presentations of facts. We shall deal here with his treatment of the nitrate problem, and shall mention in later chapters a few other items from *The Closing Circle*.

A chapter in the book called "Illinois Earth" is devoted specifically to nitrate pollution of the drinking-water supply of Decatur, Illinois. Commoner's own relations with the area health officials, city residents, and farmers of the watershed, and the research of his group, which he claims not only traced but clearly demonstrated the cause of the pollution problem in this southern Illinois county are described in the chapter. But besides this particular case history, the general subjects of natural soil nitrogen and the use of artificial nitrate fertilizers recur as themes in other parts of the book. Since an understanding of Commoner's opposition to nitrogen fertilizers requires a broader perspective than that of the Decatur case history alone, we shall try to integrate his account of the Illinois story with a summary of his more generalized views. Let us begin with his description of the overt problem and his attributions of cause:

1. Nitrate concentrations in many of our inland waters (both rivers and lakes) have been increasing since World War II.

2. For several years Commoner has been suggesting that these increases are due mainly to runoff or leaching of artificial nitrate fertilizers from agricultural lands, especially in the Middle Western states. His earlier assertions rested mainly on correlations between increase in fertilizer use and rising nitrate levels in waters adjacent to farm areas of heavy cultivation. He now claims to have proven his causal connection scientifically, at least for the Sangamon, Illinois, watershed.

3. The main reason for the phenomenon, according to Commoner, is that American farmers are applying far more fertilizer to their fields than the plants can utilize, and the excess is polluting our waters.

He discusses three principal dangers associated with this polluting practice, one bearing on water pollution per se; the second basic to his idea of the superiority of natural systems; and the third referring to a human health hazard.

1. High nitrate levels in surface waters result in eutrophication, leading to the development of algal blooms.

2. The use of artificial nitrogen fertilizers is bad *ab ovo* because it represents an interference with the natural soil cycle.

3. High nitrate levels in drinking water can cause methemoglobinemia — a dreaded disease.

Let us begin with some general discussion of nitrates in waters and their possible sources.

Looking for a Scapegoat

The generalized claim that nitrate levels have been increasing in our inland waters is partially true, depending on the area under discussion. However, any broad attempt to associate increases in nitrate concentrations with the uses of fertilizer is treated with considerable skepticism, since there are more obvious and more likely sources. Among these, one of the most important is waste effluent. Taken at a national average, the nitrate concentration is about 5 mg/l in good-quality surface waters. Nitrate concentration in the effluent of municipal waste waters after secondary treatment is 15 mg/l—a threefold increase over the background (Weinberger et al. 1966). However, figures relating to input given in relative quantities do not give the most helpful picture of actual contributions of treated wastes to local bodies of water. The impact on the receiving waters will depend on their nature, size, and condition: whether one is talking about a rapidly flowing river, a small creek, a deep lake, a shallow pond; such natural factors as the age of the body of water; and consideration of the pollutional load with other substances and from other sources.

Still, some comparative figures may help the reader to understand an initial skepticism regarding any broad claims that fertilizer is a primary cause of nitrate pollution of waters. Let us take a municipal sewage facility serving 100,000 residents as an example. If this facility is a secondary-treatment plant, the treated effluent will contain 1,200 lb of nitrate per day, discharging about 438,000 lb into the receiving waters yearly. There will also be at least 1,095,000 lb nitrate equivalent added yearly in the form of organic matter. Without sewage treatment, the proportions will be different, but the end contribution of nitrate will be about the same.

The organically bound nitrogen comes mainly from excrement; whereas the nitrate is a breakdown product of urea and other nitrogenous substances in urine. One liter of urine, for example, contains 6,750 mg nitrate equivalent.

In rural areas where the human population is limited, one cannot jump to the conclusion that addition of nitrates comes from fertilizers either, for the potential contribution of farm-animal excrement has to be considered. According to Weiss and Okun:

> The magnitude of this problem can be vividly stated. For example, a cow generates as much manure as sixteen and one half humans while one hog produces as much waste as nearly two people. On an equivalent basis, seven chickens are equivalent to one human. In total numbers, the farm population of the United States, for instance, produces ten times as much waste as the human population.[*]
>
> Not only are surface waters affected but ground-waters also receive pollution from disposal of livestock and poultry waste as indicated by undesirable changes in taste, odor and color of the water. Improperly handled manures may contribute high nitrate levels to immediately adjacent water supplies. . . . This problem is becoming even more acute as animals are maintained on a production basis confined to areas, pastures or poultry houses. Some examples of the latter now house more than 100,000 birds in a single establishment. The wastes from such a production unit are equivalent to a community of nearly 15,000 people. . . . (Weiss and Okun, 1967, p. 198)

[*] This number is now much higher than it was in 1967, since the farm-animal population has increased exponentially in comparison with the human population during the past five years.

Certainly nobody would deny that nitrate concentrations in waters are to some degree enhanced by soil erosion, fertilizer runoff, and soil nitrogen in subsurface drains; the question is what is the contribution of these sources in relative terms? Further questions arise from comparison of differing reports, even granting a large margin of variability reflecting regional conditions and practices. Consider, for example, that in the Yakima River basin irrigation-return-flow drains, the nitrate concentrations are given as 1.5 ppm in surface drains and 2.6 ppm in subsurface drains (MacKenthun, 1965). Kohl, Shearer, and Commoner (1971), on the other hand, give figures for the Illinois subsurface drains which range from 27 to 76.5 ppm! These determinations may be correct, but their magnitude tends to make one think that several independent investigations should be made to confirm them.

One could say, to be sure, that these numbers are supported by one independent report, since Commoner states that the initial readings in Decatur's tap water by the city health department—which triggered his more detailed study—were 45 ppm. However, doubts have been raised by others about the accuracy of 30 ppm readings in shallow well waters (Waring, 1949), in which circumstances the quantities of nitrogen required to achieve the reported levels are minimal compared with those which would have to be added to an entire reservoir in order to reach 45 ppm concentrations. Without knowing the size and volume of the reservoir, one cannot figure the dispersion; but since nitrate determinations by analytical techniques can be rendered inaccurate by various interfering factors, it might be of value to the people of Decatur to verify the existence of an actual problem of severe drinking-water pollution by calculating how much nitrogen fertilizer, deliberately dumped into the reservoir, would be required to attain a concentration of 45 ppm.

That we should raise doubts about the base measurements involved in the Decatur pollution story may strike the reader as unduly unkind, but, as we shall demonstrate in Chapter 17, accurate determinations of water constituents are not so simple as people generally imagine; and the frequency with which completely erroneous figures are encountered in nearly all pollution studies (those of the period in which such studies had no glamour value whatsoever, as well as in the present era of high-interest environmentalism) tends to make any knowledgeable researcher consider the *probability* of determinations—including his own—before accepting them as correct. In 20 years of study of highly polluted waters all over the world, some of them draining cultivated fields in European countries where the farmers use much higher quantities of artificial fertilizer than those of Illinois, the senior author has never encountered nitrate concentrations even approximating those reported for Decatur. This alone seems sufficient reason for entertaining at least a measure of doubt about the dramatically high levels in the reservoir of the Illinois city.

Having aired this question, we shall assume, for the rest of this chapter, that these determinations are correct, and that the people of Decatur do have a real problem. There still remain to be discussed Commoner's claims about the source of the pollution, the dangers associated with it, and the wisdom of his proposed solutions.

The Proof of Specific Cause

In his popular account of the Illinois research, Commoner tells his readers that he had been concerned for some time about the nitrate pollution of the rivers of the Middle West, and that the data on increased fertilizer use correlated well with the increase in nitrate levels. Such results were, however, "open to criticism so long as there was no information which literally traced the movement of fertilizer nitrogen from the point of application in the soil to the river itself. What was needed was some way to distinguish between nitrate in the river originating in artificial fertilizer and nitrate originating from the breakdown of humus and other organic materials" (Commoner, 1971, p. 88).

There is already a serious omission in this initial explanation: namely, although other passages indicate that he probably knows better, Commoner implies that virtually all the nitrates present in soils which are not fertilized with chemicals originate from organic materials. We shall see that this error is central, and that it is perpetuated in the formal scientific paper in which the information literally tracing "the movement of fertilizer nitrogen from its point of application in the soil to the river itself" is reported.

The popular account continues:

> In nature, the nitrogen atom exists in two forms which are chemically identical and differ only in their atomic weights. One of them, nitrogen 14 (weight: 14 atomic units), makes up about 99.6 per cent of all natural nitrogen; the other form, nitrogen 15 (weight: 15 atomic units), makes up the remaining approximately 0.4 per cent. The ratio between the prevalence of the two forms of nitrogen can be determined with remarkable precision in an electronic instrument, the mass spectrometer.
>
> From mass-spectrometer measurements we soon learned that whereas the artificial fertilizers used in Illinois all had nitrogen isotope ratios approximately the same as that found in the air (a natural consequence of the fact that they were made, chemically, from air nitrogen), nitrogen in soil, manure, and sewage was considerably enriched in nitrogen 15. This meant that measurements of the isotope ratio

in nitrate taken from the Sangamon River, or from soil drainage water, might show whether the nitrate was derived from artificial fertilizer or from organic matter in soil, manure, or sewage. (*Ibid.*, pp. 88–89)

He then describes how samples were collected from the outlets of subsurface tile drains on some of the farms of the region, and the conclusions that were reached.

It was found that those drains yielding high nitrate levels were low in nitrogen 15 content and vice versa. This meant that whatever source was responsible for high nitrate levels in soil drainage water must have itself been relatively low in nitrogen 15 content. The only possible nitrogen source with that characteristic is artificial fertilizer nitrogen. Other, more detailed, studies confirmed this conclusion and showed as well that a minimum of 60 per cent of the nitrate in Lake Decatur is derived from fertilizer used on the adjacent farms. There is now little doubt that the nitrate problem in Lake Decatur arises from the intensive use of artificial fertilizer nitrogen on the neighboring farms. (*Ibid.*, p. 89)

Now this is a very strong claim which has serious implications with respect to fertilizer use. Just one page earlier, Commoner had been discussing the supreme importance of open discussion and publication in science, since he admits that scientists are not always objective and do make mistakes. "Science gets at the truth not so much by avoiding mistakes or personal bias as by displaying them in public—where they can be corrected"(*ibid.*, p. 87). That is a fine statement, which seems also reasonable and modest; but one must ask why Commoner felt compelled to publish a popular book in which he states definitively that "the nitrate problem in Lake Decatur arises from the intensive use of artificial nitrogen on the neighboring farms," *prior* to publication of the formal research in a scientific journal? The paper, written by Kohl, Shearer, and Commoner, appeared in the December 24, 1971 issue of *Science*. We here offer the invited correction of one or two fundamental mistakes incorporated in this latter publication.

This research actually consists of two sets of findings: those relating to establishment of an inverse correlation between nitrate levels and proportions of ^{15}N in the samples; and those purporting to demonstrate that all "natural" sources of nitrate—manure, decaying humus, and *the soil nitrate typical for the region*—are enriched in ^{15}N relative to artificial nitrate fertilizers. It should be made clear that even if we accept the first claim as having been established by the research, this would not constitute proof that artificial fertilizer is the main source of nitrate enrichment in the waters unless the second claim has also been demonstrated. (There would be the disturbing suggestive evidence that a system of subsurface tile drains with outlets to a river which feeds a drinking-water reservoir is a bad plan, if all the measurements are accepted as accurate.) As Commoner explained in his popular account, the main problem was to find a way of distinguishing the contribution of artificial nitrogen fertilizers from the various naturally occurring nitrate compounds. It can be accepted that organically bound nitrogen and nitrate from urine will be enriched in ^{15}N relative to fertilizer nitrogen. Thus, even if one maintains faint doubts about the statement of the authors that there are no significant sources feeding nitrogen into the river or lake other than erosion or those directly related to cropping (a very clean watershed indeed!), these doubts do not bear significantly on the proof.

A central difficulty in the research, which the authors themselves recognized, was to show that naturally occurring soil nitrogen is also enriched in ^{15}N, and can thus be distinguished from artificial fertilizer. They used two methods to substantiate their claim that this is the case: one theoretical, and one utilizing soil samples. They also attempted to show mathematically the insignificance of the contribution of those natural nitrates which they recognized as *not* ^{15}N enriched.

Their principal theoretical explanation for the claim that natural soil nitrates are enriched with ^{15}N is the following: "This probably results from the fact that nonsymbiotic nitrogen fixation does not significantly fractionate the isotopes . . . , while denitrification favors ^{14}N, which leaves soil nitrogen enriched in ^{15}N" (Kohl et al., 1971, p. 1332). The two halves of this sentence are individually correct, but neither constitutes an explanation of why one should expect an ^{15}N enrichment in *agricultural* soils. In fact, one would expect the opposite, because once a field has been planted with legumes, *symbiotic* fixers will dominate the system. These *do* fractionate the isotopes, bringing ^{14}N into the soil and leaving ^{15}N behind in the air. Thus, even if it is true that *virgin* soils are enriched in ^{15}N, after rotational planting with legumes, enrichment should diminish, with or without fertilizer use.

The practical proof of their premise that soil nitrogen is ^{15}N-enriched consisted in sampling untreated soil and comparing the ratio of $^{14}N/^{15}N$ in the samples with that of fertilizer nitrogen. Reading the text of the paper, their results seem quite convincing, since they report that the soil samples from "fields in the study region" averaged $+13$ enrichment with ^{15}N, whereas the ratio in fertilizer is $+3.7$. If, however, one reads the notes at the end of the paper, it emerges that their soil samples were taken from *one point* in the 576,000-acre watershed, and that they sampled *only virgin soils*. The assumption that the $^{14}N/^{15}N$ ratio in their limited soil samples characterizes the soils of the whole

region is essential for the acceptance of their interepretation of basic findings—
i.e., the negative correlation of nitrate concentrations with ^{15}N enrichment.
Hence they support this assumption with two further claims (still in the footnote).
They state that the soils of the watershed are relatively uniform, which might be
true in terms of some parameter, but *would be disputed by every practical agronomist with respect to ^{15}N enrichment.* They also claim that their limited samples
must be taken to be representative of the soils of the whole watershed, since the
values obtained for the Sangamon River and Lake Decatur fall on the regression
line established for the negative correlation between nitrate concentration and
^{15}N enrichment. However, for this to be meaningful to their argument, one must
first accept their interpretation that the finding of the negative correlation demonstrates that the decrease in ^{15}N enrichment is due principally to application
of fertilizers. Since this interpretation in turn depends on the assumption that
natural soil nitrogen in *both* virgin soils and those which are cultivated (without
fertilizer) will be ^{15}N-enriched, the argument is completely circular. It is tantamount to saying: "If B is correct, then A $= X$; and since we have demonstrated
that A $= X$ (on the assumption that B is correct), B then must be correct." On
this ground alone the "scientific proof" falls.

    Another core difficulty with their proof, as the investigators clearly recog-
nized, is that there *are* natural processes which *do* favor the accumulation in soil
of nitrogen with low ^{15}N enrichment. One of these is rain; the second—far
more significant—is symbiotic nitrogen fixation during alternate-year planting
with legumes (in these fields, soybeans).

    With respect to rain they write: "Preliminary measurements (9 for nitrate
and 19 for Kjeldahl nitrogen) made under conditions certain to maximize the
concentration of nitrogen suggest that rain may contribute 12 to 17 percent as
much nitrogen as is put on the land as fertilizer. If instead one uses Aldrich's
estimate . . . for this region of 5 pounds of nitrogen per acre added in rain, the
value is about 8 percent of the fertilizer nitrogen applied in 1970" (*ibid.*, p. 1333).

    These figures do not bear significantly on the problem, but they are useful
because they indicate that the 1970 applications of fertilizer nitrogen to the corn
crop averaged about 62 pounds per acre (if 5 $= 8$ percent, then 62 $= 100$ percent). This figure is nowhere mentioned in the paper, possibly in part because it
is actually a relatively modest application rate. In fact, one generally irritating
aspect of this publication is that practically no data are expressed in terms of
absolute quantities and no information is supplied about the differences between
the sites sampled; everything is expressed in ratios, parts, percentages—a well-
recognized method of providing one's critics with as little as possible to work
with.

    The authors are not completely covered, however. Here is their comment on the "negligible" contribution of nitrogen fixation: "Under the assumption that 75 pounds of nitrogen is fixed per acre and that the partition between harvested crop and stubble returned to the land is 86:14 [ref. 8, Weber, 1966], nitrogen fixation by soybeans contributes less than 10 percent of the quantity of nitrogen added by fertilizer" *(ibid.).*

On reading this sentence, we were confronted by a puzzle in elementary arithmetic. How could 75 (pounds nitrogen fixed per acre) plus 14 percent of x (amount of nitrogen in the stubble) be equal to less than 10 percent of 62 (pounds of fertilizer nitrogen added to an acre of corn)?

From a later sentence in the text it becomes clear that the authors understood the partition figure—14:86—given by Weber to mean that only 14 percent of the 75 lb of nitrogen fixed by the soy crop/acre/year would be retained in the soil. We, on the other hand, understood that the 75 lb/acre referred to a *net gain* of nitrogen in the soil after harvesting the soy crop, to which could also be added the 10.5 lb in the soy stubble. (Note that even 14 percent of 75 lb equals 10.5 lb, which is definitely *more* than 10 percent of 62 lb.) It is generally accepted that the *minimum net gain* of nitrogen from a season of planting with legumes is about 60 kg/ha, or 54 lb/acre (Schmitt, 1965, p. 706); while from certain legumes net gains as high as 315 lb/acre of nitrogen occur (Delwiche, 1970). We therefore think it most unlikely that the Weber citation could represent a genuine substantiation of the argument that only 6 lb/acre of nitrogen (less than 10 percent of 62 lb applied as fertilizer) are gained through the soy planting. Even commonsense reasoning belies this claim, for if it were true that the soy crop takes up all but a small fraction of the nitrogen made available by symbiotic fixers in the soy roots, then the centuries-old practice of rotating grain crops with legumes would not make any sense at all.

Lastly, had the authors considered the corn crop yields, they would have had to recognize their error, or to explain how such yields could have been produced by such minimum nitrogen input. If 62 lb of nitrogen are added through fertilizer applications and only another 8 percent from rain (i.e., 5 lb) and less than 10 percent from soy stubble (i.e., 6 lb) can be reckoned in addition, the 73 lb total (*much* of which, it should be remembered, the authors claim is being lost in runoff or seepage) would have to account for the corn yields. These were reported to average from 90 to 130 bushels/acre in the area for 1971.[*] Taking an average of 100 bushels/acre, considering the nitrogen content of the grain alone rather than the whole plant, and calculating from a lower protein content in corn than that typical of today's varieties, one arrives at a figure of 77 lb/acre nitrogen removed in the corn crop. Comparing this with the 73 lb/acre total input emerging from the

[*]Personal communication, C. A. Black.

authors' figures, it would seem obvious that the claim that the Illinois farmers are applying *excess* quantities of nitrate fertilizer would have to be dropped altogether. On the contrary, the fields would be showing a negative nitrogen balance.

It is really no wonder that agriculturists become impatient when environmentalists invade their area of expertise, especially if the latter not only suggest that the use of the favored and vital tools of agronomy should be curtailed, but also either cannot or will not evaluate correctly the literature which they cite to support their contentions.

To sum up: the tracing of nitrate contamination in Lake Decatur to artificial fertilizer has *not* been proven by the methods and data reported in this paper at all. The basic premise that only the artificial-nitrogen chemical fertilizers are low in ^{15}N enrichment is, to begin with, untrue. When the authors admit that soil nitrogen from symbiotic nitrogen fixation might also be low in ^{15}N, they attempt to dismiss this contribution as insignificant—less than 10 percent of the quantity applied in the form of fertilizer. However, both data widely available in the literature and consideration of the corn yields in these fields indicate that the nitrogen enrichment contribution of symbiotic fixers may be as great or greater than the quantity applied in the form of artificial fertilizer. Since this type of natural soil nitrogen does not differ significantly in ^{15}N content from that of fertilizer nitrogen, the former cannot be distinguished from the latter by analytical techniques. The "final proof" of Kohl et al. rests on the assertion that they were able to distinguish clearly between artificially produced and naturally occurring nitrates in the soil, and since this assertion does not stand up to scrutiny, one cannot accept the claim of the authors that they definitely traced the source of Lake Decatur's nitrate pollution to artificial fertilizers. Nevertheless, Commoner's readers and lecture audiences have been led to understand that proof positive has been provided; and we may undoubtedly count on being informed henceforth—at least by lay environmentalists—that there is a sound scientific case against the use of artificial nitrate fertilizers.

We would surmise that U.S. soil-science specialists will have a good deal more to say about the faults in both techniques and reasoning in this study by Kohl, Commoner, and Shearer. However, we have ventured to offer our criticisms here, even though neither of us is such a specialist. If the nitrate issue follows the pattern of other environmentalist issues, one may predict with reasonable certainty that the genuinely knowledgeable specialists will be more or less ignored by the press and the lay public and that even many legislators will be more impressed by such dramatic findings and charismatic presentations than with the scientific refutations of the specialists.

The Manure Solution and Water Pollution

The immediate solution proposed by Commoner to protect the water supply of the city of Decatur is that the farmers in the watershed should cut back on their use of artificial fertilizers, even at the risk of sizable economic losses. (We shall see shortly on what basis Commoner carried on his persuasive discussions with the farmers of the region.) In the long run, however, the message of his book seems to be that we should give up artificial fertilizers altogether and "reclose the natural cycles" by establishing a system which will permit us to return all organic garbage and human and animal wastes to the farm, where it will be used as fertilizer instead of the cheap and handy chemicals. In other terms, a national compost heap with quite a lot of city sewer sludge in it, carried back to the farm by one modern element in the plan—long-range piping. Unlike many Americans, we have no aesthetic objections to reusing human wastes; we do, however, have *ecological* reasons for rejecting this "natural" proposal—reasons which are intimately related to the first of the bad effects Commoner associates with nitrate fertilizers: their use is contributing to the eutrophic conditions of our inland waters.

It is to Commoner's credit that in discussing the causes of eutrophication, he at least does not single out merely one nutrient as the sole root of the problem, as have many of the "ban-phosphate" crusaders. He does explain that the roles played by phosphate and nitrate in stimulating the growth of algae represent complex interacting balances and he mentions the sizable contributions of phosphate and nitrate from sewage which has undergone secondary treatment. (However, he quite incorrectly implies that such treatment is "modern." It is, though not *yet* in use by the majority of U.S. municipalities, a 120-year-old system.) Rather than discussing our water-pollution problems in the context of really modern waste-water treatment, he proposes three completely regressive solutions: give up detergents and return to soap; give up secondary sewage treatment and recycle all wastes to the land; and give up artificial fertilizers, for which the garbage and wastes can be substituted.

In connection with water pollution and eutrophication, he makes several other errors which are typical of many of the people he criticizes for blaming only one pollutant. He overestimates the significance of abundant algal growth as an indicator of water pollution and simultaneously grossly underestimates the importance of dissolved organics. He describes algal growth, in connection with Lake Erie, for example, as "the acknowledged *source* of most of the . . . problem," which is complete nonsense; and he perpetuates a misconception shared by many American scientists as well as laymen to the effect that algae deplete oxygen. In very special and rare circumstances they may do so temporarily, but the fact is that algae, even when present in the form of a massive bloom, contribute *net gains* in oxygen to a lake ecosystem.

In order to clarify some of the misunderstandings about water pollution which come up in connection with both phosphates and nitrates and to explain why implementation of Commoner's recommendation that we should use sewage as fertilizer would be ecologically disastrous, we should like to elaborate somewhat on the Kolkwitz saprobic system which we mentioned in Chapter 7. This system is used widely by European limnologists to characterize the pollutional status of fresh waters by determining the qualitative and quantitative composition of the aquatic community.

Around the turn of the century, algologists investigating the influence of untreated municipal wastes on receiving waters (rivers and lakes) found that around sewer outfalls, where the wastes were highly concentrated, the species composition of the normal community was severely decimated. All photosynthesizing organisms were completely absent where the organic load was extreme, with a few colorless algae present in huge numbers.

When Kolkwitz became interested in the characterization of polluted waters in the 1920s, he coined the term *polysaprobic* to describe the conditions of such grossly polluted waters. He found both flora and fauna to be composed of very few species, all in tremendous abundance. The forms present were specifically adapted to the high inorganic and organic contents of the waters, especially the latter. Typical for such communities are huge quantities of bacteria in the bottom sediment, mainly anaerobic forms; and tube-dwelling annelids. In the water there will be protozoans feeding on the large numbers of bacteria, and colorless algae (flagellates and apochlorotic blue-greens). The organic load and resultant low oxygen levels are conditions unsuitable for the vast majority of other aquatic organisms. The severe species decimation and concurrent foul conditions of the water are indeed serious signs of deterioration of an aquatic ecosystem; however, such conditions can develop only where the *organic* load is high, and the frequently heard predictions that DDT or phosphates or mercury will cause similar destruction have no foundation.

If a substantial amount of the organic load is eliminated from such waters — by secondary treatment, for instance, which removes about 80–90 percent of the total organic matter — an immediate improvement will ensue. Kolkwitz designated these less polluted waters as *alpha-mesosaprobic*. These are the most productive waters, and very large numbers of species will establish themselves at the primary and secondary trophic levels. *Beta-mesosaprobic* conditions, where the organic contents of the waters are still lower, support even more species.

Such waters are, however, somewhat less productive and fewer species are found as dominating organisms.

Finally, if the waters are completely renewed (as can be done with advanced waste-treatment systems), or if one starts with pristine waters, the conditions are termed *oligosaprobic*. In these waters relatively few species are found and their numbers will be low.

Kolkwitz found that determination of the species composition of a community, identification of the particular dominant organisms, and establishment of their numbers could serve to characterize the degree and nature of water pollution. Algae, rotifers, protozoa, and bottom-dwelling annelids were the groups most useful for this characterization. But as the system became more developed (cf. Liebmann, 1960–1962) it became clear that it is sufficient in certain cases to examine only one of the first three groups in order to define the nature of the general community. Thus a rotifer specialist, once he has enough data on his group, can predict which algae and protozoa should also be present and in what approximate numbers, or an algologist can characterize the protozoa and rotifers, after investigating the algal composition. When classifications are made from study of the algal community, the basic categories will show the following very general picture:

1. Oligosaprobic: About 300 algal species will be seen in the course of the whole year. Blue-green and green algae and flagellates will be more common than under the other categories, and there will be proportionally fewer diatoms. No great abundance of any species will be found.

2. Beta-mesosaprobic: 600 to 900 algal species will be present,* more than 50 percent of them diatoms. About 40 to 80 species will be abundant, depending on the season and climate. The dominant species may attain numbers of 2,000 to 3,000 per liter.

3. Alpha-mesosaprobic: 500 to 600 species will typically occur, about 20 of them dominant. Dominant species may attain numbers of 15,000 to 20,000 per liter. These conditions are those where "blooms" are most likely to occur. When there is a bloom, individual numbers of 1 to 10 million per liter may be counted.

4. Polysaprobic: 0–12 photosynthesizing algal species, in small numbers,

---

* Some specialists may object, claiming that floral lists for fresh waters do not contain anything like these numbers of different species. As far as some printed lists are concerned, this is true, but is no proof that the algae are not there. In 1958–1959, for example, I worked on the Potomac River with C. Reimer and we identified nearly 800 species (Claus and Reimer, 1961); and in 16 months of work on the Danube in 1957–1958 I identified 659 fresh-water species (Claus, 1961). G. C.

and two or three colorless algae will be present in huge quantities (more than 1 million per liter).

An experienced saprobiologist can tell a great deal about the condition of waters without even doing lengthy identifications. For example, when a few species associated with polysaprobic conditions are seen in waters which are supposed to be completely free of organic load, he can sample inlet streams and quickly find the source of the contamination—often, in rural areas, an old outhouse or drainage from fields containing animal excreta. This contamination may be so slight that it will not be noted by standard chemical techniques. With experience, he may also be able to characterize with reasonable accuracy the chemical constituents of the waters without analyses, or his predictions of these constituents may be used as a check against chemical determinations (Cholnoky and Claus, 1961).

Knowledge of the system can also alert one to errors in reports of floral counts which are incompatible with known conditions. For example, Commoner and several other environmentalists have used daily algal counts from the data of the Cleveland Waterworks to counter the argument that Lake Erie was already well on its way to advanced age before human abuses worsened its condition. We do not intend to enter into a lengthy discussion of Lake Erie, about which probably more silly and dramatic statements have been made than almost any other environmental subject. However, the matter of natural aging of the lake and the kinds of data used to refute the argument that Erie was already "old" before man began polluting it serve as an excellent illustration of the difference between the available information about the behavior of natural systems which represent hard data (with obvious implications) and that sort of information which is recorded in print but has to be rejected by anyone with experience in the field, because it cannot be reconciled with the real behavior of the system.

It is obvious that man has used Lake Erie without much thought for the quality of the water. He has added an enormous pollutional load to some parts of the lake in the forms of raw sewage and industrial effluent, and he has also filled it with various forms of junk. However, the basic argument that the lake would not live long even if unpolluted by man is a sound one, whatever one may think of its overtone of rationalization. One needs only one datum to substantiate the argument: the *natural* sedimentation rate adds 5 million metric tons yearly to this shallowest of the Great Lakes, and as this rate is constant, one can predict that in less than 500 years it will be completely filled, regardless of human intervention.

The counterargument, as presented by Commoner, consists first of the completely unsubstantiated claim that there is, *ab ovo*, no such thing as natural aging of lakes—a statement which would elicit unified opposition from all the divergent schools of ecological thought. The data used to support this counter-argument is the information that in 1927, the annual average daily algal count in the Cleveland city water-supply intake was 100/ml; whereas in 1945 it was 800/ml and in 1964, 2,500/ml. About these data, Commoner writes: "The 1927 count is typical of a 'young' non-aging lake; there is no evidence here that Lake Erie was aging before 1927" (Commoner, 1971, p. 107). On reading this con-clusion, one wonders whether Commoner confused milliliter with liter, or whether he is ignorant both of the algal counts typical for "young" lakes and of the kinds of counts that are within the realm of possibility. Let us explain: 100/ml is the same as 100,000/l. If we take this reading at face value, it suggests beta-mesosaprobic conditions, and it is certainly *not* characteristic of an oligotrophic lake. The 1964 count, on the other hand, which reports an average of 2,500,000/l, is clearly impossible and must be rejected as erroneous. If it were correct, it would indicate a 365-day perpetual bloom—a phenomenon which has never been seen on Lake Erie nor, for that matter, anywhere else.

If we return now to the saprobic system, we may draw two lessons—one theoretical and one practical—from the studies which have been carried out on these four categories of aquatic conditions. In some respects, the study of aquatic communities seems at least partially to support the theory that more diverse communities are more stable, although these observations have nothing to do with either succession or climax. In these fresh-water ecosystems, both oligo-saprobic and polysaprobic communities are highly unstable. A slight addition of appropriate nutrients into the pure waters or a slight lessening of the organic load of the most polluted ones will lead to sudden and quite dramatic changes in the species composition of the system. Communities characterized as beta- or alpha-mesosaprobic, on the one hand, are quite stable, moving over into the next pollutional stage or reverting to a cleaner one only when there is a sub-stantial change in the base conditions of the water.

More important, from a practical point of view, is that this system indicates that inorganic nutrients alone will never cause either alpha-mesosaprobic or polysaprobic conditions. For these to develop, *there must be substantial quan-tities of dissolved organics present.* It is vital that this should be understood, because there is at the present time a vast amount of confusion about the very definition of water pollution; and it is obvious that when a problem is not cor-rectly defined, it cannot be solved. The central and simplest key to the definition is the early observation that around municipal sewage outfalls, the aquatic communities were severely decimated. In other terms, it is raw sewage—human and animal wastes and other organics—which are most detrimental to inland waters.

Now let us consider some of the implications of Commoner's proposal that one way to handle simultaneously the problem of wastes—human, animal, and vegetable—and the problem of nitrate pollution of waters is to recycle all the wastes to the farm and use them in place of artificial fertilizers. We shall ignore the problem of how the sludge would be sterilized (with chlorine, or heat, or cobalt, all of which are on his long list of Very Bad Things) as well as the complex organizational problems which such a system would entail in a large country like the United States. We want to consider only questions bearing on the quantities of organic wastes which are involved and what would be the ecological effects of sending them back to the land.

To begin with, we should like to consider some quantities. We will confine ourselves to the matter of human and animal wastes alone. The farm-animal population of the United States, counting only cattle, hogs, sheep, and poultry, produces about 480 million tons of solid wastes and 2.7 billion tons of liquid wastes annually. The contribution of the human population is probably not more than 150 million tons yearly, if we calculate only urine and excrement and exclude garbage. To give the reader an idea how much this 3.3 billion tons is, let us suppose that we were to spread it over the entire land surface of the continental United States, including all cities, personal property, highways, wilderness areas, and so on. From these wastes alone there would be 1.5 tons per acre. Spread on the cropped acreage presently under cultivation, the figure would be about 22 tons per acre. Now admittedly much of this is water, and if dried, such quantities could be distributed on the farm lands, although the handling would be awkward and expensive. On the other hand, if all the garbage (carefully separated organics, of course) were also put on cropped acreage, the quantities would become unmanageable. Apparently practical considerations were not on Commoner's mind when he wrote: "Particularly important is the retention of animal manure in the soil and the similar utilization of every scrap of vegetable matter—including the return to the soil of the garbage generated in the cities by the food produced on the farm" (ibid., p. 147).

However, let us ignore the practical problems entailed in treatment, transport, and spreading which such a plan would involve in a large country like the United States. Let us consider how much organic waste would have to be spread on farmed acreage in order to have a nutrient input equivalent to 62 lb/acre of fertilizer nitrogen. Simple calculations show that one would have to apply approximately 30 tons (wet weight) of manure to each acre to reach the nitrogen equivalent value.

Leaving aside the probable objections of the farmers, who don't seem to count much anyway, what would be the impact of these materials on inland waters? If one-tenth of this quantity were to run off or seep into receiving waters (as some estimates for fertilizer indicate), about 3 tons of organic matter would enter the waters from every acre of cultivated land, compared with 6 lb of fertilizer nitrogen. (Actually the runoff from manure is likely to be a much higher proportion of the material applied than that from chemical fertilizer, since much of it would be spread in the late winter months on the ground surface and carried off in melting snow and spring rains.) In each ton of this organic matter there are about 100 kg of carbon atoms. Five oxygen atoms are required for the full oxidation of one organically bound carbon atom, which means that 0.5 ton of oxygen would be depleted from the receiving waters in order to oxidize the run-off from only 1 acre. Natural waters usually contain about 5 mg/1 oxygen, which means that 100,000 m^3 water would be needed for this oxidation process. Put in other terms, there is not enough water, and there is not enough oxygen in the waters. Furthermore, even if the use of manure were more limited and the grain yields accordingly drastically reduced, a return on a large scale to the use of animal wastes as fertilizer would result, not merely in algal nourishment, but in polysaprobic conditions in those of our inland waters which are adjacent to farms. The "solution" would be a national ecological disaster!

Commoner's book gives an impression of being fairly well reasoned, if the reader does not scratch the surface. Unlike many environmentalists, he is not just advocating bans; he is talking about looking at problems as wholes and seeking solutions which will "reclose the circle which we have broken with natural cycles." His general message may sound good to some, but his "natural" fertilizer plan is illustrative of a failure to think through the ultimate implications of the proposed solution.

An "Ecologically Disruptive Sequence"

Commoner's second major claim about the deleterious effect of fertilizer use is by far the most puzzling from the scientific point of view; for this has to do with the ruination of the soil itself, the probable destruction of naturally occurring nitrogen-fixing microorganisms, and the relationship between the efficiency of plant uptake of nutrients and the humus content of the soil. Unless one is particularly focused on soil science, it is possible to read Commoner's book and hardly perceive his message on this subject, perhaps because of its very strangeness.

In a chapter called "The Technological Flaw" the following passages on the use of artificial nitrate fertilizers are representative:

> When, as it has been in much of the Midwest, the soil is used for intensive grain production rather than pasturage, the humus content is depleted; farmers then resort

to increasingly heavy applications of inorganic fertilizer, especially of nitrogen, setting off the ecologically disruptive sequence that has already been described. . . .

The reason for the disparity between the increase in fertilizer and in yield is a biological one: the corn plant, after all, does have a limited capacity for growth, so that more and more fertilizer must be used to force the plant to produce the last few bushels of increased yield. Therefore, in order to achieve such high yields the farmer *must* use more nitrogen than the plant can take up. . . .

Before the advent of inorganic nitrogen fertilizer, the farmer had to rely heavily on nitrogen-fixing bacteria to maintain the soil's fertility. These bacteria naturally inhabit the soil either in or around the roots of plants and can make up for the inevitable loss of nitrogen in food shipped off the farm for sale or otherwise lost by natural processes. The bacteria are a free economic good, available at no cost other than the effort involved in crop rotation and other necessary husbandry of the soil. . . .

Under the impact of heavy use of inorganic nitrogen fertilizer, the nitrogen-fixing bacteria originally living in the soil may not survive, or if they do, they may mutate into nonfixing forms. (Commoner, 1971, pp. 149, 150, 152; author's emphasis)

At first we thought these passages represented merely another expression of nostalgia for the good old days, when the small farm was a more natural and more integrated community in itself, combined with a sort of pseudological but not too serious attempt to explain why increases in fertilizer applications are not linearly related to increments in per-acre yields. But the reference to depletion of humus (mentioned several other places as disastrous), and mention of "forcing" higher plant productivity by using more nitrogen than the plant can take up, gave us pause. (The possibility that natural nitrogen-fixing bacteria might not survive is presented mainly as a speculation, and it seems so unlikely to be taken seriously that we do not think it worthy of a rebuttal.) We recalled that Commoner had discussed the nitrogen soil cycle in the first—more theoretical—chapter of his book. We decided to have another look at his explanation of how the natural cycle proceeds:

About 80 per cent of the earth's nitrogen is in the air as chemically inert nitrogen gas. Of the remaining 20 per cent, a good deal is a part of the soil's humus, a very complex organic substance. Another significant fraction is contained in living things— almost entirely as organic compounds. . . .

Nitrogen can enter the soil through nitrogen fixation, a process carried out by various bacteria and algae, some of them living free in the soil and others associated with the roots of legumes such as clover or with the leaves of some tropical plants.

Nitrogen also enters the soil from the decay of plant matter and of animal wastes. Much of it eventually becomes incorporated into the soil's humus. Humus slowly releases nitrogen through the action of soil microorganisms, which finally convert it into nitrate. In turn, the nitrate is taken up by the roots of plants and is made into protein and other vital parts of the crop. . . .

By far the slowest step in this cycle is the release of nitrate from humus. As a result, the natural concentration of nitrate in the soil water is very low and the roots need to work to pull it into the plant. For this work the plant must expend energy, which is released by biological oxidation processes in the roots. The required oxygen must reach the roots from the air, a process that is efficient only if the soil is sufficiently porous. Soil porosity is very dependent on its humus content, for humus has a very spongy structure. Thus, soil porosity, therefore its oxygen content, and hence the efficiency of nutrient absorbtion by plant roots are closely related to the humus content of the soil. The efficient growth of the plant reconverts inorganic nutrients into organic matter (the plant substance), which when decayed in the soil contributes to its humus content, thus enhancing the soil's porosity and thereby supporting efficient plant growth. (*Ibid.*, pp. 24, 25)

In the first parts of this long lecture on the nitrogen cycle in soil, the description is relatively accurate, although there are some minor mistakes and omissions. (For instance, there is no known free-living alga in soil which would be capable of fixing atmospheric nitrogen; and considerable amounts of nitrogen enter the soil from the atmospheric reservoir through rainfall.) However, the point where Commoner's lay lecture turns into speculation unrelated to soil science is when he begins to define the importance of humus in soil structure conditioning and its role in permitting efficient utilization of nutrients by the roots of plants. We realized that it must be his notions that natural humus is the best source of nutrients for plants and that humus, by increasing soil porosity, also increases the availability of oxygen, which lay behind his later claim that substituting artificial fertilizers for "organic" humus destroys soil structure and decreases the efficiency of nutrient uptake. As we were reading, it seemed to us that this pronouncement had a familiar ring, although it was certainly not from agronomy. It is probably a strange historical coincidence that Commoner's precursor seems to be none other than Lysenko's soil-science counterpart in "creative biology," the "progressive Soviet scientist Academician, Vil'yams, reformer of the decadent Western bourgeois podology." Zhores Medvedev offers a fitting description of the ideas of Vil'yams, contrasting them with the genuine scientific efforts of Pryanishnikov and his school.

Without any factual basis, Vil'yams considered fine-textured, lumpy soil to be the only kind that is fertile, and soil texture to be the most important factor for good crops. According to him, a soil with indiscernible horizons or a weak profile could not produce good yields even with added fertilizers and adequate irrigation. Hence Vil'yams considered it useless to fertilize that type of soil, which, according to him, constituted most of the tilled land in the country.

His claim that, merely by including in the rotation a 30 to 40 per cent mixture of legumes and cereal grasses (for induction and maintenance of soil texture), yields could be increased tenfold was pure fantasy: behind those figures there were no experiments, no data. They were arrived at from abstract considerations of water-holding capacities of different kinds of soils. And yet there were people who believed him and oriented the whole of the country's agriculture along this unscientific and irresponsible path.

The foregoing illustrates the essence of the differences between the Vil'yams and Pryanishnikov schools. The latter insisted on the development of mineral fertilizers, one-year planting of clover without cereal grass admixture (thus improving the nitrogen balance of the soil), and the intensification of agriculture by introduction of high-yielding varieties in the rotation, as was done in Western Europe. This method had historical and practical foundations, backed by extensive factual material from experiments and experience. Pryanishnikov insistently pointed out that the development of chemical industry and chemical fertilizers was highly important. . . .

Vil'yams, on the other hand, proposed not to develop the fertilizer industry, to expand clover planting to two or three years running, and only in mixtures with timothy and other cereal grasses (thereby reducing the nitrogen-fixing effect of clover); and to reject the use of various agricultural equipment (for instance, harrows and cultivators), which allegedly destroy soil texture.

Other differences between the two men were apparent. Pryanishnikov's path was that of a real scientist and patriot. Vil'yams, on the other hand, was a cabinet theorizer, dreamer, and fanatic who, under cover of loud phrases about fatherland and socialism, concealed the aim of establishing the supremacy of his own ideas in science and in practice by all available means. (Medvedev, 1969, pp. 89–90)

Vil'yams thought that the soil structure as it determines the water-holding capacity of the soil was all-important, whereas Commoner maintains that the availability of plenty of oxygen, dependent on the porosity of the soil structure, is the central key to plant growth.

Neither of these points is completely untrue. That is, when one grows plants in soil, the texture of the soil has some importance both with respect to its capacity to hold water and a sufficiently porous structure to permit oxygen to reach the roots, although the primary energy source is the photosynthetic activity of the aboveground parts of the plant. Nobody would deny the importance of soil husbandry, and modern farmers certainly do make efforts to maintain soil conditions which will permit maximum efficiency of nutrient uptake. The problems with Commoner's view have to do with his emphasis on the *primary* importance of soil texture and with the completely erroneous implication that decaying organic substances such as manure and vegetable compost are a *better* source of plant nutrients than inorganic fertilizers.

For readers who are still somewhat lost the simpler account of Commoner's teaching as rendered by Paul Ehrlich may clarify matters:

> Unthinking use of chemicals is the rule today, and it's a dangerous rule. Farmers, for example, have been encouraged to increase production by relying heavily on inorganic nitrogen fertilizers. As is usually the case when such artificial factors are introduced into the environment, the results have been bad as well as good. The good effects of nitrates were immediately obvious. Long soil-building processes involving decay of organic matter, building of humus and nitrogen fixing by certain crops were short-cut in a single planting season as farmers used the inorganic fertilizers and reaped high yields. But, as always, it wasn't quite that simple. When the normal soil-building processes were avoided, organic soil nitrogen was lost and the earth became so compacted that root systems had difficulty absorbing nutrients. This resulted in ever-larger requirements for synthetic fertilizers; their use has increased 12 times in 25 years.
>
> Dr. Barry Commoner has said that farmers are "hooked on nitrates like a junkie is hooked on heroin." One price of this addiction is increased water pollution, for a great deal of the fertilizer that's added to farmlands runs off the surface of the land and into lakes and rivers. In the absence of proper soil-building practices, farmlands in this country have lost around 50 percent of their original organic nitrogen. Commoner says that in 25 to 50 years, the fertility of the soil will be so low that the ultimate food crisis will occur unless inorganic nutrients are used to a degree that would cause an insoluble water-pollution problem.
>
> Animal manure, on the other hand, is a soil *builder*. If we stopped treating the waste from animals as something to be disposed of—a pollutant—and used it, instead, as a fertilizer and soil builder, we'd be a long way toward solving one of our most critical pollution problems. Building soil in this way, of course, is a long, tedious process, and it may cost more than the present system of garbage disposal and chemical fertilization, but the country will save in the long run—in human as well as natural resources. (Ehrlich, 1971, pp. 95-96; author's emphasis)

The crude analogy to drug addiction seems to be a favorite one with environmentalists, as it is commonly used by anti-pesticide campaigners as well. It strikes us as illustrative of the contempt with which they regard the farmer, as well as of their complete disdain and distrust for anyone remotely connected with the chemicals industry—obviously the "suppliers" and "pushers."

But let's get back to theory. Where could Commoner have derived his notion that humus is the *most important factor* in maintaining a healthy soil cycle and that it is the best source of plant nutrients? Perhaps it stems from the observation that soil which is completely compacted or completely dry is not the best kind on which to drop seeds if you expect them to take root and grow. However, since any amateur gardener knows this, it does not really serve to illuminate Commoner's thought processes. We strongly suspect that the central problem in his theory has to do with attachment to the words "organic" and "natural," two words which carry highly positive connotations in the current climate of lay opinion, but which have very little to do with science. For the last 100 years or so, plant physiologists have been coming to the recognition that the *primary* factors for plant growth are inorganic nutrients (in addition to illumination), and that plant productivity is enhanced by the direct application of inorganic salts to the medium in which the plant is grown, the source of these nutrients being a matter of complete indifference. The idea that the slow conversion of organic materials in the soil into inorganic nutrients suitable for uptake by plants is superior to direct application of inorganic nutrients to the soil is strictly folklore. As a scientific view, it belongs to the mid-eighteenth century.

It should also be pointed out that although humus plays some role in the husbandry of many kinds of agricultural soils, it is in no sense absolutely essential for plant growth. One of the most fertile soils, for example, is loess (accumulated glacial dust), which contains no humus whatsoever. For that matter, plants rooted among pebbles can be grown very efficiently, if they are offered the right kind of nutrient solution. Finally, if one bears in mind that one of the most efficient ways of growing plants is through hydroponic techniques—where the plants are immersed in a liquid-nutrient solution—it becomes clear that Commoner's emphasis on the *primacy* of the role of humus is erroneous.

It was our general impression that all Western scientists were more or less in agreement that the provision of inorganic nutrients is of central importance to plant growth and that although soil husbandry dictates the maintenance of a reasonably porous soil structure, neither soil fertility nor plant productivity are dependent on the presence of *organic* humus as a central factor. Since Commoner is a plant physiologist by training, we were greatly surprised to learn that he maintains a view about the essentials of plant-nutrition different from that of his contemporaries among botanists.

We shall now leave the realm of soil-science theory and return to Commoner's account of "Illinois Earth." Of particular interest is the question: On what grounds can a farmer be persuaded to kick his nitrate habit?

Bottle-fed Babies

Had Commoner gone to the Illinois farmers to discuss his theory that humus is of primary importance in plant nutrition, or had he attempted to persuade them that their applications of nitrate fertilizer should be cut back so as not to nourish greater numbers of algae in the river, it seems to us unlikely that they would have given him a hearing. As things developed in Decatur, however, it was the local public health officials who first alerted Commoner to the nitrate pollution of the city reservoir, and it is the conflict between a "healthful water supply" and the farming practices of the region that is played up in his chapter on the Illinois problem.

Strictly speaking, the appearance of nitrates in drinking water is not a public health problem. The USPHS nitrate standard of 45 mg/l and the corresponding WHO limit of 50 mg/l are completely arbitrary. According to McKee and Wolf (1963), there is no rational limit for nitrates. In adults and in children over ten weeks of age, no conditions of ill health are known to be associated with any amounts of nitrates in drinking water or food (with the exception of isolated individuals in some inbred Indian tribes and among the Eskimos).

Infants, on the other hand, seem to be susceptible to elevated nitrate concentrations in their food. Since the exposure must be direct, only bottle-fed babies and only those given formula made up from water containing more than 10 ppm nitrates are at risk. Under these very special circumstances, infants can develop a condition called methemoglobinemia, in which the oxygen-carrying capacity of the blood pigment is impaired. If the intoxication lasts long enough, the baby will become blue, and signs of slow asphyxiation will be seen. The reason for the special susceptibility of very young infants is that the pH of their intestinal contents is relatively high and the composition of their bacterial flora is both qualitatively and quantitatively different for the first few weeks of life. The predominance of *E. coli* and the higher pH value will effect the reduction of nitrate into *nitrite,* which is the actual toxic substance. Beyond the first few weeks of life, this process no longer takes place.

Commoner does mention at one point that the specific danger is to infants, although he delineates neither the age limit nor the qualification that breast-fed babies, as well as bottle-fed infants whose formula is made from a source other than the nitrate-contaminated waters, will be exempt from any threat to health. Throughout the rest of the chapter, he continuously writes about the conflict between a healthful water supply and the economic benefits to farmers (and the people of Decatur as well, whose prosperity is closely linked to that of the farmers) derived from fertilizer use. In the end, he gives the impression that the nitrate contamination of the water supply represents a serious and imminent danger to the health of the populace, which could only be resolved by sacrifice on the part of the farmers: i.e., reduction in fertilizer applications.

One has to admit that from Commoner's account in *The Closing Circle* one cannot glean exactly what happened in the Sangamon River watershed area; nor do we know what the people of Decatur and the farmers of the region might have done in the meanwhile. From the book one gathers that the original alarm about the health dangers of nitrate pollution in the reservoir was kept in the forefront of public attention, and that after the scientists of Commoner's group had supposedly proven that runoff of fertilizer from the surrounding farms was the primary source of the water contamination, he met with local groups, including the farmers, and found the latter to be highly cooperative and concerned. There are many things one would like to know which are not mentioned in the book. Were independent analyses performed of the constituents of the drinking-water supply? What else is in the waters, in addition to high nitrate concentrations? Were the people of the area informed properly about alternative solutions for purifying their water supply, or were they simply programmed to begin thinking of chemical fertilizers as Bad Things?

We should like to make a few simple points here to underline the onesidedness of both the description of the problem and the discussion of its solution which Commoner presented in the book.

1. Respecting the threat of methemoglobinemia, the medical literature refers to 10 ppm nitrate concentration as the upper limit for safe consumption by infants under ten weeks of age (Rosenfield and Huston, 1950). It therefore seems meaningless that a big hue and cry was made only when a 45 ppm reading was reported in the water supply, even though this figure happens to coincide with the arbitrary PHS standard.

2. In any region where drinking-water supplies contain nitrate concentrations above 10 ppm, a first and obvious preventive step to be taken by public health authorities is to warn mothers that newborn infants should be breast-fed, or, if not feasible, that the water used for formula should originate from certified sources. Since the danger represented by nitrate pollution per se is circumscribed and ill effects are preventable through education, there is no reason for intense, emotion-ridden campaigns to try to eliminate the source of the contamination with all haste.

3. As far as the city populace is concerned, there are a number of considerations of which they should be advised:
(a) The accuracy of nitrate determinations is notoriously questionable, and the improbably high readings suggest that these ought to be confirmed by several independent laboratories, preferably not having prior information

about the readings reported earlier. This is not strictly a subjective judgment on our part, but is reflected in the latest edition of the *Standard Methods for the Examination of Water and Waste Water* (1965) where, because of the multitude of known interfering substances, several proposed alternatives to the standard method are discussed. If the high nitrate concentrations can be confirmed, then a thorough study of the other constituents of the water should be undertaken. It is almost unheard of that a body of water should show an excess in only one of the common constituents, and it is conceivable that the contamination of Decatur's drinking water is much more generalized than revealed by Commoner's studies.

(b) Should it turn out that the Decatur drinking water supply does indeed contain such consistently high levels of nitrate, even drastic curtailment of fertilizer applications would be unlikely to improve the situation appreciably. Only one genuine, long-term solution can be proposed: installation of a total water-renewal system, through which both the drinking-water supply and waste waters could be channeled. In the short term, this would be costly for the taxpayers and property owners of the region, but it represents a genuine forward-looking solution, which could make of the area one of the most advanced communities in the nation. Interestingly, Commoner admits that the economy of the city of Decatur is largely dependent on the prosperity of the farmers, and he also recognizes that their narrow profit margin has necessitated pushing yields to the utmost, for which their present applications of fertilizer are the minimum requirement. It then seems fairly obvious that the solution he proposes—a cutback in fertilizer use in the interest of a healthful water supply—could spell economic disaster for the whole region. On the other hand, the costs of constructing a genuinely modern water-renewal system, while sizable, could be borne by a farsighted community without undue economic strain in any one sector. Implementation of such a technological solution would have the added advantage of being an early realization of a system which will very likely become a pressing necessity for other communities in the very near future anyway.

4. Lastly, as far as the farmers are concerned, if one is going to advocate an economically suicidal curtailment of fertilizer application, it seems highly sophistic to do so on the basis of a health issue, which, even if genuine, is not put into proper perspective by Commoner's account. If given all the facts, it seems to us likely that the farmers might cooperate with the city in terms of tax contributions to help pay for a water-renewal system, particularly if they were allowed to grow their crops in accordance with accepted modern agricultural practices and in the hope of realizing a decent profit from their yields. It does not seem at all in accord with the spirit of science first to instill a sense of guilt in the farmers about the

possible infant deaths to which their practices might lead and then present them with a single alternative to alleviate their guilt feelings—particularly when it is a program which is likely to create more problems than it solves.

Food and Fertilizers

We hope we have made it sufficiently clear that where water pollution and waste management are concerned, we are cognizant of the existence of many real and pressing problems. While we retain some doubts about the nitrate levels reported in the Decatur reservoir, we would not deny that contamination of our inland and coastal waters with all sorts of pollutants can be said to be a serious matter of environmental deterioration. It takes us no closer to a solution of these problems, however, to read a book like *The Closing Circle,* for while Commoner points the finger of blame in a number of different directions—industrial efflu-ents, phosphate detergents, nitrate fertilizers, pesticides, inorganics from municipal sewage plants, and so on—he does not seem to recognize the central importance of organic materials in polluting the waters, and he makes rec-ommendations which would probably worsen the situation, were they to be implemented.

With respect to the particular subject of nitrate fertilizers, there are more specific objections to be raised to Commoner's stance, especially on the part of agronomists and nutritionists. For even if one were to grant that the work of his group in Illinois had succeeded in proving that the nitrate contamination of the Decatur reservoir is caused primarily by runoff of fertilizer from farms, and even if one were further to grant that rising nitrate levels in midwestern rivers do result from an increased use of fertilizer, one would still not have settled the question of which has priority: higher productivity on the farms or assurance that a natural water supply will remain uncontaminated with materials used to achieve this higher productivity.

In the United States, in a normal social and intellectual atmosphere, the attempt to define the priorities would probably rest primarily on economic grounds and consideration of viable alternatives. And in such an atmosphere, there is not much question that persons in decision-making and advisory positions would opt for a "technological fix" to purify the water long before they would consider recommending that the farmer curtail his applications of fertilizer.

But the prevailing atmosphere is an irrational one, in which consideration of priorities seems to depend more on the opinion of a few self-appointed experts and self-anointed saviors than on rational evaluation of real problems and the formulation of solutions directed toward the greater social good.

If agricultural specialists have become nervous about Commoner's rather unique attack on nitrogen fertilizers, it is probably not so much because they think he has a case as because they have learned something from the successes of the anti-pesticide campaign and even the anti-detergent campaign. They have recognized that even in cases when environmentalists are scientifically in error, or their alternative programs are inadequate or perhaps even disastrous, they may still win the right to impose their own programs on society, or at least to block those of competent specialists in relevant fields.

Like the anti-pesticide campaigners — although in a much less strident tone — the anti-fertilizer campaigners imply that it is the agrichemical industry which is responsible for encouraging the "excessive" use of fertilizers. The public is all too seldom reminded that enthusiasts for and defenders of chemical fertilizers can be found among the most disinterested and humanitarian of our globally oriented intellectuals. We should therefore like to close where we began, with some comments on world food-productivity potential in relation to agricultural technologies. The citation is from a public affairs lecture of the Columbia University Department of Biological Sciences: "Toward a Non-Malthusian Population Policy," given by nutritionist Jean Mayer, professor and member of the Center for Population Studies at Harvard University and a widely recognized authority on the nutritional problems of the United States and of underdeveloped countries:

> The biggest potential increase of food production does not . . . come from the extension of the area under cultivation, but from the increase in the use of fertilizers. The phenomenal increase in food production in this country has actually been performed with a reduction in acreage farmed. By pre-World War I standards of cultivation, it took one-and-one-half acres to support an American. If such standards prevailed today, we would need to add at least 40 million acres to our farm area every ten years, or the equivalent of an additional Iowa every decade. In fact, we use fertilizers instead. One ton of nitrogen is the equivalent of 14 acres of good farmland. The use of between two and three hundred thousand tons of nitrogen (and corresponding amounts of other necessary elements) per decade has obviated the need to discover another Iowa. And our use of fertilizer is less intensive than it is in Japan, where it is well over twice ours, or in Western Europe. . . . India, Africa, and most of Latin America use only an infinitesimal fraction of Japanese or Western amounts of fertilizer, or none at all. Garst has estimated that an expenditure of ten dollars an acre per year for fertilizers would alone add 50 to 100 per cent to the low yields in underdeveloped countries. Applying this investment to an area of 1.5 billion acres would be the equivalent to adding at least 750 million acres to the crop areas of these countries, the equivalent of a continent bigger than North America. (Mayer, 1969, pp. 10–11)

11

THE TOCSIN OVER TOXINS

The truth is, the science of Nature has been already
too long made only a work of the brain and the fancy:
It is now high time that it should return to the plainness and
soundness of observations on material and obvious things.

ROBERT HOOKE

Although it would seem obvious that investigations in natural
sciences fall into two broad categories—descriptive, interpretive investigations and experimental studies—these two categories seem sometimes to be confused. We apologize to the reader for taking him into a discussion of the most elementary levels of the philosophy of science before getting into the specific topic of this chapter, but it seems to be essential to get down to basic definitions in order to assure that misunderstandings do not arise simply from disagreements about terminology.

Both broad categories of Western natural science attempt to establish casual relationships among phenomena. However, the descriptive, interpretive branches of science (which include such disciplines as animal and plant taxonomy, descriptive astronomy, anatomy, and so on) attempt to determine the *manner* in which the causes or conditions of a phenomenon operate; whereas in the experimental branches of the natural sciences, an attempt is made to determine the causes or conditions for the *production* of a phenomenon. In this chapter, we will deal mainly with some aspects of *experimental investigations* which can be carried out in the life sciences fields.

Elementary Starting Points

Experimental techniques differ in various scientific disciplines or subdisciplines, but there are nevertheless certain basic terms, as well as assumptions about what makes experimentation meaningful, which are common to them all. To begin with, a few simple dictionary definitions:

1. fact: a thing that has actually happened or is true.
2. phenomenon: any observable fact or event that can be described.
3. truth: conformity with fact, or an established fact.
4. evidence: the state of being evident or something that makes another thing evident.
5. proof: evidence that establishes the truth of something.
6. theorem: a proposition that can be proved from accepted premises.
7. hypothesis: an unproved theory tentatively accepted to explain certain facts.
8. theory: a formulation of underlying principles of certain observed phenomena which has been verified to some degree.
9. principle: a fundamental truth, law, on which others are based.
10. law: a sequence of natural events occurring with unvarying uniformity under the same conditions.*

Starting with these definitions, we can now very briefly sketch the basic processes which take place in experimental scientific studies. (1) The scientist observes facts or events. (2) He notes relationships—or possible relationships— among phenomena. (3) He formulates a hypothesis which tentatively explains, in causal terms, how one phenomenon may produce another. This hypothesis is formulated in such a way that it can be tested experimentally. (4) He performs

---

* We have taken these definitions from a simple pocket dictionary, *Webster's New World Dictionary* (1968 ed.), because we found that the definitions available from philosophical dictionaries, dictionaries of science, or even the unabridged dictionaries of the English language become too complicated, or would require elaborate qualifications and explanations.

experiments, and in this way gathers evidence to prove or disprove the hypothesis. (5) In order to be acceptable as proof of the hypothesis, the evidence must represent truth. (6) If the scientist finds adequate proofs to support his hypothesis, he then publishes his results, opening his investigations to critical scrutiny. (7) If the hypothesis is significant (or for some reason of particular interest), other investigators may perform experiments specifically designed to prove or disprove the hypothesis. (8) If all the experimental evidence gathered in this way confirms the hypothesis, then it becomes a theory.* (9) On the other hand, no matter how many proofs have been supplied in support of a hypothesis, a single refutation (publication of either contrary experimental evidence or of material pointing to facts which contradict the hypothesis) is sufficient to destroy the basic truth-value of the hypothesis, indicating that the proofs previously gathered were not correctly interpreted or the evidence was incomplete. Since facts represent truth, they cannot be molded to fit the hypothesis; rather, the hypothesis must be so formulated as to account for all relevant facts.

Advancing new ideas about casual relationships among phenomena is one of the basic processes by which scientific knowledge expands. However, these ideas must stand up to the test of repeatable experiments and rigorous scrutiny before they can be incorporated into the body of scientific knowledge as accepted theories.

The Threshold Principle

As understanding is broadened in specific areas of investigation, it may eventually become apparent that several independent theories are interrelated through common denominators—or principles—which express generalized truths.† One of the most basic of these common denominators operating in nature is what is usually called the "threshold principle." This principle states that, even where cause-and-effect relationships are known to operate (where one phenomenon is known to give rise to a second phenomenon), the causative agent has to be present in a *quantity exceeding a known minimum* in order to produce the effect. In other terms, no matter how many times subthreshold quantities are applied, the expected effect will not become manifest. When the quantity of

---

* In usage, even among scientists and philosophers of science, the distinction between "hypothesis" and "theory" seems to have dissolved to the point where the two terms are often used as though they were synonyms.

† Scientific laws, as distinct from principles, while they may also be expressions of generalized truths, can be derived only when three conditions are fulfilled: they must involve a temporal sequence of events; this sequence must be repeatable; and it must be predictable under unvaried conditions.

the causative agent or source is below the threshold, one speaks of the "no-effect level." In nature, the threshold principle operates equally in the realms of atoms, of cells, of whole organisms, and even in ecosystems.

An explanation of how this principle is manifested at the atomic level is given by Victor Weisskopf, the great contemporary theoretical physicist:

> Quantum theory tells us that an atom is a non-divisible entity, *if* the energies applied to it are below a certain threshold. If the processes inflicted upon the atom are below a certain threshold, the atom is really indivisble, in the real sense of the word. It means that if atoms collide with energies less than the threshold, they bounce off completely unaffected, in exactly the same state that they were before. This is the new idea. That's the quantum idea. . . . However, when you are way above the threshold, the atoms go to pieces, and they behave like ordinary classical systems containing parts and particles. (Weisskopf, 1963, p. 92; author's emphasis).

At the level of cellular organization, the threshold principle was recognized in both muscle- and neurophysiology around 1920. Warburg termed it the principle of "all or nothing." By this phrase he was referring to the fact that subliminal stimuli, when applied to muscle cells or nerve fibers, will produce no effect whatsoever; nor will such low-level stimuli show summation when repeated.

With regard to whole organisms, recognition of a no-effect level goes back to Paracelsus, who first formulated this concept in 1562, and elaborated it further in 1574, when he wrote: "All things are toxins, and there is nothing which would not be toxic; it is only the dosage which makes a thing a toxin" (p. 167, our translation). In the section headed "Drugs and organisms" we shall discuss this concept in some detail.

At the level of ecosystems, it has long been acknowledged that below a certain threshold, environmental pollution does not represent a problem. We can even find this principle being vehemently defended by two modern environmentalists, Paul Ehrlich and John Holdren. "Below a certain level of pollution trees will survive in smog. But, at some point, when a small increment in population produces a small increment in smog, living trees become dead trees. Five hundred people may be able to live around a lake and dump their raw sewage into the lake, and the natural systems of the lake will be able to break down the sewage and keep the lake from undergoing rapid ecological change. Five hundred and five people may overload the system and result in a 'polluted' or eutrophic lake" (Ehrlich and Holdren, 1971, p. 1213).

This statement should be contrasted with the following passage from one of Barry Commoner's books, which represents a clear denial of the operation of the threshold principle in ecosystems: ". . . extreme caution ought to be the rule in the early uses of pesticides and other novel substances that contaminate the environment. . . . A similar approach is, I believe, equally applicable to most other pollution problems. Since they are all large-scale effects and influence a wide variety of living organisms, on statistical grounds alone it is probable that the *smallest detectable pollutant level represents some hazard,* however slight, and that the risk will increase roughly with the level" (Commoner, 1963, pp. 97, 98; our emphasis).

On the other hand, according to a footnote in the Ehrlich and Holdren paper cited earlier, Commoner appears to have at least partially changed his mind, since the two authors report that in his unpublished testimony before the President's Commission on Population Growth and the American Future, Commoner *acknowledged* the operation of threshold effects!

There is only one exception to this broad threshold principle which is widely accepted, operating at the macromolecular level and referring to the effects of ionizing radiation. The hypothesis that there is no threshold for the effects of ionizing radiation (that is, no safe level of exposure, however minute) was first proposed in 1937. Since that time the so-called "linearity theory of radiation effects" has been more or less widely accepted, and acknowledgment that there is no threshold for radiation effects is implicit in all the calculations which underlie the setting of allowable standards for radiation exposure. In the last few years some doubts have again been raised about the validity of viewing radiation as an exception to the threshold principle, and we shall review the basis for these doubts in Chapter 12 in our discussion of mutagenicity. At the same time, some scientists—impressed with certain similarities in organismic responses between mutagenic or carcinogenic chemicals and ionizing radiation—have introduced the term "radiomimetic drugs," by which phrase they mean mainly to emphasize that such chemicals resemble ionizing radiation in that they are capable of inducing mutations, cancer, or terata. In more recent developments, this term also has served to promote the notion that for such chemicals, the "theory of linearity" applies—i.e., they have no threshold dose. Quite aside from the fact that the latter claim cannot be supported on scientific grounds, the creation of such neologisms as "radiomimetic chemicals" serves to pollute the language, for such a general rubric tends to break down the distinctions among the qualities of different compounds and the varying quantities at which they may represent potential danger.

Drugs and Organisms

It is practically impossible to completely separate toxic materials from ordinary substances by definition. When Paracelsus said that all things can be toxins, he was undoubtedly referring to the fact that such essential substances as table salt, oxygen, or water, if administered in large enough quantities, will cause acute toxicity and may even result in death. On the other hand, many compounds with notable toxic potential are used in small quantities as medicines. Other substances recognized as intoxicants—such as alcohol—are deliberately ingested by humans in the hope of reaching a pleasurable state of toxicosis. There are still other substances, useful for many purposes, which are recognized as dangerously poisonous when ingested. These are usually required by law to carry warning labels on their packages reading: "Poisonous if taken internally! Do not swallow," or some equivalent cautionary note. However, even for compounds recognized to be highly toxic—such as hydrogen cyanide, for instance— there exists a level of concentration below which no toxic effects will be manifested.

In order to facilitate the understanding of what is meant by toxic threshold,* and also to differentiate more clearly among the various kinds of toxicoses recognized in modern medicine, we are going to use a highly simplified pictorial analogy of an "organism," consisting of two tanks or reservoirs, closely surrounded by a kind of flexible balloon, which may be imagined as a heavy rubber membrane. A drawing of the model "organism" appears below as Fig. 1. In the discussion of how toxic materials behave in the model "organism," we will deal

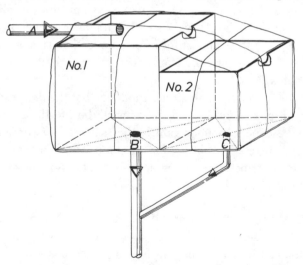

Figure 1.   *DYNAMIC MODEL OF AN ORGANISM*

---

* "Toxic threshold" should not be confused with "threshold of drug action," which refers to the minimal dosage required to bring about a desired therapeutic effect.

mainly with the question of quantity or dosage; although it is well recognized in toxicology that many other important factors—such as duration of exposure (in the case of gases, for instance), the dispersion of the materials (in the case of heavy metals), and the physiological state of the organism which receives the toxin—will influence or decide the ultimate response elicited by the agent.

The model system depicted in Fig. 1 has to be described in some detail. It is composed of two tanks of unequal size, number 1 and number 2. They are so located that at the top of tank number 1 there is an overflow outlet leading into tank number 2, which we call the "depot." A large-diameter inflow pipe *(A)* passes through the enclosing flexible membrane into tank number 1. Both tanks have normal outflow tubes at the bottom (*B* and *C*), the diameters of which are individually and in combination smaller than that of the inflow tube *A*. Finally, there is an overflow outlet from tank number 2 which leads into the virtual space between the tanks and the enclosing membrane. Since intoxication is a *process,* we had to design our model so that it would be analogous to a dynamic rather than a static system.

In this model, the inflow tube *A* represents the administration of toxic materials to the system (organism), and the outflow tubes *B* and *C* are analogous to elimination of the toxin through excretion or detoxification. It should be obvious that as long as the quantity of inflowing material is not greater than that of the outflow, there will be a steady state in the system. Rate of elimination, however, is conditioned by the relatively small diameter of tube *B,* compared with *A*. Therefore, in even the simplest forms of intoxication, such as that resulting from consuming several beers, one can become intoxicated at a faster rate than one can be "detoxified."

Another thing to bear in mind about the model is that the dimensions of the two tanks will vary in proportion to each other according to the characteristics of the toxins involved. Especially important is the fact that for some toxins the depot (tank number 2) is relatively large; for others, it is extremely small.

We now wish to describe materials which may enter this model system in terms of three separate categories:

1. Toxins with short residence time—i.e., those which are rapidly eliminated from the system.
2. Toxins with long residence time, but for which there is a large depot.
3. Toxins with long residence time, for which there is only a small depot.

In all three categories, the quantity of the toxin entering the system will condition the resultant responses.

1. Toxins with Short Residence Time

The majority of materials which we call medicines fall into this category. To begin with, one should imagine that both tanks are empty. When a drug is administered in therapeutic dosage, tank number 1 usually does not fill up entirely, and after inflow ceases, rapid and complete elimination will ensue. However, even if tank number 1 becomes filled up and some material spills over into tank number 2, both tanks will drain naturally after administration is stopped. For example, when tetracyclines (antibiotics) are given in therapeutic dosages, tank number 1 would be represented by the body fluids—mainly blood—while the bones, which are the depot for tetracyclines, are analogous to tank number 2. When administration is stopped, the blood level of the tetracyclines drops close to zero within 24 hours, whereas they remain present in the depot for another eight to ten days.

With all drugs, tanks number 1 and 2 together represent the threshold dose for toxicity. In other terms, even though the drug is administered in levels where it is pharmacologically active, as long as the material does not spill over from the second tank into the "balloon," there will be no toxic manifestations.

In another case, a drug in this same category may be administered in such quantities that a small overspill from tank number 2 results. This represents what is usually called "subacute toxicity." After the cessation of administration or intake, one may have three possible effects, depending on what happens to this material which has spilled out from tank number 2 and now occupies the space between the tanks and the membrane.

(1)The flexible membrane contracts—either by itself (spontaneous recovery) or with the aid of external help (antidotes) or other adjuvant measures—and presses the overspilled material back into the tanks, from which it will be eliminated. In these cases there is no permanent change in the organism. (2) The balloon may react with the spilled materials and bind them in a neutral form. This is what happens, for instance, in subacute argyrosis (silver toxicosis), where elemental silver will become transformed into black, inert, insoluble silver sulfide and be deposited in mucous membranes and the skin. Aside from the aesthetically unpleasant discoloration of the skin, this bound silver represents no further hazard to the individual. (3) The spilled material may make a small, permanent "corrosion spot" on the membrane itself, before being eliminated. This is typical, for instance, in subacute carbon monoxide toxicosis. If, however the individual is frequently exposed to subacute toxic levels of the gas, the repeated small effects of the toxin will be additive. This is called "summation of effects," since while the toxic material itself will be eliminated, some permanent minor damage remains.

Finally, in cases where the system is suddenly overwhelmed by a very large dose of toxin, both tanks will fill rapidly and sizable quantities of the material will spill over into the balloon. This is called "acute toxicosis." Again, several possibilities may develop. (1) The balloon bursts—the organism dies. (2) The balloon contracts—usually in these cases with external help, such as administration of an antidote—and the material is forced back into the tanks and eliminated. (3) Large portions of the membrane are taken up as binding sites for the overspilled material, which will decrease the future ability of the organism to handle even very small overspills. (4) If there is permanent damage to the membrane, it may be in the form of "large scars," rather than small "corrosion spots." An example of such major irreversible damage is the possibility of permanent blindness following on an acute toxic episode from ingesting methyl alcohol.

2. Toxins with Long Residence Time and Large Depots

There are some compounds which are eliminated from the body comparatively slowly. In the case of these substances, our model would have tubes B and C of much smaller relative diameter than that shown in the figure. However, some of the compounds not rapidly detoxified have a very large body depot—hence tank number 2 will be considerably bigger. DDT and other chlorinated hydrocarbons are prime examples of materials in this category, since their storage depot is the body fat.

With toxins of this group, when administration is continuous and at a constant level, the first tank may overspill, but very large amounts must be taken in before the depot, or tank number 2, will fill up. It has been shown, for instance, in experiments on man, that even administration of 35 mg of DDT daily for many months will result only in the development of a steady-state situation—that is, excretion will eventually correspond to intake (Hayes, 1966). Unquestionably, the level of DDT residues in the body fat of the subjects of this experiment reached much higher levels than those in the normal population; still, they showed no signs of toxicosis.

Here, too, as in the first category, it is possible to produce toxic effects by raising the dosage to the point where both tanks overspill. However, for this group, where the depot is large, continuous and prolonged overspill of the second tank at a *low* level is rather unlikely; hence chronic intoxication with these kinds of substances is almost unheard of. On the other hand, a single administration of a very large dose will cause acute toxicity. In one history of accidental poisoning, 28 men ingested 20,000 mg of DDT each. They suffered various kinds of acute toxic reactions, but all recovered within 48 hours to 5 weeks (Garrett, 1947). Thus, the pattern followed by the overspilled material was that of the balloon contracting until the toxin was pushed back into the tanks, from whence it was gradually eliminated.

3. Toxins with Long Residence Time and Small Depots

This group of compounds resemble those in the last category in the sense that their elimination from the system is rather slow. However, poisons in this category would have a very small second tank, in our pictorial model. Typical representatives for this group are the heavy metals, such as mercury and lead. We shall use lead to illustrate their behavior in the system.

The daily average intake of lead in food is 0.1 mg. The depot (the bones, in this case) can handle up to 1 mg per day intake without overspill. If daily administration rises above this level, a slight but continuous overspill of tank number 2 will occur, resulting in what is termed "chronic lead intoxication" (plumbism). This overspilled material may bind with the membrane and/or cause some kind of permanent damage to it. If the chronic, low-level intoxication continues for a long time without increased elimination, then enough material may become spilled into the ballon to cause an acute exacerbation. Such an instance would be a *real* example of the accumulation of a toxin in the organism. The term "cumulative toxin" should be restricted to this type of accumulative behavior; it is falsely used when it designates materials building up in tank number 2 or substances which have been bound to the membrane in an inert and harmless form.

As in both earlier categories, acute toxicity will also result here when a very large dose of the toxin is administered suddenly.

The "New Toxicology"

The schema which we have just described was not meant to be a complete pharmacological or toxicological classification system, but was rather used to facilitate an understanding of the development of different kinds of toxic manifestations. Recently it has become fashionable in environmental circles to classify drugs under three categories different from those which we have just mentioned. This "new toxicology" can be seen to have some relation to one area of the classical discipline, i.e., the investigation of the effects of *repeated drug administrations.*

In the 1971 edition of the comprehensive *Toxikologie* by Wirth, Hecht, and Gloxhuber, the authors write: "The manifestation of effects of repeated ad-

ministrations is determined by whether or not the effect of a single dose is completely, partially, or not at all reversible. The latter is presumed for carcinogenic
materials" (Wirth, et al., 1971, p. 12; our translation). Accordingly, one may
presume that there are three different types of toxins in this context. (1) Those
whose effects completely disappear. (These show the typical dose-response
relationship.) (2) Those which produce some minor but lasting change, and
whose effects are therefore cumulative when repeatedly administered. (These
are drugs exhibiting summation of effects.) (3) Those for which the effect is
thought to be not only irreversible, but a possible starting point for the initiation
of further damage. (The carcinogenic substances are supposed to be such noxious
agents.)

In the above citation from Wirth, et al., three basic ideas are implicit, which
if not borne in mind may lead to improper evaluation of toxicological problems.

1. The authors are referring to the repeated administration of *single doses
with effect*. In other terms, it is understood that the concept of threshold applies.
Frequent exposure to dosages below the subliminal dose *will have no effect*,
in any of the three categories.

2. It is the accumulation of the *effects*, and not of the drugs themselves,
which are under discussion. In order to produce a lasting damage, no matter how
slight, the determining factor, besides dosage, will be frequency of administration, which has to overtake the rate of elimination. When damage is produced,
the effects of repeated administrations will become summated.

3. It is only *presumed* that with respect to carcinogenic materials, one
single exposure to a dosage at or exceeding the threshold *may* serve as the
starting point of a "chain reaction," which might lead eventually to the development of a malignancy. This point is currently under hot debate, and is far from
being settled.

With all three types of drugs, the fundamental principal of existence of an
effect threshold is taken for granted.

In the current "new toxicological" usage, drugs are categorized similarly
to the three types discussed above, with some subtle but extremely important
differences. The new interpretation of toxicology stems from the work of An
der Lan (1962), whose ideas are widely echoed by environmentalists, without
crediting him. The new system is summarized most concisely by Kühnelt in the
following manner:

. . . we should remember that there are three different types of toxins. (1)
Concentration poisons: their effects increase in proportion to the dose. To these be-

long the largest majority of all known toxins, and also such materials which are usually regarded as nonpoisons, which can, however, in large quantities also produce toxic manifestations (e.g., table salt). (2) Cumulative poisons: they do not produce in small quantities any observable poisonous manifestations, but they become stored in organisms and show their effects when they have reached a certain concentration or when, through a change in the metabolism, they are mobilized. To these belong, for instance, DDT, which is stored in the body fat: also chlordane, aldrin, and dieldrin. For these materials there is therefore no tolerance dose because each uptake of the toxin, no matter how small, adds to the cumulative effect, which, in the course of time, must become manifest. (3) Summation poisons: they are destroyed or eliminated from the organism, but they cause—even in very small amounts —tissue damages which are definitely irreversible and which will be exacerbated through further doses. Such materials act mainly as carcinogens. For these, there is absolutely no harmless, minimal dosage. (Kühnelt, 1971, pp. 318–319; our translation)

Now, if we compare these two classifications, there does not seem at first reading to be a substantial difference between them, and the reader may wonder why we place such emphasis on their discussion. The crux of the matter lies, however, in the omissions and/or false conclusions in the second description of drug types. Attention should be called to the following points:

1. The existence of threshold is recognized only in the first category, that is, in the concentration poisons.

2. The negation of a tolerance (or threshold dosage) for group 2, and the assertion that "each uptake of the toxin, no matter how small, adds to the cumulative effect, which . . . must become manifest . . ." denies the possibility of elimination or detoxification of these compounds.

3. The statement that there is absolutely no safe minimal dosage for summation poisons borders on the ludicrous.

In connection with the claims about cumulative poisons, the following should be considered:

People trained in the biological sciences are generally familiar with the fact that compounds which are absorbed tend to reach a steady state of storage and that for each compound the storage at equilibrium corresponds to dosage. People not trained in the biological sciences are usually unfamiliar with these facts and suppose that compounds are of two distinct sorts, those that are stored and those that are not. They suppose that compounds that are stored at all continue to accumulate indefinitely with no tendency to reach a steady state in which the amount lost each day is equal to the amount absorbed. It may seem odd to mention this folklore . . . but the views of the public are a most important factor. . . . (Hayes, 1967, p. 102)

One must unfortunately conclude from the "new toxicology" that this folk-lore has taken hold not only of the public but also of a number of scientists trained in the biological fields.

The third claim—that there is absolutely no safe minimal dose for summation poisons—will be discussed in subsequent sections insofar as it refers to recognized or supposed carcinogenic chemicals. It should here be pointed out that many of the substances which show summation of effects are not carcinogenic. We have already mentioned that carbon monoxide is the most typical substance in this class. All the addictive drugs—including alcohol—can show such summation effects, if they are used in excess and physiological addiction develops. It would be patently ridiculous to claim that there is no safe level of intake for these substances, since the toxic threshold for carbon monoxide can be calculated, and the "no effect" levels of the addictive drugs can be defined experimentally.

While the idea that accumulation of stored compounds is a continuous process may have taken hold of biologists and laymen interested in environmental medicine—but not trained in pharmacology and toxicology—it is not taken seriously by specialists. Such a claim can be refuted by authoritative statements like that of Hayes cited above, for it *is* folklore. Or, put in other terms, known and accessible facts contradict the hypothesis, and there is thus little room for argument.

When it comes to exposure to carcinogenic substances, on the other hand, there is some disagreement among specialists as to whether a "no effect" level can be defined. We shall elaborate on this disagreement, but in order to understand its basis, we must first discuss the dose-response curve in relation to the pharmacological activity of drugs.

The Dose-response Phenomenon

Thus far we have been talking about the phenomenon of threshold as a general principle, operating at various levels in nature, and we have specified some differences in the way drugs behave in organisms when they are introduced in excess of the toxic threshold. Both in pharmacology and in toxicology it is of fundamental importance to define at what level of administration a certain compound will act as a therapeutic agent, and when it will become toxic to the organism. Paracelsus already recognized that the same drug in small doses could have no effect or a minimal one, that larger doses were needed to cure a specific condition, and that still larger doses could be toxic or even fatal.

By the end of the last century, animal experiments finally became acceptable and were widely undertaken in physiology and medicine; and at the same time drugs were isolated (mainly from plants) and made available in purified, quantifiable forms. This made possible the initiation of large-scale quantitative experiments to determine the smallest effective dose of a given drug and the largest dose which would not give rise to overt toxicity. For medicines, the range between these two levels is called the "therapeutic index"; and it was established that the broader this range, the safer the compound for medicinal purposes. During the course of such studies, it was observed that after the threshold of therapeutic effect had been reached, increasing doses showed roughly proportional increments in their effects, until such a level where either toxic manifestations set in, or a saturation plateau was reached.

The phenomenon of dose-related effect is a fundamental principle of pharmacology, and all studies concerned with drug action—even if they do not deal with immediately observable effects—have to be designed and evaluated in the context of dose response. When an experiment designed to test the effects of a drug fails to show a direct relation between dose and effect (if, for example, a greater effect is recorded in the results from a small dose than from the next larger one), such data indicate that an unknown variable is operating and that the experimental results cannot be taken to represent the drug effect *per se*. We shall see later that this failing characterizes many of the experiments which deal with feeding of DDT to birds to test its effects on reproductive performance.

In order to lend a visual dimension to this discussion, we have reproduced below a dose-response curve recorded on a coordinate system (Fig. 2). The curve

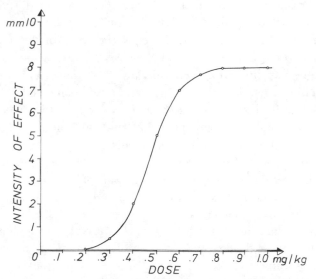

Figure 2.   *THE EFFECT OF DIGITALIS ON THE FORCE OF CON-
TRACTION OF THE ISOLATED FROG HEART.*

refers to the effect of digitalis on the force of contraction of the isolated frog's heart. The incremental doses are shown on the abscissa (x axis) and the corresponding responses on the ordinate (y axis).

Several features of this curve are noteworthy. First of all, it is not a straight line, but has the shape of an "S", indicating that relatively small doses have an insignificant effect, while too high doses no longer will produce further increments in the response. The bottom of the curve starts from the x axis; for the threshold of therapeutic action lies somewhere between 0.2 and 0.3 mg/kg. Beyond 0.7 mg/kg, where the curve again levels out, the organ becomes, so to speak, saturated with the drug. At the 1 mg/kg level, the heart may go on beating for a while with maximum force; however, it cannot maintain the high energy output this requires and will eventually stop altogether. This plateau phenomenon is characteristic for drugs, and if it is not taken into account in testings involving long-term observations, it can easily obscure the results. For instance, if a drug is investigated for carcinogenicity during lifetime administration to mice or other laboratory animals (one currently accepted method), the use of too large doses may emaciate the animals to such a degree that they either die due to direct poisoning or become excessively vulnerable to intercurrent diseases, making subsequent evaluation of the results with the surviving animals more or less meaningless.

This example of the relation between digitalis doses and the force of contraction of the frog's heart is quite typical of the dose-response curves for therapeutic agents. Similarly, curves can also be constructed for organismic responses to toxic chemicals where the distance from the origo to the starting point of the curve represents the threshold of toxic action rather than of therapeutic effect, and the upper portion an acute state of toxicosis leading to death. The exact shape of these curves differs for each individual substance, but they all begin somewhere on the x axis, since there is always a dose below which no effect can be noted. In testing for long-term effects, such as carcinogenicity, dose-response curves can also be established, provided that the compound in question is administered at a number of different dose levels (which, unfortunately, is frequently not the case) to several groups of animals. Disagreements begin, in this area of research, over the meaning of the lower part of the curve and specifically over whether it is practically possible to establish a dose level which would show no effect in a very large population.

Here, in somewhat condensed form, is the nature of the problem. In carcinogenicity testing, one is dealing with long-term developments rather than with immediate, measurable short-term effects. If one tests a particular substance at several dose levels, let us say, using 50 test animals for each dose, positive results can be expressed in a dose-response curve, and the points on the curve will represent percentages of the test animals which developed malignancies. However, even if one knows that at a given dose 50 percent of the animals got cancer, at a lower one only 10 percent, and at a still lower one none, this lowest dose cannot be regarded as a "no-effect" threshold for induction of cancer in whole populations, since the results tell us only that none of the 50 test animals developed cancer at that dose rate. If it has been shown that a substance can act as a carcinogen at some level, and if one assumes that the animal experiments can be extrapolated to humans, the argument runs, then one must seek a way of determining the lowest dose which would be safe for—not 50 people, but at least a million, or in the conservative view, 100 million. Although there have been proposals to set up testing systems using millions of animals, everyone with any common sense realizes that this is not only impracticable, but that both the possibilities of error in experimental work and the "background noise" with huge numbers are so great as to preclude meaningful results. It is largely because of this problem of numbers that the dose-response testing procedures of classical toxicology have been called "crude and insensitive," when applied to carcinogens, by some investigators engaged in cancer research.

To circumvent this inability to determine the possible effects of very small doses on a very large population through experiment, it has been suggested that if a dose-response curve can be obtained for the carcinogenic potential of a chemical in the range of doses where effects are observable, even with a relatively limited number of test animals, the dose which should produce only one tumor in a population of 1 million, or even in 100 million, could be calculated by mathematical extrapolations from the observable range. However, such a method has also been rejected as unreliable by some scientists. The reasons for the doubtful validity of such a method are treated in detail in "The Report of the Carcinogenicity Panel" (in *Report of the Secretary's Commission on Pesticides*, 1969; hereafter referred to as Mrak *Report*), whose members cite materials from "The Report of the Subcommittee on Carcinogenesis of FDA Committee on Protocols for Safety Evaluation" (1969), and announce that "the concerned statisticians at the National Cancer Institute concur" with the skepticism expressed in the FDA report.

We here reproduce a few paragraphs of the text and two tables which the Carcinogenicity Panel reprinted from the FDA publication.

"It might be thought that the basis for such an extrapolation could be provided by observations in the observable range. To show how far from being the case this actually is, we give below three different dose-response curves, mathematically defined over a dosage range of 256 fold. All three have the same TD_{50} [dose which results in tumors in 50 percent of the animals] and TD_{16} [tumor dose for 16 percent of the animals]. The first is a probit curve, the second a logistic curve, and the third the so-called one-particle curve.

EXPECTED PERCENT OF ANIMALS WITH TUMORS

Actual dose TD_{50}	Probit curve	Logistic curve	One-particle curve
16	98	96	100
8	93	92	99+
4	84	84	94
2	69	70	75
1	50	50	50
½	31	30	29
¼	16	16	16
⅛	7	8	8
1/16	2	4	4

It will be noted that below the TD_{50} the three curves differ by little and that in any experiment of practicable size (say less than several thousand animals) it would not be possible to conclude from the actual observations which one of the three best described the data. As shown below, however, the $TD_{.0001}$ (one in a million dose) and the $TD_{.000001}$ (one in a hundred million dose) obtained by extrapolation of these three curves differ markedly. Thus,

EXTRAPOLATED VALUES OF "SAFE" DOSES FOR THREE DIFFERENT DOSE-RESPONSE CURVES DESCRIBING OBSERVED RESPONSES IN THE 2 PERCENT TO 50 PERCENT RESPONSE RANGE EQUALLY WELL

	Probit curve	Logistic curve	One-particle curve
TD_1	.040	.022	.0144
$TD_{.1}$	.0155	.00315	.00144
$TD_{.0001}$	.00136	.0000098	.00000144
$TD_{.000001}$	.000412	.00000016	.000000014
TD_1	—	—	—
$TD_{.000001}$	100	100,000	1,000,000

The one in one-hundred million dose, which Mantel and Bryan call the 'virtually' safe dose is one-hundredth the TD_1 using the probit curve, one-hundred thousandth using the logistic and one one-millionth using the one-particle curve." (Mrak *Report*, 1969, pp. 493–494)

Since the two tables are not consistent with each other in their original form, we have recompiled them, in Table 3, to make it somewhat easier for the reader.

One point to be emphasized is that the numbers listed under "Dose" are strictly abstract proportions. "One" stands for the dose which would produce tumors in 50 percent of the test animals, and all the other numbers represent multiples or fractions of that dose.

Table 3. *RECOMPILATION OF TABLES FROM THE*
"REPORT OF THE CARCINOGENICITY PANEL"
(after Mrak Report, 1969, p. 494)

Probit curve	Dose	Logistic curve	Dose	One-particle curve	Dose
98.0	16.0	96.0	16.0	100.0	16.0
93.0	8.0	92.0	8.0	99.0+	8.0
84.0	4.0	84.0	4.0	94.0	4.0
69.0	2.0	70.0	2.0	75.0	2.0
50.0	1.0	50.0	1.0	50.0	1.0
31.0	0.5	30.0	0.5	29.0	0.5
16.0	0.25	16.0	0.25	16.0	0.25
7.0	0.125	8.0	0.125	8.0	0.125
2.0	0.062	4.0	0.062	4.0	0.062
1.0	0.04	1.0	0.022	1.0	0.0144
0.1	0.0155	0.1	0.00315	0.1	0.00144
0.0001	0.00136	0.0001	0.0000098	0.0001	0.00000144
0.000001	0.000412	0.000001	0.00000016	0.000001	0.0000000144

The panel and the FDA statisticians argue that from data in the observable range, it would be very difficult to decide which of the three curves most accurately represented the experimental results, and extrapolation downwards to a "virtually safe dose" is therefore not a reliable method. The agnostic position of both publications is summarized in the following: "Clearly extrapolation from the observable range to a safe dose has many of the perplexities and imponderables of extrapolation from animal to man and it would be imprudent to place excessive reliance on mathematical sleight of hand, particularly when the dose-response curves used are largely empirical descriptions, lacking any theoretical physical or chemical basis" (Mrak *Report*, 1969, p. 495).

Variations on this kind of argument have been presented for the last 15 years or so by proponents of the "no safe dose for carcinogens" school of thought. On the face of things, it would seem that the agnostic stance taken by the authors rests on genuine "unknowables," and a general conclusion that the only way to protect the public is through zero tolerances expresses an attitude of prudence in the best tradition of preventive medicine.

There is, however, one fallacy in this argument which is almost universally overlooked. In order to produce an effect, *any* material has to be present in a minimal number of atoms, molecules, subatomic particles, or photons. In the case of chemicals, the probability that one or even a few hundred molecules of a compound will have a deleterious effect on an organism is zero.

The Mathematics of the Knowable

We should now like to carry out a few calculations, feeding some real numbers into the abstract structures of the three curves which yielded such proportionately different estimates of a "virtually" safe dose. If we look at Table 3, it can be seen that on the probit curve, the TD_1 is 4/100 of the TD_{50}; on the logistic curve, it is 2/100; and on the one-particle curve the TD_1 is 14/1,000 of the TD_{50}. If we had an actual TD_{50} dose for a carcinogen, we could calculate the $TD_{0.000001}$ (one in one-hundred million dose) by dividing the TD_{50} with 2.5 $\times$ 10^3 on the probit, 6.2 $\times$ 10^6 on the logistic, and 7 $\times$ 10^7 on the one-particle curve. A summary of this and subsequent calculations is given in Table 4.

Table 4. *SUMMARY OF CALCULATIONS.*

Difference between TD_1 *and* TD_{50}			*Probit curve*	*Logistic curve*	*One-particle curve*
Probit curve	0.04	1.0	25		
Logistic curve	0.022	1.0		45	
One-particle curve	0.0144	1.0			70
Difference between TD_1 *and* $TD_{0.000001}$					
Probit curve	0.04	0.00041	100		
Logistic curve	0.022	0.00000016		137,500	
One-particle curve	0.0144	0.0000000144			1,000,000
Total difference (virtually safe dose) $\times$ less than TD_{50}			2,500 or 2.5 $\times$ 10^3	6,187,500 or 6.2 $\times$ 10^6	70,000,000 or 7 $\times$ 10^7
TD_{50} of DDT = 6.8 $\times$ 10^{19} molecules/kg					
Virtually safe dose in molecules/kg			2.7 $\times$ 10^{16}	1.1 $\times$ 10^{13}	1 $\times$ 10^{12}
Virtually safe dose in 70 kg man in molecules			1.9 $\times$ 10^{18}	7.7 $\times$ 10^{14}	7 $\times$ 10^{13}
Virtually safe dose in 70 kg man in weight			1.1 mg	450 ng	40 ng
1 kg liver tissue has 3 $\times$ 10^{11} cells					
Virtually safe dose in molecules/liver cell		or	9 $\times$ 10^4 90,000	4 $\times$ 10^1 40	3.3 $\times$ 1 3.3
Whole body has 1.4 $\times$ 10^{14} cells					
Virtually safe dose in molecules/body cell		or	1.3 $\times$ 10^4 13,000	5.5 $\times$ 1 5.5	5 $\times$ 10^{-1} ½

In order to give some meaning to these figures, one has to know four things: (1) A supposedly known carcinogen for which the TD_{50} has been established; (2) How many molecules are present in the quantity of the carcinogen represented by the TD_{50} dose; (3) How many cells are present in the organism for which the "virtually" safe dose needs to be established; and (4) The minimum number of molecules per cell the presence of which will be registered by that cell.

It has been claimed recently that DDT is a carcinogenic agent, and, according to the Bionetics Report (Innes et al., 1969 — to be discussed in detail in Chapter 14), the TD_{50} of DDT in mice is about 40 mg/kg. We propose to take DDT as our example for downward extrapolation, even though we entertain serious doubts that it has actually been demonstrated to be carcinogenic. We shall consider the quantities which would be predicted as safe for 100 million persons from all three curves.

The Italian chemist Avogadro (1776–1856) proposed in 1811 that one gram-molecular weight of material, regardless of what it is, contains an equal number of molecules. This number was later determined theoretically by Cannizzaro in 1858 and experimentally by Birge in 1941, and since the turn of the century has been called the Avogadro number. For any conditions encountered in environments suitable for life, the number is 6.02×10^{23}. The gram-molecular weight of DDT is 354.5, and simple calculations based on Avogadro's law will tell us that 1 mg of DDT contains 1.7×10^{18} molecules, while 40 mg of DDT equals 6.8×10^{19} molecules. A summary of assumptions and values used in the following calculations may be found in Table 5.

Table 5. *SUMMARY OF ASSUMPTIONS AND VALUES USED*

Gram-molecular weight of compounds contains	6.02×10^{23} molecules
Molecular weight of DDT	354.5 g
1 gram of DDT contains	1.7×10^{21} molecules
TD_{50} of DDT = 40 mg/kg. It contains	6.8×10^{19} molecules/kg
1 liver cell weighs (according to Dinman)	7×10^{-9} g
1 liver cell weighs (according to our calculation)	3.5×10^{-9} g
1 red blood cell weighs	9×10^{-11} g
1 average body cell weighs	5×10^{-10} g
1 bacterial cell weighs	4×10^{-11} g
In 1 kg of liver tissue there are	3×10^{11} cells
In the human liver there are	5×10^{11} cells
In human blood there are	3×10^{13} cells
In the human brain there are	3×10^{11} cells
One average man weighs	7×10^{4} g
In the human body there are	1.4×10^{14} cells

If we accept that the TD_{50} of DDT is 40 mg/kg, we can further calculate the "virtually" safe dose which would be derived from all three of these curves on the basis of the numbers of molecules of DDT per kilogram of body weight. For this we have to divide 6.8×10^{19} (the TD_{50} expressed in molecules) by the differences between the TD_{50} and the $TD_{0.000001}$ for each curve. The results are 2.7×10^{16} molecules/kg for the probit; 1.1×10^{13} molecules/kg for the logistic; and 1×10^{12} molecules/kg for the one-particle curve. Expressed in compound weight, the whole-body dose for a man weighing 70 kg would be 1.1 mg from the probit; 450 ng from the logistic; and 40 ng from the one-particle curve.

We now want to consider how many cells there are in the human body. Different types of cells vary quite considerably in size, but their weight can be calculated. Dinman (1972) for instance, came to the conclusion that a typical liver cell weighs 7×10^{-9} g. From his data, however, one gathers that he assumed spherical cell shape. Using a more realistic cylindrical form, we arrived at half of his value: 3.5×10^{-9} g for the average liver cell. A red blood cell, which is much smaller, weighs only 9×10^{-11} g. The weight of an average body cell should be very close to 5×10^{-10} g. There are approximately 3×10^{13} red blood cells alone in the 6 l of blood in the human body. The weight of a 70 kg man can be expressed as 7×10^{4} g, which, divided by the average cell weight, gives the total number of cells for humans as 1.4×10^{14}. One can take different approaches in estimating the total number of cells in the human body, from which one arrives at almost the same figure, so we may take this to be a good approximation.

Let us now consider the fourth question which we raised earlier: namely, how many molecules are needed just to be registered* by a cell.

There are several lines of evidence which all point towards the same basic figure: 10^{4} molecules per cell—that is 10,000 molecules for every cell.

As early as 1964, G. Evelyn Hutchinson compiled the numbers of different atoms in one liver cell. (These can be precisely determined by spectrography.) From his compilations it becomes evident that the atoms with the least numbers per cell which can be said to have a biologically demonstrable function are present in quantities of 10^{6} to 10^{8}. Since atoms per se do not occur in biological systems, but are usually bound in molecules, the least numbers of molecules which are active will be smaller. From such stochastic† considerations, Hutchinson came to the following conclusion: ". . .there might be too many commoner,

---

* It should be noted that this term has nothing to do with an effect which can be measured, either deleterious or otherwise. It is slightly awkward, but we wanted to avoid such anthropomorphic alternatives as "noticed by the cell," which conveys the meaning with more linguistic smoothness but has the disadvantage of implying that there is some kind of conscious recognition involved.

† Stochastic considerations refer to such processes where, through sampling of known reactions, the probability of another reaction taking place can be predicted.

accidentally and potentially interfering materials (or sites?) around in the cell for any very important substance to work practically at a concentration of less than 10^4 atoms or molecules per cell" (Hutchinson, 1964, p. 931).

The same conclusion was reached by Bertrand Dinman in 1972, discussed in a lead article in *Science* called " 'Non-Concept' of 'No-Threshold': Chemicals in the Environment." Using both Hutchinson's approach and also enzyme inhibition studies, in which the most potent inhibitors were tested, Dinman showed that about 4×10^4 inhibitor molecules per cell are required to produce a minimal inhibition. He concludes:

"To believe that a single molecule's presence in a cell implies a definite potential for deleterious effect disregards stochastic considerations . . . . While the construction of stochastically sound model is remote, the reasonableness of the hierarchy of cellular element concentrations as these relate to metabolic function suggest that a threshold for biological activity exists within a cell at 10^4 atoms . . . . The cellular organism operates within a quantitative rate limit that transcends any statements having only qualitative bases. Thus concepts concerning encroachments on response capabilities over a lifespan are inadequate descriptors of biological activity in the absence of quantitative qualifiers. (Dinman, 1972, p. 497)

Taking a completely different approach, we also arrive at basically the same figure of 10,000 molecules per cell. Let us consider LSD-25—accepted as the compound of which the least quantities are needed to produce a recognizable effect. (In the case of this drug, "effect" refers to reports of subjective changes from the recipient since the alterations in brain chemistry cannot be measured in human subjects.) In a few highly sensitive individuals, a dose of 20 μg of LSD-25 is sufficient to elicit reports of altered perceptions. Since LSD-25 activity seems to be localized in the brain, one may be justified in the assumption that the total dose is transported to the brain by the bloodstream. There are approximately 3×10^{11} cells in the brain, and in 20 μg of LSD-25, there are 3.8×10^{16} molecules. If each brain cell were equal in size and equally responsive to the substance (which is clearly not the case), 9×10^4 molecules would be available for each cell. However, it is thought that only the neurons of the brain are involved in neurological activities, whereas the glia cells serve mainly a supporting function. Thus it is conceivable that a mere 20 μg of LSD-25 is sufficient not only to be registered by the neurons, but to alter their chemistry.

Now let us go back to the figures for DDT derived from downward extrapolation of the curves to the one-in-100-million dose.* The probit curve gave us

---

* One should bear in mind that the TD$_{50}$ of DDT was derived from mouse-feeding experiments. A mouse eats approximately one-third of its own body weight per day (at least according to the Bionetics Report), whereas a man takes in only about 1/46 of his weight in food daily (excepting water). Thus the figures given above and in the following pages for molecules per cell are probably too large, and for extrapolation to man should be divided by approximately 15.

2.7 × 10^{16} molecules/kg as the "virtually" safe dose. If we consider this dose dispersed in 1 kg of liver tissue—which contains 3 × 10^{11} cells—there would be 9 × 10^4, or 90,000 molecules per cell. This is enough to register, but the nature of the effect need not be deleterious. We can put this figure in perspective by considering that calculations based on the data of Gabliks and Friedman (1969) show that cytotoxicity was reached at 1.4 × 10^{12} molecules of DDT per Chang human liver cell in tissue culture. In other terms, it took 10 million times more DDT molecules per cell to bring about toxic manifestations in them. Furthermore, DDT is dispersed throughout the body; it does not have a specific affinity for liver cells. If we take the whole-body dose of 1.1 mg per man and divide it into the number of cells in the body, the result is 13,000 molecules per cell, which is just about enough to register.

Similar considerations applied to the figures derived from the logistic curve bring us down to 40 molecules per liver cell, and five molecules for each average body cell. From the one-particle curve safe dose, there would be only three molecules per liver cell, and one molecule for every two cells in the whole body. These calculated "virtually" safe doses are not only clearly safe, they are ridiculously safe.

If we now use the same approach to investigate the significance of the daily intake of DDT in man's food, we find the following: At the present time the U.S. population, on an average, is taking in 0.02 mg DDT. This corresponds to 3.4 × 10^{16} molecules. Assuming the worst—that all of this DDT reaches the liver at once—we can calculate how many molecules would be present for each liver cell. Since the whole human liver contains approximately 5 × 10^{11} cells, this divided into 3.4 × 10^{16} would give almost 7 × 10^4 molecules per liver cell. This is just about the minimal level which would be registered by these cells. But, dispersed throughout the whole body, this current intake would result in only 240 molecules per cell, probably not enough even for uptake from the intestinal tract. This fact may very well account for the observation that body-residue levels of DDT in the U.S. population are continuously declining.

Now it should be added that there are also compounds which are normally in circulation within the body, and in the case of some of these, very minute quantities may be sufficient for uptake. For example, the average daily intake of vitamin B_{12} is only about 1 μg whole-body dose, which amounts to 4.5 × 10^{14} molecules, or only 3 molecules per cell. However, this quantity is added to the average amount of the vitamin stored in the body, which is about 2.5 mg (6 × 10^{17} molecules), half of it in circulation in the blood. The small concentrations of vitamin B_{12} present in the daily diet can be taken up by man because it immediately complexes with several molecules of intrinsic factor; thus at the site of uptake in the ileum, concentrations of more than 10^4 molecules per cell *are* present. On the other hand, if the normal circulation of vitamin B_{12} in the blood falls below 10 percent of the normal value ($< 6 \times 10^{16}$ molecules in the total circulation, or 2×10^3 molecules per red blood cell)—as is the case in pernicious anemia, for instance—then the therapeutic doses recommended to restore normal circulating levels are from 30 to $100\,\mu g$/day, intramuscularly. This amounts to between 500 and 2,000 molecules per red blood cell, and since excretion of the vitamin is minimal, within a few days such administration should bring the blood level above 10^4 molecules per erythrocyte.

Immaterial Essences

We must apologize to the reader for these several pages of numerical considerations, which we realize do not make the most fascinating reading. We have included them because the authors of the Carcinogenicity Report, the FDA Report, the "concerned statisticians" of the National Cancer Institute, and a number of other scientists who propagate the notion that we cannot define safe exposure levels for carcinogenic chemicals all seem to have fallen into the same trap: they forget that man is a whole organism whose body contains quadrillions of cells, and that even a single one of these cells will not be affected by the presence of the most potent of chemicals unless a certain minimum quantity of the compound is involved.

Actually, one should not be too hard on the mathematicians and statisticians, since it is not in their field of expertise to evaluate the biological meaningfulness of data, and their conclusion that downward extrapolation from three similar but slightly different dose-response curves yields markedly variant calculated safe doses is correct in a purely abstract sense. But the life scientists involved in these reports must be faulted for emphasizing the "imponderables" and the unreliability of "mathematical sleight of hand," while ignoring stochastic considerations altogether. Once one takes into account the molecular quantities of a particular compound, the phenomenon of dispersion, and the threshold of response at the cellular level, it becomes apparent that these gentlemen, in worrying over the differences among the calculated safe doses derived from various curves, are effectively concerned about "degrees of nothingness." This is not to say that even the 40 ng quantity of the most conservative whole-body dose is not "something" in the chemical sense; but biologically, it is nothing as far as the whole organism is concerned. Even prudence has its rational limits; and, we remind the reader, the quoted authors are not acting as private individuals, who may indulge themselves in hypochondriacal notions; they are professional researchers who are being paid to assess the public health dangers which may be represented by environmental contaminants.

All this unease about minute and even infinitesimal quantities of drugs is curiously reminiscent of the early days of homeopathic medicine, introduced by the German physician Friedrich Hahnemann (1755–1853) at the end of the eighteenth century. According to his dictum — *similia similibus curant* — diseases should be treated with an infinitesimally small fraction of a drug, which, if it were administered in large quantities to a healthy man, would cause symptoms similar to those characterizing the disease. Hahnemann and his followers worked out rigorous techniques for preparing the "effective" doses. They began with a 10 percent alcohol extract of the material (usually from plants), and from this "original" or "primeval tincture," they prepared dilutions with water or lactose through constant mixing, grinding, and shaking, until they arrived at a 10^{30} dilution, which was designated as T_{30}. The supposition was that a drug had an etheric component which was responsible for its therapeutic effect, and that the more dilution, grinding, and shaking employed during its preparation, the more effective would be the liberation of this immaterial essence from its bondage in the starting substance. Since we know today that any one grammolecular weight compound contains 6.02×10^{23} molecules, we can be sure that these preparations diluted to a phenomenal 10^{30} were indeed liberated from bondage to matter, for in such dilutions there would not be a single molecule of the starting substance left.

Dilution, dispersion, the principle of threshold, and the principle of dose-response relationships will not serve to protect people from toxicoses or other kinds of damage arising from exposure to substantive quantities of chemicals. On the other hand, if these basic principles are ignored in scientific medical research, we may well find that we are fleeing from phantoms and tilting at windmills. May the ghost of Hahnemann rest!

12

PANDORA'S BOX

Keep your head cool, your bowels
open, your feet warm, and don't
give a damn for doctors!

The complete sealed testament of
HERMAN BOERHAAVE, the most eminent
physician of his period (1668-1738).

It is an obvious fact that man lives in a chemical and physical
environment and that throughout the millennia of his existence
on Earth, he has interacted with that environment, which has included, long
before the development of an industrial civilization, many challenges as well as
very real threats to his existence.

Even in a pristine environment, it is not easy to establish where the lines
should be drawn among the supportive aspects of this interaction, those aspects
which are not completely "healthful" in a literal sense, but may serve to stimulate
the homeostatic mechanisms of the human body or to challenge man's intellect,
and those which are clearly threats to human health or existence. Nature obvi-

ously supports human life by providing supplies for man's needs: food, water, sunlight. She challenges him in various ways. If the human body were not constantly being forced to react to external influences, and to readjust itself, life would cease as we know it, since by definition life is dynamic rather than static. Such simple factors as changes in temperature challenge the human intellect to create artificial environments where homeostasis can be maintained at less drain of bodily energy. That nature can be seriously threatening to life is obvious when one considers the dangers of natural cataclysms; but it is often forgotten that insidious or subtle dangers are also present in a pristine environment. Overexposure to ultraviolet radiation from sunlight, which is a strong carcinogenic factor, and unrecognized heavy exposure to arsenic from natural sources are just two examples. There are pristine environments — untouched by human activity — but these environments are not "pure," or danger-free, in the chemical and physical sense.

When one hears such expressions as "pure food" or "pure water," one must ask "pure in what sense," "devoid of what"? Since about 80 of the 100 or so known elements occur in every bite of food and in every drop of water and are present in every cell of living organisms, there is no such thing as an organism which is "pure" in the sense of free of the presence of heavy metals, for instance. Whenever any question arises about contamination of food, water, or air, it is essential that one should ask about the quantities involved and compare them to the naturally occurring levels.

There are approximately 2 million organic compounds known. The majority of them are natural, but some have been produced in man's laboratories. It is often stated that there is a clear difference between man-made chemicals and those which occur naturally, but the borders are actually fluid, and as we shall show in a later chapter, many chemicals which were synthesized and first identified in laboratories were later found to occur in nature. Again, the principal questions to be considered when talking about contamination with organic compounds are: how great are the amounts to which humans are exposed and what are the relative risks when compared with "natural" contaminants?

The same quantitative and comparative considerations apply to physical factors in the environment, of which ionizing radiation is one of the most important. There are no radiation-free spaces in the Earth environment, and discussions of man-created sources and release of ionizing radiation should be carried out in the perspective of the natural background. Only when expressed in quantitatively defined and comparative terms can any meaning be attributed to statements that a nuclear power plant will release radioactivity in its cooling water effluents. In what increase above the background will this result? And what is the significance of, let us say, an increase of 1/500 of the yearly average in ionizing radiation influx, when it is known that at times of heavy sunspot activity the intensity of cosmic rays hitting the earth might be 10,000 times greater than usual?

Now it may seem rather simpleminded to mention these facts, but there appears to be an increasing amount of confusion among people about the degree of danger associated with human exposure to chemicals which can be toxic to man, as well as about human exposure to radiation. There are also a great many misunderstandings about the difference between local pollution and global pollution. Sometimes, these two subjects come together.

As an example of how findings about a source of heavy local pollution can be incorrectly extrapolated to a global basis, and how at the same time a contaminant which can indeed represent a human health hazard under certain special conditions and in a particular form can be turned into a terror element through inappropriate publicity, consisting exclusively of frightening possibilities not put into the perspective of facts, we should like briefly to recall the big mercury scare epidemic which peaked in 1970 and 1971.

The mercury question came to public attention in the spring of 1970, when a Norwegian graduate student working at the University of Toronto discovered "alarmingly high" concentrations of mercury in fish. The fish came from the Saint Clair River, where indeed there are a number of chemical plants which discharge large quantities of spent mercury into the river. His findings were immediately released to the press, resulting in a prompt ban on the sale of fish from the area. Subsequently, a great number of investigators occupied themselves with measuring mercury levels in fish. Tuna originating from Japan, swordfish from South America and both coasts of North America, game fish in Lake Huron and Lake Michigan: all appeared to contain levels dangerously close to or higher than the permitted concentration (according to the standard of the U.S. Public Health Service, which is 0.5 mg/kg in fish).

Chronic mercury poisoning may occur in populations exposed to the ingestion of food permeated with certain mercury compounds. In the whole of the literature on the subject, however, only two histories of such chronic poisoning are documented, both having occurred in Japan. The first such incident was recorded in 1953. Since at that time the cause of the disease was not known, it was called Minamata disease, after the name of the bay area in Japan where the outbreak took place.

In the Minamata Bay outbreak, 111 people became ill, 41 of whom died. Since the symptoms were not identical with typical cases of acute mercury poisoning, it was not recognized until 1959 that the disease was caused by chronic exposure to methyl-mercury. The source was finally traced to a plastics plant which was discharging huge quantities of methyl-mercury into the bay (Gold-water, 1971).

When the reports of Minamata disease were publicized in the United States 15 years after its outbreak and 10 years after it had been identified as a form of mercury poisoning, the emotional climate of the American public was such that only the frightening implications of the actual death toll were emphasized, while the circumstances which led to the outbreak of the disease were not fully reported. The residents of the impoverished fishing village of Minamata subsisted largely on fish and shellfish taken from the immediate bay area. Those who were not fishermen were for the most part workers in the local plastics factory which was the source of the mercury effluent. It has been shown that the fish and shell-fish taken from this immediate area contained 20 to 50 times the amount of mercury considered safe for consumption. In addition to eating this heavily contaminated fish with great frequency and to being generally malnourished as a consequence of lack of a balanced diet, many of the workers were apparently exposed directly to mercury vapors in the factory. Lastly, as a further tragic coincidence, the waste from the factory appeared to have consisted almost entirely of methyl mercury, which is recognized as being the most dangerous form of the metal. It is highly improbable that a similar combination of conditions would arise anywhere in the United States, even among those who are fond of eating the types of fish regarded as most suspect.

In the case of the mercury pollution of the Saint Clair River, later investigators found that the mercury deposits are relatively localized and do not spread like water-soluble compounds or oil slicks. At the site of dumping, where for the past 20 years 11 tons of pure mercury per year have been discharged from a single chemical plant, excessively high mercury concentrations in the sediment are to be found *only* in an area 5 miles long and 300 feet wide.

This is not to say that dumping large quantities of mercury into waters is not dangerous. However, the future dangers from the current concentrations have clearly been exaggerated and tend to distract from the real solution, which would appear to be quite simply a matter of eliminating the practice of discharging the spent mercury into natural waters (Turney, 1971).

We now want to consider the difference between mercury in the oceans and mercury as a pollutant of localized aquatic environments, like Minamata Bay and the Saint Clair River. It will be remembered that at the height of the mercury scare, vast quantities of oceanic fish were confiscated. Their mercury content exceeded the USPHS allowable limit; but in the general atmosphere of crisis then prevailing, no one took the trouble to separate the inorganic mercury from the organic fraction, and it was implicitly assumed that the contamination of these fish was due to industrial effluents which were spreading throughout the world's oceans. Allen L. Hammond wrote a sober evaluation of the environmental mercury problem in *Science* pointing out that "it does not seem likely that man could have increased [mercury] concentrations in the sea by as much as 1 percent" (Hammond, 1971, p. 789). His arguments are based on known distributional values of mercury in the Earth's crust and its utilization by mankind since 1900. This assessment has been strengthened by three independent lines of investigation. Albany scientists working for the New York State Department of Environmental Conservation have found mercury levels in a 43-year-old preserved fish that are twice as high as those found in fresh fish condemned by the FDA. Another group working on the fish collection of the American Museum of Natural History found that tuna caught as long as 90 years ago contained quantities of mercury equal to or higher than recently caught specimens. Finally, if one consults one of the basic works on the distribution of the elements in marine biota (Vinogradov, 1953), one learns that the larger the animals, the higher the mercury concentration. Both swordfish and tuna were reported in this study to contain several parts per million of mercury, while seals and whales may have as high as 60 ppm. Vinogradov's monograph also mentions certain kelp in which concentrations of 140 ppm mercury were found. Since this book was compiled during the 1940s when mercury scares were not yet in the public mind, one can hardly accuse the scientist of being a bandwagon extremist. On the other hand, it is unfathomable that this standard work was not consulted before the whistle was blown, and the news spread that man's industrial effluents were contaminating even the oceans and their fauna.

It is interesting to note that of late FDA scientists are no longer finding the supposedly high toxic levels of mercury in their fish samples. According to their data, large fish weighing more than 23 kg average about 0.25 ppm of mercury, while those smaller than 12 kg average only about 0.13 ppm. These findings seem curious. How do they relate to the earlier FDA measurements of mercury levels? If the mercury contamination were truly as widespread as was earlier alleged, then the FDA should still be finding "alarmingly high" concentrations in the marine products they are continually testing. After all, the fish are coming from the same oceans. Is it possible that the earlier measurements were in error? Or could it be that the mercury concentrations in tuna and swordfish are still above the 0.5 ppm level, but that they are no longer interpreted as dangerous by FDA scientists? Since Vinogradov found that larger marine animals contain proportionately higher quantities of mercury, it would seem likely that swordfish or tuna may accumulate mercury in their tissues in the 2 to 4 ppm range. Instead, however, of adjusting the sacred (though arbitrary) standard of 0.5 ppm, it may be simpler to measure quantities of mercury falling within that standard.

There are several rational steps which might have been taken in this regard. First, it would be possible to establish two separate mercury standards: one, which is more generous, for the relatively inert forms of the element, and a second for the methylated organic form, for which the 0.5 ppm standard is probably correct. This, of course, would necessitate the employment of more complex detection techniques, which is a bother. A second step would have been to provide lengthier, reasoned explanations in the public media of why the tuna and swordfish are again being permitted to reach the market. However, it is probably simpler for everybody concerned for the FDA to simply state that the fish are safe.

The mercury scare and the immediate banning of certain foods for consumption led to serious economic losses in the ailing domestic fishing industry. The cost of the mercury scare to the swordfish industry was about $750,000 in domestic sales, to which must be added the loss of $12 million in import sales. It was, however, not only the commercial fisheries which were hurt by the mercury warnings. The resort businesses centered around sport fishing lakes in many states, among them New York, also reported heavy losses. It is not, then, surprising that on May 21, 1971, Henry Diamond, New York's Commissioner of Environmental Conservation, issued a revised warning. He was quoted in the *New York Times* as saying, "In the earlier warning last year we erred on the side of health."

To many people the news that a regulatory body should have "erred on the side of health" may seem only right and fitting, and most would feel that, in any event, the economic problems of one or two industries are completely dwarfed by considerations of what might have happened had the fish continued to be sold and eaten by the American public. But the phrase "what might have happened" is at the same time exceedingly vague and broadly comprehensive in the imaginative sense; and if we consider the vast number of substances to which fear of "what might happen" is attached in one way or another, the notion that excessive prudence is synonymous with wisdom becomes more and more questionable. After all, going beyond the specific matter of chemical contaminants in food, all of life entails risks; and if people were to focus their attention on the potential dangers involved in every step that must be taken merely to function in day-to-day terms, they would be completely paralyzed by anxiety.

We are of the general opinion that, indeed, more caution should be exercised in arriving at regulatory decisions bearing on human health. However, from our point of view, the time for increased care is not at the standard-setting stage, but rather in the design and execution of experimental research and, even more importantly, in the evaluation of the accuracy, consistency, and significance of both research results and reports from the field.

On the other hand, the press-conference approach to the release of findings about environmental contaminants, as well as the emphasis on public participation in regulatory processes, tend to work against careful, reasoned evaluations and to encourage precipitate decisions. And even where regulatory action is not yet in question, much of the publicity generated about environmental contamination tends to play heavily on fear reactions, sometimes to an extent where one may fairly question whether the mental health of the populace is not at much greater risk from sensationalism than is its bodily health from pollution. This possibility has not escaped the attention of some observers, although it has unfortunately been given very little consideration by professional psychologists and psychiatrists. Canadian journalist Peter Desbarats, writing at the height of the mercury scare, is among those who have objected to the aspects of environmentalism which play on fear. In an article called "Pollute Me No More Pollution," he wrote:

> Most campaigns are based on fear and fear is a dangerous element, probably a lot more hazardous than a little mercury in the diet. Nowadays we scoff at the old-time preachers who used to put fear of God into our parents; but at the same time we listen with moronic attentiveness to every new variety of ecological doomsday prophet. It's the new puritanism of the twentieth century, and I think it's as harmful as the old variety. . . .
>
> Studies have shown that a majority of patients who consult doctors have nothing physically wrong with them. I wonder how much of this useless worry is created by fear deliberately engendered by well-intentioned campaigns of one sort or another. How many innocent pleasures have been tainted? . . . Remember — it's dangerous to walk in the city at night. It's dangerous to cross the street. It's dangerous to eat well. It's dangerous to have children. It's dangerous to go swimming.
>
> It's also dangerous to blindly ignore danger, of course, but there are various approaches to social problems. Surely it isn't necessary to terrorize people to persuade them to support sensible environmental measures, many of which have become necessary only within the past few years. The element of persuasion by fear which is evident in many campaigns is anti-life. I regard it as an attempt to pollute *me* with neurotic apprehensions. (Desbarats, 1970, pp. 16, 17; author's emphasis)

To Desbarats' personal rejection of those aspects of environmentalism which play on fear, one may add that not only does it seem unnecessary and unhealthy to "terrorize people to persuade them to support sensible environmental measures," but that the result of fear campaigns — most of which consist of identification of certain specific "dangerous agents" and of mobilizing efforts to battle against their further use—is almost invariably adverse to rational decision making. In no area of environmental concern is this more apparent than in discussions and campaigns which center on radiation sources or on those chemicals found in foods, in drugs, and in the general environment which are thought to be capable of inducing cancer, giving rise to mutations, or causing fetal defects.

One can hear and read with considerable frequency these days that it is impossible to expect people to consider topics involving carcinogens, mutagens or teratogens from an objective or rational standpoint. To a certain extent, such attitudes are understandable in the lay public, for fear runs very high around such subjects. But if we accept that the lay public is anxious about these matters, we have to face up to the questions of what are the proper ethical and practical approaches to be taken by those members of the scientific community involved in relevant research and also by those agencies of the federal government which are charged with the responsibility of setting standards or tolerances for substances suspected to be carcinogenic, mutagenic, or teratogenic. These are not easy questions and they cannot be answered definitely or comprehensively.

We shall be dealing with some broad issues in the public domain which bear on these subjects, as well as such matters as experimental procedures utilized in the testing of chemicals, controversies over particular substances, and so on. However, since this area of concern is one in which emotions run high, and since many people appear to be distressed at the very suggestion that such subjects should be reviewed and evaluated rationally, we should like first to devote some space to a discussion of emotion and reason.

About the Paranoid Streak

In his highly perceptive essay *The Ghost in the Machine* (1967), Arthur Koestler provides a masterful exposition of what he terms the "paranoid streak" in mankind. To the development of this characteristic peculiar to man he attributes most of the worst ills of past history as well as those of our present predicament as a species. On the basis of Paul MacLean's pioneering work respecting the neuroanatomical seats of emotion in the brain and the relationship between the limbic system (or "old brain") and the neocortex (the "new brain"), where these responses are analyzed and integrated with cognitive rational processes, Koestler attempts to give an anatomical explanation for the "paranoid streak." Since the two parts of the brain are relatively autonomous and the interconnections between them are quite tenuous, rationality has but limited influence on actions motivated by strong emotions. In fact, Koestler sees in this anatomically defined disparity between emotion and reason the source of the present threat to the survival of humanity, for now that we have the weapons-capacity to virtually wipe mankind from the surface of the Earth, the danger of "thinking with the guts" has taken on altogether new dimensions. If, as he claims, the paranoid streak derives from an evolutionary gap—the lack of balance between the old and the new brains—then world leaders are no less subject than the rest of us to being overwhelmed by sudden emotional responses; and improvements in actual relations among the nuclear powers, while not to be disparaged, cannot be said to have removed the threat. After painting this grim picture, Koestler ends his essay on an optimistic note, expressing the hope that "it will be soon within our reach . . . to counteract misplaced devotion and that militant enthusiasm both murderous and suicidal, which we see reflected in the pages of the daily newspaper" (Koestler, 1967, p. 379). The particular potential developments on which he bases his hope are fascinating, but since they are not relevant to our discussion, we shall leave it to the interested reader to look into them himself.

It ought to be made clear that the paranoid streak in man as it expresses in "misplaced devotion" and "militant enthusiasm" is not to be mistaken for aggression. On the contrary, Koestler insistently points out that those who think he is talking about some sort of basic animal-like aggressive behavior (which he in any event rejects as being neither basic nor typical for animals) have completely misconstrued his ideas. His reference is rather to that kind of emotionally derived ideation which permits man—alone among animals—to kill or oppress his fellow humans in the name of love of the church, loyalty to flag, devotion to secular belief systems, and other such "good causes." In reference to his own essay, he stated during a discussion at the 1969 Alpbach Symposium that his intent was to draw "some theoretical conclusions regarding the conflict between emotion and reason, and about the ways in which emotive belief-systems compel the neocortex to provide spurious rationalizations for these emotive beliefs" (Koestler, 1969, p. 276).

At this same Symposium, MacLean gave a paper on "The Paranoid Streak in Man" in which he undertook an exposition of its sensory-perceptual basis and attempted to disentangle the general affective phenomenon from its multitudinous manifestations. In his view, it is *uncertainty* in all its forms which is at the base of those vague anxieties which find expression in paranoid states—both "normal" and pathological.

> Man . . . relies largely on vision to relieve his uncertainty about the nature of things. Poorly visualized objects are under suspicion until he can bring them clearly into focus. But perhaps his greatest suspicions are aroused by things he cannot see at all. Consequently darkness has always held its particular terrors for him. Unex-

plained muted house sounds at night become amplified in the mind into the footsteps of a burglar. The faint smell of smoke explodes into a blaze of fire . . . . Repeated exposure to something that cannot be seen predisposes to a state of chronic suspicion. . . .

There is yet another form of the unseen that besets man and distinguishes him from all other animals. This is the poorly outlined and uncertain picture of future events which he is forever striving to see. When nature gave him the prefrontal neocortex for anticipation and connected it with his visual cortical areas, she failed to provide a radar antenna and viewing screen. Consequently, all his probings into the future must be done with obscured, remembered images of the past combined with his picture of the present. As the future is always generating more "futures" *ad infinitum* it is apparent why its uncertainties are responsible for most of man's chronic forms of suspicion. . . .

Stripped to nakedness, the paranoid demon steps forth from the foregoing analysis as *a general affect characterized as an unpleasant feeling of fear attached to something that cannot be clearly identified.* Seen in this pristine state, he is hardly an impressive figure. The thing, obviously, that gives him mystique is his capacity to assume as many disguises as there are individuals. He could thus be compared to a plot that lends itself to as many stories as there are potential authors. (MacLean, 1969, pp. 261, 262, 263; author's emphasis)

MacLean then goes on to speak about how this generalized unpleasant affect can become manifest in whole societies as well as in individuals. The collective appearance of the paranoid demon is characterized by widespread feelings of uneasiness which cannot be identified or clearly associated with any root cause. At such times, he writes, "leaders step in and attempt to explain to individuals what they cannot see for themselves" (*ibid.,* p. 275). Since the poorly discriminating "old brain" is dominant in such periods, there is a grave social danger that people will be inclined to mistake the caricature of a leader for a real leader. Such "false leaders" play on the element of fear, and while they may bring some temporary relief by exposing and bringing into clear focus the identity of fear-provoking agents, they may also mobilize an emotion-ridden battle against the "enemies," in an atmosphere where rational evaluation of the true nature and scope of the danger becomes exceedingly difficult if not impossible.

If one accepts that these concepts of Koestler and MacLean have at least descriptive value for the understanding of mass psychological responses, it is not too difficult to see how they can be applied to the problem of attitudes towards dangerous chemicals and radiation. Surely most people would agree that we live in a time when feelings of uneasiness and uncertainty are widespread. If Mac-Lean is right that things which cannot be seen or clearly identified tend to arouse vague feelings of suspicion in man, and that the sense of uncertainty which necessarily attaches to the unfolding of future events is one of the most powerful sources of generalized anxiety, then it is apparent that compounds suspected of causing cancer, genetic damage, or fetal deformities fit perfectly as fear-provok-ing agents, for they are hidden from view, and at the same time the element of danger associated with them lurks in the unverifiable future.

By singling out a few of these substances, or single sources for them, it is possible to give some temporary relief to public anxiety through "knowing the enemy" and identifying the unseen threat. It thus becomes possible to direct the aroused wrath of "misplaced devotion" and "militant enthusiasm" of the paranoid streak into the battle against the identified danger. Identification, or even a successful public campaign to ban the particular dangerous agent, brings only a temporary relief from suspicion, however; for there always seems to be a new source of danger to be pointed out: new fears are generated and the whole pro-cess snowballs. This kind of approach to informing the public about the dangers of hidden contaminants is clearly false leadership.

There is a second approach to leadership on these questions which may appear to be a more responsible one, but which is really not much more condu-cive to rational evaluation than the "single substance as the threat of the moment" kind of campaign. It may be summarized as the view that whenever an agent has been shown to be capable of producing one of these three dreaded effects, in whatever dosage, its uses should be severely restricted, and there should be no tolerances allowed for it in human foods. This has been the attitude taken by a number of scientists working in the field of environmental carcinogens, and it lies behind a piece of legislation called the "Delaney clause," to which we should now like to give some attention.

The NAS in a "Partisan Role"

Written as part of amendment to the Federal Food, Drug and Cosmetic Act, the Delaney clause was enacted in 1958, since which time rivers of ink have flowed in the debates over its wisdom as well as its applicability. It stipulates: "That no additive shall be deemed to be safe if it is found to induce cancer when ingested by man or animal, or if it is found, after tests which are appropriate for the evaluation of the safety of food additives, to induce cancer in man or animal" (FFDCA, 1958, Section 409 (c)(3)(A)).

The law effectively states that there should be no permissible tolerance levels in food for any material which can be considered as a food additive, if it has once been shown to be a carcinogen. The term "food additive" seems to have a rather loose definition in application, since it encompasses any compound which may be introduced into food during production or processing.

Since the time of its introduction, opponents of the clause have repeatedly objected that it places unnecessary restrictions on scientific judgment. One of the classic arguments against it is commonly called the "single rat argument." Critics claim that even though the clause includes the phrase "after tests which are appropriate," rigorous application of it could imply that if cancer were produced experimentally in a single animal, using any route of administration, with any quantity of the substance in question, the compound would have to be banned.

A more important objection is based on the fact that in recent years sophisticated analytical methods have made possible the detection of materials in exceedingly minute quantities. As a result the clause has really lost any meaning it may once have had, because trace quantities of even clearly proven carcinogenic chemicals — both natural and man-made — can be detected in practically all foods; but these trace quantities may be so small as to have no biological effect.

Another problematic aspect of the clause is that it cannot be applied to carcinogens which occur naturally, but may also enter food through processing. As an example, let us consider benz(o)pyrene. This chemical has been recognized as a highly potent carcinogen for almost 50 years. It has been recently demonstrated that it is an essential hormone for the growth of higher plants (*Der Pflanzenarzt*, 1971). All food derived from plants will thus contain benz(o)pyrene in minor quantities; but since it is a natural material rather than a food additive, the clause should not apply. A second source of benz(o)pyrene in food is the process of broiling meat, when it is formed by heat-caused chemical reactions in components of the fat. In such a case the impossibility of defining "additive" arises, for if one broils purchased meat at home, the clause should not apply, but broiled meat served in a restaurant might be subject to confiscation, because it could be claimed that the benz(o)pyrene was "added" during "processing." The situation is even worse with charcoal-broiled meat and *all* smoked products: meat, fish, cheese, and so on. Since smoke contains benz(o)pyrene and since it will become incorporated during the smoking process into the product, strict adherence to the Delaney clause should require that no charcoal-broiled or smoked foods should be sold, since in this case the benz(o)pyrene is definitely an "additive" caused by the smoking process. So far as we know, no one has ever suggested that the Delaney clause should be invoked to ban all foods containing benz(o)pyrene of "unnatural origin," but such a hypothetical possibility illustrates the impracticability of the clause, even from a legal point of view.

Or let us consider peanut butter, that great staple of the American diet. There is a mold called *Aspergillus flavus,* which grows preferentially on peanuts. While they are in storage, it is impossible to prevent a certain amount of molding of peanuts, and this particular mold secretes aflatoxin, which happens to be the most potent of the known chemical carcinogens. When the peanuts are processed into peanut butter, a certain amount of aflatoxin may be incorporated into the product. Should the Delaney clause be invoked in this case, and peanut butter banned? Both the mold and the toxin are natural, but it could be argued that the manufacturers are negligent in permitting molding during storage to take place and that the natural carcinogen is "added" to the end product as an indirect result of this negligence.

It would thus seem fairly obvious that, beyond the issue of restriction of scientific judgment, the clause has serious practical shortcomings and that advancing knowledge and improved detection techniques are making it less useful as a regulatory law with the passage of time.

The supporters of the Delaney clause in the scientific community rest their case almost exclusively on the "no safe dose for carcinogen" argument which we discussed in the previous chapter. We have already made it fairly clear that in our opinion many statements issued by scientists about the "unknowns" involved in the ingestion of exceedingly minute quantities of known or suspected carcinogens are less an expression of admirable prudence than of not so admirable failure to think with the neocortex. Consider, for example, that in connection with one of the hottest food additive issues of recent years—that surrounding use of the growth hormone DES as an additive in cattle feed—witnesses from the National Cancer Institute are reported to have stated that *no one knows* whether or not regular exposure of people to quantities of DES in the range of 0.3 micrograms (whole-body dose) represents a cancer hazard, but that it would be prudent to avoid such exposure (see Wade, 1972a). On a molecular-weight basis, such a dose comes out to a total of about 3×10^{12} molecules of DES. We believe it can be stated with complete confidence that not only will such exposures not cause cancer, but are insufficient to show any biological effect.

Now it should be understood that we are not defending the use of DES in cattle raising. Such uses have already been banned, in any case, although with apparent reluctance on the part of the FDA. We refer to this specific issue because in this instance the Delaney clause was invoked. While the decision was pending, a good deal of interest was again stirred up over the years-old controversies surrounding the clause, and environmentalists used the issue to publicize their view that those who defend the Delaney clause are the true protectors of the public interest, whereas those who oppose it are either not knowledgeable about the subtleties of cancer research, or may be biased in favor of the food industries to the point where they would protect special interests at the expense of the public health. In general, journalists had a field day with the DES question.

The ban came in early August, 1972, and shortly thereafter, Nicolas Wade, who is one of the journalists reporting in the "News and Comment" pages of *Science*, wrote an article called "Delaney Anti-Cancer Clause: Scientists Debate on Article of Faith." Here is his opener: "When the carcinogenic beef additive diethylstilbestrol (DES) was banned earlier this month, there was little rejoicing in the halls of the Food and Drug Administration (FDA) that a threat to public health had been forestalled. On the contrary, FDA Commissioner Charles C. Edwards explained apologetically that he had 'been left no choice' but to ban DES under what he implied were the unreasonable dictates of the law known as the Delaney anticancer clause" (Wade, 1972b, p. 588).

Following some general discussion of arguments over the value of the Delaney clause, Wade defines the opposing camps:

> The debate on this issue has not only divided the scientific community, but in an interesting way has become institutionalized, with the National Academy of Sciences (NAS) cast in the curiously partisan role of bandleader for the anti-Delaney forces and the National Cancer Institute (NCI) playing the somewhat more fitting part of chief defender of the clause. . . . The dispute between the two institutions in fact stretches back at least to 1960, and its continued existence is an interesting instance of the scientific method, supposedly pure and impartial, failing to triumph over the particular perspectives of its practitioners. The NAS is involved in the issue through its Food Protection Committee, a branch of the NAS's operating subsidiary, the National Research Council. Critics of the Food Protection Committee allege that scientists who work or consult for industry are overrepresented on the committee, and those concerned with the environmental aspects of cancer are underrepresented. (*Ibid.*, p. 589)

In comparison with some of Wade's articles on other subjects involving health agency decisions, the language here is relatively restrained. However, one must ask on what grounds he uses the phrase "curiously partisan role of bandleader for the anti-Delaney forces" to describe the NAS position, whereas the NCI stance is "more fitting"?

One gathers from the use of these phrases that, even though he had just reviewed some of the practical objections to the clause which we discussed, Wade himself believes that a regulatory approach to enforcing zero tolerances for carcinogens in foods is a workable method for protecting the public from undue exposure to them. Or perhaps he believes that, workable or not, support of such an approach is the correct ethical stance to be taken by responsible professionals in the biomedical fields. The NAS position, on the other hand, is described as "partisan." But partisan towards whom? Or what? There is, of course, the indirect implication that the Food Protection Committee of the National Research Council is weighted too heavily towards industry, but Wade neglects to mention that members of the committee as such are not working for the food industry but for the NRC.

The suggestion of bias is spelled out in a somewhat different fashion in Wade's description of the distress of Umberto Saffiotti, who is the associate scientific director for carcinogenesis of the National Cancer Institute, about the composition of the NRC's Food Protection Committee.

> Saffiotti's disagreement with the Food Protection Committee extends to the composition of its members, who include several scientists employed by industry but none who can be regarded "primarily" as cancer experts. The Food Protection Committee is supported by grants from the food, chemical, and packaging industries. . . . "I am worried personally about the way the committees of the National Research Council are set up," Saffiotti told *Science*. "We all know that you can always set up a committee of scientists to reflect a certain trend. I have been concerned about the fact that in a number of advisory committees—and I don't think the Food Protection Committee is totally exempt—there have been people who represent certain sectorial interests. This is not to imply that people are put there to defend their products— I don't think this is the case—but the question is, what is the function of these groups? If the function of the Food Protection Committee is one of developing safer food supplies, they may very well give little emphasis to the problems of toxicology and food safety." (*Ibid.*, p. 591)

We have to ignore the last sentence attributed to Saffiotti, because it is meaningless as printed, and there is no way of knowing whether it reflects Saffiotti's style of thinking, Wade's methods of transcription, or an editorial slipup on the part of *Science*. There are, on the other hand, two issues raised here to which we should like to give some attention: the matter of committees which "reflect a certain trend" and the question: "What is the function of these groups?"

It is fairly evident that if Saffiotti and some of his like-minded colleagues had a majority on the Food Protection Committee, the "trend" would be in the direction of recommendations for the withdrawal of many more additives which are suspected of being chemical carcinogens, however uncertain the proofs. In the last chapter we dropped a few uncharitable asides about hypochondria and belief in ghostly essences, and we should like to qualify that a bit here. It seems to us that whereas charges of bias are regularly leveled at any scientist who has even the vaguest sort of connection with industry or government, all too little attention is given to the psychological bias which affects the way any researcher evaluates the importance of his own field of inquiry and to those factors of individual "self-interest" which make it exceedingly difficult for the majority of intellectuals to admit that their past interpretations or judgments were erroneous, or, even worse, that a piece of work into which they have thrown a great deal of time and energy has been shown, in the light of later developments, to be without meaning. A second psychological factor may also operate at even more subtle levels, especially when the specialist's field is one which involves—as does the experimental study of chemical carcinogenesis—constant attention to an area of possible but subtle human health hazards. There is a psychosomatic reaction which is known in common parlance as "medical student syndrome," which means roughly that while studying some awful disease in great detail, the student may tend to imagine that he is experiencing some of its symptoms, or that he notes its manifestations in various persons in his surroundings. Now we do not really think that those members of the National Cancer Institute who have a somewhat exaggerated or distorted view of the dangers represented by various environmental chemicals are genuine hypochondriacs; but it is worth considering the possibility that their constant focus on these problems may exert a distorting effect on judgment, exaggerating the tendency to interpret any kinds of positive findings as indicative of human hazard.

We now turn to the matter of the "functions of these committees." The functions of the Food Protection Committee are multiple, but we assume that Saffiotti's primary concern in raising this question in the interview he gave to Wade is their function in evaluating the carcinogenic hazards which might be represented by a food additive, so we shall focus on that question. The two primary functions of the Committee in this respect are to review the relevant literature *critically,* and to come to a judgment as to whether positive findings have any meaning in terms of human exposure or extrapolation to humans. This is not such a simple matter as might be supposed, for a good review should not take conclusions in the published literature at face value merely because they have appeared in print. There may be experiments reported in older papers which purported to show carcinogenicity but which could not be repeated by later investigators. These then have to be discarded as "proofs." Then there is the matter of evaluating the appropriateness of various approaches to animal experimentation. This goes way beyond the problem of "one tumor, in one rat, at any dose, by any route." There is, for example, at the present time, serious doubt as to whether the mouse is an appropriate animal for obtaining meaningful results in carcinogenicity testing—a subject which we shall discuss in more detail in Chap-

ter 14. Since the largest proportion of animal experiments on chemical carcinogens have been done with mice, a review committee would be justified in evaluating the findings from such experiments with considerable skepticism. Two
further interpretive problems arise from testing techniques and from the manner
of reporting results. For example, some researchers maintain that it is not only
legitimate but necessary to use the largest dose which will not kill the animals
and to administer it over the whole lifetime in order to find out whether a chemical with "weak" carcinogenic potential can produce tumors or not; whereas others insist that when such large doses are used it is impossible to tell whether or
not the effects produced are expressive of specific drug action. NRC committees
are not the final arbitrators of such disagreements, but they have to take them
into account in formulating their recommendations to regulatory authorities.
Lastly, many studies on chemical carcinogens in laboratory animals report increases in the numbers of undefined tumors as being indicative that the chemical
is positive for carcinogenicity; whereas there are many scientists—including
cancer research specialists—who insist that malignant tumors, metastases, or
other definite indications of *cancer* must be demonstrated before one can properly state that the chemical is a cancer-causing agent. And then, on top of all of this,
there are those papers in the literature which are cited as proof of carcinogenicity, but which—even though they may never have been properly criticized—
are found on critical review to be clearly bungled jobs which should never have
been published in the first place. It makes no difference whether somebody else
is willing to testify before a congressional committee that such a paper is proof
of carcinogenicity and represents sufficient reason to evoke the Delaney clause
and withdraw the chemical in question, it is still the correct peer-review procedure for an advisory committee to eliminate such papers in making its judgment about whether the chemical represents a risk.

These are only some aspects of what is meant by the need for latitude in exercising scientific judgments, but they may make it somewhat clearer to the
reader why such an august body as the National Academy of Sciences should
have consistently opposed the Delaney clause as legislation which imposes undue
and unnecessary restrictions on the exercise of informed judgments. If the
Academy's role in this years-long debate has indeed been "partisan," we would
suggest that it has been partisan towards rationality—surely a "fitting" part for
the NAS to play.

The Consumer's Role

Since we have already indicated that we believe neither judicial decisions
nor overly restrictive legislation to be wise approaches to the settling of strictly

scientific controversies, it should not come as too great a surprise to our readers to learn that we do not favor scientific truth by referendum either. We recognize that in many controversies surrounding technological applications of scientific advances there are "transscientific" issues involved, in addition to debates about strictly scientific matters. Clearly the public has the right to participate in the former and to make its desires known. But, undemocratic though it may sound, we do not see how the involvement of the lay public can serve either to advance science or to settle arguments among scientists about such matters as to how data should be interpreted, whether or not certain findings are relevant to the assessment of human hazard, and so on. Nor can the nonscientist — no matter how well informed he might be — pass judgment on the accuracy of any particular piece of reported scientific work.

By analogy, if a municipality is planning to build a new bridge across a river, the community has the right to reject the project altogether, or to propose alternative sites, and in some cases to choose among several possible designs. But surely no one would suggest that engineering decisions about the structure can be made by persons who are not trained engineers. Although it would seem equally obvious that the judgment of whether the presence of a certain compound in foods is hazardous should be left in the hands of scientists, and that any disagreements must be worked out among themselves, some sectors of the consumer-protection movement seem to feel that they can properly arbitrate scientific disputes and that in so doing they are serving consumer interests. Since we don't believe this to be sound scientific practice, we oppose such intervention from consumer-protection groups.

On the other hand, we should like to make it clear that we are very much in favor of public involvement in those issues where protection of the consumer's interest may, indeed, depend on the exertion of a certain amount of pressure or publicity. With respect to food additives and food quality, the consumer movement *is* serving the public in bringing demands for accurate labeling, fair pricing, and honesty in advertising, and we are in favor of their continuing to do so.

It is also to be hoped that perhaps in the future the food industries will discover new and more responsive ways to find out what the larger public really desires. It should be possible to eliminate certain additive practices which are not necessary — though they may be safe from the health standpoint — without turning them into scientific controversies. For example, while it is improbable that the food dyes presently permitted for artificial food coloring are dangerous to health, it may very well be that the populace is now less impressed with the appearance of groceries in the store and is more interested in paying specifically for nutrition than for aesthetics. If so, and if the food industries are unaware of this change in values, then consumers must devise means to communicate their wishes to the industries. Personally, we would have no objection to eating bottled cherries which are not "cherry red," if the cherry canning industry stops coloring them simply because buyers no longer want them to be dyed. But, as scientists, we would be most unhappy to see a contrived health-hazard crusade initiated against the coloring agent used.

We hope that this brief aside will compensate in part for the objections we raise about intervention in strictly scientific issues from consumer-protection groups. We want now to return to some general comments about cancer.

Knowns and Unknowns

Probably one of the reasons that fear of cancer is so great—over and above the fact that its more dramatic manifestations involve great suffering—is that most people have only a very vague idea of what cancer is, of what goes wrong in the body to permit the proliferation of malignant cells. Unfortunately no definitive explanations are possible, since even scientists specializing in the field have no clearcut understanding either of the etiology of different types of cancer or of the underlying biochemical processes of malignancies.

Discussion of different schools of thought on carcinogenesis can be very confusing unless one is familiar with at least some terminology. With the exception of cancers of the blood cells—such as leukemia—the term "cancer" is usually thought incorrectly to be synonymous with tumorous growths. Tumors, however, may result from two quite different processes. (1) Localized enlargement of cells may occur in an organ—in which case there is no increase in the number of cells. This is called hyperplasia. (2) Local cellular proliferation takes place which produces an increase in new cells in the area. This is called neoplasia. The first kind of growth is never malignant, and even neoplasms are not necessarily cancerous. Some are; some are not. Even among scientists these terminologies are used loosely and sometimes incorrectly, which certainly does not contribute to lucidity in discussions about tumorous growths and cancer.

One can speak about established cancerous growths or malignant tumors only if the histopathological picture of the tumor shows certain characteristics specific for cancerous growths; and in some instances even this is not enough to be certain that one is dealing with a malignancy. Then the only true indicator is to ascertain whether the tumor is metastasizing—that is, to find proliferating cells in other organs which resemble those of the original focus of tumor growth.

Whole libraries have been written on the subject of cancer, and it should be borne in mind that there are many schools of thought on the subject, the school claiming that the majority of cancers are caused by environmental agents being only one among many. Much current research is being directed to elucidate the role played by viruses in human cancers, for instance; and it is by now recognized that at least four types of cancers have a viral etiology. Another area of major research effort is the investigation of the immunobiology of cancer, since cancerous growths are not under the control of the normal immune mechanisms of the body. Then there is the genetic school, which postulates that some change takes place at the molecular level in the DNA of cells, leading to the back-transformation of these cells to an embryonic state, with subsequent autonomous growth. Still another possibility is that a local mistake occurs in the overall regularity mechanisms of the body, or of a particular organ, and certain cells will then be able to take up a quasi-autonomous existence. In this context hormonal, humoral influences are thought to be important. The school emphasizing stress as a causative factor in the development of cancer also hypothesizes hormonal imbalances, since stressful conditions are known to induce serious changes in the normal hormonal equilibria of the body.

Researchers working on chemical carcinogens may also give varied explanations as to *how* the exposure of an organism to the cancer-causing agent leads to the malignancy. Some think that the chemicals influence the DNA of the cells directly; some that latent viruses are activated; and some that the exposure interferes with regulatory processes, both on the tissue level and on the higher level of hormonal controls.

It is evident that the whole question of cancer etiology is a complex one, and that science is still rather far from being able to offer a clear picture of the processes involved in carcinogenesis.

What Is Dangerous?

In experimental carcinogenicity studies, so many agents and techniques have given rise to positive findings that if we were to accept all of them as relevant and would attempt to eliminate them all, life would come to a complete halt. Cancerous growths can be induced, for instance, by such simple methods as repeated burning of the skin of an animal at the same site, or even the subcutaneous injection of physiological saline solution in the same locale repeatedly for 20 to 30 days. It is obvious that in these cases it is not a substance which causes the cancer, but rather continued mechanical irritation.

Some of the known carcinogens will cause malignant neoplasms only through specific routes of introduction to the organism. For example, inhalation of arsenates or chromates over an extended period may lead to the development of lung cancer. On the other hand, if you eat these substances, you might suffer from toxicosis or even die with a high enough exposure, but it is highly questionable whether small amounts taken orally can cause cancer. Butter yellow (a common dye) will not cause cancer if painted on the skin, but can become carcinogenic if ingested over a long period of time.

Still other cancer-causing substances — such as carcinogenic hydrocarbons — may act through several routes of introduction. Benz(o)pyrene, for instance, can induce cancer if its vapors are inhaled, or if it is painted on the skin, or if it is ingested.

Among the carcinogenic agents are found both man-made and natural chemicals, and contrary to popular impression, some of the most widespread and most potent carcinogens are not man-made. Aflatoxin and benz(o)pyrene, which have already been discussed, are completely natural and are powerful carcinogens. Then there is a whole array of natural chemicals which have shown weak carcinogenic potential in testing. These are probably not really hazardous to man, but if one were to take all the results for weak carcinogens as indicators of hazard, we would be in serious trouble even if the entire chemical industry were shut down. Safrol, for instance — a common constituent of the transudates of ericaceous trees and bushes — could endanger the lungs of the most careful health food faddist and nonsmoker, if he were to spend too much time camping in areas where he would be likely to inhale these vapors. Heated cholesterol, which occurs in large quantities in fried eggs; sesame seed oil; and even desoxycholic acid — a common constituent of bile which aids the digestion of higher animals and man — have all been shown to have carcinogenic potential (Steiner et al. 1942; Klein, 1963). And such a favored item as Vitamin C is also on the list (Dobrovolskaia-Zavadskaia, 1935).

Unquestionably, too, the most abundantly available cancer-causing agent is sunshine, since both the ionizing radiation component and the ultraviolet rays to which one is exposed in direct sunlight can give rise to cancer of the skin. Most medical testbooks include some variant of the following description, taken from *The Merck Manual:*

> Chronic exposure to sunlight has a distinct aging effect on the skin; in some individuals the atrophic effects may resemble those seen after X-ray therapy. A more disturbing consequence of many years of overexposure is the frequent appearance of precancerous keratotic lesions. . . . They frequently occur in young persons. Blonds and redheads are particularly susceptible. . . .

The incidence of squamous and basal cell carcinoma of the skin in the general population is directly related to the amount of yearly sunlight in the area in which the population lives. Such lesions are especially common in sportsmen, farmers, ranchers and sailors. Anyone who makes a fetish of sun worship at every given opportunity through a lifetime will almost certainly develop epitheliomas in later years. (*The Merck Manual*, 1966, p. 1173)

In addition to the fact that not all tumors are cancerous, certain tumors, such as goiter, may develop for want of a compound (in this case, iodine). This particular kind of tumor will disappear when iodine is supplied. Other types of nonmalignant tumors which are due to the administration or presence of an agent will disappear when the causative agent is eliminated from the body. Examples of such externally induced but nonmalignant tumors are warts, which are caused by viruses, or hepatomas (nodules in the liver) which can be induced with administration of large quantities of compounds like DDT or barbituates, but which will disappear if administration is withdrawn.

Finally, there are fibrous growths which are not malignant, although these usually do not disappear spontaneously when the causative agent is no longer being taken in. Inhalation of quartz dust in large concentrations over a period of many years may lead to a syndrome called silicosis, which never develops into a malignancy. (It may, on the other hand, predispose the individual towards tuberculosis.)

Now none of this is meant to imply that when an agent has been demonstrated to be a *strong* carcinogen—whether natural or man-made—that people should not be protected from exposure to it or warned properly about the risks involved. The major disagreements among scientists come up in connection with assessing the significance to humans of chemical carcinogens with weak potential to induce tumors, and arguments about whether or not the tumors produced are cancers. Since we are going to discuss this problem at considerable length in Chapter 14 in connection with the alleged carcinogenicity of DDT, we shall here terminate our remarks on cancer and go on to the next frightening subject: agents which may damage the embryo during its life *in utero*.

Teratogens

Teratogenic agents are those which can cause malformations of the fetus when the female is exposed to them during pregnancy. It has been known since time immemorial that malformed individuals are occasionally born, both to animals and to man. These forms were described and classified, but their causation was unknown, and experimental investigations designed to produce malformations in the laboratory began only around 1945. Interestingly, the first compounds which showed high teratogenic activity were such essential materials as the vitamins A, D, and E in excessive quantities. Soon the experiments were extended to the study of alkylating agents and antimetabolites, many of which turned out to be strongly teratogenic. It was also established early on that ionizing radiation can induce fetal damage — that a single medical X-ray, for instance, given to a pregnant woman, may suffice to induce the development of a malformed child, if given at a critical time during gestation.

This whole study procedure became known as the scientific subdiscipline: experimental teratology. One unexpected result of this work was the recognition that there are certain "susceptible periods" during gestation, when the embryo is much more sensitive to these influences than at other times. It was found that both in mice and rats this period is from the sixth to the fifteenth day, and in man from the fourth to the tenth week of pregnancy. By now thousands of papers have been written dealing with this subject, but the true mechanisms of action and reasons for the formation of certain types of terata are understood in relation only to a few specific drugs.

In the last decade — in particular since the thalidomide tragedy — a great upsurge of interest and research has been devoted to this problem. Although some definite advances have been made during this period, it has also become evident that the causes underlying these phenomena are multifaceted and more complex than was thought earlier. The often contradictory results found in the literature respecting the same compound can be traced to the fact that in many instances only one of the several variables which may be operative has been tested for. It is unfortunate that exactly at the time when it began to be generally recognized by specialists that experimental designs with adequate complexity are essential in order to obtain any meaningful results, many researchers entered the field who were in a great rush to test medicines and all sorts of environmentally occurring chemicals for teratogenicity; and in their haste, they have often used such simplified and even simpleminded approaches to testing as to generate more confusion than accurate information.

In order to illustrate why adequate complexity of design is so important, we shall enumerate some factors which have been shown experimentally to cause terata. Brown et al. (1970) found that air transport of mice on the twelfth and thirteenth day of pregnancy will increase the number of malformed fetuses; and as early as 1959, Kalter and Warkany demonstrated that fasting for 24 hours during the critical period resulted in defects. We have already mentioned that excesses of certain vitamins are active teratogens but it has also been ascertained that even transitory deficiency of one of several vitamins or minerals can result in malformations (Tuchman-Duplessis and Mercier-Parot, 1956). Restriction of movement or fright (Rosenzweig and Blaustein, 1969), a too warm or too cold environment (Kalter and Warkany, 1959), giving a diet of German raisins for a single day during the critical period (Peters· and Strassburg, 1969), and subcutaneous injection of sodium chloride—table salt—to mice (Nishimura and Miyamoto, 1969) have likewise led to fetal deformities.

In 1967 Bergström et al. showed that a single injection into the yolk sac of chick embryos of the essential amino acid leucine was four times as teratogenic as thalidomide in the same dosages. Even though quantified, this finding obviously cannot be taken as an indication that a little leucine is more "dangerous" than a lot of thalidomide. Since it has also been found that a few grains of sand implanted into the incubated egg will cause malformations (Miding, 1969), one can effectively say that the chick embryo technique—unfortunately a favorite one among hurried researchers—is not a very informative test.

None of the separate results just discussed can be extrapolated to pregnant women. If one can draw any inference from these experiments, it is that nonspecific factors acting through stress mechanisms may create some metabolic imbalance which could result in malformed embryos. But the role of nonspecific stress has been ignored in the design of all too many experiments dealing with the teratogenicity of environmental contaminants. Likewise, in recent epidemiological studies of human terata, it has become fashionable to ascribe effects to a single compound, without giving due consideration to the possible role of concurrent stressful conditions.

In general, in teratogenicity testing, it is more common to get false-positive results than it is false-negative. In some cases, one or several of the stress factors may be operating as unrecognized variables. For instance, mere handling of pregnant mice may suffice to increase the number of malformed offspring. Therefore, in a good test design involving mice, there should be, in addition to the usual control group, a second group of controls to which no drug is administered, but for which the handling is identical with the experimental groups. Another possible false-positive result can come from the use of too large doses that may overwhelm metabolic pathways, causing physiological dysfunctions in the mother, which in turn lead to malformations not expressing specific drug activity. One must also be wary of inappropriate routes of exposure. One current recommendation—coming from the Panel on Teratogenicity of Pesticides of the Mrak *Report*—claims that "parenteral administration is an appropriate test route for pesticides to which humans are exposed by inhalation, or for pesticides which are systemically absorbed, following ingestion" (Mrak *Report,* 1969, p. 660).

The confusion to which application of this recommendation can lead is illustrated by the conflicting results found for the same compound using oral and injection routes. The fungicide captan can be used as an example. Varrett et al. (1969), FDA scientists, have claimed that captan is strongly teratogenic when injected into the air cell of incubated chick embryos. They might have questioned the validity of their own results from the fact that they found *no* dose-response relationship, but instead Dr. Varrett cheerfully announced during a discussion at the New York Academy of Sciences that "the incidence of abnormalities is exactly the same at this low level [3 ppm] as it was at 18 to 20 ppm" (Varrett, 1969, p. 412).

On the other hand chickens *fed* captan by Industrial Biotest Laboratories in Illinois had no malformed chicks (Kraybill, 1969, p. 412).

Even more interesting are the contradictory results on captan obtained in the Biometics study of pesticide teratogenicity, where *both* routes of administration were used by the same experimenters, working with mice (see Mrak *Report,* 1969, pp. 670–673). By the oral route, 100 mg/kg administered to C57 mice was *negative* for teratogenicity. In the same strain of mice, however, when 100 mg/kg of captan was injected subcutaneously, *all* litters showed malformed fetuses, with 58 percent of the total newborns affected, which figure is duly starred and noted as being "significant at the .01 level." This marvelously transparent obfuscation follows only nine pages after the brave recommendation cited above (favoring the injection route), and is found in tables compiled by the same panel members who made the statement. Since nobody in the human population is injecting himself with captan, we would regard it as negative for teratogenicity —at least on the basis of these two sets of data—whereas this expert panel lists it as a teratogenic pesticide.

While we bring attention to several possibilities of false-positive results in teratogenicity testing, this also should serve as a reassurance that when a dose-response curve has been established and a threshold level—using oral administration—is defined, one can be quite confident that doses below the threshold will not cause malformations. Of course, one can never be certain that results with test animals can be extrapolated to man, but that is true of all experiments with lower mammals and has to be accepted as one of the unavoidable limits to the information which can be gained from animal test systems.

There are some further problems involved in interpreting the meaning of results from teratogenicity testing, even where unquestionably positive findings have been obtained. For example, if a thyroid-suppressing drug which is known not to be capable of crossing the placental barrier is administered to the pregnant female, malformations will occur in the fetuses, resulting from induction of a hypothyroid state in the mother. In such a case the drug would not qualify as a teratogen, in the strict sense. It can nevertheless be named as a secondarily causative agent, since it is involved in the production of ill effects, although it does not cause them directly.

In this connection we would like to say a few words about thalidomide. This drug is now generally regarded in scientific as well as lay circles as the *prime example* of a true teratogenic agent, the potentially damaging effects of which were unsuspected until they appeared in the affected children. In addition to subsequent animal testing, one of the reasons advanced for the certainty that thalidomide was the cause of the malformations was that in about 200 cases throughout the world these manifested in the bizarre and seldom encountered form called phocomelia, or, roughly, truncated limbs. However, there are a number of specialists who quietly entertain reasonable doubts as to whether the drug is really a direct teratogenic agent, or whether the terata resulted from its secondary actions. There are several lines of evidence behind these doubts.

1. Only a very minor fraction of the pregnant women who took thalidomide during the first trimester gave birth to defective children.

2. At the time of the thalidomide events, there was an increase in several types of human malformations, including phocomelia, in a number of countries, even in some where thalidomide had not been marketed, such as Czechoslovakia and Hungary.

3. It has been demonstrated and confirmed that thalidomide is an immuno-suppressive agent. This has several implications: (a) When immune responses are suppressed, an intercurrent viral infection, which normally would not manifest in any clinical form, could cause a mild infection adequate to produce malformations in the fetus. (The role of viruses in producing terata is well established.) (b) The studies of Carr (1965) on spontaneously aborted human embryos indicate that the largest proportion of these have defective chromosomes or are malformed. A conclusion was reached that in higher mammals there is a mechanism operating which prevents the maturation of the majority of seriously deformed embryos. This is usually ascribed to immune incompatibility between the embryo and the mother. If an immunosuppressive agent, such as thalidomide, is administered to a mother who is carrying a malformed fetus, spontaneous abortion may be prevented and the child carried to term.

4. Finally, thalidomide seems to have some antioxytocic (that is, anti-uterine contracting) effect, which would also tend to prevent spontaneous abortions.

(The interested reader may want to have a look at Sjöström and Nilsson's *Thalidomide and the Power of the Drug Companies* (1972), which treats the thalidomide court trials exclusively from the point of view of the prosecution, but nevertheless contains some information from the defense arguments which strongly suggest many unanswered scientific questions.)

In considering animal experiments, one also has to take into account that lower mammals—such as rodents—do not abort, but, if an embryo dies early during gestation, it will be resorbed; or if death occurs in late pregnancy, the dead fetus will be delivered at term. For this reason, thalidomide experiments with lower mammals may tend only to show different *proportions* between resorbed or dead fetuses and live deliveries in the control and experimental groups. In the experimental groups, there may be a larger proportion of living malformed to normal offspring, whereas in the controls the numbers of deaths or resorptions will be greater. If the investigator is merely noting malformations and not observing proportions in the litters, he may become easily convinced that he is dealing with a strong teratogenic agent in the literal sense and conclude that the drug exerts a direct deleterious effect on the developing fetus.

Now we should like to make it absolutely clear that, in raising these matters of doubt over whether thalidomide has been demonstrated once and for all to be a true teratogen, we are *not* suggesting that it is a safe drug for pregnant women, as we might with respect to some chemicals which have recently been claimed to be teratogenic on the basis of what we described as "false-positive" findings earlier on, or others which may show teratogenic effects at very high doses in laboratory animals, but to which humans are exposed only in trace quantities. Whether the mode of action of thalidomide was to cause directly the defects with which the children were born, or whether it prevented the abortion of imperfectly formed embryos, obviously has no bearing whatsoever on the issue of safety to the user. Nor do we wish in any sense to minimize the personal tragedies of the families and children involved in the thalidomide episode.

If we dare to raise these doubts—which is almost to break a taboo—it is because thalidomide has already been incorporated into the textbooks as a classic example of an agent which typifies the true teratogens; and those who might wish to further elucidate its pharmacological mode of action are looked at askance, even by their own professional colleagues. In addition, the drug is now widely used as a so-called "positive control" in experiments designed to test other drugs for teratogenic potential; and in the event that it should be found at some later date to be a strong antiabortivum rather than a true teratogen, the possibility that the results of some of these current experiments may be incorrectly quantified cannot be discounted.

These are points of importance only for the scientist. For the lay public, the thalidomide case remains and will be remembered for a long time to come an example of the dreadful developments which may ensue when drugs which possess unforeseen potential for harm are permitted to reach the consumer. If there is reason for the layman to temper his fears that among our vast armamentarium of drugs and chemicals there may be one which will affect his own children in a similar manner with at least a grain of good sense, it is not because he needs to understand how thalidomide acts, but rather because he should not permit its example to make him equally receptive to every crusader who speaks out against some chemical in the name of the physical integrity of the unborn.

2,4,5-T

We move now to a topical issue which may be of more direct interest to the American reader: the recent controversy over the chlorinated phenoxyacetic acid herbicide: 2,4,5-T. This compound was synthesized in 1948, and has been applied with great success as a weed killer in both agriculture and horticulture. It also has applications in emergency situations—such as the control of forest fires, where it can be used to accomplish relatively rapid defoliation of an encircling zone to contain the fire. Unfortunately, it has been extensively used as a defoliating agent in the Vietnam War, being the major component of the infamous "Agent Orange," which has been applied by aerial spraying both in jungle terrain and on food crops supposedly controlled by or serving the Viet Cong. (Actually the principal herbicides used on food crops were "Agent Blue," an arsenical, and "Agent White," picloram.)

The herbicide is effective mainly against broad-leaf plants, and it acts as a plant growth hormone (like naturally occurring auxins), causing the plants to outgrow themselves, so to speak. When it is used against nuisance weeds, it produces very elongated young plants which cannot support themselves and will eventually die off. Unlike DDT and some of the other chlorinated hydrocarbon pesticides, 2,4,5-T has a relatively short duration of activity; it breaks down in the environment and it is not commonly found as a trace contaminant in foods.

Attention to the possibility that the uses of 2,4,5-T might involve some measure of danger to humans came in the late 1960s, simultaneously from two different types of inquiry. One involved experimental teratogenicity studies of the herbicide in several U.S. laboratories; the other, information emerging from the interest of a group of scientists in the ecological damage and inhumane practice represented by the use of chemical-warfare agents in Southeast Asia. Both inquiries require some background information. We shall begin with the latter.

As most people are aware, the use during World War I of various gases as weapons agents resulted in more than a million casualties and accounted for at least 100,000 deaths. Following the war, prohibitions against chemical warfare were worked out and formulated in the Geneva Protocol of 1925. This protocol has been ratified by 84 nations, including all the major powers excepting the United States. The earlier failure of the Senate to ratify the agreement involves political complexities we need not go into here; however, the massive applications of chemical defoliants and also the use of the so-called antiriot gases in Vietnam have once again made the issue a live one. In 1966, two Harvard scientists, John Edsall and Mathew Meselson, threw their weight behind a campaign initiated by a staff writer for *Scientist and Citizen,* Milton Leitenberg, and an anti-chemical warfare petition signed by 5,000 scientists was presented to President Johnson. There was no reaction from the White House at that time, but the Nixon administration attempted in 1969 to persuade the Senate to ratify the protocol, with, however, the proviso that herbicides and "riot gasses" were not comprehended in the list of chemical agents proscribed. Shortly thereafter, in a vote taken at the United Nations, 80 countries opposed this interpretation of the protocol, with the United States' position being supported by only Australia and Portugal. In view of this problem of how broadly the protocol should be interpreted, the Senate has taken no action.

In the meanwhile Meselson formed an ad hoc committee through the American Association for the Advancement of Science (AAAS) called the Herbicide Assessment Commission. This group was interested in investigating all aspects of the use of herbicides in Southeast Asia which could be called inhumane in terms of destroying the environment of the inhabitants, as well as their food crops. One special aspect of these investigations which was brought to attention, however, was that an increase in stillbirths and birth anomalies had been reported from the Mekong Delta area, and the question of whether this epidemiological observation might be causally related to exposure to chemical herbicides was raised (Boffey, 1971).

The first experimental indications that 2,4,5-T might cause terata emerged from a general pesticides screening study undertaken by the Bionetics Laboratories under contract to the National Cancer Institute, beginning in 1966. By 1968, a report had been submitted indicating that the herbicide could indeed cause serious malformations in mice, by both oral and subcutaneous administration, at dose rates up to 113 mg/kg/day for nine consecutive days. This same study showed 21.5 mg/kg/day to be the "no ill effect" level. The report was available to the FDA, where in-house studies using the chick embryo technique had also shown some teratogenic activity. For reasons which we shall detail later, not much attention was paid to this material within the government agencies. Around October, 1969, the results of the Bionetics study implicating 2,4,5-T as a potential teratogen were brought to the attention of Meselson, who immediately contacted officials in the White House and stirred a considerable reaction. On October 29, Lee DuBridge, who was then the presidential science advisor, announced the findings and stated that the Department of Defense would restrict the deployment of the herbicide in Vietnam to areas remote from populations. He also made what proved to be a precipitate promise that by January of 1970, the Department of Agriculture would issue a cancellation order for the use of 2,4,5-T on domestic food crops.

The ensuing events are rather complicated, but we shall try to summarize them as clearly and simply as possible.

On April 15, 1970, a cancellation order for the use of 2,4,5-T on crops, near water, and around the home was issued. About the same time the results of the Bionetics study were finally published in *Science* (Courtney et al., 1970).

Exercising their rights under the Federal Insecticide, Fungicide, and Rodenticide Act, the two major manufacturers of the herbicide—Dow Chemical Company and Hercules Inc.—petitioned for a review of relevant data by a scientific advisory committee. The nine-member committee was duly selected by the Department of Agriculture from a list of names supplied by the National Academy of Sciences. (At the time of committee selection, pesticide safety evaluations were reviewed under the Department of Agriculture, whereas before the "Report of the 2,4,5-T Scientific Advisory Committee" had been submitted, that function had been transferred from USDA to the newly created Environmental Protection Agency [EPA].)

During the period from January, 1970, to April, 1971, considerable additional experimental work was performed on 2,4,5-T by government agencies, industrial laboratories, and private laboratories under contract, most of which threw into quite a different perspective the original reports about its possible teratogenicity.

On review, analysis of the batch of 2,4,5-T which had been used in the original Bionetics experiments revealed that it was heavily contaminated with a "dioxin" (a commonly used though technically incorrect abbreviation for a group of highly toxic molecules which can be formed as by-products in the manufacture of several chlorinated compounds). In the case of 2,4,5-T manufacture, the particular dioxin molecule involved is 2,3,7,8-tetrachlorodibenzoparadioxin. The usual degree of contamination of technical-grade 2,4,5-T is less than one part per million of dioxin (and in current manufacturing, *well* under 1 ppm), whereas the material used in the Bionetics study apparently contained about

30 ppm. It was therefore suggested that the teratogenic findings were due to the impurity and not to 2,4,5-T itself.

Emerson et al. (1970) did some experiments with rats using "pure" 2,4,5-T introduced by gavage (stomach tube) and found no teratogenic effects in doses ranging up to 24 mg/kg maternal weight.

Also in 1970, Sparschu et al. administered pure dioxin to pregnant rats. They found that 0.125 μg/kg/day was toxic to the fetus, and 8 μg/kg/day to the mother. However, they could establish 0.03 μg/kg as a dose where neither teratogenic nor embryo-toxic effects were observed.

The National Institute of Environmental Health Sciences (NIEHS) carried out some work using much higher doses of "pure" 2,4,5,-T on both pregnant rats and mice. Oral doses of 150 mg/kg with rats were negative; but in mice, subcutaneous administration of 100–150 mg/kg dosages did produce terata.

Within the FDA, some investigations of 2,4,5-T were undertaken on pregnant hamsters, with administration by oral intubation on days six through ten of gestation (Collins and Williams, 1971). The experimenters used both "pure" 2,4,5-T and batches of the herbicide to which the dioxin impurity was added in varying quantities. At 40, 80, and 100 mg/kg of the compound "contaminated" with 45 ppm of the impurity, fetal mortality was extremely high — 100 percent at the highest dosage administered for five consecutive days. With the pure compound, on the other hand, effects listed as terata appeared in significant numbers *only* at the 100 mg/kg level (also given for five days), and in one of these series fetal mortality was also high — about 56 percent. Because of the high fetal deaths and the magnitude of the dose, one would tend to regard the effects as an expression of overloading the metabolic pathways of the dam, rather than as direct effects on the embryo, with the compound as the causative agent.

Hercules Inc. then contracted with Bionetics to conduct a second series of investigations, using "pure" 2,4,5-T and attempting to repeat the NIEHS study which had shown effects at high doses. The results were negative; however, it was subsequently discovered that the laboratories had made a decimal-point error and had actually used doses which were one-tenth those of the NIEHS group. In a third attempt, Bionetics did partially confirm NIEHS findings that 100 mg/kg of "pure" 2,4,5-T produced malformations in mice. (The reader may have the impression that the Bionetics Laboratories do not seem to be the most reliable source of accurate findings. This may in part reflect the enormous scope of the projects which they undertook simultaneously during this period, further aspects of which will be discussed in Chapter 14 in connection with DDT and studies of the carcinogenicity of pesticides.)

This mass of rather confusing data certainly did not make the Advisory

Committee's task of review and evaluation an enviable one. The indications seemed to be that 2,4,5-T alone is not teratogenic, except in doses which are high enough to produce artifacts through a general disturbance of maternal metabolism which therefore might not be drug-specific; or through the sub-cutaneous route employed, which could have introduced artifacts from the injection technique. Furthermore, the doses reported to be effective are so far in excess of any possible human exposure—except that resulting from accidental ingestion of a massive quantity of the pure compound—that they are meaning-less when extrapolated to man. (The amount for a pregnant woman weighing 50 kg equivalent to the 100 mg/kg dose which was effective, subcutaneously in mice, would be 5,000 mg.)

Thus, the findings seemed to point either to artifacts or to dioxin contamina-tion as the source of positive effects, and since there were several studies which indicated that there is a "no ill effect" dose which is orders of magnitude higher than probable human exposure, the Committee could have been justified in concluding that 2,4,5-T—at least in crop uses—represents no hazard to human embryos. However, since there was some confusion surrounding the early re-sults and claims, the chairman of the Committee—A. J. Wilson, a pioneer in the field of experimental teratology—decided to perform some experiments of his own before coming to a final judgment.

In May, 1971, the Committee submitted its Report to the Environmental Protection Agency, recommending that the cancellation order on registered uses of 2,4,5-T be lifted. Respecting the reported rise in stillbirths and birth defects in the Mekong Delta, they went so far as to state: ". . . any attempt to relate birth defects or still births to herbicide exposure is predestined to failure" (cited in Wade, 1971, p. 614). The inclusion of this statement in their Report was undoubtedly a psychological error, but since the subsequent attacks on the Committee's conclusions were focused on their recommendations to lift the *domestic* cancellation orders, it is unlikely that the exclusion of these remarks would have made their Report acceptable to its critics.

A Minority View

In addition to Wilson, the nine-man Committee was made up of seven other life scientists—toxicologists, pharmacologists, oncologists—plus one applied mathematician: T. D. Sterling of Washington University, St. Louis. Sterling did not agree with the evaluations of the other members of the Committee, and his dissenting view was broadly publicized.

In July, 1971, a press conference was arranged by the Committee for Environmental Information and Ralph Nader's Center for the Study of Responsive Law at which attention was brought to various criticisms of the Advisory Committee's Report. The two principals were Dr. Samuel Epstein and Harrison Wellford, a well-known member of the Nader group. Shortly thereafter, a full-blown controversy broke loose which culminated, after considerable testimony before congressional committees and much journalistic activity, in a decision on the part of William Ruckelshaus, then newly appointed EPA chief, to ignore the recommendations of his 2,4,5-T Scientific Advisory Committee and keep the cancellation orders on the herbicide in force.

We now want to consider the views of some of the Advisory Committee's chief critics.

Sterling, the dissenting member, had two major complaints about the deliberations of the Committee and the kinds of data on which their final recommendation was based. He faulted them for not seeking more data on the possible effects of low doses of the herbicide. However, in the published version of his dissenting opinion (which appeared in the December issue of *Science*) one discerns both internal logical contradictions and evidence of a lack of fundamental understanding of the methodologies of experimental teratology. In the publication it is asserted, for example, that ". . . there is the observation that every known substance (including water and oxygen) is harmful and may even have teratogenic, mutagenic, and carcinogenic effects if given in large enough doses . . . . As a consequence, it may be unclear what the meaning is of a toxic response in an animal system to a very high dose of an agent" (Sterling, 1971, p. 1358).

Now this is very interesting because, while it is a statement which would probably meet with general agreement from most classical toxicologists and teratologists, it expresses a point of view which Epstein, a major champion of Sterling's minority view on this particular issue, dismissed during the Consolidated DDT Hearings as "complete rubbish" (Epstein, 1972, p. 7323). To the teratologist, the problem involved with responses which appear only at high doses is that they may very well be only artifacts, not expressive of specific drug activity at all. However, Sterling looks at it another way. "Thus, the major utility of an animal experiment is to ascertain whether or not the reactions to relatively high doses can serve for extrapolating a dose-response function that will reveal the occurrence of a zero or nontoxic response to some dose or whether the agent may be toxic at any dose" (Sterling, 1971, p. 1358).

Here Sterling is discussing a question which is similar to that reviewed in the previous chapter regarding the difficulties of establishing a "virtually safe dose" for carcinogens, with a slight variation in that he makes it clear that he thinks that *if* an adequate number of animals were to be used in testing and *if* the armamentarium of sophisticated statistical analyses were to be applied to the results, a correct extrapolation to a dose with zero effect could be made. But unfortunately he is making a major error, for teratogenicity studies do not involve lifelong administration of chemicals as do carcinogenicity investigations, but are more comparable to acute toxicity testings, wherein a "no ill effect" dose can be fairly easily established within the observable experimental range. Even in the rather extremist report of the "Panel on Teratogenicity of Pesticides" of the Mrak Commission, this classical view seems to be accepted. One may read: ". . . teratogens may be effective only at a certain dose range, whether high or low, narrow or wide, below which development is apparently undisturbed, and above which death *in utero* results" (Mrak *Report,* 1969, pp. 658-659). In other terms, when experiments with suspected teratogens give a defined dose-response curve and a "no ill effect" level falls on that curve, one may say with reasonable confidence that the drug is not teratogenic below that level — allowing, of course, for a margin of safety to express the possible differences in response between humans and the test animals used.

Sterling's second major objection was that the experiments considered by the Committee did not incorporate sophisticated statistical analyses; ". . . not a single one of these experimenters subjected his data to the robust and generally available technique of analysis of variance" (Sterling, 1971, p. 1359). As it stands, this statement does not seem to correspond to the facts. On June 29, 1970, Haseman and Hogan of the Biometry Branch of NIEHS submitted the results of their statistical analyses on 11 studies involving 2,4,5-T and dioxin, which included a Kruskal-Wallis one-way analysis of variance for all "variables of interest." If, however, these analyses did not satisfy Sterling, who is an applied mathematician, one may fairly ask why he did not gather the data and perform this work himself? After all, if Wilson took the time to run his own laboratory experiments, Sterling might have contributed his efforts instead of merely complaining that the statistical work was "simplistic." One may also point out that there are instances (as we will show in Chapter 14 in connection with the famous Bionetics carcinogenicity studies) when such sophisticated and robust techniques as analysis of variance are used by clever statisticians to prove a point which is simply *not* supported by the data, looked at in the light of such old-fashioned methods as calculating standard deviations. This should not be taken as an indication that we deny the value of modern statistics in general. Nor do we object to the idea that a statistician should oppose the interpretations of a whole panel of life scientists regarding biological experiments, if his objections really bear on the validity of the interpretations. However, in the matter of 2,4,5-T's teratogenicity, there is a pretty good case to be made for the argument that the tests used by the rest of the Committee in their analyses of the data were indeed adequate for arriving at an understanding of the results.

Suppose we accept that 24 mg/kg maternal weight per day was a fairly well established "no ill effect" dose for 2,4,5,-T—allowing for some differences between mice and rats, which were the principal experimental animals—and consider how this dose compares with the human exposure to the chemical through foods and water. In 1,145 water samples surveyed by the USDA, none was found to contain 2,4,5-T; and the solubility of the compound in water is so low that even massive further analyses would be unlikely to turn up any significant contamination of drinking water. In a two-year period the FDA conducted 24,000 determinations for the herbicide from their "market basket" survey, and came up with a total of three positive samples. The highest residue was 0.19 ppm found in a sample of milk fat (Kearney and Tschirley, 1970). If we supposed that all milk was equally contaminated (which it isn't), and if we suppose a 4 percent butterfat content in the milk, a few calculations indicate that a pregnant woman weighing 50 kg would have to drink 150,000 l of this contaminated milk daily before she would reach the *no* ill effect intake level of 2,4,5-T. Other possible sources of exposure—such as inhalation while applying the herbicide personally—might increase the intake considerably, but the margin of safety with relatively pure 2,4,5-T is so enormous that we really cannot see any room for disagreement with the opinion of the majority members that 2,4,5-T does not represent a teratogenic hazard for humans.

The Dioxin Question

Probably the commonest and most important criticism of the Advisory Committee's Report raised by outside scientists (and also by Sterling, though not in his written dissenting opinion) is that they failed to deal adequately with the question of whether the minor quantities of dioxins associated with 2,4,5-T might be capable of accumulating in the environment or in food chains. It does indeed seem as though members of the Committee were somewhat casual in their treatment of this possibility; for they suggested future studies to determine whether there is a buildup of these toxins, and at the same time announced that the quantities of dioxin impurities in the herbicide were negligible and would be further reduced through future controls on manufacturing standards. This certainly left them open to criticism, and it also opened the door for the presentation of a series of dioxin scare stories which may very well have been the deciding factor in Ruckelshaus' decision to ignore the advice of the Committee. One does have to recognize that dioxins—aside from the issue of teratogenicity—are acutely toxic in minute quantities, both to adult mammals and to the embryo *in utero*.

Two different kinds of speculations have been advanced about the behavior of dioxins in the environment to support the idea that they might accumulate. The first is that they may be persistent and could become magnified through the food chain. The second is that they may be formed under environmental conditions from the breakdown products of 2,4,5-T or other chlorinated phenolic chemicals, thus permitting much larger quantities to accede into the environment than are in the original compounds as manufacturing by-products. Both possibilities have been investigated and discounted, but since the Advisory Committee seems not to have made use of certain information available even at the time of their deliberations, it is to a certain extent understandable that the scare stories about dioxins took hold in connection with the 2,4,5-T controversy.

The question of the persistence of dioxins in natural conditions has been studied in considerable detail by Crosby and his coworkers. Their published results did not appear until August 23, 1971—about ten days after Ruckelshaus announced his intention to keep the cancellation order in force. However, a preliminary account of their work had been presented a year earlier at the 160th Meeting of the American Chemical Society (Crosby and Wong, 1970), and the Abstract of the presentation was available well before the Advisory Committee began to meet.

Crosby et al. (1971) showed that dioxins—far from being persistent— are highly labile in the presence of sunlight and hydrogen donors, which effectively means under most natural conditions. They undergo very rapid decomposition through photolysis, 100 percent breakdown occurring in about seven hours. The experimenters demonstrated that this reaction will fail to take place if hydrogen donors are not available, as, for instance, in distilled water, in desert sand, or on completely bare concrete surfaces. On the other hand, since distilled water does not exist in nature and since there would be no reason to spray an herbicide on a desert or on a barren concrete wall, the likelihood of accumulation of dioxins introduced through 2,4,5-T applications seems to be nil. The authors wrote: "Such [hydrogen] donors could be represented environmentally by the waxy cuticles of green leaves, surface slicks on water, or the spray oil or aromatic solvent so often incorporated into 2,4,5-T formulations. Despite the limited solubility, the organic coating of most leaves should provide adequate solvent power for the maximum of 0.27 ng/cm^2 of compound I (2,3,7,8 tetra-chlorodibenzo-p-dioxin) which could result from a normal application of 2 pound/acre (2.25 kg/ha) of 2,4,5-T containing even 10 ppm (10 mg/kg) of the impurity" (Crosby et al., 1971, p. 749).

The second speculation—that dioxins might be formed under natural conditions from the decomposition products of 2,4,5-T or similar chlorinated phenolics—was investigated by Plimmer and Klingebiel (1971). The possibility that two molecules of one of the breakdown products (2,4,5-trichlorophenol) of 2,4,5-T will combine and thus form chlorinated paradioxins under natural conditions had to be taken into account, however unlikely it might seem. It was known that this phenomenon occurs under high-temperature, high-pressure conditions of the manufacture of 2,4,5-T, and that this is how the dioxin impurity is formed. Simulating natural conditions in the laboratory, the experimenters were unable to detect any such by-products. They concluded: "The failure to detect chlorinated dibenzo-p-dioxins may result from the rapid photolytic breakdown of the lower chlorinated dibenzo-p-dioxins. Under environmental conditions, dioxins are unlikely products of the lower chlorinated phenols or phenoxyalkanoic acids" (Plimmer and Klingebiel, 1971, p. 407).

Translated into somewhat simpler terms, this means that, in the authors' view, if dioxins are formed at all from chlorinated phenoxyalkanoic acids such as 2,4-D and 2,4,5-T, then the step from dioxin formation to dioxin breakdown is so rapid that they were unable to detect it with analytical methods. It is rather difficult to imagine how these compounds, which are so labile that the chemists cannot follow the speed of their breakdown processes, could manage to accumulate in the general environment or in food chains.

We rather suspect that the sizable number of professional worriers who have suffered mentally over the possible potential environmental buildup of dioxins from 2,4,5-T uses have possibly read these two articles and are digesting their "treated" vegetables much better these days. But what about the lay public—the vast numbers of people who were exposed to the printed speculations of these worriers? They are most unlikely to have read these two technical articles on the processes of chemical breakdown, and are probably still convinced that even "pure" 2,4,5-T may be forming those awful and very dangerous things called dioxins, while the manufacturers have the gall to continue to fight the cancellation order in hearings and appeals processes. One of the most distressing aspects of those environmental concerns which are raised by scientists and publicized widely is that even where there is little question of the sincerity of the individuals involved, and even if there is at least some speculative basis for a real concern, it almost never seems to occur to those who explained the nature of the possible threat to the lay public when it was a mere speculation that they have an equal obligation to summarize reassuring findings to that same public, when such become available. Nowhere have we seen these two articles discussed in popular or semipopular terms in the mass media. As a beginning, we should like to suggest that Philip Abelson, the editor of *Science*, who wrote an editorial in the October 30, 1970 issue summarizing the then current concerns about the possibility of dioxin buildup in the food chain, ought to be the first to offer a semipopular account of the present, less scary view of how these toxic compounds behave in the natural environment.

Comment on "News and Comment"

The last critical view of the Advisory Committee's recommendations on 2,4,5-T which we want to discuss came after the EPA decision to keep the cancellation order in force. It deals with a whole spectrum of questions bearing on government policy, agency responsibility, the motivations of the committee members, supposed suppression of reports, and other matters related more to the social than the strictly scientific issues of the controversy. In the August 13, 1971 issue of *Science* Nicolas Wade wrote a five-page "News and Comment" article called "Decision on 2,4,5-T: Leaked Reports Compel Regulatory Responsibility." As the title suggests, great emphasis is placed on the supposed suppression of reports or secrecy practices within government departments and agencies—a not too suprising journalistic twist, in view of the fact that Daniel Ellsberg's release of the Pentagon Papers to the press and subsequent related events were among the major news stories of the summer of 1971.

According to Wade's account, the FDA had been in possession of the first Bionetics report on 2,4,5-T's teratogenicity for several years, and failed to do anything about it until this "secret" information was "leaked" by someone (unnamed) inside FDA to a member of the Nader center, who in turn handed it over to Meselson in late 1969, providing the impetus for Meselson's call to the White House which finally set in motion the process of cancellation orders. Wade states directly that the FDA was negligent, and he implies that the Bionetics findings were deliberately kept secret. This second point is most debatable, since the Mrak Commission on Pesticides had these materials at their disposal at the beginning of their deliberations in early 1969 and duly incorporated a summary of the Bionetics study in one of the appendices of their final report, which admittedly did not appear in print until December, 1969, but was hardly a secret proceeding. Any member of the Commission could have publicized the 2,4,5-T teratogenicity findings, had he thought them of importance. In fact, the cochairman of the Teratogenicity Panel of this Commission was Samuel Epstein, who later became a central figure in the opposition to the Advisory Committee, and he could very easily have informed Meselson about the materials involved many months before the reported "leak" from FDA, had he so desired – particularly because at that time both scientists were at Harvard. If there was any reason for the unidentified FDA "whistle blower" to turn first to the Nader center, it was not because there was any real question of secrecy, but most probably because such an approach has clear dramatic value.

As for the "negligence" of the FDA, it should be remembered that even the original Bionetics study, which was made with heavily contaminated 2,4,5-T, showed a "no ill effect" level for mice of 21.5 mg kg. This is not the sort of material about which any FDA scientist who is a realist would get excited. It should be borne in mind that pregnant women do not *eat* 2,4,5-T, and that the substance has not been found as a food residue except in three isolated cases, even given the highly sophisticated analytical techniques employed for residue detection. If the Bionetics finding had concerned a drug which might be taken by a pregnant woman in gram quantities, we feel reasonably confident that the FDA would have pursued the matter *post haste*. After all, the FDA did *not* license thalidomide for sale in the United States, despite what are reported to have been intensive "sales" efforts on the part of the manufacturers, whereas Sweden, England, Japan, and Germany did. But Wade, in attempting to reinforce the impression of FDA negligence on 2,4,5-T, mentions that O. G. Fitzhugh, an "old FDA hand," had had these materials at his disposal for a year and a half prior to the cancellation order and had done nothing about them. Furthermore, Fitzhugh was the chairman of the EPA in-house special pesticides-review group which looked over the Advisory Committee's Report and found it satisfactory. Wade writes: "Fitzhugh's own attitude to toxicology is refreshingly simple. 'As a scientist,' he told *Science*. 'I believe that anything is safe if you go low enough, and anything is toxic if you go high enough'" (Wade, 1971, p. 612).

Wade later mentions that the Committee, like Fitzhugh, "implicitly assumed" that there is a level below which exposure to both 2,4,5-T and its dioxin impurity is safe. But, as we have already pointed out at great length, this is *not* an implicit assumption on the part of only the Committee members and of Fitzhugh, as Wade tries to imply, but rather is the accepted view of scientists in all relevant fields of inquiry. The "no safe dose for carcinogens" stance, which is also a minority rather than a consensus opinion, has at least *some* arguable basis; but it is completely irrelevant to discussions of the teratogenic activity of chemicals.

When one reads the articles of journalists like Wade over a period of time and with a critical eye, one cannot avoid the impression that they tend to make an "implicit assumption" that all environmentalists and consumer protectionists are always right, even when they reverse their own earlier positions as the wind takes a new turn. In the case of Fitzhugh and the value of FDA studies, for example, it is of interest to note that whereas in Wade's article he is said to be both "irresponsibly casual in his attitude towards protection of the public health" and "rather simplistic in his scientific thinking," only six months later he became a minor hero of the environmental cause, when Samuel Epstein resurrected two forgotten studies done by Fitzhugh on DDT-induced tumors in mice and rats in support of his own statement in testimony at the Consolidated DDT Hearings that DDT has been demonstrated to represent a carcinogenic hazard to humans. Epstein is the most extreme champion of the "no safe dose" opinion, and he certainly would have rejected Fitzhugh's statement to *Science* cited above; but he seemed to be quite willing during the Consolidated DDT Hearings to elevate to the level of "first-class work" these two inconclusive studies of the FDA toxicologist.

Wade's second "secrecy in government" theme concerns the public release of the text of the Advisory Committee's Report. He writes that "the old policy, which was followed when pesticide affairs were handled by the Department of Agriculture, was to suppress the reports, even after a decision on their recommendations had been taken" (*ibid.*, p. 610). Ruckelshaus, on the other hand, has ordered that similar reports submitted to the EPA should be made public as soon as they are completed. Wade then tells his readers, in something of a logical non-sequitur, that the report of the EPA Advisory Committee on 2,4,5-T was "leaked" to the press in June, 1971, which event unleashed the second stage of the controversy over the herbicide in the public domain.

Wade's particular choice of words is crucial to the impression he wishes to convey, which appears to be that the Department of Agriculture is as impenetrable as the walls of the Pentagon. But the truth of the matter is that there was never any question of *suppressed* documents. It was quite simply not government policy to make public such advisory documents in *any* department within the administrative branch. If this policy is now being gradually changed, it is not because of Ruckelshaus' honest stance in contrast to the furtive paper shredding and supposedly locked files in the USDA or the FDA which Wade conjures up in his readers' imaginations. It is because the public is now increasingly demanding that they have the right to know about all documents and data which underlie agency decisions, excepting those which are correctly defined as classified, and the practices are changing accordingly, with varying degrees of rapidity, in most arms of the executive branch—with the notable exception of the Department of Defense.

Finally, Wade lashes into the Advisory Committee itself, portraying Sterling, Epstein, and Wellford as the heroes of the affair, and implying that the Committee was selected with a clear bias towards the food chemical industry and produced a Report which was not only "scientifically undistinguished," but was actually a "whitewash" job. Several passages are worth quoting to give an idea of the vehemence of his attack.

> Why did the EPA advisory committee on 2,4,5-T fail so badly to reach a verdict that would be generally acceptable to the scientific community? . . . It has been remarked of the 19th century English moralists that they argued from premises that were largely false to conclusions that were in harmony with the interests of the middle classes. Substitute manufacturers for middle classes and the same description — together of course with the same lofty purpose — seems applicable to the thought processes of the EPA advisory committee on 2,4,5-T. (*Ibid.*, p. 612)

And in his final paragraph:

> The history of the 2,4,5-T episode is cogent evidence of the shambles into which the official decision-making machinery has lapsed. At two crucial points — the springing of the suppressed Bionetics report and the exposé of the EPA advisory committee's whitewash — the intervention of outside scientists has been essential in keeping the government machinery on the rails and in motion. And only through by-passing the existing machinery of the advisory committee's report and the review of it by the EPA Office of Pesticides did Ruckelshaus and his aides arrive at the "correct decision" to maintain the existing restrictions. In short, the established machinery for protecting the public health has failed, and failed ignominiously. (*Ibid.*, p. 615)

Anyone reading Wade's article who had no prior information about the individual parties involved in this controversy and no access to the scientific information per se would certainly come away with the impression that had it not been for the stubborn dissent of Sterling, the activism of Meselson, the willingness of an outside scientist like Epstein to volunteer his opinions and give his time in testifying before congressional committees, the concern of Wellford and others in the Nader group, and the readiness of the press to publicize the views of the critics, a dangerous fraud might have been perpetrated on the American public, reflecting not only the failure of the health agencies to safeguard the physical well-being of the unborn, but also a successful persuasion of the scientifically naive Ruckelshaus — new at his post — by a Committee who had bungled their job and perhaps even callously sold out to special interest pressures. What reader would not feel grateful to the dissenters and to those who helped them to be heard? And who might have imagined, from Wade's account, that there was quite another side to this story which was worthy of attention? Certainly not the lay readers of *Science,* and probably only those scientist readers who already knew the other side of the story, or who have accustomed themselves to reading such journalistic accounts skeptically.

A full 13 weeks later, the following letter appeared in the "Letters to the Editor" column, signed by all nine members of the council of the Society of Toxicology:

> We, the council of the Society of Toxicology, should like to register our displeasure with the skillful selection of facts and opinions employed by Nicolas Wade to support his point of view on 2,4,5-T. We acknowledge the editorial policy of *Science* to publish minority, points of view, but we cannot allow to go unchallenged such unfounded attacks on the integrity of toxicologists and other scientists in government, universities, and industries.
>
> The 2,4,5-T controversy involves a fundamental issue in safety evaluation. The issue is simply whether or not demonstration of a teratogenic effect in some species of animal, at a dosage level far in excess of any possible human exposure, constitutes scientific grounds for banning the chemical. A small minority of toxicologists believe in the affirmative, but the overwhelming majority do not. The EPA scientific advisory committee on 2,4,5-T, which included several toxicologists and teratologists, specifically endorsed the majority opinion. To accuse the scientific advisory committee of "bias" for defending a commonly held scientific principle is unwarranted. To select a committee of ten experts who might share the opposite "bias" would be extremely difficult if not impossible.
>
> Wade attacks government and specific government scientists by saying "government regulatory machinery has taken almost no initiative to safeguard the public health—except in response to external pressure." Such a statement fails to credit government scientists with repeatedly making judgments, supported by majority opinion of the toxicology profession, that the teratology data did not justify a conclusion of health hazard to the public. It is true that "external pressure" forced the government to reverse its position, but to waste public health funds to protect the public from imaginary hazards is an unwanted consequence that Wade overlooks.
>
> Wade describes the advisory committee report as a "whitewash" job and asks the question, "Why did the EPA advisory committee on 2,4,5-T fail so badly to reach a verdict that would be generally acceptable to the scientific community?" Let us assure you that the "verdict" of the committee does indeed represent the majority view of toxicologists.
>
> The tragedy of the whole controversy is that the EPA, by Wade's own admission, set aside the recommendations of the scientific advisory committee "in response to external pressure" and continued the ban on 2,4,5-T. In so doing, the administrator

of EPA has done a disservice to his own scientific staff and has shaken the confidence of toxicologists in the scientific integrity of his agency. Must the majority membership of a scientific profession resort to "external pressure" to obtain sound judgment in government, rather than being permitted to devote full time to the investigation of real health hazards?

Joseph F. Borzelleca
Victor A. Drill
Kenneth P. DuBois
John P. Frawley
Leon Goldberg (sic)*
Wayland J. Hayes, Jr.
Donald D. McCollister
Robert L. Roudabush
Robert A. Scala
(1971, pp. 545–546.)

Three Trans-scientific Matters

We are shortly going to end our 2,4,5-T discussion and leave the subject of teratogens altogether. However, we should like to make three further points, all of which are about science and society rather than technical matters.

The appearance of the article on 2,4,5-T by Wade and the response in the form of a letter from the Society of Toxicology seems to be rather typical of the situation in which we now find ourselves as far as media information about controversial issues in science is concerned. Journalists present a great case for the point of view of environmentalists and consumer protectionists, and the public is given the impression that the opposition consists exclusively of special interest groups or of individuals who are biased towards those groups and do not have the public welfare as their primary concern. If the opposition is heard at all by the public, it is usually in the form of letters, occasional concessions to equal-space principles in "Op-Ed" pages, and so on. However, there is a major difference between reporting found in the pages of *Science* magazine and what goes on in the popular press. One can enter a plea, as we did in Chapter 2, for more responsible reporting in all branches of the media, but a realist must also recognize that modish writing on topical subjects, occasionally spiced with sensationalism, does sell newspapers, and newspapers are businesses as well as information channels. *Science* magazine on the other hand is not a business undertaking; it is the publication of the largest scientific organization in the United States, the American

---

*Dr. Golberg's name was misspelled in the publication.

Association for the Advancement of Science (AAAS). While obviously not all the members of such a large organization can be pleased with the contents of each issue, members have both the right and the responsibility to consider and review at regular intervals whether the editorial policies and practices of the magazine are serving the interest of the advancement of science. In a March, 1971 editorial, Philip Abelson reviewed some of the complaints which came in to the magazine regarding its contents and policies. He acknowledged that it is the policy-oriented materials, especially those which bear on political issues of the moment, which arouse the most tension and the strongest emotions. He then went on to say: "But the future of civilization is dependent on the wise use of science and technology, and members of AAAS cannot responsibly avoid participation in some of the opinion-making and decision-making processes. *Science's* policy in this matter is to attempt to give fair representation to the broad spectrum of views" (Abelson, 1971, p. 1101). Now that seems like a fair enough statement, and we would agree with Abelson that contemporary scientists do have a responsibility to interest themselves in the social aspects of scientific and technological developments. But, one must ask, where is the broad spectrum of views he refers to in the "News and Comment" pages of *Science?* There are usually six or seven journalists writing for these pages, and while some of the material in them is news of a nonpolemic nature, Nicolas Wade is by no means the only one of these writers whose accounts of highly emotionally charged science controversies with far-reaching social implications are one-sided. Where is the balance? For that matter, where is the debate? If those who represent a point of view which differs from these writers — or have even been quite viciously attacked by them in an article — have recourse only to writing a letter to the editor which appears weeks and sometimes months after the original account, one must conclude that this is *not* an effective fairness policy. If the "News and Comment" pages are to be a forum in *Science* where polemic issues are aired, then let it be one in which both parties to a debate are given equal voice. The days when environmentalists and consumer protectionists had a hard time being heard are quite obviously over. We think it is time that Philip Abelson should look around for at least one, if not three, intelligent hard-nosed reporters who would be capable of giving fair representation to the opposition point of view in these controversies, preferably on the same subject and in the same issue of the magazine where articles biased towards environmentalism appear. The question is, if such reporters presented themselves to Abelson, would he take up the challenge? Is he ready to extend the principle of representing a broad spectrum of views to the "News and Comment" pages, or is he satisfied that the performance of his current staff is responsible to both the lay readers of the magazine and the membership of AAAS?

Our second general point has to do with the matter of responsiveness versus responsible decisions on the part of the government health agencies and standards-setting bodies. We agree with the spirit of the letter of the toxicologists, as well as with their specific defense of the integrity of the Committee members who were so shoddily treated by Wade. It is somewhat embarrassing, however, to find ourselves in the position of defending agencies and government scientists in general, just as it is not particularly comfortable to us, subjectively, to appear to be defending industrial interests. Probably if both were not under such heavy and often unfair attack from the whistle-blowers, we would not be doing so, since after all, all the big bureaucracies in the government have serious problems of inefficiency, and certainly there is great inequality of performance among scientists in government employ, as elsewhere. However, we do agree with the toxicologists that on the whole the agencies and committees responsible for guarding the public health do a remarkably good job; that when a real danger appears, they take appropriate steps to safeguard the public; and that where they err, it is much more often on the side of overcaution and unnecessarily hasty regulations than in terms of neglect. We think it is important to make a distinction between decisions which are responsive to public opinion and those which are responsible to the public interest; for although there may be instances where an exposé could lead to attention to a hitherto neglected health danger, the record of the last two years seems to suggest that some of the agencies are becoming overly concerned with their "image," giving in to the pressures of publicity and extremist views, and making decisions which are without scientific merit, as well as frequently being economically unsound and unenforceable.

Our last point is an entirely different sort of matter altogether, and takes us back to the beginning of the 2,4,5-T discussion. In all of the excitement over the possible teratogenicity of 2,4,5-T and/or its dioxin impurity, the issue of the use of herbicides in warfare seems somehow to have been submerged. True, the United States forces, in principle, ceased to use Agent Orange for defoliation in Indochina, but nobody is saying that our allies are not availing themselves of the supply which is still stockpiled in South Vietnam, and there are always Agent White and Agent Blue, which were not under discussion as public health hazards. What happened to all the attempts to put pressure on the Administration to alter its stance on the permissibility of herbicide uses in warfare? And what happened to the Senate discussions of the ratification of the Geneva Protocol? Although we would hardly be ready to claim that this half-century-old argument would have been settled had the 2,4,5-T issue not been blown out of proportion as a health hazard, we do think it is a rather good example of how the frustrations of the anti-war groups, the generalized anger at Pentagon practices, and widespread feelings of moral indignation about U.S. involvement in Southeast Asia can get deflected into a much narrower focus where the villains of the piece are far easier to battle: two chemical corporations, one nine-man committee of scientists, and a lowly herbicide.

Are We Endangering the Stock?

The third and most terrifying of the fear-provoking subjects surrounding environmental contamination is the concern that human uses of radiation and chemicals will lead to an increase in mutations, thus endangering the genetic heritage of our species. In the mind of the layman, even a suggestion of possible genetic damage conjures up all sorts of horrifying images. Some may imagine that our children's children could literally mutate into two-headed monsters. Others may think in terms of a general deterioration of mankind, comprised of feeble-minded weaklings, exhibiting genetically determined defects. Some who are more sophisticated speak about a tremendous increase in the numbers of genetic deaths, often, however, without knowing what this term means. It is precisely because the imagined manifestations—whatever they might be—will show up only in generations to come that the subject of mutagens arouses even more undefined anxieties than does talk about carcinogens or teratogens.

With respect to cancer, for instance, risks taken by the individual are more defined in his own psyche, and they refer to his own body. If people in general were really convinced, for example, that cigarette smoking inevitably leads to lung cancer, then there should have been a marked decline in cigarette sales since the time of the announcements—known to practically everybody—that smoking may represent a cancer hazard. But on the contrary, even though some individuals have quit smoking on this account, the general sales continue to rise. The possibility that in a family a malformed child may be brought into the world is somewhat more frightening, and the suffering of those families in which a defective child is being raised is both very real and associated with many complex ramifications. But such a problem still remains within one generation of a family, if the malformation was caused by an agent acting on the fetus during gestation, rather than by a genetic defect. Although anxieties may prevail during pregnancy, people who have produced normal children are less vulnerable to exaggerated claims about teratogenic agents than they are to statements that the whole genetic heritage of the race may be at risk.

It is impossible, of course, to disprove in scientific terms any general claims advanced about what might happen in the unforeseeable future; after all, no scientist can state authoritatively that the telluric catastrophes predicted by Edgar Cayce will not take place. However, on the basis of scientific knowledge, it is possible to give some idea of the probability that any particular agent present in known quantities represents a risk to the genetic heritage of whole populations, and it is also possible to clarify some known facts about the mechanisms of mutagenicity.

One speaks about mutation when a change is brought about in the genetic material of a cell. Mutations are usually induced by an external agent—a mutagen—the prime example being penetrating ionizing radiation. In this strict definition of the word "mutation," the change has to be localized in the individual DNA strands. The causative agent must therefore be able to pass through the cell material and reach the DNA, which is located in the nucleus or nuclear equivalent of the cell. True mutagens thus act on the macromolecular level. In addition to penetrating radiation, certain chemicals, such as nitrites and some of the so-called alkylating agents, may act as mutagens.

If a compound affects only one base out of the millions which are present in a single DNA strand, one speaks about "point mutation." On the other hand, if an external molecule becomes incorporated into the DNA strand as a replacement for the required base, one talks about "base substitution." (For instance, a symmetrical triazine substituting for uracil, which is one of the bases.) Both of these are genic effects, which means that the expression of individual genes will be changed. But it does not mean that there will necessarily be any phenotypic manifestation of such mutations. In order to ascertain experimentally the occurrence of mutations, one usually has to effect scores of bases in the DNA molecule; otherwise no phenotypic change will take place.

There is also the possibility of inducing gross changes with certain chemical agents in the genetic material at the time the cell is undergoing its replication process, leading to cell division. During this process several highly regulated sequences occur, and a considerable number of substances are capable of interfering with completion of one or several of the steps involved. Some of these materials are able to block the completion of the intracellular process leading up to cell division. These are called "cytostatic" agents, an example of which is colchicine, an alkaloid of the autumn crocus. Other substances may bring about aberrations in the normal course of the process, and abnormal chromosome types (nondisjunct, ring-formed, broken, supernumerary, etc.) may result. These chemicals are referred to as "clastogens," or as agents causing "chromosome mutations."

But neither the cytostatic agents nor the clastogenic chemicals are true mutagens, in the sense of producing genic manifestations. Cells under the influence of such compounds may or may not survive. In the case of clastogens it is true that if germ cells are affected and if they do survive and undergo reproduction, they may give rise to genetically damaged progeny. However in higher life forms, where sexual reproduction occurs, the abnormal offspring will not necessarily transmit a chromosomal defect to the next generation, because in many instances spontaneous chromosomal repair takes place. By way of contrast, true genic mutations are always hereditarily transmitted, except in cases where back mutation occurs. Still, they are usually recessive genes, and will only very rarely give rise to any phenotypic expression.

Radiation Studies

The potential of ionizing radiation to induce mutations was first investigated by Herman Muller in the 1920s, using X-rays. Since that time tremendous quantities of data have been collected on the effects of acute and chronic irradiation, both in the laboratory and in nature. The discovery of the mutagenic effect of ionizing radiation enabled scientists to calculate the mutational frequencies which were due to background radiation, and to determine how these frequencies were altered, in a variety of organisms, by exposure to different radiation levels. Radiation biology became a scientific discipline in its own right, and its literature fills a small library. With the advent of more precise instrumentation suitable for the measurement of minute quantities of ionizing radiation, it became possible to establish both the spatial and temporal fluctuations of the background levels in nature and of low levels resulting from human activities. In many senses then it may be stated that we know more about radiation effects at both high and low levels than we do about any other environmental factor, although new assessments and new interpretations are constantly being made.

Penetrating ionizing radiation, such as X-rays, gamma rays, neutron flux, and cosmic rays, possesses a quality which makes it completely different from mutagenic chemicals. The latter must somehow be introduced into the body—through the alimentary tract, skin absorption, etc.—and they will be diluted and dispersed through the bloodstream before reaching individual cells, where they still have to cross the cellular boundaries and the protoplasm before even the possibility of affecting the nucleus can arise. On the other hand, radiation can directly penetrate to the interior of the body and can easily reach the nucleus of a cell. For this reason, among others, unquantified comparisons between the mutagenic potential of chemicals and of ionizing radiation serve only to obfuscate issues when clarification of degree of risk is what is most needed.

After some ten years of experimentation, the idea that ionizing radiation represents an exception to the threshold principle was proposed; and by the end of the 1950s, this had become a generally accepted concept. The "linearity theory of radiation-induced effects" states that no matter how small a quantity of irradiation reaches an organism, a deleterious effect may result. This hypothesis accepts the thesis that the natural background radiation levels—together with other factors—are continuously causing mutations, and that most of these mutations are detrimental, even though it is also accepted that mutations serve evolutionary purposes. The implication is that *any* addition to the natural background levels will increase the probability of radiation-induced effects. For more than 20 years this hypothesis has been elevated to the level of an accepted theory, with only a handful of dissenters. Where arguments have arisen about man's contributions to radiation in the environment, they have been about the degree of risk to the human population represented by small increases in radiation exposure over the natural background.

As we mentioned in Chapter 1, there was great interest aroused in radiation contaminants during the period when both the United States and the Soviet Union were engaging in atmospheric testing of nuclear weapons. After the Atmospheric Test Ban Treaty was achieved, however, generalized fears about low-level radioactivity in the environment died down for some years. In the fall of 1969, J. W. Gofman and A. R. Tamplin—two scientists working at the AEC's Livermore Laboratories—received considerable publicity which served to stir up these fears once more. Their calculations led them to conclude that unless the permissible radiation-exposure standards from nuclear power generators were reduced tenfold, large numbers of future genetic deaths and cancer occurrences in the hundreds of thousands could be predicted for the human population. They testified before the U.S. Senate Public Works Subcommittee on Air and Water Pollution, and their presentation was incorporated into the *Congressional Record.* Although the basis of their calculations was immediately refuted by other scientists, some errors in their mathematics pointed out, and their conclusions thrown into considerable doubt, the two scientists nevertheless initiated a public campaign demanding a reduction in the AEC radiation-exposure standards.

Now it is true, as with other kinds of contaminants, that there are certain human applications and man-made sources which *substantially* increase human exposure to radiation. The contribution of operating nuclear power generators, however, is not among them.

Each day, through X-rays, thousands of Americans blithely permit themselves to absorb ionizing radiation doses, often exceeding ten times that needed for diagnostic purposes. While no definite figures are available, many health physicists suspect that this superfluous radiation accounts for somewhere between 3,500 and 36,000 deaths, in the form of mutations, leukemia, thyroid cancer, bone cancer and general life-expectancy foreshortening. This may seem a small price to pay considering the benefits of radiation diagnostics. But, even these fatalities could all but be eliminated with extra care.

A survey by the U.S. Public Health Service indicates that 105 million radiographic examinations were taken in 1964. In addition there were 53.6 million dental, 10.5 million fluoroscopic and 3.4 million therapeutic examinations. Also, the use of such medical applications for X-rays is doubling every 13 years or less.

It is a statistical fact that mortality from leukemia among children whose mothers had undergone X-ray diagnosis during the fetal period is 40% higher than among comparable groups not so exposed.

An interesting sidelight to the promiscuous use of X-rays for examinations is that blacks are being exposed to as much as 50% more radiation than other races. Many technicians falsely believe that a black's bones are generally denser and harder and that their skin is less pervious to radiation than a white's. Actually, it might be best if technologists and radiologists were "color-blind."

Perhaps the most widely publicized electronic unit that can produce X-ray exposure is color television . . . . [They] may produce some 70 genetic deaths per year assuming that 14 million color television sets in the U.S. are operated at the maximum limit set by the NCRP [National Council on Radiation Protection] and that these sets are viewed on the average of 20 hours per week each by two persons at a distance of eight feet. Actually, many TV sets emit radiations *in excess* of the NCRP standard. A survey conducted last year indicated that 6% of 1124 sets surveyed exceed the NCRP recommendation and two sets overpowered the test meter, indicating at least 25 times the permissible dosage. (Morgan, 1969, pp. 47, 48; author's emphasis)

This lengthy quotation is from an article by Dr. Karl Z. Morgan, president of the International Radiation Protection Association. He estimates further that the genetic damage due to X-rays could be reduced to about 300 per year if proper precautionary measures, such as high-speed films and collimated X-ray beams, were used. On the other hand, to Dr. Morgan's calculations in relation to X-ray exposure one has to add the unknown but probably far greater number of people who are exposed to increments of radiation through home appliances such as microwave ovens, or as the result of the operation of radar, lasers, industrial X-ray equipment, and high-voltage vacuum switches.

It certainly does not seem that Dr. Morgan could be described as a scientist who is indifferent to the health hazards represented by radiation. In effect, he has for ten years been issuing warnings against the unnecessary exposure of people to diagnostic X-rays. Yet his calculations of the radiation risk to the population from the operation of nuclear power reactors are very slight indeed. "At present the radiation risk to the population from all AEC operations (including national laboratories, all other contractors, and licensees) and nuclear power reactor operations (but excluding fallout from weapons tests) would appear to account for no more than 18 deaths per year and perhaps by the end of the century to no more than 360 deaths per year (or 2,800 deaths per year if one includes future-generation genetic deaths). This is a very small and acceptable price to pay in view of the benefits derived and the magnitude of other risks which we commonly and willingly assume " (Morgan, 1971, p. 131).

Now both the calculations of Morgan and those of Gofman and Tamplin are based on acceptance of the linearity theory of radiation effects. Morgan's figures have been accepted by the majority of scientists, whereas those of Gofman and Tamplin have been repeatedly challenged, both on the basis of their assumptions and of errors in their mathematics. And yet the latter scientists have become heroes of the environmental movement, leading some phases of the battle against the construction of nuclear power facilities, while Morgan's voice has been drowned out. But certainly he is neither callous nor complacent about hazards to humans. He attempts to make quantitative distinctions between those human uses of radiation sources which may represent a real and unneccesary hazard to the human population, and those uses where the risks are very small and the benefits very great. He also proposes methods by which the risks from X-rays, for example,. could be substantially reduced. It is exactly this sort of approach that we would term responsible communication by a scientist to the lay public.

Doubts About the Linearity Theory

There have been all along a few persons who have doubted whether, in fact, there was no threshold level at some low dose even for ionizing radiation.

Investigating the mutagenic effects of ionizing radiation presents problems in downward extrapolation similar to those discussed in connection with "weak" carcinogens. In order to establish dose-response curves for low levels of radiation, exceedingly large numbers of experimental organisms would have to be investigated. Whereas for medium-range doses, such as 100 to 10,000 roentgens, dose-response curves can be relatively easily constructed for various organisms, to establish a relation between dose and effect at 5 r already requires over a million test specimens. Because there did not seem to be any evidence pointing to a no-effect level in the case of radiation, the majority of scientists have accepted the no-threshold idea. There are, however, some data pointing towards a threshold—or at least to the nonapplicability of the linearity theory at low dose ranges.

We want to mention briefly three lines of evidence related to this question. Until 1956 it was thought that mutations could not be induced in blue-green algae by radiation, since all attempts to do so up to that time were negative. It turned out, however, that earlier investigators were using subthreshold doses, which explains why they could not show an effect. It is now known that for several filamentous *Cyanophyta* 2,000 r will produce minimal mutations, and a dose-response curve can be observed at higher irradiation levels (see in Demeter, 1956). In general, blue-green algae are not radiosensitive. However, in principle, if a threshold can be shown for one group of nonsensitive organisms, there should be threshold levels for other groups of organisms, even though these might be orders of magnitude lower.

A second line of evidence may be drawn from observations on the effects of differing background radiation levels on whole populations. Background levels of terrestrial radiation show extreme spatial variations, which depend largely on the local distribution of radioactive material in the Earth's crust. For example, the usual background level in the River Thames is only 0.01 picocurie per liter; whereas in certain hot springs in Japan levels as high as 700,000 pCi/l may be found.

The mutational effects of terrestrial radiation have been extensively investigated during the past ten years. The results are not yet complete, but a number of very interesting observations have been reported. One of the most comprehensive studies was conducted by a British team on a population of wild rats which inhabit an island strip off the Malabar Coast of India (Grüneberg, 1964). This small island is covered with monazite sand, which is highly enriched with natural radioactivity originating from thorium. The background levels are about 7.5 times higher than those found on the subcontinent. The island is too far away from the mainland for the rats to swim across the water, and it is therefore certain that they have been isolated for at least several centuries from the mainland Indian population of the same species.

Exposure to the higher levels of radiation on the island for 500 rat generations should involve the cumulative effects of 500 r of gamma radiation in the strip population as against 67 r for that on the mainland. This is a considerable difference, which, according to expectations, should have resulted in a marked increase in mutation rate and easily observable phenotypic changes in the strip population. Investigations of the island rats and their counterparts on the mainland, however, did not establish any differences, although about 450 animals from each group were compared in terms of 47 separate traits.

The experimenters also investigated pregnant females in both populations for the numbers of living embryos, dead implants, and corpora lutea. (From such data one can calculate the rate of embryonic mortality both before and after implantation.) "The overall fertility and embryonic mortality was just about the same in both groups of populations," they concluded (Grüneberg, 1964, p. 224). Here again, the expectation that the island rats might show higher levels of embryonic mortality was not confirmed.

The British team left open the question of whether there is a "no effect" level for rats which is higher than the exposure even on the strip, or whether natural selection completely counterbalanced any effects which might have taken place. Nevertheless, the finding that even after several hundreds of generations of exposure to significantly higher radiation levels the island rat population showed neither phenotypic changes nor increased reproductive failure is an important one.

The third question bears on whether the linearity theory of radiation effects can be applied to exceedingly minute exposures as the cause of tumors or of cancer. In a recent paper, Rossi and Kellerer (1972) reported their assessment of dose-response curves which they established from data in the literature dealing with the induction of tumors in rats by relatively low doses of fission neutrons or X-rays. Since their report contains some complex mathematical proofs, we shall not bother the reader with the details. However, although the authors do not claim to have established a threshold at which radiation exposure will not induce cancer, they have shown that the extreme interpretation of linear radiation effects—one photon → one cell → tumor—cannot be correct. In their discussion, they write: ". . . it must be concluded that in the dose range investigated the carcinogenetic process cannot reflect radiation injury to individual cells in a population of noninteracting cells. . . . The process must therefore involve energy absorption by more than one cell, and the situation is too complicated to warrant a linear extrapolation to low doses" (Rossi and Kellerer, 1972, p. 202).

Chemical Mutagens

We turn now to the specific subject of chemical mutagenic agents, with the first point of discussion being how mutagenic chemicals can be quantitively compared in their activity with the effects of radiation. The standard procedure for establishing comparisons is to irradiate a test organism—usually *Drosophila* (common fruit fly)—with a known radiation dose and then to test different dosages of the mutagenic chemical on separate groups of the organism until the same effects are achieved as those produced by the radiation. It is customary to express the mutagenic activity of chemicals in comparison to 1,000 r, on a milligram-per-kilogram basis. Thus, for instance, Fahmy and Fahmy (1969) compiled a list of chemicals, most of them alkylating agents, in terms of 1,000 r activity. From their list we offer two examples. They give the activity of 10 to 100 mg/kg of nitrogen mustard as equivalent to 1,000 r. TEPA (triethylenephosphoramide)—an experimental insect sterilant—is much stronger, with the 1,000 r equivalent at 1 to 5 mg/kg.

To put these figures into some perspective, we should mention that a man exposed to normal radiation background originating from both cosmic and terrestrial sources, plus exposure to medical X-rays and other sources of radiation from the modern technical environment, accumulates approximately 5 r during his 30 years of reproductive life.

Since it is customary to express chemical mutagenic activities in terms of radiation exposure—for which the linearity theory is generally accepted—one should perhaps not be too surprised that scientists working with chemical mutagens are championing the idea that the concept of linearity of effect should be extended to include these agents as well. The Fahmys claim that they have demonstrated the validity of this concept, at least as far as the strong mutagens are concerned. However, whatever experimental, mathematical, or verbal manipulations are used to defend such a thesis, in the context of mutational effects due to natural background the thesis loses its meaningfulness, since linearity implies zero effect at zero dose, and there is no zero mutagenic dose in nature.

It would seem in order to review what is known about random mutation rates in man due to background radiation. It is thought that the approximate rate is one point mutation for every five individuals in one human reproductive generation, which is 30 years. The new mutations will be added to those already in the gene pool, which are inherited from previous generations, and eventually in some individuals the load of genetic disabilities will become high enough either to cause death (usually intrauterine) or, if they survive to maturity, to cause sterility. This is what is meant by genetic death. It is also calculated that the frequency of genetic extinction in man is one individual in 200 per generation. In this context it can be seen that the figure given by Morgan of 18 genetic deaths per year (in a population of 200 million people) due to emissions from nuclear power generators is indeed minuscule.

In order to give a quantitative expression to the potential damage of radiation, it is customary to speak about the "doubling dose," by which term is denoted the exposure in roentgens which would be required to double the natural mutational rate in the genetic constitution of man. Different authorities give estimates varying from 35 to 70 r. If we accept the lowest value, it means that exposure of both parents to 35 r will result in the doubling of the spontaneous mutation rate in their offspring.

In an interview in the *New York Times* (cited in Fahmy, 1969, p. 406), Dr. Fahmy stated: "The amount of pesticide chemicals man is now absorbing from his environment is enough to double the normal mutation rate." To begin with, there is no evidence whatsoever to substantiate this statement. Dr. Fahmy, who works mainly with strong alkylating agents—which are not permitted for general pesticide use at all—was apparently extrapolating his own findings on the most powerful of these chemicals to the general distribution of any and all pesticides in the environment, which is a totally unjustified example of non-think. When challenged about this remark at the New York Academy of Sciences meeting on "The Biological Effects of Pesticides in Mammalian Systems" on the same day of the press release, he qualified his statement: "One has to differentiate between a word of caution and a shriek of alarm. . . . I must emphasize that doubling of the natural mutation rate in the human population may not be a very serious situation. A great many such naturally occurring molecules as histones, DNA, and RNA are released in the body, through degeneration of cells, in amounts that probably more than double the spontaneous mutation rate in man" (*ibid.*, p. 406). Now it is all very well that Dr. Fahmy explained to his scientific colleagues that even had he been correct, his remark to the newspaper was really not significant or meaningful in terms of human development, but why did he not tell that to the *New York Times* interviewer, if he did not mean the original statement as a "shriek of alarm"? The implication of his qualification is that even in the purest environment, man's own body releases enough chemicals to more than double the rate of radiation-induced point mutations.

The problems involved in testing minute quantities of compounds which are found in the environment in small amounts, and are suspected of being weak mutagens, are similar to those surrounding the low-activity environmental carcinogens. Sanders (1969), while discussing the possibility of showing the mutagenic effects of chemicals on the human population, pointed out that because of the extreme complexity and variability of the human genetic material, investigations of a closely controlled population of 20 million people studied over a period of 25 to 50 years would be necessary to supply rigorous proof that any one of the suspected chemical mutagens actually causes genetic damage in man. His numbers are based on the assumption that overt expression of such damage would occur in 1 out of 1,000 births; whereas it is usually assumed that overtly expressed genetic damage occurs only in approximately 1 in 100,000 births.

Since such observations of the human population are not feasible, one must turn to test systems, if one is persuaded that the question is an important one to investigate. During the past 40 or so years a number of test systems have been worked out to ascertain whether or not a particular chemical can induce mutations, and if so, how it acts. Most of these deal with viruses, bacteria, yeasts, or higher plants such as onion root tips, barley, and *Tradescantia*. None of these tests was initiated for investigating the significance to man of low levels of possible environmental mutagens. They were designed to elucidate genetic mechanisms and, in more recent years, they have served to establish the molecular biological basis of genetic research. Tests were also developed in which the cytogenetic effects of clastogens on tissue cultures derived from higher animals could be studied.

Over the course of time, dose-response curves in these various test systems have been established for a number of chemicals with mutagenic potential. It was found, for instance, that the absolute minimum number of nitrite molecules which could induce a point mutation in a single cell is about 10^8. (This is four orders of magnitude greater than the quantity of any substance needed for its presence to be registered by the cell.) And, according to a statement by Ercegovich(1969, p. 410),4.9×10^{14} molecules of symmetrical triazine are needed to achieve base substitution leading to a defined phenotypic effect in an *E. coli* bacterium. If Ercegovich is correct, this means that the *E. coli* cell must be surrounded by 1,000 times its own weight of the pure compound in order to achieve such an effect. In other terms, base substitution only takes place with this kind of compound if the cell is literally swimming in what are vast quantities, on a cell-weight basis, of the chemical. It should be obvious that the results from such kinds of testing have no meaning whatsoever with respect to the question of human mutagenic hazard from use of small quantities of the chemical in the environment. Such studies are useful only to investigate the theoretical aspects of base substitution and, as Ercegovich himself pointed out, they are not relevant to conditions encountered in nature, or even in a man-influenced environment.

The "Relevant" Tests

For every field of specialization in the life sciences, it appears that there are at least a handful of professional worriers who have doctoral degrees and who manage to keep public anxieties alive rather than allaying them when possible, or just doing their research quietly when they are working on unknowns. Inquiry into the risks represented by chemical mutagens in the environment is no exception. In fact, it is one of the more fashionable areas for concerned scientists to get involved in these days. The worried and supposedly prudent point of view on this subject is voiced by the "Panel on Mutagenicity of Pesticides" of the Mrak Commission, whose members wrote: "We must remember . . . that genetic damage is irreversible by any process that we know of now. The risk to future generations, though difficult to assess in precise terms, is nevertheless very real" (Mrak *Report.,* 1969, p. 571).

We want to discuss just how these risks are being assessed, but we should first like to comment on the opening sentence. It seems very peculiar that a panel addressing itself to questions of mutagenicity and being supposedly composed of persons with some knowledge of the field could write that genetic damage is "irreversible by any process that we know of now" in the year 1969. Six full years earlier Russell's volume called *Repair from Genetic Radiation* (1963) had appeared, in which the subject of cellular repair—both DNA and chromosomal—after induced damages was treated in great detail. This monograph and subsequent work on the same theme have given clear indications that the self-repair capability of organisms after genetic injury is enormous. True, the resilience of organisms in effecting self-repair certainly should not be taken as an indication that people can expose themselves blithely to quantities of agents which are really mutagenic, but the information about self-repair is as important as information about damage, if one's task is to assess risks. Not only does this panel fail to mention self-repair; they make a statement which directly contradicts facts recognized by everyone in related fields. What could be their reasoning, or their purposes?

This same panel, in recommending mutagenicity testing on a vast scale for all pesticides now licensed or under consideration for use, wrote that there are a battery of tests for mutagenicity which are "entirely practical and feasible . . . precise, efficient, and relatively inexpensive . . . practical, sensitive, and relevant" (*ibid.,* p. 572). But, after reviewing the available tests, one is left with the impression that while many of them may indeed be relatively inexpensive and not too difficult to carry out, there is only one which has some relevance to human conditions, and that is the approach called testing for "dominant lethal mutations," which was originally developed by A. J. Bateman (1966).

The dominant lethal assay has as its basis the consideration that, if a mutagenic agent is administered to male animals during their cycle of spermiogenesis and the animals are then mated with untreated virgin females, those sperm cells carrying seriously damaged chromosome compartments, fertilizing the female ovum, will result in nonviable offspring: i.e., the embryos will not survive to term. After having been mated with the treated males, the pregnant females are sacrificed around the fifteenth day of gestation, and the implantation sites, live embryos, late fetal deaths, and corpora lutea are counted and compared with those of the controls (females mated with untreated males). From these counts, the total number of preimplantation and postimplantation deaths can be determined. If the total of preimplantation and *early* postimplantation deaths is significantly higher in the experimental females than in the controls, this should be an indicator of dominant lethal mutations induced by the chemical in the male spermia. On the other hand, if it is mainly the preimplantation losses which are high, the indication may be interpreted as nonmutagenic sperm damage and/or the induction of male sterility. It is therefore important to count the corpora lutea, which appear as small yellow protuberances on the ovary, since these indicate the number of ripened ova which were available for fertilization. The preimplantation loss refers to the *difference* between the number of implants in the uterus and the number of corpora lutea.

Most of the work using this method for mutagenicity testing has been carried out by Samuel Epstein and his coworkers. We should therefore like to comment on some of his publications and on his application of this technique.

In discussing the kinds of information which can be derived from the dominant lethal test, Epstein and Shafner wrote in 1968: "The diversity of chemical potential mutagens to which man is exposed urges the development of practical screening procedures. The dominent lethal test seems suitable, especially because 80 per cent of gene mutations in man are attributable to dominant autosomal traits. The test, however, provides *no information on point or recessive mutations nor on non-mutagenic sperm damage, which may, nevertheless, modify nucleic acid bases"* (Epstein and Shafner, 1968, p. 386; our emphasis).

By 1970 Epstein had apparently forgotten his own qualifications about the limitations of what can be learned from the test, as well as some of the interference factors, such as nonmutagenic damage to spermia, which he mentioned in the 1968 paper. By that time he had also abandoned one important but troublesome aspect of Bateman's original design for the dominant lethal test — that is, the counting of corpora lutea. The apparent reason behind this "simplification" of the test is Epstein's agreement with the following statement by the Mrak Commission Mutagenicity Panel, which he cochaired: ". . . corpora lutea counts, which are notoriously difficult, laborious, and inaccurate in mice and afford a measure of total fertilized zygotes, can be omitted and numbers of total implants in test animals can be related to those in controls, thus affording a simple measure of preimplantation losses" (Mrak *Report,* 1969, p. 597).

Corpora lutea counts in mice are indeed "notoriously laborious," as anyone who has ever performed them would attest. But the method is not an inaccurate one if it is carried out properly. Inaccuracies in such counts reflect performance capabilities of individual researchers and are not inherent limitations in the method itself. It is certainly not good science to abandon a technique merely because people are trying to cut corners or have difficulty seeing in the dissecting microscope. On the other hand, the suggested substitute *is* inaccurate as a method, since it rests on the totally false assumption that in each female mouse an equal number of ova are ripened and fertilized.

We wish now to examine a publication by Epstein and his coworkers (1970a) in which the authors report that they demonstrated the mutagenicity of TMP (trimethylenephosphate), a gasoline additive, on the basis of the dominant lethal assay. Since several aspects of this study indicate hurried and imprecise work, we shall have to explain in some detail what the experimenters did and why the reported conclusions cannot be accepted.

The investigators administered doses from 500 to 2,000 mg/kg of TMP in single intraperitoneal injections to seven groups of male Swiss mice; and to two other groups they gave 500 or 1,000 mg/kg daily, by gavage, up to total doses of 2,500 and 5,000 mg/kg respectively. These doses are described in both the abstract and in the conclusion of the paper as *subtoxic,* which is a serious misrepresentation, as the higher doses are in the sublethal or lethal range (Jackson and Jones, 1968).

Both the injected and gavaged doses were dissolved in 0.1 ml of distilled water. The highest injected dose would amount to 100 mg in total for an adult mouse weighing 50 g. This dose was "diluted" in 0.1 ml of distilled water and injected intraperitoneally. (The dilution in this dose range must have been very slight indeed since TMP is a liquid and, though somewhat heavier than distilled water, 100 mg of the substance would approach 0.1 ml in volume.) We calculated the osmotic pressure of this solution, which would be about 180 atmospheres. That of physiological saline is 2.68 atmospheres. Since every lab technician should know that one cannot inject intraperitoneally solutions which exceed much more than double the osmotic pressure of saline without serious risk of causing peritonitis and local necrosis, both the high-dose injected series (where the osmotic pressure was 67 times that of saline) and the middle dose could have caused any number of artifacts invalidating the results—including nonmutagenic sperm damage. The oral doses were also concentrated enough to cause gastritis and possible ulcerations.

In any event, whatever the general condition of the animals might have been, the experimenters went ahead and mated them for eight weeks, caged with three virgin females weekly. Since no attempt was made to observe the appearance of vaginal plugs, conception was estimated at midweek and the pregnant females were sacrificed somewhere between the ninth and fifteenth days of gestation. Corpora lutea were not counted, and the data were reported in terms of total implants and early fetal deaths. In Table 1 of the publication, where the early deaths were tabulated for the different dosage groups, only in the second week in the females mated with males which received intraperitoneal injections was there a suggestion of a dose-response relationship. The expected picture of variation between the controls and the low-dosage groups showed no pattern, with one exception. There, however, the high fetal death rate occurred at the eighth week after treatment, which contradicts the emphasis in the text on effects during the first three weeks. It is also interesting to note that occasionally the high-dosage groups showed considerably fewer fetal deaths than the low-dosage groups, even in the first weeks after treatment. One can compare, for instance, results from the gavage experiment in the second week, where no fetal deaths occurred with the 1,000 mg/kg dose; whereas at 50 mg/kg the table shows 4.08 fetal deaths—the highest mean reported.

The results showing "mutagenic" effects mainly in the first three weeks are also surprising, since Jackson and Jones, when testing the same compound on mice at about half the highest dose used by the Epstein group, found complete sterility (no offspring) in matings during the first and second week after treatment, and greatly reduced fertility during the third week. Jackson and Jones also used radioactively labeled TMP to trace the metabolism and excretion of the compound. They found that its elimination occurs very rapidly when administered orally (in about 3 hours), while it is much slower when administered intraperitoneally, and "metabolites could be found up to 16 hours in the urine" (Jackson and Jones, 1968, p. 591).

The Epstein group, on the other hand, wrote that the effects of TMP are cumulative and depend on total dose administered, irrespective of route. There is nothing in their data to support this claim.

Jackson and Jones were cited as a reference by Epstein et al., but there are at least five major discrepancies between the two sets of findings, and none of these was explained or discussed. The most important is that Jackson and Jones repeatedly pointed out that TMP's "predominant effect is a 'functional' type of sterilizing action involving post-meiotic cells (spermatids and spermatozoa), so that *intact* motile sperm remain available, but are rendered incompetent" (*ibid.,* p. 591).

Despite contradictions with earlier findings, serious technical flaws, and unconvincing results, Epstein et al. conclude that "subtoxic concentrations of trimethylphosphate administered orally or parenterally to male mice, produce mutagenic effects, dependent on dosage, in the dominant lethal assay" (Epstein, et al., 1970a, p. 168). Although they admit that not enough is known about human exposure to assess the "potential human genetic hazard due to TMP" they end by suggesting that further information about TMP's biologically active products in automobile exhausts—among other things—should be made available.

The pyrolosis product of TMP is known and it is known to be inert. However, Epstein could have estimated the human genetic hazard from unburned gasoline had he wanted to accept at least one of Jackson and Jones' data, which is that in rats—much more sensitive to TMP's spermatogenic inhibitory effects than mice— the minimal amount required for action is 100 mg/kg by stomach tube for five consecutive days. Since according to Epstein TMP concentration in gasoline is 0.25 grams per gallon, a human male could reach the minimal effective dose by drinking 28 gallons of gasoline daily for five consecutive days—provided that man is as sensitive as the rat.

Two years later, Dean and Thorpe (1972), taking the results of Epstein et al. at face value, attempted to use TMP as a positive control in the testing of dichlorvos with the dominant lethal assay. They were working with CF1 mice, and they did not go above the 2,000 mg/kg level of administration. To their surprise, they lost 50 percent of the mice within a week after dosing at this level, and one mouse given 1,000 mg/kg also died. Furthermore, only two of the females mated with the remaining males became pregnant during the first week and there were no pregnancies in the second week. It would thus seem that these findings confirm those of Jackson and Jones, who described 2,000 mg/kg as about the LD_{50} in mice and who found antifertility rather than mutagenic effects from high doses of the compound.

Exactly how Epstein et al. managed to keep their animals alive and get them to breed at such extremely high reported doses is difficult to fathom, especially when one adds to the high doses the factor of osmotic pressure in their injected series. Perhaps the dilutions were incorrectly prepared and the researchers were not actually working in the dosage ranges reported. In any event, the discrepancies with the two other publications are too great to be explained merely as a reflection of using a different strain of mouse.

We have reviewed this study of Epstein and his coworkers on trimethyl phosphate not because TMP is an important compound but because, having granted that the dominant lethal assay is the mutagenicity test which comes the closest to having some relevance to humans, being at least an *in vivo* mammalian test system, it seems important to point out—though it should not be necessary to do so—that the experimental technique is worthless unless it is properly executed. Epstein himself is a talented and well-trained research scientist. However, in the last few years he has taken an extremist stance on environmental chemicals and become something of a crusader. While the quality of this particular paper may not be typical of all of his work, its sloppiness, imprecision, and inconclusiveness are indicators that when scientific researchers embrace highly emotional positions about environmental threats, they may become so anxious to demonstrate that one or another chemical is dangerous that the quality of their experimental work deteriorates.

One can also state that even had the experiments been carried through correctly, and even if one could accept that Epstein et al. did demonstrate TMP to be mutagenic at "subtoxic" levels, the relevance to the human population of applying the dominant lethal assay to the study of a chemical to which man is exposed only in trace quantities must be subject to the same qualifications as those discussed in connection with carcinogens and teratogens. We have said this before, but at a risk of being repetitive, we again remind the reader that chemicals do not act like ionizing radiation, which can penetrate through the body and through cell walls. They must enter the organism through ingestion, inhalation, or absorption; they will be dispersed before they have any opportunity to reach the reproductive cells, and they must be present in substantial molecular quantities in order to cross the cell barrier and interact with nuclear material.

It is unlikely that Epstein would accept the importance of these qualifications, and he seems to be persuaded that testing for the mutagenicity of chemicals is now reliable and that the available test systems are practical, relevant, and informative enough to serve as the basis for regulatory decisions of a highly restrictive nature. Illustrative of his current crusade in favor of extreme prudence about chemicals are the following comments on extending the Delaney clause, which he set down in a 1970 editorial in *Nature:*

> . . . the Delaney amendment represents protection vital to the safety and interest of consumers. Special pleadings that this amendment is unduly restrictive reflect an apparent failure to comprehend the potential human hazards involved. Indeed, there are compelling reasons for extending the Delaney amendment to other categories of synthetic chemicals besides food additives, and to teratogenicity and mutagenicity besides carcinogenicity. Due consideration should also be given to applying the concept of the Delaney amendment, extended to include mutagenicity and teratogenicity, to undefined or partially defined mixtures of pollutants, such as automobile exhausts. (Epstein, 1970, p. 819)

It does not take much reflection to conclude that such a proposition would include all combustible materials (coal, gasoline, other fuels, and even leaves), since undefined mixtures of air pollutants are produced by burning, and among the products are some agents which would be regarded by certain researchers as "active" in one of the three categories discussed above. The same would hold for all waste effluents. Furthermore, there is not a single pesticide or fertilizer which has not been described by someone using one of the current methods for carcinogenicity, mutagenicity, and teratogenicity testing as showing some effect at some level in some species in at least one of these systems. Were such an extended safety clause to be enacted, and provided that one accepts at face value the conclusions of all publications in the literature, these substances would have to go as well. One thing is sure; between the time of enacting and enforcing such a piece of legislation and the time when economic ruin would inevitably set in, there would be plenty of opportunities for independent scientists to test the effects of the thousands of individual compounds and their combinations.

Perspective

In raising doubts about the validity or the relevance of many of the current claims about the subtle, long-term human hazards associated with modern technologies, we have taken the risk in this chapter, perhaps more than in any other, of appearing to be the devil's advocates. But as it has oft been said that the devil appears in many guises, who can know for a certainty the identity of his spokesmen?

Here, as throughout much of this book, we have been concerned with matters of precision in scientific work, as well as with assessments of the meaning or significance to man of findings which emerge from well-executed research. But if we have written unkindly about the "professional worriers," it is not alone because we sometimes find their thinking undistinguished, but more importantly because we believe they do a disservice to the people in spreading abroad the theme that man's activities have released the lid of a whole new Pandora's box of human ills. We do not wish to minimize real dangers, but rather to suggest that in most cases plagues of the mind are more in question than bodily hazards. Besides, even in Pandora's box there was hope at the bottom, while our modern spokesmen for extreme caution seem all to often to be submerged in their own gloom.

In our usual manner, we have introduced some polemic elements even into our discussion of these terrible topics. We should like to close with a citation which summarizes the principal thrust of our argument in this chapter, but does so in the tone of sweet reason, if you will. The passage is taken from the main body of the Mrak Report on Pesticides—quite another sort of document from the three special panels on the carcinogenicity, teratogenicity, and mutagenicity of pesticides which we have criticized—even though the latter appear in the same volume.

The members of the "Subcommittee on Effects of Pesticides on Man," chaired by Leon Golberg, wrote a subsection called "The Need for Perspective," from which we quote. Although the remarks of the authors are, of course, specifically about pesticides, they can equally well be applied to most other forms of environmental contaminants.

> Some general explanatory comments are needed on the subject of irreversible long-term effects of pesticides. From the standpoint of the toxicologist all such effects are equally undesirable, whatever their nature, or whatever organ system involved. In other words, to the expert in the field, the hazard of development of peripheral neuropathy or aplastic anemia must be taken just as seriously as risks of carcinogenesis, teratogenesis, or mutagenesis. There is a tendency on the part of the lay public, the news media, and even among some scientists who specialize in the areas of cancer, or birth defects, or genetics, to regard these particular hazards as transcending all others and, therefore, claiming most immediate and urgent emphasis.
>
> Whatever one's point of view, there is an inescapable factor in this situation that is often overlooked. This is the difficulty of establishing with any certainty carcinogenic, teratogenic, or mutagenic potential for most compounds that are only weakly active in one or other or all these directions. A powerful carcinogen such as diethylnitrosamine or aflatoxin (or unequivocal mutagens such as some alkylating agents), presents no difficulty in clear-cut characterization of effect in animals and in assessment of the carcinogenic hazard presented to man. But pesticides do not pose such straightforward problems. Methods for detecting weak carcinogenic potency are still inadequate to provide unequivocal results and hence leave room for differences in interpretation. Methods for evaluating weak mutagenic potential in mammalian systems are even more primitive, and the results even more difficult to apply for practical purposes. Even in the area of teratogenesis it can be said that extrapolation of animal results to man is fraught with great uncertainty.
>
> Such being the present parlous state of the art, one need hardly be surprised that differences of opinion should exist among scientists knowledgeable in the field of toxicology. Even more diverse are the views expressed regarding regulatory action to be taken on the basis of experimental findings. It may be argued that any well-founded suspicion against a compound should suffice to have its use restricted or totally prohibited. Prudence, it would seem, demands no less. At the risk of appearing to be imprudent, one must point to the inescapable fact that there is no chemical present anywhere in our environment, and especially any natural compound of our diet, that is incapable of yielding alarming results in some biological systems at high enough levels of exposure. Consequently, the circumstances of exposure are of fundamental importance in assessing safety.

Viewed in this light, the attitude that it is impossible to define a safe level for man of a weak carcinogen, or a weak mutagen, is a retrogressive approach to a problem that will not be solved by prohibiting from use every compound possessing an index of suspicion, however low. The argument is indisputable that, despite our state of ignorance, or even because of it, we ought not to add to the existing burden of carcinogens, or mutagens, in our environment. But a generalization of this sort must be tempered by quantitative considerations. If the additional hazard represented by a compound is in all probability trivial, then we have a responsibility to weigh those benefits conferred by use of the compound against the hazard that its presence in the environment represents.

The key issue posed by this line of reasoning is the determination of what constitutes a trivial addition to the existing burden in the environment. The sad fact we have to face is the almost total absence of information on the existing burden of carcinogens, mutagens and teratogens *naturally* present in food, drink, water, air, etc. Not the smallest effort has been made to assess this background, using the available tests, so as to achieve some perspective in judging the results of these same tests with new compounds. Man's exposure over countless generations to a wide variety of naturally occurring toxicants, and the known effects of such exposure (in terms of morbidity and mortality) should be used as a firm baseline from which to judge additional hazards. For example, we know that man and animals constantly ingest in food and drink a variety of agents that are liver toxins and carcinogens. One might therefore anticipate that liver cancer would be a major problem throughout the world. In fact it is so rare that those localized areas of high incidence are almost certainly attributable to special circumstances peculiar to the regions involved. In the United States the incidence of liver cancer is low and there is no evidence that it is rising. Thus, despite lifelong exposure of the entire population to numerous weak — and even potent — natural carcinogens in food and drink, the actual hazard in practice is, as far as we can tell, very small. It is background information of this sort that is urgently needed before assessment of hazard to man from new compounds can be based on realistic judgment. (Mrak *Report*, 1969, pp. 261–263)

PART III

THE PESTICIDE BUGABOO

Throughout the first chapters of this book we have here and there made serious allegations about the scientific judgments and motivations of some of the leaders of the environmental movement who are members of the scientific community. In order that the reader should not be put in the position of merely weighing our words against those of the environmentalists we intend to devote the whole of this section of our book to a detailed documentation of one particular environmental issue: the claim that nature has been 'and is being seriously contaminated by the use of synthetic chemical pesticides, especially those which persist for a relatively long period before degrading into nonactive metabolites.

277

In the next chapters we shall be dealing principally with the well-known and by now infamous compound: DDT. However, as some mention will be made of other insecticides, pesticides, and methods of pest control, we shall begin with a few general remarks on this broad subject.

The word "pesticide" denotes a large number of chemical, physical, and biological agents. In professional usage it is interchangeable with the term "economic poison." This term is defined in the Federal Insecticide, Fungicide, and Rodenticide Act (FIFRA) as: ". . . any substance or mixture of substances intended for preventing, destroying, repelling or mitigating any insects, rodents, nematodes, fungi, or weeds or any other forms of life declared to be pests; any substance or mixture of substances intended for use as a plant regulator, defoliant or desiccant." While many laymen tend to think of pesticides in terms of insecticides only, this definition tells us that in its broad usage, the word includes also rodenticides, herbicides, fungicides, and nematocides.* It also comprehends some methods, such as the use of repellents, which do not involve direct application of a chemical to destroy the pest. Some approaches to pest control (the old-fashioned mouse trap or the contemporary effort to develop crop strains resistant to certain common pest infestations) do not involve the use of a substance at all; which of these one views as part of professional methods for pest control is best left to common sense.

It ought to be obvious that because of the very large number of agents which can be used to achieve any of the objectives enumerated in the above definition, it is highly misleading to discuss issues bearing on the subject of pesticides without focusing on one specific agent, or at the very least, on a group of similar agents. Space does not permit enumeration, much less description, of all the compounds which are licensed for use in the United States or elsewhere in the world at the present time for pest control. However, we shall be writing about insecticides in some detail, and for the reader's reference, we are including on the following pages two tables (Tables 6 and 7) which may be helpful. The first is a compilation of the most important diseases carried by pest vectors and those pesticides used for their control, identified according to type by one of the Roman numerals in the categories below. The second shows the agricultural uses on a global basis (excluding the United States) of the organochlorine insecticides.

Modern insecticides are conveniently grouped into five major categories, the first three of which refer to chemical affinities.

I. Chlorinated hydrocarbons, such as DDT, dieldrin, endrin, toxaphene, BHC, heptachlor, and so forth.

---

* One has to point out, on the other hand, that while many of the most commonly used medical drugs, such as antibiotics, might seem to be included in this broad definition, they are not subsumed under the term "economic poisons."

Table 6. *DISEASES, THEIR VECTORS, AND PESTICIDES USED FOR CONTROL*
(after Galley, 1971)

Disease	Vector	Pesticide	Method of use and comments
Malaria	Mosquitos Anopheles spp	DDT (I)	(1) Adulticide—sprayed on interior of dwellings. (2) Larvicide—sprayed on water courses.
Yellow fever (Africa) Hemorrhagic dengue (Asia)	Mosquito Aedes aegypti	Malathion (II) Abate (II)	(1) Larvicide—sprayed on water courses. (2) Adulticide—aerosol fogs.
Filariasis	Mosquito Culex fatigans	Fenthion (II) Dursban (II) Malathion (II)	Larvicide—where it can be afforded; sprayed on polluted-water breeding sites. Larvicide—sprayed on polluted-water breeding sites. Adulticide—ULV application.
Sleeping sickness	Tsetse flies Glossina spp	DDT, dieldrin (I)	Adulticides—residual application on selected vegetation (resting sites of the fly).
Onchocerciasis	Black flies (Simulium spp	DDT (I)	Larvicide—applied to river streams. (Use of methoxychlor, dursban, and abate being investigated.)
Bubonic plague	Oriental rat flea (Xenopsylla cheopis)	DDT (I)	10% dust to rat runways.
Typhus	Body louse (Pediculus humanus)	DDT (I) BHC (I)	10% dust DDT or 1% dust BHC applied inside clothing: if resistance to these is present. Carbaryl or Malathion dusts are used.
Leishmaniasis	Sandflies (Phlebotomus spp.)	DDT (I)	Adulticide—sprayed on interior of dwellings.
Chagas disease	Reduviid bugs (Triatoma spp)	Dieldrin (I) BHC (I)	Adulticide—sprayed on interior of dwellings.

Table 6. *(continued)*

Disease	Vector	Pesticide	
Bilharziasis	Aquatic and amphibious snails	Copper sulfate (IV) Pentochenophenol (IV) Bayluscide (IV) Frescon (IV)	Snail-infested waters treated with solutions, suspensions, and emulsions of active materials. No concerted international program yet in existence. (Bayluscide and frescon very much more active than copper sulfate or pentochenophenol.)

Table 7. *USE PATTERN OF PERSISTENT ORGANOCHLORINE INSECTICIDES ON MAJOR CROPS (after Ling, Whittemore, and Turtle, 1972)*

Crop	Areas of major use of organochlorine insecticides	Insecticides	Pests
Cotton	Mexico, Nicaragua, Egypt, Sudan, Brazil, Guatemala, Colombia, Australia, Turkey, Uganda, Ivory Coast, El Salvador	various	Boll weevils, leafworms, lace bugs, stinkbugs, cutworms, thrips, jassids, cotton stainers, tortrix larvae, lygus, mites, armyworms, whiteflies, aphids, pink bollworms, spiny bollworms, loopers.
		cyclodienes	Soil insects.
Rice	Japan, India, Indonesia, Cambodia, Colombia, Venezuela, Taiwan, Brazil, Spain	BHC	Stem borers, armyworms, hoppers, beetles.
		endrin	Stem borers, hoppers, rice bugs, gallflies, jassids.
		DDT	Cutworms, armyworms, flea beetles, loopers, paddy borers, paddy rice jassids, leafhoppers.
		toxaphene	Cutworms.
		aldrin	Termites, rice water weevils, *Gryllotolpa*, *Tipula*, paddy root weevils, paddy grasshoppers.

Table 7. *(continued)*

Crop	Areas of major use of organochlorine insecticides	Insecticides	Pests
Other cereals (corn, small grains, sorghum, etc.)	India, U.K., Mexico, Upper Volta, Niger, Turkey	BHC	Crickets, cutworms, wireworms, myriads, lepidopterous larvae, *Tipulidae*. Soil pests.
	France, Colombia, Chile, Mexico, Turkey, Spain, India, Argentina, Japan, Greece, East Africa	cyclodienes	
Vegetables (excluding potatoes)	India, Japan, Mexico, Spain	BHC	Vegetable pests, generally.
	Mexico, Spain, Japan, India, Chile, U.K., Thailand, South Africa	DDT	Cutworms, bollworms, whiteflies, jassids, fruit borers, webworms, cabbage moths, flea beetles, weevils, armyworms.
Onions, tomatoes, chilies, cabbage	Japan, Italy, Spain, France, Portugal	cyclodienes	Soil pests.
Potatoes and sweet potatoes	France, Spain, Brazil, Colombia, Peru, U.K., Japan, Greece, Taiwan	cyclodienes	Wireworms and other soil pests.
	Brazil, Colombia, Mexico, Australia	DDT	Thrips, tuber moths, armyworms, blister beetles, flea beetles, Colorado beetles.
Sugar beets	Belgium, Italy, France, Spain, Greece, Chile, Turkey	aldrin heptachlor	Soil and ground-surface pests, e.g., *Agriotes, Agrotis, Gryllotolpa, Melolontha, Millipedes, Lixus, Cleonis, Pegomyia*.
Sugarcane	Mexico, Australia, India, Brazil	BHC lindane	Leafhoppers, whiteflies, termites, soldier flies, borers, cane beetles.
	Ivory Coast, Taiwan, India	endrin	Borers.
	South Africa	dieldrin	*Heteronychus licas*.
	India, Brazil, Mexico, Pakistan, Taiwan	aldrin heptachlor	Soil pests.
Tobacco	Mexico, Australia, South and East Africa	DDT	Leafworms, bollworms, thrips, hornworms, flea
	Mexico	BHC cyclodienes	beetles, leaf miners, stinkbugs, cutworms.
	Japan, Italy, South Africa, Mexico, Colombia, Greece, Spain		Various soil pests.

Table 7. *(continued)*

Crop	Areas of major use of organochlorine insecticides	Insecticides	Pests
Oil seeds (sesame, soy-beans, peanuts, sunflower, etc.)	India, Japan	BHC	Various.
	Argentina, Brazil, India, Japan, Colombia, Nica-ragua	DDT	Various.
	Colombia, France, Brazil, Venezuela	toxaphene	Lepidopterous larvae, earworms, armyworms, loopers.
Crops in general	Asia and Africa	dieldrin BHC	Locusts.

II. Organophosphate esters, such as parathion, malathion, TEPP, systox, etc.

III. Carbamate derivatives, such as sevin or zectran.

IV. Other chemicals not falling into one of the above categories, such as copper sulfate, nitrophenols, and so forth.

V. Some naturally occurring compounds or agents like rotenone, pyrethrum, nicotine, and *Bacillus thuringiensis.*

Of the groups of synthetic organic pesticides, the first to find wide applications after World War II were the organochlorines (another term for the chlorinated hydrocarbons). DDT was the first of these to be used on a broad scale for disease control, in agriculture and in forestry, and it remains a favored insecticide, as it is highly efficient, safe to use, and inexpensive to produce. After the introduction of the chlorinated hydrocarbons, the more dangerous and persistent inorganic substances like lead arsenate were almost completely eliminated from use.

The organophosphate compounds were discovered in Germany prior to World War II, and they were manufactured on a large scale as part of the German war effort, for possible deployment as nerve gases. Their uses in pest control, however, began only in the late 1940s.

The carbamates are often called "second-generation pesticides," since they were developed and introduced only in the 1950s. Actually, most members of the carbamate group are used as fungicides and herbicides, but those which are applied as insecticides were synthesized to achieve both high target specificity and low nontarget toxicity.

Although the activities, physico-chemical behavior and uses of individual compounds within these categories are by no means identical, a few generalizations can be made about the first three groups. The way in which characteristics common to each group are evaluated depends on the specific purposes for which they are being used, as well as on the point of view of the person who is discussing them.

The organochlorine compounds have a broad spectrum of target organisms and a relatively long residence time. This broad spectrum, however, is restricted specifically to the arthropods and, more closely, to insects in the arthropod phylum. In concentrations effective against insect species, they have practically no effect on any of the other major phyla, including the two most important: the mollusks and the vertebrates. Furthermore, the toxicity of DDT, the prime representative of this group of compounds, shows a negative correlation with temperature (that is, the higher the body temperature of the organism, the less toxic DDT will be for it). It has long been recognized that bees do not seem to be much affected by DDT, but the reasons for this were not clear. Recently, however, it has been shown that bees and wasps, unlike other insects, are able to regulate their body temperature, maintaining it at around 27° C, or from 5 to 15 degrees above the ambient (Heinrich, 1972). This factor of relative exemption from DDT toxicity is exceedingly important, for in addition to the economic value of bees as honey producers, bees and wasps are invaluable in their roles as pollinators.

The long residence time or persistence in nature of the chlorinated hydrocarbon group indicates that these compounds are degraded into nonactive metabolites only relatively slowly. In combating disease vectors this is a tremendous asset. In malaria control programs, for example, while six or more applications per year would be needed of the less persistent insecticides against the *Anopheles* mosquito, when DDT is used, two yearly applications are usually sufficient for complete control, even in tropical areas. At the same time, this factor of persistence is one of the major arguments raised against the organochlorine insecticides, because it is thought that it permits their unlimited accumulation in the biotic environment. Later we shall deal specifically with this matter of accumulation and with what is known about the time required for degradation of these chemicals under various conditions.

The organophosphate insecticides have even broader target spectra than the organochlorine compounds; this target spectrum includes the vertebrates, among them, man. Since their toxicity is not inversely related to body temperature, they may be highly destructive to bee colonies. These compounds are much more toxic in general than any of the former group (with the exceptions of malathion and dimethoate), and hundreds of human poisonings have been reported as a result of their careless application. Parathion, for example, one of their most toxic representatives, can be fatal to a man who absorbs a single drop of it through the skin. Where it is used, safety precautions for appliers are elaborate, and it may be dangerous also to persons entering the fields following sprayings. From the environmentalist standpoint, the supposed advantage of this group of chemicals lies in the fact that they degrade rather rapidly in nature (from several hours to several weeks) and do not, therefore, accumulate. This "advantage," however, makes them virtually useless in large-scale operations for the control of disease vectors, since they must be frequently applied and each application involves some degree of direct danger to man and other mammals.

The carbamate insecticides have selective and rather narrow target spectra. They are therefore less toxic to nontarget organisms; they also decompose relatively rapidly. Unfortunately, however, they are also much less effective in general than the compounds in either of the two other groups. In disease-vector control programs, they do not represent serious direct danger to man, but on account of their rapid degradation, they must be applied repeatedly, which makes them expensive and impractical as alternatives to the organochlorines, even when their effectiveness against a particular vector insect has been shown. Their principal value seems to be in combating strains which have developed resistance to other major insecticides.

The Idyllic Past

Although the synthetic organic pesticides of the post–World War II period have found far wider applications than any of the compounds used in the past, it is worthwhile, for the sake of perspective, to take a fleeting look at the historical picture. Insects and other pests have been plaguing man for millennia, and pesticides or pest-control methods as such are not new. The most ancient practices designed to achieve some degree of chemical pest control are the various techniques of fumigation, some of which go back at least to the time of the Romans. Fumigation with sulfur, for instance, in the orchards of ancient Rome, and with cinnabar (mercury oxide) in Hispania, was practiced extensively. The former technique remained common up until World War II.

The use of sea salt (basically a mixture of magnesium and sodium chlorides) as a weed killer may also be traced back to antiquity. The Middle Ages knew the efficacy of lime or lime sulfur suspensions for insecticidal purposes, and lime was also used in "privies" until the era of running-water toilets. Its widespread application in the form of whitewash has a purpose beyond aesthetics, for it has some bactericidal and insecticidal properties in this form—especially against the eggs of common houseflies.

The end of the eighteenth century saw the introduction of the famous "Bordeaux mixture" for the protection of grapes. Vintners are still using this mixture of lime and copper sulfate in many parts of the world.

With the expansion of urbanization, bedbugs and cockroaches became rampant, and extreme methods were undertaken to control them. After the discovery of arsenical dyes, such as Schweinfurt green, a powder made from this highly toxic compound was spread copiously along the baseboards of walls in city apartments against the ubiquitous and most unpleasant cockroach infestations so common in old buildings. One approach to the bedbug problem was to soak furniture, walls, and even linens in generous quantities of petroleum lamp oil or, later, gasoline. Needless to say, the odor of the protective agent remained for the duration of the effective control period, and there were probably some people who preferred the bugs to the treatment. Around the time of World War I, a more modern approach was taken: fumigation with hydrogen cyanide was introduced for control of both cockroaches and bedbugs. The technique involved vacating the apartment for two to three days while exterminators sealed off all windows and doors and then generated the hydrogen cyanide in the rooms, making a rapid exit themselves. When the gas had done its job on the bugs, the exterminators opened the dwelling wearing protective gas masks, and they aired it thoroughly before the family was allowed to return.

Several other practices involving considerable risk to humans might be mentioned in connection with varied kinds of pest control. Schweinfurt green, for example, enjoyed favor as a paint material because its arsenic content was active as a fungicide and provided some protection against mildew. Unfortunately, however, in humid climates where mildew is a serious problem, enough arsenic can be vaporized from such paints to cause chronic arsenic poisoning in the inhabitants.

In agriculture and horticulture another early insecticide was made from a decoction of tobacco leaves. This was used mainly as a miticide, but since the quantities of the active ingredient—nicotine—could not be controlled in these simple formulations, it frequently happened that the concoctum caused the leaves of the plants to shrivel as well as killing the mites. By the first decade of the twentieth century, inorganic arsenicals (lead arsenate, etc.) came into widespread use, especially in orchards. While the bad reputation of the modern chlorinated hydrocarbon insecticides is in large part predicated on their relative persistence, it is often forgotten that the inorganic arsenicals have a far longer residence time, accumulate in the soil, and are toxic to mammals.

To show how desperate the battle with bugs could become, one has only to be reminded that fumigation with naphthalene was used against outbreaks of June bugs in orchards, and fumigation with phosgene (the poison gas of World

War I) was employed to protect vineyards. With the latter method, if the wind turned, it was simply *pech* for the local residents.

With respect to personal hygiene, some readers will certainly remember that until the introduction of DDT during World War II, the classic remedy for hair or body lice was liberal and repeated applications of kerosene oil to the skin and body hair. To soldiers in the trenches, to whom the odorous treatment was usually not available, there was nothing for it but to suffer and pray that they would not develop typhus, a louse-borne disease. We do not wish to judge the efficacy of invoking divine protection, but the statistics of World War I indicate that more soldiers died of typhus than were killed in battle.

For those who are enthusiasts of "organically grown foods," it may be of interest to learn that one of the most ancient types of seed coating—thought to promote sprouting—was a completely natural product: the urine of women or, when an adequate supply was lacking, of mares. In modern times a similar technique was promoted in slightly disguised form by Lysenkoist biologists, who claimed that manure seepage was one of the best of sprouting agents.

Finally, we wish to mention some substances used for the control of rodents. The proliferation of rats and the dangers of the disease vectors they carry (such as fleas which transmit the causative organism of bubonic plague) have always been a problem to human populations. Thus the discovery of effective rat poisons was regarded as a great boon, despite certain dangers connected with their use. In the early decades of this century, the agent most widely used for rodent control was yellow phosphorus, prepared in a form which looked very much like a cheese spread and had a garliclike smell. This preparation was both highly toxic to rats and attractive to them, but its resemblance to cheese also entailed dangers to small children and even adults, with accidental ingestion frequently resulting in death.

Yellow phosphorus as a rodenticide was finally replaced by thallium salts, which are also highly toxic to humans, but were less likely to be eaten by accident, as the white powder form in which they were applied did not resemble food. Today, neither is used, the preferred treatment for rat infestations being the newer anticoagulant substances.

These brief comments on man's historical battle with the bugs are admittedly incomplete; nevertheless, a few points can be drawn from them. To begin with, one must deny the ridiculous notion propagated by some environmentalists that insects and other pests did not really constitute a problem in the more "natural" past periods. The desperate techniques resorted to in agricultural practices alone indicate that, quite to the contrary, our recent and more distant ancestors were well aware of the serious competition between man and pests for the fruits of the harvest. Against the much more serious problem of insect-borne diseases, our forebears were in large part helpless, for, although some of the methods mentioned—fumigation, for example—could be employed as temporary measures giving partial protection against infestations, none was suitable for large-scale public health applications.

But perhaps what is most obvious about the methods of pest control employed before the era of the synthetic organic pesticides is that those techniques which were effective in any measure nearly all entailed significant risks to the human population, and with some compounds, to the permanent status of the environment as well. The reader might keep this fact in mind when considering the arguments put forth by environmentalists about the dangers associated with the use of DDT and other organochlorine pesticides.

13

A COMPOUND
WITH A HISTORY

If a steady observer really looks
at life, he will see that men never
think if they can help it.
WALTER BAGEHOT

DDT was first synthesized in 1874, but not until 1940 was it
patented as a contact insecticide in Switzerland by Dr. Paul
Müller. During World War II, it was used extensively by the Allied forces to combat disease vectors: especially mosquitoes, various flies, ticks, and lice, which
are carriers of malaria, typus, river blindness, yellow fever, trypanosomiasis,
plagues, and encephalitis.

By 1946, it was recognized that DDT is one of the most important disease-
preventing agents known to man; and in 1948, the Nobel Prize in medicine was
awarded to Dr. Müller. In his presentation speech, Professor G. Fisher of the
Karolinska Institute concluded his introduction with the following words: "Dr.
Paul Müller. Your discovery of the strong contact insecticidal action of dichloro-

diphenyl-trichloromethyl-methane is of the greatest importance in the field of medicine. Thanks to you, preventive medicine is now able to fight many diseases carried by insects in a way totally different from that employed heretofore" (Fisher, 1948, p. 226).

DDT has been subject to so much bad publicity over the last decade that many people find it difficult to imagine why anyone should still defend it, and why a Nobel Prize in medicine should have been given to the discoverer of its insecticidal properties.

Probably few people in the United States are aware that malaria has been known, since the beginnings of historical time, as the greatest of the killer diseases, and that it is even today the single largest cause of death on a global basis. In Cecil and Loeb's *Textbook of Medicine* (1971), Phillip Marsden begins the "General Considerations Introducing the Protozoal Diseases" with the following sentence: "Malaria remains the greatest challenge in parasitic disease both in terms of prevalence (1038 million people still live in malarious areas) and in the amount of morbidity and mortality caused by this infection" (Marsden, p. 700).

In the detailed description of the disease given by L. J. Bruce-Chwatt, Professor of Tropical Medicine in London, we may read the following: "References to intermittent fevers exist in the ancient Assyrian, Chinese, and Indian medical texts, but the clinical entity of malaria was established in Greece by Hippocrates only in the fifth century B.C. The Romans knew it well, associated it with marshy areas, and attempted to control it by drainage. . . . Epidemics of malaria, so common in the past, are now exceptional. One of the greatest epidemics of malaria in modern times struck the Soviet Union after World War I; more than 5 million cases were reported in 1923, and there were at least 60,000 deaths" (Bruce-Chwatt, p. 701).

Malaria, caused by protoza of the genus *Plasmodium,* is a vector-borne disease transmitted by anophelid mosquitoes. The disease is endemic both in temperate and tropical regions; thus roughly two-thirds of the world population — that is, about 2 billion people — live in areas where malaria is indigenous.

The clinical manifestations of the disease and its course are rather varied, but Bruce-Chwatt gives a relatively condensed description of the typical paroxysmal attack:

THE ATTACK. Preceded by various premonitory signs such as headache, malaise, and nausea, an attack of malaria consists of several short febrile paroxysms recurring every second day (tertian or vivax malaria) or every third day (quartan malaria); falciparum malaria produces either daily or irregular fever.

A *typical paroxysm* starts with a feeling of chill accompanied by shivering (rigor), pallor, cyanosis, and, at times in children, by a convulsive seizure. Other symptoms comprise severe frontal headache, myalgia of the lower back, neck, and legs, dizziness, and general malaise. The pulse is usually fast, but this is not constant. . . . During the "cold stage," lasting up to one hour, the temperature rises slowly, and in the subsequent "hot stage" may go up to 104 to 106°F (40 to 41°C) and higher. In this stage the patient feels very hot and restless, his respiration is fast, his skin is dry and flushed, his pulse is full and bounding, and headache, thirst, and vomiting are common. After two to four hours comes the "sweating stage": the patient breaks out in profuse perspiration, and his temperature falls to normal or below, at times with a suddenness that may lead to near collapse; later the pulse rate becomes normal, and the drowsy and weak patient usually falls asleep. (*Ibid.*, p. 705)

If the disease is untreated or poorly treated, the attacks described above usually recur more or less regularly for a period of a few months. Afterwards, a relatively symptom-free period may ensue, but then relapses will begin to take place; and these may go on, depending on the type of malaria involved, for from one year to more than ten years. Thus, for those who survive the initial attacks, the debilitating effects of the disease may be manifest for a very long time. Since the disease is transmitted from infected pregnant women to unborn children, infant mortality is exceedingly high in malarious areas. When public health authorities speak about the vast social benefits which follow malaria control, they are not referring only to decreases in mortality from the disease, but also to the increased capacity of peoples freed from these persistent symptoms for energetic work and an optimistic attitude toward building a better society.

Before the introduction of DDT, the malaria problem could only be attacked by indirect preventive measures and palliative treatment of symptoms in the stricken. Since elimination of the mosquito itself was not feasible, prevention was restricted to the destruction of breeding grounds. Two practices were used on a large scale in the developed countries. Lakes and other open water surfaces were flooded with oil to form a continuous surface slick, which prevented the mosquito larvae from breathing. This practice was continued from the early spring to the fall in areas where there was no other possible approach to the problem. These bodies of water were obviously not utilizable for any purposes. The other approach was to drain and dry out swampy areas or shallow lakes. Where irrigation channels were needed for agricultural production, the mosquito fish, *Gambusia affinis,* was introduced at tremendous expense. First, however, the indigenous catfish populations had to be eradicated, or they would have devoured the smaller *Gambusia.*

With the exception of the boot of Italy, where vast expenditures over 15 years under Mussolini's regime led to eradication of malaria, no other areas of the world are known where the disease was indigenous and where these measures succeeded in eliminating the mosquitoes. Even the partial success in Italy was only temporary, and by 1945 the disease was again widespread there.

Until the 1940s, on a world basis, 200 million people were stricken with malaria annually, with an average of 2 million deaths per year. DDT applications for control of the *Anopheles* mosquito began shortly after the end of World War II. In the course of a few years endemic malaria was completely eradicated from most countries in the temperate zone. In the United States the eradication campaign was carried out between 1948 and 1952.

In tropical countries, however, the battle against malaria is far from over. Of the estimated 1,724 millions now living in 124 tropical countries, 37 million people live in areas where eradication has been achieved, and 1,230 million in areas where extensive eradication programs are currently under way (Executive Board, WHO, 1971).

Some data on individual countries may help to make these very large figures more comprehensible. In Taiwan, for instance, there were more than 1,000,000 cases of malaria reported in 1945. In 1969 there were only nine cases, and in 1971, none.

In Venezuela, more than 800,000 cases were reported for 1943. In 1958, the figure was 800. In Turkey, 1,200,000 cases in 1950 were reduced to 2,900 by 1969.

The case of Ceylon is particularly instructive as an example of what can happen when DDT is withdrawn for dubious political reasons from a malaria eradication program. In 1946 there were 2.8 million cases of malaria annually in Ceylon.

> Following a countrywide malaria eradication campaign in the 1950's and early 1960's, the number of confirmed malaria cases reached lows of 31 in 1962 and 17 in 1963, when full-scale house spraying was partially withdrawn, and subsequently terminated in 1964. The cases increased annually thereafter, numbering 150 in 1964, 308 in 1965, 499 in 1966, and 3466 in 1967, most of them occurring in the last few months of that year. In 1968, the epidemic flared rapidly — 16,493 confirmed cases being reported in January and 42,161 in February. No DDT supplies were on hand with which to reinstate the house spraying program on the wide scale needed, and months were required for the procurement and delivery of them. As a result, *more than a million cases of malaria* occurred throughout the country in 1968. (National Communicable Disease Center, 1969, p. 8; our emphasis)

By 1969 the epidemic in Ceylon had grown to 2.5 million cases.

The Ceylon story ought to be taken as an object lesson, for even where malaria has been officially declared as eradicated, unless the means are on hand to control an outbreak, epidemics can flare with great rapidity. In the United States, malaria morbidity amounted to 2,686 cases in 1968, 3,806 in 1969, and 1,559 in the first four months of 1970. This increasing trend is usually ascribed to the increased volume of international travel and to the return of military personnel from Southeast Asia. However, Marsden points out that "At the time of writing (1970) there have been a few cases of indigenous vivax malaria recognized in the United States. Epidemiologic work has revealed vector *Anopheles* in the area" (Marsden, 1971, p. 700). Clearly, there is no reason for domestic complacency even about malaria; other mosquito-borne diseases, such as encephalitis, are on the rise, too. In tropical countries, the chances of a repeat of the Ceylon disaster are very high. Those environmental organizations urging a total ban on DDT manufacture and use have been shockingly silent about the likely epidemics affecting millions of people which would follow, were they to achieve their goal.

It is not only malaria among the vector-borne diseases which can be controlled partially or completely with DDT. In a 1959 volume, Simmons listed 30 diseases the vectors of which are sensitive to DDT. Among them are a number of mass killers and highly debilitating illnesses: viral encephalitis, yellow fever, typhus, plague, trypanosomiasis (sleeping sickness), and onchocerciasis. The last of these is commonly called river blindness, and, although the disease is not too familiar to North Americans, the number of victims in Africa and Middle America is 40,000,000 per year.

With the introduction of DDT to control the vectors of these diseases, it seemed, for the first time in human history, that man could look forward to a life of dignity, freed from the scourges of maiming diseases and famine. It is no wonder, then, that its applications were greeted with general high enthusiasm.

A few evaluations by health authorities made at different stages of DDT's history may give some further perspective on who defends DDT and why. S. W. Simmons, of the U.S. Public Health Service, wrote in 1959:

> The total value of DDT to mankind is inestimable, and is comprised of health, economic, and social benefits. Health benefits are both direct and indirect and fall into three principal categories: (1) direct control of vector-borne diseases such as malaria, typhus, etc., and of insect pests, by the use of DDT for destroying the insects concerned; (2) use of DDT in agriculture for crop pest control, resulting in an increased food supply, often where malnutrition is the principal health problem;

and (3) an increase in resistance to non-vector-borne diseases through better health as a result of freedom from malaria and other vector-borne diseases and malnutrition . . .

Raising the health standards of the people has resulted in better agricultural and industrial production. Much land has been reclaimed, new factories have been built, and more goods have been made available for sale as well as home consumption. There has been a significant decrease in absentee workers in countries where malaria has been controlled, and this has enabled higher earnings, with an increase in economic status for both individuals and the community. . . .

The sociological changes brought about by DDT are only beginning to be apparent. . . .

Except for the antibiotics, it is doubtful that any material has been found which protects more people against more diseases over a larger area than does DDT. Most of the peoples of the globe have received some measure of benefit from this compound, either directly by protection from infectious diseases and pestiferous insects, or indirectly by better nutrition, cleaner food, and increased disease resistance... (Simmons, 1959, pp. 251–252)

With reference only to India, R. Pal wrote:

Estimates of actual morbidity and mortality [from malaria] are difficult but it would appear, from the available data, that malaria in India has been reduced from 75 million cases to less than 5 million. A new era in economic development and social progress has been initiated with its beneficial transformation of the life of the people. The average span of life in India is now 47 years, whereas before the eradication campaign began it was 32 years. The improvement has resulted in better agriculture and industrial production. In the Terai region (Uttar Pradesh), land under cultivation and food grain production has increased and this region, once abandoned by its inhabitants because of the high incidence of malaria, has become a beautiful and prosperous area. (Pal, 1962, p. 6)

In 1969, the Director General of the World Health Organization, Dr. M. Candau, made the following comment: "DDT has been instrumental in controlling some of the most important vector-borne diseases of man; the concept of malaria eradication rests completely on its continued use. The record of safety of DDT to man has been outstanding during the past 20 years and its low cost makes it irreplaceable in public health at the present time" (Candau, 1969, p. 1096).

In 1971, the then Surgeon General of the United States, Dr. Jesse Steinfeld, stated:

DDT has been instrumental in literally changing the course of history for many nations and continues to do so today. Its use in the eradication and control of disease has meant the difference between hunger, despair and poverty, and good health, hope and the promise of a better life to billions of people throughout the world. DDT has been responsible for returning to man the use of agriculturally rich lands, thereby making possible improvements in nutrition, providing in turn the energy and strength for social and economic development. It has had a tremendous impact on the health of the world and few drugs can claim to have done so much for mankind in so short a period of time as can DDT. (Steinfeld, 1971, p. 1136)

It is noteworthy that while Rachel Carson sermonized at great length in *Silent Spring* about the sanctity of life, nowhere in her book did she so much as mention the role of DDT in literally saving millions of human lives and alleviating the miseries of untold numbers.

Food, Fiber, and Forestry

In the foregoing, we have elaborated at some length on DDT's extreme importance in disease control, because no discussions of the pros and cons of DDT use can be meaningful without this perspective. It should not, however, be forgotten that the pesticide is also vitally needed in food and fiber production and in forest management.

In the first years after its introduction, because of its broad spectrum and low toxicity, DDT was used on practically all crops, and was widely applied in forestry. By now, other, more specific pesticides have replaced it in many instances. However, there are a considerable number of pests for which no other good alternative insecticide has been found.

In forestry, for example, DDT is essential to control the spruce budworm and the large pine weevil which flourish happily when other pesticides are used, as Sweden found out after its ban. In cotton farming in the southeastern United States, it is needed against bollworm, and in other parts of the world it controls various pests on cotton crops. There is no substitute for DDT against cutworms, as Canada learned the hard way, when a whole season's onion crop was nearly lost following a hasty ban on DDT, which was then quickly reinstated. In the Far East, rice crops are protected from a number of pests by DDT, and it is also important in soybean cultiviation.

Officials of the United Nations Food and Agriculture Organization (FAO) have frequently emphasized the need for DDT in food and fiber production in the underdeveloped countries. In an interview given to the *Wall Street Journal* on February 16, 1970, they stated: "If the proportion of cropland protected by pesticides—mainly DDT—in India is increased from 10% to 20%, India can grow an extra 1,400,000 tons of rice, 100,000 tons of peanuts, 65,000 tons of sorghum, 250,000 tons of sugar, 46,000 tons of corn, and 200,000 tons of potatoes every year. . . . To the gathering pro-DDT forces, the issue is clear. It is hard to talk about pesticide contamination in food to a man who is starving to death."

Dr. Whittemore, Head of the Crop Protection Branch, further emphasized: "DDT is urgently needed for the next 10 to 15 years, at the least. There are numerous insecticides that kill insects as well as DDT does, but many of them are much more acutely toxic than DDT . . . and most of them are far too expensive for use in underdeveloped lands. DDT costs around 15 cents a pound. Some alternative chemicals cost as much as a dollar a pound, and a few run as high as $15 a pound" (Whittemore, 1970).

Besides those aspects of insect control in agriculture where DDT has no effective substitutes, the economic and safety factors favoring its use have to be taken into account. DDT is both the cheapest of the synthetic organic pesticides and one of the easiest and safest compounds to apply. These considerations are usually minimized by environmentalists—most of whom are middle- and upper-class Americans. But in a world where vast numbers of people still live in abject poverty, to ignore the central role of economic considerations is morally unacceptable. When listening to American environmentalists voicing slogans deriding big business, bureaucracy, and establishment science, it is instructive to attend to the echoes, which often come out sounding like "Let the people eat cake."

In an impassioned speech in Rome in November, 1971, at a conference of the United Nations Food and Agriculture Organization, Norman Borlaug attacked those who seek bans on DDT and other essential pesticides as irresponsible. His words were strong and unequivocal: "If agriculture is denied their [chemicals] use because of unwise legislation that is now being promoted by a powerful group of hysterical lobbyists who are provoking fear by predicting doom for the world through chemical poisoning, then the world will be doomed not by chemical poisoning but from starvation" (Borlaug, 1971).

At the same meeting, an official of FAO made the following statement: "As FAO has said before, until cheap, safe, and efficient substitute pesticides are produced and made easily available, there is no alternative to the judicious use of DDT, especially in the developing world, to increase agricultural productivity to feed the growing number of people on our planet" (*San Francisco Chronicle*, Nov. 9, 1971).

What Is a Contact Poison?

After hearing about so many beneficial uses, the reader may be curious about why DDT is so effective. We cannot explain the biochemical mode of action by which DDT kills insects because, curiously, 30 years of research has not yet settled this question. On the other hand, there is a vast literature on DDT which treats both detailed and very basic questions relating to its activity.

The insecticidal action of the compound is summarized in Goodman and Gilman's *Pharmacological Basis of Therapeutics* in the following:

> Insecticidal Action: DDT is toxic to many species of insects and various other arthropods. The LD_{50} for most insects, when expressed in terms of body weight, differs little from the intravenous LD_{50} for mammals. However, DDT is as toxic to an insect following topical application as following injection. The high susceptibility of many arthropods to locally applied DDT is due to the ability of the compound to penetrate the chitinous exoskeleton. . . . Following the intravenous administration of emulsified solutions of DDT in peanut oil, signs of intoxication are evident within 5 to 10 minutes; the LD_{50} for most species is around 50 mg/kg. (Goodman and Gilman, 1970, p. 1062)

From this it follows that since a mosquito, for instance, weighs only a few milligrams, exceedingly minute quantities of DDT are sufficient to kill it. It should be emphasized, however, that in insects DDT acts as if it had been injected intravenously. In mammals, the difference between the effects of intravenous injection of DDT and feeding DDT is at least tenfold. Thus, the safety factor for mammals is not only a factor of body size, but also the route of exposure.

In disease prevention, DDT can be safely sprayed on the interior walls and ceilings of dwellings, where its residual action continues to be effective for several months, on contact, against insects. Hence the terms "contact poison" and "residual insecticide." Because of its low toxicity to man, its residual activity, and its proven effectiveness, the introduction and widescale deployment of DDT was welcomed as an almost magical panacea for the solution of all problems created by pestiferous insects.

Abuses and Checks

The tremendous initial enthusiasm for DDT had, to be sure, some negative aspects. The prospect of eradicating the most damaging pests sometimes led to the use of unwarranted quantities of the insecticide. In some cases, innocent excesses stemmed from the general assumption that "if one pound per acre can do a good job, then surely two pounds would be better." In other cases, not so innocent industry salesmen recommended application levels three to five times those needed in order to increase their sales. Sprayings were advocated two to three times in one season, when it was known that a single deployment would be sufficient. Commercial crop dusters, who were paid according to the number of gallons of pesticides they dispensed rather than by acreage treated, sometimes sprayed the same areas two or three times running.

Inevitably, too, there were some accidents due to carelessness: instances in which pesticide wastes were dumped in open waters without dilution or prior treatment; cases of leakage from containers; and similar events which have no bearing on proper use or on labeling regulations. Careless handling or gross dumping without concern for the consequences to the local environment are, of course, not specific to DDT or to pesticides. Nevertheless, one has to admit that these things happen, and that excessive quantities of DDT have been dumped in local waters and, on occasion, have resulted in detrimental environmental effects.

Errors were also made in certain kinds of applications sanctioned by government agencies in the early days of DDT use. It was sometimes recommended for use against types of insects which were not sensitive or were only partially sensitive to it. Other mistakes involved the mode or medium of attack against certain species. For instance, in the famous Clear Lake incident—an affair which the environmentalists will never allow us to forget—DDD was added in soluble form to the waters of the lake for the control of gnats. The gnats were eliminated, but considerable damage to other organisms in the lake also resulted. When this incident is recounted, it is usually not mentioned that labeling regulations no longer permit such direct applications to open bodies of water. In effect, the early abuses have been corrected by a series of regulatory changes limiting the recommended uses for the pesticide and also delineating proper modes and quantities of application for the remaining essential uses.

We mentioned in Chapter 1 that some of the reviewers of *Silent Spring* may have hoped that Carson's book would serve to alert regulatory agencies to abuses in pesticide applications, and that the public would not be too greatly affected by those aspects of her message which consisted of exaggerated claims and untenable pseudoscientific views. Had this been the case, one would have supposed that tightening of the controls regulating the proper uses of the chemicals would have quieted the critics, and Carson's book would have faded into oblivion as just another statement from a romantic and rather extremist naturalist. But this is not what happened, for it was Carson's second principal theme of gradual contamination of the environment with man-made chemicals which took hold of the public and made of her book a perennial best seller. "Chlorinated hydrocarbons" were household words long before Earth Day and the burgeoning of public interest in "ecology." The campaign against pesticides was on, and among this large group of agricultural chemicals, it was DDT which became the central symbol: a Very Bad Thing, indeed.

Crusaders

During the five years following the publication of *Silent Spring,* the principal participants in the DDT controversy were enraged members of the lay public and conservation-oriented wildlife biologists on the side of the opposition, with the agencies responsible for regulating agricultural practices and the pesticide manufacturers on the defense.

At this stage, the arguments of the defenders of chemical pesticides were often primitive. In the first place, they were unprepared for open controversy, having grown accustomed to the enthusiasm and general public acceptance of pesticides as beneficial substances. Secondly, both the manufacturers and the regulatory agencies had eventually to admit that there were some abusive or unwise practices involved in certain kinds of pesticide applications; but they often treated their opponents in a high-handed manner, failing to recognize the extent to which Carson's book had generated fear reactions in the public.

Their opponents, on the other hand, were thoroughly irrational. The anti-pesticide movement began to assume the charismatic tone of a holy crusade. Reasonable reassurances from agencies like the U.S. Public Health Service fell on deaf ears, for Miss Carson's followers were, for the most part, whether laymen or scientists, "true believers." As Eric Hoffer has written: "It is the true believer's ability to 'shut his eyes and stop his ears' to facts that do not deserve to be either seen or heard which is the source of his unequaled fortitude and constancy. He cannot be frightened by danger nor disheartened by obstacle nor baffled by contradictions because he denies their existence" (Hoffer, 1958, p. 76).

We intend to devote considerable attention to the social and scientific claims advanced by Carson and by the contemporary environmentalists who oppose DDT; and we shall be underlining some of the contradictions in logic, uncomfortable facts, and problems with numbers which confront these believers. Here we would like to bring the reader's attention to one of the nonscientific methods favored by environmentalists to discredit the arguments of those who defend DDT or other agricultural chemicals. This tactic consists in ad hominem attacks on the spokesmen themselves, and amounts, in essence, to labeling all opposition statements as "the work of the devil."

The attitude of Miss Carson's followers toward any and all of her detractors has been documented in Frank Graham's *Since Silent Spring*. In it one may read, for example, that Dr. Robert White-Stevens is "American Cyanamid's all-purpose spokesman" (Graham, 1970, p. 82). It is true, as Mr. Graham mentions, that White-Stevens worked for some years in the research and development department of American Cyanamid; but it would seem important also to mention that he is a professor of biology at Rutgers University, and Chairman of the Rutgers Bureau of Conservation and Environmental Science.

Similar tactics of guilt by association are directed at Thomas Jukes, a professor of medical physics from the University of California at Berkeley, who has been one of the most outspoken defenders of DDT in public health and agriculture during the past decade. Replying to an article in the *New York Times* in which Dr. Jukes had said that withdrawal of DDT from the WHO malaria eradication programs would be "tantamount to genocide," R. A. Cameron of the Environmental Defense Fund described Jukes as "having worked for over 20 years for the pesticide industry" (*New York Times*, August 18, 1971). What Dr. Jukes actually did during those 20 years was to direct the Department of Nutrition and Physiology Research at Lederle Laboratories, a subsidiary of American Cyanamid, where work was performed on vitamins, antibiotics, and anticancer substances. In these innuendo attacks on the two scientists, it is of course never mentioned that American Cyanamid has never produced DDT (they manufacture, in fact, several of the proposed substitutes). If there had been any pressure exerted by company executives on Jukes and White-Stevens, it would much more logically have been an attempt to quiet their recommendations of a competitor's product.

The most recent such attack appeared in the *New York Times*, reporting an interview with Robert Arbib, editor of *American Birds*. Mr. Arbib had written a strong protest in a recent issue of the magazine to the "misuse" by the "pesticide industry's scientist spokesmen" of the data resulting from the Audubon Society's annual Christmas bird counts. He said that such "spokesmen" were "lying" when they stated that bird life in North America is thriving despite the use of DDT. He did not identify the persons under attack in the original publication, but to the *New York Times* interviewer he said they included Robert White-Stevens, Thomas Jukes, Norman Borlaug, J. Gordon Edwards, and Donald Spencer.[*]

---

[*] White-Stevens, Jukes, and Edwards have commenced a libel action against the *New York Times* and the National Audubon Society based upon the magazine article and the subsequent interview. The defendants have asserted many defenses (including freedom of the press), and no disposition of the action has occurred as of the date of this writing.

Mr. Arbib claims that the increased numbers of birds observed during the Society's Christmas count is a reflection of more and better birders rather than of more birds. (Curiously, when fewer birds are observed by the amateurs, the survey is always taken to be accurate, though another argument raised against using these counts in the current controversy over DDT is that they are not scientific.) He goes on to say that there is now abundant evidence to *prove* that bird species high on the food chain are suffering serious declines in numbers as a *direct result* of pesticide contaminations. "'Anytime you hear a "scientist" say the opposite,' he continued, 'you are in the presence of someone who is being paid to lie . . .'" (Devlin, 1972). Exactly what is meant to be implied by the quotation marks around the word "scientist" escapes us, for Mr. Arbib is referring to men of considerable eminence, some of whom have been slandered before, but whose titles have never been questioned to our knowledge. But the desperate reaction to which some environmentalists are driven when their claims are refuted by their own data is illustrated in this nasty and incredible piece of name-calling. We wonder whether Arbib really expects people to believe that these gentlemen, a Nobel laureate included, can be bought for a few pieces of silver.

That whole universities may be labeled as lackeys of the chemical industry can also be gleaned from Graham's book. In the following, his own text is combined with a citation from a *Science* journalist, as well as a disclaimer from a faculty member of the university in question:

> In Delaware, one occasionally hears pesticide advice and information discounted by conservationists because of the close relationship there between the University of Delaware and the world's largest chemical complex, E. I. du Pont de Nemours and Company. Nine of the fourteen trustees serving on the university's executive committee in 1968 were members of the du Pont family or were associated with the company.

> "According to many faculty members and students," a reporter wrote recently in *Science,* "the university . . . has been 'distorted' and 'intimidated' by the du Pont presence. . . . It is perhaps not surprising that a Delaware faculty member felt no qualms about publicly criticizing Rachel Carson's attacks on pesticides and the chemical industry, but when two faculty members asked permission to give testimony that was expected to be adverse to industry at a pollution hearing last year they were advised by the university administration to submit remarks in writing but not to testify in person."

> However, Dale F. Bray, head of the University's Department of Entomology and Applied Ecology, is unaware of any pressure by du Pont upon his department. "If such exists, it is far too subtle for me and my colleagues to detect," he says. (Graham, 1970, p. 218)

Miss Carson made equally sweeping indictments in her attempt to explain
". . . the otherwise mystifying fact that certain outstanding entomologists are
among the leading advocates of chemical control. Inquiry into the background
of some of these men reveals that their entire research program is supported by
the chemical industry. Their professional prestige, sometimes their very jobs
depend on the perpetuation of chemical methods. Can we then expect them to
bite the hand that literally feeds them? But knowing their bias, how much credence can we give to their protests that insecticides are harmless?" (Carson,
1962, p. 229).

The commonsense point of view that, whether or not funded by chemical
companies, experienced entomologists may favor chemical pesticides because
they represent the best and most workable method of pest control, is apparently
deemed unworthy of consideration.

Miss Carson also reminds us that entomologists are, in general, narrow specialists who are not qualified by training to discover and interpret wildlife losses.
The professional wildlife biologist, on the other hand, is accepted as an unbiased
and objective interpreter. In the later stages of the anti-pesticide movement,
we shall see that *only* those professional wildlife biologists who agree that the
chemical pesticides are seriously damaging to wild species can be regarded as
objective and unbiased. When the statistical observations or controlled studies
of some Fish and Wildlife Service biologists fail to support the arguments of the
anti-pesticide crusaders, they are automatically relegated to the biased group,
along with the more specialized entomologists. Or, the converse: certain entomologists who are on the "right side," such as Paul Ehrlich, LaMont Cole, Robert
van den Bosch, and David Pimentel, are seen as "qualified observers."

Wildlife biologists and especially ornithologists were, indeed, the first of
the professional scientists to join in the anti-pesticide battle. Prominent among
them was Britain's D. A. Ratcliffe (a botanist turned ornithologist), who had
already attempted in the 1950s to establish some relationship between the introduction of the chlorinated hydrocarbon pesticides and his observations of
eggshell thinning in 17 species of British birds. During the 1960s, any number
of amateur and professional naturalists joined in this field observation and on-
the-spot interpretation game. These were, for the most part, sincere lovers of
birds and animals who quite naturally and innocently, from observations of population decline or reproductive difficulties, inferred a cause-and-effect relationship between pesticides and the problems suffered by wildlife populations. Their
observations were sometimes correct and sometimes false, but in either case,
the less sophisticated among them did not stop to consider the fact that they
were arriving at conclusions from circumstantial evidence alone, and the public

was deluged with more "information" about the deleterious effects of chlorinated hydrocarbons on fish, wild animals, and especially on birds.

The Battle Is On

From 1967 on, the pace of the anti-pesticide campaign quickened, and a number of new elements entered. Scientists opposing DDT went from the field into the laboratory, and in 1968 reports of "controlled experiments" indicting DDT began to appear in scientific journals. The Environmental Defense Fund (EDF) was formed in 1967, and began to initiate legal suits demanding bans on DDT.

The first such suit, as we mentioned earlier, was brought against the Suffolk County Mosquito Control Commission in 1966, with Victor Yannacone leading the attack. The trial was financed by the Rachel Carson Memorial Fund of the National Audubon Society. In 1967, after incorporation of EDF, a similar suit was brought against nine municipalities in Michigan, followed by further actions in 1968 throughout the state of Michigan, one of which involved dieldrin, another important chlorinated hydrocarbon pesticide. Although these suits were not entirely successful, a great deal of public concern was generated through the press, and, in the spring of 1969, Michigan banned the sale of DDT within the state. In the same year, the Wisconsin Department of Natural Resources held an administrative hearing on the effects of DDT in the environment, and both EDF and the opposing forces ("the task force for DDT") arrived on the scene to participate, with EDF joining the Wisconsin chapter of the Izaak Walton League and the local Citizens Natural Resources Association. The Wisconsin hearings have frequently been characterized as a "circus," with Yannacone's histrionic techniques of cross-examination and the parade of assembled anti-DDT scientists clearly stealing the show. As Bruce Ingersoll reported in *BioScience,* while the decision was being awaited: "For . . . the conservation-minded everywhere, round one [the anti-DDT testimony] was a time when their doubts about DDT crystallized, when their worst fears were substantiated by scientific fact. Reports of testimony against DDT and its metabolites were then disseminated across the nation by journalists clambering aboard the accelerating band wagon of environmental awareness. Many people heard the indictments and tuned out, not waiting to hear the defense" (Ingersoll, 1969, p. 735).

The indirect outcome of the Wisconsin Hearings was the passing of a bill by the Wisconsin State Legislature outlawing the sale and distribution of DDT in the state, with an amendment allowing for emergency use of the compound to control an epidemic disease outbreak among people or domestic animals, or an epidemic outbreak of plant pests threatening the loss of a significant portion of a crop.

Similar suits brought in the states of Washington and California were less successful for the environmentalists in terms of achieved legislation, but the adverse publicity about DDT generated by the press continued to accelerate. When public interest flagged, the "concerned scientists" took to calling press conferences, making excellent use of two studies published in 1969 which purported to show that DDT causes cancer in mice (Innes et al., 1969; Tarján and Kemény, 1969; see our Chapter 14 for discussion).

By 1971, a thorough job of educating the public had been done, with most informed laymen possessed of the *knowledge* that DDT is one of our most serious environmental pollutants, and that it may very well endanger the human race. It seemed obvious that only persons whose financial interests were at stake would stoop to defend such a heinous substance, and that, at the very least, its continued domestic uses ought to be prohibited forthwith.

Late in 1970 the Environmental Defense Fund brought suit in the U.S. Court of Appeals, District of Columbia, against the Environmental Protection Agency (which, since its creation in 1970 has taken over from the Department of Agriculture the regulatory controls governing pesticide registration and use), demanding suspension of the remaining registrations for DDT uses in the United States. On January 7, 1971, the Court ruled that the Administrator of EPA, William Ruckelshaus, must either implement cancellation procedures against the few remaining registrations of DDT in the United States or show cause for a decision that the continued use of the insecticide under the limited current registrations does not constitute an imminent hazard to the public. (*Environmental Defense Fund, Inc.* v. *Ruckelshaus,* U.S. Court of Appeals, District of Columbia, No. 23,813; decided January 7, 1971.) Shortly thereafter cancellation procedures were implemented.

The EDF, together with the Sierra Club, the Audubon Society, and other conservation organizations, were not satisfied with this ruling, since cancellation procedures permit manufacturers and users of the product in question to appeal through due process against withdrawal of the labeling, whereas the environmentalists sought a suspension order, which would immediately halt the sale and use of DDT. They therefore brought another court of appeals suit to this end.

In response to the cancellation order two moves were undertaken by the DDT defense. The Montrose Chemical Company (sole remaining manufacturer of DDT in the United States) requested that EPA appoint an advisory committee to evaluate the status of DDT. The U.S. Department of Agriculture, together with about 30 formulators of products containing DDT, requested a formal hearing before a U.S. government examiner for a review of the case. Such a proceeding is a quasi-judicial affair, conducted under legal rules of evidence and entailing examination and cross-examination of witnesses, but carried out under the auspices of the administrative rather than the judicial arm of the federal government. This hearing began in August of 1971, and at this writing is in process. Although the original injunctions leading up to the cancellation order involved EDF versus EPA, in the Consolidated DDT Hearings, the EDF and the conservation organizations are joined with the EPA as Intervenors, while the Agriculture Department and the manufacturers together represent the Group Petitioners.

In appointing the EPA Scientific Advisory Committee on DDT, the EPA requested that the Committee should "provide its expert, independent judgment on the issue of whether products containing DDT constitute an imminent hazard to the public."

Montrose objected to the inclusion of O. L. Loucks on the Committee, on the grounds that his prior bias had been established.* Dr. Loucks had testified at the Wisconsin DDT Hearings for the Environmental Defense Fund; and he had coauthored a report (Harrison et al., 1970), together with several EDF members, called "Systems Studies of DDT Transport" (a paper which takes such an extreme point of view that even other anti-DDT environmentalists have objected to it—see our Chapter 17). Even more to the point, he had signed an affidavit in February, 1971, which was sent by Dr. Charles Wurster to the Committee on Agriculture, House of Representatives, on March 4. It stated: "I therefore conclude that all registered uses of DDT should be suspended at once." That Loucks had made a commitment to a course of action prior to the deliberations of the independent committee would seem to be an undeniable fact. Nevertheless, objections to his inclusion were not acted upon.

On September 20, 1971, the Advisory Committee issued a 43-page report on DDT. With respect to the "imminent hazard" question, the Committee wrote:

A. The present reported annual usage level of DDT does not present an imminent hazard to human health in terms of individual bodily functions and safety.

B. DDT and its derivatives are serious environmental pollutants and present a substantial threat to the quality of the human environment through widespread

---

* The substantiation of this statement can be found in: *Before EPA, Group Petitioners' Brief in Opposition to Respondent's Exceptions to the Examiner's Decision and Brief in Support Thereof* (I. F. & R. Docket No. 80, May 26, 1972, Washington, D.C., pp. 120), where on pp. 72–75 the *Advisory Committee Report* is discussed.

damage to some nontarget organisms. There is, therefore, an imminent hazard to human welfare in terms of maintaining healthy desirable flora and fauna in man's environment. (Advisory Committee on DDT, 1971, p. 43)

This partial qualification of the concept of "imminent hazard," wherein a substance can be declared not to represent an imminent hazard to human health in terms of individual bodily functions and safety, but may still be declared an indirect hazard to human welfare because it threatens the quality of the human environment, is an interesting development—one which was most welcomed by the EDF and other conservation groups battling against DDT.

We do not know the extent to which other members of the Advisory Committee were influenced by Loucks' opinions in making their evaluations nor whether they were cognizant of his EDF associations. Many of the statements in the Report are cautious, and the recommendations are, on the whole, measured. However, a good many of the more extremist claims from publications indicting DDT are incorporated in it, and it has been subsequently cited as a semiofficial document in which the case against DDT as an environmental pollutant is summarized. It is evident, for example, that the Committee relied heavily on a recent National Academy of Sciences pamphlet, "Chlorinated Hydrocarbons in the Marine Environment," accepting its major conclusions at face value and assuming that the paper is objective. The fact is that this publication is replete with distortions (which we shall be discussing at length in Chapters 16 and 17), many of which were taken over in the Advisory Committee's Report.

It is time, now, for us to begin consideration of the claims on which the case against DDT is built—a consideration which will carry us through the last part of this chapter and the four which follow it.

The Modern Case and the Early Views

The claims which have been advanced at one time or another to justify the demand for cessation of DDT use are so numerous, and some are so out-of-date, that to cover them all would be beside the point. For instance, in 1953 Biskind asserted that DDT causes poliomyelitis. After effective vaccines were developed against the causative viruses, this claim was quickly dropped, never to be heard of again. The most common of the relatively current claims against DDT can be summarized in the following fourteen points:

1. The persistent pesticides remain indefinitely in the biosphere and are steadily accumulating.

2. The persistence of DDT (or its active metabolites) in the environment is so great that even if we do not now identify it in living organisms, we may expect them to take it up in the future and be endangered because it is available in reservoirs where it has accumulated. Thus, even an immediate and total ban on DDT production and use would not remove the danger to living forms for some years to come.

3. DDT is ubiquitous in the environment. It has been detected in living organisms from all parts of the globe.

4. Because DDT persists in active form, it can find its way in large quantities to organisms high on the food chain through the process of biomagnification.

5. DDT is carcinogenic. It is present in small quantities in the human diet, and through accumulation may cause cancer in people.

6. DDT may selectively inhibit the growth of certain algae, favoring undesirable species.

7. DDT inhibits the photosynthetic process of marine algae and may thus interfere with the production of oxygen by plant photosynthesis.

8. DDT is an active estrogen, and this is how it interferes with reproduction in general.

9. DDT is responsible for the thin eggshells observed in certain birds in the wild.

10. DDT leads to thin-shelled eggs in exposed populations of birds because it inhibits the enzyme carbonic anhydrase.

11. DDT blocks one of the "pump" enzymes, an ATPase.

12. DDT induces nonspecific liver enzymes which break down indigenous steroid hormones.

13. DDT causes hyperthyroidism in birds.

14. DDT is a nerve poison; this is how it kills insects, fish, birds, and mammals.

These points will all be discussed in the course of the next four chapters.

There are, however, some claims which, although no longer raised by the scientists among the anti-DDT campaigners, are still considered to be valid by many laymen, largely as a result of the phenomenal success of *Silent Spring*. (One should not forget that although ten years have passed since its publication, the book is still selling well and is recommended reading for many high school and college courses.)

One of the major points developed by Carson is a broad generalization about the possible extinction of all living species on Earth, including man himself, because of the unrestricted use of unnatural chemicals. She referred to this process of extinction by the word "sterility," by which she meant reproductive failure of whole species. "The shadow of sterility lies over all the bird studies, and indeed lengthens to include all living things within its potential range" (Carson, 1962, p. 101). This threat encompassed all the invertebrate and vertebrate phyla, in her view. There were no exceptions. Mollusks, crabs, fish, birds, and even small mammals were perishing, she thought. She was quite convinced that certain bird species were to face their ultimate day in the near future: "We plunge vast segments of our bird populations into the night of extinction" (ibid., p. 99). The robins were most affected but "the populations of nesting birds in general have declined as much as 90 per cent in some of the sprayed towns" (ibid., p. 103). "Pheasant sickness became a well-known phenomenon. Birds seek water, become paralyzed, and are found in the ditchbacks and ricechecks quivering" (ibid.; p. 117).

In man she assumed the effects would not be attributable so much to direct poisoning but rather to the hidden, insidious accumulation of the compound, which will cause cancer and mutations, maiming unborn generations.

Although it was difficult to explain how DDT could bring about all these terrifying effects, Carson felt the necessity to put forth some scientific-sounding explanation. She gave a rather lengthy description of the supposed mechanism of action, thinking that pesticides, especially DDT, interfere with cellular respiration.

> We have seen that each step in oxidation is directed and expedited by a specific enzyme. When any of these enzymes — even a single one of them — is destroyed or weakened, the cycle of oxidation within the cell comes to a halt. It makes no difference which enzyme is affected . . . DDT, methoxychlor, malathion, phenothiazine, and various dinitro compounds are among the numerous pesticides that have been found to inhibit one or more of the enzymes concerned in the cycle of oxidation. They thus appear as agents potentially capable of blocking the whole process of energy production and depriving the cells of utilizable oxygen. This is an injury with most disastrous consequences. . . . (Ibid., p. 183)

Basically the same mechanism, in less acute manifestation, was supposed to be responsible for DDT's carcinogenic properties: ". . . most pesticides meet the criterion of the perfect carcinogen too well for comfort. As we have seen in the preceding chapter, many of the chlorinated hydrocarbons, the phenols, and some herbicides interfere with oxidation and energy production within the cell. By this means they may be creating sleeping cancer cells, cells in which an irreversible malignancy will slumber long and undetected until finally — its cause long forgotten and even unsuspected—it flares into the open as recognizable cancer" (*ibid.*, p. 207).

Scary, isn't it? Unfortunately, these poetically expressed nightmares are so far from anything resembling knowledge that no scientist today, however committed to the environmental cause, would support such views.

With respect to the general, indiscriminate poisoning of wildlife, a perusal of official U.S. wildlife statistics quickly dispels Carson's apocalyptic vision. Let us review just a few of the data.

Wild Things

If we treat the different animal groups separately, we can find the following:

Among mollusks, oysters are able to concentrate 70,000 times the environmental levels of DDT in their bodies. In spite of this, no large-scale oyster mortalities have been ascribable to the pesticide. Historical catch statistics show fluctuations in oyster and clam production, but there are no overall declines in the postwar period. In those localized areas where the catches have decreased dramatically in recent years, the declines have been attributed to sewage, industrial waste, or overfishing. In Great South Bay, Long Island, where a sharp drop in oyster production occurred at the end of the 1940s, the cause was clearly traced to effluents originating from duck farms on the eastern end of the Island. The decrease in the Chesapeake Bay production was due to disease and, to a lesser degree, to industrial (phenolic) pollutants. The disappearance of the Olympia oyster in Washington State resulted from overfishing. Similar explanations are given for declines in the stone crab and blue crab catches. Almost invariably when drops in the catch figures were reported, they were found to be related to gross industrial pollution or to natural events, such as hurricanes.

Major fish kills in both the fresh-water and coastal environments are compiled annually by the Federal Water Pollution Control Administration. In 1967, which was a peak year for fish kills, only 3 percent of these could be traced to pesticides, and even this small percentage originated either from applications contrary to labeling instructions or from usage which has been subsequently suspended—that is, direct spraying of waters with chemicals inappropriate for this purpose.

Birds do not seem to be universally affected either. Robins, depicted so eloquently by Miss Carson as a species already doomed, have exhibited a phenomenal increase of 1,000 percent in the years from 1940 to 1960, according to the Audubon Society's bird counts. It does not seem to have been DDT which was behind the "quivering" of the pheasants depicted by Carson, either; for DeWitt

(1955) has shown experimentally that these birds can resist the fantastically high dosage of 10,000 ppm of DDT, with 15,000 ppm the dose lethal to half of the test animals. Similar results were obtained on quail and domestic hens, all of which prompted Charles Wurster (1970) to state that gallinaceous birds represent a family exceptionally resistant to DDT.

That birds can become serious pests is, of course, a well-recognized fact, although urban dwellers often forget this, unless they have personally experienced an infestation in great numbers. Recently, two towns in the southeastern United States faced serious problems in dealing with pesty starlings and blackbirds:

> RADFORD, Va., Jan. 19 (UPI).
> Officials of this southwest Virginia city plan to exterminate 150,000 starlings whose presence has been called a health hazard.
> The city council voted to have wildlife specialists spray the birds with a detergent foam solution that would leave their feathers matted and expose them to weather, resulting in their death.
> The decision was greeted with cheers from most residents, who had been demanding a solution to the starling problem. They complained that the birds' droppings have covered their lawns, trees, houses, and cars.
> "It smells like a steaming barnyard," said one woman.
> Glen Dudderar, a Virginia Tech wildlife specialist, said the droppings could also carry encephalitis and other diseases.
> The city said the extermination will be carried out within two weeks. (*International Herald Tribune,* Jan. 20, 1972, "City in Virginia Plans to Destroy 150,000 Starlings")
> An even worse infestation of birds bedevils Scotland Neck, N.C. (pop. 2,869). There, perhaps 20 million blackbirds are jammed into 60 to 85 acres of pine and hardwood trees. Branches have broken under the weight of the birds, and the accumulated carpet of guano in some sections of the woods is a foot thick. No one can figure out why the birds chose this particular town or how to drive the intruders away. (*Time,* Feb. 7, 1972, "The Bird Plague")

One has to admit, of course, that no sophisticated contemporary environmentalist would support Miss Carson's fears for the robins or the pheasants; and certainly they have no great fondness for starlings or blackbirds, either. Somewhat more embarrassing to environmentalist arguments are recent population explosions reported for the herring gull. In many areas bordering the Great Lakes these birds became serious pests, and the Fish and Wildlife Service quietly undertook their extermination.

Even more shocking was the announcement in the spring of 1971 that the

Audubon Society itself planned to poison herring gulls occupying Tern Island in the Nantucket Sound area. Apparently the herring gulls, which are on the State of Massachusetts' protected list of seabirds, have taken over the traditional nesting grounds of the local terns, and the Audubon Society had received permission from the Massachusetts Department of Natural Resources to exterminate them from this particular island (reported in the *New York Times,* April 15, 1971). But what of the famous balance of nature? If the herring gull is a protected species, it can hardly be called a general pest like the starlings and the blackbirds. Human intervention in this case seems to be a matter of eliminating one desirable species from a certain locale in the interest of another desirable species.

At the present time, it is only a few of the great predator birds which environmentalists claim are suffering from DDT effects: those high on the food chain, such as some of the hawks, eagles, large owls, and fish-eating pelagic birds. These species are said to accumulate high DDT residues from their prey, which are already several steps up the food chain, and to lay eggs with abnormally thin shells. Both Wurster and Graham write that the American red-tailed hawk, the golden eagle, and the great horned owl are exempt from these effects because they feed on rodents, which are in turn herbivores, and hence only a two-step food chain is involved. Birds like the bald eagle or the brown pelican, on the other hand, are said to be seriously endangered because they are "top predators." We don't know whether Miss Carson would have been displeased or relieved to learn that robins, are, after all, *not* headed for extinction. Her followers, however, seem to be curiously upset when it is pointed out to them that one of the bird species they have described as endangered turns out to be doing reasonably well; or they evidence the sort of deafness phenomenon characteristic of the "true believer." In November, 1969, record numbers of bald eagles were observed in Glacier National Park (*Crazy Horse News,* 1972), just at the time when Dr. Wurster was giving frequent lectures (Wurster, 1969; 1970) in which he explained in great scientific detail that this species was declining according to expectation, being one of those top predators in which pesticides accumulate through biomagnification. The Anacapa brown pelicans, which Robert Risebrough described in 1969 as "extinct," and Michael McCloskey of the Sierra Club mentioned as late as February, 1971, as "doomed," have made an embarrassing recovery, too. The California population of brown pelicans apparently did lay abnormally thin-shelled eggs and experienced considerable reproductive failure for at least two seasons, but the reasons for this have not been causally established, despite numerous statements and publications attributing the birds difficulties to DDT (or its metabolite, DDE). At the present time, the only way Risebrough—who has made a great case out of the plight of the pelican— can save the hypothesis that the thinning was caused by DDE is to throw out the subtle and pervasive oceanic-food-chain-magnification theory so favored by Wurster and claim instead that it was gross pollution of southern California coastal waters with sewage effluents containing DDT which was responsible for the birds' bad seasons (Risebrough *et al.*, 1972). Now that this situation has been corrected, Risebrough explains in all earnestness, the birds are beginning to recover. As we shall see later, the explanations of *how* all kinds of environmental damage attributed to DDT could be wrought by the compound often change with great rapidity; so fast, in fact, that environmentalists working in the same problem area frequently cannot keep up with each other's latest hypotheses. However, we are getting ahead of our story, and we want to return to the old claim that all wild things are in danger of dying out as a result of the use of the postwar pesticides.

Actually, one would expect that small wild mammals and big game should be declining in the developed countries — pesticides or no pesticides — since man has long been encroaching on their territories, turning previously wild woods, meadows, and swamps into suburban developments, and building superhighways through their haunts. Industrial operations have also reduced the acreage of available habitat for wild things. Strangely enough, however, the numbers of many species seem to be increasing rather than decreasing, in some cases at astounding rates. According to official wildlife surveys, animals are thriving to the point where hunting no longer represents any threat to most species, and at the same time, record harvests of all kinds of game are reported. Big-game populations have doubled in the United States since 1948. Beavers, which were once regarded as in danger of extinction because trappers sought them for their valuable fur, have become so numerous that in certain areas they constitute pests requiring special management. Antelopes have rebounded from near extinction in the early part of the century to levels where they can again be hunted.

The situation is similar in Europe, too. Even in highly industrialized, extensively cultivated, and supposedly overcrowded West Germany, the forests teem with wildlife. In the period between 1939 and 1969 the numbers of deer have grown by 23 percent, roe by 52 percent, and moose by 968 percent. There are about 18 percent more each of pheasants and quail, and 272 percent the number of ducks (Cramer, 1971).

In effect, if one reads *Silent Spring* with care, one comes across passages which would seem to indicate that Carson was not all that convinced herself that the use of pesticides was causing permanent, long-term deleterious effects on wild things. She wrote, for instance, the following: "To the bird watcher, the suburbanite who derives joy from the birds in his garden, the hunter, the fisherman or the explorer of wild regions, anything that destroys the wildlife of an area for even a single year has deprived him of pleasure to which he has a legitimate right. This is a valid point of view. Even if, as has sometimes happened, some of the birds and mammals and fishes are able to re-establish themselves after a single spraying, a great and real harm has been done" (Carson, 1962, p. 84). What is really interesting about this passage is not so much the tacit admission that wild species may very well be able to rebound from any temporary ill effects associated with pesticide use. It is rather the underlying assumption that the private pleasure of the individual suburbanite is a right which takes precedence over such public matters as disease control and the production of food, fiber, and housing for a world where the many do not live in the suburbs and may even lack the energy or leisure to take pleasure in wild things. The environmentalists usually strike a stance of moral righteousness, and on first impression they seem always to be on the side of the angels. But we invite the reader to take a fresh look at the arguments and to form his own judgment as to who are the real humanists in the battle over pesticide uses.

Trees

Before quitting the subject of the general status of wildlife, we want to remind the reader that the coin has a second side, and that there are cases illustrating the ill effects on wildlife which may ensue when pesticide programs are *suspended*. Most people are aware that the northeastern United States has been faced with a serious infestation of gypsy moths in the last several summers, but probably few realize the extent of the damage which has been wrought by this pest to the forests of this region.

There has been a great hue and cry raised in opposition to aerial spraying of woodlands, based mainly on the assertion that the natural ecological balance of the forests is disturbed by the spray programs. It is by now clear, however, that even the most ill-conceived and poorly executed spray program imaginable could not rival a large infestation by gypsy moths in terms of ecological disturbances. These pests, though children of nature, devour *all* the foliage of trees, especially oaks, and in large enough numbers they can destroy entire stands, leaving the other living things in the woodland devoid of food and habitat, and altering the ecology of whole watersheds. For lack of shade and food, the fauna either perish or migrate from the denuded woods. This can be unpleasant and even dangerous for nearby communities, as when, for instance, large numbers of copperheads and rattlesnakes migrated into suburban areas in northern New Jersey.

People who lived through the summers in locales of infestation probably need no reminders of the extent of the destruction, but for others, a few figures referring to the acreage defoliated might be useful (Table 8).

Table 8. *DEFOLIATION CAUSED BY GYPSY MOTHS: 1968-1971*

State	Year	Acres defoliated
New Jersey:	1968	5,000
	1969	38,000
	1970	129,000
	1971	180,595
Pennsylvania:	1968	80
	1969	800
	1970	10,000
	1971	655,000
Connecticut:	1970	369,000
	1971	655,000

In Suffolk County, New York, alone — the Long Island community which was the focal point of many of the early public protests against spray programs — 25,000 acres were stripped, prompting officials to declare a state of emergency in the summer of 1971.

By the spring of 1972, of the 113,000,000 acres of northeastern woodlands susceptible to gypsy moths, more than 2,000,000 acres had been defoliated, and sizable proportions of the trees have been permanently destroyed.

It is with a certain irony, then, that we consider the public statement of a New Jersey anti-pesticide activist that the gypsy moth is merely a "cosmetic problem" and that tree loss by this pest is of "no consequence."*

"Super Bugs"

Another of Miss Carson's arguments against chemical pesticides like DDT — one which is kept at least partially alive today — is that insect resistance makes chemical control impractical, uneconomic, and dangerous. We shall explain later the particular kind of danger which she associated with insect resistance.

Resistance does, of course, develop among insect populations exposed to pesticides. Nobody denies this. Resistance to chemicals is a generalized biological phenomenon, common to all groups of organisms from bacteria to man; it is part

*See "Note added in proof," p. 332.

of the natural adaptive process. Carson's particular explanations both of how this phenomenon occurs and what it implies are, however, completely erroneous.

In her view, resistance is an expression of the Darwinian notion of "the survival of the fittest." She thought that the chemicals would eliminate the weaker members of a given pest population, and that the survivors would represent the strongest specimens, those best able to recover from the attack. These survivors would then transmit their "strong" genotype, giving rise to progeny composed mostly of these "strong" types. Each new assault on the population would thus favor the selection of superior specimens, leading eventually to the creation of a population of "super bugs." She claimed that, since these new variants would be hardier, combating them would lead to a process of escalation in which ever more toxic chemicals would have to be found. Given her view of stronger and stronger pest specimens evolving after chemical control, it follows that she envisioned a vicious circle. In agriculture, the use of pesticides would inevitably lead to economic difficulties. In public health programs for disease-vector control, it would result in exacerbation rather than relief of endemic vector-borne diseases.

Now let us consider what actually happens in the development of resistance. First of all, resistance is neither an expression of mutation nor of selection of the strongest specimens in the population. Within a given population, resistance may arise if that population includes individuals in whose DNA the genetic components defining the mechanism of resistance are *already present.* As the compound kills all those individuals in the population that do not possess the resistant trait, those which live may give rise to a new population which consists only of resistant individuals. However, it is quite untrue that the resistant strains represent some kind of "super bug"; on the contrary, they are usually weaker than the population which has been eliminated, because the random mutations which at one time gave rise to the trait permitting resistance had to become manifest at the detriment of another trait more typical for the population as a whole. Thus, as a rule, resistant populations can be eliminated with a usually weaker but more specific pesticide than the one to which resistance has developed.

Even LaMont Cole, who is among the biologists who gave *Silent Spring* a rather warm review and whose articles are written in an equally alarmist tone as Miss Carson's book, could not let her views on resistance stand unchallenged. "I do not for a moment believe that the chemicals are producing super insects," he wrote in 1962 (Cole, 1962, p. 178).

The argument that the use of broad-spectrum chemical pesticides leads to falling profits for the farmer is not, as one might imagine, one of those which has dropped into oblivion. On the contrary, it is constantly brought up by environmentalists as a reason for turning away from these "crude ecological poisons."

Wurster and van den Bosch, for example, wrote recently: "The farmer, faced with nightmarish insect problems, finds himself addicted to more and heavier insecticide treatments, often at the urging of pesticide salesmen. With rising pesticide bills and falling crop yields, he is on a treadmill to economic disaster" (Wurster and van den Bosch, 1972, p. 6).

These statements, written in the popular press, are not documented with any economic references, and one would suspect that the writers do not know any farmers. On the other hand, economic analyses of returns from pesticide investment have been carried out with some frequency, and the figures stand in marked contradiction to the assertions of these self-proclaimed experts. According to Headley (1968), the return on every dollar of pesticide investment is $4.16. In 1963, pesticide expenditures on crops totaled $436 million, while the increase in returns amounted to $1.8 billion. Naturally, there are fluctuations in the annual yields of particular crops in particular regions, but there are absolutely no indications of the overall "falling crop yields" mentioned by the two environmentalists.

We must give some further consideration to Carson's statement that the phenomenon of insect resistance involves "dangers." She writes that, although most farmers and agriculturists go blithely on putting their faith in chemicals, inviting "further disasters," "those concerned with disease-carrying insects seem by now to have been thoroughly aroused to the alarming nature of the situation . . ." (Carson, 1962, p. 233). She supports this subjective assessment with a citation from WHO which does not mention alarm, but states that insect resistance has become the most important problem facing vector-control programs. (In 1962 this was probably true; by now it would seem that "environmentalist resistance" has become at least as serious an obstacle to these programs.) She then goes on for several pages writing about specific areas where certain target pests have developed resistance to the chemical of choice in the program. The general impression left with the reader is that chemicals for vector control have failed ignominiously in their purpose: the alleviation of the human misery caused by diseases such as malaria, typhus, plague, and so on. To the malaria problem, she devotes a mere half a page, wherein she recounts the obstacles encountered in Greece from DDT-resistant *Anopheles sacharovi*. She comments, "This was a portent of the extremely serious situation that has now developed" (*ibid.*, p. 237). The final message impressed on the readers of these pages is that the use of chemical pesticides in disease control is actually creating new and more serious epidemics than those which characterized the prewar era.

To a certain extent we are inclined to excuse Miss Carson's mischaracterization of the causes and nature of the resistance phenomenon on grounds of ignorance. But the complete misrepresentation of the status of public health programs throughout the world can on no account be excused, for her book involved a great deal of library work, and there is no question that the data on the vast successes of the disease-vector control programs were available to her. Her treatment of the relation of DDT and the other organochlorine pesticides to problems of human health must be described as deliberate misrepresentation of hard facts and figures, and conscious distortions by omission. So long as her book continues to circulate, it is essential that protests be repeatedly raised against this serious falsification.

We have given earlier a few figures relating to the numbers of lives saved and the numbers of people living in areas where the malaria eradication programs have been carried through to success. Readers who are interested in further facts and figures for other vector-borne diseases should consult the bulletins of the World Health Organization.

How Passable Is the Less Traveled Road?

Rachel Carson was clearly alarmed about the spread of man-made chemicals in the environment, and the basic message of her book concerned the long-term dangers of approaching insect control with chemical weapons devised in the laboratory. In some parts of her book she minimizes the damage and dangers associated with insect pests, asserting that pesticides wreak havoc on the environment merely in the interest of controlling "a few unwanted species." Nevertheless she does not advocate passive submission to an insect-filled world. She devotes an entire chapter called "The Other Road" to discussing an alternative to chemical control about which she is most enthusiastic. This "other way" is usually called either "biological control" or "natural control." In its purest version—that is, using no chemicals at all—the natural control method includes three basic techniques: the release of sterile males, the use of insect pathogens, and the introduction of natural insect parasites.

The first approach is often called the Knipling technique, after its originator, E. F. Knipling. This involves the release into the environment of large numbers of sterilized males of a particular insect species. In the first variant of this approach males are sterilized by exposure to a cobalt source for irradiation with gamma rays. The sterile males are then released into the environment during the breeding season in numbers which would result in a ratio of sterile to nonsterilized males in the natural population of 3:1. It is then expected that the sterilized males will successfully compete with the untreated males in mating with females of the species and that fertilization will thus be prevented. Even under ideal conditions with a relatively small starting population the practice has to be continued for a minimum of several years in order to reduce reproduction to zero, for some of the untreated males will continue to locate female partners.

This technique definitely holds a certain promise for pest control. It has been successfully employed to eradicate two species: the Florida fruit fly and the screwworm. It is very costly however, even when only one or two species are involved. It also becomes complicated when the pest in question is ubiquitous, like the common housefly, for example. Think about it. Three times the normal male population of houseflies would have to be released each year for a number of years, and these hundreds of billions of flies would have to be released more or less simultaneously throughout the whole country for the program to be effective. We would also have certain problems in border areas, since it would be difficult to patrol the whole of the Mexican border against contamination by virile Mexican flies.

The cost would escalate tremendously if we were to attack all pests in this manner. Although environmentalists frequently remind us that only one-tenth of 1 percent of the insect species are pests, since there are nearly three million species, this small fraction still adds up to 3,000 species, and this figure does not include those pests which are not insects, such as mites, lice, scorpions, ticks, and so on. Since the universities clearly could not manage the task of producing billions of sterilized males for each of these 3,000 species, it would probably be necessary to set up special hatcheries for each species, staffed by highly specialized entomologists. These hatcheries would have to be equipped with a cobalt-60 radioactive source, which introduces some danger of environmental radiation leakage, although we do not regard this as a serious hazard, provided that careful precautions are taken. The sterilized males of flying insects could be released into the environment by fleets of airplanes. The nonflying pests, however, would present a special problem, since many of them, like mites, fleas, bedbugs, and ticks, do not move any appreciable distance during their lifetime; thus the females would have to be precisely located so that the sterilized males could be deposited in their vicinity. This might be accomplished by eliciting the cooperation of the general public. The sterile males could be distributed to individual households by Boy Scouts and Sierra Club members in small, reusable containers, and the people themselves could join in the fight by distributing these specimens at sites of probable female inhabitants. For a few years people would have to contend with a higher population of all the nuisance organisms, but perhaps for many, the moral satisfaction of eliminating pests without resorting to chemical means would more than compensate for this. Personally, we still prefer the faster and tidier chemicals.

There is a variant on this technique which is somewhat less expensive and less complicated. This consists of applying chemosterilants to native populations in their own environment, and allowing the treated insects to disperse and breed with the rest of the untreated population. It is one of the curious inconsistencies in *Silent Spring* that in a book devoted to the supposed dangers of many relatively innocuous pesticides Miss Carson could write so casually and even hopefully about the use of chemicals for insect sterilization, since all substances known to achieve this end are dangerous. Recognizing the practical problems which would arise from attempting to control common flies by hatching and releasing huge numbers of sterile males, she wrote: "A chemical sterilant, on the other hand, could be combined with a bait substancce and introduced into the natural environment of the fly; insects feeding on it would become sterile and in the course of time the sterile flies would predominate and the insects would breed themselves out of existence" (Carson, 1962, p. 249).

It should be added that Carson expressed some awareness that presently known chemosterilants, such as the alkylating agents, are not substances to be introduced casually into the environment. Most knowledgeable people—even those hardened "Philistines" who still favor the judicious use of broad-spectrum insecticides—are exceedingly wary of any suggested uses of chemosterilants other than those in which treatment of organisms is confined to a laboratory and carefully controlled.

A second natural control method—the one most highly favored by the real purists—involves the identification and introduction into the environment of natural predators and parasites of damaging pests. The principle that even parasitic pests have natural enemies has, of course, been recognized for many years. However, identification of useful predators and parasites which are really effective in controlling a pest is not such a simple matter. During the 90 or so years that this method has been of interest, the concentrated efforts of the world's entomologists have resulted in the discovery and successful establishment of a little over 100 such beneficial insects, but only 20 of these have provided significant control of some of the more destructive pests (Huffaker, 1971; Irving, 1970). Professionals are hard at work in the search for predators and parasites which might help in the control of the remaining 2,980 pestiferous species.

The third completely natural method involves the use of insect pathogens. *Bacillus thuringiensis*, a bacterium which has been recognized for over 60 years as a possible means of causing fatalities in some insects, constitutes one of the two partial successes up to now on the insect pathogen front. The other is the milky-spore disease of the Japanese beetle. Carson also mentions experimental work with insect pathogen viruses and with other microbes as hopeful. She assures her readers that none of these microbial insecticides is dangerous to non-target organisms. "In contrast to chemicals, insect pathogens are harmless to all but their intended targets" (Carson, 1962, p. 256). The statement illustrates Miss Carson's appalling ignorance on this subject matter, and also speaks very poorly for her sources. Without turning to recondite references, we can enumerate several microorganisms which are pathogenic to both insects and vertebrates: *Proteus, Actinoplaca, Bacillus chitinovorus, Saprolegnia, Laboulbenia, Microsporidium*, to name a few. *Saprolegnia* is, for example, the cause of a fungal disease which affects insects and fish—being responsible for large-scale fish kills. *Microsporidium* can attack any type of insect; but it also causes a fungal disease of large domestic animals and man.

As for the target specificity of the virsuses in experimental insect control methods, it is most unlikely that officials will ever give their seal of approval to this technique. In general, viruses are prone to mutations, and fears that large quantities of them released into nature could mutate into forms with an altered host specificity are well grounded.

Even with the bacteria, there is no assurance of target specificity, simply because it is impossible to test the whole scale of possible hosts. There are further good reasons why the supposed promise of the techniques employing insect pathogens is questionable. An analogous procedure was tried in the Soviet Union in the late 1940s, in experimental attempts to control human bacterial infections by administering specific bacteriophages. The results were discouraging, with improvement noted in only a small percentage of patients. There were many reasons behind this failure which we shall not detail here, but what became apparent from these experiments as a general principle is the following. If the virulence and infectivity of a microbe is high enough to cause a fatal disease in a target organism, then it will not restrict its activity to that species only, but will attack other related forms. If its virulence is not high enough to produce an immediate kill, the body defenses of the target species will overcome the infection. Were one to resort to the use of highly virulent microbial strains to combat insect pests, a nearly complete eradication of all insects might ensue, leading to unforeseeable consequences. (*Bacillus chitinovorus* would be a good candidate for such a program. It solubilizes the chitinaceous exoskeleton, a feature common to all arthropods.) But such an approach would obviously not be favored by either the natural-control enthusiasts or the technologically oriented agriculturists. The risks are just too great.

We do not wish to give the impression that we are against efforts to achieve successful biological controls for some insect species; but we feel that it is deceptive to place too great hopes in the feasibility of these methods, and that talk of biological controls as a panacea is irresponsible.

Approximately the same holds true for the concept of "integrated control," at least when this is used to refer to methods where minimal amounts of target-specific pesticides are used together with the whole armamentarium of the biological control techniques. There is probably nobody who would oppose such a method as a theoretical ideal. Unfortunately, however, neither the scientific basis nor the economic means are presently adequate to make such programs workable on a large scale. With regard to some of the problems which remain to be solved, one may consider this summary by George Irving of the USDA Agricultural Research Service:

> Integrated control is a compatible system of insect control in which various methods are used in proper sequence and timing so as to create the least hazard to man and the environment and to permit maximum assistance from natural controls. . . . Much research is needed, because for several major insect pests pertinent information is lacking on the life history, host plants, flight habits, population dynamics, role of natural enemies, numbers of different stages of insects per acre, nutritional requirements, requirements for mass rearing, comparative vigor and competitiveness of reared insects and native strains. . . . Much more information about the insects is required for development and application of integrated control methods than is generally required for use of insecticides. Areawide programs in which billions of sterilized insects, or biological control agents, or large quantities of natural sex attractant are used, will require housing facilities, development of suitable rearing media, and automated techniques for mass production of insects. (Irving, 1970, pp. 1422–1423)

About a year later, E. F. Knipling, the father of the "sterile male technique" and a man who could hardly be labeled as an "agricultural technocrat," gave an interview to *Environmental Science and Technology* in which he offered a similar assessment of the practicability of the methods involved in integrated control: "Although many of the alternative controls have shown promise in limited tests or practical use, the majority of pest control methods is still relatively in the future. 'We still need to rely on proved pesticides,' says Knipling. 'The alternatives are going to come slow, and will take time' " (Miller and Knapp, 1971, p. 403).

After these sober assessments in the scientific press, it comes as something of a surprise to read, only a few months later in the *popular press*, that according to Wurster and van den Bosch, integrated control methods have not only been thoroughly worked out to the point where they are effective as alternatives to the use of persistent pesticides, but also that they are now *economical.* In the same newspaper article in which they referred to the "economic disaster" experienced by the farmer who uses broad-spectrum insecticides like DDT, they wrote: "Entomologists have developed effective, economical and ecologically sound integrated control programs for a number of the world's major crops . . ." (Wurster and van den Bosch, 1972, p. 6).

One would think, then, that in the space of a few months, all the problems had been solved, and we could cheerfully abandon the persistent pesticides, having found safer means of dealing with pests which are equally as effective and economical. That is exactly the point that the two scientists hoped to put across; but, unfortunately, there are good reasons to suppose that in this article the gentlemen were not speaking solely as scientists, but also as advocates. The context in which the article was written was at the height of the Consolidated DDT Hearings, where one of the major points at issue was the suspension of DDT registrations for use on cotton crops. There are no known effective natural methods or narrow-spectrum, target-specific chemicals which can control the cotton bollworm, a pest which creates serious problems for the cotton farmers of the southeastern states. The only available substitute for the control of this pest at the present time is parathion, which has a much broader range of targets than DDT and is exceedingly toxic to man. None of these facts are mentioned in the article, which was clearly designed to give the public the impression that anyone who contends there are still legitimate needs for pesticides like DDT is very much behind the times. The writers began, in fact, by describing Nobel Laureate Dr. Norman Borlaug, the father of the "Green Revolution," as a man whose "expertise is non-existent or 20 years out-of-date" *(ibid.).*

May not one fairly ask, in any case, who are these people either as men of import or as scientists that they dare to pass such a judgement about one of the greatest personalities of our age? What are their concrete contributions to the welfare of mankind that they should speak up—dressed in the cloak of righteousness—against a benefactor of the whole of humanity? Where are their discoveries, and what is the nature of their achievement? How much have they done to alleviate human misery, and on which side do they stand in the battle of the poor and of the third-world peoples against hunger? *Quo usque tandem abutere patientia nostra?* To what limits will their audacity carry them before they arouse the ire of the populace? It is a near certainty that Dr. Borlaug will not stoop to answer such absurd charges on the part of his individual detractors, for he is too busy carrying on his work in the fields of the Philippines, of Mexico, of Malaysia. As the Arabs say: "The dog howls—the caravan proceeds."

If environmentalists are willing to discredit their opposition in such a crude fashion, then, it seems to us, there can be only two possible interpretations of such moves: either their case against DDT is so horrifying that they are willing to go to any lengths to carry it to a righteous conclusion—or they have no case against DDT at all.

It is time, then, that we examine the current arguments about this famous and infamous pesticide in more detail.

Note Added in Proof

Since this book was completed, an even more widespread and economically far more significant devastation of high-value timber forests by a tussock moth infestation has developed in Washington, Oregon, and Idaho. Millions of acres of prime Douglas fir have been destroyed, with direct damages estimated, as of December 1973, at more than $300 million. Two years of efforts on the part of local residents to lift the ban on the use of DDT—the only effective way known to control the moth—have thus far had no result, although it is known that the House Committee on Forestry is considering the introduction of a bill which would grant authority to the Secretary of Agriculture to permit deployment of DDT in cases of agricultural or forestry emergencies. To date, however, no action has been taken, as the matter is still under the jurisdiction of the Environmental Protection Agency. New Hearings on the issue are scheduled to begin on January 19, 1974.

14

OF MEN AND MICE

"Have you an umbrella in your house?"

"I think so."

"I wish you would bring it out here,
and walk up and down with it, and
look up at me every now and then,
and say 'Tut-tut, it looks like rain.'
I think, if you did that, it would help
the deception which we are practising
with these bees."

Pooh to Christopher Robin

A. A. MILNE

Question: Would you give us your professional opinion, if you have one, on whether the presence of DDT in the human environment represents a significant carcinogenic hazard to man!

Answer: I can only answer that qualitatively, and the answer is yes, DDT has been shown to be carcinogenic in a series of well-designed experiments on the basis of standard toxicological carcinogensis procedure and philosophy . . . . I would attach a high degree of importance in terms of the decision-making process to such experiments on DDT because we are dealing with a material which not only is carcinogenic but also is highly persistent and cumulative.

323

Question: In your professional opinion, can a man be safely exposed to any level of DDT?

Answer: The answer is no.

(Epstein, 1972b, p. 7322)

The statements above were made by Samuel Epstein as part of his testimony on behalf of EDF at the Consolidated DDT Hearings, on January 14, 1972. Consistent with the past pattern of widespread press coverage of any utterance by a scientist that DDT is harmful, Epstein's opinions were picked up immediately by the popular press. This citation and other quotes from his testimony were also published in the "Point of View" column in *Science* (Epstein, 1972a). None of the papers saw fit to grant equal space to the testimonies of several other prominent experts: among them Jesse Steinfeld, the U.S. Surgeon General, and John Higginson, Director of the International Agency for Research on Cancer, both of whom expressed the judgment that DDT is not a human carcinogen. And *Science,* although quick to print Epstein's comments as a "point of view," turned down a letter from W. H. Butler of the British Medical Research Council (who also testified at the Hearings) in which he had expressed an opposing opinion.

Since Epstein was the star witness for the EDF with respect to the claim that DDT is a carcinogen, we should like to examine in some detail what he said and on what he based his interpretations. Going over Epstein's arguments can serve as the basis for a review of the literature dealing with DDT and cancer. We also wish to bring attention to some sweeping generalizations he made during the course of his testimony which we feel cannot be substantiated, for although his right to hold his own opinions and make dissenting evaluations cannot be questioned, his views cease to be mere private judgments when he either claims or implies the agreement of his scientific colleagues and speaks for them in a public forum. It then becomes a matter for public argument whether he represents properly what is in the literature and whether he describes accurately the consensus among scientists.

Among the broad, general statements made by Epstein during the course of his testimony are the following:

1. The consensus of disinterested scientific opinion on, I think, a universal basis is that there is no such evidence which would support the concept of a safe level of a carcinogen. . . (Epstein, 1972b, p. 7322)

2. As far as negative experiment is concerned, all one can say is, under those particularly artificial conditions of test, bearing in mind the gross insensitivity of the procedure, all one can say is that there was no evidence—that these experiments have not provided any evidence of carcinogenic hazard. (*Ibid.,* p. 7328)

3. It has been commonly and repeatedly stated that carcinogenicity can be induced nonspecifically. There is no evidence whatsoever in the literature that this is the case. (*Ibid.*, p. 7324)

4. I would say that there is a consensus, which I share, that the majority of human cancers are environmental in origin. (*Ibid.*, p. 7336)

1. With respect to Epstein's first generalization, the reader is asked to refer back to some of the basic concepts of toxicology which we discussed in Chapter 11, in particular to the topic of toxic threshold. We do not wish to repeat that material again, but it ought to be pointed out here that Epstein is, in our opinion, misusing the word "consensus" when he claims agreement with his views on this matter of no-safe-exposure level for a carcinogen. If anything, the consensus would seem to favor the converse and one would probably be hard put to find more than a small number of scientists who accept the "no-safe-exposure" view.

The general opinion among "informed laymen" might, on the other hand, favor the "no-safe-limit" concept, for the public has been largely educated by journalists, who have in turn taken much of their most interesting and frighteningly impressive copy from just that small number of scientists who intepret certain experiments as indicating that DDT is a carcinogen and, at the same time, hold to the idea that there is no safe exposure level for any material which has been shown to cause cancer in animals, by whatever method.

2. In emphasizing that negative experimental results cannot be taken as an assurance that a chemical is not carcinogenic, Epstein appears to imply that all chemicals must be held suspect until demonstrated to be innocuous. Since there is no way to arrive at a final negative proof through the experimental method, such a stance, extended ad absurdum, would indicate that there are no safe compounds. With reference to this problem, Golberg has written: ". . .should it happen that a chemical agent turns out negative in all the tests applied, it remains under suspicion until such time as someone can discover an organism, devise a route of administration or achieve a sufficiently heroic dose to produce some positive biological result, however bizarre. Thus there is an obvious premium on ingenuity and persistence!" (Golberg, 1971, p. 205).

3. In claiming that there are no data in the literature which would indicate that carcinogenicity can be induced nonspecifically, Epstein again makes a broad generalization which seems without foundation. Under cross-examination he admitted that there are a number of definitely noncarcinogenic substances which, when tested by the subcutaneous route, will cause malignant tumors in rats or mice. Production of subcutaneous malignant tumors by such common substances as table salt and sugar—precisely the two compounds which Epstein mentioned could never cause cancer—has been shown. A host of other common

nutrients, and even water, can also result in malignancies by this route (Grasso and Golberg, 1966, p. 269). In the article cited earlier, Golberg wrote further: "It is safe to predict that, by appropriate choice of dose, concentration of solution and frequency of administration by the subcutaneous route, any chemical agent can be shown to be a carcinogen in the rat and probably also in other species of laboratory rodent" (Golberg, 1971, p. 206).

When confronted during cross-examination with material from the literature on this subject, Epstein hedged, stating that the subcutaneous route is not the proper method of administration to test compounds such as food additives or pesticides for carcinogenicity.

However, the subcutaneous route is not the only means by which nonspecific carcinogenicity has been demonstrated. For example, when pellets of paraffin wax, cholesterol, palmitic acid (an ubiquitous component of all fats), or even glass beads are inserted into the bladders of either mice or rats, carcinoma of the vesicle develops in a large percentage of the test animals (Bryan and Spring-berg, 1966; Ball et al., 1964). It seems unlikely that anyone would claim that glass or palmitic acid are specifically carcinogenic.

Furthermore, skin cancers can also be induced by nonspecific substances. It was shown in 1925 that both dilute hydrochloric acid and sodium hydroxide produced carcinoma of the skin when applied repeatedly to the epidermis (Narat, 1925). Dilute hydrochloric acid is one of the major components of the stomach juice in humans.

Lastly, even by oral administration, such common food items as honey and egg yolk have been shown to induce cancer of the stomach in mice when the diet was not a balanced one (Crosby, 1966; Colorado Extension Service, 1970). It could be argued that there might be some potent, specific carcinogen in both honey and egg yolk. Nevertheless, that would not alter the point of the finding, which is that these two foods have been eaten by millions of people throughout their lives and are considered to be perfectly safe. On the other hand, the point of Epstein's generalization was that one can clearly distinguish between com-pounds which do and do not induce cancer, and if a substance can be shown to be carcinogenic, it is not safe.

4. Epstein's statement that he shares the "consensus" opinion that most cancers are environmental in origin is so controversial that it is not worth argu-ing about. There hardly can be a consensus about a mechanism (the origin of cancer) which is as yet completely unknown and which still defies the attempts at clarification of thousands of scientists throughout the world.

The "Total Available Literature"

We come now to the specific evaluation in Epstein's testimony of the literature on the role of DDT in carcinogenesis.

Although he himself has neither conducted experiments involving the carcinogenic effects of DDT on test animals nor been involved in epidemiological studies of populations exposed to DDT, Epstein's testimony on these subjects was fluent and confident, and while reading through it, one gets the impression that he must be as thoroughly familiar with the pertinent literature as almost anyone. He stated that he had had occasion to review "some time ago what I consider to be the total available literature on carcinogenicity of DDT, and I'm willing to discuss aspects of this . . ." (Epstein, 1972b, p. 7341).

In his oral evaluation of the DDT-carcinogen question, he refers to a total of 18 studies, 11 of which he dismisses as suffering "from such serious defects of design, conceptually and informationally and in other aspects . . . that it is impossible to use these in any way to make judgments on carcinogenic or other hazards of DDT . . ." *(ibid.).* According to him, all of these 11 "inadequate" studies either used too low a dosage, or too short an exposure period, or too small numbers of test animals or subjects. He separates these 11 reports into two categories: epidemiological and strict toxicity studies.

To begin with, let us consider some of the work which has been carried out on humans exposed to DDT.

Twenty-five Years of Safe Use

Since the time of the discovery of the active properties of DDT, many studies have been conducted on its toxicity for man and other mammals. Some of these have used human volunteers; some have followed the health records of pesticide factory workers and spraymen; still others have involved laboratory experiments with test animals.

Hayes and his coworkers reported in 1956 the results of several experiments with human volunteers. Six people ingested 35 mg of DDT per man per day for 12 months, and three volunteers took the same dosage for 18 months daily. Another six volunteers ingested 3.5 mg of DDT per man per day for 12 months, and six others the same dosage for 18 months. In a second study (Hayes et al., 1961) similar doses were given for 21 months to 24 volunteers. The subjects reported no complaints and the researchers could find no damage ascribable to DDT. To get some idea of the quantities involved one should consider that the

1968 average daily intake of DDT in foods for the U.S. population was 0.02 mg per man per day. This is 1,750 times less than the amount of DDT ingested by the volunteers taking the higher dose in Hayes' experiments. In a five-year follow-up (Hayes et al., 1971) on the high-dose volunteers, no adverse effects were noted.

In a study on the epidemiology of pesticides, Hayes compared the incidences per 100,000 population of different types of cancers in all areas of the United States from 1927 to the early 1960s, noting regional variations. He could not find any correlation between DDT use patterns, its quantities in food, or in human tissues, and the incidence or fluctuations of cancer types (Hayes, 1964).

Special studies of persons exposed to DDT for periods of many years are also available (Laws et al. 1967; Wolfe et al., 1959; Ortelee, 1958; Davignon et al., 1965). Laws, for example, reported an extensive investigation of 35 men who had been employed from 11 to 19 years in a plant that had produced DDT continuously and exclusively since 1947. The exposure tolerated by these workers was calculated to be 18 mg per man per day—that is, from 600 to 900 times more than the daily intake of the general population. No complaints or symptoms of illness attributable to DDT could be identified. In an article by Ortelee on clinical and laboratory examinations of 40 workers who had been exposed to DDT (and in many cases simultaneously to other pesticides) no ill effects were reported, and at least one of the subjects had tolerated DDT exposure of 42 mg per day for eight years.

Wolfe and his coworkers studied several thousand people in tropical and subtropical countries who had been frequently and liberally dusted with DDT. They also examined applicators who had been working for years in a virtual cloud of the compound. The only health abnormalities which they observed were some cases of dermatitis among the applicators; and these rashes were ascribed to the kerosene solvent rather than to the pesticide itself.

More recently, Wolfe has mentioned that extensive studies of high-exposure individuals in the United States are in progress through the Division of Community Studies of the FDA. There are 15 of these projects in areas of heavy pesticide use. In each group, 100 selected high-exposure individuals are being compared with a control of 100 persons from the same community with minimal pesticide exposure. One of the purposes of the investigation is to look for gradual, delayed, or subtle changes (Wolfe, 1969).

A paper of a different nature (the therapeutic use of the chemical) reporting that there were no deleterious effects from extensive oral exposure of humans to DDT is that of Thompson et al. (1959). These investigators administered about 200 mg of DDT per man per day as a treatment for congenital jaundice. This value is 7,500 times greater than was the intake of the pesticide in the general

U.S. population at that time. The DDT treatment was highly beneficial for the jaundice, and no adverse effects were noted.

Two of the earliest studies of human volunteers deal with exposure to DDT through the inhalation route. Neal et al. (1944) reported on the continuous daily exposure of volunteers to aerosols, mists, and dusting powders of DDT for several months. Although the exact amount of exposure was not measured, it was sufficient to leave a white deposit of DDT on the nasal passages of these subjects each day. In 1945, Fennah conducted a self-experiment, during which he inhaled daily 100 mg of DDT for a total of 11.5 months. In addition to this, to test the simultaneous action of ingested DDT, he drank water dusted at the rate of 3,240 mg/m^2. With the exception of minor, local irritations in the nose, neither Neal's volunteers nor Fennah observed any ill effects.

In all the chronic exposure studies of humans, the investigators have specifically looked for the occurrence of cancer. Laws underlines, for example, that among the 35 DDT plant workers whom he investigated there were no cases of cancer, whereas it has been shown that among selected groups of industrial workers the probable incidence of cancer is nearly 5 in 100 (Birks, 1960).

The fact that neither experimental nor occupational exposure has given rise to any reports of chronic toxic effects from DDT has led researchers involved in such studies to state that DDT is safe for humans, even in amounts substantially in excess of those to which the general public is exposed.

Epstein objects strongly to the fact that DDT has been declared safe on the basis of these studies. However, in his oral review of the DDT literature, he mentions only three of the 12 papers we have just enumerated, which list is by no means comprehensive. To carry the matter a little further, an extensive list of epidemiological works is given for the United States alone in the *Report of the Secretary's Commission on Pesticides and Their Relationship to Environmental Health* (1969), to which body Epstein served as an advisor in three separate capacities, according to his own statement. On pages 359-360 of the report one may read:

> Epidemiological searches for chronic DDT effects have been carried out with negative results in the Northwest (Summerford, 1953; Hayes, 1957; Hayes, 1958; Durham, 1964; Durham, 1965), the Southwest (Hartwell, 1965; Rappolt, 1968), the Southeast (Fowler, 1953; Hayes, 1955; Quinby, 1958; Ortelee, 1958; Witter, 1959; Hayes, 1965; Davies, 1966; Fiserova-Bergerova, 1968; Davies, 1968), in Hawaii (Casarett, 1968), in Alaska (Durham, 1961), and in the United States (Hayes, 1963; Hayes, 1968; Dale, 1963; Durham, 1965a; Durham, 1965b; Foter, 1966). These studies have been summarized recently (Hayes, 1967; Hayes, 1969).

From the whole of Hayes' work on DDT, much of which clearly relates directly to epidemiological investigations, Epstein mentions only the two studies with volunteers in his testimony. He dismisses these in the following terms: "I would submit that any further discussion on the appropriateness of this paper to assessing of epidemiological hazards or carcinogenic hazards of DDT to man is clearly irrelevant" (Epstein, 1972b, pp. 7361-7362).

In addition to not citing Hayes' extensive work on the epidemiology of pesticides per se, Epstein also does not mention the Wolfe studies of exposed populations in the tropics, which involved very large numbers of people; and he does not seem to be aware of the FDA epidemiological studies in progress, from which some results are undoubtedly available by now.

About the Laws study of the Montrose factory workers he says: "On the basis of this period of observation [11 to 19 years of exposure] Laws makes the claim, no cases of cancer or blood dyscrasia were recorded. These papers [those of Hayes and Laws] have been cited repeatedly . . . to indicate that DDT has been used in humans with no evidence of carcinogenic hazard, and I would represent that such claims are a travesty of the scientific data" (ibid., p. 7362).

Here there should not be any misunderstanding of his meaning, for he later amplified his statement and made it clear that it is the claims of Hayes and Laws in their papers which he considers a travesty. If we understand correctly the implication of the above citation, it means that it is a travesty of scientific data evaluation to declare a substance safe just because one has not identified any carcinogenic effects among heavily exposed humans after many years.

In general, it would seem that Epstein's review of the literature of human exposure studies was less than thorough, since he also stated, most emphatically: "In the case of pesticides, where inhalation is a very significant mode of human exposure, there are in the literature no data whatsoever—and I repeat, there are in the literature no data whatsoever on chronic inhalation studies of any pesticides, be it DDT or dichlorvos or any other pesticide—so we have no intimation on the basis of which to assess hazard or by [sic] one route to which human exposure is significant" (ibid., p. 7315).

What of the studies of Neal and of Fennah? Or the British researchers, Cameron and Burgess (1945)? Are they no longer in the literature? And if those experiments do not satisfy Dr. Epstein's criteria for chronic exposure, one could point him toward some data in the literature on inhalation experiments of other pesticides. He should be more careful when using phrases like "no data whatsoever" and "any pesticides," if he wants to avoid the embarrassment of direct contradiction. (See the literature in Hayes, 1969a.)

"Irrelevant" Experiments

The other eight papers dismissed by Epstein as irrelevant or inappropriate are "strict toxicity studies"—i.e., experiments with laboratory animals. While one could argue with him on a number of grounds about whether all eight can be summarily discarded, even using his own criteria for appropriateness and relevance, we do not propose to do so. We should like to bring up some studies not referred to by him, however, and provide a few further comments from one that he does mention (Cameron and Cheng, 1951), since these are pertinent to discussion of the reports which Epstein classifies as either firm proof of DDT's carcinogenicity or as being "highly suggestive" of the same.

From the earliest days of acute and chronic DDT exposure in experiments with test animals, there have been reports that if the dosage is high enough, liver damage is observed. A sizable number of studies were done in the mid-1940s in both the United States and the United Kingdom in which large doses of DDT we ᴧ fed to all kinds of animals: mice, rats, guinea pigs, rabbits, chickens, dogs, cats, cows, sheep, and horses. In all of these animals except chickens, damage to the liver was reported after prolonged exposure to large doses. The liver damage involved fatty or parenchymatous degeneration, with centrolobular or focal coagulation necrosis. Smith and Stohlman (1944) found that when rats were fed 1,000 ppm DDT daily, all died from 18 to 80 days after onset of the experiment; but those fed 500 ppm survived beyond 3 months. Their experimental animals were worked up for histopathology by Lillie and Smith·(1944). The animals which succumbed to the 1,000 ppm DDT administration showed the liver pathology mentioned above. However, in the group of rats on 500 ppm for 3 months, the liver pathology was relatively minor.

In a more extensive study, using approximately 400 animals, the British researchers Cameron and Burgess (1945) did both single- and repeated-dose toxicity studies using all possible routes of administration. Pathological examination of animals which died from a single lethal dose of DDT revealed little change in the organs, showing no specific and distinguishing pathological alterations. On the other hand, in those which received repeated administration of the LD_{50} dose (800 ppm), a different pathological picture was seen. Especially striking was the severe damage to the liver.

> Numerous areas of focal necrosis or large areas of centrolobular necrosis are uniformly distributed throughout the organ. . . . There is much fatty degeneration, with cloudy swelling of liver cells surrounding the necrotic areas. Bile ducts are not affected. Polymorphonuclear leucocytes infiltrate the dead tissue in the early stages; later, mononuclear cells may be numerous. The degree of liver injury is sufficient to

account for death. In less severe cases, and especially if D.D.T. be discontinued, necrotic material is removed in the course of a week or two by autolysis and solution as well as by phagocytic activity. Repair is complete, no fibrosis developing even when exposure to D.D.T. is prolonged. Calcification is sometimes seen in some of the necrotic areas. (Cameron and Burgess, 1945, p. 867)

To explain exactly what these changes entail is really not too important. What is germane is to bear this description in mind for a later discussion, and to note that in the animals which survived, complete repair of the liver damage took place.

In a 1950 publication, Laug and his coauthors referred to experiments in which they had fed various amounts of DDT to several types of animals. After histopathological examination, they reported minimal hepatic cell changes in rabbits, rats, mice, and guinea pigs, even at such low doses as 5 ppm. However, these changes were not observable at any dose range tested in chickens, dogs, cats, monkeys, pigs, or sheep.

In 1951, Cameron carried out another study together with Cheng, the results of which they published under the title "Failure of Oral D.D.T. to Induce Toxic Changes in Rats." They had fed albino rats dosages of 3.5, 35, and 350 ppm DDT, for 33 to 63 weeks. They could find *no* pathological changes in the livers of these animals, and they came to the conclusion that previous authors who had described liver damage in rats at these or lower doses of the pesticide may have been dealing with fixation artifacts. In other words, in their judgment the preparations for histopathological examination of the supposedly damaged livers may have been faulty. They stated that neither Laug et al. nor Fitzhugh and Nelson (the authors of one of the "highly suggestive studies" which we shall come to shortly) could be confirmed. Epstein dismisses the work of Cameron and Cheng on the grounds that the experimental periods were too short and that there was an episode of infection in one group of experimental animals. However, the observations on histopathology are noteworthy, and we shall come back to this paper later.

In two further experiments with nonrodent species, Lehman and his co-workers (using dogs) (1952) and Durham et al. (using monkeys) (1963) gave up to 5,000 ppm DDT per day to some of the animals, without getting the kinds of tissue changes which had been reported in mice livers, and occasionally in rats.

By the mid-1960s the suspicion that alterations in liver tissue associated with DDT feeding are peculiar to rodents—and perhaps only to mice except at very high dosages—had become established as the accepted interpretation of the variable results of these animal feeding experiments. In 1965, Arnold Lehman, then Director of the Division of Pharmacology, Bureau of Scientific Research, Food and Drug Administration, reviewed the literature on DDT carcinogenicity and concluded simply, "DDT is not a carcinogen" (Lehman, 1965). So far as we know, his evaluation met with little or no opposition. It would have been difficult, in any case, to dismiss Lehman's opinion as biased in favor of the agricultural chemicals industry—the now all too familiar ad hominem argument raised against most of the scientists who defend DDT—since he was responsible for a study showing that the miticide aramite is carcinogenic in rats (Lehman, 1951).

Before turning at last to the papers which Epstein regards as positive for or suggestive of DDT's carcinogenicity, we want to mention one more negative study reported recently in a German publication. This is actually a series of extensive, long-term experiments with mice and other laboratory animals which involved the feeding of various chlorinated hydrocarbon insecticides at several dose levels. DDT, dieldrin, heptachlor, DDT + dieldrin, toxaphene, and aldrin were tested. Also investigated were the effects of phenobarbital on mice, with the results compared to those of the insecticide-fed groups. In this review article in 1970, Van Raalte described the histopathological findings of these experiments in the following:

> [Earlier] work was scrutinized and confirmed in our Tunstall laboratory, where it was found that:
>
> a. With feeding of dieldrin (or DDT, or both), one can initiate the development of noduli in the mouse liver.
>
> b. Histologically and in behavior, these noduli differ both from spontaneously occurring hepatomas and from carcinomas, such as those to which butter yellow (dimethylaminoazobenzol) gives rise.
>
> c. It was possible to induce similar early damage in the livers, leading to the development of noduli, with phenobarbital.
>
> d. These noduli do not show infiltrating growth; they do not metastasize; they do not grow autonomously; they cannot be transplanted; they have a tendency to decrease in size when [the pesticide] is withdrawn from the feed; therefore, they are not malignant.
>
> With endrin, it was not possible to produce such liver noduli in mice. In other animals, neither noduli nor tumors could be initiated with either dieldrin or DDT. (Van Raalte, 1970, p. 67; our translation)

In connection with this citation, three points should be emphasized.

1. The finding that phenobarbital induces the same kind of liver nodules as do DDT and dieldrin is in accord with the statement of Hayes about these liver

alterations: "The changes are not really characteristic, but essentially identical with those produced by the drug phenobarbital, the botanical insecticide pyrethrum, and a number of other materials" (Hayes, 1969b). To this list one can also add ethanol (alcohol), oxidized fats, and several antioxidants (common preservatives in margarine, oils, and other shortenings).

2. The use of the word "nodules" (or noduli) has apparently been deliberately chosen here instead of hepatomas. We shall discuss the reason for this shortly

3. There does not seem to be any question that these researchers felt confident they were not dealing with malignant growths.

One Real Result

Seven studies remain from the eighteen which Epstein describes as representing the total literature on DDT and carcinogenesis. These seven he separates into two groups: (1) those which he regards as "highly suggestive," but which suffer from some defect of design or statistical analysis, and (2) those which provide "conclusive evidence" that DDT is a carcinogen. The first category includes an experiment conducted by Halver (1967) on rainbow trout; a 1947 paper by Fitzhugh and Nelson on rats; and the multigenerational studies on mice by Tarján and Kemény (1969). In the second category he places two current investigations under the auspices of the World Health Organization being conducted by the International Agency for Research on Cancer in Milan, Italy, and in Lyon, France; some unpublished experiments from an in-house FDA study which Epstein calls the "second Fitzhugh study"; and, finally, the Innes or Bionetics Report.

Of these seven studies, we shall immediately eliminate three from further discussion, for the following reasons:

Had Epstein reviewed the literature thoroughly, it seems unlikely that he would have taken Halver's work on DDT and trout seriously, for it is highly improbable that the experiments, even as described by Epstein, could have been carried through with any live fish. He states that Halver fed 75 ppm DDT daily to the trout for 20 months and that more "liver cancers" were found among the experimental fish than the controls. Actually Halver's reported dose ranges (according to the text of his paper, p. 80) are from 38 ppm all the way to 9,600 ppm daily, beginning from the time the young fish began to feed (Halver, 1967). All other investigations on the effects of DDT on various species of freshwater trout suggest that these fish are extremely sensitive to the pesticide. Holden, for instance (1965, 1966), found that trout exposed for 100 days to a concentration in the waters of 1 ppb DDT accumulated enough pesticide to cause their death. This concentration is 27,000 times less than that mentioned by Epstein as having been *fed* in the Halver experiment. Admitting that absorption through the gills and ingestion are quite different routes, it still does not seem very probable that the rainbow trout could tolerate such large doses. Using cutthroat trout, Allison reported that among fish fed 3 mg/kg *per week* for five months, the mortality was 60 percent (Allison et al., 1964). Macek (1968) described some species differences in the sensitivity of inland trout to DDT, but nothing to suggest that any species would survive 75 ppm daily intake for more than a short period. Unless all of these investigators were in error, we have to dismiss the alleged results of the Halver study as impossible.

The two investigations now in progress under WHO sponsorship, on the other hand, are not yet complete, although some Progress Reports have been released. We would represent, to borrow Epstein's phraseology, that to claim on the basis of these Reports that DDT is carcinogenic is a travesty of data evaluation.

We do want to devote some space to the Tarján and Kemény experiments, however, since they gave rise to considerable discussion within the international scientific community and have also have a direct effect on the decision-making process in Hungary, where they were performed.

The results of these multigenerational experiments have been published in several versions, the most widely known being a paper in *Food and Cosmetics Toxicology* (1969). The researchers used very small concentrations of DDT, compared with most other studies of the compound's carcinogenic potential in test animals: about 3 ppm in the food per day. This dose was fed to five generations of inbred Balb/c mice. A greater incidence of leukemia and malignant tumors was reported in the DDT group over the controls, attaining significance in the F_3 and F_4 generations—that is, the third and fourth progeny. The level of significance reportedly increased progressively up to the fifth generation. The authors also described the incidences of leukemia and of tumors in their controls and in their breeding-stock animals. One very puzzling fact was their report that the tumor incidence was lower in the controls than in the breeding stock. Furthermore, although the authors claimed that the mice used were a leukemia-free strain, there was leukemia among controls as well as the treated animals. Lastly, some skepticism was aroused merely by the fact that no incidences of cancer of any type have been reported by any other investigator working with comparable dosages with animals of any species or strain.

An investigation of the questions to which this study gave rise was undertaken by the WHO. Some problems in experimental design were uncovered, and it was also shown that all of the findings might be explainable by spoiled food contaminated with aflatoxins. (As has been noted, aflatoxins are among the most widespread and most potent of known carcinogens to be found in the natural environment. They are a secretory product of a common mold, *Aspergillus flavus.*) The supposition of aflatoxin contamination of the feed would explain both the unexpected incidence of leukemia in the breeding stock, and also the variability of the results over the course of time.

By now everyone is in agreement that something must have gone wrong in the Tarján and Kemeny experiments, although exactly what is still a matter for speculation. Nevertheless, one very concrete result can be directly associated with these studies and the publicity they received: Hungary was the first among the Eastern bloc nations to ban DDT, together with the other chlorinated hydro-carbon insecticides. Earlier DDT was manufactured in Hungary, but the organophosphates and carbamates now being used have to be imported from the West. Hence the added cost of the ban on DDT to the agricultural sector includes not only handling and base price increases, but also tariff charges. The economic consequences of this ban were felt almost immediately. However, even though within Hungary it might be readily admitted that the ban was overhasty and ill-founded, the chances of reversing the official decision seem to be slight.

Did Someone Say Liver Dumplings?

As the third of his "suggestive" studies, Epstein goes back to an early paper by Fitzhugh and Nelson, in which several experiments with oral administration of DDT to Osborne-Mendel rats were reported. In two experiments, the investigators fed dosages ranging from 100 to 800 ppm DDT to the animals for 24 months. In a third one, they fed 1,000 ppm DDT daily to female rats for a period of 12 weeks, withdrew the surviving test animals from the pesticide for an 8-to-10-week period, and then sacrificed and examined them.

Evaluation of the long-term feeding experiments is difficult, as Epstein himself admits, since more than two-thirds of the test animals were lost during the course of the study, and the effects of DDT on the livers of the survivors were reported with all test groups lumped together. Briefly, 75 out of 228 test animals, originally divided into 12 groups, survived. Of these, four had hepatic adenomas and 11 others showed "varying amounts of nodular adenomatoid hyperplasia." The authors concluded: "Taken together, the 15 rats having either liver tumor or nodular adenomatoid hyperplasia are numerically enough to strongly suggest a distinct although minimal tumorigenic tendency of DDT" (Fitzhugh and Nelson, 1947, p. 25). While the original researchers used the phrase "numerically enough to strongly suggest," Epstein took these same figures and stated that a finding of four animals out of 75 with adenoma compared with 1 percent in the controls represents a statistically significant occurrence of tumors in the DDT-fed rats. This is definitely *not* a permissible conclusion, since the positive animals came from different test groups, and particularly as the study failed to describe any relationship between the dosages used and the effects.

Now, what were the kinds of hepatic alterations reported by Fitzhugh and Nelson? They first gave a generalized description which they claimed to be typical for DDT liver damage.

> The lesion consisted principally in hypertrophy and increased cytoplasmic oxyphilia of the centrolobular hepatic cells, plus increased basophilia and margination of the cytoplasmic granules, and a tendency to hyalinization of the remainder of the cytoplasm. . . . The increased weight of the livers of the treated animals could easily be explained on a basis of centrolobular cellular hypertrophy, when it is considered that doubling each dimension of the hepatic cell would increase its volume approximately eight times; and increase in the number of hepatic cells would not have to be invoked. (*Ibid.*, p. 24)

The four tumors were described as:

> from 5 to 12 mm. in diameter, paler than the surrounding liver tissue on gross examination, not sharply circumscribed microscopically, and composed of cells larger than those in the rest of the liver. Lobular architecture was almost obliterated. Mitoses were not noted. Some cells had foamy cytoplasm; some cells showed DDT changes of a degree greater than that elsewhere. Tumors of this type are not a sharply defined entity, and the question of their nomenclature cannot be treated here. They would probably be generally called adenomas because of their relative size, discrete gross appearance, and almost total loss of lobular architecture. There might be almost as much justification for considering them low grade hepatic cell carcinomas. (*Ibid.*, p. 25)

Let us compare these descriptions with those of the liver alterations seen in the female rats fed 1,000 ppm for 12 weeks.

> Changes were almost entirely confined to the liver, in which there was an enlargement of the centrolobular hepatic cells, with more oxyphilic cytoplasm and more distinct large basophilic granules than in the slightly atrophic cells of the peripheral halves of the lobules. There was a slight tendency to cytoplasmic hyalinization and peripheral segmentation of the basophilic granules in the centrolobular cells. (*Ibid.*, p. 27)

Lastly, we should consider the picture given by Laug, Nelson, Fitzhugh, and Kunze of liver patterns seen at the 5 ppm level and higher.

The changes consisted of hepatic cell enlargement, especially centrolobularly: increased cytoplasmic oxyphilia with sometimes a semihyaline appearance; and a more peripheral location of the basophilic cytoplasmic granules. Nuclear size was increased little if any, and there were none of the common nonspecific degenerative changes such as necrosis. (Laug et al. 1950, p. 271)

What is notable is that the alterations described in all four of these quotations are basically the same. The authors (whom, the reader will note, all work together) claimed that such hepatic changes are *the* characteristic manifestations of chlorinated hydrocarbon insecticide effects. The difference between the low-dose findings and even the four tumors that Fitzhugh and Nelson reported was one of degree only, but not of kind.

There are two things to recall from the earlier experiments. Even at 1,000 ppm DDT for 12 weeks, which dosage was lethal to 100 percent of the rats in Smith and Stohlman's experiments, the Fitzhugh and Nelson rats not only lived for 12 weeks, but did not show any liver cell necrosis. Thus, this "typical DDT pattern" seems to be characteristic only for their laboratory: Lillie and Smith (1944) and Cameron and Burgess (1945) found massive necrosis, sufficient to cause the death of the animals at this dosage.

This evidently was distressing to Cameron, who set out with Cheng to replicate both these studies, again using rats. They wrote in the introduction to their 1951 paper: "The conclusion they [Laug et al.] drew that as little as 5 p.p.m. of D.D.T. in the diet can produce recognizable changes in the structure of the hepatic cells of the rat has obvious and serious implications bearing on the question of what should be the maximum permitted limit of D.D.T. in foodstuff for human or animal consumption" (p. 819).

We have already mentioned that Cameron and Cheng failed to find these "characteristic DDT changes" described by both Laug et al. and Fitzhugh and Nelson. In their discussion, they stated:

No rat showed any histological evidence that could be called characteristic of chronic D.D.T. poisoning. The findings of Fitzhugh and Nelson (1947) and Laug *et al.* (1950) have not been confirmed. . . . Basophilic cytoplasmic granules are often observed in the normal rat liver cells. Margination of basophilic cytoplasmic granules are common fixation artifacts. They are seen especially in formalin-fixed tissues and are more marked if the tissue is deliberately badly fixed. Formalin is not a suitable fixative for cytological study. The photo-micrographs that illustrate the paper of Laug *et al.* (1950) suggest badly fixed tissues. (Cameron and Cheng, 1951, p.   281)

This very strongly worded refutation requires some comment. The reader should not get the impression that Cameron was just put out because his American colleagues reported quite different results from his own earlier findings (Cameron and Burgess, 1945). The Americans apparently did not know of his extensive investigations on DDT effects, since they failed to refer to them. Neither is it likely that Cameron would have gone so far as to imply that the tissues might have been "deliberately badly fixed" out of mere pique, for his reputation was certainly not dependent on the Americans' opinions. He was a Fellow of the Royal Society, a Fellow of the Royal College of Pathologists, holder of several honorary doctorates, and was shortly afterwards knighted for his fundamental scientific contributions in pathology. It is our conjecture that an Englishman of his stature would not use such strong language unless he felt it necessary to check the spread of a concept which could only generate confusion. Unfortunately his critical comment apparently went unheeded. In 1972, the four tumors described by Fitzhugh and Nelson were declared by Epstein to be *malignant*—a strong "suggestive proof" that DDT is a carcinogen. How he came to this conclusion from the description is hard to fathom, since even the authors had stated that the growths failed to show evidence of mitotic activity (rapid division of cells)—a characteristic typical of malignant neoplasms.

After establishing the "statistical significance" of these four tumors, Epstein came to the core of his argument with other interpreters about the third series reported in the Fitzhugh-Nelson paper: i.e., the one in which rats were fed 1,000 ppm DDT for some weeks and then withdrawn from the pesticide regime. This experiment, it should be remembered, was essentially the same as those of Lillie and Smith in 1944 and Cameron and Burgess in 1945. Such studies have been cited by various investigators as evidence that DDT alterations of liver tissue are reversible, and some have further inferred from this that where nodules, liver tumors, or hepatomas have been observed, these are probably benign growths, even if not specifically described as such.

The exact wording of Epstein's objection to the fact that results from one of the Fitzhugh-Nelson experiments have been cited in support of this nonmalignancy interpretation is rather important:

It has been claimed on the basis of the Fitzhugh Nelson paper that hepatomas are reversible. This is completely untrue. What Fitzhugh and Nelson did was . . .

They did an additional experiment where they exposed rats for 12 weeks only to [1,000 ppm] DDT, and at the end of that time, they looked at some of the rats and there were *minimal toxic changes* in the liver, things like *centrilobular necrosis* and phasecilia [?]*—early toxic changes in the liver. They took the rats off at 12 weeks and it then subsequently disappeared. Now, to suggest on the basis of a reversal of minimal toxic and necrotic changes in the liver, to suggest that hepatomas are reversible, is clearly a gross distortion of the Fitzhugh and Nelson concept. In this connection, I may say, I know of no information in the total literature that hepatomas are reversible. (Epstein, 1972b, p. 7355; our emphasis)

Since the publication does not delineate specifically just what was the "Fitzhugh and Nelson concept," we have to admit that Epstein could be correct in stating that the interpretations of other scientists have distorted this "concept." All the other statements in this paragraph, however, rest on a semantic game— a game which permits Epstein to reject out of hand, on the authority of the literature, the notion that hepatomas can. ever be reversible; to minimize at the same time the nature of those liver-tissue alterations which have been shown to be reversible; and to imply a general level of incompetence on the part of his own adversaries among toxicologists and pathologists.

First there is the question of the definition of "hepatoma." The literal meaning of the word is liver tumor, and a tumor is, by definition, merely a localized enlargement in tissue. A tumor may be benign or malignant. When it has been shown to metastasize, it is usually designated as a carcinoma of the liver, so that there should be no question about the fact that it is malignant. "Hepatoma" is sometimes used to refer to tumors which may or may not be malignant. To avoid all this confusion, those liver growths which are not suspected of being malignant are often called nodules, as we have seen from both the English- and German-language literature. Elsewhere in his testimony, however, Epstein stated that by *his* definition all hepatomas are malignant; that is, when he uses the word he is referring to carcinomas. If one grants his definition, then it is a true statement that there is nothing in the literature to suggest that such growths are reversible. However, when Hayes and Van Raalte and others have spoken about the reversibility of the liver nodules produced by DDT feeding, they were not talking about hepatomas in Epstein's sense. Hence it seems clear to us that he is playing with words in an effort to discredit those who disagree with him.

That various kinds of cell proliferations in one organ can be differentiated from one another would seem to be so obvious that it does not require documentation. Epstein, however, says: "Hepatomas in mice, one makes no distinction

---

* Basophilia?

between benign and malignant. . . . I am speaking for a wide consensus of the scientific community . . . that distinctions between benign and malignant hepatomas lack validity" (*ibid.*, p. 7344). Here is that word "consensus" again, but we do not even know what it is that we all agree to, for one cannot tell for certain whether he means that practically no one distinguishes benign from malignant growths in the mouse liver, or that hepatomas, being by definition malignancies, cannot be separated into benign and malignant categories. If the latter, he is making a meaningless, redundant statement; if the former, an invalid one, for many pathologists *do indeed* make this distinction. In fact, in the study we shall discuss next, which Epstein regards as a good piece of work, the histopathological evaluations include a careful differentiation of benign and malignant tumors, for the liver as well as for other organs.

A further semantic problem in the long passage quoted earlier arises from Epstein's description of the alterations in liver induced by the feeding of 1,000 ppm DDT as merely "minimal toxic changes" or "early toxic changes," the reversal of which means nothing. These "minimal toxic changes," according to him, include centrolobular necrosis, and if so would be the same kinds of changes described by Cameron and Burgess in their 1945 paper—changes which led to the death of many of the animals. In short, whatever the Fitzhugh-Nelson concept might have been, it seems that the data they reported for this third series do, after all, support the interpretation that the reversible tissue changes associated with extremely high doses administered for shorter periods can be extrapolated to the nodules produced by longer feeding with DDT at moderate dosages.

Finally, one has to ask why Epstein should have brought up this old study as "suggestive evidence" when it does not even meet his own criteria for meaningfulness (too many animals died during the course of the experiment, etc.). One suspects that he needed this study in support of his argument because it was the only chronic DDT experiment which was at least slightly positive for tumorigenicity in *rats*. His acceptance of the Halver work on trout—which strains credibility more than a little—may also make some sense if one considers that all four of the "clear proof" studies to which he refers were performed with *mice*, and Epstein is well aware, and in fact states elsewhere in his writings, that positive findings with *at least two* species of test animals should precede any declaration that a substance is a carcinogen.

An In-house Secret

When testifying about the well-designed, well-executed studies which he regards as definite proof that DDT is a carcinogen, Epstein sprang a complete surprise on the DDT defense. He introduced into evidence some data from an in-house FDA experiment, about which no one had heard earlier. This study was performed between 1964 and 1969 under the title "Chronic Toxicity of Chlorinated Hydrocarbon Pesticides." Epstein calls it the "second Fitzhugh study"; however, the preliminary report carries the names of the project leader, Walter Hansen, and the pathologist, Kent Davis. Fitzhugh's name appears elsewhere as a toxicology advisor, but in order to avoid confusion with his earlier work, we shall refer to this study as the Hansen et al. (1969) Report.

Epstein speaks about this as an excellent piece of work and expresses great puzzlement that the results have never been published. As we shall see later, there are probably several explanations for this failure on the part of the investigators to get the material into print.

The experiments involved testing of DDT (at 100 ppm) and methoxychlor (at 750 ppm) in the feed of two strains of inbred mice for two years. All the animals were autopsied, either at death during the course of the feeding study or after sacrifice at two years. The records and the preserved animals were then sent over to the pathology laboratories, where approximately 600 selected animals were worked up and examined in detail for histopathology.

At the time of Dr. Epstein's testimony, only three pages of materials dealing with this study were introduced into evidence, and it was not until the day before the summation arguments that other documents—such as two in-house memos from Davis and Gross respectively—were made available to the defense. Whether or not Epstein had these memos in his possession before he testified is a question which cannot be answered from the record, but it is probable that he did, for the figures mentioned in his testimony correspond to tables included in the Gross memo (1969) but not to the tables from the Preliminary Report of 1966.

In any event, these memos are now available in the public record, and it is worthwhile to consider some of the terse comments written by Davis in 1969 on submission of his pathology report.

1. Preliminary surveys show that in this study neither of these pesticides were carcinogenic . . .
2. Despite individual caging there was not random distribution of either mortality or pathology.
3. These 1200 mice are approximately one-fourth of the total animals processed through the Division of Toxicology pathology laboratory in the three years of its existence hence represent a large expenditure of taxpayers' funds on a project which is twenty-five years too late to serve a useful FDA regulatory purpose.

4. The biological significance of malignant tumor in the mouse is not clearly delineated.

5. These data do not differentiate between mice dying of tumor and those dying with tumor.

6. The effects of the acid fast bacterial infection on this study or its hazards to caretakers has not been determined . . . (Davis, 1969)

One does not have to be terribly perceptive or knowledgeable to glean from these remarks Davis' general opinion about the value of this study. However, we want to amplify somewhat two of his statements.

Davis' last comment refers to an acid-fast bacterial infection of the animals — something we have not found mentioned anywhere else in the reports. This might have been a tubercle bacillus, and since he expressed concern about its hazard to caretakers, one supposes that it might have been a form pathogenic to humans. The occurrence of such infectious disease among the animals could have had a considerable effect on the final mortality rates. In effect, Epstein disregarded the results with the strain-A mice because of high mortalities among that group, but he did not disclose at the Hearings whether he had any information about the causes of this high number of deaths.

A second possible contributing factor to high mortality among the strain-A DDT-fed mice is mentioned in the preliminary Report of 1966, where it is stated that at about the sixty-seventh week, a mistake was made in the preparation of the feed, and 300 instead of 100 ppm of the pesticide was incorporated into the diet for an unspecified period of time. It is not known, however, whether the strain-B animals also were fed the erroneous dosage, and, if so, why they did not show the same high mortality rates.

In spite of the general confusion surrounding these two interfering events and the cryptic or casual manner in which they are mentioned by the investigators, they constitute adequate explanation of why the entire study was never published.

Taking into account both that Davis was apparently aware of these problems which had arisen during the feeding stage of the study and also that the histopathological findings on the pesticide-fed animals did not seem to indicate significant increases in malignancies above the controls, one can better understand his relatively impatient remark in statement number 3. But perhaps it would also aid the reader to have some information on what is involved in the histopathological work-up of 1,200 mice.

The first step is selecting the animals, in accordance with the autopsy reports of grossly observable lesions and tumors, from which organs are to be taken for embedding, sectioning, staining, and microscopic examination. If one assumes that only one organ was serial-sectioned from each of the approximately 600 animals Davis selected for detailed examination—a most conservative assumption—this alone would result in about 480,000 microscopic sections. Thorough scanning and evaluation of that many sections could easily take two man-years. Since Davis' team looked at all sorts of lesions, it is not too surprising that he stated that the work had occupied one-fourth of the efforts of his laboratory for three full years.

The memo which Davis attached to the report of this three years of work was condensed onto a single page. The second memorandum, on the other hand, which was addressed from M. Adrian Gross to O. G. Fitzhugh, is a rather lengthy statistical analysis of the data. In general, one can summarize Gross' opinion as contradicting that of Davis. He claims that in spite of the obvious mistakes made during the feeding stage, the results of these experiments can be meaningfully interpreted, and the study may be said to demonstrate the tumorigenicity of both compounds tested, at least in certain sex-strain subgroups.

Let us now see what were the actual results of all this effort. From various interoffice memoranda, we compiled Table 9 on page 345, showing the tumor occurrences in DDT-fed mice compared with controls. On gross inspection it would seem obvious that if one takes the two strains together, the number of tumors in both male and female mice was higher in the control groups than in the experimental animals (males: 66 versus 63; females: 82 versus 73). If one considers only the strain-B animals, there appears to be a very slight increase in the total tumors of the pesticide-fed mice over the controls (males: 42 versus 39; females: 50 versus 49).

The only significant increase in tumors among the DDT-fed mice is seen among the strain-B females, in the numbers of *benign* liver tumors. It is precisely this single subgroup and this one type of tumor which Epstein mentioned in his testimony as proof of the carcinogenicity of DDT. That such apparently selective data evaluation is misleading and not scientifically permissible ought to be recognized by someone of Dr. Epstein's training. If it were meaningful to thus select out a single subgroup, one could, by the same token, claim that this study demonstrated DDT's anticarcinogenic properties, since in the strain-B female controls ten *malignant* uterine tumors were reported, whereas in the DDT group there were only three.

While in our judgment this study does not advance in one way or another knowledge about DDT's toxicological properties, Epstein classifies it as a well-designed, well-executed, definitive experiment. One would naturally presume that he includes the findings on methoxychlor in his evaluation. Although we have not discussed these results it may be said briefly that the data show an

Table 9. *TUMORS IN MICE FED 100 PPM DDT FOR 2 YEARS*
(from the unpublished results of Hansen et al. 1969)

Strain	A				B			
Sex	Males		Females		Males		Females	
Treatment type	Control	DDT	Control	DDT	Control	DDT	Control	DDT
Total positive animals	20	19	32	19	36	37	42	43
Total number of tumors	27	21	33	23	39	42	49	50
Liver tumors	3	2	4	4	30	33	9	24
benign	3	1	3	4	28	31	8	24
malignant	0	1	1	0	2	2	1	0
Ovarian tumors	. . .	. . .	1	2	. . .	. . .	11	5
benign	. . .	. . .	1	2	. . .	. . .	10	1
malignant	. . .	. . .	0	0	. . .	. . .	1	4
Uterine tumors	. . .	. . .	0	0	. . .	. . .	10	3
malignant	. . .	. . .	0	0	. . .	. . .	10	3
Testicular tumors	8	4	. . .	. . .	0	0	. . .	. . .
benign	7	4	. . .	. . .	0	0	. . .	. . .
malignant	1	0	. . .	. . .	0	0	. . .	. . .
Lung tumors	14	11	13	7	7	5	5	4
benign	0	0	1	1	1	0	1	0
malignant	14	11	12	6	6	5	4	4
Other tumors	2	4	15	9	2	4	14	14
benign	2	0	0	0	0	1	0	0
malignant	0	4	15	9	2	3	14	14

overall *higher* tumorigenic tendency from this compound than from DDT. As a consequence, one would expect Epstein to object strenuously to its use. In 1970, however—presumably at about the time he completed his review of the DDT carcinogenicity literature—he wrote the following, in a general editorial called "Control of Chemical Pollutants": "Once carcinogenicity has been determined, similarly efficacious but non-carcinogenic alternatives are usually available, for example, 'methoxychlor' can replace the persistent and carcinogenic DDT" (Epstein, 1970, p. 817).

Since the self-contradiction in positions here is glaring, one would like to know Epstein's latest opinion regarding the conclusiveness of the work by Hansen et al.

The Best Proof

Although Dr. Epstein's hand as we have presented it thus far has a certain amount of flash, it is not strong enough to account for his singular air of confidence, unless he is holding a more powerful card. And, indeed, there is one more study which we have not yet touched on—the real winner in this game, the backbone support for Epstein's conclusion that DDT is a carcinogen: the Bionetics Report of 1969, sometimes referred to as the Innes paper, after the name of its first author. It is this report which has been the principal source of the media articles of recent years in which DDT is branded as a carcinogen. It is this report which has made even the most ardent defenders of DDT take on a distressed look while rearranging their own hands. In the pages which follow we shall endeavor to show that this much publicized and much lauded study is really the joker in the deck, in this game, we hasten to add, where nothing is wild. First, however, we think it might be useful to give some idea of the nature, magnitude, and sponsorship of the Bionetics effort, so that it may be more easily grasped why nearly everyone has been to some degree impressed by this particular study.

The work as proposed was let on a contract basis by the National Cancer Institute to Bionetics Laboratories, a subsidiary of Litton Industries. According to Epstein, Bionetics received $5.5 million for the carcinogenicity studies alone—only one aspect of the complete proposal. Lest this strike the reader as far too large a sum, we ought to give some idea of the scope and logistics of the study.

The experiments and evaluations, which were conducted in at least eight stages, involved the testing of 123 chemical compounds in bioassays with close to 20,000 mice of two hybrid strains. For each test compound (with three exceptions), both oral and single-injection intraperitoneal routes were used. In addition to the test compounds, seven positive control chemicals were also administered.* There were five groups of negative controls: four receiving normal treatment and one to which the gelatin used as a vehicle for intubation of some of the chemicals was given. According to the publication, all the mice from both the oral and injection experiments, plus those from the five negative and seven positive control groups, were autopsied on death or after sacrifice at the end of 18 months. A blood smear was taken from each mouse. "Histologic examination of major organs and all grossly visible lesions" was then performed. (This means the pathologists must have worked up at least a minimum of seven organs per mouse,

---

* In a positive control, an experiment is carried out with a compound whose effects are known already from previous studies, and the results are compared with the protocol for the test compound.

plus the lesions.) "The entire carcass and all internal organs were fixed and have been saved" (Innes et al., 1969, p. 1103).

In stage 1, the compounds, which had been obtained from industrial sources, were rechecked as to identity by various chemical assay methods. The hybrid mice were bred by Bionetics in this stage also.

During stage 2, the maximum tolerated dose (MTD) was established for each compound. The MTD was defined in this paper as the highest dose which resulted in zero mortality in preliminary experiments with 19 daily doses. In the subsequent feeding experiments, the test animals were given the MTD of each chemical for approximately the full life span of a mouse: i.e., from age 7 days to about 80 weeks. For DDT, this dose was determined to be 46 mg/kg body weight, or 140 ppm in the feed.

One aspect of stage 3 involved single injections of the MTD, followed by feeding without added chemicals until sacrifice of the animals. This experiment would have required 9,720 mice.

The second aspect of stage 3 involved the feeding by intubation (stomach tube) of 8,710 neonatal mice for three weeks: from age seven days to 28 days. (Actually, in order to have the necessary number of mice intubated with the proper chemicals, the investigators would probably have had to use a much larger number of neonates, since it is *inevitable* that one loses some of the baby mice in intubation experiments.) To the lay reader, the complexity of gavaging neonatal mice may not be apparent. A few numbers, however, may elucidate the magnitude of the task. One can estimate that during this three-week period alone the intubation of approximately 9,000 baby mice would have entailed a minimum of 400 man-hours per day. In other terms, 50 trained technicians doing *nothing but* gavaging the mice and cleaning their cages for eight hours a day would have been needed.

Stage 4 was the long-term feeding experiment of the neonatal mice which had received the chemicals by intubation. This went on for about 75 weeks. There were 18 mice in each sex-strain subgroup, giving 72 mice for each compound.

Stage 5 was the necropsy of all surviving mice from all groups, experimentals and controls, orally fed and injected. Necropsy included gross examination for lesions, blood smears, choice of organs to be examined microscopically, preservation of other organs and carcasses. The investigators mention, in passing, that the logistics of necropsy of so many mice were somewhat difficult. One can imagine! Even though not all mice were sacrificed at the eighty-fourth week, as called for by the experimental design, there must have been a period of four to five weeks during which they were performing necropsies on 600–1,000 mice per day. Taking a minimum of 30 minutes per mouse, 600 necropsies would require 300 man-hours per day, or at least the labor of 40 skilled technicians.

During stage 6, the major organs and the visible lesions were embedded, stained, sectioned, and placed on slides.

Stage 7 was by far the biggest job: the scanning of the slides and recording of histopathological evaluations for all 20,000 mice.

To someone familiar with the procedures involved in this type of animal study the description thus far should be sufficient to convey the impression of a tremendously complicated and time-consuming piece of work. However, to the general reader it may still not sound like $5.5 million worth of effort. We should therefore like to elaborate a little on the probable man-hours involved in stage 7 —admittedly the hardest part of the job if one is thinking in terms of time and attention.

One has to picture that there should have been around 48 million sections prepared, which could have been placed on 2,400,000 slides, in turn contained in 60,000 boxes. A pathologist who wants to look at each section and to give careful consideration to slides on which he sees something notable probably would not work up more than one—or at the most two—boxes in any one day. If the pathologists at Bionetics had proceeded at such a pace, completion of the work would have taken from 100 to 200 man-years, or 50 to 100 pathologists working full time during the approximately two years allotted for the histopathology phase.

Since it seems unlikely that Bionetics employed 50, much less 100 such professionals, we have to consider how the work might have been done faster.

Let us assume that the pathologists examined only one section from each organ and lesion of each mouse: *a method which would not yield meaningful results v nder any conditions,* but would shorten the task. This would give only about 160,000 sections to be checked. If we allow the pathologist only six minutes in which to place each slide in the microscope, focus, scan, evaluate, and record what he sees, the working up of these absolutely minimal 160,000 sections would require four men working at breakneck speed for every hour of every working day for two full years. It is impossible to imagine even the most dedicated professional working at such a pace. It seems more reasonable to suppose that at least ten pathologists would have been needed even to get a cursory idea about the tumorigenicity of these 130 compounds. One would like to know how many sections were actually made, and how many trained specialists were employed to evaluate them.

In stage 8 the mass of resultant data was evaluated statistically, both by computers and by the investigators, and the test compounds were classified in 3 groups: (1) 11 showing significant increases in tumorigenicity above the negative controls; (2) 20 which were not clearly positive, but which were indicated as subjects for further study; and (3) 89 which did not show any increase in tumors.*

Finally, the report had to be prepared. It appeared in April, 1969, under the title "Bioassay of Pesticides and Industrial Chemicals for Tumorigenicity in Mice: A Preliminary Note." This publication was signed by seven researchers from Bionetics: Innes, Ulland, Valerio, Petrucelli, Fishbein, Hart, and Pallotta. It also carried the names of six officers of the National Cancer Institute, U.S. Department of Health, Education and Welfare: Bates, Falk, Gart, Klein, Mitchell, and Peters.

Despite the ambitiousness of this project and the semiofficial nature of the preliminary publication, the Bionetics Report has not been without its serious critics, even at the time of its appearance. C. S. Weil (1969, 1970), for example, who was a member of the "Panel on Carcinogenicity of Pesticides" of the Mrak Commission, pointed out in his dissenting opinion that the experimental design was faulty in several respects. He objected that the statistical analyses applied were meaningless, since the researchers did not assure random distribution of the litters. In this study litter mates were exposed to the same compound, and he insisted that they should therefore have been treated as a single experimental unit in statistical evaluation. (It is recognized that genetic factors contribute heavily to tumor occurrences in mice, and where only members of the same litter are involved in a test, the genetic factor may mask the results.)

Some of his further criticisms bear on the general incidence of tumors, and are based on material not contained in the publication, but reported to the National Cancer Institute. He wrote in the Mrak *Report:*

> While gastric papillomas might not have been accurately counted, they were recorded in Vol. 1 of the report by the Bionetics Research Laboratories to the National Cancer Institute. They were, furthermore, listed on pp. 45, 46, and 47 of that report as being one of a "class of tumors requiring virtually no explanatory comment." The incidence of gastric papillomas was statistically significantly higher in the female B6C3F1 negative control mice than in eight of the 11 "experimental compounds which resulted in an elevated tumor incidence" in table 2 of the Innes, *et al.* publication. Therefore, some doubt is cast on the significance of the increase of hepatomas when the gastric papilloma incidence is concurrently decreased. (Weil, 1969, p. 487)

His final conclusion reads: "As the hepatomas were generally not considered cancers, and as the incidence of lymphoma was quite low compared to the controls in each sex of each strain, and could have been the result of litter effect

---

* The results and classifications mentioned apparently refer only to the orally fed mice.

(already described), none of the materials have been definitely 'found to induce cancer when ingested by man or animal'—Section 409(c)3(A) of the Food, Drug and Cosmetic Act—in this study. Therefore, no action is required by the Secretary of the Department of Health, Education, and Welfare" *(ibid.).*

Wayland Hayes (1969b) questioned the authors' conclusions on the grounds that they failed to distinguish between malignant liver tumors and benign nodules. They stated that "metastasizing hepatic cell tumors were rare" in the study. Nevertheless, they concluded: "'Hepatoma' as used in this manuscript should not be considered as implying that these tumors are benign. Indeed, it seems more reasonable to conclude that the great majority had malignant potentiality" (Innes et al., 1969, p. 1114). What "seemed more reasonable" to the authors has, however, been judged by a number of other interpreters to be a highly questionable supposition.

Leon Golberg has attacked the conclusions of the study on two grounds: that the researchers did not study and describe the liver tumors in any detail, and that they used only the "maximum tolerated dose" in a single level of exposure. In a 1971 article, he wrote: ". . . the conclusions based on the Bionetics study (Innes *et al,* 1969) are subject to dispute . . . on such questions as the interpretation of liver nodules without antecedent study of their pathogenesis, without looking for possible regression on discontinuing administration of the test compounds, without adequate attempts to transplant the hepatic nodules, without trying to grow the cells making up the nodules in tissue culture . . . and without detailed attention to pulmonary metastases, both in controls and test animals" (Golberg, 1971, p. 205). And further: "The insistence on administration of a 'maximum tolerated dose' may also be misleading if this is the only dose tested, as in the Bionetics study (Innes *et al.,* 1969). No justification is forthcoming for abrogating the need to establish a dose-response relationship, which is fundamental to all toxicological endeavour" *(ibid.,* p. 206).

In this connection it may be useful to point out that the DDT dosage fed to the mice in the Bionetics study would correspond to an intake of about 3 grams per person per day in humans, or 75 kg over the course of a lifetime. This figure is approximately 100,000 times higher than the average daily intake of the pesticide residues in food.

It has been further pointed out by Hayes and others that the so-called "positive controls" are questionable as true chemical carcinogens. And to all of these general objections referring to experimental design it must be added that 18 mice in each subgroup is too small a sample number to obtain meaningful results. We are certain that on this point Dr. Epstein would agree, since he quite pointedly disregarded the findings of several studies *negative* for the tumorigenicity of DDT on the specific ground that the group sizes were too small to attain statistical significance.

Now all these general objections would be sufficient to put many a published experiment on the back shelves, never to be heard about further. The psychological impact of the Bionetics Report and the publicity it received in the news media seem to have assured its staying power and, as evidenced by Epstein's 1972 testimony, scientists contending that DDT is carcinogenic can still rely on it as having proven this to be the case. We shall now propose to take a closer look at the detailed contents of the publication itself.

Methinks, Thou Dost Protest Too Much

With regard to the negative controls, it seems to us that a few comments comparing the claims in the text of the publication with the reported data are in order.

As we have already mentioned, five groups of negative controls were used in this study. Each consisted of 18 strain-X males, 18 strain-X females, 18 strain-Y males, and 18 strain-Y females. The authors devote one-seventh of their written text to a discussion of the homogeneity of these five groups, reporting that several types of statistical tests were performed to determine the variability among all subgroups in the controls, with consideration given to the incidence of three types of tumors and also of total mice with tumors. They write: ". . . the conclusion was reached from the several analyses performed that there was no significant evidence of difference among negative control groups. In subsequent comparisons . . . the five negative control groups were lumped together" (Innes et al., 1969, p. 1102).

This statement struck us as remarkable, for the first thing we noticed on observing the data was what appeared to be a rather notable variability among the groups of controls, at least as far as the incidence of total tumors is concerned. We compiled in Table 10 on page 352 the results of strain-X only, for the five controls and the DDT-fed mice. The reader can see at a glance that the percentage of mice developing tumors in the controls varies from 0 to 41.2 percent in the males and from 0 to 16.3 percent in the females. Had the authors calculated the standard error for the total animals with tumors in the five control groups, they would have found that it is 14.4 percent in the males—slightly more than half the mean value of 27.7 percent. For the females, the standard error is 5.6 percent, well over half the mean value of 8.9 percent. From these figures it should have been obvious that the variation among the controls was indeed

Table 10. *TUMORS IN STRAIN-X CONTROL
MICE COMPARED WITH MICE FED 140 PPM DDT
(after Innes et al. 1969)*

	Control 1		Control 2		Control 3		Control 4		Control 5		DDT	
Sex	M	F	M	F	M	F	M	F	M	F	M	F
Total mice necropsied	17	18	15	18	14	18	17	17	16	16	18	18
Total mice with tumors	6	3	5	2	4	2	7	1	0	0	11	8
Percentage of mice with tumors	35.3	16.3	33.3	11.1	25.0	11.1	41.2	5.8	0.0	0.0	61.1	27.7

Mean male control mice with tumors: 27.7% ± 14.4%
Mean female control mice with tumors: 8.9% ± 5.6%

significant, since a standard error greater than 50 percent of the mean does not arise in a homogeneous population.

We recognize that this is old-fashioned reasoning, and that with computerized stastistics, commonsense observations can be circumvented. Nevertheless, even at the risk of being called "simplistic," we would like to pursue this train of thought further.

If the standard error is now added to the highest percentage of tumor occurrence—41.2 percent—in the control stain-X males of group 4, the resulting figure is 55.6 percent. The percentage of animals with tumors in the DDT group of strain-X males is 61.1 percent, the highest found among the DDT animals. Thus, the increase in tumor occurrences which could be attributed to DDT amounts to 5.5 percent. Where the controls show such variability, no statistical methods or manipulations could show this to be significant. The situation is equally disastrous with the strain-X females, for if one applies the same method, the increase in the percentage of tumors above the highest control value plus the standard error is only 5.8 percent.

Although we have tabulated and discussed only the results of the strain-X animals, we would like to point out that this selectivity is favorable to the authors. In strain-Y, application of the same reasoning would result in higher tumor percentages in the controls than in the pesticide-fed animals.

Taking into consideration this variablity factor among the negative controls, the results for all of the other ten compounds claimed by the Innes group to be tumorigenic are equally unconvincing. On these grounds alone, all but one of the 11 chemicals which they found to "increase tumorigenicity significantly" would have, at the very least, to be moved into the second classification of "doubtful tumorigens, but suspect."

Mention of these groupings brings us beyond statistical juggling to our next subject: the specific composition of the three lists classifying the tested compounds as "tumorigenic," "suspect," and "safe."

On the List

Having had more than a measure of skepticism aroused by the several questionable points we have just discussed, we decided to take a look at the long lists in the Bionetics Report that classify the 120 test and seven control chemicals as "tumorigenic," "doubtfully tumorigenic" or "not tumor-producing" —i.e., safe. After having only scanned them, we began to wonder why we had not heard any objections raised about the composition of these lists. However, it has to be admitted that they are almost impossible to read, there being no apparent organizing principle to the order in which the compounds are placed within each category. In addition, the authors frequently employed an unconventional chemical nomenclature, so that rapid scrutiny was made extremely taxing. For the convenience of those who may wish to make some comparisons of their own, we have entered about a third of the compounds in Table 11 on pages 354-357 according to their chemical affinities.

In pharmacological and biochemical research, the basic importance of structure-functional relationships of any compounds being tested is well recognized. The authors of the Innes paper selected their materials "on the basis of chemical structure suggesting possible carcinogenicty" (p. 1102). When they got around to reporting their findings, however, any structure-functional relationship—or lack thereof—was completely masked by the haphazard way in which the chemicals were listed.

Once they are presented in an ordered way, some puzzling patterns emerge. One should have liked the authors to explain their findings in comparative terms and offer at least some guidelines as to why certain compounds were found to be carcinogenic, whereas their congenitors were declared safe. Looking at a few of the carbamates in the table, one might ask why the monosodium salt (No. 049) is a probable carcinogen, the disodium salt (No. 079) is safe, and the dipotassium salt (No. 170) is definitely carcinogenic. The two zinc salts, methyl zimate (No. 132) and ethyl zimate (No. 070), are not carcinogenic. Neither is methyl selenac (No. 133). Ethyl selenac (No. 129), on the other hand, is highly carcinogenic. If the latter finding is meaningful, would the authors attribute

Table 11. *SELECTED PESTICIDES, THEIR STRUCTURE AND "CATEGORIES"*
(according to Innes et al., 1969)

No.	Name	Not carcinogenic	Probably carcinogenic	Carcinogenic
	Metallo carbamates			
049	SDDC		$(C_2H_5)_2 NCS_2 - Na$	
079	Nabam	$CH_2 - NHCS_2 - Na$ $CH_2 - NHCS_2 - Na$		
170				$CH_2 - NHCS_2 - K$ $CH(OH)NHCS_2 - K$
056	Maneb	$CH_2 - NHCS_2$ $>$ Mn $CH_2 - NHCS_2$		
063	Ferbam	$[(CH_3)_2NCS_2]_3 \equiv Fe$		
140	Vanguard N	$[(C_3H_7)_2NCS_2]_2 = Ni$		
099	Cumate	$[(CH_3)_2NCS_2]_2 = Cu$		
132	Methyl zimate	$[(CH_3)_2NCS_2]_2 = Zn$		
070	Ethyl zimate	$[(C_2H_5)_2NCS_2]_2 = Zn$		
125	Butyl zimate	$[(C_3H_7)_2NCS_2]_2 = Zn$		
051	Zimeb	CH_2NHCS_2 $>$ Zn CH_2NHCS_2		
133	Methyl selenac	$[(CH_3)_2NCS_2]_2 = Se$		
129	Ethyl selenac			$[(C_2H_5)_2NCS_2]_2 = Se$
136	Ethyl cadmate	$[(C_2H_5)_2NCS_2]_2 = Cd$		
068	Ethyl tellurac		$[(C_2H_5)_2NCS_2]_2 = Te$	
088	Ledate		$[(CH_3)_2NCS_2]_2 = Pb$	
082	Bismate	$[(CH_3)_2NCS_2]_2 = Bi$		
143	.....	$(C_2H_5)_2NCS_2 - N(CH_3)_2$		

Table 11. (continued)

No.	Name	Not carcinogenic	Probably carcinogenic	Carcinogenic
	Other carbamates and urea compounds			
034	Urethane			HNH—CO—O—C₂H₅
048	IPC	⟨C₆H₅⟩ NH—CO—O—iC₃H₇		
150	CIPC	Cl⟨C₆H₄⟩ NH—CO—O—iC₃H₇		
047	Sevin	CH₃NH—CO—O—⟨naphthyl⟩		
149	Zectran		CH₃NH—CO—O—⟨C₆H₂(CH₃)₂⟩—N(CH₃)₂	
059	Monuron	Cl⟨C₆H₄⟩ NH—CO—N(CH₃)₂		
053	Diuron	Cl⟨C₆H₃⟩Cl NH—CO—N(CH₃)₂	Cl⟨C₆H₄⟩ NH—CO—O—N(CH₃)₂	
	Thiuram group			
075	Unads	(CH₃)₂C(S)N—S—N(S)C(CH₃)₂		
058	Thiram (tuads)	(CH₃)₂C(S)N—S—S—N(S)C(CH₃)₂		
123	Vanguard G. F.			
134	Ethyl tuads		(C₂H₅)₂C(S)N—S—S—N(S)C(C₂H₅)₂	
	Safrole group			
162	Safrole			⟨methylenedioxybenzene⟩ CH₂—CH=CH₂
161	Isosafrole			⟨methylenedioxybenzene⟩ CH=CH—CH₃

Table 11. (continued)

No.	Name	Not carcinogenic	Probably carcinogenic	Carcinogenic
	Safrole group (continued)			
160	Dihydrosafrole			
092	Butacide (piperonyl butoxide)			
027	Piperonyl butoxide			
028	Piperonyl sulfoxide			
	Chlorophenol and nitrobenzene groups			
050	Dowcide 7			
097	Dowcide 25			
060	PCNB			
081	Vancide PB			

Table 11. (continued)

No.	Name	Not carcinogenic	Probably carcinogenic	Carcinogenic
		Chlorophenol and nitrobenzene groups (continued)		
101	...	O_2N—⟨ring⟩—NO_2 CH_3 — CH — CH_2CH_3		
		Diphenylamine and naphthylamine group		
093	Botran	O_2N—⟨ring⟩ Cl, NH_2, Cl		
128	...			
077	Dicryl	Cl, Cl —⟨ring⟩— NH — CO — $C = CH_2$ / CH_3		
080	Agerite DPPD	⟨ring⟩— NH —⟨ring⟩— NH —⟨ring⟩		
130	Agerite white	⟨ring⟩— NH —⟨ring⟩— NH —⟨ring⟩		
137	Agerite 150	⟨ring⟩— NH —⟨ring⟩ CH_3 HC — O —⟨ring⟩— NH —⟨ring⟩ CH_3		
083	Redax		⟨ring⟩— N — $N = O$ —⟨ring⟩ ⟨ring⟩— O —⟨ring⟩— NH_2	
102	Agerite powder			
		Some other noteworthy compounds		
057	Maleichydrazid	⟨ring with O, N—H, N, O⟩		
071	Phenylisothio-cyanate	⟨ring⟩— $N = C = S$		
115	Cacodylic acid	$(CH_3)_2As(O)OH$		

the carcinogenic activity to the substitution of the methyl by the ethyl group? And if so, why is ethyl zimate then nonactive?

For the general reader, it would take us too far afield to explain in detail why such findings seem unlikely, or at the least puzzling, but we should be pleased if those interested in the structure-functional relationships of chemical carcinogens would pursue further the elucidation of these lists of compounds. Perhaps someone can rationalize their inconsistencies in a way that we cannot.

Several other matters not requiring detailed knowledge of organic chemistry ought also to be raised in connection with these classifications. It is startling, for example, to find tetraethylthiuramdisulphide in the group of the possible carcinogens. Since the DDT results from this study have received so much attention, why was this finding not equally publicized? Did nobody recognize the compound—here listed as a fungicide called ethyl tuads—as exactly the same substance which has been given to millions of alcoholics for the past 20 years under such common names as Antabuse, Abstensil, or Noxal? Surely the investigators must have known what they were investigating—or did they? If Antabuse were a suspected carcinogen, one should have heard about this, since humans are directly subjected through chemotherapy to doses of 10 mg/kg/ day—quantities far in excess of any conceivable human exposure to the pesticide DDT under proper use conditions—and it would be of the greatest importance to seek confirmation of this finding as soon as possible.

Listed as an innocuous herbicide is maleic hydrazide (No. 057), a substance which Epstein supposedly showed to be both a powerful mutagen and definitely carcinogenic (Epstein et al., 1967). Does his endorsement of the Bionetics study mean that he is retracting his own earlier work?

The two herbicides IPC (No. 048) and CIPC (No. 150) are also listed as safe. They may very well be so, but Rachel Carson made a big point of the fact that Van Esch (1958) had shown them to produce skin tumors on oral administration. "These [arsenics, aramite] are by no means the only known carcinogens among pesticides. . . . Two herbicides belonging to the carbamate group, IPC and CIPC, have been found to play a role in producing skin tumors in mice. Some of the tumors were malignant" (Carson, 1962, p. 200). And later, "The herbicides IPC and CIPC may act as initiators in the production of skin tumors, sowing the seeds of malignancy that may be brought into actual being by something else—perhaps a common detergent" (ibid., p. 212). The winds of fashion are apparently not blowing much attention toward these two lowly herbicides, as the public was not informed that the Bionetics Report had vindicated them.

Considerably more puzzling is the inclusion in the safe category of several substances which are widely regarded as probable chemical carcinogens. Among these are a diphenylamide compound (No. 137), cacodylic acid, an arsenical (No. 115), and phenylisothiocyanate (No. 071), commonly known as phenyl mustard oil!

But there is one last discrepancy which is so glaring that it makes one wonder whether these lists were compiled from data or were just compiled. The authors state in the text that three compounds were tested in two different commercial preparations: Nos. 069 and 126; 093 and 128; 027 and 092. Compound No. 126 is missing altogether, but the other two pairs can be found, 027 and 092 both being piperonyl butoxide.

In the list of doubtful carcinogens, one finds piperonyl butoxide as No. 092 and piperonyl sulfoxide as No. 029. These two compounds were described by Epstein et al. (1967) and by Falk* and Kotin (1969) as cocarcinogenic. On the grounds of their structural affinities to the three safrole compounds used as positive controls, one wonders why these two chemicals were not found to be definitely carcinogenic, unless, of course, the safrole group does not really belong in that classification either.

The crowning insult is that the second entry for piperonyl butoxide (as Butacide, No. 092) is on the safe list. We would like to know how the 13 authors —who specifically pointed out in the body of the text that they had tested some compounds twice—could have expected that any of their results should be taken seriously when they have listed the *same* compound under two separate classifications. There would seem to be only two possible interpretations for such an error: either that the data did not reflect anything meaningful or that the lists do not represent data. *Parturiunt montes: nascetur ridiculus mus.*

All in the Family

Since we have criticized Epstein for misusing the word "consensus," it would not be fair to imply that he is the *only* scientist around who regards the Bionetics study as an important and meaningful piece of work. Nor would it be accurate to state that the findings were kept alive in the popular press even after being criticized on serious grounds by other scientists, without adding that the results were taken most seriously by the majority membership of the "Panel on Carcinogenicity of Pesticides" of the Mrak Commission, whose evaluations and recommendations were published by HEW in December, 1969, as part of the *Report of the Secretary's Commission on Pesticides and Their Relationship to Environmental Health.*

This 677-page volume is the result of deliberations and literature reviews of five subcommittees of the Commission and four separate advisory panels.

---

* It should be noted that Falk is one of the coauthors of the Bionetics Report. Epstein, according to his own statement, although not directly involved in the work, reviewed the findings before publication.

The five subcommittees addressed themselves to the uses and benefits of pesticides, environmental contamination, effects on nontarget organisms other than
man, effects on man, and criteria for regulation and recommendations. The four
special panels treated pesticide interactions, carcinogenicity, mutagenicity, and
teratogenicity of pesticides.

There are striking differences in the evaluations and recommendations of
the main subcommittees and those of the three last panels. The "Subcommittee
on Effects of Pesticides on Man," whose review constitutes more than 200 pages
of the Report, explicitly state that they were *not* responsible for the conclusions
of the special panel reviews incorporated into the Report (p. 243). If, then,
the "Panel on Carcinogenicity" endorsed the Bionetics study, it should be
clearly understood that this does *not* imply the acceptance of their evaluation by
the "Subcommittee on Effects on Man."

Now let us see how the "Panel on Carcinogenicity" deals with the Bionetics
Report. They refer to it as the "National Cancer Institute Study," and at several
places make general admiring comments about the research. For instance: "In
recognition of the prominent position which the National Cancer Institute
Study occupies in the spectrum of efforts to characterize the carcinogenicity of
pesticidal chemicals, the Panel believes it appropriate to address a few remarks
to the methods employed in this study" (Mrak *Report*, 1969, p. 481). There
then follow comments expressing approval of the method of selecting the
chemicals studied, the dosages used, the techniques of administration, and the
selection of test animals—all of which have been criticized above. "A major
test of the validity of a system employed as a measure of the tumorigenicity of
specific pesticidal chemicals in animals is the consistency of its results with what
has been found in other animal systems which have been and continue to be
accepted as valid. In this study the test system responded to the negative and
the positive controls in the appropriate manner" (*ibid.*, p. 483). And finally,
". . . the National Cancer Institute Study should be regarded as a fine-meshed
screen designed to identify as many as possible of the carcinogens submitted to it.
It has performed this task with considerable success" (*ibid.*, pp. 482–483).

Despite these laudatory comments, however, the panel members apparently
recognized that there were shortcomings in the written version of the Bionetics
Report, which was published at the time of the deliberations of the Panel. In a
special appendix, they addressed themselves to many of those problems which
we have raised, especially in connection with the relationship between chemical
structure and tumorigenicity. They begin with the flat statement: "In general,
the data obtained in the National Cancer Institute Study show a consistent relationship between the chemical structure and tumorigenicity" (*ibid.*, p. 488).
This seems to promise clarification of the haphazard compilation of the chemicals

in the Bionetics tables and possible explanation of the apparent lack of structure activity relationships. Unfortunately, upon reading through the later materials, one is not enlightened. "Several chlorophenols exhibited borderline activity [actually only two], but an insufficient number of compounds of this class was included in the test to lend importance to this observation" (ibid., p. 489). Indeed, the third compound tested which belongs to this group was not found carcinogenic. "Also, many pesticides which are potential biological alkylating agents were inactive in the test circumstances. . . . These results seem inconsistent with prior data, since some biological alkylating agents have been shown to be carcinogens as well as carcinostats" (ibid., p. 490). Contrast this with their earlier statement that a major test of validity is consistency with earlier results in other animal systems. "The activity among the carbamates was not consistent" (ibid., p. 491). "An insufficient number of urea derivatives was evaluated to give a clear picture of their activities" (ibid., p. 492). "Hydrazine has been reported previously to produce hepatomas in mice. In this study N–(2–hydroxyethyl) hydrazine was found to be tumorigenic, but maleic hydrazide was not. If free hydrazine were liberated enzymatically, tumorigenicity should ensue. It may be that animals differ in their abilities to liberate free hydrazine from maléic hydrazide. This could account for the conflicting reports which appear in the literature on the effects of maleic hydrazide" (ibid., p. 492).

This "if . . . may be . . . could account" rationalization should be contrasted with the definite statement made in a study which did show positive results for tumorigenicity of maleic hydrazide, authored by Epstein, Andrea, Jaffe, Joshi, Falk, and Mantel, bearing in mind that Epstein and Falk were nonmember participants on this Panel: "The complete absence of pulmonary carcinomas and multiple adenomas in these experiments makes it improbable that the carcinogenicity of maleic hydrazide is caused by a presumptive ring scission in vivo to yield hydrazine . . ." (Epstein et al., 1967, p. 1390).

One must ask what is meant by "animals differ" in the Panel's statement? Since both the Bionetics group and Epstein's team used mice and the results were inconsistent, are we to understand that they refer to individual differences among test animals? If such rationalizations have to be used to explain away poor results, then where do we stand?

What we considered as the final insult in the Bionetics Report classifications was apparently observed by the Panel members, too. They devote a lengthy footnote to the interesting fact that the same compound under two different names is classified under two different categories. "Piperonyl butoxide was also tested as Butacide (piperonyl butoxide in a solvent vehicle). Because of the presence of the solvent, they were given at different gross dose levels. The difference in category assignment . . . comes about because for piperonyl butoxide,

5 of 15 strain-X male mice developed lymphomas . . . and for Butacide, 3 of 16 animals (strain-X male mice) developed lymphomas" (*ibid.*, p. 492).

This is not an explanation; it is a tautology. They are basically stating that the categories differed because the results differed, which is the central problem needing explanation.

What kind of an expert panel is it that can not only so warmly endorse this ambitious but dismally sloppy study and dignify it with the name of the NCI, but also provide rationalizations for its obvious weaknesses? The Panel was not unanimous in its approval, for one member was so distressed at the evaluation that he insisted on his five-page dissenting opinion being printed in the final version of the Report (see Weil, in Mrak *Report*, 1969, pp. 483–488), but the majority view was that this study represented one of the most significant and meaningful efforts to determine the carcinogenicity of pesticides. Can it be completely a matter of indifference that of the six members of the National Cancer Institute who signed the original Innes publication, five were either full Panel members or nonmember participants, and that of seven other persons who advised the Bionetics researchers and/or reviewed the results, five were also involved in the deliberations of this Panel? *Similes similibus gaudent.*

Retirement for the Mouse?

After having been subjected to this rather detailed account dealing with a number of inconclusive experiments in which DDT's carcinogenic properties were tested on mice, the reader may be wondering how it is that all of this extensive, time-consuming, and expensive work does not seem to have produced meaningful results. This is certainly a legitimate question to raise.

During the course of his testimony, Epstein stated that mice are ideal animals for these kinds of studies. They are cheap, easy to maintain in large numbers, and they have a conveniently short life span; and since in the course of time, intensive in-breeding has been carried out, genetically homogenous populations are available for experimentation.

Recalling, however, that in the experiments described a large percentage of the control mice developed the most varied types of spontaneous tumors—in some instances not differing statistically in number from the tumor occurrences in the experimental animals—one has to pause and ask whether mice are, in fact, ideally suitable for experimental carcinogenicity studies.

During the past 20 years, huge quantities of data have been accumulated on both spontaneous and induced cancers in the mouse. In reviewing these studies, it has become more and more apparent that large proportions of murine cancers are virally induced. Already in 1967, Kaplan sounded a warning about the ubiquity of lymphoma-causing viruses in mice: "There is increasing reason to believe that such leukaemogenic viruses are ubiquitous among many and perhaps all laboratory strains of mice and they may be the causative agent of the lymphomas developing after treatment of such strains . . ." (Kaplan, 1967, p. 1325). Since that time, several experiments have shown that many of the substances earlier classified as carcinogens act in the mouse as "promoters" of other tumorigenic agents—in many cases, indigenous viruses—while the substances alone may or may not be cancer-causing. One of the most interesting studies in this respect was performed by Roe and Grant (1971). The researchers compared the effects on mouse livers of some carcinogenic compounds in germ-free mice and in mice with "minimal disease." The two controls, the germ-free animals and the minimal-disease mice showed approximately the same percentage of spontaneous hepatomas. When they administered dimethylbenzanthracene, a well-established carcinogen, to the gnotobiotic animals, it caused a liver-tumor occurrence of from 6 to 37 percent. In the minimal-disease mice, the same treatment resulted in 44 to 63 percent developing hepatomas. The authors came to the conclusion that the induction of hepatomas was the result of a cocarcinogenic effect—that is, not true carcinogenesis. It was the appearance of bacterial saprophytes in the minimal-disease mice together with the chemical agent which led to the increased occurrence of liver tumors.

In a 1971 editorial in the BIBRA* *Bulletin* attention was called to the questionable usefulness of the mouse as an experimental animal for carcinogenicity studies. After reviewing the literature dealing with the spontaneous and induced occurrences of tumors in the mouse, the editors stated: "There are already some indications that because of the peculiar susceptibility of the mouse to virus-induced tumours, findings of a significant production of tumours in long-term tests are being disregarded unless other species, usually the rat, also show similar results. Certainly the time is now ripe for a retrospective survey to identify the influence the results of mouse testing have had on the making of decisions" (Editorial, 1971, p. 116). About a year later an even more strongly worded review was published by Grasso and Crampton. The authors showed that practically any type of tumor occurrence in the mouse which has been claimed to result from administration of a specific carcinogen is subject to considerable doubt. They write about lymphomas, for instance: "The widespread presence of leukaemogenic viruses in mice, and the apparent ease with which they can be activated by immunosuppressive agents invalidates the induction of lymphomas and leukaemias as an index of carcinogenic activity" (Grasso and Crampton, 1972, p. 425). They also express a most skeptical attitude about the value of not-

* British Industrial Biological Research Association.

ing mouse hepatomas as a criterion of carcinogenicity. "It . . . appears that factors unconnected with the administration of the test compound may have a considerable influence on the incidence of hepatomas in mice, so that other evidence is required if claims of carcinogenicity based on the induction of this type of tumour are to be seriously considered" (ibid, p. 423).

In their final conclusion they point out that the use of mice, *even in conjunction with a second species,* such as rats, would not lead to decisively meaningful results in carcinogenic studies. They seem to favor the retirement of mice for this purpose altogether.

> It is doubtful, therefore, whether the use of the mouse, without data from a second species, is a reliable method for detecting carcinogenic activity. Results from the use of a second species, such as the rat, would be required to confirm either a positive or negative effect in the mouse. At best, confirmation would be obtained, but at the worst a state of confusion would result from a positive effect in the mouse and a negative effect in the rat. Hence the practical attractions of the mouse, in terms of size, reproduction and economy, may constitute very tenuous premises for its use in carcinogenicity testing. (*Ibid.,* p. 425)

In view of these widespread doubts about the usefulness of the mouse for carcinogenicity testing, one wonders why the idea of the so-called "megamouse" studies is still currently fashionable. The rationale behind the notion that the subtle effects of a compound could be tested if one used a million or more mice was put forth a few years ago. It has been claimed that the carcinogenic or mutagenic effects of environmental contaminants, if tested at levels comparable to environmental exposure, would become manifest only in very small numbers of the test animals, and that in order to obtain data showing statistical significance compared with naturally occurring variability, one would have to utilize at least a million mice. This kind of project, when dressed up in high-sounding scientific justifications, might seem to have some appeal. At the very least it may be seen as one way out of the objectionable "maximum tolerated dose" approach to testing. Unfortunately, however, it fails to take into account several problems of a practical nature.

To begin with, the discovery that mice carry numerous cancer-causing viruses seems to be a strong indication that this animal is, sui generis, unsuitable for the testing of carcinogens. One has only to consider that a single virus, such as the polyoma virus, can cause 23 different types of tumors in the animals.

Secondly, it strikes us as highly doubtful whether those projecting studies of this sort have taken into account the tremendous logistic problems which would arise working with 1,000,000 mice. Even given that the histopathological procedures for screening purposes could be very much simpler than those usually performed, the personnel requirements for both professionals and care-takers would be enormous. And the screening of these million mice would give only preliminary indications regarding a single compound.

With respect to mutagenicity, the megamouse concept does not seem to be too practical either. Recent calculations indicate that in order to detect a genetic change in mice resulting from administration of a minimal but still effective level of a chemical compound, not 1 million but 8 million test animals would be required (Weinberg, 1971). It is obvious that it would be impossible to ex-periment on such numbers of animals. Finally it should be pointed out that even if one or the other type of study could be carried out and statistically significant results were to be achieved, there would still remain the nagging question of whether the findings could be extrapolated from mouse to man.

If the megamouse concept is logistically nonsensical, and if, at the same time, results from the testing of smaller numbers of animals with maximal tol-erated doses are rejected by many toxicologists as unreliable, the reader may very well ask what kind of studies *can* be performed to provide answers to anxi-ety-causing questions about which environmentally ubiquitous chemicals—naturally occurring or artificial—are potentially dangerous to man.

To answer this question we have to return once more to the time-honored concept of the toxic threshold and the meaningfulness of dose-response rela-tionships. When these concepts are applied to carcinogenesis, a substance will be described as a cancer-causing agent if it can be shown to produce cancers in one or two species of appropriate laboratory animals and if, at the same time, a relationship between the doses tested and the observed effects can be estab-lished (Weil and McCollister, 1963; Weil, 1970). After all, as W. H. Butler has pointed out: "From the Public Health point of view, a distinction should be made between chemicals that only induce benign neoplasia of one species (for example, the mouse) and those that induce frank carcinoma either in the mouse or in other species. A chemical can hardly be labeled a carcinogen if, in fact, it does not induce carcinoma" (Butler, 1970, p. 40).

We are aware that the testing methods built on these concepts of classical toxicology have been described by Epstein as "insensitive," and we are by no means in favor of retaining older methodologies merely because they are time-honored. However, in the matter of toxicological studies of carcinogenicity, a perusal of the literature of the last ten years suggests that the applications of newer, more "sensitive" methods has resulted in a state of generalized con-fusion and a failure to clarify the question of fundamental importance to the welfare of the public: which substances, in what quantities, are dangerous to humans, and to which can the population be exposed without fear of harm?

It has to be said once again that the experimental methodologies applied in the life sciences cannot, by definition, yield a negative proof. It will, therefore, always be possible for an individual scientist or layman to state that there is *no* proof that DDT, or any other compound, is *not* a carcinogen, at some dosage. However, the methods of testing used in toxicology can provide assurance that DDT does not produce the effects associated with known carcinogenic substances, under any reasonable testing conditions with proper experimental animals. Since its introduction into use as a pesticide in 1945, DDT has been repeatedly subjected to such tests, and in evaluating these, public health authorities, toxicologists of world renown, officials of the World Health Organization, and spokesmen of various national medical associations and international research organizations have over and over again declared that DDT is not carcinogenic to man. Having reviewed the materials on which the dissenting opinions are based, we think the public may rest assured that these pronouncements of safety are expressions of well-considered and responsible evaluations.

Fertility Games

While not so dramatic as the cancer materials, there is one other claim about DDT's harmful effects on humans which is notable for its persistence. This is the allegation that the pesticide may render women sterile and reduce the sexual potency of human males.

One source of the supposition that DDT might affect human fertility is the slight similarity of its chemical structure with that of stilbestrol, a compound recognized for its estrogenic activity. Stilbestrol and some of its congenitors have been widely used in human and veterinary medicine to cure hormonal insufficiencies and in animal husbandry to obtain weight gain. Since these compounds are artificial estrogens, they are capable of affecting the uterus directly and they can also interfere with the action of male hormones. In large enough quantities they can be used for chemical caponization or to induce sterility in female animals.

The estrogenic property of DDT was first demonstrated in birds by Burlington and Lindeman, in 1950. Their paper did not arouse any particular concern about such properties of the compound, but shortly thereafter attempts were made to incorporate the pesticide into pigeons' feed, in the hope that the pests could be controlled through reduced fertility. These experiments were completely unsuccessful. During the subsequent decade, the estrogenic properties of DDT were largely ignored, although Fischer and his coworkers (1952) did attempt to demonstrate such activity in rats. They were unsuccessful, even when 45 mg of technical DDT was injected intraperitoneally into adult female animals.

More recently, Bitman et al. (1968), Welch et al. (1969), Bitman and Cecil (1970), and Cecil et al. (1971) have shown, using more refined techniques, that the o,p'-isomer of DDT induced increased weight, glycogen content, and RNA synthesis in the uteri of rats. The minimal effective dosage was 0.4 mg intraperitoneally or 250 ppm orally. Cecil et al. (1971) reported that the estradiol potency of o,p'-DDT is 1 to 10,000 — that is to say, it is ten thousand times weaker than the naturally occurring estrogenic hormone.

In contrast with o,p'-DDT, the much more frequently encountered p,p'-isomer has been shown recently to possess antiestrogenic activity (Welch et al., 1971).

It was claimed at one time that the p,p'-DDT isomer could be converted into o,p'-DDT *in vivo* (French and Jeffries, 1969), but recent work indicates that this is not the case; nor is o,p'-DDT converted to the para, para isomer (Bitman, et al., 1971). Since the o,p'-isomer accounts for only 10 to 20 percent of technical DDT, and since it shows only very weak estrogenic properties, the chances that the human population will be effected appear to be nil. Some simple arithmetic indicates that in order to arrive at an intake of o,p'-DDT through diet which is comparable to the *minimal* oral dosage in rats, one would have to consume around four million times as much food as usual. We may be a nation of overeaters, but. . . .

In spite of all these serious qualifications regarding DDT's estrogenic potential, attempts are made every now and then to impute damaging uterotropic effects to the pesticide. One of the latest was a study reported in *Science* in 1971 by Heinrichs and his coworkers. The paper was called "DDT Administered to Neonatal Rats Induces Persistent Estrus Syndrome."

The authors started with the known premise that exogenous sexual hormones such as estrogens or androgens can induce permanent sterility after administration to newborn female rats. Assuming that the o,p'-isomer of DDT acts as a weak estrogen, they injected the neonatal rats (subcutaneously) with 1 mg of the pure o,p'-isomer on the second, third, and fourth days of life. It should be kept in mind that this is an enormous quantity: equivalent to 666 mg/kg, since the average weight of a neonatal rat is 4.5 g (Witschi, 1956). Had they used technical-grade DDT, they would have had to administer at least 3,500 ppm of the pesticide in order to reach an equivalent dose of the o,p'-isomer.

The abstract of the publication reads: "The o,p'-isomer of the insecticide DDT when injected into neonatal female rats significantly advanced puberty, induced persistent vaginal estrus after a period of normal estrus cycles, and caused the ovaries to develop follicular cysts and a reduced number of corpora lutea. The uterotropic response to administered estradiol was reduced, and the female pattern of mating behavior was slightly disturbed. Residues of DDT in ovarian, brain, and adipose tissues of the adult animals were the same in both treated and control groups" (Heinrichs et al., 1971, p. 642). The concluding paragraph is the following: "These data show that DDT, in addition to sex steroids, can induce the constant estrus syndrome with permanent sterility. The similarity between this syndrome in rats and the polycystic ovary syndrome found in women has been described. . . . The oligo-ovulation and relative sterility in the human syndrome could be related to the presence of DDT in the fetal environment . . . , but the relationship remains to be established" (*ibid.*, p. 643).

If one considers these two citations together with the title, one would understand the authors to have demonstrated that o,p'-DDT acts very much like the sex steroids and is capable of inducing constant estrus syndrome *with permanent sterility,* and further, that there may be a cause-and-effect relationship between the presence of DDT residues in the human fetal environment and the polycystic ovary syndrome found in women.

We again remind the reader that when scanning the vast amount of literature arriving on his desk weekly, a scientist frequently reads only the abstract and the conclusions of papers which are not of special interest to him. It is therefore crucial that the titles and abstracts of publications should be precise and that the concluding statements should reflect the data reported in the body of the article.

These criteria are not met by this publication. To begin with, the title is misleading, for the investigators did not, in fact, demonstrate a "persistent estrus syndrome" effect.

The authors report that the ovaries of the animals were removed, weighed, and prepared for histological examination on the 120th day of life. They found that the ovaries of the treated rats contained large cystic follicles, and that these histological findings were reflected in slightly decreased ovarian weights of the treated animals compared with controls. These decreases were, however, only of borderline statistical significance. They write: "Since the high incidence of cornified vaginal smears was occasionally interrupted by 1 or 2 days of diestrus and the differences in ovarian weight of the groups had only a borderline statistical significance, it is likely that our animals were in the early stages of the development of this syndrome. Had the observation period in this experiment been extended, a longer absence of ovulation and greater regression of existing corpora lutea would likely have yielded a more dramatic diminution in ovarian weight" (*ibid*).

This rather strange passage deserves some attention. The fact that the "high incidence of cornified vaginal smears was occasionally interrupted by 1 or 2 days of diestrus" means that persistent estrus syndrome was *not* produced by the treatment, since by definition this syndrome means no diestrus. The results reported by the authors suggest some disturbance of the estrus-diestrus rhythm, but this is a very long way from permanent sterility!

In the second sentence of the above citation, the authors are saying in effect that they terminated the experiment too soon, but had they continued it longer, they have faith that they would have achieved the ovarian weight reduction to be expected from a genuinely active agent. We are sorry to say that the data they reported do not, in our view, represent firm predictive values, and that their rationalization represents a thinly veiled admission that they did not complete the experiment, but printed only partial findings. When both researchers and the editors of *Science* seem satisfied with this kind of "proof," it is, indeed, late in the day.

The most important comment on this study is yet to come, for we have to go back to a consideration of the dosage used in these experiments, particularly in view of the authors' speculation that their "results" might have implications for human females, who could be exposed to DDT in utero through the placenta. Recall that the researchers injected 666 mg/kg into their newborn rats. Since a human baby would not be subjected to such treatment under any conditions, her exposure would have to come from the mother ingesting huge quantities of DDT at the end of pregnancy. If we assume that about 1/600 of the DDT taken in by the mother could pass the placental barrier, a dose of o,p'-DDT equivalent, in a human infant of normal birth weight, to that of the test conditions, could only result from the mother *eating* about 1½ kg of the pure o,p'-isomer, or 7 to 8 kg of technical grade DDT! These quantities are so astronomical as to make the speculative extrapolation to humans an intellectual outrage.

This publication is one of those which we mentioned in Chapter 3 as having roused the ire of several scientists not otherwise concerned about the literature indicting DDT. Once having studied the paper, they were indignant about the misleading statements in the conclusion and the meaningless extrapolation to human females. We also might mention that we wrote a letter to the editor of *Science* objecting to these two factors; a wasted effort, apparently, as it was duly returned. It was not the rejection of our letter per se which we found disturbing—after all, perhaps our plea for reason was not put with sufficient eloquence—but rather the growing impression that whereas it is very easy these days to get anything published which implies that DDT is a Bad Thing, critical analyses of such publications are printed only rarely.

We want finally to mention that there are experiments indicating that when relatively high dosages of DDT are incorporated into the feed of female rats and dogs, enhanced rather than reduced fertility results. In a recent series of well-designed experiments, Ottoboni (1972) showed that female rats receiving 20 ppm DDT had a significantly longer average fertile life (14.5 months) than did their litter-mate controls (8.9 months). Eight of the DDT-fed rats became pregnant after the normal age for menopause (17 months), whereas only one of the control rats conceived at this age; and some of these very fertile female rats had several pregnancies after 17 months.

Perhaps the next claim against DDT will be that it acts as a fertility drug and is responsible for the population explosion. For the moment we shall conclude this argument by stating that attempts to prove that DDT causes sterility seem about as sensible as setting out to discover the West Pole.

15

WURSTER'S SENSATIONAL SCIENCE STORY

No error will be changed into truth
by constantly believing, nor by
persistently declaring it as truth.

KARL MÖBIUS

We have seen that many of the earlier claims against DDT are
rarely voiced these days by those of its opponents who are professional scientists. The scientific case against DDT now rests primarily on the
assertion that it endangers nontarget organisms—especially in subtle and insidious ways—and that the presence of its residues in the environment represents an indirect but imminent hazard to human welfare.

In the course of the next three chapters, we shall be examining in some detail three major topics central to understanding the foundations of this assertion.
These are:

371

1. Data allegedly demonstrating that DDT and its residues, either in the field or under laboratory conditions, are deleterious to wildlife—in particular to the reproductive success of birds of prey and certain fish.

2. The supposed biochemical mechanisms of DDT's mode of action, whereby it affects the reproductive performance of animals.

3. The chemical and physical mechanisms which have been postulated to account for the worldwide dispersion of DDT, and the methodology underlying estimates of the amounts of DDT residues which are contaminating different reservoirs of the biosphere.

In approaching our first major topic, we shall use as our point of departure the text of a lecture given in 1970 by Charles Wurster. We selected this presentation in part because it represents a good summary of the arguments bearing on insidious damage to wildlife, and in part because Wurster, as chairman of the Scientific Advisory Committee of the Environmental Defense Fund and one of the founders of this organization, is perhaps the best known of all the anti-DDT spokesmen. We shall discuss some of the specific claims made by Wurster in the lecture, and in some cases we shall want to examine in detail the studies which form the basis for these claims. In addition, we should like to call the attention of our readers to the manner in which the presentation is delivered: to the style, the tone, and the underlying psychology that characterizes Wurster's mode of expression in the public forum.

The Storyteller

Charles Wurster is an organic chemist by training, who began his professional career working for the Monsanto Chemical Company, sole U.S. manufacturer of the now infamous polychlorinated biphenyls. At the present time he is an associate professor of biology at the State University of New York at Stony Brook, Long Island. Although he is probably the most articulate foe of DDT, his own scientific research carried out on the ecological effects of this compound is surprisingly slight. Since 1967, as far as we have been able to ascertain, he has written one paper and been a coauthor of six others which actually deal with research on DDT and related compounds. The remainder of his publications consist of reports of political and legal developments regarding the registration of DDT uses, printed versions of public lectures, general reviews about DDT, and publicist statements.

The specific text we shall use as the basis for our analysis was originally an oral presentation, delivered as part of the Yale School of Forestry's symposium series: "Issues in the Environmental Crisis." The lecture was entitled: "DDT and the Environment." We have taken the text from a book called *Agenda for Survival* (1970, ed. H. W. Helfrich), which consists of reprints of the entire lecture series for the academic year 1969–1970. It seems that Wurster has given almost identical versions of this same lecture before a number of other forums, and there also exist printed summaries of the DDT problem under his signature which contain very similar material. It would, therefore, seem fair to assume that this presentation is typical of Wurster's style and its contents representative of his point of view, despite the fact that it is slightly dated.

He begins with a general statement of his purpose: "to attempt here to define the pesticide problem—particularly as it concerns DDT." He suggests that environmental contamination with DDT may serve as a model for the understanding of other sorts of chemical pollutants and states his opinion that DDT "is a particularly serious pollution problem—indeed, one of the worst we have."

In order to give his audience some idea of why the widespread use of DDT has given rise to so many serious and unforeseen effects, Wurster embarks on a lengthy theoretical discussion, in which he considers the physical and chemical properties of the molecule itself, in relation to its behavior in the environment. We cite from this part of his discussion at some length:

> The environmental behavior of DDT can be explained by the presence of four properties, all combined in one molecule. Modification of any one property would produce a very different situation in terms of environmental behavior.
>
> 1. DDT is a biologically active material in two different ways:
>   a. It is broadly active within the animal kingdom, being either toxic or active in one way or another to a great diversity of animals, ranging from the target insect to all the insects, the rest of the arthropods, and all five classes of vertebrates: fish, amphibians, reptiles, birds, and mammals. There is even some activity within the realm of plants.
>   b. Its activity is broad not only in terms of animal species, but also in terms of mechanisms. DDT is a nerve poison; it unstabilizes nerves. A high enough dosage produces tremors and death. This mechanism is how it kills insects, birds, and other organisms. In the last ten years other mechanisms in addition to nerve toxicity have been found. We now know that DDT is an active estrogen. (This fact may or may not be of much environmental significance; my own opinion is that it is not.) It is also an enzyme inducer. It induces liver enzymes—a fact that would appear to be of considerable environmental significance. It inhibits certain other enzymes—and this fact, too, may have environmental importance. DDT is also carcinogenic—capable of producing cancer; the significance of

that finding is obvious. We have a molecule, then, that is enormously active biologically. If we contaminate living systems with it, we may not know *what* is going to happen, but we can very well predict that *something* is likely to happen.

2. DDT residues are very stable or persistent materials. They do break down, but not fast enough to keep us out of environmental trouble. Once we have used DDT, its residues remain in the environment, and we tend to be stuck with them for a long time. Nobody really knows their exact half-life in the world environment, but it is clearly many years.

3. The mobility of DDT residues is quite significant. One might hope that an insecticide will stay on the target area, but DDT departs. Although it has a finite vapor pressure and water solubility, both are extremely low. Initially these traits gave people the impression that DDT would stay where it was put because it would not wash away. They overlooked, however, the earth's enormous volume of air and water, which can carry quite a bit of DDT at exceedingly low concentrations over a period of time. Other properties substantially enhance the ability of air and water to carry the material. Since suspensions are formed in both air and water, DDT does not have to be in solution to move. It also adsorbs to particulate matter, especially soil particles, which can erode and wash downstream in the watershed, eventually reaching the oceans. Similarly, particulates are picked up by the winds and carried about the world in the atmosphere. Finally, the material has the interesting property of co-distillation with water. If we placed a beaker of water on a bench and suspended in it ten parts per billion of DDT, by this time tomorrow there would be only about five parts per billion; the other half would have escaped into the air as the water evaporated.

We therefore have a number of ways by which DDT residues can be transported by air and water currents to all parts of the earth. It comes down in the rainfall, and it occurs in the air wherever anybody has looked, even in remote areas. Contaminated Antarctic animals afford an example of the material's capability for distant journeys. The air over Barbados, after filtration and analysis, disclosed the presence of DDT, DDE, and dieldrin, even though this air had traversed several thousand miles of ocean. [Riseborough et al., 1968a.] Similar cases have been recorded in a number of other circumstances and locations. It is therefore hardly surprising that DDT is distributed all over the world.

4. The solubility characteristics of DDT are environmentally important. We cannot minimize the importance of the fact that DDT is a material with an extremely low water solubility—one of the lowest known for any organic chemical—while it has a very high solubility in lipids (fatlike organic materials). As a consequence, DDT is not going to remain in the inorganic environment but will be transferred into the organic. Because all living organisms contain lipids in which DDT is more soluble, they accumulate it. Therefore,

it will not get lost in the oceans or remain in the soil and air but, instead, will be funneled constantly into food chains.* Organisms thus become contaminated from an environment that may often appear to be uncontaminated but actually contains a very low amount of DDT.

Obviously we have a molecule with a rather unusual combination of properties, posing a unique problem. (Wurster, 1970, pp. 38-41; author's emphasis)

We do not intend here to analyze these passages point by point, since a few of the specific statements made by Wurster have already been discussed in part, while most of the others will be dealt with in considerable detail in the following chapters. We have included this lengthy citation for the purpose of giving our readers an idea of the psychological effect such a technical description may have on the audience as a whole. Wurster is a chemist by training and a professor of biology. He is usually introduced as one of America's most knowledgeable experts on DDT. His initial discussion sounds highly scientific and is delivered in a detached, objective tone. True, one or two of his specific statements might be questioned by a handful of his listeners: for instance, the allegation that DDT is carcinogenic might be recognized as an unproven speculation. But as we have already seen, this allegation has been around for such a long time that most people are either convinced that it is true or pay little attention to it, and it is always worth throwing in as an impressive and frightening remark, even at the risk of being challenged. In the particular audience for whom this presentation was intended—which presumably consisted in large part of students from the School of Forestry—there might also have been one or two skeptics who would have wondered about Wurster's manner of summarizing DDT's toxic properties, since it is rather widely recognized that DDT is not toxic to mammals under any ordinary conditions of use. However, he does not actually state that the compound is toxic to mammals, but uses the vague expression "being either toxic or active in one way or another to a great diversity of animals." In general, it would seem not at all unlikely that the majority of listeners in Wurster's audience would be psychologically prepared, following on such a long and seemingly objective theoretical description of the properties of DDT, to accept rather uncritically the contents of the main part of his presentation, which he refers to as cases illustrating "how DDT and its residues actually work in the real world."

---

*See pages 500-501 and compare this unequivocal description of how DDT becomes funneled into the lipid-rich biota with the more recent statement by Woodwell et al. (1971) to the effect that this expected funneling process, for some inexplicable reason, does not seem to be "working well" in the biosphere.

Adaptability as a Prerequisite of Survival

The first "case" he discusses deals with the phenomenon of biological magnification through the food chain. His material is derived almost exclusively from research which he performed together with George Woodwell and Peter Isaacson on DDT residues in a Long Island marsh (Woodwell et al., 1967). In describing their work, Wurster states:

> We ran something in excess of 200 analyses in the summer of 1966 on soils, grasses, and many kinds of organisms. The marsh averaged about a pound of DDT per acre. In the whole group of analyses there was but a single zero—only one analysis in which we could detect no trace of DDT. It was a sample of mud from forty centimeters under the surface of the marsh.
>
> We estimated that in our own marsh the water contained fifty parts per trillion of DDT. Two steps up the food chain the zooplankton contained a hundred times more DDT than the water, while shrimp feeding on zooplankton were four times higher in DDT content than were the zooplankton. Smaller fish, such as minnows and silversides carried about one-fourth to one part per million (ppm) of DDT— concentrations five to ten times higher than the zooplankton on which they were presumably feeding. The larger fish, among them pickerel and needlefish, have one or two ppm of DDT—again five or ten times higher than the small fish. Birds such as terns contain from three to ten ppm of DDT, about ten times higher than the small fish on which they feed. Finally, at the top of this particular food web, we see the large diving ducks, such as mergansers and cormorants, which contain from twenty to thirty ppm of DDT, about ten times higher than the larger fish they eat. (Wurster, 1970, pp. 42, 43)

Wurster's statement in the first paragraph to the effect that the marsh contained an average of about one pound per acre of residues proved to be a point of acute embarrassment to George Woodwell, the first author of the 1967 publication on this marsh, since in the original paper they had written: "DDT residues in the soil of an extensive salt marsh on the south shore of Long Island average more than 13 pounds per acre (15 kilograms per hectare)" (Woodwell et al., 1967, p. 821).

On January 12, 1972, when confronted during the consolidated DDT Hearings with the fact that Wurster had spoken and written about a *one* pound per acre average in this same marsh, Woodwell said: "That is a true statement in my experience. I didn't know that Dr. Wurster had said that, but that is true . . . (p. 7236) . . . It is also true that this sampling [referring to the original data reported for the marsh] is *deliberately biased** in order to find the highest residues we could find" (Woodwell, 1972, p. 7235; our emphasis).

There are a number of other discrepancies between the residue data which Woodwell et al. reported in their 1967 publication and those which Wurster speaks about in the presentation under discussion. There are also discrepancies within the second paragraph of Wurster's speech, cited above, between the mathematically calculated values he suggests and the "actual" residue values to which he refers. For instance, he says that five to ten times more residues occur in small fish feeding on zooplankton than within the zooplankton. He then states that "this is one-fourth to one part per million of DDT." He has already told us that the zooplankton contain about 5 ppb (100 times the 50 ppt level in the water). Five to ten times 5 ppb would equal 25 to 50 ppb, instead of the stated 250 to 1,000 ppb (the same as ¼ to 1 ppm). These differences between the proposed magnification calculations and the values he states as typical for each trophic level may be found throughout the whole food-chain summary.

The differences between his stated values and the data published in 1967 are also astonishing, particularly at the lower trophic levels. In this lecture Wurster tells his audience that zooplankton contain 5 ppb, and shrimp, one level up in the food chain, 20 ppb. In 1967, on the other hand, these levels were eight times higher: 40 and 160 ppb respectively. The reader will find on page 379 a representation in Fig. 3 of a simplified marine food chain, with Wurster's theoretical magnification potentials expressed in parts per billion DDT residues. Table 12 compares Wurster's theoretical values, the values he mentions in the 1970 oral presentation, and correlative data drawn from the 1967 publication with Woodwell.

That Woodwell was never informed of Wurster's "adjustments" in a downward direction of the residues they reported in 1967 is apparent not only from the testimony at the Consolidated DDT Hearings, but also from Table 1 in Woodwell's more recent publication on DDT residues (Woodwell et al., 1971)—to be discussed in detail later—in which he duly records estimated DDT residues in the biomass of marine arthropods as 0.1 ppm (100 ppb).

Several questions come to mind immediately. Did the residue data reported in the 1967 publication represent typical averages or did they not? If they did not, and further samples were taken in the same marsh by the same investigators, yielding lower averages, why were these not reported in a formal scientific publication? If Woodwell is still convinced that their 1967 measurements were

---

*Lest even one pound per acre strike the reader as very high, it should perhaps be explained that these analyses were made around sites where DDT stocks were being dumped, a practice which is obviously not encouraged or related to proper use.

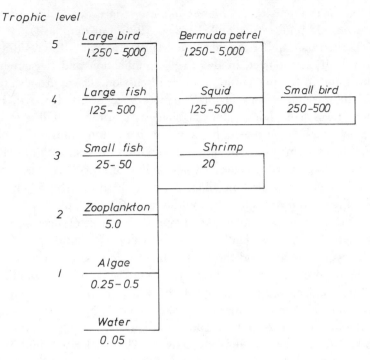

Figure 3. *SIMPLIFIED MARINE FOOD CHAIN*
(after Wurster, 1970).
(Numbers = DDT residues calculated from data presented in above article, in ppb)

Table 12. *COMPARISON OF RESIDUE LEVELS IN MARINE ORGANISMS*
(all values expressed in ppb)

Trophic levels, organisms	Wurster, 1970: proposed calculated magnifications	Wurster, 1970: stated values	Woodwell, et al., 1967: published data. . . . . . .
1. Algae	0.25– 0.5	. . .	88
2. Zooplankton	5	5	40
3a. Shrimp	20	20	.160
3b. Small fish	25 – 50	250– 1,000	230– 940
4a. Small bird	250 – 500	3,000– 5,000	1,480– 9,600
4b. Large fish	125 – 500	1,000– 2,000	1,330–2,070
5a. Large bird	1,250 –5,000	20,000–30,000	22,800–26,400
4c. Squid	125 – 500	. . .	. . .
5b. Bermuda petrel	1,250 –5,000	6,400 (in eggs and dead chicks)	. . .

correct and meaningful, why should Wurster have felt the need to alter the data? Did he not clearly state that they derived from the analyses made by himself and Woodwell in the summer of 1966? Could it be that he perceived that the residues reported for living organisms from the lower trophic levels were just too high to be credible?

In his lecture Wurster conveys the impression that, whereas government agencies charged with the responsibility of monitoring pesticide residue levels fail to take into account the phenomenon of pesticide magnification through the various trophic levels of the food chain, environmentalists have long been aware of the importance of this phenomenon and understand it well. Unfortunately, a rhetorical declaration of the clarity of this process is not convincing; one has only to take into account the conflicting and often confused reports, for the most part supplied by environmentalists, to see just how unclear this whole process is.

Let us examine a few examples of residue data published for various trophic levels.

Level 1: Algae

1. In 1967, Woodwell and his coworkers reported 88 ppb in *Cladophora*. (This is higher than their figure for the grazers, or zooplankton, which are at trophic level 2.)

2. Cox (1970b) found 750 to 1,000 ppb residues in algae in Monterey Bay, California. (This is approximately the same as the residues mentioned by Phillips (1970) for anchovies in the same bay. Anchovies are at trophic level 3, and thus theoretically should have residues from 50 to 100 times higher than those found in algae.) (In a second paper, Cox (1970a) reported residue levels of only 40 ppb in anchovies taken from the Gulf of California.)

Level 2: Zooplankton

1. "Calanoid copepods show significant mortality at 5 ppt (parts per trillion)." (Menzel, Anderson, and Randtke; unpublished data 1970a, cited by SCEP panel, p. 128).

2. In 1967, Woodwell, Wurster, and Isaacson reported 40 parts per *billion* in *live* organisms from this group.

3. In 1970, Wurster estimated that there should be about 5 ppb at this trophic level.

4. If Menzel et al. really have shown significant mortality of these organisms at 5 ppt, and if the estimates of the SCEP panel that there should be an average concentration of 5 ppt DDT dispersed in the mixed layer of the oceans* were to be taken seriously, then the greatest proportion of marine zooplankton should already be dead.

---

* To be discussed later.

Level 3a: Shrimp

Data are available on both brine shrimp and edible shrimp. Let us first consider brine shrimp.

1. In 1967, Grosch reported 39 percent mortality among brine shrimp exposed for 21 days to 1 ppt DDT. This datum was cited by Wurster in 1969 in an article entitled "DDT: Danger to the Environment." If this were true, then there should be no brine shrimp left at all in San Francisco Bay, where the 1963 DDT levels were reported at 100 ppt, and concentrations in 1970 were still at 10 ppt. "Luckily," the brine shrimp are still there.

It seems fairly likely to us that Grosch's original report was in error — that he perhaps confused 1 ppt with 1 ppb. One cannot, of course, be certain, but to borrow a phrase from the environmentalists, "the evidence is highly suggestive." In a follow-up study published in 1970, Grosch made this remarkable report. He had introduced 3 nanograms of DDT, or 1 ppt, into one of his 3 liter jars (his culture number 3) of sea water containing brine shrimp. Three years later, he analyzed the total contents of the jar and found that "apparently, a fraction of our original dose has persisted as a toxic residue deposit despite losses by (a) co-evaporation; (b) shrimp transfer for subculture and pair mating tests; and (c) conversion by yeast and other microorganisms." (Grosch, 1970, p. 913). This remaining "fraction" was reported as "0.10 micrograms per 3 liters," which happens to be 33 nanograms per liter, or 33 *times more* than he originally added to his culture! One is forced to conclude either that there was something wrong with Grosch's measurements, or that Wurster left out of his list of DDT's amazing properties its most astonishing characteristic: by some mechanism not yet understood by chemists (or anybody else, for that matter), DDT multiplies itself while just waiting quietly in a jar of seawater.

2. Edible (Penaeid) shrimp. According to Nimmo, Wilson, and Blackman (unpublished data, 1970, cited by the SCEP panel, p. 129) "continuous exposure of shrimp to DDT concentrations of less than 0.2 ppb caused 100 percent mortality in less than 20 days.

If we presume that shrimp are able to utilize nourishment dispersed in 0.5 liters of water per day, and also presume 100 percent efficiency of uptake, then in 20 days, with a background of 0.2 ppb, the maximum body burden of the dead shrimp (weighing about 10 grams) should have been 200 ppb. Uptake efficiency is, however, more realistically estimated as 10 percent, which would point to a lethal body burden in shrimp of about 20 ppb.

3. In 1967 Woodwell, Wurster, and Isaacson reported 160 ppb in *live* shrimp. Perhaps the unlikeliness of such residues might account for Wurster's "adjustment" in his 1970 lecture to 20 ppb in shrimp?

Finally, shrimp are scavenger/predators. If either algae or zooplankton actually contained more than 0.2 ppb of DDT residues, shrimp should not survive at all. Are we to conclude from this that the reported shrimp catches of recent years are false propaganda, and that all the shrimp we have been enjoying as food were really frozen before 1947?

Level 3b: Small Fish

As already mentioned, anchovies are variously described as having residues ranging from 40 to 750 to 1,000 ppb DDT residues. This is not far from the range of measurements Woodwell et al. reported for small fish in 1967. However, it is not at all in accord with the measurements reported for shrimp, which are at the *same* trophic level.

In view of these many inconsistencies, although we do not outrightly deny the possibility that DDT may be magnified up the food chain in some cases, we would submit that the environmentalists have not demonstrated any clear idea of how or in what circumstances this supposed process operates.

DDT and Phytoplankton

Wurster's next example of DDT's behavior in "the real world" consists of a brief summary of experiments he performed at Woods Hole in 1968 testing the effects of various concentrations of DDT in water on algal photosynthesis, together with a few remarks on the possible implications of his results. He tells his audience the following:

A few years ago I did some studies at the Woods Hole Oceanographic Institution in which the photosynthesis of marine phytoplankton was measured where DDT had been added to the water in the parts-per-billion range. . . . The data indicated that as DDT was added to the water, the rate of photosynthesis was decreased. (Photosynthesis is the process whereby green plants absorb carbon dioxide and the energy from sunlight, producing organic nutrients and oxygen. All animal life on earth is dependent on this process.) By the time we reach eight or ten parts per billion of DDT in the water, the photosynthetic rate is diminished to about three-quarters of normal; as the DDT concentration goes higher, the photosynthetic rate goes lower. Since these experiments were done, others who have worked in the field have confirmed the findings in both marine and freshwater systems.

What are the environmental implications of these results? (I find it difficult to extrapolate from an Erlenmeyer flask to an ocean.) There is no evidence that DDT is reducing the rate of photosynthesis in the ocean, nor that DDT is present there in comparable concentrations. In local areas, I think it means that if DDT reaches these concentration ranges, it will inhibit the whole base of the food chain. I believe it also indicates a likelihood of manipulating the species composition of the phytoplankton community because it is selectively toxic. Since it does not exert the same toxic stress on all species, it could aggravate problems of eutrophication (overenrichment that leads to algal blooms). It could increase algal-bloom problems where certain species that are not good food organisms could become predominant. If this should occur, the species composition of the whole food chain might be changed. (Wurster, 1970, p. 44)

We wish to make some specific comments on the design of Wurster's experiment, and on the investigations of those "others who have . . . confirmed the findings" since 1968. Before entering on a technical critique, however, a few general comments are in order on the manner in which Wurster is here describing what he "thinks" might be the implications of his own findings.

First, perhaps, the reader should be told that after the publication of this experimental work, there was a tremendous flurry of excitement among pollution alarmists, which included speculations that the presence of DDT in the aqueous environment might be depressing the rate of photosynthesis on a global scale. Most of this did not come from the pen of Wurster himself, but rather from other environmentalists — among them Paul Ehrlich and LaMont Cole. It became a subject of general discussion, and some may recall that it was repeated by U Thant, then Secretary General of the United Nations. When alarmists went so far as to suggest that a serious depletion of oxygen might be imminent, there was a reaction, and a number of rather strongly worded articles were published by specialists in atmospheric oxygen and related fields, who flatly stated that no such implications could be drawn from Wurster's experiment. One finds by now that even the "Ecological Study Group" of the *Report of the Study of Critical Environmental Problems* (SCEP), most of whose members, as we shall see later, are sympathetic to Wurster's views in general, discount the ecological meaningfulness of this piece of work. "The effect of DDT on the ability of ocean phytoplankton to convert carbon dioxide into oxygen is not considered significant. The DDT concentration necessary to induce significant inhibition exceeds expected concentrations in the open ocean by ten times its solubility (1 part per billion) in water. . . . Laboratory evidence is available demonstrating its [DDT's] inhibitory effect on photosynthesis in single-celled marine plants (Wurster, 1968; Menzel, Anderson, and Randtke, 1970a). It is doubtful that these results are ecologically meaningful" (SCEP, 1970, pp. 25, 127).

These criticisms may in part account for the apparent conservatism of Wurster's statement in his lecture that he is not prepared to extrapolate from an Erlenmeyer flask to the ocean. Actually, only a few months earlier, although he did not say in so many words that his findings pointed to an endangered supply of oxygen, he did not at that time seem to find a worldwide extrapolation from his laboratory flask so difficult, for he wrote: "These single-celled algae . . . are responsible for more than half of the world's photosynthesis; interference with this process could have profound worldwide biological implications" (Wurster, 1969, p. 25).

By 1970, Wurster is quite ready to admit that there is no evidence that DDT is reducing the rate of photosynthesis in the oceans, and he also grants that it is not present there in anything like the concentrations he used in his experiment. Following these defensive admissions, however, he immediately turns the whole matter to his advantage by placing the emphasis on DDT's selective toxicity and suggesting, with a lot of subjective and conditional language, that he "thinks" his experiments "might" indicate the "likelihood" that DDT will encourage the growth of algae which are not good food organisms, and thus alter deleteriously the whole base of the food chain. These remarks are bound to make a rather dramatic impression on his audience, even supposing that some of his listeners are familiar with the argument and counterargument which arose over this whole question of the ecological significance of these photosynthesis studies.

Now let us turn to a somewhat more technical discussion of the algal experiments per se.

Wurster's primary investigations dealt with changes in the photosynthetic activity of four different species of marine algae, plus one mixed community, in the presence of concentrations of DDT ranging from 1 to 500 ppb. Since the solubility of DDT in water is only 1.2 ppb, he had to dissolve each of the quantities tested which exceeded this limit in ethanol before adding the solution to his cultures. He did not measure growth (cell division) of his algae; nor did he attempt to determine at the end of the experiment whether or not the plants had actually taken up any quantity of pesticide. The failure to do the latter seems very peculiar, since it would have been the crucial experimental step in establishing a cause and effect relationship on the *biochemical* level.

He unquestionably got some results.* His experiments showed that when about 10 ppb of DDT was added to the cultures, photosynthesis was decreased

---

* For those who might be interested, we should like to cite Wurster's interpretation of these results: "The fact that these data apparently follow sigmoid curves is typical of dose-response relations and suggests the *absence* of a threshold concentration of DDT below which no effects occur" (Wurster, 1968, p. 1475; our emphasis). This sentence is masterfully constructed. Its first half, describing a dose-response relationship in connection with DDT, is true. The existence of such relationship is the cornerstone of pharmacology and toxicology, and it is therefore only natural that it should also be applicable to DDT. The second half of the sentence, however, is untrue. Exactly from the established fact that a dose-response relationship exists, it follows that there is somewhere a point on this sigmoid curve under which a dose will be without effect—i.e., a no-effect concentration. The claim that there is an *absence of threshold* is therefore obviously false. However, after reading the first correct half of the sentence, it is psychologically quite likely that the reader, even if a scientist, may fall into the trap and accept the second, incorrect postulate without reflection.

in the tested species by about 20 percent. At concentrations of 100 ppb, photo-synthetic activity of the experimental algae was reduced by about 80 percent compared with that of the controls. As an explanation of these changes, he wrote: "Presumably the effect on phytoplankton occurs after absorption of DDT by the cells, a process to be expected from the very low solubility of DDT in water and its higher solubility in lipid-containing biological material" (Wurster, 1968, p. 1475).

This sentence would seem to imply that the DDT was taken up into the in-terior of the cells, where a biochemical reaction took place between the pesticide and the photosynthesizing apparatus of the organism. That Wurster did indeed mean this as an interpretation is made clear by another statement in the text: "It is known that DDT reduces Hill reaction activity* in barley chloroplasts" (ibid.).

However, since he did not perform any measurements which would have demonstrated that DDT was indeed within the algal cells, the basic experimental design was not adequate to yield a meaningful answer to the question raised: Is DDT a chemical inhibitor of photosynthesis?

The experiment tells us that something happened (photosynthetic activity was reduced), but it does not tell us why. The investigator assumed that the ef-fect followed on absorption of DDT by the cells, and he justified this assumption by reminding his readers that DDT is more soluble in lipid-containing biological material than in water. However, there is a problem with these unicellular algae which throws considerable doubt on this "expected process of absorption into the lipid-containing biological material"—namely, the cell walls of these organisms are mucopolysaccharides, and contain no lipids. † Since one can only "presume" why the effect took place, it would seem equally if not more legitimate to sup-pose that Wurster's findings were simply the result of the heavy precipitate of DDT falling onto the surfaces of the cells, causing them to settle, and decreasing light penetration to their interiors.

* The dark phase of photosynthesis; that is, those biochemical reactions which proceed without light.

† To be absolutely correct, it should be stated that some of these forms do not have fully developed cell walls. However, in such motile algae as Dunaliella and Primnesium, the pellicle is composed of polysaccharides, and even in the most primitive organisms the wall contains cellulose fibrils (Brown, 1969; Brown et al., 1970). The lipoprotein membrane is within this external layer, which is not easily penetrated by lipid solvents. It is a well-known fact that in order to extract hydrophobic materials—such as chlorophyll—from algal cells, even when such small molecule solvents as ethanol or acetone are used, the cells have to be broken open (mechanically or chemically) on account of the barrier presented by the highly hydrophylic external wall components against the passage of lipo-philic materials. The early lipoid mosaic theory of Overton, which assumed the passive penetration of alcohol into plant cells, has long since been overthrown. And, more in accordance with expectations from physiological facts, Peterle (1966) showed with radioactively labeled DDT that the compound is adsorbed to and not taken up by aquatic plants.

That this physical rather than biochemical phenomenon is sufficient to explain Wurster's findings is supported by the much more detailed experiments of Menzel and his coworkers (Menzel et al., 1970b), which, despite Wurster's public claims, cannot be said to have confirmed his own experiments.

Menzel's group used exactly the same techniques as Wurster to study decline in photosynthesis, with the exception that they employed a different solvent (acetone) for the addition of DDT to their cultures. Two of the algal species *(Skeletonema costatum* and *Coccolithus huxleyi)* were common to both experiments. In their series of investigations Menzel et al. also found about a 20 percent decrease in photosynthesis at the 10 ppb level in the two species mentioned. At higher levels, however, they did *not* get the marked decrease in photosynthesis which Wurster had shown.

In the Menzel paper, a second experiment is reported which has important implications. After introduction of the DDT solution to the culture medium, the investigators filtered off the precipitated DDT and studied the effect of the filtrate on photosynthesis. Although they were not able to filter off all the fine precipitates, they detected no decrease in photosynthesis at any starting concentration of DDT when the algae were cultured in the filtered solution. Since they had already established that DDT at the 10 ppb level did decrease photosynthetic activity, they concluded that less than 10 ppb of DDT remained in the filtrate.

This second experiment strongly suggests that in order for DDT to bring about a decrease in algal photosynthesis, it has to be present in the form of large precipitate flakes. Although Menzel et al. did not draw this rather obvious conclusion from their second experiment, and although they too failed to examine whether there had been any actual uptake of DDT into the interior of the algal cells in any of their cultures, the lack of effect in the filtered solution supports the contention that a simple physical process was responsible for the decrease in photosynthesis. In other terms, the same effect might have been achieved with some other substance which will precipitate in water—iron chloride, for instance. It may therefore be said that the effect has not been established as having been caused by the chemical action of DDT.

For the benefit of those without a special interest in chemistry, a simple analogy may aid in the understanding of the above discussion. Imagine that a large number of very young green pea shoots have just come up in a vegetable garden. A vigorous and rather thick sandstorm sets in. Many of the shoots will be buried by the sand and fail altogether to grow. Others will be battered and weakened, but will survive. An explanation from a gardener that both the dead pea shoots and the weakened ones had "taken up" the sand into their interiors, and in this way perished or were altered in their growth activity, would seem somewhat farfetched; and one would not be inclined to believe it, unless the gardener could in some way demonstrate that the sand particles were indeed inside the pea shoots, interacting with their internal structures.

In his 1968 publication, Wurster had speculated—without doing any experiments to test this matter—that the presence of DDT not only decreases photosynthesis, but may also inhibit cell division (growth) of some algal species, and consequently alter the base of the food chain. The final sentence of his paper reads: "Such effects are insidious and their cause may be obscure, yet they may be ecologically more important than the obvious, direct mortality of larger organisms that is so often reported" (Wurster, 1968, p. 1475). We have already noted that in the second paragraph of his 1970 lecture, it is this possibility which is emphasized, rather than a large-scale decrease in photosynthesis.

Menzel's group, however, *did* perform special experiments to test inhibition of growth per se; and in early 1972, a third study dealing with the effects of chlorinated hydrocarbons on algal growth was published, with Wurster as one of its authors (Mosser, Fisher, Teng, and Wurster, 1972). In the latter, the main object of study was the effect of PCBs (polychlorinated biphenyls) on algal growth; but since algae immersed in DDT solutions served as one of the controls, comparisons can be made.

In testing four different marine algae, Menzel et al. found no (or insignificant) retardation of growth up to the 100 to 200 ppb concentrations of DDT. Similarly, when dealing with a species common to all three studies, the Mosser group found no blocking of cell division at the 100 ppb DDT level. This should have been reassuring to Dr. Wurster, since the chances that DDT will ever be present in waters—even in highly localized areas—at more than the 100 ppb level are virtually zero.

As further comfort to Wurster, one might want to point out that one of the most nutritious and preferred algal food organisms (both for grazers and other filter-feeding planktonic or benthic animals) is the green algal flagellate *Dunaliella tertiolecta*. This species was found by both Menzel et al. and Mosser et al. to be almost completely resistant to DDT, showing neither decrease in photosynthesis nor inhibition of growth at concentrations as high as 1,000 ppb. This might at first seem to contradict our hypothesis that the effects on other organisms resulted from precipitates settling on the cell surfaces. This particular organism, however, is a highly motile, rapidly swimming form, and its tendency to remain in almost constant motion, even in the confined conditions of a laboratory culture, would either prevent precipitates from settling on its surfaces or permit the organism to wash off those which might strike it.

At about the time of Wurster's first publication on algae, a very careful study dealing with the uptake and accumulation of DDT by the unicellular green alga *Chlorella pyrenoidosa* (?) appeared in the Danish journal *Oikos*. The author, Södergren (1968), conducted his experiments at the Sanitary Engineering Research Laboratory of Richmond, California, where he investigated the fate of radioactively labeled DDT in concentrations in water well below its solubility (in the 0.6 ppb range), tracing its uptake by the algal cells both in batch cultures and in continuous-flow systems. He found that the uptake is an extremely rapid phenomenon, requiring only about 15 seconds, and he correctly ascribed it to *adsorption* to the cellular surface. Subsequently, however, he argued that this adsorption must be followed by absorption into the cellular interior, since he could not detect radioactivity in the culture medium when he transferred his DDT-labeled algae to a DDT-free medium. (One would presume—goes the argument—that if only surface adsorption took place, in a medium containing no DDT the sorbed substance should become partially desorbed, resulting in an equilibrium distribution of the compound on the surface of the cells and in the medium.) In effect, all of Södergren's experimental results, which we are not going to detail here, speak for the opposite interpretation—i.e., that we are dealing strictly with a surface phenomenon and not with penetration into the cells. For instance, he calculated the theoretical concentration of DDT which should have been reached in the lipid phase of the algae, knowing DDT's lipid solubility and the lipid contents of the plants: "The theoretical capacity of a culture with 10×10^6 cells/ml on the basis of the above assumptions is 1.6 mg/l [of DDT]. It was impossible to verificate [sic] this value experimentally...it was found that 1.9×10^8 cells with a dry weight of 1.2 mg had an absorption capacity greater than 0.38 μg C^{14}-DDT" (Södergren, 1968, p. 134).

In other terms, Södergren found only about 1/100,000 the quantity of DDT "in" the algae compared with what would be predicted, if, indeed, absorption were taking place. (1×10^7 cells have the theoretical capacity to accumulate 1.6 mg/l DDT in their lipids; 19×10^7 cells contained only 0.38 μg/l DDT, instead of 30.4 mg/l as expected.) It seems fairly clear that there is no proof here whatsoever of absorption.

The author also described some morphological changes in his cultures, expressed primarily as the clumping of the algal cells after three days of continuous administration of DDT at a rate of about 4.3 μg/l/24 hours. In this case the total of DDT for the 72 hours would have been 13 μg/l, which is well above its solubility. These quantities could easily have led to the clumping of the cells through precipitation on the algal surfaces. Again, a strictly physical phenomenon seems to be the best explanation of the findings.

It is unfortunate that these carefully executed experiments were interpreted in a way that does not follow from the results, but instead serves to substantiate a preconceived idea—i.e., that even minute concentrations of DDT may be damaging to microorganisms forming the base of the food chain in the aquatic environment.

The last paper to be mentioned here is by Vance and Drummond (1969). It is instructive to note that the authors do not refer either to Wurster's 1968 paper or to Södergren's work. They attempted to study the "accumulation" of DDT in two species of blue-green algae and in two green algae. They introduced DDT, dissolved in acetone, in quantities of 5, 10, and 20 μg/ml (the same as mg/l)—that is, *5,000 to 20,000 times higher than its solubility.* They extracted some of their samples with *methylene chloride* (!) and claimed "that the algae were able to concentrate the pesticide by several 100 folds within their cells." The absurdity of these data does not require comment.

One feature of these experiments is, however, noteworthy. The investigators also conducted studies of algal respiration in the presence of varying concentrations of different chlorinated hydrocarbon pesticides. They write: ". . . data obtained from our Warburg analyses suggests (sic) that p,p'-DDT, dieldrin, aldrin, and endrin at a concentration of 1.0 ppm or below has no significant effect on the total oxygen uptake of *Microcystis aeruginosa, Anabaena cylindrica, Scenedesmus quadricauda,* and *Oedogonium* species" (Vance and Drummond, 1969, p. 362).

Thus, although they used huge quantities of the pesticides—orders of magnitude more than their solubility—the findings of these researchers do not confirm any of Wurster's "results" respecting inhibition of photosynthesis with any of the freshwater algae named above.

Now let us summarize. DDT is soluble in water only up to 1.2 ppb. Its concentration in waters, even near sites of DDT application, is rarely even close to this maximum. Should it be present in higher concentrations in a local body of water, it will be adsorbed to soil particles. (The only exception would be deliberate or accidental addition of an oil-based preparation of DDT directly to water.) Environmentalists have frequently implied or suggested indirectly that the DDT in waters which is attached to particulate matter could become desorbed from the particles and as a result become available for absorption by the lipid-rich biota. This hinted-at speculation may also be laid to rest, however, since an excellent recent study by Huang has shown that under natural conditions DDT does *not* desorb from particulates (Huang, 1971). The minor quantity of DDT which is soluble in water neither decreases the photosynthetic rate of algae nor does it interfere with the growth of even the most sensitive species. Even under highly artificial laboratory conditions, *Dunaliella tertiolecta,* which of all the algal species tested is the *best* food organism for zooplankton, is unaffected by concentrations as high as 1,000 ppb. It would therefore seem that the time has come to bury once and for all the speculation that the ubiquitous presence of minute quantities of DDT in waters might alter the base of the food chain in some deleterious manner—unless, of course, some completely new, well-designed, and properly executed experiments are performed which really succeed in demonstrating that DDT can interfere with the growth and/or biochemical activities of algae under conditions approximating those in nature.

We hope that Dr. Wurster will sleep more peacefully in the future and will cease altogether to worry his audiences about DDT's effects on phytoplankton. As far as we have been able to determine, in the case of unicellular algae the experiments performed do not provide even sufficient "suggestive evidence" to support concern over "possible insidious effects."

At the Top of the Pyramid

Having completed his discussion of the marine food chain and of the manner in which DDT might be adversely affecting the unicellular plants at the base of this food pyramid, Wurster has prepared his listeners for the last and most important theme of his lecture: the effects of DDT residues on the reproductive performance of animals high on the food chain—more particularly, the great predator birds which are raptors or fish eaters.

He begins his comments on birds with a description of the plight of the Bermuda petrel, referring to some work which he did in collaboration with Bermuda ornithologist David Wingate. The petrel is a very rare species, indeed. It was believed to be extinct as long ago as 1630, and only in the 1950s was a small surviving colony of fewer than 100 birds identified by ornithologists, Wingate among them, on several islets near Bermuda.

Wingate wrote to Wurster, explaining, according to the latter, ". . . that the Bermuda petrel was suffering reproduction problems. He did not understand what was the trouble with this rare oceanic species, but he suspected that pesticides were somehow involved. In view of the properties of DDT and its residues and the similarity of the petrel's symptoms with those of some terrestrial birds, I suspected that DDT residues had contaminated the food chain of the petrel" (Wurster, 1970, p. 46).

Wurster was interested in pursuing the matter. He performed some DDT residue analyses on dead chicks and eggs of the species and identified pesticide residue peaks. The results were published in an article in *Science* signed by both Wurster and Wingate (1968). In his 1970 lecture, he summarizes the implication of their findings as follows: "The rate of reproduction—the percentage of birds that have been able to raise a chick—has been declining since 1958. Statistical analysis shows a declining regression, reaching zero reproduction in 1978. This time the bird may really be headed for extinction" (Wurster, 1970, p. 46).

It seems rather odd that Wurster should still be emphasizing this declining regression and imminent extinction of the petrel in 1970, since in the meanwhile his coworker Wingate publicly reported an altogether different explanation for the reproductive failure during the 1950s in the small colony. In an interview for *Sports Illustrated,* he explained that long tailed tropic birds competed for the nest burrow of the Bermuda petrel and killed their chicks. Having tried unsuccessfully to make the burrows inaccessible to the "longtails," Wingate finally resorted to direct intervention, stalked the petrel nests during the breeding season, and personally killed any longtails which tried to invade the petrel burrows (Rogin, 1968). Prior to 1958 nearly all the chicks died, but Wingate's patient protective measures seem to be bearing fruit. According to a recent statement by none other than Charles Wurster, 12 viable young were produced by the Bermuda colony in 1971 (Wurster, 1972).

In view of these developments, one might say that Wurster's account in his lecture of the situation of the Bermuda petrel constitutes a distortion by omission. However, one may perhaps excuse him on the grounds that he was trying to bring home a point, for his interest in the petrel's status is clearly quite different from that of Wingate. The latter is an ornithologist, whose activities attest to an earnest concern with the survival of this particular rare species. Wurster's focus, on the other hand, is on the general conclusion which he believes may be inferred from the very presence of detectable DDT residues in the eggs of a species nesting in an area remote from sites of DDT applications and feeding exclusively at sea. He states: "Analyses of dead chicks and eggs disclosed 6.4 ppm of DDT and its metabolites. This figure does not tell us whether or not DDT is causing the reproductive difficulties; there may be a relationship, but the DDT content is not direct evidence, and the reproductive failure could be entirely coincidental. The data do say very clearly, however, that there *is* DDT in the ocean, that it *is* moving through marine food chains, and that a surprising amount *is* present" (Wurster, 1970, p. 46; author's emphasis).

At this point Wurster enters on a discussion of the work of other investigators on the problem of declining avian reproduction, which he describes as "a rather sensational science story that has taken a long time to piece together." He tells about field observations of various birds of prey which have been exhibiting reproductive difficulties (the peregrine falcon, the bald eagle, the osprey, the Cooper's hawk, and the brown pelican). He mentions the findings of the British peregrine falcon authority, Ratcliffe, who compared the eggshells of museum-stored peregrine eggs from 1905 to the 1960s and "discovered that the thickness of peregrine eggshells had been stable until the late 1940s, around 1947, when it suddenly declined about 18 percent to a lower level, where it has remained ever since" (*ibid.*, p. 49). Investigations of eggshell changes in predator species were also carried out in the United States, and Wurster describes with considerable admiration the diligence and extensiveness of a study by two Wisconsin ornithologists.

By the latter part of 1967 a few people were beginning to put two and two together. One of them was Joseph J. Hickey, a University of Wisconsin ornithologist. His graduate student, Daniel W. Anderson, went to museums all over the United States to measure eggshells. He has measured something like 35,000 shells since then. His computer program unravels some of these data with quite interesting results. The peregrine falcon in California, half a world away from Britain, shows the same situation, with the weight of its eggshells stable since 1890 until suddenly, since 1947, the bird has been laying eggs with thin shells—roughly 18 percent thinner than they were before. (Wurster, 1970, p. 49)

In discussing the findings of the ornithologists, Wurster again emphasizes the importance of the food-chain-magnification hypothesis, pointing out that those predator species which feed on herbivores (red-tailed hawks, for example, which eat rodents, and golden eagles, whose prey are rabbits, ground squirrels, and other rodents) are *not* showing any great buildup of DDT; nor are their eggshells becoming abnormally thin. This exemption from population decline is easily understood when one realizes that they are only at trophic level 3, the chain being seeds, rodents, birds. On the other hand, those birds which feed on large fish or on other marine birds will be at trophic level 5 or even 6. He invites his listeners to consider the bald eagle as an example: "It feeds on large fish; the large fish feed on smaller fish; the smaller fish perhaps feed on yet smaller fish that feed in turn on zooplankton; the zooplankton feed on phytoplankton; and the phytoplankton absorb DDT from the water. Since this food chain contains about five steps, we should expect a steep buildup of contamination toward the top" (*ibid.*, p. 50).

Leaving aside, for the moment, the embarrassing fact that the bald eagle does not seem to be exhibiting the "expected" reproductive failure, one must admit that this is a very logical presentation and that its argument is well supported by the earlier explanation of how DDT residues are magnified through the trophic levels of the marine food chain. However, Wurster has no intention of quitting his audience having merely discussed the inferred behavior of DDT residues in biological systems and having summarized these fascinating field studies about birds of prey. Quite to the contrary, in a sudden and rather dramatic turn, he brings to the attention of his listeners that *none* of the observations he has thus far recounted constitutes scientific proof of a cause-and-effect relationship between DDT residues and the reproductive problems of certain birds. In one sentence he admits that the correlations of the timing of the introduction of DDT use with the timing of population declines (or eggshell thinning), however suggestive, could be accounted for "as just a strange coincidence." Before this skeptical disclaimer can give rise to real doubts in the minds of his listeners, he counters it with a rapid, condensed, and impressive account of the most recent work on the DDT–thin-eggshell problem. In these penultimate paragraphs of his lecture, which we shall cite in full, it seems to us that Wurster achieves a most unusual effect: to wit, a high-pitched dramatic climax is coupled with a return to the tone of scientific objectivity which dominated the first part of this presentation.

> By now I may have given you the suggestion that DDT might have something to do with the problems of these birds. Actually, what I have described so far is circumstantial evidence; all data can be accounted for as just a strange coincidence. However, there are much tighter data that establish a direct cause-and-effect relationship. Data relating the thickness of herring gulls' eggshells with the amount of DDE in ppm inside those same eggs indicate that as the DDE concentration increases inside the eggs, the shells grow thinner. There is a statistically significant relationship, with only one chance in a thousand that the relationship is based on just an accident or random phenomenon.
>
> The real test of a relationship is whether or not we can cause the effect under controlled conditions. This experiment has been attempted several times on various gallinaceous birds. Pheasants, quail, and chickens have proved to be resistant to DDT; this fact makes it difficult to detect the effect, and scientists were misled for a long time. More recently, however, controlled experiments using the mallard duck (an omnivore), our American sparrow hawk or kestrel, and most recently the Japanese quail (a herbivore) did produce the effect. . . . Control birds on clean food (without DDT) laid normal eggs and had normal reproductive success. Birds fed DDT or DDE in their diets laid eggs with shells 15 to 17 percent thinner than normal, and they did so at concentrations approximating those found in the natural food supply.
>
> These experiments settle the question of a cause-and-effect relationship: DDT residues *do* cause the reproductive problems of the carnivorous birds. (Wurster, 1970, pp. 51–52, author's emphasis)

We hope that those of our readers who have never heard Wurster deliver a discourse on the DDT problem will have gained some idea of his considerable effectiveness as a public speaker. His ardor is tempered by a logical format. Enough of his personal opinions and speculations are labeled as such to give the impression that the rest of his material is factual. The tenor of his speech moves easily among expressions of personal concern, detached observations of supposedly long-accepted scientific knowledge, summaries of his own work, homey stories of the desperate plight of rare birds, and dramatic revelations concerning recent laboratory findings. Who but the most hardened skeptic could come away from such a lecture without being impressed and at least in part convinced of the truth of Wurster's opening claim that DDT in the environment represents one of our most serious pollution problems?

Although at no point does Wurster mention the great public health benefits of DDT, it seems that many persons who are actively fighting for its continued use as an agent to control disease vectors are inclined to accept the "overwhelming evidence" that DDT residues are associated with the reproductive failures of certain species of birds. This is particularly true since 1968–1969 — the time when the publications asserting a cause-and-effect relationship appeared. Members of the World Health Organization, for example, whose official position is that the continued availability of DDT for disease control is absolutely imperative for many underdeveloped countries, appear to have accepted the validity of the laboratory studies and statistical correlations to which Wurster refers at the end of his lecture.

We should like to go on record here as declaring that the same held true for us. Although our skepticism about matters bearing on pollution of the environment by "unseen threats" had been growing rather than diminishing as we continued to read both the popular and the scientific literature on the subject, we nevertheless assumed that there *must be* some scientific basis for the case against DDT. We supposed that the investigators whose research is mentioned by Wurster had, in fact, succeeded in establishing the cause-and-effect relationship to which he refers — particularly as their results were all published in either the British journal *Nature* or in *Science,* two highly prestigious publications whose editorial policies and referee system are generally thought to be quite stringent. We decided, nevertheless, to read through the papers involved rather closely, not because we had any intent to discredit them, but so that we might refine our understanding of the case against DDT, and thus be better able to weigh in the balance the arguments of those who support motions for a complete ban on DDT production against those who defend the compound as a needed and valuable pesticide.

Fortunately, in the printed version of his lecture, Wurster gives specific references for the statements in the last paragraphs which we quoted. These are: a 1968 publication in *Science* by J. J. Hickey and D. W. Anderson (the statistically significant correlations and the extensive measurements of the thickness of muse-

um eggs); a study reported in 1969 in *Nature* by R. G. Heath, J. W. Spann, and
J. F. Kreitzer (the mallard duck experiments); a 1969 article in *Science* by R. D.
Porter and S. N. Wiemeyer (the sparrow hawk or kestrel studies); and a 1969
publication in *Nature* by J. Bitman, H. C. Cecil, S. J. Harris, and G. J. Fries (experiments with the Japanese quail).

We shall next attempt to summarize some of the startling discoveries we
made when we scrutinized these four publications.

Ornithological Juggling

The first of the four publications is entitled: "Chlorinated Hydrocarbons
and Eggshell Changes in Raptorial and Fish-Eating Birds" (Hickey and Anderson,
1968). This is not a controlled laboratory experiment but a correlative study.
In one of its aspects it deals with a correlation in time: the population crash of the
California peregrine falcon, which presumably resulted from the production of
overly thin eggshells, is related to the introduction of DDT into the general environment in the year 1947. A second correlation relates the amounts of DDE
within the eggs of herring gulls to the thickness of their shells, as determined by
direct measurements.

Hickey and Anderson reported that they found good correlations between
thinner eggshells and declining populations. They pinpointed 1947 as the specific
date when the "population crash" had its onset. Actually, the only evidence they
produced to support the importance of this particular date was a sudden change
between about 1941 and 1951 in the eggshells of *one* population (California) of
one species (peregrine falcon); but more about that later.

They selected for study six species of raptorial and fish-eating birds: the
peregrine falcon, the osprey, the bald eagle, the red-tailed hawk, the golden
eagle, and the great horned owl. Three of the six species are *not* declining in
population (red-tailed hawks, great horned owls, and golden eagles). However,
as Wurster pointed out, this can easily be explained by the fact that they feed on a
two-step food chain (rats, rabbits, and other herbivores), whereas the three declining species (bald eagles, peregrine falcons, and ospreys) are at the top of a
five-step food chain.

In the very broad conclusions of the paper, which we cite below, the authors
place strong emphasis on the chlorinated hydrocarbons as *the* causative agent
of eggshell thinning. They also imply that the population losses among raptors
in both Europe and America must have had a common physiological basis, although their paper in no way demonstrates this.

(i) many of the recent and spectacular raptor population crashes in both the
United States and Western Europe have had a common physiological basis; (ii) egg-

shell breakage has been widespread but largely overlooked in North America; [The logic here is very subtle, for it is difficult to see how, if it has been overlooked, the authors could know after the fact that it has been widespread.] (iii) significant decreases in shell thickness and weight are characteristic of the unprecedented reproductive failures of raptor populations in certain parts of the United States; (iv) the onset of the calcium change 1 year after the introduction of chlorinated hydrocarbons into general usage was not a random circumstance; and (v) these persisting compounds are having a serious insidious effect on certain species of birds at the tops of contaminated ecosystems. (Hickey and Anderson, 1968, pp. 272-273)

Let us see what Hickey and Anderson did which led them to these far-reaching conclusions.

One of their principal activities involved examining 1,729 blown eggs of the six species of birds in museum collections in various parts of the United States. Some of these eggs dated from as early as 1885, and they represented various local populations of the species. The authors present a table showing some of the data resulting from these observations. However, they state that for five of the six species "the data do not permit a precise delineation of the onset of the change in calcium metabolism." Only for the California population of peregrine falcons can they show a clear relation in time between the decrease in weight and thickness of the eggshells and the beginnings of DDT use. They therefore emphasize this particular population, tabulating in considerable graphic detail the mean eggshell thickness measurements, mean weights, and mean thickness indices for ten-year periods from 1890 through 1952.

The latter is a ratio which was devised by Ratcliffe for the comparison of museum eggs under study. Underneath the graphs in their Figure 1, Hickey and Anderson write: "The thickness index, calculated as ten times the weight divided by the product of the length and breadth (in mm) of each egg, was devised by Ratcliffe [1967] for the study of museum eggs. . . ." If one looks at Ratcliffe's article in *Nature,* however, it is evident that he did *not* multiply the weight of the eggshells by ten or by any other number. He simply converted it from grams into milligrams (a conversion of 1,000 which is not a multiplication process at all), before he divided it by the length and breadth in millimeters. One would expect that Hickey and Anderson's thickness indices should vary from those of Ratcliffe by a factor of 100, *if* they performed their calculations as reported. However, by some miracle, they managed to get a close approximation of the British researcher's results for these indices — perhaps by making a concomitant but appropriate error in their measurements of length and breadth?

In any event, they present three very small graphs representing the findings on the California peregrine in terms of the three mentioned parameters, one beneath the other, in order to illustrate that in all three parameters there is a sudden drop in the period 1946–1952.

This is essentially the only evidence presented in the study which substantiates the statement in the conclusions that ". . . the onset of the calcium change 1 year after the introduction of chlorinated hydrocarbons into general usage was not a random circumstance. . . ."

Now a few remarks on these graphs.

The accuracy of the graph representing the thickness indices is uncertain because of the authors' failure to apply correctly Ratcliffe's method of calculating it.

The graph plotting the direct measurements of the thickness of the shells is scientifically meaningless, because the standard error shown for most of the ten-year periods involved is ± 0.030 mm (i.e., 0.060 mm), whereas the "great drop" from the highest average in 1900 to the lowest in the 1946–1952 period is only a matter of a 0.040 mm difference.

In addition, the three graphs are not covariant—that is to say, there are some years when the average weight goes down, the thickness remains steady, and the index goes up. The only possible explanation for this would be the laying of considerably smaller eggs (size of the eggs is not reported), and this is in contradiction to Ratcliffe's findings. We are not impressed, therefore, with the reliability of any of these plottings. However, since shell weight is the parameter which can be most easily measured, we have taken it to be the most accurate of the three.

If one looks at the figure as the authors have drawn it, one does indeed get the impression of a slightly fluctuating but fundamentally steady shell weight up to the period 1947–1952, when there is a sudden drastic decline. If one takes the trouble to magnify the figure, however, it is possible to read off the ordinate values for each ten-year period and replot the means in the form of a line graph, or a regression line. We have done so with the result shown in Fig. 4, the x marks representing the mean shell weights. If one looks at the regression, it then becomes apparent that a gradual but steady decline in eggshell weight has been occurring in this population of California peregrines since 1900. There is, indeed, a sharp increase in the decline between 1940 and 1950. However, it need hardly be pointed out that a number of other events took place affecting the State of California in that ten-year period in addition to the introduction of the chlorinated hydrocarbon pesticides. Reproductive failures among wildlife populations may be related to any number of factors—among them the encroachment of humans on their breeding territory. The circle points on the graph represent the increases in the human population of California during the same periods for which the shell weights are plotted. It is clear from the two regression lines that the steady minor decrease in eggshell weight corresponds very nicely with the

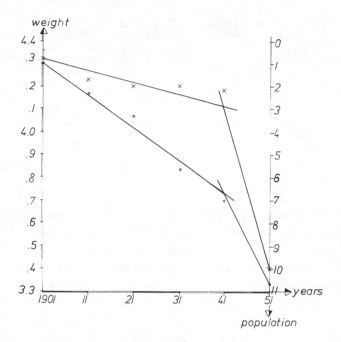

Figure 4. *TRENDS IN CALIFORNIA PEREGRINE FALCON EGGSHELL
WEIGHT DECREASE AND IN INCREASE OF CALIFORNIA HUMAN POPULATION
(Shell data; in grams; after Hickey and Anderson; 1968)
(Population data; × 10⁶; Encyclopedia Britannica; 1968)*

increase in the human population; while the marked changes in both parameters during the period 1940 to 1950 also correlate remarkably well. (During the ten years from 1940–1950 the human population of California increased by 53 percent.) We are not presenting this as "proof" that the sudden expansion of the human population is the "cause" of the lighter eggshells and presumed subsequent population decline among these birds, but it could have a bearing on the matter, and it actually correlates much better with the shell-weight statistics of Hickey and Anderson than does the timing of the introduction of DDT.

Now what is this tremendous population crash referred to? One would imagine that tens of thousands of birds disappeared. As it turns out, the whole California breeding population amounted to between 30 and 40 pairs. Table 13 shows the number of eggs collected from 1891 to 1952 and kept in museums or by private individuals which were available to Hickey and Anderson for comparative studies.

Taking an average of 2.3 eggs laid by a pair of birds yearly, and assuming an adult population of 35 pairs, it can be seen that during each ten-year period until

Table 13. *PEREGRINE FALCON EGGS IN CALIFORNIA*
COLLECTIONS INVESTIGATED BY HICKEY AND ANDERSON (1968)

10-year periods	1900	1910	1920	1930	1940	1950
Eggs investigated	95	80	65	108	192	74
Percentage of eggs laid by 35 pairs	12	10	8	13	24	*
Corresponding number of clutches	41	35	30	47	83	32

*By 1950, the "crash" was supposedly well under way, and therefore the assumption of 35 pairs laying 805 eggs no longer applies.

1940, between 8 to 24 percent of the eggs of the breeding population were officially collected and stored. This does not include any eggs which may have been destroyed by other animals or the parent birds, or collected privately but not made available to the investigators. These numbers suggest that, in addition to the general human encroachment on breeding territory, the penchant of ornithologists and bird lovers for stealing the eggs of rare species may have contributed significantly to the population decline of the peregrine falcon in California. Another important factor to be considered is hunting. As Robert Risebrough has observed, "Despite official protection surviving birds are still subjected to shooting by sportsmen and to harassment at the eyries. If this could be effectively reduced the population might yet survive" (Risebrough et al., 1968b, p. 1099).

In order to substantiate their own findings further, Hickey and Anderson refer to a study by Enderson and Berger (1968), in which quantities of pesticide residues in the peregrine falcon population of northern Canada were reported. "For nine surviving adult peregrines in Canada's Northwest Territories in 1966, the data are reported to have averaged 369 parts per million (ppm) (fresh weight) in fat" (Hickey and Anderson, 1968, p. 272). However, they neglect to cite the further observations of Enderson and Berger, which stand in marked contradiction to their own implied certainty that high DDT residues are causally related to reproductive failure. The earlier study reads: "Total residues in 11 birds that are potential Peregrine prey averaged 27.1 ppm, about twice that found in Peregrine eggs in Britain. A seemingly normal average of 2.3 viable eggs or young, or both, was found near the time of hatching in the 15 sites that we observed. All these data suggest that adult Peregrines in northern Canada carry high levels of organochlorine residues acquired over a period of many months, that their eggs bear about twice the levels found in eggs from the stricken British Peregrine population, and that even with these precariously high levels the Canadian Peregrines appear to be reproducing normally" (Enderson and Berger, 1968, p. 153).

Since critics have often pointed to the fact that the Alaskan and Canadian peregrine populations are *not* declining, in spite of high DDT residues, techniques similar to those of Anderson and Hickey have recently been employed by Cade and his coworkers to attempt to demonstrate that the Alaskan population is also *on the verge* of reproductive failure (Cade et al., 1971). Here again the field methods of scientists who claim to be concerned about a rare and endangered species give rise to wonderment. The authors state that the Colville (Alaska) population of peregrines, while it has not previously shown the marked effects of pesticide poisoning seen in the United States mainland populations, must now have reached the threshold level which will lead to reproductive failure, for the birds "did not do well in 1970." This 1970 difficulty is not too surprising to us, however, for if one reads the fine print, it emerges that during the two previous years, from 13 reproductive pairs, which should have laid 38 eggs in each year according to their figures, the investigators collected a total of 23 eggs for DDT analysis, which amounts to one-third of the young for each year. Although some ornithologists claim that a second clutch will be laid if the nests are robbed early in the breeding season, this does not seem to have happened in Alaska, since Cade gives the number of young fledged in 1969 as 26, which is exactly 12 less than the expected 38. Perhaps, in the interest of the survival of rare species of birds, ornithologists should be banned! (Excepting, of course, the David Wingate variety. See the earlier discussion about the plight of the Bermuda petrel.)

With regard to declining populations of predator birds, two last puzzles should be mentioned. We have seen that the golden eagle is not declining in the United States, the explanation being that its favored food involves only a two-step food chain. On the other hand, the British ornithologist Ratcliffe reported a severe population crash among British golden eagles. The osprey, which is declining in the northeastern states, is doing well in Alaska despite high DDT residues (Graham, 1970, p. 150). In England, herons seem to be holding their own, whereas in the United States they have been reported as declining. No really satisfactory explanation has as yet been offered for these differences in response to DDT in the environment on the part of birds of the *same* species, with approximately the same food habits.

The second puzzle is that Hickey himself, who has been interested in the problems of the peregrine for a very long time, studied various factors involved in the extirpation of the East Coast population of the birds as early as 1942, some time before the introduction of DDT as a pesticide. These two puzzles alone make it seem very strange that Hickey and Anderson can conclude with such confidence that the population crashes of raptors in Western Europe and in America have had a "common physiological basis."

Enough for the moment about declining reproduction of birds high on the food chain. Declines do seem to be occurring locally, and these might, indeed, signal the pending extinction of at least the rarest among these birds. If so, this would be a sad development, as is the disappearance of any interesting plant or animal species. But to this point we have not advanced very far towards answering the particular question which concerns us: Is there any relation between man's use of chlorinated hydrocarbon pesticides and the reproductive difficulties of birds?

Actually, if the reader turns back to the final citations from Wurster's lecture, it will be noted that although he admires the diligence of Hickey and Anderson in tracing down and examining such large numbers of museum eggs, he does not include these correlations of peregrine eggshell changes with the year 1947 in his list of *genuinely scientific* proofs of a cause-and-effect relationship. The aspect of the Hickey and Anderson paper which he singled out as "more than coincidence" and "much tighter data" was the *second* correlation: that is, the correlation of the mean amounts of DDE residues in the eggs of herring gulls from five states with the mean thickness of the shells of the eggs. We want to discuss this correlation and see how well it stands up to scrutiny, but first we must digress briefly on the technique which is commonly used to measure eggshells and the quantities involved in the reported differences in thickness. This consideration of shell-measurement technique is pertinent not only to the studies of Hickey and Anderson but also to the reports of many other investigators concerned with avian reproduction. We therefore believe that the technique itself ought to be carefully appraised.

The Turning of the Screw

In the Hickey and Anderson article, the range of thickness reported for peregrine falcon eggs is from about 0.29 to 0.42 mm, if we take the very lowest and the very highest individual extremes recorded on the graph. The range for the means of 10-year periods is from 0.32 to 0.37 mm. This represents a difference of 0.05 mm, which may also be expressed as 50 micrometers or, more commonly, 50 micron (μm). Ranges reported for the shell thickness of other species of birds may, of course, be somewhat different, depending partly on the size of the birds and their eggs. Nevertheless, we have nowhere seen reports of changes in shell thickness of any species which exceed 50 to 60 μm (0.05 to 0.06 mm); and in some cases, differences of from 5 to 7 μm have been reported as "significant" decreases.

The question to be raised is: How can minute differences in thickness be measured at these levels? Nowhere in their paper do Hickey and Anderson mention the precision of the instruments which they used in measuring the thickness of either museum eggshells or the herring-gull eggs. What they do say is: ". . . we were able to insert a micrometer through the hole drilled by the collector at the girth of the shell and to take four measurements of thickness 7 mm from the edge of the blow hole; these were then *averaged* to the nearest 0.01 mm for each shell. Thickness in each case then represented the shell itself plus the dried egg membranes" (Hickey and Anderson, 1968, p. 271; our emphasis).

In some of the later papers dealing with eggshell thinning, we are told that each shell was measured with a micrometer *to the nearest 0.01 mm*, quite a different matter from speaking of averaging to 0.01 mm.

It is important first to get an idea of the dimensions under discussion before we consider whether it is possible to measure at these levels with a mechanical instrument. One thousandth of a millimeter is equal to one micrometer. This is about half the size of a well-developed bacterium. A human red blood cell measures approximately 8 μm. We assume that every schoolchild knows that neither a bacterium nor a red blood cell can be seen with the naked eye. In fact, the resolving power of the human eye is not much better than 100 μm, or 0.1 mm. If one were looking at something thinner than that—let us say, a human hair (which might range in thickness from around 50 to 80 μm) or an even thinner wire— one would be able to see the hair or the wire on account of its length, but could not see its thickness. The same holds true for extremely thin sheets of metal foil, or of paper, which the eye may perceive in the two dimensions of length and breadth, despite their thinness.

The eggshells described in the majority of these scientific articles are approximately from 300 to 400 μm, or 0.3 to 0.4 mm, thick. The shells of ordinary domestic chicken eggs are in the same general range. If one breaks a shell of these dimensions, one can indeed see it edge on—that is, one can get an impression of its thickness. However, while the eggshells measure altogether about 300–400 μm in cross section, the differences here being discussed in various publications (the "measured" thinning phenomena) are in the range of 2 to 50 μm!

To obtain a direct visual measurement of the difference between one eggshell which is 0.378 mm in thickness and another of 0.380 mm, a change of only 2 μm, it would be necessary to embed chips of the two shells in plastic, section them, and examine the sections under a high-power oil immersion light microscope with a minimum magnification of 1,000×. Even at that, estimates of thickness differences in this range would require a person with a great deal of skill and experience at working in small dimensions under the microscope. Obviously, a change of 40 μm could be much more easily observed under the microscope, but again, to ascertain whether the observed difference was one of 36 μm or 42 μm one would have to be an experienced microscopist and use a high-power objective. (Of course, none of the scientists describing eggshell changes is referring to direct visual observations or measurements under the microscope, but we are using these illustrations to give the reader some concept of how very small are the reported changes.)

Let us now consider the possibilities of mechanical measurements.

There are basically two types of instruments available that are designed to measure very fine differences in thickness, both being compound tools in which the differences are magnified on a readout scale through mechanical means.

The first type are the pantographic-type micrometers. These are relatively large instruments which are not suitable for eggshell measurements. Their primary use is in the determination of thickness of very fine wires or thin foils.

The second type are the dial or screw micrometers. In this case, the object to be measured is inserted into a miniature vise. Magnification of small differences is achieved by the spiral construction of the screw leading to the readout scale. These dial or screw micrometers may be sensitive enough to show differences of about 50 μm with reasonable precision, anything less than that generally being an estimate.

In the very recent literature, some investigators are reporting the use of Starrett® micrometers graduated to 0.01 mm.* Such instruments are useful mainly for measuring the thickness of very thin sheets of metallic foil. With thin materials such as paper — or *eggshells* — which are compressible substances, the determination of the end point becomes a matter of subjective feeling. With metal foils, the end point can be determined when the sheet being measured no longer falls out of the vise under the force of gravity. Paper or eggshells, on the other hand, might stay in the vise when the dial is not turned far enough to give a correct reading, since the friction between the material and the two sides of the vise can "hold" the material without an absolute end point. One may also turn the dial too far, beyond the real end point, because the material can be compressed to some degree by the vise without being crushed. There is therefore no objective way of determining the end point. The range of error which may be involved in this matter of "turning the screw" is probably somewhere between 10 to 30 μm.

Lastly, in connection with eggshells there is an additional problem: unless the membranes have been removed and the shells have been subsequently dried

---

* See "Note Added in Proof," pp. 421-422.

at a minimum temperature of 80°C for several hours, the presence of water in the shell itself and in the membrane, which is strictly dependent on ambient humidity, will cause a considerable variability in both the weight and the thickness of the same eggshell. As much as a 20 percent variation in the weight of the same museum egg has been observed.*

None of this, of course, is a denial of the possibility that observations may be made indicating that one eggshell is thinner than another. If you go into your kitchen to make an omelette and open two cartons of eggs, you may very well find that one group of eggs seems definitely to have thinner shells than the other. What we are bringing into question is *how precisely the exact degree of thinning can be measured when one is employing a micrometer*. This may seem to be a picayune matter, but it is extremely important when scientists write about the percentages of thinning which occurred in an experiment; and when they begin recording their data on computers and performing elaborate statistical analyses on their measurements, one would like to be certain that the "statistically significant" results they are reporting have reference to something better than guesswork or subjective determinations.

As evidence that, at least in the measurement of the shells of museum eggs, the second decimal place in the millimeter measurements (the 10 to 90 micron range) is not very precise, we can compare the results of two environmentalists reporting on museum-stored California peregrine falcon eggs. Hickey and Anderson's averages for the shell thickness before 1947 are all 0.36 mm or above; whereas Risebrough et al. report that the average shell thickness before 1947 for the same population of the same species was 0.34 ± 0.015 mm (Risebrough et al., 1968b.) Since all of the results reported on eggshell thinning affect only the second and in some cases only the third decimal place (the 1 to 10 micron range), one wonders why the meaningfulness of this technique was not questioned much earlier.

Now let us return to the Hickey and Anderson publication and consider the "real scientific" correlation—i.e., the graph showing the excellent correspondence between the DDE residue levels and eggshell thickness in herring gull populations from five eastern and middlewestern states. The authors' graph appears to show convincingly that the higher the DDE residue in the eggs, the thinner they become. The graph is reproduced on page 404 as Fig. 5. There is no denying that the computed regression line, as drawn, shows an almost perfect correlation between the two variables, r (the correlation coefficient) being -0.98, with a one in a thousand probability that this is a chance occurrence, as

*Personal communication, A. Festetics.

Wurster pointed out. There is, however, one minor problem with this excellent result: namely, where do the points on the graph come from? Presumably they are the result of eggshell thickness measurements. But unfortunately the precise measurements represented cannot be performed with the techniques described by the authors. If one looks at the graph, it can be seen that most of the dots are placed at positions requiring measurement at the 1 μm level. For instance, the Wisconsin population is said to have eggshell thickness of 338 μm (or .338 mm) while that from Michigan is shown as 345 μm. Just a little less compression of the screw, or an increase in the humidity of the laboratory, and these measurements might easily have been 370 or 380 micron, or the same as those reported for the Rhode Island population, in which case there would have been no correlation, no regression line, no statement of statistical significance.

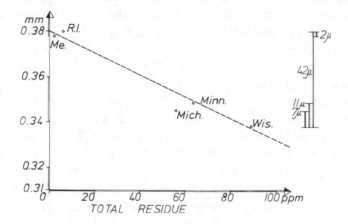

Figure 5.   *VARIATION IN SHELL THICKNESS AND DDE CONCENTRATIONS*
IN THE EGGS OF HERRING GULLS
(after Hickey and Anderson, 1968).
Bars on the right represent 500-fold visual magnification of the changes expressed,
since 1 micron(μ) is plotted as 0.5 millimeter (mm)

Even if we grant that an eggshell which has not been carefully dried and which includes the membrane *might* be measured to the nearest 0.015 mm—which is pretty generous—there would still be only two points left, since the Rhode Island population and the Maine population are separated by only 0.002 mm, and the three middlewestern states show a maximum difference of 0.011 mm. This reduction to two points would also eliminate the regression line and the statement of statistical significance. The best the investigators could then get out of their "correlations" would be a vague statement about trends, or something comparable to the observation you can make in your own kitchen.

Presumably what Hickey and Anderson did in order to arrive at these fine differences at the third decimal place in the millimeter range was to add up the thickness measurements of individual eggs from each state, divide the sum by the number of eggs involved, and then arbitrarily decide to round off the results to the nearest 0.001 mm, forgetting that they could not possibly measure single eggs with that degree of sensitivity and therefore cannot legitimately express their averages in that range. Or perhaps it was the computer which caused them the trouble. It might have fed them means for each group with seven digits after the decimal point, making the third decimal place seem like a fair and reasonable place to round off their numbers. We do not know exactly how they did it, but we do know that the result as published in *Science* is a beautiful example of a perfectly lovely correlation with the highest statistical significance, based on absolutely nonmeasurable quantities which have been accepted by the readership as standing for precise, careful measurements.

Aesthetically, this publication is most satisfying. Scientifically, it leaves much to be desired.

Troubles at Patuxent

We turn now to the mallard duck study (Heath et al., 1969) and the kestrel paper (Porter and Wiemeyer, 1969), both of which were controlled feeding experiments, and both carried out at the Patuxent Wildlife Center in Laurel, Maryland.

Heath and his coworkers actually performed two experiments with their mallards, extending altogether over a period of four years: 1965–1968. During the first two years they used four groups of birds: a control group, and three experimental groups fed 2.5 ppm DDT, 10 ppm DDT, and 40 (1965) or 25 (1966) ppm DDT daily.

In 1967 and 1968, they used five groups of birds: controls, birds fed 10 ppm DDE, another group fed 40 ppm DDE, one fed 10 ppm DDD, and a fifth fed 40 ppm DDD. DDE and DDD are metabolites of DDT, and presumably the experimenters reasoned that in the wild the food of these birds might be contaminated with residues already metabolized to DDE or DDD. The authors state that they regard 10 ppm as a residue easily encountered in the natural foods of mallards (which are omnivores); and, although this is a highly debatable point, one may accept it at face value for the purpose of examining the study. It should, however, be borne in mind that the amounts mentioned above were fed to the experimental birds *daily* for a period of two years.

The title of the paper reporting the results of these lengthy experiments is "Marked DDE Impairment of Mallard Reproduction in Controlled Studies." As the title implies, the findings of the investigators pointed to DDE as the metabolite of DDT which "caused the effect"—to use Wurster's phrase. Basically, they found no results of any significance in the DDD-fed birds, and we shall therefore have nothing further to say about them.

The authors do not summarize all of their claims in one concluding passage, but the most important may be stated as follows:

1. Embryo mortality increased 30 to 50 percent after DDE feeding.
2. The number of 14-day-old hatchlings per hen was one-third to one-half that "expected" after DDE.
3. Duckling production per hen was reduced by as much as 75 percent.
4. In the DDT-fed experimental birds, 2.5 ppm and 10 ppm had no measurable effects on reproduction.
5. In the high-dose DDT group (40 ppm in 1965, reduced to 25 ppm in 1966), a qualified observation of effect is made without claiming statistical significance: ". . . the 50 percent deficit in ducklings per hen approaches significance but fails because of variation in pen fertility rates" (Heath et al., 1969, p. 48).

Since these investigators had two groups of identical control birds, it seems peculiar that no one has previously objected to the large variations between the controls on many of the parameters studied. For instance, the number of eggs laid per hen in one control group is 39.2, whereas in the other it is 16.8. This difference alone is far in excess of any of the differences cited as "effects" among the experimental birds. The difference in the number of live 14-day-old ducklings per hen in the two control groups is 16.1 versus 6.0. The 50 percent deficit in ducklings per hen noted for the birds fed on the highest DDT diet is still less than this normal variation among the two controls (69 percent). This is particularly important, since it is the end point of the experiment: that is to say, the real measure of reproductive success.

On the basis of these absurd differences between the reproductive performances of the two control groups, the entire study becomes meaningless, and all of the conclusions presented by the authors have to be discarded. Since this is a very strong statement, it is perhaps necessary to explain that when the variations among the controls are larger than the variations between control and experimental animals, then it should be obvious that a factor other than the specific variable which is being tested (in this case DDT, DDE, and DDD intake through food) is operating, which unknown variable is affecting both the control and the experimental groups. The need to be alert to such unknown variables, which may spoil an experiment, is an absolutely fundamental principle of experimental studies.

The authors themselves obviously noticed that something was wrong with their data; hence the rather lame excuse about "variations in pen fertility rate." This might have accounted for unsuccessful embryonation in one of the control groups and therefore reduced the total number of live ducklings per hen at the end of the experiment. On the other hand, it cannot explain the difference between the number of eggs laid per hen in the two control groups (16.8 versus 39.2). Furthermore, when, in the DDT series, the *control* birds showed 17 percent less fertilization than the experimental animals, this is "explained away" as a variation in pen fertility rate. On the other hand, when the *experimental* birds on doses of 10 ppm DDE showed 35 percent less fertilization than the controls, this is no longer a variation in pen fertility rates, but a statistically significant "effect" attributed to the DDE. No explanation is offered for the curious fact that in the same series, the 40 ppm DDE dosage "caused" only a 21 percent decrease in fertility.

Fundamentally, what we have here is a four-year-long experiment which failed disastrously. What other researchers would probably do in such a case is either file the data in a bottom drawer and turn to other questions, or do further experiments designed to find out what happened. One of the things they might have wanted to investigate is why, in their 1966 control group, they got a 70 percent loss from the incubation stage to the live 14-day-old ducklings.

Instead, Heath and his coworkers attempted to salvage their work and duly published their findings. In the text of their article they bring attention only to those data which seem to support their contention that DDE is the causative agent in the reproductive failures they observed.

It would have been equally feasible, on the other hand, to use the same data tables to show that DDT feeding markedly *improved* reproductive success in mallards, had one wished to do so. For instance, when fed 2.5 ppm or 10 ppm DDT (10 ppm being the amount claimed by Heath et al. as approximately what might be found in the natural food of mallards in the wild), the percentage of embryonated eggs is 17 and 7 percent higher, respectively, than in the control birds. The number of the normal hatchlings alive after 14 days was greater than the controls by 7 percent at 2.5 ppm and 10 percent at 10 ppm. Finally, the birds fed 2.5 ppm DDT produced 36 percent more 14-day-old live ducklings per hen than the controls, and those on 10 ppm 23 percent more! This last parameter is the clearest test of reproductive success, and the figures would seem to indicate that the authors erred when they stated that the effects of the two low dosages of DDT on reproduction were not measurable. Perhaps what they meant to convey was that the *anticipated* negative effect was not measurable. But the positive gain from control birds to experimental birds is not only obvious and measurable, it could even be described as statistically significant — at least if one were willing to employ the same methods of evaluation as those used by the authors. Actually this increase of 36 percent greater reproductive success among experimental birds should not be ascribed to a positive "effect" of DDT feeding, but should rather serve as a clear indicator that the experimental data are meaningless because of the interference of some unknown variable.

How this paper could have been passed for publication in *Nature* is unfathomable, for even a rapid scanning of the tables presented in the article should have made it immediately evident to the referees that the data for the two series of control birds invalidate the whole experiment. On the other hand, once in print, any scientist who merely read through the text itself would definitely get the impression that this study succeeded in demonstrating, under controlled laboratory conditions, a cause-and-effect relationship between intake of metabolites of DDT and reproductive difficulties of mallard ducks. Since its publication, this study has remained virtually unchallenged, and it has become one of the most frequently cited references in support of the hypothesis that chronic exposure of animals to sublethal concentrations of DDT in the environment can be held responsible for declines in wildlife populations.

For those environmentalists who are concerned in particular with the effects of chlorinated hydrocarbons on *raptors* in the wild, the experiments of Porter and Wiemeyer (1969) were perhaps even more important than the one we have just reviewed, for these two researchers worked with kestrels (also called sparrow hawks). This species is closely related to the peregrine falcon, but unlike the latter, it has been successfully bred in captivity, and it is not so rare that the survival of the species would be affected by capture of birds for purposes of study.

Porter and Wiemeyer investigated the effects of a combination of dieldrin and DDT in their experiments, reasoning that birds in the wild would be likely to be exposed to residues of both chemicals in their natural food. They worked with two different populations of the kestrel, one originating in Florida and the other in the northeastern states. Although there is now some question as to whether the Florida birds were actually a distinct subspecies native to the southern state, they were so treated in the original experiment, and each population was divided into a control, a low-treatment, and a high-treatment group. The low-treatment group received 1 ppm dieldrin and 5 ppm DDT (wet-weight basis) in their food daily, the high-treatment group 3 ppm dieldrin and 15 ppm DDT. This high dosage "was calculated to be just short of lethal to adults," and since a number of birds died during the course of the study (apparently between 17 and 22 percent), it would appear that the high dosage fed continuously was very close indeed to a lethal quantity. The experiment went on for three years (1966-1968). In the 1968 observations, the yearlings reared from the 1967 parental groups were included. They were kept on the same diets as the parent birds and the reproductive performance of these young birds was investigated in the final year.

The major findings were summarized thus: "The influence of the pesticides on reproductive success was greatest in the yearling group. Differences between yearling control and yearling dosed birds were significant ($P < .05$) at most major points of their reproductive cycle. The same trend was apparent in the parental group in both 1967 and 1968 . . ." (Porter and Weimeyer, 1969, p.200).

The authors also investigated changes in eggshell thickness and reported that the shells of the treated parental birds were 8 to 10 percent thinner than those of the eggs laid by controls, and there was a 15 to 17 percent decrease in the shells of the eggs of experimental yearlings as compared with controls. It is not worthwhile to discuss this in detail, since the results are reported in the 0.001 mm range, although the text states that the measurements were made to the nearest 0.01 mm; thus the same criticism applies to these results as to those reported by Hickey and Anderson.

If one reads through the text of the paper, the findings seem less spectacular than those of Heath et al. since no significance greater than $P = .05$ is claimed, and the Florida population was too small to show statistically significant changes. Nevertheless, the study appears to support the hypothesis that chronic, long-term feeding of doses of chlorinated hydrocarbons presumed to be comparable to those encountered in the wild not only causes reproductive difficulties, but that these increase with time and in successive generations.

The authors claim that a crucial factor in the reproductive failure of the treated birds was the disappearance of eggs or newly hatched birds. (This was presumed to be the result of cannibalism on the part of the parent birds, although no egg-eating was observed.) Actually, however, it seems to us that embryonic mortality was a more important factor, and we have therefore tabulated this parameter (Table 14). Our table includes only the control and the high-treatment groups of the northeastern population for 1967, 1968, and the 1968 yearlings, since the low-treatment groups did not show any significant differences.

One notes that the highest percentage of embryonic mortality occurred in the 1968 *control* group, where out of 29 fertile eggs, 13 (or 45 percent) were lost.

Table 14   *EMBRYONIC MORTALITY AMONG*
PORTER AND WIEMEYER'S SPARROW HAWKS
(after Porter and Wiemeyer, 1969)

	1967		1968		Yearlings, 1968	
	Control	*High treatment*	*Control*	*High treatment*	*Control*	*High treatment*
Remaining eggs	39	24	29	15	33	30
Dead embryos	6	2	13	3	3	9
Percentage of dead embryos	15	8	45	20	9	30

In their own notations, the authors point to the nine dead embryos in the high-treatment yearling group (which represent 30 percent of the fertilized eggs) as "highly significant," whereas the 45 percent loss in the 1968 controls is not. Instead, they make a statement in the text that "reduced success in the parental group in 1968 was due mainly to embryonic mortality, which *may have been caused* by bacterial infection of the eggs" *(ibid.;* our emphasis). How do we know that the 30 percent mortality among the 1968 high-treatment yearlings was not also caused by bacterial infection, rather than being an "effect" of DDT and dieldrin intake? The answer is, quite simply, that we do not.

Now let us suppose that we accept the approach of the investigators them-selves, and figure the percentage of the losses from the original eggs laid to the live hatchlings, which means that the disappearance of eggs would be included. It does seem to be true that there was more egg disappearance among the ex-perimental birds (although there is no certainty that the increased cannibalism is an effect of pesticide dosage, it being a factor little understood when wild birds are raised in captivity). Still, there is something peculiar about the observa-tions of the investigators, for a 46 percent loss in the high-dosage group in 1967 is marked as significant, a 62 percent loss among the high-treatment yearlings is highly significant, whereas the loss of 58 *percent* of the 1968 *controls* is not significant at all. This seems to be another example of the method of Heath et al. where losses among experimental birds are called statistically significant "effects" of pesticide feeding, while high losses among control birds are either ignored or "explained away" as due to some unknown variable—in this case, bacterial infection of the eggs.

In addition to the paucity of real results and the unorthodox methods of presenting and interpreting data common to both of these "controlled" feeding experiments, it seems to us that there must be some rather serious survival problem for animals kept at the Patuxent Wildlife Center, if the controls are showing more variations and as great or greater losses than the experimental animals. That this appears to be a persistent difficulty at Patuxent is evident from information contained in a more recent publication to come from researchers there, a paper on the effects of mercury on avian reproduction by Spann, Heath, Kreitzer and Locke (1972). We do *not* intend to review this paper, but it is worth noting that during the second half of the experiment, during which period none of the experimental birds died, the reader is informed that "mortality among the controls was *routine"* (Spann et al., p. 330; our emphasis). This routine death among the control birds amounted to 5 out of 23 hens! Is not Patuxent ripe for a general housecleaning?

Desperation Science

The last of the three papers mentioned by Wurster as demonstrating the "effect" on avian reproduction through experimental studies is one by Bitman and his coworkers, which appeared in the same issue of *Nature* that carried the mallard article by Heath et al. This study is entitled: "DDT Induces a Decrease in Eggshell Calcium" (Bitman et al., 1969).

The birds used in this experiment were Japanese quail, divided into 3 groups of 14 birds each: controls, birds fed 100 ppm o,p'-DDT, and birds fed 100 ppm p,p'-DDT. It should be noted that the o,p'-DDT isomer constitutes less than 20 percent of commercial DDT and that it breaks down quite quickly. There is therefore no reason to suppose that birds in the wild will take in any appreciable quantities of this isomer in natural food. Furthermore, the 100 ppm dosage of even the more persistent and common isomer is in excess by a factor of ten of the amounts thought by Porter and Wiemeyer to be reasonable estimates for residues in natural food of raptors.* In general, these quantities are probably on the order of 100 times higher than residues in the natural environment. As if this exceedingly high dosage were not enough, the experimenters introduced a "calcium stress" situation by feeding the birds (controls included) a diet which was markedly deficient in calcium. (The calcium content of the feed was 0.56 percent, whereas a normal diet should contain about 3 percent calcium.) The feeding lasted for 45 days, after which time the birds were sacrificed. Many parameters were investigated, including egg production, egg weight, eggshell thickness, eggshell calcium content, calcium circulating in the blood, and the calcium content of the medullary bone.

---

* Quail, of course, are not raptors. In fact they are three levels lower on the food chain.

The principal conclusions were stated thus: "[1] Our experiments confirm previous reported correlative evidence that DDT and related organochlorine compounds induce a decrease in eggshell calcium. . . . [2] By incorporating DDT into the diet of Japanese quail, we have demonstrated directly, that o,p'-DDT and p,p'-DDT produce thinner eggshells" (Bitman et al., 1969, p. 46).

Both of these conclusions are without real basis. Given the design of the experiment, one would, of course, expect both the control and the treated birds to have overall low calcium levels. The question raised is: Did the feeding of these rather massive dosages of o,p'-DDT and p,p'-DDT exacerbate any problems of calcium depletion which might have been caused by the calcium stress imposed on both the experimental and the control birds? The authors claim that it did, on the basis that the eggshells of the birds fed the pesticide showed a decrease in calcium content in comparison to the controls. They admit, however, that there were "no significant differences in blood calcium concentrations at the end of the experiment." The calcium content of the shaft of the femur and the amount of medullary bone was also reported as the same in the three groups. Since the calcium reserves of the parent birds seem to have been unaffected by the pesticide feedings, it seems odd that the shells of their eggs should have had significantly less calcium than those of the controls. Yet Table 1 of the publication shows the shell calcium as having decreased from 2.03 percent in the eggs of control birds to 1.95 percent and 1.96 percent in those of the o,p'-DDT fed group and the p,p'-DDT fed group, respectively. Both these differences are indicated as significant at the $P<0.01$ level.[*] However, there is a small and important footnote in the same table which reads: "The entire eggshell was analyzed for calcium and the value obtained was expressed as a percentage of the fresh weight of the egg." We must demur: this is *not* a meaningful way to compare the percentage of calcium in the eggshells. The weights of the shells are not given, and there is every possibility that, even though the eggs of the experimental birds were reported as being somewhat smaller and hence presumably lighter in total weight than those of the controls, the shells of those eggs might have been heavier. From the data presented, one cannot tell whether the percentage of eggshell calcium was reduced or not.

As for the other most significant finding—that the eggshells of the experimental birds were thinner than those of the controls—we must refer back to our earlier discussion about the measurement of eggshells and consider the actual

---

[*] It should be noted that from the strictly mathematical point of view, these claims of statistical significance are correct. However, they were reached by applying a method of statistical evaluation inappropiate for the experiment as designed, since the observations were not independent, but correlated with each other.

quantity involved in the thinning. The investigators measured the shells with a micrometer, after removing the membranes. We are not told whether or not the shells were dried before measurement, nor is the precision capability of the instrument reported. The results are expressed in terms of inches $\times 10^{-4}$. The difference between the average shell thickness of the controls (69.5×10^{-4} inches) and the mean for the o,p'-DDT group (66.7×10^{-4} inches) is 2.8×10^{-4} inches. The p,p'-DDT eggshells (mean thickness 65.6×10^{-4} inches) were 3.9×10^{-4} inches thinner than the controls. Both these differences are described as *highly* significant, with $P < 0.001$.[*]

If one merely looks at the numbers given, it does seem as though the decrease from 69.5 to 65.6 might mean something, although it amounts to only a 5.6 percent drop. But the quantities involved are very strangely expressed, and once converted, another picture emerges: 69.5×10^{-4} inches is equal to 0.00695 inches; the *largest* decrease reported is equal to 0.00039 inches.

If we convert all figures into the metric system, we find that the decrease in the thickness of the o,p'-DDT shells compared with controls amounts to 0.007112 mm; and that of the p,p'-DDT group to 0.009906 mm. The last three digits are below the resolving power of the light microscope. If we eliminate them, we get decreases of 7 and 10 μm in the two experimental groups. These quantities are *not* measurable with any mechanical instrument, even with ideal preparation of the shells. Nevertheless, they are reported and have been accepted as highly significant statistically!

A few remarks concerning experimental design and presentation of data in this publication: as we have already noted, the investigators created a calcium stress situation for all birds by feeding a diet exceedingly low in calcium. The question which was supposed to be answered by the experiment was whether DDT has an influence on calcium metabolism. Even if they had obtained some results that pointed to a decrease in calcium levels among the exposed birds, this question would not have been answered by the study. As performed, this experiment is analogous to withholding vitamin C from the diet of both control and experimental animals and, finding that scurvy developed in all, but was slightly exacerbated in the pesticide-fed groups, reaching the conclusion that DDT is the cause of scurvy.

One can perform an experiment in which a critical variable, such as a calcium-depleted diet, is tested simultaneously with the effects of pesticide feeding, but in order to do so, one needs more groups for comparison: at least one experimental group, for example, where pesticides are added to a diet containing normal levels of calcium. Since Bitman et al. failed to do so, two

* See previous footnote.

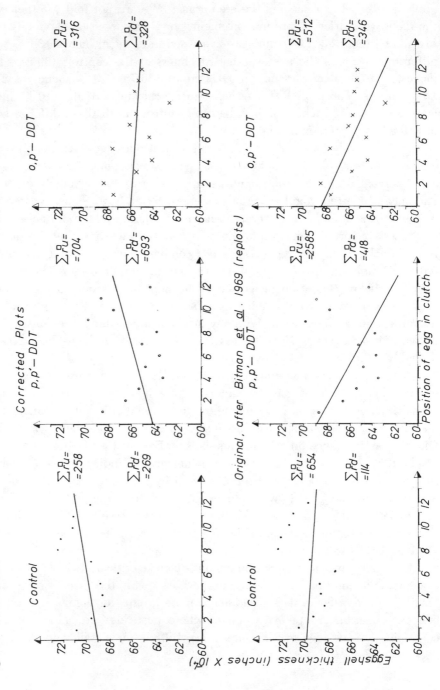

Figure 6. CORRECTED AND ORIGINAL REGRESSION LINES OF EGGSHELL DATA IN BITMAN, CECIL, HARRIS, AND FRIES, 1969.

other investigators, Tucker and Haegle (1970), performed studies in which the experimental design was more meaningful in terms of this question. Briefly, they treated several groups of quails and mallards, some kept on a normal calcium diet to which DDT was added, some on a low-calcium diet without DDT, and some on low-calcium diet with DDT. They found that the low-calcium diet with or without DDT was sufficient to explain the eggshell problems; whereas the diet normal in calcium levels to which DDT was added failed to cause any significant effect. In other terms, they showed that calcium problems in eggshells are caused by calcium depletion—a not too surprising finding.

Beyond the matter of lack of results and poor experimental design, there is one last problem with the Bitman paper that is exceedingly serious from the point of view of scientific ethics. The authors state: "Individual records revealed that as successive eggs were laid in a clutch, there was a decrease in thickness and in percentage content of shell calcium in the groups given o,p'-DDT and p,p'-DDT, but only a slight decrease in eggs of the control quail. . . . A consideration of the data according to the position of the egg in the clutch makes this effect readily apparent. . . shell thickness (Fig. 3) declined sharply in the groups given o,p'-DDT and p,p'-DDT, with only a slight decrease in control shell thickness as clutch size increased" (Bitman et al., 1969, p. 45).

These statements are reflected in two graphs, in which the mean values for eggshell thickness (Figure 3) and for calcium content (Figure 2) are plotted for all three groups according to the position of eggs in the clutch, and regression lines are drawn.

At considerable expense of time and energy, we have completely replotted Figure 3 from the Bitman text and drawn the regression lines according to the accepted method of the least-square technique. The reader will find the graphs as Figure 6 on page 414. The lower series show the original plots and lines of Bitman et al., except that in our figure each plot is shown separately, whereas in the original all were represented on a single graph. The upper series gives the corrected regression lines. It should be obvious that both the control and the p,p'-DDT groups have a positive slope, while the very slight negative slope of the o,p'-DDT group is insignificant. It is not even necessary to perform the mathematical calculations involved in arriving at the most accurate regression line to recognize that the trend of the slopes must be upward, for anyone can see that some of the points plotted for the last six eggs in these two series are clustered at much higher positions on the graphs than those of the first six eggs. In the publication, however, where all three regression lines are represented on one tiny graph, it is not so visually apparent that they are incorrectly presented. The regression lines of their other figure are also improperly drawn, and, in addition, there is such a wide scatter of points that the very attempt to represent trends as regressions is questionable.

We ought to make it clear that we do *not* accept the eggshell thickness values for which we have recalculated the regressions as representing meaningful data. Nevertheless, in drawing their regressions, Bitman and his co-authors were using points which they had described in their text as meaningful, and they still had to present them in a fashion not warranted by the positions of the points in order to support their claims. We cannot imagine in this case that the regressions as originally drawn could have resulted from methodological misunderstandings alone, for one would assume that any scientist who has decided to represent his data in terms of regression lines must have some idea of how to construct them.

It might be possible to explain the mistakes of the first three papers discussed as unfortunate examples of what results when less-than-clear thinking and enthusiasm for a good cause are combined. But this paper, in which misrepresentation is a possibility, may be said to signal a real danger to the future of American science.

Poorly designed experiments which produced no meaningful results but were reported as supporting preconceived ideas through manipulations of the data were typical in biological works that appeared during the Lysenko era in the Soviet Union. Let us hope we are not in for thirty years of this sort of thing; for while the cause of saving wildlife may seem like a Good Thing in comparison with supporting Stalinist ideology, distortions are distortions under any banner, and no system of science can avoid being drastically weakened if too many errors and falsifications are allowed to stand in its literature as "demonstrated facts. "

More Little Fishes

Before quitting our discussion centered on Wurster's lecture, we should like to touch briefly on one last subject, which the reader will probably be relieved to learn, has nothing to do with eggshells. As we mentioned in Chapter 7, the claim that DDT in waters is responsible for massive fish kills is no longer raised so frequently by environmentalists—probably not so much because it is ill supported by facts, as because of a certain embarrassment that arose in the wake of the response to the much publicized Mississippi fish kill of 1963, which turned out, after all, not to have been caused by pesticides. The emphasis has now shifted to the indirect, more subtle, but ultimately more threatening damage to the reproductive performance of fish exposed to sublethal quantities of pesticides —just as in the case of birds.

At the very end of his presentation, almost as an aside, Wurster says: "I have made no mention of fish, but they can also have very serious reproductive problems caused by DDT. In some cases 100 percent mortality of the fry occurs. This finding has been confirmed with controlled experiments similar to those described for birds. . . . The DDT concentrations that cause the effect are frequently found in the fresh-water environment and are approached—and in some case equaled—in the ocean" (Wurster, 1970, p. 53).

It is probably no exaggeration to state that we have read in at least 50 different places about a report of 100 percent mortality of lake trout fish fry related to DDT, but we have never been able to learn who it was who originally published this finding. It seems to be such a "well-known fact" that it no longer requires a reference.* For example, in both the SCEP DDT case study and the National Academy of Sciences Committee on Oceanography publication *Chlorinated Hydrocarbons in the Marine Environment* (which are substantially the same, and which will be discussed in some detail in the next two chapters), one may read: "In the speckled sea trout on the south Texas coast, DDT residues in the ripe eggs are about 8 ppm. This level may be compared with the residues of 5 ppm in freshwater trout, which causes 100 percent failure in the development of sac fry or young fish. There is presumptive evidence for similar reproductive failure in the sea trout" (SCEP, p. 127).

Both publications, in which the passage above appears in exactly the same wording, inform us that the presumptive evidence regarding the reproductive problems of Texas coast sea trout stems from a report by Butler in *BioScience* (1969). It is recognized by a few people who keep up with developments that this presumptive evidence has evaporated without trace because, after all, the sea trout are now reproducing normally, residues or no residues. However, that is an aside. The point we wish to mention here is that neither of these august scientific publications offers any reference for the information that 100 percent of freshwater trout eggs containing 5 ppm DDT residues failed to develop into mature fish. Even as one turns to the 1969 Butler article, where this mortality of sac fry in trout is also mentioned, one cannot learn who reported it, for Butler did not do the work himself, and there are only three references in his paper— all, curiously to Butler. We were, therefore, delighted to note that Wurster provided a precise reference for the mentioned "confirmation" in controlled experiments of this famous sac-fry mortality observation—thinking that from his citation we could learn all about the matter. And, indeed, we found the paper noted to be most instructive.

* The event apparently referred to took place in 1955 in the trout hatchery at Lake George, N.Y. But who did the analyses, and where were the findings published?

The publication to which Wurster referred is a study by Kenneth Macek entitled "Reproduction in Brook Trout *(Salvelinus fontinalis)* Fed Sublethal Concentrations of DDT" (1968). In addition to providing a detailed report on his own experiments, Macek reviews the literature on exposure of fish to DDT, and from this review, a number of interesting facts emerge.

A report of 100 percent mortality of sac fry was made by Burdick et al. in 1964, but these losses, although supposedly correlated with DDT residues, do not seem to have had anything at all to do with the oft-quoted figure of 5 ppm. Macek comments that no data were available on the mortality of the adults from which these eggs were obtained, and that it is therefore impossible to determine whether or not sublethal concentrations of pesticide were involved. Much more important, however, are the quantitative data reviewed. Macek writes: "Burdick et al. (1964) indicated that a concentration of 10 ppm DDT or more in lake trout eggs produced 50% or greater mortality of fry; 4.75 ppm or more usually resulted in at least 15% mortality" (Macek, 1968, p. 1795). Now 15 percent mortality at 5 ppm residues is a far cry from 100 percent losses; *n'est-ce pas?* Nevertheless, the word has been spread, and is now accepted as gospel.

Macek also has some qualifying remarks to make about earlier attempts to perform controlled laboratory experiments on the effects of DDT feeding on fish reproduction. He points out that previous investigators concerned with chronic exposure of fish to sublethal concentrations of pesticides (Mount, 1962; Allison et al., 1964; Andrews et al., 1966) have always lost considerable numbers of their adult fish during the course of their experiments, and that the concentrations they used cannot therefore be correctly described as sublethal. With this we would heartily agree.

The dosages which Macek used evidently were genuinely sublethal, for at least his adult fish did not die. He fed 3 groups of fish with 0.5, 1.0, and 2.0 ppm DDT weekly, for a period of 156 days. The matings combined control males with pesticide-fed females, both male and female controls, both pesticide-fed parents, and so on, in all possible combinations.

Some exceedingly interesting observations were made, aside from the general conclusion, which we shall get to shortly.

1. Females fed 0.5 and 1 ppm DDT had significantly more mature ova than the controls (1,711 and 1,733 respectively, compared with 1,590). Females fed 2 ppm had fewer mature ova than the controls (1,510 compared with 1,590).

2. The treatments did not appear to effect the viability of the gametes.

3. Male fish from the treated groups tended to be longer than the controls. In the high-treatment group they were significantly longer. Macek goes so far as to suggest that this may be a direct effect of the pesticide feeding.

4. The percent of fertilization achieved with sperm from treated males was similar to that of controls.

The author's own principal conclusion, quoted below, is expressed in a way which appears to indict DDT as an agent which may reduce reproductive success of brook trout. "The cumulative mortality of fertilized eggs and fry to the swim-up stage was higher when one or both of the gametes were from a DDT-treated fish than when both gametes were from control fish" (*ibid.*, p. 1791).

But how much higher was this cumulative mortality? The results are expressed on a graph in terms of the percentage of loss from fertilization of eggs to the fourteenth week. On reading the figure, one learns that where both gametes were from control fish, just over 2.5 percent of the fry were lost. The highest loss was 8 percent, in fry from control males mated with females fed 1 ppm DDT; the second highest was 7 percent, where both parents were fed 2 ppm DDT; and the third highest was 6.5 percent, where both parents received 1 ppm DDT.

The difference between the normal 2.5 percent loss and the highest loss in the experimental groups, although not spectacular, does seem to support the general hypothesis that DDT intake may reduce productivity in brook trout. However, if one recalls that the females fed 1 ppm DDT laid considerably more eggs than the control females, the results shape up in a fashion which is quite contrary to "expectations."

Calculating from the numbers of eggs,* an 8 percent loss from the females fed 1 ppm would leave 1,595 little fishes, compared with 1,520 among the controls—a *net gain* of 75 brook trout. The 6.5 percent loss in the group where both parents were fed 1 ppm DDT would give us 1,629 little fishes, 119 *more* than for the controls. Only in the group where both parents were fed 2 ppm DDT would there be a net loss of fry, 1,404 compared with 1,520 in the controls. On the whole, considering his caution when compared with the bird experimenters, we feel fairly certain that Macek would agree with us that even though 2 ppm DDT per week is a sublethal dosage for brook trout, it is *not* a quantity which would be commonly encountered by the fish under natural conditions. We therefore have to conclude that this experiment does not indicate, as Wurster implied, that chronic exposure of fish to sublethal quantities of DDT may cause

---

* As Macek does not report the number of *fertile* ova per female, we have taken these figures from his table for the number of ova, corrected for size. This is probably not precisely correct, but since he stated that there were no changes in the viability of the gametes in control and experimental fish, and that the percentage of fertilization from treated males was the same as control, it seems fair to assume that the percentages of fertilized eggs should be about the same.

100 percent mortality of the young, but rather that it may lead to *more* little fishes, and, as an added boon to trout fishermen, *longer* adult male fish.

More Sensational Correlations

Having reviewed these five fundamental contributions to the scientific case against DDT, we are afraid that we must strongly disagree with Dr. Wurster's opinion that the question of a cause-and-effect relationship between intake of sublethal quantities of pesticides and reproductive problems of birds and fish in the wild has been settled. It does not appear to us to have been settled at all. Furthermore, Wurster's assertion that "Control birds on clean food (without DDT) laid normal eggs and had normal reproductive success. . ." is completely false as far as both the Heath et al. and the Porter and Wiemeyer experiments are concerned. We would agree with his general statement that the real test of a relationship is whether or not it can be demonstrated under controlled conditions. So far, the only one of the studies reviewed which may be correctly described as a controlled study demonstrating a cause-and-effect relationship between DDT feeding and reproductive performance is that of Macek; and, as we have seen, at all but the highest dosage the positive effects (more eggs) appear to more than cancel out the negative ones (less survival of progeny).

We are aware, of course, that since Wurster's lecture a number of other articles have appeared which either report controlled feeding experiments or correlations between DDT residues and eggshell thinning in wild populations. We have examined as many of these as we have been able to obtain, and so far, we have not yet found one which would stand up to close scrutiny. One of the most recent of these, for example, is a publication by Blus, Gish, Belisle and Prouty called "Logarithmic Relationship of DDE Residues to Eggshell Thinning" (1972), which purports to demonstrate that the eggshell thinning of brown pelican eggs from various local populations shows a good concentration-effect relationship to the DDE residues in the eggs, if these residues are expressed on a logarithmic scale. There are no tables in the article, all the data for three separate populations being once again shown on one tiny figure. The authors claim that a single regression line is adequate to express the relation of residues to variation in eggshell thickness for all three populations. This seemed to us questionable, and we set about to replot the data on a larger graph in order to be able to examine the slopes of the three regressions separately. The task proved to be impossible, however, since in order to read off ordinate values, one needs a graph constructed according to the customary *right angle,* and in their graph the axes are drawn at an angle of about 93 degrees.

Another paper involving some of the same authors was published in late 1971—also dealing with brown pelican eggshell thinning and DDE residues (Blus, Heath, Gish, Belisle, and Prouty, 1971). It contains the following puzzling paragraph:

> Although the percentage of variability accounted for by DDE in the Southeastern eggs seems low, [the highest was 27.3% on the shell thickness parameter] the shell parameters of individual eggs ranged from approximately 35% less to 15% greater than the pre-1947 means listed by Anderson and Hickey. . ., the pre-1947 means being exceeded by a few of the Florida eggs. *Since* the parameters of pelican eggs collected prior to the usage of organochlorine insecticides *varied by as much as 30%,* the percentage of variability accounted for by DDE *does not appear low* in light of these qualifications. (Blus et al., 1971, p. 1214; our emphasis)

If any reader can fathom the meaning of these sentences, we should appreciate being enlightened. While we await such clarification, however, we are absolutely certain that there have been no fundamental changes in plane geometry, and that 90 degrees is still the definition of a right angle. At times, however, in the course of our reading, we have been overtaken by doubts, and we wonder if there might not be some new logic now accepted by almost everybody, in which we alone are deficient.

Note Added in Proof

After having completed the writing of this chapter, we decided to purchase a fine mechanical micrometer, as we did not want to appear prejudiced in favor of microscopy as the only way of determining accurately such minor variations in the thickness of eggshells as those reported in the literature reviewed in the foregoing. Sparing no expense, we bought a Starrett ® Friction Thimble Micrometer, their latest model, claimed to be graduated to 2 μm. (The word "graduated" should not be confused with the word "calibrated," as is frequently the case. With a large enough screw, such an instrument could be graduated down to Ångströms, which still would not mean anything in terms of calibration.) In the instruction manual, one may read: "Caution: Do not force measurement—light contact pressure assures correct reading. After some practice, you will develop a measuring 'feel' that will give your readings automatic accuracy" (Starrett Co., Ltd., 1955, p. 7).

We conducted some experiments with friends innocent of the problem at hand, having them measure the thickness of different pieces of paper, normal hens' eggs dried with the membrane, and broken eggshells which had been dried and from which the membrane had been removed. It is true that after some practice each individual began to get a "feel" of what he thought should be the end point; for particular persons, the readings for high-quality Austrian paper (which is rather thin) became consistent within about 18 μm, while with high-quality American paper (which is considerably thicker) the variations for one individual were as great as 24 μm. Measuring membrane-free eggshells, the variation was around 36 μm, and eggshells dried with membranes yielded results varying from 38 to 52 μm. Pooling the samples for types of paper and eggshells for all tested individuals, the variance was, unfortunately, close to 60 μm. Now we certainly do not wish to claim any statistical significance for these minor experimentations, but we felt confirmed in our impression that something was amiss with all the eggshell thickness measurements using screw micrometers.

We also located a 1970 paper by Lewin in which he described "A Simple Device for Measuring Eggshell Thickness." He wrote: "While conducting research on the effects of pesticide residues on eggshell structure it was apparent that conventional calipers were unsuitable for making thickness measurements. These instruments either have parallel jaws, which cannot be used to determine the thickness of a curved plane, or points which were found to be widely inaccurate due to either poor alignment or point flexibility which varied according to the pressure applied" (Lewin, 1070, p. 305).

The special instrument he constructed to circumvent these problems has a highly polished ball bearing as one of the "jaws," which is helpful in measuring curved surfaces, and a spring device which eliminates subjective differences in the "end point feel." With this special instrument—not suitable for measuring museum eggs—he claims accuracy *can* be reached in the 10 μm range.

16

EXPERTS

That in our day such pygmies
throw such giant shadows only shows
how late in the day it has become.
ERWIN CHARGAFF

    In the summer of 1970, a sizable number of scientists, engineers, attorneys, and professionals in other disciplines assembled at Williams College, in Williamstown, Massachusetts, for a month of intensive interdisciplinary discussions on global environmental problems. Six of the eleven members of the Steering Committee which planned the study were from the faculty of the Massachusetts Institute of Technology, and the reports resulting from the deliberations of the several study groups were published by the MIT Press under the title: *Man's Impact on the Global Environment,* with the subtitle, "Report of the Study of Critical Environmental Problems." Although 13 federal agencies and 4 private foundations were directly or indirectly involved in sponsorship of the program, the close cooperation of Massachusetts Institute of Technology has led many people to refer to the publication as "the MIT Study." However, to avoid confusion with a more recent book also coming out of MIT — *The Limits to Growth*, by Meadows et al. — we shall designate this earlier publication as the Report of the Study of Critical Environmental Problems, hereinafter referred to by the acronym SCEP.

In the spring of 1970, the National Academy of Sciences' Committee on Oceanography (NASCO) established the "Panel on Monitoring Persistent Pesticides in the Marine Environment," with Edward D. Goldberg as its chairman. The deliberations of this panel led to certain conclusions which appeared in 1971 in the form of a small monograph: *Chlorinated Hydrocarbons in the Marine Environment*. Six of the seven panel members working on this monograph also participated in the 1970 SCEP meeting in Williamstown, contributing to the so-called "DDT Case Study" which is incorporated as a part of the "Report of the Ecological Work Group" of SCEP. The material in the two publications dealing with DDT is substantially the same — almost word for word. Although the NASCO publication is more recent, we have decided to use the SCEP version as the basis for our discussion in the next two chapters, principally because the latter is in far wider circulation, both in the United States and abroad.

The NASCO panel members who came to Williamstown were E. Goldberg, P. Butler, P. Meier, D. Menzel, R. Risebrough, and L. Stickel. The full-time participants on the SCEP Ecological Work Group who joined in the preparation of the DDT case study were — besides E. Goldberg — D. Jenkins, P. Kearny, J. Reid, and G. Woodwell. Three other scientists also took part who were not full-time members of either panel: G. Ewing, M. Ingham, and B. Ketchum.

Before we get into the content of the DDT case study report, some discussion should be devoted to SCEP as a project and to the printed version of the study.

One of the principal motivations for convening SCEP was the recognition by the Steering Committee that insufficient material was available on those of man's activities which might be creating pollution problems on a global scale: that is, anything which might be affecting world climate or the large terrestrial and oceanic ecosystems. According to the Preface, it was felt that the SCEP discussions, in focusing on global environmental effects, could help in raising the "level of informed public and scientific discussion and action on global environmental problems" (SCEP, 1970, p. xiv), could provide important input for the 1972 United Nations Conference on the Human Environment and similar international meetings, and, more generally, "could provide citizens, public policy makers, and scientists with an authoritative assessment of the degree and nature of man's impact on the global environment and with specific recommendations for new programs of focused research, monitoring, and action" (*ibid.*, p. xi).

The volume called *Man's Impact on the Global Environment,* which constitutes the original SCEP report, is now in fact in the hands of many citizens, public policymakers, and scientists, who seek to find in it reliable information about the status of our understanding of global pollutants and their possible effects. It is recommended with the highest praise, for example, by Mr. Edward Goldsmith, editor of the British journal *The Ecologist.* This gentleman, who refers to himself as an ecologist although he has no scientific training as such, appears to regard it as a sort of combination of basic science textbook and revealed Word: the lay ecologist's Bible, if you will. Public policymakers who turn to the SCEP study are generally not so rhapsodic about its contents; but they naturally assume, since the book is for the most part written in a dry, scientific style, that they have in their hands authoritative assessments and objective compilations of scientific opinions on the subjects treated.

In view of the lofty aims and far-reaching questions to which the study is addressed, it is natural to expect that all the SCEP participants would have prepared their reports as thoroughly and as objectively as they were able — emphasizing the gaps in their knowledge when these made definitive assessments of problems impossible, and giving equal space to conflicting opinions wherever they were aware of a lack of consensus in the evaluations of the effects of a particular form of pollution. This is precisely what many of them did. The result in most of the seven work group reports is that information gaps were emphasized, and the recommendations consisted largely of suggestions for better monitoring programs and improved methods of information storage and exchange. Nevertheless, most of the panels did a creditable job of evaluating with caution whatever material was available to them and of writing their reports in a reasonable tone, without obfuscation of the issues involved.

Unfortunately, much of the material in the "Report of the Ecological Work Group" fails to conform to these standards of careful appraisal.

Anyone who reads critically will note that the tone in which the report of this group is written is different from that of the others in the same volume. Initially, one may get the impression that it is an objective review, simply because it is replete with scientific jargon, numbers, tables, and summaries of work on several specific pollutants. However, on close reading, it becomes evident that the *evaluations* of available information on nearly all of the ecological problems which might be described as current "hot issues" are nothing better than thinly disguised repetitions of the *opinions* of the handful of scientists who are in the vanguard of the environmental movement. Although admitting that nearly all the data and tables which they present are filled with uncertainties and lacunae, this panel does not seem to feel that the recognized gaps in information should preclude expression of far-reaching generalizations about the probable deleterious effects of man's activities. And with respect to some problems, they write confidently of *inevitable* global effects, even ,though they are unable to document their predictions. For example, world population growth is *not* one of the subjects which they treat. They present no demographic arguments whatsoever, partisan or otherwise. Nevertheless, the implicit assumptions that the world population will double in the next 35 years and that it will continue on its exponential growth curve are behind their general contention that "relations between man and the biosphere are approaching a stage of crisis" (*ibid.*, p. 114). Growth rate in general is later described as "frightening," and they are moved to write that, although "an intractable crisis does not now seem to exist . . . the risk is very great that we shall overshoot in our environmental demands (as some ecologists claim we have already done), leading to a cumulative collapse of our civilization" (*ibid.*, p. 126).

Furthermore, sandwiched in among the tables, "case studies," and monitoring recommendations are a number of sections which are both unnecessary and inappropriate in a publication of this sort. One of these is an eight-page "treatise," consisting of highly oversimplified ecological theorizing. These pages, brief though they are, compete with a number of full-length books popularizing the science of ecology when it comes to distortion beyond recognition of certain ecological concepts and the presentation of exceedingly questionable hypotheses in the guise of well-founded theories.

[As an aside, it may also be noted that neither these theoretical sections nor other parts of the ecological work group's output seem to have been proofread. Here is one of our favorite sentences: "Forests are familiar with the consequences that may follow cleaning out underbrush, selectively removing tree species, or growing single-aged, one-species stands" (*ibid.*, p, 122).]

Other inappropriate inclusions deal with ethical and moral problems. Readers are treated, for instance, to a brief discourse on ecology and life-style. While the continued exponential growth of the human population is assumed to be unavoidable, the panel states that we can and should curb the rising material standard of living, which for some odd reason is referred to as "ecological growth." Readers are flatly informed: "A basic change in values in which increase in material wealth is not so highly rated must accompany any solution to the problem of ecological growth" (*ibid.*, p. 158). The level of comfort at which people ought to cease placing such a high value on increases in material wealth is not specified. In other terms, both the genuine pressing human needs of individ-

uals with empty stomachs, and the very natural growth expectations of underdeveloped and developing nations — where increases in material wealth may be
justifiably described as fundamental to survival — are blithely ignored.

Once having got onto the question of values, the writers must have worked
themselves into a sort of frenzy of moral righteousness, for they follow their
comments on life-style changes with a section called "Pesticide Addiction." This
terrifying tale, typifying the "errors of man's ways," we should like to cite in full.

> Realization that the use of pesticides increases the need to continue their use
> is not new, nor is the awareness that the constant use of pesticides creates new pests.
> For many of our crops on which pesticide use is heavy, the number of pests requiring
> control increases through time. In a very real sense, new herbivorous insects find
> shelter among our crops where their predator enemies cannot survive.
>
> Fifty years ago most insect pests were exotic species, accidently [sic] imported
> to a country lacking their natural enemies. More recently many of the pests, including
> especially the mites, leaf-rolling insects, and a variety of aphids and scale insects,
> have been indigenous [sic].
>
> Thus pesticides not only create the demand for future use (addiction), they also
> create the demand to use more pesticide more often (habituation). Our agricultural
> system is already heavily locked into this process, and it is now spreading to the
> developing countries. It is also spreading into forest management. Pesticides are
> becoming increasingly "necessary" in more and more places.
>
> Before the entire biosphere is "hooked" on pesticides, an alternative means of
> coping with pests should be developed. At the very least this will include crop breed-
> ing for resistance, changes in crop patterns that may not be so well suited to mechani-
> zation, massive developments in the techniques of managing predators, parasites,
> and diseases for use in control, relaxed acceptance values for blemished fruit, and a
> general acceptance of low levels of insects as a situation we do not have to fight.
> (*Ibid.*, pp. 158-159)

To begin with, there are several matters of factual accuracy to be questioned
here. Does the phrase "in a very real sense" in the first paragraph mean what one
would naturally suppose that it means — that is, "in reality"? If so, we should like
to know what are the *new* insect species which are finding shelter among our
crops. To our knowledge the first and last observation of an insect speciation
process in historical times was the emergence of a moth subspecies, described
by Goldschmidt in the mid-1920s. If "new insects" are appearing as a result
of pesticide use, environmental scientists reporting such events in an offhand
manner ought perhaps to be reminded of the vital significance of such phenomena for the validation of evolutionary theories. It is remarkable that the

scientific community at large has been kept in the dark, if such amazing events are indeed taking place.

Secondly, we should like to know the authority for the statement in the second paragraph that most insect pests were exotic 50 years ago. The writers must be very far removed from their peasant ancestors, and they must have been deprived both of the privilege of reading history and of the firsthand stories of grandparents and other elders, who remember vast crop destructions, blights, and plagues caused by indigenous pests on the rampage.

Lastly, quite aside from the loose handling of language when dealing with facts, we must object to the use of the "addiction" metaphor in this type of publication. The inclusion of this tasteless and highly charged figure of speech makes these paragraphs read like columns of a cheap tabloid or a circulating tract written by amateur sociologists. Such a soapbox sermon surely has no place whatsoever in a supposedly dispassionate assessment of global pollution problems.

The final item in the "Report of the Ecological Work Group" which we wish to bring to our readers' attention before turning to the DDT case study per se concerns the recommendations of the panel regarding future uses of DDT and other pesticides. They state that production and use of DDT (and by implication all other persistent pesticides) should be drastically curtailed as soon as possible. They claim (without offering documentation) that alternative, less persistent pesticides exist which are adequate to control insects, for both agricultural and public health purposes. They suggest that, as DDT is phased out, subsidies should be furnished to the developing nations, permitting them to employ these more expensive substitutes. (No actual cost calculations are included, although these are readily available.) They further imply that even these alternative, less persistent pesticides will still be *ecologically* dangerous (no mention is made of their greater toxicity to man and other mammals) because, according to the "theories" so succinctly summarized, the use of *any* pesticides creates "new" pests, and thus perpetuates the "addiction" situation. In their words: ". . . research and the development of new, less-persistent pesticides is an inadequate solution or rather no solution at all" (*ibid.*, p. 136). Accordingly, they recommend that funds be made available for crash programs aimed at perfecting other methods of pest control (nonchemical approaches, and the so-called biological controls). They give no evaluation of either the feasibility or the effectiveness of these "other methods."

In view of the extremist position reflected in these recommendations, and in the light of the unscientific tone and the distorted popularizations which characterize many sections of the "Report of the Ecological Work Group," we came to the conclusion that we had best examine very carefully what these scientists claim to know about the global effects of DDT uses, and also to look into the sources of their information.

We warn the reader that we are going to be merciless in what follows. It does not take the most discerning observer to realize that Wurster is dead set against DDT, and even a cursory examination of his Yale University speech (Wurster, 1970) reveals that he was dramatizing a case, emphasizing certain aspects at the expense of others. However, this lecture, analyzed in the previous chapter, was originally a semipopular oral presentation; and one may suppose that Wurster's bias as an activist is sufficiently well known that at least sophisticated and informed persons would have been inclined to take what he had then to say for what it was, rather than as a substitute for a formal research report. The SCEP publication and the National Academy of Sciences monograph,* on the other hand, purport to be *strictly scientific reviews* on the environmental effects of the chlorinated hydrocarbons. As such, they must stand up to close scrutiny and rigorous criticism. Both reviews conclude, supposedly on the evidence of the literature, that these substances are serious, persistent, globally distributed pollutants which are affecting large ecosystems. The implications of the conclusions and the recommendations are serious. Furthermore, these two documents are being relied upon heavily by government officials charged with the responsibility of deciding the outcome of the current legal battle over the registration of DDT. In view of these considerations, it is our judgment that— beyond examining the accuracy of the scientific content of these reviews—any omissions or distortions which suggest advocacy on the part of the panel members should be exposed.

A Closed Body of Experts

The first matter to be considered in connection with the DDT case study is its bibliography. This appears at the end of the complete report of the "Work Group on Ecological Effects," and publications dealing with DDT are listed together with references on other subjects, in alphabetical order. It is not difficult, however, for someone familiar with the DDT literature to separate out the publications which are specifically related to this compound. These are 42 in number—or 43, if one adds one reference cited in the text but left out of the bibliography (Risebrough et al., 1968b).

Of these 43 publications, 13 may be described as supplying data supporting statements of fact made in the case study. Three deal with physico-chemical

* The fact that the NASCO publication *Chlorinated Hydrocarbons in the Marine Environment* was sponsored by the National Academy of Sciences and published under its auspices should not be taken to mean that the membership of the Academy is in agreement with its contents.

properties of DDT, such as its solubility in water. Five papers report on DDT residues in the general environment: in rivers, rainwater, and so forth. Four others are about the biochemistry of compounds similar to DDT. The last of the 13 supporting references is the 1969 *Report of the Secretary's Commission on Pesticides and Their Relationship to Environmental Health*.

Some of the statements of fact within the body of the text are actually supported by one of the 13 "neutral" references—the solubility properties of DDT, as reported by Bowman, Acree, and Corbett (1960), being an example. Others represent distortions of the findings reported in these publications, as, for instance, when the panel cites Matsumura and Patil (1969) as a source for their claim that DDE inhibits myosin in the nerve membrane.

Only four of the cited papers which deal with either DDT residues in animals or with DDT feeding experiments were written by researchers who have not, to our knowledge, been in any way directly involved in the American legal controversy over DDT uses and registrations.

The remaining 26 of the 43 references are publications in which at least one of the coauthors is a scientific advisor to the Environmental Defense Fund (EDF), or has testified in court proceedings against DDT, or has made public statements to the effect that DDT ought to be banned. In other terms, these studies are the work of scientists who have already made up their minds about DDT. All of these papers indict (or appear to indict) the insecticide as an environmentally damaging substance.

Sixteen of the 26 papers written by DDT foes are the work of panel members. Eleven of these are listed as "unpublished" or "forthcoming," and hence were not available for scrutiny by other scientists at the time of publication.

Not a single publication containing material which might throw doubt on the claims advanced in the text is included. There are well over 1,000 articles treating the nonmetabolic breakdown of DDT in soils and sediments. None of these is listed. No references to photodegradation of DDT vapors by the action of ultraviolet light, nor to its degradation by microorganisms are to be found. Although scores of impartial, factual papers have been published that deal with DDT metabolism in higher organisms, most of these are ignored, whereas the papers in the bibliography on this subject are all studies which conclude that DDT is harmful to nontarget organisms.

It might, of course, be argued that the extreme haste with which the printed version of the SCEP report was prepared and brought out accounts for the fact that a large number of important studies on DDT were not included in its reference list. Were this the sole explanation, however, for its apparent bias, then the NASCO monograph, which was prepared at a much more leisurely pace, should have had a properly balanced bibliography. Unfortunately, it does not.

It is not worthwhile to go over in detail the composition of the reference list of this second publication, since a few comments will suffice. The bibliography is a good deal longer than that of the SCEP "DDT Study," but this is almost exclusively due to the expanded subject matter, which includes PCBs and the chlorinated hydrocarbon pesticides as a group, rather than only DDT. Also added were a few more papers indicting DDT—some of them new publications, others older works which were apparently overlooked in the preparation of the SCEP report. But studies treating the natural rates and processes by which these persistent substances break down in the environment are still conspicuous by their absence. Furthermore, even on the subject of chlorinated hydrocarbons in the marine environment—the specific theme of the monograph—there are glaring omissions. Why, for instance, did the Goldberg panel ignore completely the works of Robinson and his colleagues, who have published a number of papers on DDT residues in marine biota? Why is the old claim that the 1963 "Mississippi fish kill" was caused by endrin dredged up, with a 1966 citation from Mount and Putnicki to support the allegation, with not so much as a whisper about refutations? Even more startling is the failure to include two highly pertinent studies performed by associates of one of the panel members: one dealing with DDT effects on developing oysters (Lowe et al., 1971); the second reporting experiments on the half-life of DDT in seawater (Wilson et al., 1970)—a subject of the most vital significance in relation to the final assessments reached by the panel on the distribution of DDT residues.

The extreme one-sidedness of these two bibliographies augurs ill for an objective appraisal. Simply from noting the important omissions in the reference lists, one gets the impression that these two panels of scientists regard themselves as a sort of "closed body of experts." Both publications reflect a certitude of correctness in judgment which apparently no longer makes it mandatory to present both sides of the picture in an exceedingly controversial case, but permits selectivity in the interest of hammering out a persuasive argument. Are these two publications scientific reviews, or are they briefs summarizing the position of advocates? Apparently, wherever DDT is a subject of inquiry, this question has to be repeatedly raised. It would be well to keep this in mind while we examine the contents of the "DDT Case Study," which we are now, at long last, going to do.

The Impact

The "DDT Case Study" begins with a brief review of the effects of the pesticide on marine fauna (sic), both in laboratory and in field. This section is called "The Ecological Impact," and it has five subheadings, covering plankton, fish, crustaceans, mollusks, and birds. We have already discussed, in the last chapter, much of the material summarized in this review. However, there are a few points to which attention should be called.

1. Phytoplankton

The panel expresses doubt that the laboratory experiments on DDT and algal photosynthesis of Wurster (1968) and of Menzel et al. (1970) can be described as "ecologically meaningful," since the concentrations of the compound required to depress photosynthesis or inhibit growth exceed its solubility in water by a factor of at least ten and are far in excess of expected concentrations in the open ocean. They are not content to rest with this disclaimer, however, for they add: "However, toxicity may vary interspecifically and, if not universally toxic, may exert some control on species succession in the near-shore environment. . . . If DDT is concentrated in surface oil film, it is not improbable that concentrations there may reach levels sufficient to cause acute toxicity to plants" (SCEP, 1970, p. 127).

Both "possible effects" referred to are sheer speculations. No one has ever shown the depression of growth of *any* algal species in the near-shore environment in relation to DDT. Nor have any samples from open-ocean surface slicks ever been taken in which it has been shown that DDT is present in concentrations exceeding its water solubility, much less that it has caused acute toxicity to plants. If the panel wanted to include these speculations in connection with suggestions for further studies and monitoring, they should have listed them under "Information Needs," not under "Ecological Impact."

2. Fish

We have already discussed (pages 417–418) the panel's distorted report of 100 percent failure in the development of the sac fry of freshwater trout. It should also be mentioned that Butler, when questioned under oath during the Consolidated DDT Hearings (Butler, 1971, p. 3722), described the *mean* residues in the ripe eggs of speckled sea trout on the south Texas coast as 1 ppm, whereas here (and in the NASCO monograph) the text reads: "DDT residues in the ripe eggs are *about* 8 ppm" (SCEP, 1970, p. 127; our emphasis). Whereas the rather vague word "about" will be taken by most people to stand for "averaged," what it apparently means here is that one or two eggs were found to contain 8 ppm residues. As we shall see, this is not the only place where the panel introduces a figure representing an *upper limit* of residues found, and then either implies or baldly states that it stands for an average.

In writing about coastal fish, they mention only California mackerel, where DDT residues are reported to have exceeded FDA guidelines for human consumption (5 ppm in the edible portions of the fish). There is no reference for this information and no precise delineation of the date or the duration of this contamination. The panel lets this statement stand at the end of a paragraph, which tends to give an impression that it is a symptomatic pattern typical for all oceanic fish, which, we hasten to assure the reader, it is not.

They state next that laboratory experiments have established the concentrations of several chlorinated hydrocarbons, including DDE, that damage the reproductive success of fish, but they offer no references and do not describe what these concentrations are. They then go on to say: "Concentrations of DDT in species from the marine environment exceed those found to have deleterious effects in the laboratory and have been correlated with population decreases or reproductive failures of a number of marine species. Signs of incipient damage that can be expected to develop with continuing accumulation have also been reported" (*ibid.*, p. 128).

What species are they referring to? Who has reported these population decreases? Who has observed the "signs of incipient damage?" *No documentation whatsoever* is offered in support of these serious allegations. Scientists generally do not make statements of this sort unless they can quote, at the very least, their own unpublished data to support them; and most scientists would not consider setting down such generalities without confirmed published results. With this panel, evidently, one is simply expected to take their word for it. After all, *quod scripsi, scripsi.*

3. Crustaceans

Since crustaceans are arthropods and are known to be sensitive to DDT, one would expect that the panel would examine with some care whether there have been actual recorded declines of shrimp and crab productivity in coastal waters where these organisms are of commercial importance. It is thus rather surprising that they give no general fishery production figures for shrimp and crab, although these are readily available for years prior to and following the introduction of DDT—at least for the United States. Instead of dealing with the production records of these species for extensive areas, which would seem to be an appropriate approach in a panel concerned with *global* effects, they mention only two local areas. A decline in the production of Dungeness crab in California is said to have been associated with DDT residues. Actually, according to 1970 data the catch off the northern California coast was a record 14 million pounds, while the decline in productivity was limited to the San Francisco area and has been established as due to pollution other than DDT (*San Francisco Examiner,* November 14, 1970, p. 11). With respect to shrimp, the panel offers only a speculation, and that again in connection with a highly localized area. They report laboratory evidence that DDT concentrations of 0.2 ppb can cause 100 percent mortality of shrimp in 20 days of continuous exposure (Nimmo, Wilson, and Blackman, forthcoming). They also cite residue data indicating that "concentrations of this magnitude have been detected in Texas river waters flowing into commercially important shrimp nursery areas (Manigold and Schulze, 1969)" (SCEP, 1970, p. 129). This information is immediately followed by the sentence: "*We can be certain* that significant mortalities of juvenile crustaceans are increasing in such contaminated areas" (*ibid.*; our emphasis).

Now we would not disagree with the argument that *if* there were, indeed, steady concentrations in the ambient waters of the nursery area itself of 0.2 ppb DDT (which is not quite the same thing as an inflow into these areas of waters containing such concentrations), the probability would be very high that juvenile, and even adult, shrimp would die. But why should the panel resort to speculation about shrimp production when there is no information gap on this particular subject? Why did they not rather report the 1969 shrimp production figures for the estuary involved and compare them with other years? Or better still, why did they not simply recommend that the ambient waters of the nursery area be monitored and compared with the concentrations in the river? In general, as we implied in the last chapter, the sensitivity of shrimp to DDT—which we do not dispute—seems to argue against the likelihood of extensive contamination of shrimp nursery areas, since anyone who bothers to read the production figures will learn that they are higher now than they were in the early fifties, for instance (Fisheries Statistics of the U.S., 1969). Local and regional variations in productivity appear to follow long-term cyclic patterns unrelated to DDT contamination of waters.

4. Mollusks

Although the panel's summary of DDT's effects on mollusks is condensed into a single sentence, the way it is worded in the two versions of the report seems to support our contention that publications which fail to confirm those findings useful to the argument of the report have been ignored. In the SCEP study, the sentence reads: "DDT characteristically interferes with the growth of oysters at levels as low as 0.1 ppb (Butler, 1966) in the ambient water" (SCEP, 1970, p. 129).

In the NASCO monograph it has been changed to: "Many pesticides interfere with oyster growth at levels as low as 0.1 ppb (Butler, 1966b), in the ambient water" (NASCO, 1971, p. 10).

In the summer of 1970, a paper dealing with chronic exposure of oysters to DDT, toxaphene, and parathion was presented at the National Shellfisheries Association Meeting in Atlantic City. The researchers—Lowe, P. D. Wilson, Rick, and A. J. Wilson of the Gulf Breeze Laboratories in Florida—thanked Dr. P. Butler for his advice in connection with their experiments.

To summarize briefly, these investigators exposed developing oysters to concentrations of the three substances in flowing seawater, separately and in combination, in four experimental series. In the DDT series, the oysters were kept in water containing 1 ppb of the compound for 36 weeks, or up to the stage of sexual maturity. They were then kept in clean water for another three months, during which depuration period they completely cleansed themselves of accumulated pesticide residues (about 29 ppm DDT, wet-tissue weight). The experimenters found *no* significant differences between the weights or heights of the oysters reared in the DDT containing water and those of the control group. Furthermore, eggs fertilized with spermatozoa removed from the mature oysters at the end of the experimental period developed into normal larvae.

This lengthy and thorough experiment fails to confirm the earlier findings of Butler, which are the basis for the panel's assertion that DDT characteristically interferes with oyster growth at levels as low as 0.1 ppb. By 1971, when the NASCO monograph was published, the study of Lowe et al., was already in print. Furthermore, one of the panel members evidently followed the course of the experiment since he was thanked for his advice in conducting it.

In any respectable scientific review one would expect that the 1971 version of the DDT report would say something like the following: "Although it was earlier thought that levels of DDT in the ambient waters as low as 0.1 ppb (Butler, 1966) interfere with the growth of oysters, more recent investigations (Lowe et al., 1971) have failed to demonstrate any significant inhibition of growth from continued exposure to 1 ppb of the pesticide." But instead of including a correction of this sort—which would have conveyed a real change in our understanding about DDT tolerance of mollusks—the 1971 NASCO report merely substitutes the phrase "many pesticides" for "DDT." In this way, although they are not telling the whole truth, the panel is at least partially covered, for they could always claim that they meant "many pesticides" to include DFP, for instance, which might indeed inhibit growth.

It may seem to the reader that we exaggerate the importance of a minor point, in raising such a strong objection to the fact that the panel avoids admitting that Butler's 1966 findings have been refuted. However, this is just one illustration of the many distortions by omission which characterize both of these reviews, as we shall try to demonstrate throughout the remainder of this chapter and in the one which follows it.

5. *Birds*

The effects of DDT residues on avian reproduction are given the most attention—even more in the 1971 than in the 1970 review. In the SCEP version, the mallard duck experiments of Heath et al. are cited,[*] and another study is mentioned in which high DDT residues in dead peregrines, bald eagles, and common loons were reported (Jeffries and Prestt, 1966). The rest of the discussion is devoted to predator birds of California, where, according to the writers, the bald eagle and the peregrine falcon have disappeared from the Channel Islands, and the brown pelican and double-crested cormorant are no longer able to reproduce. *All* the references documenting these claims are listed as forthcoming or unpublished manuscripts. Four of these refer to Risebrough's work; and it seems fairly likely that he wrote this section on birds, in which the California ecosystem is presented as a symptomatic example of what is about to happen elsewhere. The discussion of birds ends with an unequivocal prediction: "Continued buildup of DDT in this ecosystem and in other marine ecosystems around the world will cause reproductive failures in these and other marine species" (SCEP, 1970, p. 130).

It should be evident to the reader by this time that the reproductive problems of the predator bird species have received a great deal of attention from those scientists who are worried about the deleterious effects of DDT residues in the natural environment. In addition to "demonstrating" the cause-and-effect relationship of DDT to avian reproduction problems in the laboratory, a number of these concerned scientists have attempted to investigate experimentally *how* DDT and its metabolites act on the biochemical level to cause the thin eggshells and other symptoms of reproductive difficulties. In their next major section, "Biochemical Effects," the panel summarizes the various mechanisms which have been postulated in connection with DDT's mode of action. We wish first to quote the whole of this summary, and then we shall break it down in terms of the different biochemical mechanisms which are mentioned, devoting the remainder of this chapter to a rather detailed analysis of this technical material.

"A Molecule That Is Enormously Active"

Several physiological effects of DDT and its residues account for shell thinning and for the abnormal behavior observed in contaminated populations. In affecting nerves, chlorinated hydrocarbons, including DDE, are believed to block the ion trans-

---

[*] The scientific value of this paper has already been discussed in Chapter 15, pages 405–408).

port process by inhibiting ATPase (an enzyme, otherwise called myosin) in the nerve membrane that causes the required energy to be made available (Matsumura and Patil, 1969). Transport of ionic calcium across membranes such as those in the shell gland of birds is also an energy-requiring process dependent upon membrane ATPase (Skou, 1965). Inhibition of these enzymes by DDE could account for the concentration-effect curves obtained for shell thickness and DDE concentration in eggs of the brown pelican, double-crested cormorant (Anderson et al., 1969) and herring gull (Hickey and Anderson, 1968). DDE has also been found to inhibit the enzyme carbonic anhydrase (Bitman, Cecil, and Fries, 1970; Peakall, 1970; Risebrough, Davis, and Anderson, forthcoming), essential for the deposition of calcium carbonate in the eggshell and for the maintenance of pH gradients across membranes, such as those in the shell gland. Inhibition of this enzyme by such drugs as sulfanilamide results in the production of thin-shelled eggs.

The chlorinated hydrocarbons, including DDE, induce mixed-function oxidase enzymes in the livers of birds and mammals that hydroxylate and render water-soluble foreign, lipid-soluble compounds (Conney, 1967; Risebrough et al., 1968). Induction is usually temporary, ending when the inducing materials are themselves metabolized. DDE is comparatively resistant to degradation by the induced enzymes, so that they may persist as inducers without being degraded. The induced enzymes may therefore become constitutive.

The steroid hormones such as estrogen and testosterone (Conney, 1967; Peakall, 1970) and thyroxine (Schwartz et al., 1969) are metabolized at higher rates when these enzymes are induced. Lower estrogen concentrations are present in pigeons fed p,p'-DDT (Peakall, 1970). Birds may also show symptoms of hyperthyroidism when fed a chlorinated hydrocarbon (Jeffries, 1969; Jeffries and French, 1969). An increasing number of instances of abnormal behavior are being reported in contaminated populations, including herring gulls and the brown pelicans (Gress, forthcoming). These abnormalities also affect reproductive success and most likely result from hormone imbalance caused by the activity of the nonspecific enzymes induced by the chlorinated hydrocarbons. (SCEP, pp. 130–131)

These three long paragraphs are supposed to represent a summary of the scientific understanding of how DDT and its metabolites act on the biochemical level, and what might be the relation between their biological activity and the chronic reproductive problems of birds which have been reported as "correlating" so well with the presence of DDT residues.

Actually, the panel is writing about four separate biochemical mechanisms of action:

1. Blocking of ion transport—calcium—through inhibition of ATPase.
2. Inhibition of carbonic anhydrase.
3. Induction of mixed-function hydroxylases, which break down circulating steroid hormones.

4. Production of hyperthyroidism.

It is, in itself, somewhat unusual that there should be four separate biochemical mechanisms postulated, all of which are needed to explain the supposed disturbance in calcium metabolism ultimately leading to "shell thinning and abnormal behavior in contaminated populations." But, as we have already learned from Dr. Wurster, DDT is biologically one of the most active molecules known.

We should like to treat these four cited mechanisms separately, beginning with the matter of enzyme induction and steroid hormone breakdown.

Something out of Nothing

The sections of the citation pertinent to discussion of the first mechanism are the second paragraph and the first two sentences of the third paragraph. To begin with, it has to be pointed out that the third sentence in the second paragraph does not mean what it says. As written, according to standard English grammar, it implies that the induced enzymes will persist as inducers without degrading. Since this is complete nonsense, one must suppose that the authors meant the "they" in the second clause to refer to the subject "DDE," even though the latter is singular.

Secondly, the claim expressed in the fourth sentence to the effect that the induced enzymes may become constitutive is impossible. By definition, no induced enzyme can become constitutive. An enzyme is *either* constitutive *or* induced; and the synthesis of constitutive enzymes is carried out by organisms quite independently of the presence or absence of inducers.

Perhaps haste in preparation of the manuscript could account for these two errors.* Still, the concepts involved in this postulated biochemical pathway have to be examined with some care. What is the significance of the induction of nonspecific hepatic enzymes? Does the ability of DDT to induce enzymes have anything to do with eggshell thinning or other reproductive problems?

Many lipophilic compounds—especially those which contain benzene rings—have to be made water-soluble after getting into an organism, in order that they may be eliminated from it. In higher animals, this natural detoxification function is carried out by the liver. In the liver cells, there are small bodies called microsomes, which produce microsomal enzymes. These enzymes are not substrate-

---

* In the 1971 NASCO publication, the grammatical confusion has been straightened out, but the other, more important error, remains.

specific, but will hydroxylate (make water-soluble) a great number of different compounds. The hydroxylation process alters the molecular structure of the parent compound, changing it into what are called its polar metabolites. Since these microsomal enzymes are not automatically synthesized by the liver cells (that is, are not constitutive), their production will only take place when an inducing agent (an appropriate drug) is circulating in the blood. Even when a lipophilic compound capable of acting as an enzyme inducer is present in an organism, if it is stored in the body fat and only minor quantities are in active circulation, it will not induce these nonspecific hepatic enzymes.

Nobody would quarrel with the statement that DDT and DDE act as microsomal enzyme inducers in higher organisms, when circulating in the blood in high enough concentrations. This, in itself, however, has nothing to do with reproductive problems or abnormal behavior. It merely represents evidence that the organisms are capable of detoxifying these substances.

The connection made by the panel between reproductive and/or behavioral difficulties and the induction of these enzymes is expressed solely in the first two sentences of the third paragraph, where the claim is put forth that the steroid hormones, estrogen and testosterone, and the thyroid hormone, thyroxine, are metabolized at higher rates when these enzymes are induced. Let us see where these ideas came from.

Four specific references are given in the passage: Conney, 1967; Risebrough et al., 1968; Peakall, 1970; and Schwartz et al., 1969.

The Conney work is a review article on the pharmacological significance of microsomal enzymes, in which the breakdown of such steroid hormones as estrogen, testosterone, progesterone, and desoxycorticosterone by these enzymes is treated. (This is one of the 13 bibliography references cited as supporting evidence.) Conney and his coworkers have carried out investigations on steroid hormone breakdown by DDT-induced microsomal enzymes; however, this particular review deals with several drugs influencing the catabolic pathway of the steroid hormones.

The publication by Schwartz and his coworkers, another of the 13 neutral papers, does not deal with DDT at all. Its subject is *phenobarbital* as an enzyme inducer. These researchers showed that, when relatively large doses of the drug were administered to rats, microsomal enzymes isolated after sacrifice of the animals produced an increase in the deiodination of thyroid hormones, *in vitro*.[*]
The connection between this work and the supposed hormonal disbalance of

---

[*] The term *in vitro* experiments refers to investigations carried out in the laboratory using certain extracts obtained from previously treated and sacrificed animals. *In vivo* experiments refer to observations and measurements conducted on living animals after appropriate treatment.

living birds exposed to DDT is entirely imaginary. However, *if* it were permissible to extrapolate from rats to birds, and from barbiturates to DDT, and *if* this phenomenon were to occur *in vivo,* one would expect the behavior of affected animals to be typical of hypothyroid conditions—that is, the birds would be sluggish, rather than nervous and excited. By including this reference, however, the panel is nicely covered: after all, tomorrow's wildlife problem may very well be sluggish birds laying thick-shelled eggs!

The studies of Peakall and of Risebrough et al. do deal with DDT, and they are worth examining.

The first paper Peakall published on this general subject, "Pesticide-induced Enzyme Breakdown of Steroids in Birds" (1967), is not the same as the one cited by the panel as a reference. We do not know exactly why they failed to mention this earlier Peakall work, but it may have been an oversight due to haste, as evidenced by the fact that the 1968 Risebrough et al. paper is cited but not listed in the bibliography. In any case, it is important to review the earlier Peakall paper, not only because of its relevant subject matter, but also because it introduces a very special kind of methodology which is used in the later paper with Risebrough, of which Peakall is one of the coauthors.

Since, as we have already seen, the first papers establishing "proof" of a cause-and-effect relationship between DDT residues (or sublethal exposures) and reproductive problems in birds appeared only in 1968 and 1969, Peakall's attempts as early as 1967 to explore the biochemical mechanisms leading to eggshell thinning were definitely pioneering. He wrote: "It has been thought that these decreases [in bird populations] are caused by pesticides, but concentrations of pesticide residues found are often low compared with a toxic dose. There is evidence from laboratory studies that gross blockage of the reproductive system does not occur except at concentrations approaching toxic doses. More subtle effects on the breeding cycle caused by changes in hormonal concentrations and neurotoxic effects may be important" (Peakall, 1967, p. 505).

Peakall decided to investigate whether DDT might cause come changes in hormonal concentrations which could, in turn, possibly account for "more subtle effects on the breeding cycle." Briefly, this is how he proceeded. He fed king pigeons the relatively "low" dose of 100 ppm DDT and 2 ppm dieldrin, both separately and in combination, for one week. Afterwards, he killed the birds, separated the induced liver enzyme fraction, and added to it either radioactively labeled testosterone (the male sex hormone) or radioactively labeled progesterone (one of the female sex hormones), in order to establish how they would be broken down by the induced enzymes. He then separated the unchanged parent compounds—testosterone and progesterone—and their respective polar metabolites. He determined the radioactivity of each of the fractions obtained, which he reported in terms of counts per minute,* showing these counts on graphs as Figures 1 and 2 in his publication.

In his text, Peakall claims that after DDT and dieldrin treatment, or both together, far greater quantities of polar metabolites were formed from the hormones than in the control, indicating that the induced enzymes increased the rate of metabolism of progesterone and testosterone. He even calculated the exact amounts of these metabolites for comparative purposes, expressed in millimicromoles in his table. His basic conclusion reads: "The experiments demonstrate that relatively small amounts of DDT and dieldrin can induce increased rates of metabolism of steroids by induction of hepatic enzymes" *(ibid.)*. In the very next sentence, however, he admits that the relation of elevated steroid metabolism *in the liver* to the concentration of *circulating* steroids was not established by his experiments. Still, this minor gap in information apparently did not strike him as too important, and by some mysterious process he manages, after a few remarks concerning field observations of avian reproductive problems, to arrive at his more generalized, speculative conclusion that "observation of the decrease in weight in recent years of the eggshell of some birds of prey could be explained by increased metabolism of *oestrogen* induced by hepatic enzymes"*(ibid.*, p.506; our emphasis).

We shall come back to these conclusions shortly, but first let us look at the graphs. Peakall's original figures are here reproduced in two different forms on pages 442, 443, and 444, first approximately as they appeared in *Nature* (Fig. 7), to scale, and then with each of the curves drawn separately (Figs. 8 and 9). In the original versions, as the reader will easily perceive, it is a bit difficult to determine exactly what values are represented by the curves, since they are all shown together in a mass of overlapping lines. As soon as they are separated, however, it becomes immediately obvious—at least to a scientist—that there is something very wrong with the data, for in both series there is an increase in the total amount of radioactive material. The "gain" from the controls to the two DDT curves can be seen at a glance, since the peaks of unaltered parent compounds are nearly identical, while the peaks representing the polar metabolites show considerably more metabolized material in the DDT curves than in the controls. Although the increases in the dieldrin and the dieldrin + DDT curves are not quite so apparent visually, a quick addition of the ordinate values from the graphs indicates an ever greater gain in material.

It should perhaps be made clear for the general reader that Peakall added

---

* Radioactive decay is proportional to the concentration of the starting material. The decay of atoms can be registered by appropriate instruments, which will give the radioactive counts. Decay per unit of time—counts per second, counts per minute, etc.—is a convenient measure of the concentrations present.

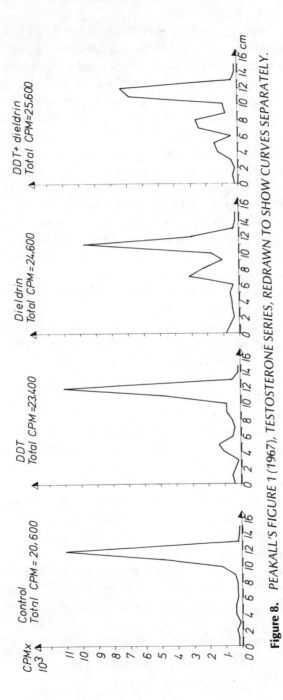

Figure 8.   PEAKALL'S FIGURE 1 (1967), TESTOSTERONE SERIES, REDRAWN TO SHOW CURVES SEPARATELY.

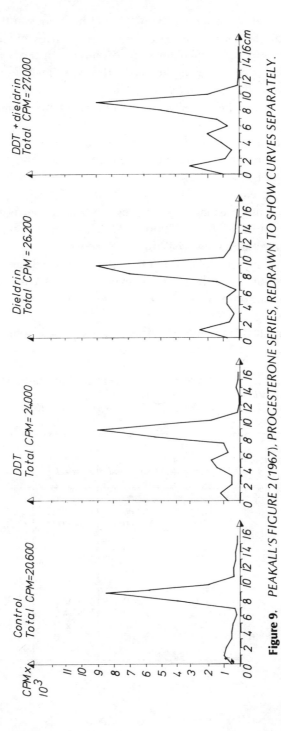

Figure 9. PEAKALL'S FIGURE 2 (1967), PROGESTERONE SERIES, REDRAWN TO SHOW CURVES SEPARATELY.

exactly the same amounts of radioactively labeled hormones to the controls and the three experimental series. No matter what differences might occur in the quantities or types of polar metabolites formed, the *sum* of the parent compound plus its metabolites (as expressed at the end of the experiment in terms of counts per minute) *has to be the same in all four.* This is not an experimental variable, nor is it a matter over which there can be any arguments about technique or interpretation.

The counts, as read off from the graphs, are summarized in Table 15. In both series, there is a remarkable progression. The control total in the testosterone series is 20,600 CPM; the DDT total is 23,400 CPM; the dieldrin total is 24,600 CPM; and that for dieldrin + DDT is 25,600 CPM. In the progesterone series the results are even more astonishing, progressing from a control total of 20,600 CPM to that of dieldrin + DDT: 27,000 CPM. This indicates that a net gain of 6,400 CPM over the starting material—or one-third again as much as the amount of radioactive hormone which he added to begin with—has been "achieved" by Dr. Peakall, all within a few hours. (This even surpasses Grosch's record, who needed three years in order to generate 33 times as much DDT as he added to his jars!)

The source of all this radioactivity is a mystery, unless some new principle

Table 15.   *TABULATION OF PEAKALL'S RESULTS (1967)
AS DERIVED FROM HIS GRAPHS, SHOWING GAINS IN HIS
RADIOACTIVITY COUNTS OVER HIS CONTROL.*

Testosterone series	CPM			
	Unaltered	Metabolite	Total	Net gain
Control	17,300	3,300	20,600	. . .
DDT	16,800	6,600	23,400	2,800
Dieldrin	14,500	10,100	24,600	4,000
DDT + dieldrin	15,200	10,400	25,600	5,000
Progesterone series				
Control	14,800	5,800	20,600	. . .
DDT	16,500	7,500	24,000	3,400
Dieldrin	16,500	9,700	26,200	5,600
DDT + dieldrin	17,500	9,500	27,000	6,400

of pesticide-induced generation of radioactivity is postulated. Perhaps Peakall has discovered an unknown kind of controlled chain reaction which creates matter out of nothing! Or may he simply have made some mistakes?

It is peculiar that Peakall didn't notice this gain in material, since from these curves he carefully calculated the exact amounts of the polar metabolites in millimicromoles. This is even more peculiar because he had no idea about the molecular structure of his breakdown products—not having isolated and identified any of them—and therefore had no grounds for expressing their quantities in terms implying precise knowledge of molecular weights.

These completely erroneous data are the experimental results. It should be a sufficient insult to our intelligence that on these grounds we are informed that the pesticide-induced enzymes caused the tested hormones to break down into such and such increased quantities of millimicromoles of unidentified polar metabolites. But this is not enough. The implications of these nonresults are extended to a different steroid hormone which has not even been tested, and increased metabolism of *estrogen* by DDT-induced enzymes is postulated as the cause of thin eggshells. It would seem ludicrous, were it not tragic, that such a paper could ever have been published in a reputable scientific journal. This is no longer science, but an unwitting persiflage.

Inkblots

In 1968 Risebrough, Rieche, Peakall, Herman, and Kirven published a paper in *Nature* called "Polychlorinated Biphenyls in the Global Ecosystem." If the worth of a scientific publication could be judged by the number of times it is cited, this article would have to be ranked among the great biological works of the 1960s, for in the four brief years since its appearance, it has already been quoted ad nauseam.

The paper is lengthy, but its first pages deal only with comparisons of residues of PCBs (polychlorinated biphenyls, a group of chlorinated hydrocarbons widely used as plasticizers, which we will discuss in Chapter 17), DDT, and dieldrin in dead birds. These residue comparisons need not concern us here. What is important is that the article reports on some experiments, again with king pigeons, testing the effect of enzymes induced by the three substances mentioned above on estradiol—the female sex hormone about which Peakall had speculated at the end of his 1967 study.

The abstract reads: "Polychlorinated biphenyls are widely dispersed in the global ecosystem, and are powerful inducers of hepatic enzymes which degrade oestradiol. Together with other chlorinated biocides, such as DDT, they could account for a large part of the aberration in calcium metabolism which has been observed in many species of birds since the Second World War" (Risebrough et al., 1968a, p. 1098).

For these experiments, the researchers used p,p'-DDE, technical grade DDT, and PCB (Aroclor 1262), which they injected intramuscularly in the amounts of 40 ppm, 40 ppm, and 20 ppm, respectively. They claim that with the exception of injection rather than feeding as the route of administration, their experimental procedures were the same as those used by Peakall in 1967. However, the body burden of DDT in Peakall's experiment was only 8.3 ppm (as cal-

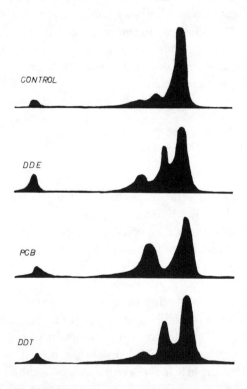

Figure 10.   *AN APPROXIMATION OF FIG. 1 FROM RISEBROUGH ET AL., 1968*

culated from the feeding data), and since this is quite different from 40 ppm, the two experiments really cannot be compared. The method of radioactive counting was, however, apparently similar; and the unidentified polar metabolites of unknown molecular weight were here also tabulated in terms of milli-micromoles.

A rendering of the authors' Figure 1, which is the only representation in the paper of the hormone breakdown by the induced enzymes, is shown as Figure 10, in the same scale and form as the original. The largest peak is unaltered estradiol.

This is not a graph, dear reader; it is a disgrace. Much more precise information can be derived from a Rorschach inkblot. Not only are the peaks represented as nondescript blotches but no coordinates whatever are given, and one must therefore take it on faith from the text of the paper that the peaks represent CPMs. However, with a great deal of patience, one can get something out of it.

In order to evaluate the meaning of this "graph," one has to consider that the dark areas underneath the peaks represent concentrations of the hormone and its metabolites. If one takes the trouble to divide these dark blots into triangles, one can calculate the area of each triangle, sum the figures, and arrive at an approximation of the total radioactivity, expressed in terms of square millimeters. Just as the total CPMs of the control and experimental series in Peakall's earlier work should have been the same, here the sum of the areas (in mm^2) covered by the peaks should be equal in all four drawings, since each of the sums is supposed to represent the same amount of starting radioactive labeled material, however metabolized.

Table 16 shows the calculated areas underneath the peaks. The totals are

Table 16. *TABULATION OF RESULTS OF RISEBROUGH ET AL. (1969) AS DERIVED FROM THEIR GRAPHS, SHOWING GAINS IN THEIR RADIOACTIVITY COUNTS*

Estradiol added	mm^2			Net gain
	Unaltered	Metabolite	Total	
Control	84.0	12.0	96.0	. . .
DDT	79.5	38.5	118.0	22.0
DDE	79.5	47.5	127.0	31.0
PCB	72.0	46.5	118.5	22.5

not equal—all three experimental series show a "net gain" over the control total. It would seem that Peakall's gift for creating something out of nothing is still active. In this paper, however, coauthored by four other scientists, the nearly indecipherable form of the data presentation tends to obscure the impossible findings even more than the crowded line graphs of the earlier publication.

We ought, perhaps, to comment that it is probably true that nonspecific hepatic enzymes which have been induced by a sufficient quantity of circulating DDT can, when isolated, increase the breakdown of some of the steroid hormones *in vitro*. How significant this might be is another matter, but we do not deny the possibility that the basic method of the two studies discussed could have demonstrated the phenomenon, had the work been carried out properly. As reported, however, these experiments prove nothing, except that the standards of scientific publications appear to have reached an all-time low.

Before we leave the study of Risebrough et al., we wish briefly to consider the conclusions reached by the authors, since they concern PCBs, and we shall be discussing these substances in a later chapter. They write: "On a weight basis the PCB preparation had an oestradiol degrading potential approximately five times that of p,p -DDE or technical DDT. Both DDE and PCB, which are apparently the most abundant of the chlorinated hydrocarbon pollutants in the global ecosystem, have therefore the capacity to produce sublethal physiological effects in birds" (*ibid.*, p. 1101).

The remark that PCBs are five times more effective on a weight basis in degrading estradiol is supported by a table in which the amounts of metabolites are reported in "millimicromoles." It does not seem to be borne out by the graphs, however, which suggest only twice as much activity, presuming that one can accept them as at least vague representations of some kind of measurements of estrogen metabolism.

From a historical point of view, the greater activity of PCBs is quite interesting. In 1968, PCBs were a relatively new environmental "find." They were then, and indeed still are, regarded as Very Bad Things, spread all over the natural environment as a side effect of modern man's plastic mania. At that time it was thought that they might be as responsible as DDT or its derivatives for eggshell thinning in wild birds. Now, however, at a time when DDT is under concerted attack in the courts, the role of PCBs in affecting avian reproduction is being minimized.

It will be interesting to note what develops in this respect in a year or two— assuming that some kind of legal decision will eventually be reached that will take the focus of attention off DDT. If one observes with care the way in which some of the more prominent environmentalists have shifted their emphasis from one pollutant to another, or altered their evaluations of how certain substances act in damaging the environment, one cannot but wonder if strategic considerations are not as important in these changes of stance as advances in scientific understanding of the problems.

This rather unkind remark is by way of a generalized aside, which should not be taken as a definite prediction on our part that PCBs will again, in the near future, be implicated as primary causative agents in avian reproductive difficulties. It does seem to us, however, that insofar as there are rather strong indications that many of these leading environmental scientists desire to extend their spheres of activity and influence into the political arena, there is every reason to examine whether changes in their scientific judgments are purely professional in nature, or whether these might not at times be explained in terms of politcal realism.

But now—back to biochemistry.

A Transitional Paper

We come at last to the 1970 publication by Peakall: "p,p'-DDT: Effect on Calcium Metabolism and Concentration of Estradiol in the Blood." This is a rather complicated article, in which four different experimental series are reported, with several parameters observed in each.

The first two series are those which concern us here—that is, those which deal with parameters related to the enzyme-induction–steroid-hormone-metabolism question. Peakall used paired ringdoves *(Streptopelia risoria)* in this investigation—two control groups and two experimental groups, feeding the latter 10 ppm DDT for at least four weeks. The females of one control and one experimental group were sacrificed eight days after the second mating; the others were killed after production of the clutch of two eggs.

In both the eight-day series and the complete clutch series, comparisons between the control and experimental animals were made for a number of different parameters, the most important being: (1) levels of circulating estradiol in the blood, (2) metabolic activity of hepatic microsomal enzymes, (3) bone-calcium determinations, and (4) the time between mating and the laying of the first egg. With the exception of the last factor, all these parameters were determined by taking radioactive counts. In this paper, Peakall *does not* represent his original data at all; his Table 1 shows only the final averages for comparison on each of the observations. In view of what we have seen regarding Peakall's difficulties in performing accurate radioactive determinations in earlier work, we are not altogether enthusiastic about accepting at face value the correctness of the final mean values he represents in the table. However, we shall set aside our doubts and explain what he claims to have found in this experimental series.

1. The eight-day experimental birds had significantly lower levels of circulating estradiol than the controls.

2. The same group had significantly less specific calcium activity in the leg bones.

3. Metabolism by induced liver enzymes of estradiol *in vitro* was significantly greater for experimental birds than controls in both the eight-day and the complete clutch series. (However, the metabolized fraction is reported in total nanomoles, and there is again no identification of the metabolites and no indication that the author knew their molecular weights.)

4. In the complete clutch, among experimental females, egg laying was significantly delayed.

5. At the end of egg laying, there were no significant differences in either circulating levels of estradiol or specific calcium activity of the leg bones.

If we accept that the measurements of estradiol blood levels and specific calcium activity were correctly performed and reported, then the picture that emerges is the following: The pesticide-fed females showed some depression. of blood levels of estrogen, and consequently of deposition of medullary bone calcium. Their egg laying was slightly delayed compared with the controls. They seemed, however, to "catch up," lay their eggs, and afterwards to have had approximately the same estrogen and calcium status as the controls. This suggests that the whole syndrome of induced-liver-enzyme–hormone-breakdown—if it really does occur *in vivo*—is insufficent to explain eggshell thinning in the wild, although it might explain the few days of delay in egg laying, as reported occasionally.

This is exactly the conclusion reached by Peakall: "Since the breeding cycle proceeded to the stage of egg-laying, even though delayed, it is unlikely that severe depletion of stored calcium in the medullary bone occurs. Thus, although the phenomenon of hepatic enzyme induction has an effect on calcium balance, it does not explain the extremely thin eggshells found in the brown pelican *(Pelecanus occidentalis)* colonies along the California coast" (Peakall, 1970a, p. 594).

He goes on to say that the extremely thin shells observed in this colony— where the average thinning was more than 50 percent—could not possibly be explained by induced enzymes affecting calcium balance, because a sufficient reduction of calcium supply in the body of the female would inhibit egg laying altogether, rather than result in thin-shelled eggs. He postulates that the calcium inhibition must take place near the site of eggshell formation. He then develops the idea, which had been suggested by Anderson, Hickey, Risebrough, Hughes, and Christenson in the previous year (1969), that the primary mechanism by which DDT and its metabolites act to cause thin eggshells is by inhibiting the enzyme carbonic anhydrase.

We shall shortly discuss this second postulated mechanism and will review the results of Peakall's next experimental series, in which he went ahead and "proved" that DDT does inhibit carbonic anhydrase. First, however, we want to summarize the enzyme induction matter.

DDT in sufficient concentrations does induce mixed-function oxidase enzymes in the liver. In this it resembles many other lipophilic compounds. In a recent study by Gielen and Nebert (1971) precise comparisons were made between the enzyme-inducing properties of a large number of different aromatic hydrocarbons, among them benz(o)pyrene, phenobarbital, and DDT. These investigators found that DDT was one of the least potent of the tested compounds — three times less effective as an inducer than phenobarbital, for example. The most powerful inducer was benz(o)pyrene — a naturally occuring substance known to be highly carcinogenic.

The maximum enzyme-induction effect with DDT was found to be at the 35.2 ppm level. Below 1 ppm, practically no induction could be shown. This would seem to indicate that with respect to the human population, where mean levels of circulating DDT are less than 0.03 ppm, we do not have to worry at all about these liver enzymes.

Where birds (or other test animals) are exposed through feeding experiments to high daily intakes of DDT, the liver will respond by producing these hydroxylating enzymes. Whether they, in turn, will alter steroid metabolism *in vivo* cannot be determined from the papers we have reviewed. However, even if they do so, the only relatively consistent finding which might be related to a disturbance in steroid hormone balance is delayed ovulation. Late breeding and delay in ovulation have also been reported in connection with PCBs; and in theory it is possible that a physiological change related to breeding time could be a secondary effect associated with any of the aromatic hydrocarbons which induce microsomal enzymes.* In any event, it is now agreed that the thin eggshells observed in the

---

* Although several authors have reported a few days of delay in ovulation among birds on high DDT or DDE diets, this can hardly be considered in itself as a cause of extensive reproductive failure. In most cases the same authors have shown that, by the end of the entire egg-laying period, even those experimental birds in which delayed ovulation was observed tend to catch up with the controls and to produce equal numbers of eggs in a slightly shortened time span.

wild—which are the most emphasized avian reproduction problem—cannot be explained in terms of this first mechanism of action.

In effect, there is even a chance that the induced enzymes might lead to thicker eggshells. It is known that certain polar metabolites of vitamin D mitigate calcium uptake from the intestine (Gray et al., 1971). These metabolites are formed by nonspecific hepatic enzymes. Since it is recognized that DDT can induce such enzymes, might it not be fruitful for someone to investigate whether DDT enhances calcification in the presence of adequate calcium supply? We are not really speculating that this is the case, but merely suggesting that such a hypothesis would be equally if not more logical than those which have been put forth with such certainty and pursued with such slipshod fervor by the environmentalists.

Now on to the next mode of action.

The Carbonic Anhydrase Hypothesis: Our Experts Meet Some Real Opposition

The second biochemical mechanism we wish to discuss is described by the panel in the following: "DDE has also been found to inhibit the enzyme carbonic anhydrase (Bitman, Cecil, and Fries, 1970; Peakall, 1970; Risebrough, Davis, and Anderson, forthcoming), essential for the deposition of calcium carbonate in the eggshell and for the maintenance of pH gradients across membranes, such as those in the shell gland. Inhibition of this enzyme by such drugs as sulfanilamide results in the production of thin-shelled eggs" (SCEP, 1970, p. 130).

Before we consider the two published papers which the panel cites as having demonstrated DDE inhibiton of carbonic anhydrase, a brief explanation of the functions of this enzyme and of what is known about its inhibitors is perhaps in order.

Carbonic anhydrase (CA) is a constitutive enzyme which is more or less ubiquitous in organisms throughout the plant and animal kingdom. Its major function is to speed up the process by which CO_2, one of the end products of cellular respiration, is hydrated. The chemical formula for this mechanism is the following:

$$CO_2 + H_2O \rightleftharpoons H_2CO_3$$

The carbonic acid (H_2CO_3) which results from the hydration of CO_2 will easily dissociate into a hydrogen ion (H^+) and a hydrocarbonate residue (HCO_3^-)

$$H_2CO_3 \rightleftharpoons H^+ + HCO_3^-$$

which residue is extremely important in maintaining the physiological homeostatic acid-base equilibrium in the body.

The process also works in reverse, as illustrated by the following homely example. When sodium bicarbonate is taken for heartburn, which one experiences because of an overproduction of hydrochloric acid in the stomach, the acid will be neutralized by the sodium to form sodium chloride (table salt), and the hydrocarbonate will dissociate to water and CO_2, which gas can then escape from the body by one or another familiar route: $HCl + NaHCO_3 \rightarrow NaCl + H_2O + CO_2$.

Maintenance of the acid-base balance is the major function of the carbonic anhydrase enzymes. But since they aid in the production of hydrocarbonates (hydrated CO_2) throughout the body, they also play an important role in making these residues available for calcification processes—bone building, shell formation, and so forth. The principal minerals of such calcified tissues are calcite and aragonite, and these are built through the coupling of calcium with carbonates. The speculation of the environmentalists relates to this role of carbonic anhydrase. Their reasoning is: if DDT should prove to be an inhibitor of CA enzymes, then the presence of the pesticide might block the process by which carbonates are made available at the site of shell formation, and in this way the very thin eggshells in nature might be explained. However, in pursuing this speculation, neither Peakall nor Bitman et al. appeared to have paid any attention to the extensive literature on the principal function of CA enzymes and on their known inhibitors.

In higher animals, a shift in the body's acid-base balance in the alkaline direction usually leads to diuresis, in order that the excess alkalinity may be excreted. Such a shift can also be produced artificially by the administration of agents which block carbonic anhydrase, and CA-inhibiting drugs are used in medical practice when it is therapeutically essential to induce diuresis. On account of the medical importance of CA inhibitors, and because of the very basic and vital physiological functions of the CA enzymes in general, the structural and functional relationships of those drugs that can inhibit CA have been thoroughly investigated.

Sulfanilamide, for example (the substance mentioned in the panel's final sentence on this second mechanism), is known to inhibit carbonic anhydrase, although its medical applications are primarily for other purposes. It has the following structure:

$$H_2NSO_2 \langle \rangle NH_2$$

Nierexone, which is a much more potent inhibitor of the enzyme, looks like this:

$$H_2NSO_2 \langle \rangle \underset{H}{C} \underset{H}{C} \langle \rangle SO_2NH_2$$

(Sulfanilamide may be thought of rather loosely as representing one-half of the Nierexone structure, and, indeed, its activity as a CA inhibitor is about 50 percent that of the latter drug.)

Here is the structure of DDE:

$$Cl \langle \rangle \underset{\underset{Cl - C - Cl}{|}}{C} \langle \rangle Cl$$

If this is now compared with the structure of Nierexone, it will be seen that there is a superficial resemblance between the two. DDE has two benzene rings connected by a carbon bridge, and at the end of each ring there is a chlorine atom. In Nierexone, one also sees two benzene rings, but instead of a chlorine atom, the so-called N-sulfamyl group ($-SO_2NH$) is found at the end of each of the rings. This same group may be seen on one side of the sulfanilamide structure, which does not resemble the DDE molecule, even superficially.

What is important about these structural pictures is that it has been for some time established that a compound will not be an effective inhibitor of CA unless the N-sulfamyl group is present. One may read, for example, in Goodman and Gilman's monumental work, *The Pharmacological Basis of Therapeutics*, "The most important structure-activity relationship is that, for all practical pur-

poses, carbonic anhydrase inhibitory activity is abolished by N-sulfamyl sub-
stitutions" (Goodman and Gilman, 1970, p. 859). This means that where the
$-SO_2NH_2$ group has been replaced on the compound by some other group, such
as the Cl atoms found in the DDE structure, there should be no CA inhibitory
activity. How was it then possible that the authors of these two papers, which
were cited as references for the panel's second major claim about how DDT
(or DDE) acts biochemically, *demonstrated* carbonic anhydrase inhibition with
DDE? Was the established view of the world's best biochemists in error? Had
the Bitman group and Peakall succeeded in showing that carbonic anhydrase
could be inhibited without the presence of the $-SO_2NH_2$ group?

On the basis alone of the fact that the structure of the DDE molecule
speaks against a CA-inhibitory function, it seemed to us unlikely that either
of these investigations was carried out in such a way as to demonstrate the claim,
since there is a measure of consistency in biochemical interactions which allows
for considerations of probability, even though these interactions are not quite
so tidy and controlled as those of forces in classical mechanics, for example.
Nevertheless, accepted scientific ideas are constantly being overthrown, and lack
of experience in a particular area of research does not preclude the possibility
that some young or previously unknown investigator might be responsible for
performing crucial work pointing to the inadequacy of accepted concepts. One
must therefore examine how Peakall and the Bitman group carried out their
proofs that DDE inhibits carbonic anhydrase.

It will be remembered that Peakall's dissatisfaction with the induced-enzyme
activity of DDT was that this mode of action could not account for the extremely
thin shells observed in the wild, which suggested to him some kind of sudden
and extreme interference with the calcification process during the period of
shell formation. In his report in *Science*, Peakall did not specify exactly why
he decided to test CA activity, but he did do so in a *Scientific American* article
which he published one month earlier: "Pesticides and the Reproduction of
Birds." There he wrote: ". . . if the pesticide produced an effect, it would be not on
the stored supply [of calcium] but on the delivery of calcium to the eggshell,
which as we have noted is laid down within 20 hours of the laying of the egg. And
with regard to delivery it was known that an enzyme, carbonic anhydrase, plays
an important role in making *calcium* available to the eggshell in the oviduct. One
could therefore look for a possible effect on the activity of this enzyme" (Peakall,
1970b, p.77; our emphasis). If one examines this explanation, it becomes evident
that Peakall's hypothesis rests on a false understanding of the role of CA in shell
formation. It is *not* the availability of calcium, but of carbonate, which is influ-

enced by the enzyme. Nevertheless, as we shall see shortly, Peakall was certain that he had found the clue to the biochemical effects of DDT metabolites in affected bird populations. The experimental series which he designed to test this hypothesis were reported in the same 1970 *Science* paper which we have already discussed in part.

Peakall's procedure was as follows. On the day before his female ringdoves were expected to lay their first egg, he injected one group of experimental birds (intraperitoneally) with 150 ppm DDE, and a second group with 30 ppm dieldrin. After the production of the clutch, these birds and three control females were sacrificed immediately and the oviducts removed for pesticide analysis and determination of CA activity. In the DDE series, he found an average of 76.9 ppm pesticide in the oviduct, and he reported a more than 60 percent reduction in CA activity compared with the controls. In the dieldrin series, 4.6 ppm was the mean residue in the gland, but there was no significant reduction of CA activity. Those parts of his conclusions which relate to CA activity were very definite and confident. He wrote: ". . . carbonic anhydrase activity was markedly reduced in the oviducts of birds receiving DDE but were [sic] unaffected by dieldrin. Thus, a relation of eggshell weight to carbonic anhydrase activity has been established. The inhibition of carbonic anhydrase could explain the extremely thin eggshells found in California. Inhibition of this enzyme would prevent utilization of calcium in the oviduct even though the bird was otherwise in normal calcium balance" (Peakall, 1970a, p. 594).

The 1970 study of Bitman, Cecil, and Fries—"DDT-Induced Inhibition of Avian Shell Gland Carbonic Anhydrase: A Mechanism for Thin Eggshells"— appeared in the same issue of *Science* as the Peakall paper, although from all indications the investigations were independent of each other. The authors begin by citing the feeding experiments of Heath et al., Porter and Wiemeyer, and themselves as having confirmed the correlative evidence of Ratcliffe and of Hickey and Anderson "that DDT and related organochlorine compounds decrease eggshell thickness" (Bitman et al., 1970, p. 594). This kind of opener is part of what we like to call the "it-has-been-shown" pattern, standard in scientific papers, but which on this particular subject—in view of the fact that it has *not* been shown—may be said to be equally if not more problematic than the supposed "raptor-pesticide-thin-eggshell" syndrome. They also cite the work of Keller (1952) as supporting evidence that DDT inhibits bovine erythrocyte (red blood cell) carbonic anhydrase, even though several attempts to repeat Keller's work have yielded negative results.

In investigating CA activity in the avian shell gland, Bitman and his coworkers used Japanese quail to which they fed 100 ppm p,p'-DDT or 100 ppm p,p'

DDE for three months. In addition to these massive dosages, half the experimental birds were fed a low calcium diet (0.6 percent calcium), while the other half received the pesticides together with a diet adequate in calcium (2.5 percent). By the time the authors got around to making up the two tables in which they summarized their results, they had apparently forgotten about this variable, because the data were reported only in terms of three groups: controls, birds fed p,p'-DDT. and birds fed p,p'-DDE. As a consequence, it is impossible to evaluate the averages represented in the tables because one cannot tell what the relative effects of the calcium stress situation might have been. In this experiment, Bitman's group improved on the design of their earlier investigation (see page 413), but their failure to show data which reflect effects of all the experimental variables obliges us again to point out that these results are meaningless — especially those relating to calcium content.

With respect to the matter of CA inhibition per se, these authors have a better theoretical grasp of the possible role of the enzyme in shell formation than Peakall, and, at the same time, their concluding statements are much less dramatic and sweeping than his.

> Treatment with DDT results in decreased CA activity in the avian shell gland. This demonstration in vitro does not preclude normal functioning of the CA enzymatic machinery in the intact tissue in vivo. Under the conditions of our experiments, however, the percentage declines in shell gland CA activity were 16 to 19 percent, amounts which could account for observed decreases in eggshell thickness of 10 to 15 percent in birds treated with DDT or DDE. The limitation by carbonic anhydrase of carbonate ions needed for the deposition of the calcium carbonate of the shell could provide the mechanism by which chlorinated hydrocarbons affect eggshell thickness. (Bitman et al., 1970, p. 595)

The authors' qualifications are important, for it is indeed uncertain whether this apparent inhibition of CA *in vitro* (in their experiments carried out on oviduct and blood of birds sacrificed 6 to 8 hours before oviposition) has anything at all to do with what goes on in living birds, particularly at exposure concentrations in nature, which in the worst imaginable circumstances would not even approximate a continuous intake of 100 ppm DDT daily for three months, nor the sudden impact of an intraperitoneal injection of 150 ppm the day before egg laying. Nevertheless, if one considers the psychology of environmental scientists who are fighting to achieve a ban on DDT, it is not difficult to understand why they would accept these two papers as important demonstrations of how DDT acts on the biochemical level to cause thin eggshells. In the first place, they are sure that DDT is the causal agent; they never seem to be bothered much by considerations like the improbability of the chemical structure of the molecule as a CA inhibitor; and they do not appear inclined to examine the publications of their colleagues for technical and methodological flaws, nor even to inquire whether the data support the conclusions.

At the time of the SCEP deliberations, these two papers had been in print for only two or three months, and had not yet been challenged. In 1971, however, two refutations appeared, and we feel it is appropriate to turn to them in discussing what is wrong with these studies, since the authors of both rebuttals are specialists on the particular subject in question.

We have already mentioned that most of the publications dealing with DDT's effects on birds have never been scrutinized or criticized with care. This is not a very happy reflection on the state of affairs in science, but it can be in part explained by the fact that most scientists assume that editorial review and screening by referees will eliminate poor material from at least the better journals, and in addition, by the probability that those skeptical types who are inclined to pore over fine print have not been much interested in reports about a few birds laying thin-shelled eggs. The bird problem in the wild and the papers on DDT and avian reproduction have simply not drawn much attention from scientists except for those specifically involved in the DDT battle on one side or the other.

However, on occasion, a study of DDT and avian reproductive problems does encounter some strong critical opposition, especially where the environmentalists have attempted experimental work which is completely out of their areas of competence. This is apparently what happened with the inhibition-of-carbonic-anhydrase hypothesis, which elicited a strongly worded rebuttal in the spring of 1971 by Dvorchik, Istin, and Maren.

The abstract of their paper, which is called "Does DDT Inhibit Carbonic Anhydrase?", reads as follows: "At a concentration of 50 to 100 micrograms per milliliter, p,p'-DDT (and p,p'-DDE) did not inhibit the rate of hydration or dehydration of carbon dioxide by carbonic anhydrase. At concentrations greater than 500 micrograms per milliliter, partial inhibition of the rate of dehydration of carbonic acid was observed, but this involved precipitation of drug in the reaction vessel. This degree of inhibition suggests that DDT may not inhibit carbonic anhydrase effectively at the usual concentrations found in tissue after exposure of organisms to DDT in the environment" (Dvorchik et al., 1971, p. 728).

In the body of the article, the authors mention the work of Peakall and Bitman and immediately raise two major objections to the meaningfulness of their

studies. On the one hand they state that even if the experiments really demonstrated 18 (Bitman et al.) or 60 (Peakall) percent inhibition of CA, this is not
enough inhibition to be physiologically significant. To put it another way, an
enzyme inhibitor that would actually interfere with the carbonate availability
at the site of shell building would have to cause at least 90 percent blocking,
and it would also have to be more or less continuously present in the circulating
blood; otherwise the CA function would be rapidly restored, since carbonic anhydrase is a constitutive enzyme which is continuously synthesized. The brief comment of these authors on this subject of the difference between an observed
percentage of inhibition of the enzyme and blocking of the physiological functions of that enzyme is a polite way of saying that Peakall and the Bitman group
apparently do not understand some of the fundamentals of enzymology.

Their second critical comment has to do with methodology. They suggest
that, if one is going to do an *in vitro* study of CA inhibition, it cannot be carried
out with a homogenate of the oviduct containing both pesticide and enzyme,
since such an analysis "dilutes and distorts the original relation" (*ibid.*, p. 729).
In other words, they are here referring to plain bad technique.

Dvorchik et al. then go on to report their own recent *in vitro* studies of the
effects of DDT on carbonic anhydrase. They attempted once again to repeat
the 1952 work of Keller on bovine CA, but their results were negative. They
found no inhibition of human red-blood-cell CA when DDT and DDE were added
to an incubation vessel, dissolved in appropriate solvents, with final concentrations of 50 to 85 μg/ml (ppm). They further noted that even when the pesticide
was added in a solvent, some precipitation of the drug occurred at concentrations
above 50 ppm.

In experiments with higher amounts, some "apparent inhibition" was observed between 500 to 2,000 μg/ml. However, the precipitation factor led them
to state, "Further clarification is required because of solubility difficulties in
the *in vitro* system" (*ibid.*). In effect, the authors are raising a question analogous
to the one we raised in connection with the algal photosynthesis experiments:
Is the observed apparent inhibition—which does not even become significant
until one reaches concentrations well over 500 ppm—the result of a genuine
biochemical interaction, or is it an artifact produced by a *physical* process—i.e.,
precipitation of the pesticide?

They end by suggesting that further investigations should be pursued which
would entail direct—*in vivo*—observations of the possible inhibition of the enzyme in the shell glands of birds. They also note, however, that "no case has yet
arisen in tissues of the vertebrate kingdom in which carbonic anhydrase inhibition by known drugs has been greater than that found against the enzyme in

red cells" (*ibid.*). This means that a proper *in vitro* experiment—or one in which known quantities of a suspected CA inhibitor are added in solution to an incubation vessel containing red blood cells—should give a sufficient answer to the question of whether or not the compound is a true CA inhibitor, since the blocking activity of the known CA inhibitors has never been observed to be greater in tissues (like the oviduct) than it is against the CA of red blood cells.

Although some of the environmentalists opposing DDT have wisely dropped the whole carbonic-anhydrase-inhibition hypothesis, Bitman, and perhaps others too, were apparently too solidly committed to it by the time the Dvorchik publication appeared to yield quietly to the opinion of the specialists. During the Consolidated DDT Hearings, when asked about prior testimony by Maren and about the article of Dvorchik et al., Dr. Bitman explained why he could not agree with the opinions expressed in the paper: "Dr. Maren's* paper is very brief. It gives no data and no facts, except that he disagrees with our work. I'm very surprised that *Science* published this paper" (Bitman, 1972, p. 6034).

Now it is true that the article by Dvorchik et al. does not present data in the form of a table, although it is certainly not true that it contains no facts. However, if the matter of "surprise" over what is published in *Science* is at issue, we remind the reader that in the last of the publications by Bitman and his coworkers which we analyzed (see pages 456–457), the authors duly included tables supposedly expressing their findings, but these were without meaning, since they did not record the data in terms of the original experimental design. One can, to be sure, understand Bitman's pique at the appearance of the article by Dvorchik and his coworkers, since these authors' irritation at having to bother to work up a rebuttal was only rather thinly disguised beneath correct scientific language.

Looking at it from the other side, however, we can understand even more readily why Maren's group may have been irritated. There is, these days, a great deal of loud wailing about the dangers of narrow specialization, the inability of specialists to see the forest for the trees, and so on. Sometimes these complaints have a point, but it ought to be remembered that the accomplished specialist usually does know a thing or two about his area of expertise and may be quite justifiably annoyed when scientists who have never before worked in the area in question perform inept experiments, betray their ignorance of basic long-established concepts, and spread inconclusive results around like proud schoolboys. Part of the problem of evaluating the tone of some of the refutations, rebuttals, and even letters to the editor which one encounters from time to time in connection with environmental questions stems from the fact that the old

---

* Although Maren was listed as the third author of the article, his reputation as one of the world's authorities on carbonic anhydrase may have accounted for Bitman calling it "Dr. Maren's paper."

standards of publication and the referee system seem no longer to be operating effectively. If, for example, the Peakall paper (1970a) and the 1970 article by Bitman et al. had been sent out for review to an enzymologist, or specifically to a specialist in carbonic anhydrase, it is almost certain that these studies would not have been passed for publication. By the same token, if an authority on single-celled algae had reviewed Wurster's manuscript treating experiments on DDT and algal photosynthesis, he would have quickly realized that the report in question evidenced little knowledge of the physiology, morphology, and taxonomy of the organisms studied. It would have been equally apparent to such a reviewer that the assumption of pesticide absorption through the cell walls was based on the false notion that these contain lipoproteins. It, too, would probably have been refused for publication, thus avoiding a great deal of unnecessary hysteria about the death of the ocean, oxygen depletion, and other nonsense, as well as obviating the necessity for strongly worded rebuttals after the fact.

Apparently what is happening at the present time is that journals using the referee system are sending out papers dealing with DDT "effects" to persons who have established reputations as being concerned with DDT "effects." This merely perpetuates the "closed body of experts" situation, and does not aid in maintaining the quality of the literature. In fact, things have gone so far that the DDT experts have managed to eliminate most witnesses in the legal proceedings regarding DDT registrations who have not worked directly with the pesticide; and they have quite frequently reacted in a most unprofessionally petulant manner to perfectly legitimate criticisms of their work by other scientists. We can only conclude that it is in the interests of good science that those who really have some expertise in a field should occasionally abandon the gentlemanly ethics to which they have been trained and attack these weak publications on whatever grounds will best bring home the point, even if this means insinuations of incompetence.

In any event, to return to the matter of carbonic anhydrase and thin eggshells, Bitman's complaint that the Dvorchik paper was brief and had no data tables does not apply to the second refutation of the CA inhibition claims. This publication—the work of Pocker, Beug, and Ainardi (1971) of the University of Washington's Department of Chemistry—is replete with tables, graphs, and methodological details. Since we have been talking about the value of experience in a special field, it may be remarked that Pocker has made some notable contributions to a broadening of the contemporary understanding of carbonic anhydrase functions.

After expressing their concern about the numerous reports suggesting that DDT and its metabolites in high concentrations may inhibit CA in birds and other animals, the authors state:

> We now report that our kinetic studies lead us to the conclusion that DDT, DDE, and dieldrin are not true inhibitors of CA action as is currently believed. We have demonstrated that these pesticides have the ability, *when added in excess of their solubility limit,* to occlude small amounts of CA from solution during the course of crystal formation. The precipitate containing the enzyme does not catalyze CO_2 hydration. Nevertheless, active enzyme can be recovered from the precipitate, proving that the observed "inhibition" is purely an interface phenomenon arising from removal of enzyme from solution.
>
> Specific effects of various inhibitors of the CA-catalyzed hydration of CO_2 have been studied with both anions and sulfonamides. We have extended these studies to DDT, DDE, and dieldrin and found no inhibition of bovine CA activity up to their respective solubility limits. However, these chlorinated pesticides are very insoluble in pure water . . . and, when introduced in excess of their solubility limits with the help of an organic co-solvent, they slowly form a precipitate or suspension that occludes erythrocyte CA from the test solution and induces an apparent "inhibition." (Pocker, et al., 1971, p. 1337; our emphasis)

It seems to us that these paragraphs need no further clarification, and that they explain adequately what happened in the experiments of Peakall and Bitman, as well as in the earlier work of Keller (1952). We should like also to cite part of the conclusion of these authors, however, since it expresses a wise warning about future work on the chlorinated hydrocarbons, which, even if not heeded by the environmentalists, might aid skeptical readers in evaluating some of their experimental work. "In conclusion, when the effects of compounds such as DDT, DDE, and dieldrin, where a very low solubility in water is encountered, are being studied one must be alert to a number of biochemical and physiological consequences that arise from a purely physical action of precipitation and occlusion" (*ibid.*, p. 1338). To date, that is pretty well all there is to say about the hypothesis that DDT or DDE are CA inhibitors, and that it is by blocking this enzyme that they lead to the laying of thin-shelled eggs.

Thicker Eggshells

The third of the postulated mechanisms we wish to discuss is something of a separate issue, involving some slightly embarrassing results which are not too often mentioned by the American bird researchers. The panel writes: "Birds may also show symptoms of hyperthyroidism when fed a chlorinated hydrocarbon" (Jeffries, 1969; Jeffries and French, 1969)" (SCEP, 1973, p. 131).

Jeffries and French are British researchers associated with the Monks Wood Experimental Station. Jeffries' first paper is entitled "Induction of Apparent

Hyperthyroidism in Birds Fed DDT" (1969). The word "apparent" in the title is important, as we shall see shortly.

Jeffries fed p,p'-DDT to 102 Bengalese finches for about nine weeks: six weeks before pairing and during the breeding period. The three-dose rates for the females are given as 50, 50 to 100, and 100 to 300 μg/day; but since the average weight of the adult birds is not given, we cannot express these quantities in terms of parts per million. It may be generally stated, however, that even though Bengalese finches are not very big, these dosages are quite modest, at least in comparison with those of Bitman, for instance.

The emphasis in the paper is on the weight of the eggs and their shells. The author states that "The weight of an egg is correlated with the order of laying as successive eggs laid in a clutch tend to be progressively heavier (Jeffries, 1969, p. 578)."* He found that this general rule applied to the eggs of both control and dosed birds. However, the dosed birds tended to lay lighter eggs, which had, at the same time, proportionately *heavier and thicker* shells. The medium-dose group, for example, laid eggs which were 9 percent lighter in total weight than the controls, but had proportionately about 13 percent heavier shells.

At the end of his paper, Jeffries writes that this finding of heavier eggshells "does not at first sight seem to support Ratcliffe's theory that organochlorines may have caused the thinner eggshells of the peregrine and sparrowhawk . . ." (*ibid.*, p. 579). He adds, however, that if DDT does affect avian calcium metabolism by acting on the thyroid-stimulating-hormone-thyroxine balance, this could have different effects in different species of birds.

We hasten to point out here that our objection to the eggshell thickness measurements in the American papers we discussed in the last chapter does not apply to Jeffries' results, because he did not attempt direct measurements with a micrometer. His method was to weigh the whole egg on the day of laying, freeze those eggs of which the shells were to be measured at $-20°$ C, remove the shells, dry them for seven days at room temperature, weigh them, and calculate the percentage of shell weight to total egg weight. This *can* be done mechanically, since scales are available which are accurate for measurements in the milligram range involved; and his method avoids both interference from friction or compression factors, as well as variability due to humidity.

It is a pity that none of the Americans performing feeding experiments attempted to use this method, at least for comparison with their micrometer mea-

---

* This statement is in direct contradiction to the report of Bitman et al. (1970), which we discussed in Chapter 15, p. 415. They had claimed that the eggs of a clutch tend to become successively lighter and lighter. However, an analysis of their data and the replotting of their regression lines (see Figure 6, p. 414) does not bear out their claim. On the contrary, their data are in good agreement with Jeffries' observation mentioned above; only their generalizations and the representation of their own data are in contradiction.

surements, for as it is we are left in the dark on the question of whether the differing results reported by them are a reflection of species-dependent responses or are merely artifacts resulting from a poor measuring technique. Jeffries' technique cannot, of course, be used on blown museum eggs. But it could have been applied to the eggs of Porter and Wiemeyer's experimental kestrels—said to be closely related to the peregrine falcon—and one might then have had some better way of judging whether the eggshell thinning observed in the wild and that reported for peregrine museum eggs bears any relation to DDT exposure.

Jeffries was led to postulate that a hyperthyroid effect might have been induced in his dosed birds precisely because it is known that feeding thyreoprotein to domestic hens causes them to lay lighter eggs, with heavier, thicker shells. He proceeded to examine several other parameters in his treated birds which might be expressive of a hyperthyroid state: the relation of heart weight to brain weight, loss of body weight, and so on. The findings were either negative or the r values too low to be statistically meaningful, and this probably accounts for the word "apparent" in his title.

A few months later, Jeffries published, together with M. C. French, the second paper cited by the SCEP panel: "Avian Thyroid: Effect of p,p'-DDT on Size and Activity" (1969).

The abstract of the paper reads: "Feeding sublethal amounts of p,p'-DDT to pigeons caused an increase in thyroid weight and a reduction in colloid content of the follicles. This may reflect a hyper- or hypo-functioning gland and may be connected with recent reductions in eggshell weights in wild birds. The effect was accompanied by increased liver weight" (Jeffries and French, 1969, p. 1278). From the title and the abstract, it is clear that the authors are no longer speculating about an apparent or possible effect. Even though they are not certain whether the "effect" represents a hyper- or hypothyroid picture, the increase in thyroid weight and the reduction of colloid area in the thyroid are said to have been "caused" by feeding sublethal quantities of DDT. The only thing left to speculation is whether the effect on thyroid activity is connected with the thin eggshells observed in wild birds.

In many respects this is the most elegant of all the papers on the biochemical effects of DDT written by environmentalists. It is well expressed; the mathematics appear to be correct; the figures are legible. The investigation involved some rather elaborate techniques and sophisticated equipment, such as a Quantimet image-analyzer computer, which was used to count and measure particles showing image contrast on microscopic sections of the thyroid glands. However, there are two major problems with this study, insofar as the authors claim to have demonstrated a cause-and-effect relationship between the administration of the drug and the abnormalities they observed in the thyroid glands of dosed birds. Both difficulties derive from the overly small size of the groups of experimental animals.

The investigators used homing pigeons *(Lonchura striata)*, force-feeding three groups of experimental birds 18, 36, and 72 ppm DDT every other day for 42 days. Each of these experimental groups consisted of four birds, with six in the control. The mean body burden of the pesticide during the course of the whole experiment was calculated to be 381, 765, and 1,517 mg/kg for the low-, medium-, and high-dosage groups respectively. Although none of the birds died, the high dosage may have been barely sublethal, since one of the birds began to exhibit tremors on the thirtieth day, and the DDT and DDE residues in the livers and brains were exceedingly high at the end of the experiment.

After the pigeons were sacrificed, brain, liver, and thyroid were weighed. Pesticide concentrations of brain and liver were determined, and microscopic sections of the thyroid glands were prepared. Measurements of the extension of the colloid areas in the thyroid, which are an expression of its activity, constituted the most complex part of the experiment, and considerable emphasis is placed on these results in the text of the article.

According to the authors, the control birds all "showed follicles containing colloid quantities within normal limits," which are shown in their table as ranging from 42,480 μ^2 to 145,800 μ^2. Furthermore, they make a big point of the fact that one of the birds in the *low* treatment group had a mean colloid area of only 2,700 μ^2. They write: "Because the liver content of this bird was only 11.4 ppm of p,p'-DDT . . . it seems likely that even the low 'background' quantities found in wild birds could have an effect on thyroid activity" *(ibid.,* pp. 1279–1280).

We do wish that Jeffries and French had refrained from making this comment, for we are now obliged to point out that it is a most unsound practice to make a sweeping generalization on the basis of *one bird*. Were it meaningful to do so, one could completely reverse their argument in the following way. Examination of the data shows that there is at least one bird in each of the dosed groups with a colloid area from 10 to 20 times that of the bird they singled out. In the medium- and high-treatment groups the liver concentrations of DDT are about 60 and 160 ppm, respectively. Furthermore, at the low and medium dosage, at least one of the treated birds shows a more extensive colloid area than the low range of the controls, which was described as "normal." On this basis, if one is permitted to use individual birds to establish a connection with conditions in the wild, one could say that even very high circulating DDT concentrations are unlikely to cause any effect on the thyroid gland, as shown by the well-developed colloid areas.

A much more sensible explanation for the anomalously small colloid area of this single bird in the low-treatment group is that it was sick before the onset of the experiment.

The use of very small sample sizes often gives rise to other problems which can invalidate an experiment, even when one gets something that appears to be an "effect." If, for instance, the experiment is designed to test the effects of one variable in increasing or decreasing quantities (as is here the case, where different dosages of the same drug are involved), it is a fundamental requirement for meaningful interpretation that the results corresponding to each level of the tested variable should be discrete. Another way of putting this is that the measurements of the parameters observed in the target organism must yield values which do not overlap from one dosage level to another, if one is going to claim that the results are caused by the administration of the drug. If these values do overlap, then it becomes evident that something was wrong in the planning or execution of the experiment, or it may be that the apparent effects are unrelated to the variable being tested.

Jeffries and French claimed that one effect of DDT feeding was an increase in thyroid weight, which is most accurately expressed, according to them, as a percentage of brain weight. We have taken the results for this parameter from their Table 1 and plotted these in Figures 11 and 12, seen on page 468. In Figure 11 the total bar represents the range of variability for each of the four groups (control and three experimental), with the means shown as heavy cross lines. In Figure 12, the means and the calculated standard deviations are expressed.

Ordinarily, when means and standard deviations have been calculated, the graphs or plots showing the data visually would be expressed only in terms of these calculations. However, attention has to be called to the fact that these researchers are dealing with groups of only four birds, and within each group there are tremendous ranges on most of the observed parameters, in some cases apparently due to one bird. In such a situation the calculation of means is more than a little suspect. It is rather like measuring the height of four adult persons, one of whom is a midget, and then expressing their average height as 4 feet 7 inches (or 132 cm). The result would not be a very meaningful indication of how tall the individual members of the sample actually were. To calculate standard deviations based on means of four such widely separated figures is even less meaningful, although it is known to be a good technique for "data improvement." On the other hand, the correct way to find out if the parameters measured for the different dosages are really discrete is to increase the number of animals in the experiment.

If one looks at the two figures we have drawn, it will be seen that in the first, Figure 11, there is a continuous overlap from one group to the next, beginning with the control in relation to the low-dosage group, and also seen between the middle- and the high-dosage group. The proper interpretation of such results is that the experiment has not shown discretely measurable results. When the same data are drawn on the basis of the means $\pm$ the standard deviation, as in Figure 12, one discrete change appears between the low- and the medium-dosage groups. Even when the data are represented in this manner, however, the overlaps between control–low-treatment and middle–high-treatment groups should be taken as an indication that something is amiss, since the experimental results do not indicate a dose-response relationship.

The data of Jeffries and French must be described as preliminary results, which cannot in any respect be said to have demonstrated a causal relationship between DDT administration and disturbed thyroid function. The paper is well written, and the technical aspects of the experiment appear to have been carried out with considerable care. The use of such a small number of experimental animals was, however, a serious error in planning, and it is unfortunate that the authors published the work and drew from it unwarranted conclusions before extending their studies to larger samples.

Out of Context

The fourth and last mode of action of DDT which we are going to discuss is actually the first one mentioned in the panel's summary of the compound's biochemical effects. We have left it to the last principally because it is the only mechanism where the main supporting reference cited deals with a subject most pertinent to a review of DDT's biological activity—i.e., how it kills insects or other organisms exposed to lethal quantities. Strange as it may seem—in the light of the extensive arguments and complicated changes of stance among the environmentalists on the subject of how DDT acts on nontarget organisms in chronic, sublethal quantities—thirty years of research has still not yielded a complete answer to the question of how it kills insects! One can, to be sure, learn from Rachel Carson or Charles Wurster that DDT is a "nerve poison," but had they been asked to define precisely what they meant by this vague term, neither of these authorities would have been able to clarify, since the biochemists who have been studying and elucidating this problem for decades have not yet completely defined the mode of action of the compound on the molecular level.

Here are the words with which the panel attempts to demystify the problem:

> In affecting nerves, chlorinated hydrocarbons, including DDE, are believed to block the ion transport process by inhibiting ATPase (an enzyme, otherwise called myosin)

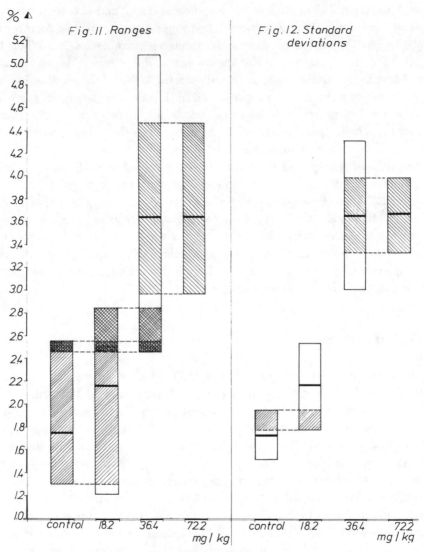

Figures 11 and 12. *PLOTS OF DATA OF JEFFRIES AND FRENCH (1969),*
SHOWING THYROID WEIGHT EXPRESSED AS PERCENTAGE OF BRAIN WEIGHT.
(Solid cross lines = means; dashed cross lines = limits of overlapping areas.)

in the nerve membrane that causes the required energy to be made available (Matsumura and Patil, 1969). Transport of ionic calcium across membranes such as those
in the shell gland of birds is also an energy-requiring process dependent upon membrane ATPase (Skou, 1965). Inhibition of these enzymes by DDE could account for

the concentration-effect curves obtained for shell thickness and DDE concentration in eggs of the brown pelican . . . (SCEP, 1970, p. 130)

Now, if one has some familiarity with scientific jargon, but not a very extensive knowledge of enzymology, one would assume that this rather complicated statement was meant to convey the following:

1. There is an enzyme—ATPase, also referred to as myosin—which plays a role in carrying the calcium ion across cell membranes.

2. Chlorinated hydrocarbons, including DDE, have been shown by Matsumura and Patil in 1969 to block this particular enzyme.

3. Skou also demonstrated, in 1965, that calcium ion transport across membranes is dependent upon membrane ATPase.

4. The blocking of this enzyme by DDE in the shell glands of birds could be the cause of the thin eggshells observed among brown pelicans.

All of this sounds, at first, rather convincing, and the two cited references are reports of solid experimental work. However, on closer consideration it becomes apparent that there are just as many problems with this "hypothesis" as with the three other modes of action which have already been discussed. The most serious difficulty is that neither of the papers referred to actually demonstrates what the panel is citing them as substantiating.

In order to get a better understanding of this fourth proposed mechanism and why it is improbable, we should like to consider some concepts regarding the transport of different ions across membranes and within cells.

It was thought earlier that ions can enter cells from the interstitium (virtual intercellular spaces and/or circulating body fluids) merely through passive diffusion; but this idea is no longer accepted as a general principle. If diffusion through a semipermeable membrane such as a cell membrane were completely passive, the diffusion process ought to lead rapidly to an equilibrium concentration of any particular ion within and outside of the cell. However, this is seldom the case. Ions quite frequently migrate against a concentration gradient (tend to move from an area of low concentration into one of higher concentration), and once this was recognized, the idea of *active ion transport* was advanced. In order to explain this phenomenon of ions moving against concentration gradients— which is more or less analogous to swimming against a current—the concept of special enzymes which perform a "pumping function" was put forth. For some specific ions, those enzymes which serve as pumps have been at least partially characterized; for others, they have not yet been described. Thus, when one speaks about the "sodium pump," one means the enzyme of which the function is to carry sodium ions across cell membranes. It is also pertinent to mention that these pump enzymes are thought to be membrane-bound.

Let us now consider ATP and ATPase. ATP stands for adenosinetriphosphate. This is a ubiquitous molecule in which high amounts of energy are chemically stored in the –P–O–P– (pyrophosphate) bonds. There are three such phosphate bonds in the ATP molecule, each liberating energy when split, which energy is then utilized for various life functions of the cells. The enzymes which split these phosphate bonds are called ATPases.

Prior to the 1960s, the *intracellular* protein myosin had been isolated from muscle cells; but it was only later that it was recognized as one of the enzymes belonging to the ATPase group. When the functions of myosin were investigated, it was found that the contractile protein of the muscle fibrils (actin) shrinks in the presence of adenosinetriphosphate, myosin, and magnesium ions. The result of this reaction is a complex of the enzyme and the protein: actomyosin + adenosinediphosphate (ADP). The energy needed for the process of muscle contraction is supplied by the breaking of the pyrophosphate bond, when ATP loses one of its phosphates and becomes ADP. Only fairly recently has it been shown that it is myosin which acts on the pyrophosphate bond in the muscle contraction process.

The awareness that calcium and some other ions are necessary both for muscle contraction and nerve conductance is not new. However, the idea that certain ATPase enzymes play a role in making these ions available to appropriate cells has been understood for less than a decade. The importance of the 1965 Skou paper cited by the panel is that he there described a differentiation among at least three groups of ATPases. He also *speculated* that these enzymes might be involved in active ion transport; but his publication cannot be said to have demonstrated the specific claim for which the panel cites his work: "Transport of ionic calcium across membranes such as those in the shell glands of birds is . . . an energy-requiring process dependent upon membrane ATPase." Skou did *not* show, as the panel implies, that any of the ATPases—much less specifically myosin—is a pump enzyme.

In referring to the 1969 work of Matsumura and Patil, the panel also grossly distorted what these two researchers actually demonstrated in their experiments. In the first place, attention should be brought to what it was they were investigating. The purpose of their experiments was to find out more about how DDT kills insects. They were not in the least concerned about the supposed chronic, sublethal effects of either DDT or DDE.

Matsumura and Patil wrote: "There are at least three different groups of adenosinetriphosphatases existing in the nervous system: $Na^+K^+Mg^{2+}$-adenosinetriphosphatases. . .; Mg^{2+} Ca^{2+}—or contractile—adenosinetriphosphatases. . . ; and Mg^{2+}-adenosinetriphosphatases. The former two enzymes may take part in the mechanism of ion transport in the nervous system" (Matsumura and Patil, 1969, p. 121).

It seems clear from this that they are merely stating their recognition that there are at least three groups of ATPase enzymes, two of which *may* play a role in ion transport. Myosin is a synonym for the second group only; it is definitely localized *within* the cell, and has nothing to do with ion transport *across* cell membranes.[*]

The experiments they performed had to do with the inhibitory activity of DDT and DDE on the first and the second of these ATPase enzymes. In separate *in vitro* preparations involving the effects of DDT and DDE on both enzymes, Matsumura and Patil's principal finding was that *DDT* is capable of blocking the first enzyme in relatively low concentrations, given the proper temperature conditions. This enzyme ($Na^+K^+Mg^{2+}$–ATPase) has been said to be involved in the transport of sodium, potassium, and magnesium. It was, however, never claimed to be involved in calcium transport, the latter function having been ascribed by some to the second enzyme ($Mg^{2+}Ca^{2+}$-ATPase).

Their next finding was that DDE could only effectively block this first enzyme in concentrations 1,000 times higher than those at which DDT was an inhibitor. This led them to presume that DDT may kill insects by blocking the first of the ATPase enzymes. When, in effect, the function of this enzyme is blocked, the magnesium ions essential both for nerve conductance and muscle contraction will not be available to the cells. Severe tremors followed by contracture are typical for organisms where magnesium is unavailable at the cellular level. Since DDT in toxic dosages is known to cause tremors and contractures, this assumption on the part of Matsumura and Patil seemed to be at least theoretically not unreasonable.

Their third finding was that although both DDT and DDE were capable of inhibiting the second enzyme (the one supposedly involved in calcium transport *within* cells), the concentrations needed were of the same order as those of DDE which could block the first enzyme—i.e., three orders of magnitude

---

[*] For the benefit of the record, one may detail the understanding about myosin's location. From the time of its isolation in the 1940s the intracellular localization of myosin was accepted. Its discovery in microtubules (Adelman et al., 1968), in the mitotic apparatus (Wilson, 1969), and in other cellular organelles cast serious doubts on the possiblity that it might be located in the cell membrane, which would be necessary if either the $Na^+K^+Mg^{2+}$– or the $Mg^{2+}Ca^{2+}$–ATPases were indeed functioning as "pump enzymes." In 1972, Gibbons and Gibbons removed the cell membrane from individual sperm cells by Triton® and found no change in the ATPase activity of the spermia. The results of this experiment make the whole matter of any further claims identifying ATPases with "pump enzymes" extremely questionable.

higher than the amount of DDT required to inhibit the first enzyme. The rather obvious implication of these data is that the organism would probably be long dead from DDT poisoning before the DDE metabolite could exert any inhibitory effect on the calcium carrying ATPase.

Finally, Matsumura and Patil demonstrated, *in vitro,* what has long been suspected from *in vivo* observations—that DDT effects show an inverse relation to temperature. For instance, the quantity of DDT which will cause 100 percent inhibition of the $Na^+ K^+ Mg^{2+}$-ATPase at a temperature of $13\,^\circ C$ produces only 10 percent inhibition at $37\,^\circ C$, and practically no blocking at all at $42\,^\circ C$. This means that exposure to DDT will not seriously affect man, whose normal body temperature is $37\,^\circ C$, and should have even less effect on birds, with body temperatures of around $42\,^\circ C$. It may also explain why DDT does not seem to be destructive to bees, for although most arthropods have low body temperatures, bees constitute a major exception. These quite vital conclusions of Matsumura and Patil's work are completely ignored by the panel.

The concluding statement of the panel's summary of this fourth mechanism of action of DDT and DDE—that the myosin-blocking action of DDE in the shell glands of birds may be the cause of the thin eggshells observed among brown pelicans—certainly does not follow from the work of the authors referred to. Even if one grants, as most environmentalists now claim, that birds at the top of a food chain are consuming in their prey primarily DDE rather than DDT, the dose-response curve characteristic for the inhibition of constitutive enzymes does *not* support the relationship postulated by the panel. There are solid reasons why Dvorchik et al. stated flatly in their rebuttal of the CA inhibition hypothesis that even 60 percent inhibition of that enzyme would be without physiological significance. On the basis of the general kinetics of enzyme inhibition, one may also say that *partial* inhibition of the $Mg^{2+}Ca^{2+}$-ATPase in the cells of birds— even in the shell gland—would not result in the laying of thin-shelled eggs. On the other hand, were enough DDE taken in by the bird to cause 90 percent or more inhibition of this enzyme for prolonged periods, the bird would undoubtedly die, leaving no eggs at all for the enthusiastic shell-measurers. Thus we see that the last and currently most favored "explanation" of how chronic exposure to metabolites of DDT leads to thin-shelled eggs is no more probable than any of the others, and it certainly has not been proven experimentally by anybody.

Who Believes in What Claim?

If the reader is thoroughly confused by now about these biochemical "effects," there is no cause for despair. Our experts are confused, too, and there is not much substance left to any of these claims, even in the inner circles of environ-

mental activists. Just to give an idea of the rapid "tacking" which has characterized their explanations, let us run down a brief chronological summary of who
said what when.

1967 Peakall postulates induction of nonspecific hepatic enzymes and subsequent steroid disturbance as the cause of the thin shells.

1968 Risebrough, Peakall, and Co. accept this mechanism, and show that PCBs
are five times more effective in inducing liver enzymes than DDT or DDE.

1969 Anderson, Hickey, Risebrough, and Co. claim that in addition to enzyme
induction, inhibition of CA is a further probable mode of action accounting
for thin shells.

1969 Jeffries "shows" that thyroid imbalance arises in birds fed DDT, which
interferes with calcium metabolism. Unfortunately, however, this particular imbalance seems to lead to thicker eggshells.

1970 Peakall admits that the enzyme-induction effect is insufficient to account
for the very thin pelican shells, and also that it is not a rapid enough mechanism to explain some of the laboratory findings. He concludes that it must
be CA inhibition which is the principal mode of action.

1970 Bitman and Co. say that CA inhibition is, indeed, the most probable explanation for eggshell thinning.

1970 Risebrough, Davis, and Anderson reject enzyme induction, as well as CA
inhibition, as the mechanisms which can explain the thin eggshells. They
also claim that PCBs do not cause eggshell thinning.

1971 Blus, Heath, and Co. state that PCBs *might* cause thin eggshells, but they
rule them out as the agent responsible for the severe reproductive problems of the brown pelican.

1971 Dvorchik, Istin, and Maren state authoritatively that DDE is not a CA
inhibitor, and Pocker et al. back this up with thorough chemical studies.

1970 SCEP panel and NASCO monograph authors enumerate four mechanisms:
1971 ATPase inhibition; CA inhibition; enzyme–induction–steroid-disturbance;
thyroid hormone imbalance. Here everything is thrown in for good measure.

1971 Bitman, during the Consolidated DDT Hearings, stands firmly behind the
conviction that it must be CA inhibition which is the true cause of the problem, not anticipating that Risebrough will contradict him in the same forum
only a few weeks later.

1972 Risebrough, who is, after all, the chief biochemist among the anti-DDT
scientists, testifies in an authoritative manner that ATPase inhibition has
now become the favored hypothesis.

In considering the mechanism whereby . . . [DDE causes thin eggshells] . . ., we ruled out the possibility that the inhibition of the enzyme carbonic anhydrase could itself account for the phenomenon, because the nature of the dose response curve was not consistent with this theory. . . . Therefore, we postulated that inhibition of a membrane-bound substance, most likely a protein involved with ion transport, possibly, or calcium transport across the shell gland membrane, was a more likely theory. (Risebrough, 1972, p. 6854)

The final stance is all quite clear by now, is it not? Or is it? Unfortunately, since Dr. Risebrough was referring in this statement to one of his review articles rather than to his own research, he seems to have forgotten that Matsumura had published a "technical note" in *Science* in 1970, in order to clear up some misreadings of his earlier paper reporting on the joint experimental work with Patil. This note contained the following qualifications regarding the possible inhibition of ATPases by DDT or DDE: "What we found was that DDT inhibits a yet unidentified $Na^+K^+Mg^{2+}$–adenosinetriphosphatase which may or may not be involved in the process of 'sodium-potassium pump.' . . . What we actually suspect, therefore, is either (i) this portion of DDT-sensitive adenosinetriphosphatase is not the 'pump' enzyme (but rather an enzyme-protein involved in the processes of conductance changes) or (ii) the adenosinetriphosphatase in question superficially resembles the actual DDT target . . ." (Matsumura, 1970, p. 1343).

In general, Matsumura's "technical note" seems to represent a plea for caution in interpretation, and it underlines that even those who are focusing attention on the biological activity of DDT — quite aside from the matter of avian reproductive problems — do *not* claim to have any definitive answers. It also seems clear that Matsumura intended to bring attention to the fact that the DDT target is *not* a membrane-bound pump enzyme involved in active ionic transport. Apparently his cautionary and corrective note failed in its purpose, and we suspect that we shall be reading for the next year or two all kinds of illuminating explanations about DDE and ATPase inhibition.

A Few Words in Summary

It ought to be borne in mind that the four paragraphs headed "Biochemical Effects" which we cited in full at the beginning of this discussion are supposed to represent a summary of *what has been scientifically established* about the modes of action by which DDT and its metabolites cause deleterious effects on nontarget organisms — particularly birds.

However, if one rereads these four paragraphs — taking into account all the important qualifications which are not stated, the errors in statements of fact, the acceptance of conclusions based on faulty experiments, the distorted references to properly performed investigations, and so on—it seems as though this section headed "Biochemical effects" was designed more to impress readers with the "amazing biological activity" of DDT and its metabolites than to elucidate known modes of action or point to gaps in information and understanding.

The task to which these scientists addressed themselves was an objective appraisal of what is know (and not known) about pollutants suspected to be of global significance. Their summary of the biochemical modes of action of DDT residues on nontarget organisms cannot be said to contribute to an assessment of whether or not some degree of contamination of the environment with the compound is a critical problem, for beyond the fact that some of the mechanisms listed are based on publications which will not stand up to scrutiny, the panel offers no evaluation of how meaningful these biochemical effects might be—if indeed they take place at all—in conditions encountered in nature.

How Important Are a Few Mistakes?

During the course of the last two chapters, we have reviewed or referred to more than a dozen papers which either report "experimental proofs" that certain undesirable effects on nontarget organisms are caused by exposure to sublethal quantities of DDT, or describe experiments purporting to demonstrate one or another hypothesis about the biochemical mode of action through which the compound produces these undesirable effects. We have elaborated on these experiments in considerable detail, going to some pains to show that they are filled with scientific errors which invalidate the conclusions: The design of the experiment is inadequate to yield an answer to the question posed; the measuring techniques defy the laws of mechanics; the statistical methods are wrong; the results do not support the conclusions; the data reveal interference from unknown variables; they are manipulated to make the results look better, or perhaps even falsified in their presentation; the results represented are impossible; the hypothesis is theoretically untenable or fails to take account of known facts; the methodology is technically faulty; artifacts are mistaken for "effects"; and so on.

The reader may be wondering why we have bothered to tear these publications apart in such detail. Are we playing a sophistic game? Have we exposed these weaknesses merely because we derive some sort of personal pleasure from catching the environmentalists making mistakes? Why are a few sloppy graphs or meaningless experiments so important, since nearly everyone seems to agree that DDT residues are the cause of avian reproductive difficulties, and perhaps are also responsible for declines in certain representatives of the marine fauna?

There are at least two good reasons why close criticism of these papers is important. The first is that there is a world of difference between "nearly every-one seems to agree" and "it has been scientifically proven." *If* there existed solid scientific proof that DDT and its metabolites are indeed the cause of the avian reproductive problems that have been observed in the field, then one might take a very different attitude toward these weak publications. It would still be generally distressing to find them appearing in renowned scientific journals, but it would probably not be worthwhile to tax the patience of our readers and to expend so much of our own time and energy merely to show that there are a few dozen bad papers on DDT effects in the literature. But *these are* the publications that constitute the supposed proof that DDT is the cause of declining numbers of certain top predators.

The second reason is that the principal argument of the contemporary "scientific case" against DDT is built on the foundation of *these* publications. The case for excessive or unwarranted applications of the pesticide has long since been invalidated by agency controls. The argument that DDT is directly danger-ous to human health is exceedingly weak and the environmentalists know it, although they are still willing to bring up the possiblity of cancer in relation to DDT, recognizing that the suggestion will have an irrational impact even if un-founded. But the real argument now is that DDT residues damage the environ-ment by endangering certain species.

This case is no longer based on "suggestive evidence" or loose correlations between observations from the field and the timing of the introduction of DDT use. Such observations—which, as Wurster himself points out, might merely result from strange coincidences—were the original basis of the *speculative* hypothesis that DDT *might* be the cause of wildlife reproductive problems. But the present allegations of the anti-DDT scientists rest on the claims that cause-and-effect relationships have been shown in controlled laboratory studies; that hard evidence may be derived from highly meaningful statistical correlations of DDT residues and declines in certain wild species; that the way in which DDT causes these problems is understood and has been demonstrated experimentally.

We should like to refer the reader back to the beginning of Chapter 11, where we offered some elementary definitions of such words as "phenomenon," "evidence," "proof," "hypothesis," and "theory," followed by a short discussion on how one goes about experimental studies designed to prove a hypothesis. Perhaps, if that discussion is kept in mind, and if we restrict ourselves to the claim that DDT residues cause thin eggshells, we can get some idea of how the whole superstructure of the broader allegation of subtle pernicious effects on wildlife was built up.

To begin with, there were some field observations. Ratcliffe noticed that peregrine eggshells appeared to be getting thinner. He made further observations of museum eggs, and noted that the shells of this species seemed to be considerably lighter in the period after 1945 than they had been earlier. He *speculated* that this might have something to do with the introduction of the organochlorine insecticides.

Hickey and Anderson picked up this speculation and formulated the hypothesis that DDT *is* the cause of the eggshell thinning. They offered what they thought to be evidence in support of this hypothesis—the famous herring-gull correlations between residues and shell thickness.

This hypothesis was attractive to a number of people, who decided to explore it experimentally. The controlled feeding experiments which followed did *not* succeed in demonstrating the truth-value of the hypothesis, because in two cases (Heath et al.; Porter and Wiemeyer) the controls failed, and in the third (Bitman et al.), the experimental design was inadequate; contrary evidence was brought forth by other investigators, and the data did not represent facts. However, some of the environmentalists had already become extremely attached to this hypothesis, and despite the obvious weaknesses of these studies, they are still accepted by anti-DDT scientists as experimental proofs of the hypothesis on the grounds that they were reported in well-known scientific journals. This favored hypothesis thus became a "proven theory" without actually being demonstrated, and it is now spoken of as a "well-known fact." By now nearly everyone is in agreement that DDT *is* the cause of thin eggshells in declining species of birds. The only problem is, that according to the standards of the experimental sciences, the theory is false. It does not even have the value of the original speculation because in the meantime too much contrary evidence has been amassed.

When pressured during cross-examination at the recent Consolidated DDT Hearings, the investigators responsible for these "well-known proofs" of the DDT–thin-eggshell hypothesis were for the most part reduced to speaking about trends. By this we suppose that they meant that, even if their results were not exactly scientific proof in the strict sense, they observed that something happened when they fed DDT to birds. Unfortunately, while trends may be of interest to field biologists, sociologists, and polltakers, they do not constitute experimental proofs. To put it in unequivocal terms, so that there is no doubt about the publications we did not review in detail, we must state that we have not seen a *single* report of experiments or correlations dealing with DDT and birds that could be said to constitute a scientific verification of the favored hypothesis.

We should like to suggest that the great difficulties encountered by those scientists who attempted to go further and show by what mode of action DDT and its metabolites cause thin eggshells might stem from the possiblity that they were not dealing with the causal agent at all. Would it not be both more sensible and scientifically more tenable to start all over again, and examine, without preconceptions, whether the phenomenon of thin-shelled eggs in wild populations could be associated with some other possible cause or causes?

If the interest of the scientists who have expended so much effort on this problem is really in the affected populations about which they write so eloquently, there would be nothing professionally shameful about abandoning the idea that DDT is the causal agent and seeking to test other possible explanations. On the other hand, if their interest is to indict DDT, even at the cost of abandoning truth, then they are not worthy of their professional titles.

> If we do not penalize false statements in error, we open up the way, don't you see, for false statements by intention. And of course a false statement of fact, made deliberately, is the most serious crime a scientist can commit. (Snow, 1934, p. 273)

17

VANISHING RESIDUES

O happy is he who still can hope
To surface from this sea of errors
GOETHE

For well over a decade now, we have been repeatedly told by
worried scientists and ecologically minded laymen that DDT,
once released into environment,* is dangerously persistent. The estimates on the
part of anti-DDT scientists with respect to exactly how long DDT and its active
metabolities remain in soil, air, fresh and sea water vary widely—from about
four years all the way to several hundreds of years. Nevertheless, there seems
to be a consensus among the scientists opposing the use of DDT that its average
residence time cannot be less than a minimum of four to five years.*

* "Consensus," as used here, refers only to the "closed body of experts," not to the scientific community as a whole.

We have also been told that DDT is remarkably mobile and, for all practical purposes, ubiquitous. It can be found virtually everywhere, even in areas remote from any application sites, such as the wilds of northern Canada and Antarctica. Its widespread distribution has led to a number of speculations about how it is transported from areas of heavy use to become dispersed around the globe.

Lastly, we are reminded that although DDT is only slightly soluble in water, it may enter the atmosphere in the form of vapors, and, since it adsorbs to particulate matter, it may be transported attached to airborne dust or aqueous sediments. In contrast with its low solubility in water, DDT is known to be highly soluble in fats. It is therefore natural to assume that where it is present in sufficient concentrations for uptake, it will be incorporated in the lipid fractions of organisms. No one questions the fact that DDT and its metabolites can be stored in the body fat of living forms (including man) at least up to a certain point. It is important, however, to bear in mind the phrase "where it is present in sufficient concentrations for uptake," for, as we shall see later, there seems to be some bewilderment on the part of environmentalists as to why only an insignificant fraction of the DDT which man has thus far released into the environment can be found in the biota.

In this section, we wish to review the issue of the estimated quantities of active DDT residues said to be in circulation on a global basis. We shall do so in terms of statements made in the SCEP case study on DDT, the papers pertinent to its dispersion cited as references by the SCEP panel, and a review of a 1971 publication by Woodwell, Craig, and Johnson entitled "DDT in the Biosphere: Where Does It Go?"

In the SCEP report, the DDT case study deals specifically with DDT in the marine environment. Consequently, in discussing its distribution in the biosphere, the panel places its emphasis on the amounts of DDT residues which may be presumed to be present in the world's oceans. The members of the Goldberg panel face a peculiar scientific difficulty in addressing themselves to this question, for although they have some data on residues in marine organisms permitting them to extrapolate a gross approximation of the amount of DDT accumulated in the biota of the oceans (603 metric tons as the most generous estimate for the total marine biomass, a figure which the panel admits is an insignificant fraction of the input of DDT into the environment), they have no data representing concentrations of DDT in the waters of the open seas.

Nevertheless, with hardly a shred of evidence, and for reasons grounded in neither logic nor common sense, the members of the panel assume that a very large proportion of the DDT released into the environment each year must end up in the oceans while still in a biologically active form. Beginning with this nonevident assumption and hampered by the limitation of having no real measurements of DDT residues in open ocean waters, they face two problems: (1) to explain how the residues get into the oceans; and (2) to find a way of estimating the quantities "present" there.

With regard to the first problem, the Goldberg group have to reject surface runoff carried by rivers as a possible route to the sea, since even according to their most generous estimates, "it seems unlikely that more than 1/1,000 of the annual production of DDT (100 metric tons) could reach the oceans by surface runoff" (SCEP, 1970, p. 132). They therefore turn to atmospheric transport as the most likely route by which DDT is disseminated.

Now it happens that the chairman of the DDT case study panel, E. D. Goldberg, and one of the other panel members, R. Risebrough, had concerned themselves with this problem some time earlier. In 1968, together with R. J. Huggett and J. J. Griffin, they published a paper entitled "Pesticides: Transatlantic Movements in the Northeast Trades," with Risebrough as first author. This was, as far as we know, the first investigation in which an attempt was made to measure pesticide residues in air over the open ocean and also to explain the mobility of these residues by postulating atmospheric transport as the most likely mode of dispersion.

Risebrough and his coworkers (1968a) took extensive samples of air carried over 6,000 km of open ocean from Europe and Africa across the Atlantic to Barbados by equatorial easterly winds. They reported the average concentration of pesticides in the air over the Atlantic as 7.8×10^{-14} g/m^3.[*] Implicit in their study was the assumption that most of the pesticide residues would be attached to dust particles, rather than being present as vapors. They reported the pesticide content in the dust to be 41 ppb by weight. They then took available data on the average sedimentation rate above these waters, calculated the area over the equatorial Atlantic involved in dissemination by the trade winds, and concluded that 600 kg of pesticide residues would be deposited yearly into the open sea of this region as a result of the rather slight degree of air contamination carried by the easterly winds.

In the Pacific, the same investigators found no detectable pesticide residues in the air over the ocean. Their explanation for this is that the sample sizes were too small (in milligram quantities of dust, as compared with gram quantities in the Atlantic). This seems rather curious, since three of the authors

---

[*] In this study, the term "pesticide concentration" refers not only to DDT and all of its breakdown products, but to dieldrin as well.

were associated with Scripps Institute of Oceanography, and presumably they would have had the opportunities and the necessary apparatus to take larger samples; but the point is unimportant except insofar as it leaves open the question of whether or not the air over the open Pacific is contaminated with approximately the same concentrations as the Barbados air. More important is the fact that they collected dust from an ocean pier at La Jolla, California, where they found pesticide residues averaging 7.0×10^{-11} g/m^3 of air: that is, 1,000 times more than in the Barbados samples. The authors explain this extreme local variation thus: "Such is the difference in pesticide load between marine air *adjacent to agricultural areas in which pesticides are used intensively* and marine air remote from sites of application" (Risebrough et al., 1968, p. 1235: our emphasis).

Now let us turn back to the SCEP report and examine how the panel chaired by Goldberg (and with Risebrough as one of its members) went about estimating the amounts of DDT residues entering the oceans from the atmosphere.

> DDT residues enter the atmosphere by several routes, including aerial drift during application, by rapid vaporization from water surfaces (Acree, Berova [sic],* and Bowman, 1963) and by vaporization from plants and soils (Nash and Beal, 1970). Once in the atmosphere it [sic] may travel great distances, entering the sea in precipitation or in dry fallout. There are few data for estimating the rates of transfer. The most extensive sampling of DDT residues in precipitation has been in Great Britain, where total accumulation was measured at 7 stations between August 1, 1966, and July, 1967. The mean concentration for all rainwater samples was 80 parts per trillion (Tarrant and Tatton, 1968). This concentration is about twice that reported for meltwaters of recent antarctic snow (Peterle, 1969). The DDT residues in South Florida precipitation averaged 1,000 parts per trillion in 18 samples taken at 4 sites between June 1968 and May 1969 (Yates, Holswade, and Higer, 1970).
>
> Total annual precipitation over the oceans has been estimated as 2.97×10^{14} metric tons (Sverdrup, Johnson, and Fleming, 1942). If this contained an average of 80 parts per trillion, a total of 2.4×10^4 metric tons of DDT residues would be transported annually to the oceans. This is about one-quarter of the estimated total annual production of DDT. Thus, the atmosphere appears to be the major route for transfer of DDT residues into the oceans. (SCEP, pp. 132–133)

If we now scrutinize these two paragraphs carefully, a number of interesting things emerge.

1. DDT residues are said to enter the atmosphere by aerial drift during spray operations, by vaporization from water surfaces, and by vaporization

---

*Beroza's name is consistently misspelled in this publication.

from plants and soils. Only indirect mention is made of dust, or of wind carrying particulate matter as a transport mechanism. Why? Two years earlier Risebrough and Goldberg thought this was the principal way in which the residues were dispersed. We shall come back to this point shortly.

2. Vaporization from water surfaces is now emphasized. For some years, it has been repeatedly stated that DDT codistills with water, and that this is a primary factor in its supposed extreme mobility. Indeed, in the reference cited by the panel, Acree and his coworkers did show that DDT codistills with water, but their experiments were performed at 114 °F (45.5 °C), a temperature seldom occurring in nature, and almost never on open water surfaces. Under more normal temperature conditions, the very low vapor pressure of DDT (1.5 × 10^{-7} mm Hg at 20 °C—or about 1/10,000 atm) will not permit codistillation to take place. Four independent studies have been conducted which failed to confirm codistillation phenomenon at lower temperatures (Anderson et al., 1963; Sutherland et al., 1970; Harris and Lichtenstein, 1961; Guenzi and Beard, 1967). Nevertheless, the codistillation-with-water hypothesis has been repeated so many times that it is not surprising to find it here presented by the panel as a *known fact* about DDT's physicochemical properties.

3. Next we learn that there are few data available for estimating the rates of transfer, but the panel makes a selection from the available studies on DDT in air and rainwater, presenting three average figures. Tarrant and Tatton found an average of 80 ppt in rainwater samples in Great Britain. About 40 ppt were found in the meltwaters of recent Antarctic snow; and 1,000 ppt was the average in the rainwater samples collected by Yates et al., in South Florida.

From the point of view of the psychology of the readers, the decision of the panel to report specifically these three average figures, before proceeding to calculate global input on the basis of Tarrant and Tatton's data, is quite clever. One very high figure is represented (Florida, 1,000 ppt). The British average of 80 ppt is lower than this by a factor of more than 10. The suggestion that it is a "reasonable" average is further reinforced by noting that it is only about twice as high as the average reported by Peterle, found in the snow of a highly remote and presumably "pure" area of the world—Antarctica. In view of these comparisons, most readers would probably accept without much question that to assume an 80 ppt concentration as an average for rainwaters falling all over the globe is not unreasonable, even though it is admitted to be a speculation.

However, if the reader happens to have some other data at hand, and if he takes the trouble to think about the relative values of these data, 80 ppt ceases to seem so reasonable as a global average in rainfall. To begin with, the Peterle report from the meltwaters of Antarctic snow seems highly suspect. Earlier investigators found no detectable pesticides in these meltwaters (George and Frear, 1966). Peterle himself admits that only one of his five filters showed measurable residues (the total quantity of which could be accounted for by two micturations into the snow). Nevertheless, from this single datum he did not hesitate to calculate that there should be about 5 million pounds of DDT in the Antarctic ice. No independent investigators have confirmed Peterle's findings. Furthermore, they simply do not seem credible as averages for that area if one takes into account other comparative concentrations reported in the literature. To mention only a few uncomfortable facts: in many American rivers near sites of heavy agricultural activities, concentrations of less than 10 ppt are reported (Weaver et al., 1965). An earlier, rather extensive sampling in England (Wheatley and Hardman, 1965) yielded average rainwater concentrations of only 3 ppt—13 times less than those reported by Peterle from the remote Antarctic area. Most impressive of all, if one converts the concentrations reported by Risebrough et al. in the air over the Atlantic near Barbados into relative parts by weight* the average amounts only to 60 parts per quintillion (pp10^{18}). This is about 1 million times less than the Tarrant and Tatton average from Great Britain.

We have to come back to the question of why Risebrough and Goldberg ignore their own data when seeking a basis for establishing an average annual input of DDT into the oceans through precipitation. We may be quite confident that they do not leave out their own findings out of modesty, for their 1968 paper is duly cited in the references, and is credited as the source for estimates of the amount of DDT carried into the Gulf of Mexico by the Mississippi River. (The credits should have been: Breidenbach et al., 1967; and Nicholson, 1967.)

As noted, in their 1968 article, Risebrough and his coauthors explained the thousand-fold difference in the pesticide concentrations of their Barbados and La Jolla dust samples as a reflection of the proximity of La Jolla to sites of pesticide application. This would seem to be a commonsense interpretation of their findings; it is also one borne out by other studies of pesticide residues in airborne dust and/or rainwater—nearly all of which show an extremely wide range of variability, the high residues correlating well with heavy pesticide use in the area of sampling or with recent spraying in the vicinity. By 1970, however, Goldberg and Risebrough appear to have forgotten their own observations regarding the extreme variability of residue concentrations, as well as their

*When converting concentrations of weight in volume units into relative parts by weight, it is necessary to take into account the specific gravity of the substance in which the parts are contained. In the case of water, the conversion is very simple, since 1 l of water (a volume measurement) is equal to 1 kg (a weight measurement). On the other hand, 1 l of air weighs only 0.0013 kg, or about 1.3 g. Thus 1 g/m³ of water is 1 part per million (ppm), whereas 1 g/m³ of air is 0.77 parts per thousand (ppth). Or, alternatively, 1.3 mg/m³ of air equals 1 ppm. (In rough calculations, one may take a ratio of 1 to 1,000 for these two common substances in order to simplify the conversion.)

interpretation of these observations, for they settle on an average from Great Britain, known to be an area of heavy pesticide applications, as an acceptable figure for global extrapolations.

Let us now make some extrapolations of our own.

If we were to calculate concentrations entering the ocean through rainfall from the Barbados data of Risebrough et al. (7.8×10^{-14} g/m^3 of air, or 6.0×10^{-11}g/m^3 of water, or 60 pp 10^{18}) we would arrive at a figure of only 17.8 kg of pesticides carried to the world's seas annually through precipitation. This figure is not only negligible; it is so small in comparison with the volume of the mixed layer that it may be regarded virtually as a zero contribution to pesticide concentrations.

What is even more interesting, however, is that Risebrough et al. reported in 1968 that they had identified averages of 41 ppb (dry weight) pesticides in their dust sample; and on this basis, they calculated that 600 kg of pesticides would enter the equatorial Atlantic yearly through dry fallout or rain, Extrapolated to the oceans of the whole globe, this figure would give an input of approximately 11 metric tons per year . . . still a negligible quantity, but, curiously, almost 1,000 times as great as the extrapolation from their reported concentrations of 7.8×10^{-14} g/m^3 in the air. This discovery led us to turn back to the 1968 Risebrough study and reexamine the figures reported in the fine print of the table, as we have had to do so often in the papers treating eggshell thinning.

If one recalculates the data presented for each sample by considering the total pesticide concentrations expressed in terms of the amount of air sampled, the gram quantities of dust used for analysis, and the concentrations found in each of the dry-weight dust samples, it becomes immediately clear that only pesticide quantities in the *parts per trillion* range will yield results agreeing with the reported concentrations per cubic meter of air. This represents a *thousandfold error* in conversion on the part of one or all of the four authors of the 1968 paper.

We now have three good reasons why Risebrough and Goldberg make no use of their earlier findings: (1) Their 1968 interpretation of the variability in pesticide residues in air is inconsistent with choosing an average from a highpesticide-use area (England) as the basis for global extrapolation. (2) Computing the input to the world's oceans on the basis of the 600 kg of pesticides supposedly entering the equatorial Atlantic each year results in less than 11 metric tons annually—an embarrassingly small figure. (3) In reviewing their own material in connection with these new speculations, they may have discovered the original conversion error in their 1968 publication and wisely decided not to make any use of their own numbers.

We do not intend to dwell at length on this thousand-fold error, since it should be obvious to anyone that scientists cannot afford to make mistakes of this order, and that something is very wrong indeed when none of the four scientists signing this publication, nor the referees who presumably scrutinized the paper before publication, noticed the error. It naturally raises the question of how accurate might be the figures reported in other papers in which the same authors are involved. Risebrough, in particular, most of whose publications of the last five years deal with pesticide and PCB residue analyses, is well known for finding concentrations in animal tissues that are astonishingly high. Is it possible that when he writes, as he has on occasion, of residues in the range of 5,000 ppm, that he has slipped a decimal point three places in his conversions, and is really dealing with 5 ppm?

But the question of why the Goldberg panel decided specifically on the 80 ppt concentrations of Tarrant and Tatton is still not quite settled. Suppose they had decided to use Wheatley's average of 3 ppt instead? Or Yates' 1,000 ppt? What would be the input into the world's oceans calculated from these data?

Extrapolation from Wheatley's average yields a mere 891 metric tons annually. Clearly, this is not enough, since the panel has already described 600 metric tons as an insignificant fraction of the total production figures.

On the other hand, had they chosen to use the averages reported from south Florida by Yates et al. they would have arrived at 297,000 metric tons of DDT raining annually into the seas. This figure is impressively large. It certainly tends to suggest that the oceans are indeed being seriously contaminated by the input of DDT through rainfall. Unfortunately, however, there is an obvious problem with this total—even for arbitrary speculators. It represents almost three times the annual world production of DDT!

If we now return to the two paragraphs cited from the text of the report, we have to admit that the panel does not at this point make a definite statement to the effect that 24,000 tons of DDT are being transported into the oceans annually through rainfall. In their second paragraph, the reader will note that they first present a completely neutral fact (an estimate of the annual rainfall over the oceans). They then state: "*If* this contained an average of 80 parts per trillion; a total of 2.4×10^4 metric tons of DDT residues *would be* transported annually to the oceans" (SCEP, 1970, p. 133; our emphasis). There is nothing like a conditional statement to make it appear that one is proceeding with caution and modesty. Nevertheless, in spite of the tremendous importance of the word "if" in the above sentence, and despite their repeated disclaimers that there are no objective data on residue concentrations in the oceans, a careful reading suggests that the members of the panel are subjectively convinced that a large part of the DDT released into the atmosphere *must* end up in the oceans.

The choice of 80 ppt as an average global concentration in rainwater is made to appear reasonable. Considering the data *not* mentioned by the panel, however, it seems more likely that the 80 ppt average was chosen because it conveniently yielded an annual input into the seas which corresponded nicely to the prior expectations of the panel—that is, 24,000 metric tons, or about one-fourth the DDT produced each year.

Having dealt with the problem of how DDT residues enter the sea, and having presented a qualified estimate of the annual input through rainfall, the panel then turns to a consideration of what happens to all this DDT in the oceans; how it is distributed, how long its metabolites remain biologically active, and so on. They are obliged to remind us again that, even if they extrapolate average DDT residues in fish and marine plankton from the highest available figures, they cannot account for more than an insignificant fraction of the residues in living organisms. This is really too bad, since it is contrary to expectations. They proceed, however, to estimate how much DDT is still actively available for uptake by organisms, for this is important with respect to their ultimate conclusions about the dangers of all this DDT "present" in the oceans, even assuming that manufacture of DDT will cease at some time in the near future.

Two pages after their tentative estimate that 24,000 metric tons of DDT residues are raining into the sea annually, they write: "If only 0.01 percent (100 metric tons) can be accounted for in pelagic marine organisms, 0.50×10^6 metric tons (one-quarter of total production) should be present in solution and in the bottom sediments. In order to balance input with accountable fractions, the surface mixed layer volume (0.025×10^{24} ml) should contain concentrations of approximately 5×10^{-12} g/ml, assuming a residence time of 5 years and an annual input of 0.25×10^5 metric tons of DDT/year" (*ibid.*, p. 135).

Now obviously the general reader may easily be put off by the rather obscure wording and the complicated numbers involved in this statement. We shall attempt to draw out some of its implications and to express the numbers in somewhat clearer terms. The panel is saying:

1. The total production of DDT to date, on a world basis, is estimated to be about 2 million tons.

2. Even though, according to expectations, DDT residues should tend to accumulate in organisms, we can account for only 100 metric tons in pelagic marine organisms, which represents a mere 0.01 percent of the amount so far produced. (Actually, 100 tons is 0.005 percent of 2 million tons, but this arithmetic error of a factor of two is not particularly upsetting when compared to many of the others we have noted.)

3. We estimate that one-fourth of the DDT produced annually is transported

to the oceans through rainfall. (See earlier discussion, and note how this has now become a "fact" in connection with their new calculations.) Since 2 million tons have been produced so far, this means that 500,000 tons (0.50×10^6 tons) must be in the oceans somewhere, either in solution or in the bottom sediments.

4. The surface mixed layer volume of the oceans (first 100 m) is 0.025×10^{24} ml, which may also be expressed as 25×10^{15} m^3, or 25,000,000,000,000,000 cubic meters. This is a great deal of water!

5. We assume a residence time of five years. (That is, we assume that DDT and its active metabolites will remain in virtually unchanged state in the surface layer for a period of five years.)

6. An annual input of 0.25×10 metric tons (which is the same as 25,000 tons) with a residence time of five years implies that there should be 125,000 tons of active DDT residues in the surface mixed layer of the oceans.

7. If we divide this figure of 125,000 tons by the total volume of the surface mixed layer of all the world's oceans, we arrive at a concentration of 5×10^{-12} g/ml. This concentration may also be expressed as 5×10^{-6} g/m^3, or 5 micrograms per cubic meter, or 5 ppt.

Although the total quantity of 125,000 tons of DDT in circulation seems impressive, if it were evenly dispersed in the mixed layer to a concentration of 5 ppt, no organism could accumulate it, as this concentration is insufficient for uptake. This problem apparently also bothered some members of the panel and may account for the mutual contradiction of the following two statements, which appear on the same page:

> A homogeneous distribution of DDT in the mixed layer has resulted from atmospheric transport from the continents.

Eleven lines later we may read:

> There is no indication, however, that DDT introduced into the marine environment is uniformly distributed in the mixed layer. Enrichment is likely to occur in the sea's surface film, which contains fatty acids and alcohols. (*Ibid.*, p. 134)

Which of these two statements do the authors intend that their readers should accept as a basic assumption?

We have already discussed the arbitrary nature of the calculations estimating the annual input of DDT into the oceans. In these new input-output balance calculations, we see that there is a second arbitrary assumption involved: i.e., the five-year residence time.

Why should the panel have chosen specifically five years as the residence time? There is no clear answer to this question, but, like the 80 ppt rainfall average, the period of five years is made to sound reasonable and even conservative, since they write themselves, ". . . The rate at which it [DDT] degrades to harmless products in the marine system is *unknowm*. For some of its degradation products, half-lives are *certainly* of the order of years, *perhaps even of decades" (ibid.,* p. 135; our emphasis).

Earlier on, the panel had reported the following information about oysters and DDT residues: "In the coastal environment DDT and its residues range from undetectable levels to 0 [sic] to 5.4 ppm in oysters (Butler, 1969). Concentrations between these limits are highly variable locally, even within the same estuary"* *(ibid.,* p. 133).

The source cited for this information is a 1969 publication by P. Butler. Butler is also one of the panel members. A residence time of five years for DDT in seawater would seem to be inconsistent with Butler's oyster findings, for in the shallow waters of estuaries a relatively quick mixing takes place. Oysters are filter feeders, and as such they serve as good indicators of the degree of pollution of coastal waters. If Butler found a variability of from 0 to 5.4 ppm DDT residues in oysters *in the same estuary,* it would seem logical to interpret these findings as an indication that DDT decays rather rapidly in sea water. Otherwise there should be a much more even distribution of residues.

But let us suppose that Butler's evaluation of these oyster data did not lead him to the above conclusion, either because he did not think about it, or because he reasons in a different fashion. Let us let him off the hook on this point.

There still remains a remarkable mystery with respect to Butler's contributions to the panel, one which can be explained only as evidence of selective memory blocking or, alternatively, as deliberate withholding of known facts which would contradict the assumptions of the panel and invalidate their final conclusions.

What is this mystery, this "forgotten" fact?

Laboratory studies *have been carried out* on the residence time of DDT in seawater. They were performed by Wilson, Forrester, and Knight in the Gulf Breeze Laboratory in Florida, of which Butler happened to be the head.

---

* The statement as here set down by the panel about the range of residues in oysters is literally true. However, for the sake of clarification, it is instructive to see how Butler described the high-range residues in the original publication cited as a reference. In discussing more than 5,000 samples from 170 stations on the Atlantic, Gulf, and Pacific coasts, he wrote: "In the estuaries of Washington, less than 3% of the samples have been contaminated and the DDT residues have always been less than 0.05 ppm. . . . In some areas that are intensively farmed, oyster samples always contain DDT residues, but the amounts of DDT plus metabolites are usually less than 0.5 ppm. *Only rarely has the residue exceeded 1.0 ppm.* The highest residue of DDT observed in oysters, 5.4 ppm, *was the result of a single incident of gross pollution"* (Butler, 1969, p. 890; our emphasis).

This work was done in 1969 and the results were published in 1970, in a U.S. Department of the Interior Circular, only a short time following the deliberations of the panel in which Butler participated.

The findings of Wilson et al.,* may be summarized as showing that;

1. When 3 ppb of DDT was added to natural seawater and kept in sealed containers (to eliminate possible codistillation), 92.9 percent of the parent compound and its metabolites (DDE and DDD) had completely disappeared from the water within 38 days.

2. The half-life of DDT in seawater is between 17 and 18 days.

Figure 13 represents a plotting of the data of Wilson et al. with the original figures shown in the upper right corner. The dotted lines represent extrapolations from the given data, which can be legitimately performed, since all three curves follow regular decay patterns, from which one could write their corresponding differential equations. By subtracting the residue concentrations measured at any particular time during the decay process from the starting concentrations, one can easily calculate the percentage of loss at that given time.

There does not seem to be even a remote probability that Butler could have been ignorant of these findings, since the study was undertaken in this laboratory and his own work has been primarily on pollution of estuarine environments; hence he should have been most interested in this research.† Whether the other members of the panel were aware of the publication of this work is anybody's guess. In any event, it should be obvious that there is a sizable difference between five years and 40 days.

Had these findings been taken into account by the panel, they might have had an excellent and logical explanation for the mysterious fact that such a

---

*It might be legitimately argued that the findings of Wilson et al., have not been confirmed by independent investigations, and on these grounds might be held to be of questionable validity, as is, in our opinion, the Antarctic snow report of Peterle. However, this is no excuse for failing altogether to mention the experiments. Furthermore, it ought to be pointed out that anyone with access to pesticide residue equipment and a few jars of seawater could repeat this experiment easily and relatively quickly, natural seawater being quite accessible compared with the meltwaters of Antarctic snow. If Butler knew about this work but judged it to be of uncertain reliability, the panel should at the very least have described the findings and recommended immediate attempts to repeat the experiments. (In the meanwhile Patil et al., 1972, have at least partially confirmed the Wilson et al. findings.)

†That Butler did indeed know about these results finally came out during his cross-examination in the Consolidated DDT Hearings. In his direct testimony he estimated DDT's persistence in seawater at 40 years. He repeated this statement during cross-examination (Butler, 1971, p. 3768). When first asked whether he knew of the work of Wilson et al., he said he had never seen the article (ibid., p. 3769). On p. 3770 (ibid.), he finally admitted that he knew that the authors had worked on this project for a total period of about 60 days.

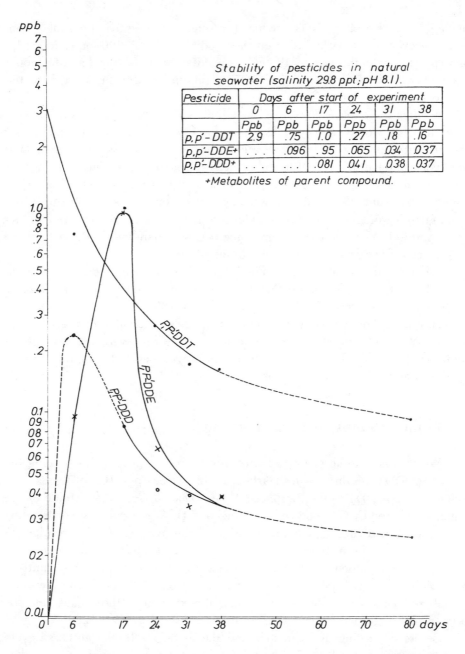

Stability of pesticides in natural seawater (salinity 29.8 ppt; pH 8.1).

Pesticide	Days after start of experiment					
	0	6	17	24	31	38
	Ppb	Ppb	Ppb	Ppb	Ppb	Ppb
p,p'-DDT	2.9	.75	1.0	.27	.18	.16
p,p'-DDE+	. . .	.096	.95	.065	.034	.037
p,p'-DDD+	. . .	. . .	.081	.041	.038	.037

+Metabolites of parent compound.

Figure 13.   *DECAY OF DDT IN SEAWATER HELD IN SEALED JARS*
(after Wilson, Forester, and Knight, 1970)

negligible fraction of the DDT produced can be accounted for in marine organisms; for even if one wished to grant the validity of the 25,000-ton estimate for annual input into the oceans through precipitation, a 17-day half-life would leave only a minuscule quantity of DDT circulating in the mixed layer of the oceans at any one time.

Reading their conclusions, it is clear that acknowledgment of such a short residence time would have been devastating to the argument of the panel, since the dramatic and frightening implications they wish to convey are predicated on a very long half-life for DDT and its active breakdown products: "If most of the remaining DDT residues are presently in reservoirs which will in time transfer their contents to the sea, we may expect, quite independent of future manufacturing practices, an increased level of these substances in marine organisms. And if, in fact, these compounds degrade with half-lives of decades, there may be no opportunity to redress the consequences.

The more the problems are studied, the more unexpected effects are identified. In view of the findings of the past decade, our prediction of the hazards may be vastly underestimated" (SCEP, 1970, pp. 135–136).

Having commented at some length on the scientific value of the "findings of the last decade" to which they refer, and having reviewed the assumptions underlying their predictions of future hazards, we need not comment further on the irony of this final paragraph.

From Calculus to Good Fortune

We turn now to an examination of a more recent publication treating the subject of DDT residues: a lead article in the December 10, 1971, issue of *Science* called "DDT in the Biosphere: Where Does It Go?" The subtitle of the paper—authored by G. Woodwell, P. Craig, and H. A. Johnson—is worth noting too: "Global modeling permits an appraisal of the hazards of DDT residues in the biosphere." The main purpose of the paper is to report on the creation of a computerized mathematical model which can be used to estimate the quantities of DDT residues circulating in four major reservoirs—the land, the lower atmosphere (or the troposphere), the surface mixed layer of the oceans, and the oceanic abyss—for any specific year from 1943 through the year 2000.

Before describing the equations and the model itself, the authors devote four pages to a general discussion of DDT. First come the familiar reminders about DDT's remarkable persistence, its mobility and worldwide distribution, its "causal" relationship with spectacular declines in the populations of certain species of fish and birds, and so on. Then comes a brief summary of the physical properties of DDT: its low solubility in water, its high solubility in fats, its tendency to accumulate in lipids and therefore in living organisms. The extreme persistence of DDT residues in nature is emphasized: ". . . estimates of their half-life range upward to 20 years, perhaps longer under certain circumstances. . ." (Woodwell et al., 1971, p. 1101). In this article, the codistillation-with-water argument is no longer mentioned; instead, tremendous stress is placed on the potential of DDT to enter the atmosphere through vaporization from plant and soil surfaces. All of this leads up to the statement that ". . . soils, air, the waters of the oceans, and the biota are all potential reservoirs for DDT residues, and the hazard to the biota, including man, hinges on the distribution of DDT residues among these reservoirs" *(ibid.)*.

A long discussion ensues which covers DDT production, DDT in soils, DDT in the atmosphere, DDT in the oceans, and DDT in the biota. We need not review these sections, except to point out that, like the SCEP panel, Woodwell and his coauthors have to admit that the estimated DDT residues in the total animal and plant biomass of the Earth are insignificant compared with production. The estimates they present are exceedingly high—six times higher, for example, for the biota of the oceans than those given by the SCEP panel. Still, their total figure for the maximum quantity of DDT residues which may be presumed to be at present in living things is only 5.4×10^9g (5,400 tons)—such a small amount that they decide to ignore it in the creation of the model which will tell them where all the DDT has gone.

[Although we have no quarrel with the authors' statement that this quantity is negligible, we do think it would be helpful if the next time they prepare a table on DDT residues in the biomass, they would at least do their arithmetic correctly. In Table 2 (*ibid.*, p. 1104), for example, there are four numbers listed in a column, which are then added. These numbers are: 0.004, 0.240, 1.814, 14.000 summed as: 15.058 instead of 16.058. This is a miscalculation which would be taken seriously only in a second-grade arithmetic class, but if the Atomic Energy Commission, under whose sponsorship this work was done, would buy these scientists an inexpensive calculator to complement their computer time, they could avoid similar mistakes in the future, where they might come into a more vital addition of numbers. The second mistake in the table is more serious, as far as these estimates are concerned. An approximation of the total biomass of humans (in dry weight) is given as 0.3×10^9 metric tons. The superscript § calls the reader's attention to the following footnote: "Bowen used .03 $\times 10^9$ tons, which seems to be about 10 times too low (G. M. W.)." It is difficult to understand why Dr. Woodwell felt the need to correct the work of a well-established authority, unless it slipped his mind that he is dealing in dry weight, or he thinks there are 30 billion people on the planet, or he calculates the average human weight at 1,520 lbs. Rough calculation of the dry biomass of humans is very simple. There are about 3 billion people on the planet (10^9 persons), each weighing approximately 70 kg, at a most generous estimate. This gives 0.07×10^9 metric tons net weight. Since at least 60 percent of the human body is water, dry weight will be 0.028×10^9 metric tons for the human biomass—or about the same as Bowen's original figure. *Si tacuisset philosophus fuisset!*]

The authors are apparently convinced that huge quantities of active DDT residues are present somewhere; hence they pose two basic questions: what amounts of DDT are in each of the four principal reservoirs, and how long do they remain in these, before finally being dissipated into the abyss?

They make the following assumptions, which serve as the basis for the model:

1. Theoretically, nearly all the DDT applied annually is capable of entering the atmosphere, except for the small amounts trapped in runoff or taken up by the biota.

2. The residence time of DDT in soils is about 4.5 years.

3. Dispersion of DDT around the globe is principally accomplished through atmospheric transport, chiefly in vapor form.

4. A mean residence time of four years is assumed for DDT in the atmosphere before it is returned to the surface of the Earth.

5. The dominant mechanism for removal of DDT from the atmosphere is rainfall. 60 ppt is accepted as a reasonable concentration of DDT residues in rainwater. This will result in a global annual precipitation content of 30,000 metric tons of residues.

6. The residence time in the mixed surface layer of DDT carried into the oceans is four years. After this period, it sinks below the thermocline and enters the abyss.

7. Biological and chemical breakdown in soils and photodegradation in the atmosphere are thought to be unimportant in comparison with transport. In other words, the authors are of the opinion that practically none of the DDT decomposes during the assigned residence times.

The results of the modeling experiments are presented in a graph, in which the concentrations of DDT residues in two of the four reservoirs—the atmosphere and the surface mixed layer of the sea—are shown, from 1940 to the year 2000. The concentrations for the period from 1970 to 2000 are presented in terms of alternate possibilities: (a) that DDT world production will be reduced to zero by 1974, and (b) that world production will increase from now up to the year 2000.

In the following, we wish to examine this model in two different ways. First we shall consider briefly two of the basic assumptions behind the model: the residence time in soil, and the average rainwater concentrations. Then we will ignore any doubts we may have about the validity of the assumptions behind the model and will merely examine whether or not the predictions resulting from the computations can be verified in terms of the model itself.

The 4.5-year residence time assumed for DDT in soil, when compared with Woodwell's previous estimates of decades (Woodwell and Martin, 1964) sounds like a reasonable figure. However, what is important to note here is the following emphasis of the authors: ". . . evaporation is a major mechanism for the removal of persistent pesticides from soil, and, despite its slowness, evaporation proceeds faster than chemical breakdown" (*ibid.*, p. 1102). The implication, of course, is that even though the residues seem to be disappearing from soils much faster than had earlier been assumed, this can be explained by evaporation rather than breakdown; thus DDT enters the atmosphere while still in active form.

In spite of its lengthy bibliography, it is notable that the paper contains no references to works describing the relatively rapid biological and/or chemical degradation of DDT in certain types of soils. Menzie has shown, for instance, that in some kinds of anaerobic soils, the half-life of DDT is only four weeks (Menzie, 1969). There are literally scores of papers which deal with the variability of the persistence of DDT, dependent on temperature, humidity, aeration, soil type, and soil microorganisms present. If indeed the residence time of DDT on land averaged five years, this would be most helpful for the worldwide malaria eradication programs, since it would only be necessary to apply the pesticide once in every five years, instead of twice yearly.

The second assumption to which we wish to call attention is the supposed average concentration of DDT in rainfall and its residence time in the atmosphere. Two of the same sources are cited as those used by the SCEP panel: Tarrant and Tatton (1968) (rainwater concentrations in England) and Peterle (1969) (Antarctic snow). Woodwell et al. also cite Wheatley and Hardman (1965) as a source for DDT residue concentrations in rainwaters of the British Isles. They state:

> In England, DDT concentrations in the range from 73 to 210 ppm have been reported in rain in areas close to regions where DDT has been used, and similar concentrations have been reported in the United States [Tarrant and Tatton, 1968; Wheatley and Hardman, 1965]. A DDT concentration in meltwaters from Antarctic ice of 40 ppt has been reported recently [Peterle, 1969]. . . . If the average DDT concentration in rainfall were 60 ppt and precipitation averaged 1 meter per year, rainfall would remove a total of 3×10^{10} grams of DDT residues from the atmosphere annually, most of that into the oceans. (*Ibid.*, p. 1103)

There are several problems with these statements. First, Woodwell and his coauthors make a serious conversion error in discussing Tarrant and Tatton's data, for they write 73 to 210 pp*m*, which is one million times too high. Tarrant and Tatton reported their results in terms of parts per 10^{12}, in order to avoid the confusion which sometimes arises from the fact that the British abbreviation for parts per trillion is often written as ppm·m, rather than the American ppt.[*] Secondly, the numbers given do *not* represent the range of concentrations in the two papers cited. Wheatley and Hardman found an average of only 3 ppt in rainwaters in Britain; while Tarrant and Tatton presented data ranging from 16 to 210 ppt, 73 ppt being their *mean*. Thirdly, there is no reference supplied for any United States data. Lastly, we have again Peterle's 40 ppt reading from Antarctic snow, the questionable validity of which we have already discussed.

The assumption of a residence time of four years in the atmosphere is equally problematic. The authors arbitrarily decided on four years, on the basis of their claim that DDT occurs primarily in vapor form in the atmosphere, although a number of studies have shown that the greatest proportion of pesticides present in the atmosphere are adsorbed to particulates (Risebrough et al., 1968; Tarrant and Tatton, 1968; Stanley et al., 1971 — all cited as references). To admit that the residues are attached to particles would destroy their whole rate-of-transfer theory, since it has been established that the residence time of particulate matter in the lower atmosphere is much less than four years. In the report of Work Group I on Climatic Effects of Global Pollution, in the same SCEP study in which Woodwell was a participant of the Ecological Group, one may read: "The average lifetimes of particles in the lower atmosphere depends on the rainfall (or snowfall) regime in which they reside. Studies using various radioactive tracers have given lifetimes ranging from 6 days to 2 or more weeks in the lower troposphere. At mid-latitudes the shorter lifetime seems to be more accurate. In the upper troposphere the residence time is probably 2 to 4 weeks . . ." (SCEP, 1970, p. 59). The discrepancy between postulated residence times and actually measured lifetimes in the atmosphere seems curiously similar to those discussed already in connection with the half-life of DDT in seawater.[†]

---

[*] It is possible that the "m" in ppm is a typing mistake. However, since the paper deals primarily in quantities, such a serious error should have been caught in the proofs.

[†] That Woodwell is well aware of the very brief residence time in the atmosphere of material absorbed to particulate matter is also clear from the following statements in one of his own earlier publications: "Radioactivity and Fallout: The Model Pollution." "First, particulate matter, introduced into the lower atmosphere, enters air currents that move around the world in periods of 15 to 25 days in the middle latitudes, sometimes less. Second, the half-time of residence (time for one-half of the material to be removed) of particulate matter carried in these currents ranges between a few days and a month . . ." (Woodwell, 1968, p. 885).

These few examples should illustrate the questionable basis on which the model is built. However, for the purpose of investigating the mathematical validity of the model itself let us now suppose that all of the assumptions are correct.

Figure 1 in the article represents the back calculations and predictions of the model for concentrations of DDT in the troposphere and in the oceanic mixed layer. Two predictive values are emphasized in the text: "If the world DDT production becomes zero in 1974, the concentration in the lower atmosphere would have reached a peak in 1966 at about 72 ppt (84×10^{-9} g/m^3). The mixed layer of the ocean would contain its maximum of 15 ppt in 1971" (Woodwell et al., 1971, p. 1104).

The authors write triumphantly that their prediction for peak atmospheric concentrations show a good approximation of DDT residue analyses of the air over nine U.S. cities as reported by Stanley et al. in 1971. The latter investigators found averages of 20 to 30 nanograms per cubic meter of air. Again, Woodwell et al. conveniently changed Stanley's data just a little, claiming that the averages were from 1 to 100 nanograms per cubic meter. Setting aside any quibble over numbers, Stanley's measurements may appear to represent a verification of the model.

However, if we substitute these figures back into the model, it emerges that something is seriously wrong. (We will not burden the reader with an analysis of the differential equations, even though they are quite simple, because standard arithmetic is adequate to illustrate our point.)

From the author's own data,[*] it can be determined that they used the figure 3.3×10^{17} m^3 for the volume of the lower atmosphere. If there were a maximum of 72 ppt DDT present in this volume, this would yield a total of 27,700 tons in circulation. This is the maximum value which has *ever* been present in the atmosphere, on the basis of their calculations. If 30,000 tons of residues are annually dissipated in rainfall out of this 27,700 tons, it is difficult to fathom how a four-year residence time can be claimed, since the latter would require that there should have been at least 120,000 tons circulating in the atmosphere.

Looking at it from another angle, if we used Stanley's high average of 30 nanograms per cubic meter in air (30 ppt) there would be only 10,000 tons of DDT residues in the atmosphere, which obviously could not result in a global precipitation of 30,000 tons per year.

It is further important to note that Stanley and his coworkers (who have conducted the most thorough study to date on atmospheric pesticide concen-

---

[*]They state that the equilibrium concentration of DDT in the atmosphere is about 3×10^{-6} g/m^3, and the saturation capacity of the atmosphere to the tropopause is about 10^{12} grams of DDT.

trations, having examined 880 composite samples) clearly established that DDT in the atmosphere is primarily attached to particulates, rather than being in vapor form. They wrote: "Appreciable amounts of pesticide were on the filter, indicating that the pesticide was probably absorbed [sic] on particulate matter trapped by the filter. . . . about 80% of the chlorinated pesticides was [sic] present in the filter . . ." (Stanley et al., 1971, p. 434). And further: "There was no apparent correlation of level with rainfall. . . . The pesticide distribution in the components of the sampling train indicates that most pesticides are present in the atmosphere as particulates" (*ibid.*, p. 435).

It has been repeatedly stated that there are no data on DDT concentrations in open ocean waters. Therefore, Woodwell and his coauthors understandably could not "verify" the predicted concentrations of residues in the mixed layer, resulting from their model, in terms of independent measurements. On the other hand, they could have tested the correctness of their predictions—at least in terms of their own assumptions—by substituting the derived concentrations back into the model.

According to the authors, approximately 25,000 metric tons of DDT reach the mixed layer per year, where it has a four-year residence time. One could, thus, have a total of 100,000 tons present in these waters. The volume of this layer is $25 \times 10^{15} m^3$. 100,000 tons of DDT residues dispersed in it would give a concentration of 4 ppt. To reach a value of 15 ppt, as predicted by the model for 1971, one would need to have 375,000 tons of DDT in circulation. If there were no loss to the abyss, one could reach this amount in 15 years, given a steady yearly input of 25,000 tons since 1956. However, because the residence time is only four years—as postulated—it is impossible to accumulate at any time more than 100,000 tons. Given all these inconsistencies, one wonders that the computer didn't break down, for the ordinary human mind boggles at such numerical discrepancies.

It should be apparent to the reader that the two studies on the distribution of DDT residues which we have discussed are rather similar, both in their basic assumptions and in their general estimates. Since Dr. Woodwell was a member of the SCEP Ecological Work Group, it seems curious that he felt the need only one and one-half years later to develop a computerized model dealing with the same basic question to which the members of the SCEP panel had addressed themselves, particularly as no new data were utilized in the design of the model. Naturally, we can only speculate here about the motives of the authors, but several things come to mind.

In October, 1970, a different mathematical model was proposed by Harrison, et al. to account for and predict the accumulation and residence time of DDT throughout different trophic levels of the food chain of the biosphere. The authors came to the conclusion that the residence time of DDT in the biosphere is in the range of hundreds of years. This study gave rise to so much serious criticism that it became more of a liability than an asset for environmentalists fighting against the future uses of DDT. Without going into any detailed criticism of the Harrison paper, Woodwell and his coauthors quietly dissociated themselves from it as follows: "Such an analysis [referring to Harrison et al.] suggests that equilibrium for the entire biota would be reached only after many decades. Movement of DDT residues to the abyss appears much more rapid than this" (Woodwell et al., 1971, p. 1105).

There are probably other more important reasons for attempting to put the whole DDT transport question into a new perspective. Since the time of the publication of the SCEP reports, there has been considerable re-examination and dissemination of information about DDT's behavior in the physico-chemical environment. For the most part, this information is contained in older publications, but it had been conveniently ignored or quoted out of context by the environmental activists. For instance, as we pointed out earlier, the oft-mentioned codistillation-with-water phenomenon simply does not occur under normal environmental conditions, and this fact has been brought to the attention of persons involved in the regulation of future DDT manufacture and use. The SCEP panel made a central point of codistillation, whereas in the study by Woodwell et al. it is not even mentioned. Similarly, although the Goldberg panel speaks of atmospheric transport as the principal route by which DDT is disseminated, they do not mention the atmosphere itself as a major reservoir for the storage of DDT residues. In the Woodwell paper, emphasis is placed on the probability that DDT in the atmosphere is primarily in a vapor phase, rather than present as aerosols or adsorbed to particulates; and this assumption permits the authors to postulate that the atmosphere is a relatively long-term reservoir for active DDT residues.

Further, the SCEP panel's conclusions differ importantly from those of Woodwell and his coauthors. The panel claimed that—even if the manufacture of DDT is halted in the near future—it will still accumulate for years in the mixed layer of the oceans (being capable of re-entering the atmosphere from the surface film) and will thus continue to endanger marine organisms. It was this kind of thinking that led them to make the alarmist declaration: ". . . we may not have an opportunity to redress the consequences." In view of the growing evidence to the contrary—that is, wherever use restrictions have been introduced, DDT residues have declined dramatically and rapidly in soils, fresh waters, estuaries, and in the whole biota, man included—the above statement seems to have lost its credibility.

The conclusions of Woodwell and his coauthors are quite another matter, for they foresee a definite decline in all reservoirs, provided, of course, that DDT production stops by 1974. In the atmosphere, they predict that the concentration will have declined to 10 percent of its 1966 peak value (72 ppt) by 1984, and in the mixed layer of the oceans, a decline to 10 percent of the 1971 peak value (15 ppt) will be reached by 1993. This is a much less pessimistic prediction.

Lastly, there is one serious unanswered question in these evaluations of DDT residue distributions: Why has only an insignificant amount of the DDT produced accumulated in the biota? The SCEP panel mentions this fact, but does not attempt to explain it. Woodwell et al., on the other hand, address themselves directly to this puzzling situation. Here it will be fruitful to consider several lengthy quotations from their paper. On page 1105 they write: "The residues presently held in the biota, and the maximum quantity that the biota could hold (not very greatly different), are so small in proportion to the total amount of DDT produced that we wonder why the biota has not been affected much more drastically than it has been—and what the future holds." In speaking about oceanic birds and mammals high on the food chain, which have been contaminated as a result of the worldwide circulation of DDT in the nonliving reservoirs, they state: "The fact that none of these organisms has yet become extinct from DDT effects is *mere good fortune:* the total amounts of DDT estimated to be circulating in the biosphere are many times greater than the amounts required to eliminate most such animals. . . . Yet, although there is no question about the devastation wrought by DDT locally and even regionally, the worldwide component seems not yet to have reached the point of widespread extinctions" (*ibid.,* p. 1106, our emphasis).

And later on the same page:

> The physical and chemical characteristics of DDT might lead one to assume that the biosphere should behave as a giant separatory funnel, gradually partitioning the lipid-soluble residues into the lipid-rich biota. Although there is no question that this process does occur, there is also no escape from the conclusion that it does not work well on the biospheric level. Most of the DDT produced has either been degraded to innocuousness or sequestered in places where it is not freely available to the biota. Recent work seems to support the latter assumption . . . [?] The fact remains, however, that, despite the abundance, peristence, and worldwide distribution of DDT residues, they are not as freely available to the biota as might be assumed . . . In this instance *man seems to have been blessed with extraordinary good fortune. (Ibid.,* our emphasis)

And in their final conclusion: "The reason for the biota's failure to absorb larger quantities and to be affected much more severely is unclear. The analysis suggests that *mere good fortune* has protected man and the rest of the biota from much higher concentrations . . ." (*ibid.;* our emphasis).

The first pages of this article give a review in high scientific jargon of the properties of DDT and a summary of what the authors believe to be important aspects of its biological actions. Then follow the explanation of the assumptions for the mathematics of the computer model, together with the precise predictions, still written in scientific style. However, when the authors deal with the implications of their findings for life, the language suddenly changes into that of faith. The use of expressions such as "man has been blessed with extraordinary good fortune" seem like a most peculiar way for scientists to explain why an expected phenomenon failed to take place. Blessed by Whom? Was it a fluke of luck, or predestined protection? We don't know exactly what the authors meant, but it is clear that they cannot give a scientific answer to the questions they raised: Why are there such insignificant amounts of DDT residues in the biota? And why are those which have been identified in living forms not more damaging?

Would it not be both much simpler and more in accord with scientific findings to consider the probability that DDT is, after all, degradable; and that in most circumstances, it disappears without a trace in a period of a few months?

To sum up: we have seen that a sizable number of persons with supposedly well-trained, critical minds have expended considerable time, energy, and expense attempting to validate a preconceived idea, and in the end, despite all their numerical jugglings, they are left with a declaration of faith.

Who Is Measuring What?

Before we leave completely this subject of DDT residues in the biosphere— those that were there, or might be there, or ought to be there, or certainly, anyway, probably will be there—we wish to raise one last question bearing on what is, in fact, being measured.

It is a peculiar irony that while many lay environmentalists share Rachel Carson's low opinion of those creative organic chemists who make new compounds in their laboratories, these same purists take as gospel the results of chemical analytical techniques, particularly when the substance identified in the biota or environment is "scary" and the quantities reported sound "threatening." It rarely occurs to anyone other than "narrow specialists" to question the accuracy of these residue determinations. We certainly do not want to cast doubt on the achievements of modern analytical chemistry in general, nor to deny that, in the right hands, the various methods for indentification and quantification of residual compounds in minute amounts are amazingly sensitive and sophisticated. However, the phrase "in the right hands" is a key one, for the methodologies used most commonly are not nearly so simple and straightforward as they are often made to sound. Rather serious errors in both quantitation and identification have been made even by highly cautious, objective specialists who are not out to prove any sort of case, and one may suspect that where doubtful "readings" are involved, accuracy is often inversely proportional to the degree to which the analyst is convinced beforehand that he will find a high degree of contamination.

Where residues of pesticides are concerned, we have seen that these are frequently reported in the parts per billion and parts per trillion range, and sometimes in even smaller quantities. To grasp what very small proportions these are, it may be useful to consider several analogies: for example, 200 loaded rail cars full of coal weigh approximately 2,000 tons. A pinhead weighs 2 milligrams. The proportion between 2,000 tons and 2 milligrams is 1 part per trillion: one pinhead to the 200 cars full of coal. Find it! Parts per million and parts per billion are not altogether large quantities, either. Considering proportions in these ranges, two participants at a New York Academy of Sciences Conference made the following comparisons: "A level of 0.01 ppm is equivalent to 1 inch in 1,578 miles or 1 second in 3.17 years, and 0.01 ppb is only 1 inch in 1,578,000 miles (over six times the distance to the moon) or only 1 second in 31.7 centuries!" (Schechter, 1969, p. 141). "The thickness of a sheet of paper is a part per million of the height of this hotel [the Barbizon Plaza in New York City]. A part per million is an extremely small proportion; a part per billion is even smaller, the relationship of one foot of distance to the distance to the moon" (Crosby, 1969, p. 203). These examples may give the lay reader a clearer idea of the minuteness of the quantities of pesticide residues which are commonly measured in waters, soils, and tissues. One may sometimes wonder about the accuracy of the quantitative measurements, since these amounts are so extremely small that even a minor error can throw off the determinations considerably.

A much more serious problem arises if one considers the underlying principles of gas chromatography, which is the favored technique employed for identification of the various pesticides and their residues. Gas chromatography is an excellent analytical technique for identifying absolutely *pure* compounds; but when samples of soil, or water, or tissues, which contain mixtures of a great number of organics are measured by this method, considerable difficulty arises in interpreting the results. Many completely unrelated compounds may produce peaks in the same location on the chromatogram; and when a great number of compounds are present in the sample, it is sometimes impossible to decide to which of them a certain peak should be ascribed.

For instance, in 1964, the Public Health Service identified endrin in fish in connection with one of the famous Mississippi fish kills. Endrin is a very complex molecule that is composed of several carbon atom rings, with six attached chloride atoms. Subsequent developments, however, indicated that at that time the agency was not equipped to measure endrin at all. They misidentified dieldrin—a similarly complex molecule—when what they were actually dealing with was chlorohydrin (McLean, 1967). The latter compound is a straight chain alcohol made up of three carbon atoms, with only one chlorine attached to it. The two molecules have absolutely no chemical affinity, yet one was mistaken for the other. The myth of this "endrin-caused" Mississippi fish kill is still being perpetrated at the present time, in spite of solid refutations. Frank Graham, Jr., keeps the story alive for laymen in several of his books, while the NASCO panel members included it in their "objective" scientific review *Chlorinated Hydrocarbons in the Marine Environment.* Once identified as such, pesticide residue reports prove amazingly persistent, not to be broken down by refutations.

Errors in identification resulting from the use of the gas chromatograph alone are not isolated incidences. In a 1969 lecture on methodology Francis Gunther, who is the editor of *Residue Reviews* and one of the world's most respected authorities on residue chemistry, repeatedly made warning statements concerning rash conclusions reached through misapplications of gas chromatography, particularly where the results refer to very small sample sizes and where there has been no confirmation based on other techniques.

> As emphasized by many authorities, gas chromatology represents both cleanup and estimation, but it is neither an identifying nor a measuring technique unless supported by multicolumn and multidectector systems and preferably buttressed by independent determinations by other methods on aliquots of the sample in question.
>
> It [gas chromatology] is obviously the most popular single technique in use in residue evaluations today, yet it can be abused unless supported by other methods and by inclusion of carefully selected samples to demonstrate integrity of results.
>
> Finally, the current fascination with everdecreasing sample size is to be deplored for many reasons: background tends to increase disproportionately, contamination becomes a perpetual problem, instrumental vagaries are exaggerated, and the interpretive skill of the analyst is strained. . . . A comfortable compromise lies in the microgram-detection region, now attainable by all "specific" detectors, as well as by emission, infrared, and mass spectrometry, polarography, fluorometry, and functional group colorimetry. Sample sizes are larger than for picogram requirements, of course, but there is a rewarding comfort in having confidence in the results. (Gunther, 1969, pp. 74, 79, 80)

Recently, some attention has been brought in the daily press to problems of residue measurement uncertainties. In considering the many inconsistent reports over mercury contamination of fish, DDT in the environment, and so on, the *San Francisco Examiner* sponsored a small experiment involving testing by three different laboratories of soil samples collected in the Bay Area for mercury, lead, DDT, and DDE. The differences in the results exceeded any normal allowances for error, and the purposes and implications of the experiment were summarized in an *Examiner* editorial:

> . . . we sought to make the point that the public should view with caution some of the flood of pronouncements currently being made in the field of environmental hazards, food and drug dangers, medical tests, etc.
>
> The fact is that the opportunities for error in most laboratory testing are quite numerous. They range from the degree of competence of the lab technicians through the purity of equipment and materials and accuracy of procedures to interpretation of results. Aware of this, a careful scientist or laboratory will order tests run over and over again, and seek to have the results duplicated in some other laboratory.
>
> But we seem to live in a time when too many researchers, in and out of government, are too eager to get before the public with scare findings of one sort or another, or findings that bolster a preconceived notion. This leads them to violate sound rules of testing. (Editorial, *San Francisco Examiner,* September 26, 1972)

After raising the possibility that too many hasty and unconfirmed pronouncements about environmental threats will lead to a loss of public support and confidence, the editorial concludes: "If that public support is ever lost, the battle of the environment will be lost too."

A Sideshow

In addition to these general problems with residue measurements, there is one particular "interference factor" involved in identification by gas chromatography of chlorinated hydrocarbon residues which has become evident in the last three or four years. In 1966 the Swedish scientist Jensen raised the issue of environmental contamination with polychlorinated biphenyls (PCBs), which the reader may recall became a subject of interest to Risebrough and Peakall two years later. By 1969, evidence was accumulating that PCBs could interfere with various pesticide identifications when the gas chromatograph was used, since the peaks typical for lindane, heptachlor, aldrin, heptachlor epoxide, and p,p'-DDT might all be manifest when PCBs were present in a sample, whether or not it contained any of the mentioned pesticides (Reynolds, 1969). Actually, things are further complicated by the fact that the PCB designation does not refer to a single compound, there being more than 200 possible combinations, depending on the numbers and locations of the chlorine atoms on the biphenyl molecule. Usually Aroclor 1254 (Monsanto) is used as a reference. This particular PCB contains about 50 percent chlorine by weight.

Figure 14 is included to provide the reader with some idea of the gas chromatographic peaks which are typical for several chlorinated hydrocarbon pesticides and to show how these compare with those of a PCB. It should be apparent that several of the pesticide peaks in diagram A seem to be present in diagram B, which in fact, however, represents only Aroclor 1254. When a one-to-one mixture of pesticides and PCB is found—as in diagram A + B—it is impossible to know what is represented by the peaks, unless some other identification technique is employed. The suspicion that many pesticide determinations which have relied exclusively on single-column gas chromatography may be wildly inaccurate because of the possible presence in the sample of one of the PCBs—or some other interference factor—has naturally been raised since this discovery of the overlap of the typical peaks. We shall return to this point shortly, but first we wish to pay some attention to PCBs as a new environmental scare.

It is likely that the PCB story is in its early stages, both as regards the involvement of environmental activists and with respect to the evaluations by cautious scientists concerned with their prevalence and behavior in nature. Some public stir has been made about PCB accidents—leakage from insulating materials into chickenfeed for example (Pichirallo, 1971)—and a few activists, Robert Risebrough and David Brower among them, have been stimulating concern about these persistent compounds as "dangerous contaminants." However, the reader who has not yet heard about them should not feel too backward, for at the moment the PCB controversy is still a minor sideshow compared with the great DDT circus.

PCBs are important industrial compounds. Their largest single use is as coolant-insulators in transformers. They are also used as plasticizers in wire and cable coatings, insulating materials for electrical wiring and fluorescent lights. They are found in polymer films, in carbonless reproducing paper, some epoxy paints, and protective coatings for wood and metal. They have been produced in Europe and in the United States since the 1930s, although their prewar applications were probably minor.

Unlike pesticides, PCBs are not deliberately released into nature. On the contrary, their uses are such that one would expect only a very small proportion of the compounds produced to find their way into the environment. There are

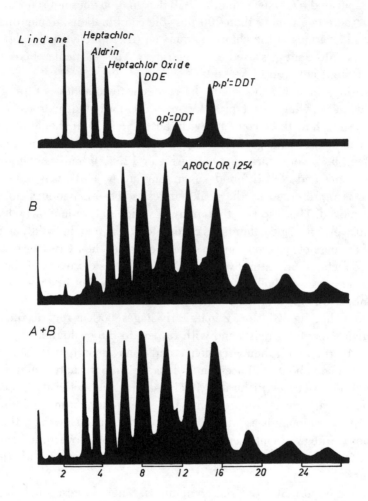

Figure 14. *GAS CHROMATOGRAM A IS OF STANDARD PESTICIDE MIXTURE, B IS TYPICAL OF AROCLOR 1254, AND A + B IS A CHROMATOGRAM OF A 50:50 MIXTURE OF BOTH (after Gustafson, 1970).*

basically three routes into the open environment: accidental leaks; incineration of materials containing them, or industrial effluents; and leaching from materials which have been "plasticized" with the compounds.

There have been indications for several years in scientific circles that small quantities of PCBs can leach out of plastic materials. For instance, a scientist at Texas A & M University who was planning to conduct some pesticide determinations on shellfish first made a routine test of some seawater in which he washed the Tygon tubing of his gas chromatographic instruments. He found to his surprise that the water contained several parts per billion of PCBs. His initial speculations about the origin of the PCBs were inconclusive—had they leached out of the plastic tubing?—but there was not much question in his mind that their presence cast grave doubts on the accuracy of earlier pesticide readings. When he exchanged the Tygon (which is standard on most gas chromatographs and other laboratory instruments) for rubber tubes, the PCB readings disappeared. This naturally heightened his suspicion that the PCBs were leaching out of the plastic tubing.* It was not long before confirmation of his experience began to come in from other scientists.

These scientists were not environmental activists; they were residue analysts, interested in making the best determinations possible of the compounds they sought to identify and quantify. Their reaction to the possibility that Tygon might be leaching PCBs was to replace it, or to calculate the errors which might have been introduced in their determinations by this contaminant. The experience also alerted them to the need for the use of multiple detection and confirmation methods.

But let us suppose they had been inclined toward doomsday prophesying. Might they not have called joint press conferences around the nation and created a colossal scare story, dwarfing all the worries about lead, mercury, pesticides, air pollution, food additives, and the other menaces with which we are said to be threatened? They probably could have done so, had they had the inclination and the properly dramatic personality types.

Think of it. PCBs are not readily degraded and they are lipid-soluble—like DDT—capable of accumulating in human fat. They are more toxic than DDT, and it would probably not be difficult to show that they are carcinogenic—especially in mouse experiments. There is already some suggestive evidence that they are teratogenic. As many commonly used items in our society are made of materials plasticized with PCBs, these deathly contaminants might be leaching out, creating a direct health hazard for man. Furthermore, other plasticizers, or even the base materials in thermoplastics (heat-polymerized compounds) have already been implicated as dangerous and unsafe agents. Phthalates, a group of chemicals most commonly used in the plastics industry in connection with the polymerization of cellulose derivatives, have been shown, for instance, to leach out from the cellophane bags in which blood for transfusion is stored. The con-

*Personal communication, S. Petrocelli, 1970.

cerned scientists (Jaeger and Rubin, 1970) who made this discovery darkly hinted at the horrifying implication that while attempting to save the patient's life through transfusion, the physician may unknowingly introduce a potential carcinogen.

The starting materials of some of the thermoplastics—vinyl chloride and vinylidene chloride—have also been shown to be "highly carcinogenic" (Viola, 1970). Such plastics as PVC and Saran, which are representatives of the two groups, are widely used as food wrappings, and it is known that some small amounts of the monomers and oligomers always present in traces in the finished compounds will migrate into the food items. Also, when PVC is used as water-pipe materials, it requires the addition of lead or cadmium salts as stabilizers, leaching of which in minor quantities into the drinking-water supply is unavoidable. Thus, we see that the other categories of plastics could be claimed to be equally dangerous as those in which PCBs have been used as a plasticizer.

Why have the environmentalists not made a major issue of this potential horror tale? Imagine the consequences of a movement to ban plastics: the rash of legal actions brought by irate citizens, the holy anger at the systematic poisoning of our plastic-packaged foods! Plastic cups, paper diapers, Tupperware, artificial fabrics . . . the list of potential dangers is endless! One can almost visualize the chaos that would ensue—not to speak of the economic disaster—from a people's movement to ban plastics. But perhaps an effort to stimulate such a movement would backfire? Perhaps people would not want to be told that myriads of items useful in their everyday lives are bad for them? We don't know why such an idea has not taken hold of environmentalists; the only talk we have heard of "replacing plastics" was from David Brower (president of Friends of the Earth) who says he is very worried about PCBs but pleased that Max Linn (president of the John Muir Institute) has suggested that a substitute for plastics should be found (Brower, 1970). We hope the gentleman is applying his intellectual powers to this challenging problem.

The "scenario" we have just described has not happened—not yet, at any rate, or perhaps we should say, not yet to our knowledge, it being somewhat difficult to keep abreast of all the scare stories about dangerous substances in our artificial world.

Instead, the environmentalists who have given their attention to PCB contamination have described the problem in terms of the ubiquity of the compounds (the route to the open environment being primarily industrial effluents and incineration); their persistence; their tendency to be accumulated in lipid tissues and magnified up the food chain; the threat to species on top of the food pyramid through effects on reproductive success. Sounds familiar, doesn't it? PCBs do *not,* however, cause eggshell thinning; not this year, anyway. In every other respect the parallels with DDT's described behavior in nature are remarkable.

One of the points most emphasized by the environmentalists concerned with PCBs is their almost complete resistance to both chemical and biological degradation, a "fact" which explains their extreme persistence. In this respect they are said to resemble DDE, the major metabolite of DDT. Recently, however, both compounds have been shown to be metabolized to a substantial degree in biological systems, DDE by common soil bacteria (Focht and Alexander, 1970) and PCBs even by higher organisms, such as pigeons and rats (Hutzinger et al., 1972). Naturally, this does not mean that there will be a retraction of claims about PCBs as "serious global pollutants." That is not the way the game goes.

In Sweden, where PCBs were first identified, the environment and the biota are said to be about equally as contaminated with them as with DDT and its metabolites (Jensen et al., 1969). They have not yet been discovered in Antarctic snow, but alarming reports have come in of quite considerable quantities found in the wilderness areas of northern and western Canada. In the summer of 1970, there were rumors that huge quantities had been identified in the Hudson, but these died out when it was noted that the amounts exceeded the solubility in water about a millionfold. To the environmentalist way of thinking, the obvious conclusion to be drawn from the information that areas remote from use are contaminated is that PCBs are dangerously persistent and are transported to wilderness areas like the forests of Saskatchewan by winds and rain. It is by this familiar route that they have become ubiquitous and serious global contaminants.

There is only one problem with this interpretation. It is almost painful to have to be so repetitive in our arguments, but there is again the question of quantities. We just do not see how there could be enough PCBs in the open environment to cause serious contamination of more than small local areas. Let us consider some numbers.

Annual production figures for PCBs in the United States are given by Goldberg as 5×10^9 g, or 5,000 tons (NASCO, 1971, p. 41). (The compounds are not manufactured in Canada or in Mexico.) While it is conceivable that the contamination of Swedish flora and fauna could reflect incineration of materials containing PCBs in continental Europe (the Swedes do have very bad luck with respect to wind currents), probably no one would maintain that the PCBs found in Saskatchewan had the same origins: they must have come from the United States.

If we suppose that *all* the PCBs manufactured in one year were to be released into the environment, and if we further suppose that they will be spread by winds and rain *only* over the continental United States, the "application rate" would be 5 grams per hectare. That is clearly not enough. We might further assume that production rates have been constant since 1932 (too high) and that none of these PCBs had degraded in any manner (clearly not true), and then we would get a figure of 100 grams per hectare. This begins to look a slight bit more like "environmental contamination," but it is still negligible compared with pesticide residues. Only if the entire production lot for the full 40 years were deliberately dumped over one state of the union could the PCB levels be high enough to account for those residues reported in some samples; and this would still not give us any explanation of how so much of the compound found its way to the Canadian wilderness.

Could it be possible that the interference readings for pesticides were not necessarily all PCBs, but may have included some other, perhaps naturally occurring substances?

Natural Interference

The possibility that there might be interference from natural compounds was raised as early as 1961, when Goodwin et al. found that aldrin-like materials originating from plants could be distinguished from insecticides in soil analysis by the use of multicolumn chromatography. In spite of the customary cleanup procedures employed in sample preparation for gas chromatographic work, interfering substances indigenous to the soil itself have also been detected on analysis. This disturbing problem was investigated in 1970 by Frazier and his coworkers at the University of Wisconsin. They obtained 34 soil samples which had been collected in the period 1909–1911 and had been stored in tightly stoppered glass jars. There could be no question about the soils being contaminated with organochlorine insecticides because they came from a time before the introduction of these compounds. Using routine sample preparation techniques and three-column gas chromatography, the authors found that all the soil extracts yielded one or more apparent organochlorine insecticide peaks. They could identify only one of the peaks as a laboratory artifact originating from the Tygon tubing used in the extraction procedure. They did not come to any conclusion as to the nature of the other interfering compounds, except to emphasize that they were indigenous to the soils.

In 1969 a review article by Hylin et al. appeared, entitled "Potential Interferences in Certain Pesticide Residue Analyses from Organochlorine Compounds Occurring Naturally in Plants." Two interesting points emerge from this review:

1. There are several classes of lower plants which produce a variety of chlorinated organic compounds. These include *Actinomycetes* or ray fungi (which

are not really fungi at all, but belong to the bacteria), lichens, and many true fungi, especially the molds and mushrooms of the class *Basidiomycetes.*

2. Many higher, vascular plants synthesize alkaloids which contain epoxides. These are groups that are very labile chemically; they can become easily chlorinated even under mild conditions, while drying at room temperature, for instance. All plants contain chloride ions in their cell sap; thus the materials for the chlorination of the epoxide alkaloids are available within the plant itself.

We should like to elaborate a bit further on the general matter of chlorinated organics in nature. To begin with, one might point out that many of the most potent antibiotics—chloramphenicol, griseofulvin, chlorotetracycline, and caldariomycin—are produced by the soil-dwelling *Actinomycetes.* Ray fungi are extremely abundant microorganisms; their weight in the top layers of soil is approximately 1,000 pounds per acre. They are also worldwide in distribution, being equally at home in arid and humid lands. Among the chlorine-containing antibiotics synthesized by ray fungi, caldariomycin is the simplest. It looks like this:

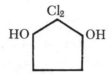

a structure which closely resembles several of the organochlorine pesticides.

The two most widespread genera of molds—*Penicillium* and *Aspergillus*—synthesize a number of organochlorine compounds. One of the metabolites of a soil-living *Penicillium* species is 2,4-dichlorophenol (Ando et al. 1970) shown below:

Although this compound was only very recently identified in nature, it was synthesized in the laboratory about 80 years ago. It was widely used as a surface disinfectant in the fairly recent past, and it forms the starting point for a whole array of chlorinated phenol compounds, among which are a number of pesticides. Its cogenitor, Dowcide 2S (2,4,6-trichlorophenol) is a useful fungicide.

Some of the naturally synthesized, chlorine-containing metabolites of these two molds are harmful to man. *Penicillium islandicum,* for example, secretes *islanditoxin*—a potent carcinogen. In spite of its name, this mold is quite common in the Far East, where mass intoxications have resulted from ingestion of rice on which it has established itself. Some authors are of the opinion that the higher incidence of liver tumors in Japan and China reflects the frequency with which the staple food of these countries is molded by *P. islandicum* (Wirth et al., 1971). *Aspergillus ochraceous,* which favors other grains like oats, also produces a highly toxic organochlorine metabolite: *ochratoxin A.* When contaminated food is ingested by higher animals or people, it causes severe damage to the liver. Although not a chlorine-containing compound, *aflatoxin* should probably be mentioned once again, since this exceedingly common metabolite of another *Aspergillus* species, *A. flavus,* is one of the strongest chemical carcinogens as yet known — a completely natural product.

Coming back to the natural chlorinated organics synthesized by plants, the higher fungus *Drosophila subatrata** is of particular interest, since it produces the chlorine-containing antibiotic *drosophilin A.* The latter is a rather simple compound that has four attached chlorine atoms. It has the structure

$$\underset{\text{Cl}\qquad\text{Cl}}{\overset{\text{Cl}\qquad\text{Cl}}{\text{HO}\!\!\left\langle\!\!\bigcirc\!\!\right\rangle\!\!\text{OCH}_3}}$$

which is remarkably similar to the fungicide-slimicide, Dowcide G.

Finally, a great many lichens of both soil-dwelling and bark-dwelling forms synthesize a large variety of organochlorine compounds. These fall into two major categories: the depsides and the depsidones, with both aliphatic and aromatic representatives.

All the particular organisms which we have mentioned so far as capable of producing organochlorine compounds are lower plants, and all are basically soil-dwelling, although some, such as the molds, migrate freely to other substrates.

But the higher plants also include some species which contain clearly identified organochlorine compounds — not just the epoxy alkaloids which may become chlorinated. One of the most common flavon pigments — malvidin chloride — is such a chemical. This substance imparts the coloring in the blue-purple-mauve range to many familiar flowers and fruits: lilac, hortensia, petunias, peonies, and blue grapes, just to name a few. The synthetic analogues of the chemical, which do not differ essentially from the natural product, are used in all kinds of dyes and paints in this color range.

The role of the soil-dwelling microorganisms is a double one. On the one hand, many of them are capable of breaking down the organochlorines — both

---

* This organism has no relation to the common fruit fly, *Drosophila melanogaster.* The similarity in the names results from the fact that the botanical and zoological nomenclatures are independent of each other. There are several genera in the plant and animal kingdoms which have the same names.

the naturally occurring compounds and the man-made chemicals—into their simplest constituents. For instance, *Hydrogenomonas* spp., which are very common soil bacteria, have recently been reported to metabolize DDT and DDE through ring fission, or breaking open the benzene rings (Focht and Alexander, 1970). On the other hand, as we have seen, the opposite process is also taking place in the soil: chlorinated organic molecules are being synthesized by microorganisms. Where higher plants that contain chlorinated alkaloids or malvidin chloride pigments are decomposing, the organochlorine compounds will either be broken down completely, or parts of them will be used by the soil microorganisms to build their own metabolites. Thus there does not seem to be much question that natural chlorinated organics are quite prevalent in soils and could interfere with organochlorine determinations aimed at identifying and quantifying the man-made products. It is also quite probable that some natural compounds of this sort exist in waters, although this area is even less explored than that of soil.[*]

The oft-repeated idea that man-made chemicals are things altogether apart from nature was stated in unequivocal terms by Carson: "The chemicals to which life is asked to make its adjustment are no longer merely the calcium and silica and copper and all the rest of the minerals washed out of the rocks and carried in rivers to the sea; they are the synthetic creations of man's inventive mind, brewed in his laboratories, and having no counterparts in nature" (Carson, 1962, p. 17).

This statement makes it appear as though nature doesn't produce any organic molecules at all, which even Miss Carson certainly knew was not the case. But what would she have said to the discovery that a simple mold, living in the soil under quite natural conditions, is capable of synthesizing a chlorinated phenol, the very prototype of the modern pesticides "brewed in man's laboratories"? For better or for worse, many of the creations of man's inventive mind do have counterparts in nature.

It would seem then that there are a sizable number of naturally occurring compounds which might interfere with gas chromatographic determinations of man-made organochlorines in the environment, particularly in soils.

We want to make it clear that, in bringing attention to these possible natural sources of interference with residue determinations, we do not mean to assert

---

[*] With respect to PCB determinations in the aqueous environment, one possible interference factor should be mentioned, although it is not "natural." Holden (1970) reported relatively large quantities of PCBs in sewage sludge in the British Isles. He assumed that the source of these contaminants must be industrial effluents entering the treatment plants, but he was unable to trace down actual discharging industries. He found no contamination of fish, nor were the liquid sewage effluents contaminated to any significant extent. Since all the supposed PCBs were extracted from the sludge, it seems strange that no investigations have been pursued to determine whether the chlorination process employed in secondary treatment could itself produce chlorinated organics.

that there are *no* residues of DDT or PCB or dieldrin, or any other of the man-made organochlorines. The more persistent compounds do remain in the environment for a period, although the time required for their breakdown in most natural systems has been grossly overestimated by the environmentalists. But the questions raised by interference factors are those of precise identity and of quantities. We are not prepared to accept the reports of PCB contamination of wilderness soils, even if such reports become overwhelming in number, unless the measurements are performed by scientists with no special interest in proving a case and are backed by careful multiple detection systems.

It is to be hoped that before the environmentalists get too carried away with stories about the ubiquity of PCB contamination and descriptions of its behavior in food webs, some critical thinkers will ask whether the areas where the contamination is reported are near enough to some actual source of the compound for the reports to be probable. We don't want to be subjected to speculative models about how PCBs get transported into the wilderness and how great are the worldwide levels of these pollutants until we are persuaded that it is really the man-made industrial materials which are being "measured," rather than some very similar compound which is part of nature's own chemical bag of tricks.

To Man's Advantage

Having considered some natural substances which might be responsible in some analytical techniques for false or faulty identifications of trace quantities of pesticides and PCBs, we should like to pursue the matter of the "counterparts" in nature from a slightly different angle—that of naturally occurring compounds as the precursors or analogues of the chemicals man brews in his laboratories.

During the 1920s, explorers reported the peculiar fact that in some regions of the upper Amazon River there were no mosquitoes. The populations of the whole insect fauna seemed thin there in comparison to those of typical rain forests. The waters had a faint yellowish coloration, and in 1937 Kalle isolated from them a pigment which is still called yellow pigment *(Gelbstoff)*. The composition of this substance is not yet completely known, but chemical analysis has related it to certain breakdown products of lignins.

The puzzling phenomenon of the mosquito-free tropical area was never satisfactorily explained. Other observations of unexpected insecticidal properties have, however, been pursued further. A few years ago, the Harvard biologist Williams and the Czech entomologist Slama were working together on the larvae of the linden bug. The larvae, which Slama had brought with him from Prague, failed to develop normally in the Harvard labs. From the behavior of the insects, which grew into juvenile monsters and then died, the scientists suspected that a juvenile hormone was operating, but careful checks failed to reveal any contamination in the seeds, the water vials, or the general environment of the larvae. After considerable experimentation, they began to suspect the paper toweling spread on the petri dishes, and they learned that the larvae would develop normally if the paper was replaced by European filters. They discovered that paper of American or Canadian origin of all sorts—everything from Kleenex to the *New York Times* and the pages of *Science*—was active in inhibiting larval development, while European and Japanese papers were inert. Further investigations led to the specific source of the active "paper factor": a terpene produced by the balsam fir (Williams, 1967).

What might have been the mosquito-killing substance in the upper Amazon? Probably another terpene, such as camphor, pinene, phellandrene, menthol, or borneol. These essential oils are produced by all kinds of plants, and form a large fraction of the organic matter in many trees, particularly the conifers. All the terpenes show some insecticidal properties (do you remember the camphor mothballs in your closet?), and all are toxic to man in varying degrees. Trees may evaporate them into the air, or extrude them as one of the constituents of gum. And beyond that, the whole tree is permeated with them.

Woody tissues contain a highly complex polymer called lignin, whose chemical structure is not yet completely defined. Its basic constituents, however, are different phenolic compounds: vanillin, coniferyl alcohol, cresol, and so on. When woods decompose to form humus, some of these phenols and the terpenes, if present, will become liberated into the soil. We have already seen that several soil-dwelling molds and even higher fungi are capable of producing chlorinated phenols, such as 2,4-dichlorophenol. To our knowledge, no chlorinated terpenes have been identified in nature with certainty, but since 2,4-dichlorophenol was synthesized in the laboratory 80 years before it was found to be a naturally occurring compound, there is no ruling out the possibility that chlorinated terpenes may also occur as a result of the natural humification process.

In general, the terpenes have some insecticidal properties in their natural state. Some of them may have evolved as part of the chemical defense system of plants. What man does when he chlorinates a terpene in the laboratory, as in the production of the insecticides toxaphene and strobane, is to increase the efficiency of the molecule to his own advantage. Toxaphene is basically a chlorinated camphor. The lethal dosage of the natural substance and that of the pesticide are exactly the same for man; but the chlorinated compound is much more toxic to insects than is pure camphor.

Consider also the fungicide pentachlorophenol (Dowcide 2S), which is a simple phenol molecule with five chlorine atoms attached. Phenol alone—which is quite ubiquitous in nature—has about twice the acute toxicity to man as the artificial fungicide. On the other hand, while phenol is reasonably effective as a surface disinfectant, it cannot compete with Dowcide 2S for protection against wood rot. To be sure, there are those who say that Dowcide 2S is a carcinogen; but so is phenol, if enough of it is injected into mice for long enough periods of time. Are we to conclude that we should ban nature?

Of course, "nature knows best," as many have been told by the learned scientist Barry Commoner, who unlike the autodidact Carson, obtained a Ph.D. In his most recent book, *The Closing Circle*, Commoner develops four "fundamental laws of ecology," the third of which concerns the superiority and ecological soundness of everything synthesized in nature, and the potentially destructive properties of most of the compounds made by man, even when he just copies nature (see nitrate fertilizers, discussed in Chapter 10). In justifying this point of view, he argues:

> . . . living cells synthesize fatty acids (a type of organic molecule that contains carbon chains of various lengths) with even-numbered carbon chain lengths (i.e., 4, 6, 8, etc., carbons), but no fatty acids with odd-numbered carbon chain lengths. This suggests that the latter have once been tried out and found wanting.
>
> Similarly, organic compounds that contain attached nitrogen and oxygen atoms are singularly rare in living things. This should warn us that the artificial introduction of substances of this type would be dangerous. This is indeed the case, for such substances are usually toxic and frequently carcinogenic.
>
> One of the striking facts about the chemistry of living systems is that for every organic substance produced by a living organism, there exists, somewhere in nature, an enzyme capable of breaking that substance down. In effect, no organic substance is synthesized unless there is provision for its degradation. . . . (Commoner, 1971, p. 44)

Fortunately for man, all three of these fundamental teachings are wrong. Commoner makes a point of confessing, in the first pages of *The Closing Circle*, that although his book deals mainly with ecological problems, he never received any special training in this subject. It appears to us that he may have also skipped organic chemistry. So as not to be charged with lack of respect, let us explain wherein he errs.

1. Odd-numbered fatty acids with from 1 to 33 carbon chains *are* synthesized by living cells, some of them abundantly, some with minor frequency. A number of these fatty acids have been known since the earliest days of organic

chemistry. The simplest among them is formic acid, which is responsible for the itching caused by insect bites. And propionic acid, for instance, is a ubiquitous compound, present in animals from mollusks to man. The penetrating odor of feline urine is due to valeric acid, which is also a common constituent of several plants. Or how about undecylinic acid, a basic ingredient of sweat, Dr. Commoner's included, presumably? All of these completely natural chemicals are odd-numbered fatty acids, but, if we are to believe the professor, they simply don't exist.

2. Unfortunately, the statement referring to the rarity of organic compounds containing attached nitrogen and oxygen atoms is not clearly expressed, and since no examples are given, there are three possible meanings: (a) that compounds with attached nitrogen atoms and also those with attached oxygen atoms are both rare; (b) that those with a nitrogen atom and also an oxygen atom separately bonded on the same compound are rare; or (c) that those with an NO group attached are rare.

If (a), then the statement is completely absurd, since there are thousands of such compounds—all fatty acids, all amino acids, most of the sugars, etc. If (b), there are a number of alkaloids containing such a configuration. Some of them are toxic, some are not. On the other hand, there are only a limited number of manufactured compounds with this type of structure, and none of them is used in the environment. If (c), we are talking about molecules occurring in intermediary metabolism of cells—not rare at all. One of these nitroso compounds is vitamin B_{12c}.

3. The third great generalization about nature's chemistry is not right either; if it were, pollen grains and spores would not be so abundant as important fossils. There is *no* known enzyme which is capable of breaking down sporopollinin, the complex organic polymer which is a major constituent of spore and pollen grain walls. Sporopollinin makes up the major fraction of bitumen and the insoluble fraction of kerogen. Here is a widely occurring natural substance which is absolutely not biodegradable; in fact, it is almost indestructible, withstanding treatment with concentrated acids and alkalis, and being broken down only at high temperatures. Sporopollinin is not only one of the commonest of organic polymers, but it is also one of the first to have developed on the planet. Over the whole course of evolutionary time, not a *single* species ever evolved an enzyme which could degrade it.

Were it not for the considerable influence Commoner exerts over the thinking of the populace, it would hardly be worthwhile to point up these fallacies, for one tends to assume that no professional could take seriously generalizations which derive from such appalling basic errors. Unfortunately, however, Commoner—probably more than any other of the heroic, concerned scientists of the environmental movement—sees himself as an educator of the masses, a man whose goal is to bridge the "two cultures." Through his organization, his writings, his lectures, he attempts to "bring science to the people." But, sadly, this worthy goal is tainted, for many of his utterances reveal that the teacher is not up to the task.

When we mentioned Commoner's "neo-Lamarckian" views on evolution (see Chapter 4), we did not fault him for holding an unorthodox opinion, since evolutionary theories still involve a great many unknowns. But on issues where known scientific *facts* are discussed—facts about which there is no dispute— we have no reason to spare him embarrassment.

Commoner's "ecological law" that "nature knows best" amounts fundamentally to the same emotional stance as that taken by Rachel Carson. It was unscientific in 1962 in her formulation, and it is equally unacceptable to the rational mind as presented in *The Closing Circle*. Beyond the lamentable fact that many of his theses are scientifically untenable, Commoner's "third law of ecology" is completely removed from the realities of life on this planet, where man, his needs, his social structures, and his ways of meeting the challenges confronted by other species *are not separate from but part of nature*.

Man, unlike other species, is supplied with very meager defenses. Without his brain, he would be most unfit for survival in the natural environment, and would undoubtedly have been a short-lived evolutionary experiment. As Nobel laureate Joshua Lederberg put it, ". . . the 'balance of nature' offers no assurance that any particular species will survive, especially not such a frail creature as man whose defenses are limited to what his wits can create" (Lederberg, 1971, p. 399).

One of man's greatest triumphs in outwitting competing organisms is represented by the synthesis of pesticides over the last 40 years. In developing these compounds, organic chemists take many different approaches, from simply simulating a natural chemical to creating entirely new molecules constructed on the basis of known structure-activity relationships. One such approach is illustrated by the development of the pesticide lindane. This compound was not originally synthesized for insecticidal purposes. It represented the product of a search for antivitamins. There is one vitamin in the B group called mesoinositol. It is not an essential vitamin for man, since it has no demonstrable function in higher animals. On the other hand, it is an essential growth factor for yeasts. It seemed obvious that, if a substance could be found which would be similar to m-inositol, but which still would be different enough not to be capable of fulfilling the physiological function of the vitamin, then the yeast cells would not be able to recognize the substance as foreign and would incorporate it, where it would block or disrupt the metabolic pathway necessary for the growth process. After several years of highly interesting experimentation (from the details of which we spare the reader), it was found that replacing the six hydroxyl groups on the *m*-inositol molecule with chlorine atoms would do the trick. Thus the first antivitamin was synthesized, and, as an unexpected bonus, it turned out to be a highly effective insecticide as well as being a yeast growth inhibitor.

Gammexane, the active ingredient in lindane, is an antimetabolite, at least for yeasts. It is not a natural compound, but rather the perfect analogue of a vitamin. Antimetabolites produce an effect precisely because they are not natural. Nevertheless, in her version of "nature knows best," Carson (who did not know that lindane is an antimetabolite) recommended them as possible substitutes for the broad-spectrum pesticides, along with lead arsenate and "safe" alkylating agents.

If we now come full circle and return to DDT, which has been, after all, our principal focus for discussion, we must confess that the DDT molecule is a human creation, too. It is not found in nature, but its discovery as an insecticide was of unparalleled importance for man in his struggle with the insects which compete for his food and transfer deadly disease parasites. The environmental activists assert, without being able to offer proof of their claim, that DDT use has disrupted the balance of nature and that even if its use is suspended, it will still remain a threat to the global ecosystem. We would counter that there is only one certain fact about DDT's disruption of nature: it has saved so many lives in so short a span of time that it has created a temporary imbalance in terms of the sudden rise in the curve of population growth. If we want to be responsible to our fellow men, it would seem that we have no real choice but to meet the challenges of the global population increase with an intensification, and not a diminution, of human technology. What the DDT story has really taught us is not that we should refrain from tampering with natural conditions, but that we cannot lose courage at the half-way point once we have begun to do so. On every continent of the globe there are peoples engaged in an immediate life-and-death struggle with hunger and disease. Would it not be more fulfilling to terminate these endless arguments over mostly imaginary and invented problems, and pitch our energies into aiding the world's poor towards victory in their very real struggle?

18

DEUS EX MACHINA

... though it grieves me to the heart,
What can we do? It is the people's voice,
And who would risk the loss of all he hath
In rash defiance of the raging tide?

IMRE MADÁCH

In this final chapter, we wish to leave the strictly scientific issues
and return to the more public side of the DDT story. We shall
begin by attempting to delineate more precisely the aims of the politically active
environmental organizations and the pragmatic stances of the defenders of DDT.

Unfortunately there is confusion in this area too because environmental
activists do not represent a unity, even with respect to their stated, immediate
goals. Nor are the defenders of DDT a single camp agreeing on all points. Nevertheless, the reader should have some idea of the positions behind this battle
before we can consider the decision-making aspects of the DDT drama. We shall
try, therefore, to formulate the demands and responses which have been most
commonly expressed.

520

Ban It!

Despite some recent disclaimers, many if not most environmental activists favor a total ban on DDT production and use, including its applications in domestic and foreign public health programs and its manufacture for export. Three major organizations are involved in the current legal actions against DDT: the Audubon Society, the Sierra Club, and the Environmental Defense Fund. The Audubon Society has advocated a worldwide ban for some time, calling on the public to collaborate in an effort to stop the manufacture and export of DDT. And the Sierra Club has at times demanded a total ban on all of the persistent pesticides.

In an article following an interview with Michael McCloskey, the executive director of the Sierra Club, John Leighty delineated the official stance of the 80,000-member club. "The Sierra Club wants a ban, not a curb on persistent pesticides, even in tropical countries where DDT has kept malaria under control" (Leighty, 1971, p. C-3). He went on to mention the possibility of using alternative pesticides in malaria control, implying that the only obstacle to developing such is one of cost. However, if Leighty's reporting is accurate, it would seem that McCloskey does not personally favor programs which save too many lives in the underdeveloped countries. "He said by using DDT, we also eliminate mortality rate of underdeveloped countries without the consideration of how to support the increase in population. He said this was going about it backwards" (*ibid.*). Although obscurely phrased, the implications of this statement are clear: saving lives with modern health-control measures exacerbates the hunger problem. That this is not the actual effect of successful malaria control is evident from the assessments of world humanitarian organizations, who have shown convincingly that healthier populations are far more able to increase their own food productivity, and that malaria control has also opened up vast areas of land for cultivation which were earlier virtually uninhabitable. Nevertheless, on the face of it McCloskey's argument may impress some people as not completely unreasonable —even people who would reject the more extreme statement attributed to another environmentalist: "To feed a starving child is to exacerbate the population problem" (cited by Yannacone, 1970, p. 4).

McCloskey repeated all the familiar arguments about DDT's damaging effects in their most extreme versions, and stated that "most critics of the fight to ban DDT act out of 'self-interest' and use unscientific arguments." He called for an immediate worldwide ban on its applications.

It perhaps ought to be explained that although the United States has no formal means of exercising control over DDT use in other countries, the largest portion of the pesticide used for both public health and agricultural purposes in underdeveloped countries is manufactured in the United States and its distribution is largely managed by such international humanitarian agencies as WHO, FAO, and AID (the Agency for International Development). Thus, were the opponents of DDT to achieve a ban on U.S. production, this would amount to virtual elimination of the supply of the pesticide for world uses.

Another typical environmentalist stance regarding the need for DDT in malaria control is that the compound is no longer really useful because of insect resistance on a broad scale. Information to this effect is frequently propagated by persons who ought to be aware of the real situation as it has been described by the WHO. While there is some resistance among *Anopheles* mosquitoes, the areas where substitutes have to be used because of resistance amount to only 1 percent of those where control programs are being carried out.

Of late, some scientist members of the EDF have taken to making public statements that they do *not* oppose the export of DDT to tropical countries for malaria control. However, as the EDF is working in close partnership with the Audubon Society and the Sierra Club in the current DDT suspension suit, one would think that these scientists, if they are sincere, could and should persuade the large conservation organizations to alter their public positions. Furthermore, the executive director of EDF, Rod Cameron, responded to an article by Thomas Jukes in which a stirring appeal was made for DDT in disease control programs with this strange remark: "Malaria is an emotional problem for Americans" (Cameron, 1971). It is most unlikely that he meant by this that any cases of malaria in the United States manifest themselves in emotional disorders. One must assume his implication to be that those North Americans who express compassionate concern for the disease victims in foreign lands are unduly influenced by emotions. Is this not a most peculiar point to be made by the leader of an organization whose members can deliver moving sermons about the tragic loss of a few birds? And is it not a highly provincial and selfish point of view? We have always been under the impression that empathy for the suffering of others is grouped among the higher emotions—those which are not very likely to interfere with soundness of scientific judgment. Without it, it would be very difficult to explain the motivations of those physicians, for example, who voluntarily forego practices which might bring them prestige or money and choose instead to work in slums, missions, and so forth.

By way of contrast with Cameron's cavalier remark, the statement issued by the Executive Board of WHO on January 22, 1971, and published in April of the same year may be considered: "It is obvious . . . that the withdrawal of DDT would indeed be a major tragedy in the chapter of human health. Vast populations in the malarious areas of the world would be condemned to the frightening ravages of endemic and epidemic malaria" (p. 182).

But why doesn't WHO seek a substitute pesticide for malaria control? The partially informed layman often asks this question. The answer is that they have done so, and thus far the efforts still point to the continued need for DDT.

Since 1960, more than 1,400 new insecticidal compounds have been tested by WHO for their suitability in vector control. While some of these can be used at relatively low doses for the control of vectors of other diseases, malaria control is a special case. A long period of residual efficacy is needed to combat the *Anopheles* mosquito. Furthermore, the insecticide is sprayed inside houses in malaria programs, and spraymen experience much heavier exposure to the substance used than in outdoor applications. Where materials more toxic than DDT are proposed as substitutes, the immediate dangers to the applicators and householders obviously must be weighed heavily.

Out of the 1,400 compounds tested, WHO found only two—malathion and propoxur—which might be suitable to replace DDT in malaria control, but neither of these is cheap enough nor sufficiently long acting to be practicable. The cost factor alone would be a tremendous obstacle. The estimates on a global basis for the replacement of DDT in the malaria eradication program *alone* indicate that the cost would escalate from $60 million annually with DDT to about $184 million per year if malathion were used and $510 million if propoxur were to replace DDT. Since training of personnel and creating safeguards for toxicity risks are complicated, these estimates are probably well on the low side.

For those aware of the importance of DDT in these worldwide disease-control programs, it came as no surprise that many of the world's leading health authorities appeared at the DDT Hearings to defend the pesticide. Were these the people to whom McCloskey was referring when he said that the critics of the fight to ban DDT "act out of 'self-interest' and use unscientific arguments?"

A discussion of the implications for human health of a total ban on DDT could be carried on in more detail, but this should suffice to give the reader one good reason why scientists with no industrial affiliations still stand up for the much maligned pesticide.

There are also many reasons why agricultural specialists worry about a possible victory for the environmentalists on the DDT issue. Some of these relate directly to the continuing need for DDT per se in the protection of many crops. However, of even greater concern is the probability that a ban on DDT would set a precedent for rather easy successes in attempts to suspend the use of other vitally needed pesticides.

Why DDT?

One question which has puzzled nearly everyone involved in the pesticide battle is why the environmental activists have chosen, from the early 1960s to the present, to concentrate their frontal attacks on DDT, since it is acknowledged to be the least damaging of the organochlorine insecticides to mammals and useful insects, and it also has the most obvious important beneficial uses, especially in connection with control of disease vectors. Various speculations have been advanced to explain this puzzle.

One of these has been characterized as the "kill the king" hypothesis. As Rappolt expressed it: "Only DDT has had the press and romance; only DDT was associated with a Nobel prize . . . Young 'crusading' scientists cannot make their reputations by calling for a moratorium on, say, lead arsenate . . . reputations are made by killing heroes . . . and DDT fulfills this imperial aura . . ." (Rappolt, 1969, p. 4).

A less elaborate explanation for the emphasis on DDT is the ease of reading and recalling its acronym. Even journalists admit that DDT fits nicely into headlines, and it would clearly have been much more difficult to impress upon the consciousness of millions the notion that, let us say, "methoxychlor is a Very Bad Thing." It's just too difficult to remember the word and keep on repeating it; whereas, as one colleague remarked jokingly: "Even a stutterer can say DDT without much trouble."

Probably the most convincing speculation about the reasons behind the focus on DDT is the so-called "domino theory," which has been articulated by many people, most emphatically by Norman Borlaug. According to this idea, DDT was chosen as the first target precisely *because* it is the most innocuous of the well-known pesticides, as well as the one with overwhelming redeeming characteristics balancing the minimal risks connected with its applications. If a ban on DDT could be achieved, the reasoning goes, then many other pesticedes could easily be eliminated as well.

In support of this view, it can be considered that the whole organochlorine pesticide group is under attack. McCloskey and many other environmentalists refer to the "persistent pesticides" as the culprits, even though most of the time they are still singling out DDT. Among the politicians who have to be counted as anti-pesticide extremists is Wisconsin's Senator Nelson, who introduced a bill in the Ninety-second Congress demanding the prohibition for sale or use in the United States of aldrin, chlordane, DDD/TDE, dieldrin, endrin, heptachlor, lindane, and toxaphene (Nelson, 1971). These compounds are coming up for administrative review in the near future, as are also the phenoxyacetic acid herbicides.

It is also quite possible that many of the less persistent pesticides will come under attack, on the grounds of hazard to human health. Most of the carbamates, for instance, have already been described as carcinogenic, mutagenic, or teratogenic by some researchers. In contrast to these possible insidious effects, the common organophosphate insecticides have high acute toxicity for mammals (with some exceptions, the most familiar of whiich is malathion) and are thus correctly described as rather dangerous to man. And even malathion—the pesticide favored by EDF as the safest for both man and the environment—has not been immune from class suit actions; for in 1969, Yannacone brought such a suit on Long Island, demanding that its use in mosquito control be suspended. If one considers the recent criticisms of Barry Commoner and his followers on the use of nitrate fertilizers in farming, it would seem that not only pesticides but agricultural chemicals in general may be vulnerable to demands for curtailment of applications.

It is not, then, particularly startling to learn that many agricultural specialists are worried that if DDT registrations are revoked in this current case, most of their important chemical tools could be withdrawn one by one, in the wake of a first major victory for the environmentalists at the federal level.

The more articulate among the anti-DDT leaders refer to this "domino theory" as "paranoid propaganda," and loudly proclaim that they are not against all pesticides. However, since agriculturalists are aware that attacks on the various chemical substances used in farming are rarely simultaneous and often come in from different directions, it would appear that the domino speculation is a justified fear rather than a paranoid reaction. Whether it will prove to be true can, of course, only be revealed by the actual unfolding of events in the course of the next few years.

In any event, whatever might be the ultimate plans of the various environmental groups regarding other agricultural chemicals, there is no question that the DDT case has become a symbolic issue and that the repercussions of its outcome will be felt in many other areas of evnironmental legislation. It is clearly a test case, and both the attackers and the defenders of the pesticide are throwing their all into the battle.

More Recent Developments

While we have been writing the four preceding chapters the seven-month-long DDT Hearings have come to an end, and we should like to bring the reader up to date on some aspects of the proceedings, findings, and rulings.

Compared with the Wisconsin Hearings, which even environmentalists willingly admit were a circus, the proceedings of the Consolidated Hearings on DDT were a model of dignity. Nevertheless, since both the attackers and the defenders of the pesticides were represented by attorneys, who attempted to show the strength of the claims of their clients and the weaknesses in their opponents' case, there were times when the process of cross-examination was unrelenting to the point of acute embarrassment for certain witnesses. Among those testifying for EDF and EPA who probably wished they had stayed home were George Woodwell, who got caught with "his samplers down," learning only in the courtroom that his coauthor Charles Wurster had stated publicly that the averages they had published together concerning residues in a Long Island marsh were not typical at all; Robert Risebrough, who was forced to admit that inappropriate statistical techniques had been consistently used to evaluate the supposed relationship between DDE residues and the thin shells of brown pelican eggs; Joseph Hickey, who was confronted with his own publications from the *pre-DDT* era documenting the decline of the peregrine falcon and the causes thereof; Philip Butler, whose several "oversights" we have mentioned in Chapters 15, 16, and 17; and Robert Heath, whose famous mallard-duck feeding study was scrutinized and found wanting. According to accounts, Heath was given the roughest drubbing; but there was evidently reason why the truth had to be "sweated out of him," since he declined to answer some legitimate questions and refused to explain his methods of statistical evaluation on the grounds that the attorney for the Group Petitioners and the Hearing Examiner would not be capable of understanding them. On that particular day in court, personal feelings were apparently running high, and Examiner Sweeney is said to have made an unkind "off the record" remark about the witness, after having been insulted from the stand. As we did not attend any of these sessions, however, and have only the transcripts from which to judge, it seems to us that Mr. Heath was indeed evasive and unresponsive and that the insistent cross-examination was evidently neccessary for the attorney of the Group Petitioners to bring home his point: viz., that the mallard-duck studies of Heath's group did *not* prove a cause-and-effect relationship between DDE feeding and reproductive failure and/or thin-shelled eggs in these birds.

There is a further ironic twist to the whole matter of Mr. Heath's statistical applications, which he, as a "biometrician," thought would be too difficult for the attorneys to comprehend. It turned out, in the final analysis, that Heath, like Risebrough and all the other "residue-shell-thickness-correlation experts," had consistently applied statistical techniques inappropriate for the analysis of their data. (Since the DDE residues in eggs do not show a Gaussian—normal—

distribution, only nonparametric statistics are appropriate, whereas all of the authors doing correlation analyses used parametric statistics.) Is it not more than a little odd that it had to be one of the attorneys for the DDT defense who finally alerted these scientists to their error?

There is one other remarkable matter in connection with Heath's testimony which needs to be brought to attention, since it supports the general contention of the DDT defense that the witnesses for the EDF/EPA deliberately withheld data which might have been damaging to their case, and it also raises some questions about the ethics of the Department of Interior, as well as the witness himself. If the reader recalls Heath's mallard-duck experiments, discussed at some length in Chapter 15, it will be remembered that he fed 2.5, 10, and 40 ppm of DDE to the birds daily for a prolonged period, which treatment supposedly led to eggshell thinning and reduced reproductive success at the higher dosage. The publication in which this work was reported did not establish the relevance of the results to actual conditions occurring in nature. Considerable data are available on DDE residues in mallards in the wild. It was therefore of obvious interest to find out what might have been the residue levels in the birds fed DDE in these laboratory studies. It was known that Heath's group at Patuxent had sent out his experimental animals for residue analysis by an independent laboratory at least 18 months prior to the Consolidated DDT Hearings. The results were repeatedly requested by the DDT defense, but all kinds of excuses were offered as to why they could not be produced, and they were not made available until *after* the Hearings had come to an end. Only when the attorneys for the defense evoked the Freedom of Information Act did the Department of Interior finally release these results, several months after the original request. The reasons behind Heath's reluctance to disclose the findings seem evident from the report. While mallards in the wild have average DDE wingtip residues of 0.01 ppm, Heath's experimental birds—even those receiving the lowest dose of 2.5 ppm, where *no* reproductive failure was claimed—had average residues of 35 ppm. These data clearly support the contention of the DDT defense that the experiments have no relevance to actual conditions in nature, even were one to accept that they were properly carried through and correctly evaluated, which they were not. Why should the Patuxent center, which is a branch of the Department of the Interior, have failed to deliver these reports until their hand was forced by an extreme legal maneuver? The event in question is one which has been kept very quiet, but it is certainly relevant in assessing which side violated the ethics of scientific debate in examining Heath and the materials he offered in evidence.

In connection with the "Heath incident," Eugene Dustman, who is the director of the Patuxent center, was quoted in the "News and Comment" pages of *Science:* "'I'm told this is a game you have to play, but I can't accept that,' he told *Science.* 'You can't treat scientists like criminals, and tear down morale like that.' Dustman says he's worried that Perry Mason tactics of cross-examination, like those permitted in the DDT hearings, will make scientists more reluctant to testify at public hearings in the future and may even cause them to shy away from research that has obvious and thorny implications for public policy . . . Dustman says he hopes the blowup will lead to some new and 'more dignified' procedures for handling expert witnesses" (Gillette, 1971, p. 1109).

To Dustman's last remark one may add a quiet "Amen," and another plea that the editors and referees of scientific journals should return to more rigorous standards, so that it is *not* left up to lawyers to expose the weaknesses of published works in the glare of the courtroom.

On the other hand, while we do not believe that the trend of settling matters of scientific import in a legal setting is a healthy one, we should like to remind everyone once again that it was the EDF and the environmentalists who initiated these kinds of advocate proceedings, and if the shoe is now on the other foot, with their witnesses being made to appear foolish by well-schooled attorneys, they have only themselves to blame for the creation of the game. In 1969, in connection with the Wisconsin Hearings, Wurster wrote the following:

> Cross-examination played a vital role in the Madison story. Conducted by a skillful attorney who understands science in addition to trial law, cross-examination *can separate fact from fiction* by "sweating the truth out of a witness." . . . Cross-examination is the acid test of relevance and competence. . . . Victor J. Yannacone, Jr., the Environmental Defense Fund's (EDF) trial attorney,* has an impressive grasp of scientific material, especially the environmental sciences. His cross-examination is usually aggressive and may be devastating where a witness takes a position that is scientifically weak. Cross-examination can be a very rough business. It gives prospective witnesses an incentive to be well prepared and confident of the validity of their testimony — *or not testify at all.* The specter of cross-examination thereby "selects" witnesses in advance, tending to separate fact from fiction. (Wurster, 1969, p. 809; our emphases)

It is interesting to note that Wurster himself, who was present on an almost daily basis during the seven months of the Hearings and whose testimony had been scheduled for January 21, 1972, decided at the last moment that he had nothing to add and would "not testify at all."

* The readers will recall that only a little more than a year later, this same "skillful attorney" was described by this same Dr. Wurster as a person who had "lost touch with reality" and whose inability to "separate fact from fiction" had accelerated (Wurster, 1971).

The EPA Ruling

Most readers will have been only dimly aware that these DDT Hearings took place at all, for they were given very little attention in the popular press during their progress. With the exception of especially interested persons it seems safe to assume that both laymen and scientists learned that DDT's fate was being weighed only after the administrator of the Environmental Protection Agency, William Ruckelshaus, handed down his decision on June 14, 1972. The newspaper accounts of Ruckelshaus' ruling varied, of course, but it is probable that many local papers carried stories based on wire-service reports and were therefore quite similar. We have chosen to cite here a good part of the report printed in the *Minneapolis Star*, as its contents seem to be typical of the kind of information imparted to the larger public.

U.S. Bans Nearly All DDT Uses

Washington, D.C. (UPI)—The government today banned virtually all uses of DDT on grounds the pesticide is uncontrollable and poses hazards to man and his environment.

The ban, announced by the Environmental Protection Agency (EPA), is effective next Dec. 31. It does not affect exports of DDT to foreign nations, many of which use it for malaria control.

DDT will be permitted in this country only for public health purposes and in three minor uses to protect crops where no effective alternatives are available—that is, on green peppers, onions and sweet potatoes in storage.

All remaining crop uses of DDT—mainly on cotton, peanuts, and soybeans—will be banned.

The decision was based on a 17-month study by EPA on the effects of the widely used chemical.

"I am convinced by a preponderance of the evidence that, once used, DDT is an uncontrollable, durable chemical that persists in aquatic and terrestrial environments," EPA Administrator William D. Ruckelshaus said in a 40-page decision.

"The evidence of record showing storage in man and magnification in the food chain is a warning to the prudent that man may be exposing himself to a substance that may ultimately have a serious effect on his health," Ruckelshaus said. "The risks to the environment from continued use of DDT in massive quantities are more clearly established.". . .

He [Ruckelshaus] said he is delaying the ban until Dec. 31 so farmers can learn how to use substitute pesticides that are more toxic than DDT although not as persistent.

The primary argument against DDT is that, unlike many other pesticides, it retains its killing power for years. The World Health Organization estimates that more than two-thirds of the DDT ever used remains in the environment.

Human harm has not been proven, and a DDT proponent once drank a cup of the pesticide on television to prove that point. He was not harmed.

But Ruckelshaus said the possibility of harm to humans cannot be ignored, particularly since other pesticides are available for most crops.

Environmentalists contend DDT kills crabs, shrimp, and most fish, and apparently causes some birds to lay eggs with shells so thin they crack before hatching. (*Minneapolis Star*, June 14, 1972)

If we list the points that are either explicitly stated or implied in this article, it will become clear how misleading the account is. The reader would naturally gather that:

1. The EPA conducted a 17-month long study on the effects of DDT.
2. It was the results of this study which led Ruckelshaus to conclude that the pesticide is "uncontrollable" and poses "hazards to the environment." These were more or less clearly established.
3. Although "human harm has not been proven," the probable, ultimate risks to human health are serious.
4. The "other pesticides" available as substitutes on crops are more toxic, but better for the environment.
5. The WHO has stated that more than two-thirds of the DDT ever used remains in the environment in active form, still capable of "killing."
6. DDT kills crabs, shrimp, and most fish.

The first statement is literally untrue. No study was carried out within the EPA; the reference is to the request for an advisory committee report and to the administrative review process of the formal hearings to which we have been referring.

The second statement implies that Ruckelshaus reached the "hazard to the environment" conclusion on the basis of the "study." The Advisory Committee Report—issued in September, 1971—did speak about DDT as a hazard to the environment, but grave doubts were raised about the validity of this contention during the course of the Hearings. The report was not admitted as evidence by the Examiner. "Clearly established" is a questionable descriptive phrase for the as yet unproven hazards to the environment from limited DDT use.

The third statement reflects widely held public fears, and not much else.

The fourth statement is misleading. It refers to the greater toxicity of the substitutes for DDT, but does not quantify these, either for beneficial animals or humans. Perhaps if people were informed that the human mortality rate from these "other pesticides" is steadily increasing, they would be more willing to live with the speculated, unproven "ultimate" hazards to human health loosely associated with DDT. After all, not every citizen is so fearful of an outside risk of cancer that he will casually discount the lives of a "few Mexican and Negro farm workers" (see Chapter 2). Furthermore, while it is true that the organophosphate substitutes are less persistent than DDT, it does not necessarily follow from this that they are better for the environment.

The fifth statement is a complete fabrication. Even the most ardent environmentalists do not make such an extreme claim, their *high* estimates for DDT residues remaining in the environment being in the range of one-quarter of the total production. The WHO has never made any estimate even remotely resembling the one mentioned, and we suspect that whoever wrote the release invented the figure, as we cannot imagine a possible source.

The sixth statement is meaningless because it is not quantified. In large enough amounts, DDT will of course kill crabs, shrimp, and fish. In the quantities present in our aquatic environments at this time, it does not do so.

The most important distortion in this newspaper account lies not in what it says, but in what is omitted altogether. There is no mention of the very important fact that the Ruckelshaus decision represented a *reversal* of all major points in the opinion handed down by Edmund Sweeney, the Examiner appointed by EPA to preside over the Consolidated DDT Hearings, excepting the need for DDT in emergency public health applications. We should have thought that such a development would be treated as "news" in any normal context of newspaper coverage, but the only American daily in which we saw this turnaround described was the *Wall Street Journal*, although obviously we did not have the opportunity to read all of them. It was not mentioned in the coverage by the major weekly news magazines either, although the last-minute reversal would seem to be at least one of the newsworthy aspects of the decision. *Newsweek* wrote that neither the environmentalists nor the defenders of DDT were entirely pleased with the ruling, and tried to leave its readers with the impression that Ruckelshaus had reached a fair compromise, acting for the greater public good, without regard to any special interest groups. Their brief article on the ban ended with a self-congratulatory citation from inside EPA: "'But it was a solid decision, a courageous decision,' said one EPA official. 'It pleased no special interest but it was the right thing to do'" (*Newsweek*, June 26, 1972, p. 30).

By the time this book is printed, the decision will be more than a year old, and the appeals filed by both the attackers and defenders of the pesticide may have been acted on as well. Nevertheless, we feel that the public deserves a somewhat more accurate description of the events immediately preceding the EPA ruling than those which have been provided by the mass media. Let us, then, have a look at how this EPA "DDT study" was evaluated.

The Examiner's "Findings"

The testimony of expert witnesses came to an end in February, 1972, and by the end of March the attorneys representing the several parties for both sides of the dispute had completed their oral summations and their written recommendations to the Hearing Examiner. On April 25 Examiner Sweeney submitted to EPA his *Recommended Findings, Conclusions, and Orders* in a 114-page opinion. This incorporated a lengthy discussion of the benefits and risks of DDT and proper uses at issue. His conclusions of law included the following points:

> DDT is not a carcinogenic hazard to man.
> DDT is not a mutagenic or teratogenic hazard to man.
> The uses of DDT under the registrations involved here do not have a deleterious effect on freshwater fish, estuarine organisms, wild birds, or other wildlife.
> The adverse effect on beneficial animals from the use of DDT under the registrations involved here is not unreasonable on balance with its benefit.
> The Petitioners have met fully their burden of proof.
> There is a present need for the continued use of DDT for the essential uses defined in this case. (Sweeney, 1972, pp. 93, 94)

He recommended no changes in the remaining uses for DDT registered under the Federal Insecticide, Fungicide and Rodenticide Act, although it was understood by all that there would be some technical changes in the labeling of the formulations containing the pesticide.

With respect to particular assertions most frequently raised about adverse effects from DDT applications, while denying that the evidence presented in the proceedings constituted proof of the "truth" of these assertions, Sweeney made a number of qualifying statements, including suggestions about the needs for continued surveillance of environmental conditions and for further research. Regarding aquatic ecosystems, he wrote: "While it is necessary to maintain a vigilant concern over the possibility of serious damage to our important aquatic life, it is questionable whether the evidence presented in this case supports a finding that, at present and foreseeable future levels, the use of DDT would cause damage to aquatic life sufficient to justify complete cancellation" (*ibid.,* p. 66).

He denied the meaningfulness of the data presented in support of the contention that DDT is responsible for subtle problems of avian reproduction. However, he recommended continued attention to the status of birds in the wild: "The evidence adequately shows that there should be a continued and extended experimentation and observation of the effect of DDT, as well as any other pesticide, on the bird populations in the wildlife; in the event that such studies might reveal more serious damage to the birds in the wild than has heretofore been shown" (*ibid.*, p. 71).

Here it ought to be pointed out that while not all the materials we have presented regarding the "eggshell-thinning hypothesis" were brought out in the Hearings, the cross-examination of Heath, Hickey, Cade, Bitman, Blus, Peakall, and Risebrough revealed, in our opinion, enough inconsistencies in the data, poor experimental designs, erroneous statistical analyses, failure to take into account facts which did not fit, and indications of fervent commitment to preconceived ideas as to not only throw great doubt on the value of the hypothesis, but also to raise serious questions about the scientific credibility of the EDF witnesses.

Sweeney devoted a number of pages to the cancer issue, bringing attention to Epstein's testimony as well as to statements by witnesses who denied the validity of the mouse experiments altogether (W. H. Butler) and to the judgment of others that the existing animal experiments are not adequate to support a conclusion that DDT is a human carcinogen. He qualified his finding that "DDT is not a carcinogenic hazard to man" as follows:

> In my opinion the evidence presented demonstrates a continuing need to pursue the truth as to the fact of DDT as a carcinogen for humans. Although the evidence at times appeared to deny the carcinogenic properties of DDT for animals and at other times seemed to confirm it, there was no showing of any evidence that man himself was not safe from cancer from the present dosages to which we are exposed. Really, it can't seriously be contended that the fact that DDT had NOT been proven NOT to be carcinogenic to man, is a logical basis for advocating a complete ban on all future uses of DDT.
>
> I give a lot of weight to the testimony of the Surgeon General, Dr. Jesse Steinfeld. . . . He has to consider the health of all the people in the United States, and judicial notice can be taken of the prompt and forthright official actions he has taken in this regard. In addition, Dr. Steinfeld is a highly competent doctor of medicine who prior to his appointment did extensive research in the area of cancer. . . .
>
> The risk of DDT as a carcinogen was presented fully by the parties, including the present levels of intake and other impacts of DDT to which the human population of this country is presently subjected. The testimony is sufficient in amount and quality to permit appropriate findings and conclusions. (*Ibid.*, pp. 58-59)

In general, Sweeney's *Findings* may be summarized as representing the view that the need for and benefits from the continued, limited use of DDT were shown by the Group Petitioners; and that the evidence presented in the proceedings did not support either the contention that the current uses of DDT represent a hazard to human health or that they cause significant damage to wildlife. He placed considerable emphasis, on the other hand, on the known facts (not contested by any party) that ethyl and methyl parathion, which are the substitutes recommended to replace DDT for most of its present agricultural applications in the United States, are much more destructive to beneficial insects than is DDT and, even more important, are so toxic to mammals that their use entails serious threats to human life for applicators, farmers, farm laborers, and even residents near sites of application.

It would seem to us that the Examiner's *Findings* were "courageous," serving "no special interests," except those of the public at large. It was an important landmark, too, considering that we seem to have entered on a period when controversial scientific issues are going to be reviewed in legal proceedings, whether or not the larger scientific community regards the courtroom as a proper forum for settling these questions. Sweeney's recommendations evidence an understanding unusual in a nonscientist of what may be properly regarded as scientifically established facts and scientific proof.

The ink was hardly dry on his papers before an appeal was filed by the attorneys representing EDF and EPA, taking exception to Sweeney's decision. This consisted mostly of attacks on the Examiner, claims that his legal rulings were prejudicial to the Intervenors and Respondent (EPA), and contentions that his decision reflected personal bias. A subsequent brief from the Group Petitioners' attorneys was submitted, in which opposition to these exceptions was expressed at some length, and certain questions posed by EPA Administrator Ruckelshaus were answered. We need not go into all of this legal shuffling. It is important, however, to consider the charge of bias.

The literal meaning of "biased" is having a prior leaning or prejudgment towards one viewpoint in a controversy. From review of the oral testimony, we see no basis for any contention that the Examiner showed such bias from the beginning. He seems to have come into the case with a neutral point of view, and, on the whole, his rulings during the course of the Hearings appear to reflect legal technicalities rather than favoritism. His final opinion was, of course, "prejudicial" to EDF, since it reflected his judgment that they had failed to prove their allegations about DDT and could not support their demand that its uses should be suspended.

The role of the EPA in the late stages of the controversy is also interesting. Early on, although EPA as Respondent in the case was technically aligned with EDF and the other anti-DDT Intervenors (as a result of the Court of Appeals ruling), a spokesman for the Agency had emphasized that the role of EPA in the Hearings was *not* to be that of an adversary but of a public servant. In the brief taking exception to the Examiner's findings, however, the counsel for the Agency stated that EDF and EPA had taken the same adversary position in the Hearings. Which was it? What is the role of the Environmental Protection Agency? Are its administrators dispassionate public servants, or is the Agency becoming an arm of the environmental movement within the Federal government? Such questions cannot, of course, be answered, but it is apparently necessary to raise them, especially as regards those environmental issues which generate strong emotional responses and opinions in the general public.

Decision Making

We wish now to consider several aspects of the *Opinion* in which Ruckelshaus reversed Sweeney's orders, and to examine some of its sociopolitical implications.

The notion that Ruckelshaus' ruling was the expression of balance and fairness would seem to derive from the fact that he retained DDT's uses in public health, even while suspending registrations for most major applications. Thus, neither EDF nor the Group Petitioners was given a total victory, and the public was left with the impression that EPA's Administrator had arrived at a compromise which would protect both people and the environment.

In general, Ruckelshaus' *Opinion* indicates that he accepted almost completely the allegations of environmentalists that DDT is a widespread global contaminant and that the presence of its residues in the environment are casually related to damage in wildlife. It may be supposed that he based this conclusion primarily on the *Report of the Advisory Committee on DDT*, which report in turn relied heavily on the review by the Goldberg panel discussed at length in Chapters 16 and 17. From the Hearings alone it would have been difficult for him to justify this conclusion, although, as we shall see shortly, he made some attempts to "explain away" facts detrimental to the argument of the environmentalists which came out during the course of the Hearings. His *Opinion* also reveals his own belief that DDT may, in the long run, represent a health hazard to man. Since the Advisory Committee had taken the view that this is not the case, Ruckelshaus must have derived his belief either from the publicly disseminated misinformation to which we have all been subject during the last ten years, or from the testimony and writings of those few scientists who contended that DDT may be a carcinogen or mutagen.

Throughout his written *Opinion* one finds a number of rationalizations, evidently introduced to justify his almost complete disagreement with Sweeney's evaluation and recommendations. Both the attorneys for the Group Petitioners and Examiner Sweeney had argued that some of the witnesses for EDF lacked credibility, to put it in polite terms. Ruckelshaus, on the other hand, wrote: "Whatever extra weight . . . might be due to findings based expressly on a credibility judgment is not appropriate in the case before me" (Ruckelshaus, 1971, p. 24). It is difficult to imagine what might be the reasoning behind such a statement. Does the Administrator think that because the witnesses were scientists, the testimony of each should have equal weight, regardless of competence? It would be ideal if we could assume that all scientists are equal in abilities and performance, but clearly this is not the case, in or out of court. The fact is that some are better than others. When a scientist evaluates conflicting opinions among his colleagues, he is just as likely as someone of any other professional group to take into account the relative talents and solidity of achievement of the individuals involved.

There also appears to be some confusion between assessments of personal credibility and matters bearing on the credibility of the data, or the manner in which they are presented. It is our impression that Sweeney raised the credibility issue mainly to bring attention to the fact that some of the EDF witnesses withheld or distorted information and failed to tell the whole truth, rather than to throw doubt on the testimony of witnesses who mumbled, appeared unsure of themselves, or just did not come across as "performers." The incident in which Philip Butler had to be forced into admitting knowledge of the Wilson study on DDT's decay time in seawater (see Chapter 17) is one good example, among many others, of the kind of behavior which distressed Sweeney.

If one carries through ad absurdum the idea that in this kind of inquiry (although in no other judicial or administrative proceeding we know of), all witnesses are to be taken as equally credible, it would seem to follow that the more witnesses who could be marshaled to appear and repeat the same claim, the more weight would be given to the allegation—regardless of its truth value. This is more or less what has been happening in the shaping of public opinion about DDT through the press, where repetition of scientific-sounding assertions all too often substitutes for reports of scientific findings. But, as distressing as this may be, the private citizen whose "scientific" views derive from the reading of newspapers does not translate these directly into public policy. One would expect that government officials charged with the responsibility for important decisions would need to be discriminating in evaluating information provided to them. Otherwise any vociferous pressure group could easily win official sanction for its own "scientific claims." Exactly this happened in the Soviet Union in 1948, when Lysenkoism triumphed through the seal of approval of the Central Committee.

That Ruckelshaus himself "weighted" the testimony—apparently on the basis of his own assessments of credibility—is evident from his references to DDT as a possible human health hazard. There are only a handful of scientists who maintain that DDT might represent a mutagenic or carcinogenic hazard for man, and the data available in the literature clearly do not support such contentions. Still, Ruckelshaus accepted the argument that even though DDT has *not* been shown to be a carcinogen in man, this does not prove that it might not, in the future, be demonstrated as such. This is no argument at all, and Sweeney was quite correct when he wrote that such statements can't be taken seriously as the basis for a logical decision. With regard to possible genetic damage, Ruckelshaus wrote: "Mutagenic effects will be apparent only in future generations" (*ibid.*, p. 18). It probably did not occur to anyone involved in this case that the issue of possible mutagenicity would influence the Administrator. The question came up mainly during Marvin Legator's testimony, and we did not even bother to discuss it, since both the techniques used in the mutagenicity testing of chemicals and the repeatability of the results are so controversial that at the present time they do not have much weight as scientific evidence. Attempts to extrapolate from these kinds of laboratory data to the natural environment are, furthermore, completely meaningless. But the tired old theme that the ill effects of our present activities may be visited only upon our progeny is one with great staying power among the lay public, and apparently Ruckelshaus felt constrained to give expression to it in his *Opinion*. If the Administrator really believes his own statement and its implications, maybe he ought to be alerted to the awful responsibilities he is facing in protecting the public from the hundreds of possible mutagens present in items with which we have daily contact. For all we know, 5-hydroxytriptamine may very well be mutagenic, but since "only future generations will experience the effect," the prudent thing would be to act quickly and ban all cheeses!

Concerning the "eggshell-thinning hypothesis"—our favorite boring subject —one may read the following incredible summary in the Administrator's *Opinion:* "Viewing the evidence as a total picture, a preponderance supports the conclusion that DDT does cause eggshell thinning. Whether or not the laboratory data . . . would sustain this conclusion is beside the point. [!] For here is [sic] laboratory data and observational data, and in addition, a scientific hypothesis, which might explain the phenomenon" (*ibid.*, p. 10). These statements indicate that the lacunae in Mr. Ruckelshaus' education are such that he should be forthwith removed from duties involving scientific questions. The laboratory data are *beside the point?* Does he not realize that the whole purpose of pursuing laboratory experiments in connection with the "eggshell-thinning hypothesis" was to test the hypothesis under controlled conditions? The experiments failed; and data showing this are very much *to* the point—the point being that causality was *not* established.

The reference to preponderance of the evidence apparently means the quantity of observational data gathered in connection with the hypothesis. But what Mr. Ruckelshaus fails to grasp is that not all reported data are meaningful. Some may be accurate but unrelated to the problem under study. Others may be great in number, but inaccurate. A good example of the latter category are the museum eggshell measurements made with mechanical micrometers. Anderson is said to have measured 35,000 such eggshells, from collections all over the United States. He is undoubtedly among the most sincere of the scientists concerned about birds, but he could have measured 35 million shells without proving anything except his diligence, so long as he continued to use an instrument that is not accurate in the range where differences are reported.

Evidently, too, the Administrator does not understand the meaning of the word "hypothesis." A hypothesis is what you start with in science; it is not a basis for conclusions. One can formulate a hypothesis on very thin evidence, or even on sheer speculation. We can set forth the sociological hypothesis that William Ruckelshaus as Administrator of EPA is leading the country on a disaster course, and future historians will be able to judge whether or not we are proven right. But the hypothesis itself is not proof, not fact, not the basis for conclusions, not scientific truth.

The inclusion in the Administrator's *Opinion* of the statements we cited above augur ill for the future, if science is to be so debased and distorted by pontificating bureaucrats.

Finally, that even in the realm of ordinary logic Ruckelshaus seems to have lost his senses on the DDT issue is illustrated by the following statement: "The Petitioner-registrants' assertion that there is no evidence of declining aquatic or avian populations, even if actually true, is an attempt at confession [?] and avoidance" (*ibid.*, p. 16). What does it mean? We tried to think like lawyers, but that didn't seem to help. If I am accused of stealing the neighbor's silverware and can demonstrate that it is still in his own cupboard, is this avoidance? Am I guilty? Or has the neighbor made a mistake, which he should be glad to have corrected without further trouble? What else can one say about this superb example of environmental non-think?

Now, having been rather hard on Mr. Ruckelshaus, we should like to let him off the hook in several respects and take into account a few of the difficulties with which he was faced in making this decision.

To begin with, he gave himself only a few weeks in which to study the massive amounts of material incorporated into records of the DDT Hearings, and to consider Sweeney's evaluation, the various briefs of the lawyers, the Advisory Committee Report, and the lengthy personal communications he is known to have received from at least one of the EDF participants. His own legal staff could hardly be of much help to him in reaching a fair decision, since the attorney representing EPA in the Hearings had taken an anti-DDT adversary position and was also clearly offended by Sweeney's ruling. Furthermore, it would seem that Ruckelshaus' entire scientific staff must have been out of town studying other environmental problems, or vacationing, or just not available to him during these weeks. Otherwise it is doubtful whether Ruckelshaus would have incorporated certain plain and rather "dumb" mistakes into his written *Opinion,* such as giving the wrong chemical designation for DDT and referring to carbaryl, which is a carbamate pesticide, as one of the organophosphates. Surely any scientist on the EPA staff—no matter what his specialty—should have easily noticed such errors and done his administrative chief the favor of editing them out of the final *Opinion.*

Secondly, nobody would pretend that the DDT case was an open-and-shut affair, even from the point of view of legal technicalities. Neither Sweeney's *Findings* nor the conduct of the DDT defense were entirely faultless, and it must have been very confusing for Ruckelshaus to have to review the legal complaints of both parties to the case in such a short period of time, when he was supposed simultaneously to evaluate a good deal of difficult and conflicting material bearing on the scientific issues.

Then there was the Advisory Committee Report, which at least gave some support to the "hazard to the environment" argument. Not being a scientist, Ruckelshaus can perhaps not be expected to have grasped the significance of the conflicting evidence which emerged about this claim during the course of the Hearings. Sweeney seemed to get the point—which is essentially that *any* new findings or proof of procedural errors that contradict a scientific hypothesis are sufficient to throw out all the work assembled to give credence to the hypothesis—but then, Sweeney had the advantage of a seven-month long special education while presiding over the Hearings.

On the general hazard to the environment issue, the scientific community has to be seriously faulted too; for there is really no justification for the fact that most of the weaknesses in the published work of the EDF witnesses were ignored until the time of these Hearings. Why should the criticism of these works have been left to the DDT defense? Or, for that matter, to us? We said earlier that scientists not especially involved in scientific questions beyond their own interest tend to assume that faulty reports are weeded out before publication by the editors and referees of the journals to which they are submitted; and we laid some of the blame at the doors of the editors for the lowering of scientific standards. But there are, after all, a number of scientists and scientific organizations highly interested in all publications dealing with DDT and reasonably familiar with the literature of the whole 30-year period since its introduction into use as a pesticide. *Why weren't they more critical?* On the subject of the ecological impact of DDT, there have been a few scientists in the direct employ of industry (as distinct from those described by environmentalists as "pesticide industry spokesmen"), like Shell's John Robinson, who have refuted one or two of the claims, such as the correlative studies associating declines in avian populations with pesticide usage. Some analytical chemists have raised questions about the accuracy of residue determinations. And, occasionally, a particular argument about possible environmental disaster has been so squarely rebutted that it died out altogether, as happened in the case of speculations concerning reduced oxygen supply in connection with Wurster's photosynthesis experiments. But the large organizations with an interest in defending DDT—USDA, FAO, WHO, and so on—did not at any time undertake a truly critical review of all the studies purporting to demonstrate DDT's adverse effects on the global ecosystem. Ruckelshaus could easily be among Norman Borlaug's admirers, and still judge it somewhat peculiar that Borlaug referred to the anti-DDT scientists as "hysterical lobbyists" at a recent FAO meeting, since after all FAO had earlier employed some of these same scientists as expert advisors on the environmental impact of DDT. And where were the critical minds at WHO when it came to careful examination of claims about global residues of DDT, its damage to birds and aquatic organisms, and so on? WHO has consistently expressed the need for continued DDT use in disease-vector control programs and has investigated with considerable care any contentions that the pesticide might be a human health hazard, but like members of the other organizations with a serious interest in retaining essential DDT uses, many WHO scientists and officials seemed to have acquiesced too readily to unproven assertions about the ecological hazards supposedly represented by the pesticide.

The role of the NASCO monograph and its influence on the members of the DDT Advisory Committee is less a responsiblity of the scientific community at large because it had only been published for a month or so when the Committee Report was written, and there had not yet been time for refutations to appear. On the other hand, it is unfathomable how such a "tract," expressing the opinion of its authors but having no objective merit, could have appeared under the imprimatur of the National Academy of Sciences.

In general, one can imagine that Mr. Ruckelshaus may have given credence to the assertion that DDT is hazardous to the environment on the commonsense grounds that other scientists with backgrounds in ecology had not thoroughly rebutted the claim in print. On this ground we also should be faulted for not bringing out our own criticisms a year or so earlier.

Lastly, one has to take into account some of the pressures which were operative at the personal level on the Administrator. During his administration of the newly created Agency, Ruckelshaus made a point of demonstrating that he is not subject to pressures from industrial lobbies—see his decisions on industrial pollutants of air and water, for example. But what about the pressure of public opinion? And the press? What would have been the general response had he upheld Sweeney's ruling? It is impossible to know exactly, of course, but there would undoubtedly have been a violent reaction from the members of nearly all environmental organizations in the country, even those not particularly concerned with pesticides. And there is not much question that Ruckelshaus would have received very bad press coverage—particularly from the major East Coast dailies, and especially the *New York Times.* As an appointee rather than an elected official, his position would probably not have been jeopardized by a drubbing in the popular press. Nevertheless, it would clearly have taken considerable courage and conviction for him to render a decision favoring the defenders of DDT.

One can thus understand some of the personal factors which may have been behind the Administrator's reversal of Sweeney's ruling. Unfortunately, these do not suffice to make his own decision either wise or just.

Ruckelshaus did not grant a total victory to DDT's attackers, but he accepted nearly all their assertions in his *Opinion,* giving thus semiofficial approval to a peculiar version of "science," wherein evidence is substituted for proof, and unsubstantiated claims are asserted all the louder when they are refuted by contrary facts. The ruling also gave a tremendous psychological victory to the environmental activists, for whom, as Wurster made clear in 1969, "much more is at stake than DDT." The real issue, according to EDF's chief scientific advisor, is one of control.

It is true, indeed, that much more is at stake than DDT. The defeat represented by this ruling is not just a defeat for the farmers, or the USDA, or the chemical companies involved in the manufacture and formulation of DDT and its preparations; it is a defeat for science. In failing to recognize that the Hearings had exposed most of the work indicting DDT as pseudoscience or ignorant bungling, Ruckelshaus has set a very dangerous precedent for the future of American biology. One can only hope that this semiofficial endorsement of our American "new, creative biology" will be challenged and countermanded, lest we find ourselves replaying the irrational and regressive drama of Soviet biology a few decades ago.

A "Special Interest Group"

While we have placed particular emphasis on the threat to the integrity of the biological sciences implied in Ruckelshaus' acceptance of the environmentalists' unproven assertions, our efforts to set the record straight on the DDT issue would be incomplete if we did not include a few further comments about the special impact of the EPA Administrator's *Opinion* on the sector of the American farm economy represented by the cotton farmers of the Mid-South and the Southeast. We mentioned earlier that DDT (usually mixed with toxaphene) has been and still is the pesticide of choice for control of the boll weevil and the bollworm, which insects represent particularly knotty problems for cotton growers in the southeastern states. We are willing to admit that, in general, an advanced country like the United States, with a highly developed agriculture, may survive economically when much more expensive pesticides are substituted for DDT, if these are effective. However, this generalization does not apply to the region in question. Ruckelshaus' *Opinion* granted exceptions to a total ban on crop applications of DDT only for green peppers, onions, and sweet potatoes in storage. On the other hand, the largest portion of the pesticide still being applied in domestic agriculture up to the time of these Hearings (99 percent of the remaining registered uses) was for combating cotton pests in the fields of the Mid-South and the Southeast.

The Administrator's *Opinion* included statements to the effect that appropriate, economical pesticides are available to substitute for DDT, and that these are safe when applied in accordance with labeling instructions.

With respect to the cotton farmers of the southeastern region of the United States, however, all three of these points are seriously debatable. The only presently available substitute which is effective against the boll weevil–bollworm problem in these states is parathion (ethyl or methyl), which is certainly not economical for small growers, and the effectiveness of which is also questionable. From the experience of Texas and Arizona farmers, it appears that resistance to parathion develops much more rapidly than to DDT, and the high toxicity of the organophosphate substitute to bees and wasps has by now been recognized as a serious problem. But leaving aside the issues of effectiveness or appropriateness, it is the economic impact on the farmers of the South to which we wish to bring attention.

Cotton is one of the principal traditional crops grown in the Mid-South and the Southeast. In these states a large number of cotton farms are owned by small farmers, many of them holding less than ten acres of land. These farmers are for the most part already operating at a subsistence level, and they can afford neither the hiring of professional applicators dictated by the marked acute toxicity of parathion, nor the purchase of the elaborate safety equipment which they would need were they to apply the organophosphate themselves. (The DDT-toxaphene mix which they have been using can be applied without hazard from simple backpack spray units.)

It seems to us that this information came out quite clearly during the course of the seven-month-long Consolidated DDT Hearings, which incorporated testimony from individual cotton farmers of the region in question, as well as those of USDA experts. One gets the impression from his written *Opinion* that if Ruckelshaus read the transcripts at all, he apparently missed this testimony and accepted instead the opinions of one or two California entomologists, who were unfamiliar with the insect problems typical in the Southeast and who worked in a state where there are also fewer small-acreage cotton farmers. The Administrator also revealed his almost complete ignorance of the general agricultural situation in the South, as well as of the importance of cotton to the national economy. Whereas one would expect the EPA chief to know that cotton is a major crop for both the production of domestic fiber and for export purposes, Ruckelshaus naively questioned the Group Petitioners at one point as to whether some other crop might not be grown in the fields of this extensive region!

Shortly before Ruckelshaus handed down his decision canceling any further use of DDT against cotton insects, the Economic Research Service of USDA (1972) published some estimates regarding the probable impact of such a decision. To begin with, it should be remembered that the United States is the world's largest cotton-producing country. Cotton is the fifth most valuable domestic crop, with a farm value of about $1.3 billion per year. In the southeastern states, about 500,000 people are directly involved in growing cotton, and an additional five million are either directly or indirectly dependent on cotton for their living. In these states there are at least 120,000 cotton farms which are smaller than ten acres. Many of these operate at a marginal profit level, and the USDA estimated that about 90,000 of them would not be able to sustain economically a changeover from DDT to parathion. Should these 90,000 farmers be bankrupted, 270,000 people would be directly deprived of income, and another one-and-one-half million could become unemployed. This severe economic stress would affect a region which is, in any case, relatively impoverished in comparison to other areas of the nation. None of these facts or probabilities was apparently deemed worthy of consideration by the Administrator in formulating his decision.

We have already spoken about the acute toxicity of parathion to useful insects, higher animals, and man. It is perhaps necessary, however, to mention this once again, and to question the Administrator's judgment that the greater dangers associated with the application of highly toxic substitutes should be regarded as an occupational risk for farmers and applicators. In general, it has been estimated that for every 500 tons of parathion applied, there is one *human* fatality (Burnside et al., 1970), and these are on the increase, not only among farmers and spraymen, but also in the general populace. In 1952 there were four human deaths caused by parathion; in 1961, 18; in 1967, 36; in 1970, 58. By mid-1972, estimates of the number of human deaths caused by parathion had jumped to 118 for the first half of the year.

May one not fairly ask if the small cotton farmers of the Mid-South and the Southeast, who may risk their lives or lose their livelihood as a result of the Administrator's "courageous" decision, are to be included among those "special interest groups" who were not pleased by his *Opinion?*

That some members of Congress are not too satisfied with the manner in which EPA officials are exercising their relatively new powers of environmental regulation is evidenced by the following. Shortly after Ruckelshaus handed down his *Opinion,* the House Committee on Appropriations for the Department of Agriculture, and Environmental and Consumer Protection, held hearings in which they considered the objections of some of those most affected by Ruckelshaus' DDT decision. Following these hearings, they wrote:

Information provided to the Committee has indicated that in some cases the Environmental Protection Agency may be experiencing a lack of technical expertise in some areas. The need for expert advice was particularly evident in the recent highly publicized decision on DDT. The report demonstrated a regrettable lack of information on the costs, supplies and programs for cotton. The report indicated that information on costs of production were not available. The Department of Agriculture has made numerous cost studies and findings on this crop. The report indicated supplies were plentiful, while the Department of Agriculture, which is officially charged with the responsibility, reports that cotton is now in short supply and that we are not meeting minimum export demands. The report indicated that Federal cotton programs are designed to provide producer profits, while the Congress has carefully written programs to provide the differential between U.S. costs, including a reasonable return on investment, and the world price. To compound this show of lack of knowledge of the crop which will take the brunt of increased costs and greater dangers in handling substitutes, the administrator made reference to a "per bushel subsidy," a measurement which has never been used for this commodity throughout history. Due to the enormity of impact of EPA's decisions on the citizens of the country, it is essential that only the very best qualified personnel be available to the Agency. (U.S. House of Representatives, 1972, p. 7)

Whence Their Zeal?

During the past two years, we have had occasion to discuss the DDT affair and other emotionally charged environmental campaigns with a number of people, and to show them some parts of our manuscript during its composition. These discussions have been with laymen and scientists, Americans and Europeans, young and old. Almost invariably, no matter what the original persuasions of the individuals, and regardless of the degree to which they found our arguments convincing, certain insistent questions were raised. The knottiest among these bore on the possible motivations of the scientists who have been directly involved in the most extreme kinds of environmental campaigns—those in which the search for truth seems to have been abandoned in favor of the popularization of views with most dubious scientific merit. We have been repeatedly asked: "How could trained scientists bring themselves to violate the basic ethics of their profession? What might motivate them to advocate half-truths, withhold or ignore information damaging to their arguments, play on public fears, and, in some cases, even make conscious use of 'advertising techniques' either to discredit their opponents or to persuade the public that their slogans and pronouncements are supported by facts? What could they stand to gain? How could they be so convinced, and convincing, unless they are clearly in the right? And are not at least some among them sincere in their concerns for the integrity of natural ecosystems and the protection of flora and fauna from the dangers of environmental contaminants?"

From the nature of these questions, it seems fairly apparent that people are most puzzled by two matters which have nothing to do with the scientific arguments involved in the DDT case or in similar issues. The first is whether one is to suppose that all the scientists arguing against DDT are consciously exaggerating their materials, or whether at least some among them might be perfectly sincere and well meaning in intent. The second suggests that even persons who perceive indications that some findings have been consciously manipulated, or pseudoscientific views propagated, cannot imagine what an American scientist could gain from so doing.

(It is noteworthy, on the other hand, that the same people do not seem to find the motives of Lysenko and his followers hard to fathom. This may derive from that fact that people in the West who know anything about Lysenko at all, mistakenly assume that the "creative biologists" had, from the beginning, the full support of the party bosses in their campaign to discredit Russia's "Establishment" biologists. Only a few are aware that it was after nearly 20 years of generating publicity about the superiority of their own approach to agronomy

and to plant genetics—using any and all means to denounce their opponents—
and after making concerted efforts to win the support of the populace, that the
Lysenkoists finally were granted official sanction and became established as the
controlling element in Soviet biology.)

We had had no intention of addressing ourselves directly to this matter of
motives, but since those with whom we have discussed our materials have raised
these questions repeatedly, we shall offer a few remarks.

Even when all the separate issues and themes are taken together, the number of professionals who are committed to the idea that contamination of the environment represents a serious threat to the biosphere is a relatively small fraction of the working community of scientists from all disciplines. Nevertheless,
in terms of absolute numbers, there are quite a few people involved in "ecological
scares" who have earned advanced degrees in science and hold teaching or research posts. There are, in addition, the biologists and biomedical researchers
whose principal concern is with the possible human health hazards of pollutants.
Among these, medical researchers are only rarely directly involved in activist
organizations, but it is fairly evident to anyone who examines the literature and
present funding programs that there is a "bandwagon" effect operating in the
environmental health fields, too.

Now clearly, only a few of the scientists appearing suddenly aboard the
environmental bandwagon are manipulators, consciously willing to distort science for their own personal gain. Most are obviously sincere in their concern
for the integrity of the natural environment. We would be inclined to suppose
that the majority of wildlife biologists involved in these issues have good intentions. That in the DDT case some of them came to believe that the pesticide
is a "villain" threatening certain species, and that some showed apparent un-
willingness to evaluate the facts anew, does not speak well for their abilities
to think scientifically. But on the whole, these "natural historian types" have
tended to be followers rather than leaders in the groups of ecologically alarmed
scientists, and it is quite likely that they have not given much consideration to
the ethics and/or motives of the leading figures, whom they more or less automatically would assume to be "on the right side."

A small number of the alarmed scientists fall into a different and special category. These are persons who are subjectively so thoroughly caught up in "doomsday feelings" that many psychologists would not hesitate to render a diagnosis
of rather severe depression-anxiety neurosis. This is not to say that they are necessarily so ill as to be incapacitated, but they may do considerable social harm
by projecting their own fears into vague scientific formulations. The result is
that generalized anxieties which are based on *feeling states* rather than findings

are spread among the populace. Such individuals probably gain very little from their involvement in activist programs, and it is unlikely that they are more than dimly aware that they might be misusing their scientific titles. There is really not very much one can say about these spokesmen except that it would probably be better for all if they were granted lengthy leaves of absence.

Then there is the group of scientists who might be characterized as the "newly important small people." These are persons who may be aware, to some extent, that they are not behaving *quite* according to strict professional ethics, or may even be deliberately altering their data just a little bit, but who have too much to lose at this point to back down. Most have worked for many years in areas of science with very little prestige and had not been earlier accorded any measure of public recognition or attention from colleagues, until the burgeoning of the environmental movement. Such simple motives as ego-enhancement and the flattering feelings of importance associated with their new center-stage roles may be sufficient to explain why they are willing to go to considerable lengths to defend their allegations, even when these have been squarely refuted. It is apparent that there are a number of such researchers who have come into the limelight in the last few years, but who would fall back into obscurity were they to retract their claims about one or another environmental hazard "discovered" by them.

That there are probably a rather sizable number of environmental scientists in both the ecological and the health-related fields who are honest, but simply not too talented, is also fairly evident to anyone who familiarizes himself with the literature. Why this should be the case at the present time is not too difficult to understand either, for there does not seem to be any other field of science where funding is so readily granted for insignificant or redundant research projects, and papers of questionable quality are so readily accepted for publication. This is not to say that there are no other fields of science where public funding is capricious or poor publications appear, but at the moment the environmental sciences seem to be leading the field in terms of the churning out of work which is "relevant" but "irreproducible."*

Basically, then, our answer to the question of whether most or all of the "concerned" scientists can be regarded as conscious manipulators is a definite "No." Probably most of them are well meaning, or, even if they distort just a bit, cannot help themselves for one reason or another. It is unlikely that there are

---

* Most of the reports of such work would not, however, be accepted for publication in the *Journal of Irreproducible Results,* since this official organ of the Society for Basic Irreproducible Research has high standards of cleverness (see, e.g., Williams, 1971).

any more than a very small number of scientists in the movement for whom personal gain takes precedence over commitment to scientific truth or ethics.

But what kind of people are such scientists? What is their game? What do they hope to gain? These questions are easier to consider if one grants that the environmental movement as a social phenomenon is essentially political in nature. If one stops thinking of the scientists whose ethics seem most questionable as professionals, and regards them instead as politicians, then their behavior is not so difficult to comprehend. The passionate expression of emotionally loaded slogans; testing "which way the wind bloweth" before making any new pronouncements about the state of affairs in society; emphasis on charismatic personal power rather than the substance of ideas—these are, after all, sadly admitted by most realists to be essential constituents of the way of politics. It is not difficult, either, to perceive that the ultimate gains from this game of "relevant science politics" can be very high. The stakes include the acquisition of personal power and prestige, dependent on neither exacting work nor brilliant ideas; the mobilization of masses of loyal followers; the possibility of exercising considerable social control through direct influence on decision-making bodies; and ready access to sizable portions of the national scientific budget, with which empires can be built.

For some of the leaders of the movement, there is also the special reward that comes from fulfilling the passion for teaching—a drive which Eric Hoffer (1964) has described as much more powerful than the passion for learning. And if it seems curious and ironic that those who are most obsessed with the desire to teach the masses "all about ecology" are often ill equipped to do so, one might want to consider the rather fitting descriptions offered by Hoffer of the kinds of people who tend to participate in mass movements and the nature of their typical leaders.

The slipping author, artist, scientist—slipping because of a drying-up of the creative flow within—drifts sooner or later into the camps of ardent patriots, race mongers, uplift promoters and champions of holy causes. . . .
The quality of ideas seems to play a minor role in mass movement leadership. What counts is the arrogant gesture, the complete disregard of the opinion of others, the singlehanded defiance of the world. . . . Charlatanism of some degree is indispensable to effective leadership. There can be no mass movement without some deliberate misrepresentation of facts. . . . The leader has to be practical and a realist, yet must talk the language of the visionary and idealist. (Hoffer, 1951, pp. 38, 107)

On the Uses of Criticism

This completes our review of the DDT issue, as it has developed up to mid-1972, the time of this writing. It will undoubtedly be said that we have told a one-sided story, and to a certain extent this is true. However, we have tried to tell that side of the story which has not yet been told, that which exposes the falsities and exaggerations in the assertions of activist environmentalists about the pesticide. The environmentalist point of view has been repeated so often on this particular issue we think it is fair to say that they have been heard by all but the indifferent. One can go further and state that public opinion about DDT has been formed by environmentalists, who have publicized their assertions so effectively that the majority of laymen accept claims which amount to nothing more than unproven allegations put forth by a small minority as scientific facts. Against this background we felt that it was not only justifiable but necessary to undertake this rather unpleasant task of exposing the weaknesses of the case.

It was also our judgment that the anti-DDT scientists had succeeded so well in establishing their own public image as "heroes of a good cause" and "experts" that to write a purely dispassionate critique in a neutral scientific tone without bringing attention to matters of questionable ethics, or to professional incompetence, would have made of our book an exercise in futility. We are well aware that many scientists will object to the facetious and ironic tone we have sometimes employed; but we ask our readers to bear in mind that we are not writing from the cool perspective of history. The environmental movement is in full swing as a "movement for the 1970s," and its scientific leaders are only now beginning to experience tangible successes in the political forum. Now—and not 20 years hence—is the time for the citizenry, the members of the scientific community, and government leaders to ask themselves who among these activist scientists are responsible, competent professionals, and who are not.

In emphasizing the DDT case in these long chapters, our purpose has been not so much to defend DDT per se, or even the use of synthetic pesticides in general, as to defend the scientific process. We chose the DDT issue as the focus for analysis because it is thoroughly documented and because it is probably the issue on which the environmentalists have best succeeded in establishing in the mind of the public, that *their* opinions represent scientific truth and that any opposition may be written off as mere noise made by "industry spokesmen" or people with vested interests in "agribusiness."

Perhaps this is the place to state once again that we have nothing against minority opinions in science as such. The history of science is replete with examples of individuals or groups of scientists who have been opposed in their own times by diehard Establishment conservatives, only to be vindicated by posterity as visionaries whose ideas were more representative of truth than those of their opponents. Unquestionably, minority views and stubborn dissent in science are frequently the seeds of progress in understanding. If we have taken the view that the environmentalists' case against DDT is more akin to Lysenkoism than to a genuine scientific revolution, it is not because the interpretations of these activist scientists differ from those of the majority of their colleagues, but rather because their work is hasty, sloppy, and inadequate to support their contentions and because, for want of real scientific proofs of their preconceived ideas, they have turned to manipulation of public opinion and attempts to discredit their opponents through slander.

In short, we would contend that allowing distortions and bad experiments to stand unchallenged in an area of science which involves vital decisions and has drawn a great deal of public attention threatens to poison the well of rational discourse—a threat which holds far greater dangers to the welfare of society than any of the alleged ill effects of DDT on the environment.

All critical thinkers are aware of the difficulties associated with the search for truth, whether this be defined scientifically or in more philosophical terms. Much has also been said about the increased complexities of the scientist's task introduced by the contemporary "explosion of knowledge." But in our age, the fundamental need to exercise intelligent skepticism in seeking the truth has been minimized altogether too much, with the result that elements of unnecessary confusion have been introduced by a corollary "explosion of ignorance." One antidote to ignorance is, of course, the acquisition of correct information; but another, equally important, is the dispelling of half-truths and falsities which do not stand the test of critical examination.

Let us end with the words of the great eighteenth-century skeptic, Jonathan Swift. His devastating remarks here border on cynical despair; nonetheless, they seem sadly applicable to human affairs, as much in our times as in his own.

> Few lies carry the inventor's mark, and the most prostitute enemy to truth may spread a thousand without being known for the author: besides, as the vilest writer has his readers, so the greatest liar has his believers; and it often happens that, if a lie be believed only for an hour, it has done its work, and there is no farther occasion for it. . . . Considering the natural disposition in many men to lie, and in multitudes to believe, I have been perplexed what to do with that maxim so frequent in everybody's mouth, that truth will at last prevail. (Swift, 1711, pp. 86–87)

BIBLIOGRAPHY

Part I. A MASS MOVEMENT FOR THE SEVENTIES

SELLAR, W. C.; YEATMAN, R. J. 1930. *1066 and All That.* Penguin Books Ltd. (11th printing, 1971), Harmondsworth, pp. 124.

SHKLOVSKII, I. S.; SAGAN, C. 1966. *Intelligent Life in the Universe.* Dell Publ. Co., New York, pp. 509.

Chapter 1. EXPOSITION AND VARIATIONS

CARSON, R. 1962. *Silent Spring.* Fawcett World Library (11th printing April 1970), New York, pp. 304.

COLE, C. L. 1968. Can the World be Saved? The New York Times Magazine, March 31.

DUBOS, R. 1968. *So Human An Animal.* Charles Scribner's Sons, New York. pp. 269.

FULLER, R.B. 1969a. *Operating Manual for Spaceship Earth.* Pocket Books (Nov., 1970), New York, pp. 127.

————1969b. *Utopia or Oblivion: The Prospects for Humanity.* Bantam Books, Inc., New York, pp. 366.

————1971. The City of the Future. In: *Project Survival.* Editors of Playboy: 221-238. Playboy Press, Chicago, pp. 255.

GRAHAM, F., Jr. 1970. *Since Silent Spring.* Fawcett World Library, New York, pp. 288.

McELHENY, V. K. 1971. Insects: Progress Toward Hormonal Control. Technol. Rev., July-August: 12-13.

MEDAWAR, P. 1969. On the Effecting of All Things Possible. Nature, *223:* 895-898.

POLÁNYI, M. 1966. *The Tacit Dimension.* Anchor Books (1967), Garden City, pp. 108.

REICH, C. A. 1970. *The Greening of America.* Bantam Books, Inc. (5th printing, 1971), New York, pp. 433.

SEABORG, G. T. 1971. Science, Technology, and the Citizen. In: *It's Not Too Late.* Eds.: Carvell, F.; Tadlock, M.: 153-167. Glenco Press, Beverly Hills, pp. 232.

SHEPARD, P. 1971. Ecology and Man—A Viewpoint. In: *It's Not Too Late.* Eds.: Carvell, F.; Tadlock, M.: 210-222. Glenco Press, Beverly Hills, pp. 232.

WATTS, A. 1971. Wealth Versus Money. In: *Project Survival.* Editors of Playboy: 165-184. Playboy Press, Chicago, pp. 255.

Chapter 2. CITIZENRY AND SCIENCE

GRAHAM, F., Jr. 1970. *Since Silent Spring.* Fawcett World Library, New York, pp. 288.
JANSSEN, P. R. 1970. The Age of Ecology. In: *Ecotactics: The Sierra Club Handbook for Environmental Activists.* Eds: Mitchell, J. C.; Stallings, C. L.: 53-62. Pocket Books, New York, pp. 288.
RIDGEWAY, J. 1970. *The Politics of Ecology.* E. P. Dutton and Co., Inc., New York, pp. 223.
WAYS, M. 1971. How to Think About the Environment. In: *It's Not Too Late.* Eds.: Carvell, F.; Tadlock, M.: 168-188. Glenco Press, Beverly Hills, pp. 232.
WOLFENDEN, J. 1963. The Gap—and the Bridge. In: *The Languages of Science.* Ed.: Le Corbeiller, P.: 19-34. Fawcett World Library (June, 1966), New York, pp. 176.
WURSTER, C. F. 1969. DDT Goes to Trial in Madison. BioScience, *19* (9): 809-813.
YANNACONE, V. J. 1970. In: *Highlights 70,* Congress for Recreation and Parks, Philadelphia, Pa., p. 24 (Sept. 27–30, 1970).

Chapter 3. O TEMPORA! O MORES!

BITMAN, J.; CECIL, H. C.; HARRIS, S. J.; FRIES, G. J. 1969. DDT Induces a Decrease in Eggshell Calcium. Nature, *224:* 44-46.
HEATH, R.G.; SPANN, J. W.; KREITZER, J. F. 1969. Marked DDE Impairment of Mallard Reproduction in Controlled Studies. Nature, *224:* 47-48.
HEINRICHS, W. L.; GELLERT, R. J.; BAKKE, J. L.; LAWRENCE, N. L. 1971. DDT Administered to Neonatal Rats Induces Persistent Estrus Syndrome. Science. *173:* 642-643.
POLÁNYI, M. 1966. *The Tacit Dimension.* Anchor Books (1967), Garden City, pp. 108
SNOW, C. P. 1934. *The Search.* (1958 ed.) Charles Scribner's Sons, New York, pp. 343.

Chapter 4. THE PROSTITUTION OF SCIENCE

BELKAP, M. 1971. The American Way of Life: Is It Killing Us? The New York Times, April 18.
COMMONER, B. 1963. *Science and Survival.* The Viking Press, Inc. (7th printing, March, 1970), New York, pp. 150.
LAKUBTSINER, M. M. 1952. Materialy k voprosu o nakhozdenii zeren rzhi v kolos'iakh pshenitsy. [Materials on the Questions of the Occurrence of Rye Seeds in Wheat Ear.] Agrobiologiia, (1): 1-34.
JORAVSKY, D. 1970. *The Lysenko Affair.* Harvard University Press, Cambridge, pp. 462.
KARAPETIAN, V. K. 1948. Izmeneniie prirody tverdykh pshenits v miagkie. [The Transformation of Hard Seed Wheat into Soft Seed Wheat.] Agrobiologiia, (4): 5-21.
KOZO-POLIANSKII, B. M. 1951. Protiv idealisma v morfologii rastenii. [The Fight Against Idealism in Plant Morphology.] Bot. Zhurn., (2): 115-179.
LYSENKO, T. D. 1951. *Novoe v nauke o biologicheskom vide.* [A New Characterization of the Concept of Biological Species, or the Fight Against the Ideological Basis of the Reactionary Mendel-Morgan Theories, the Falsification of Darwin's Teachings.] In: *Agrobiologiia: raboty po voprosam genetiki, selektsii i semenovodstva.* [Agrobiology, Contributions to the Problems of Genetics, Selection and Breeding for Improved Seed Varieties.] Lenin Akad. Agr. Nauk, Moscow, pp. 604.
MEDVEDEV, ZH. A.1969. *The Rise and Fall of T. D. Lysenko.* Columbia University Press. New York, pp. 284.
POLÁNYI, M. 1966. *The Tacit Dimension.* Anchor Books (1967), Garden City, pp. 108.

Chapter 5. POWER FOR THE PEOPLE

ALLEN, A. A.; SCHLUETER, R. S.; MIKOLAJ, P. G. 1970. Natural Oil Seepage at Coal Oil Point, Santa Barbara, California. Science, *170*: 974-977.

ANONYMOUS. 1970. Der Konsumentenbund für den Bau von Atomkraftwerken. Neue Züricher Z., *193* (261): 33, (Sept. 23).

ANONYMOUS. 1970. Neues Bundesgesetz über den Schutz der Gewässer. Höhere Subventionen und gestrafte Vorschriften. Neue Züricher Z., *191* (243): 33, (Sept. 4).

BROWN, R. P.; SMITH, D. D. 1969. *Marine Disposal of Solid Wastes: An Interim Summary.* Dillingham Corp., Appl. Oceanography Branch, La Jolla, pp. 8.

KLEIN, D. R. 1971. Reaction of Reindeer to Obstructions and Disturbances. Science, *173*: 393-398.

MADDOX, J. 1972. *The Doomsday Syndrome.* Macmillan London Ltd., London, pp. 248.

MANIAK, U. 1970. Water Pollution Regulation in West Germany and the Rhine River Problem. Proc. Conf. Internatl, Interstate Regulation Water Poll. School of Law, Columbia Univ., New York, N.Y., March 12-13: 50-58.

MEADOWS, D. H.; MEADOWS, D. L.; RANDERS, J.; BEHRENS, W. W. 1972. *The Limits to Growth.* Universe Books, Washington, D.C., pp. 205.

PRO AQUA. 1970. *Wasser und Luft in der Industrie. Bericht über die internationale Vortragstagung Pro Aqua 1969 Basel.* Oldenburg Verl., München, Wien, pp. 314.

U.S. DEPARTMENT OF THE INTERIOR. 1968a. *The Cost of Clean Water. Summary Report, 1*: 1-39, F.W.P.C.A., Washington, D.C.

—— 1968b. *Summary Report, Advanced Waste Treatment, July 1964-1967.* (WP-20-AWTR-19): 1-96. F.W.P.C.A., Washington, D.C.

Chapter 6. REVOLUTION, ANYONE?

CHRISMAN, R. 1970. Ecology, a Racist Shuck. Scanlan's, *1*(6): 46-49.

COMMONER, B. 1971. *The Closing Circle.* Alfred A. Knopf, New York, pp. 326 + x.

EHRLICH, P. R. 1968. *The Population Bomb.* Ballantine Books, New York, pp. 223.

—— 1971. Playboy Interview: Dr. Paul Ehrlich. In: *Project Survival.* Editors of Playboy: 65-111, Playboy Press, Chicago, pp. 255.

——; HARRIMAN, R. L. 1971. *How to be a Survivor. A Plan to Save Spaceship Earth*: Ballantine Books, Inc., New York, pp. 208.

JÓCSIK, L. 1971. *Az öngyilkos civilizáció.* [The Suicidal Civilization.] Közgazdasági és Jogi Könyvkiadó. [Economics and Juristics Publishing House.] Budapest, pp. 276.

MAO TSE-TUNG. 1949. Speech Made on Sept. 16. Quoted by Myrdal and Kessle (1972), p. 67.

MYRDAL, J.; KESSLE, G. 1972. *China: The Revolution Continued.* Vintage Books, New York, pp. 210.

NORMAN, G. 1971. Project Survival. In: *Project Survival.* Editors of Playboy: 11-25. Playboy Press, Chicago, pp. 255.

PADDOCK, W.; PADDOCK, P. 1967. *Famine–1975! America's Decision: Who Will Survive.* Little, Brown and Co., Boston, Toronto, pp. 276.

YANNACONE, V. J. 1971. Remarks at Paper Industry PR Luncheon Group, Union League Club, New York, N.Y., May 20, 1970. In: U.S. House of Representatives. Hearings Before the Committee on Agriculture; 92-A, 58-542, p. 267; and a Copy of Mr. Yannacone's Filed Speech. U.S. Govt. Printing Office, Washington, D.C.

Part II. THE STAYING POWER OF HALF-TRUTHS

Chapter 7. THE SUBJECT OF ECOLOGY

ALLEE, W. C.; EMERSON, A. E.; PARK, O.; PARK, T.; SCHMIDT, K. P. 1949. *Principals of Animal Ecology*. Saunders Co., Philadelphia, London, pp. xii + 837.

BALOGH, J. 1958. *Lebensgemeinschaften der Landtiere*. Ung. Akad. Wiss., Budapest, pp. 482.

BARLOW, E. 1970. The *New York* Magazine Environmental Teach-In. *New York magazine*, March 30: 24-30.

CLEMENTS, F. E.; SHELFORD, V. E. 1939. *Bio-ecology*. Wiley and Sons, Inc., New York, pp. vi + 425.

DOWDESWELL, W. H. 1952. *Animal Ecology*. Methuen and Co., London, pp. 207.

EHRLICH, P. R. 1971. Playboy Interview: Dr. Paul Ehrlich. In: *Project Survival*. Editors of Playboy: 65-111. Playboy Press, Chicago, pp. 255.

FREITAG, H. 1962. *Einführung in die Biographie von Mitteleuropa, unter besonderer Berücksichtigung von Deutschland*. G. Fischer Verl., Stuttgart, pp. 214.

GLEASON, H. 1926. The Individualistic Concept of the Plant Association. Bull. Torrey Bot. Club, 53: 7-26.

HAECKEL, E. 1870. Über Entwicklungsgang und Aufgabe der Zoologie. Jena. Z. Natur W., 5: 353-370.

HAFNER, E. M. 1969. Toward a New Discipline for the Seventies: Ecography. In: *Ecotactics: The Sierra Club Handbook for Environmental Activists*. Eds.: Mitchell, J. G.; Stallings, C. L.: 211-219. Pocket Books, New York, pp. 288.

HARDIN, G. 1970. To Trouble a Star: The Cost of Intervention in Nature. In: *It's Not Too Late*. Eds.: Carvell, F.; Tadlock, M.: 192-199. Glenco Press, Beverly Hills, pp. 232.

HESSE, R. 1924. *Tiergeographie auf ökologischer Grundlage*. G. Fischer Verl., Jena, pp. 613.

——; DOFLEIN, F. 1935. *Tierbau und Tierleben in ihrem Zusammenhang betrachtet*. (2nd ed.), Vol. I: *Der Tierkörper als selbständiger Organismus*. pp. 878. Vol. II: *Das Tier als Glied des Naturganzen*. pp. 828. G. Fischer Verl., Jena.

KNIGHT, C. B. 1965. *Basic Concepts of Ecology*. (7th printing, 1970), The Macmillan Co., New York, pp. 468.

KOLKWITZ, R. 1950. Ökologie der Saprobien. Über die Beziehungen der Wasserorganismen zur Umwelt. Sch.-r. Ver. Wasser-Boden-Lufthyg., Berlin-Dahlem, 4: 1-64.

KORMONDY, E.J. 1969. *Concepts of Ecology*. Prentice Hall, Inc., Englewood Cliffs, pp. xiii + 209.

KÜHNELT, W. 1965. *Grundriss der Ökologie, unter besonderer Berücksichtigung der Tierwelt*. VEB G. Fischer Verl., Jena, pp. 402.

——. 1970. *Grundriss der Ökologie, unter besonderer Berücksichtigung der Tierwelt*. (2nd ed.), VEB G. Fischer Verl., Jena, pp. 443.

MÖBIUS, K. 1877. *Auster und die Austernwirtschaft*. P. Parey Verl., Berlin, pp. 126.

ODUM, E. F. 1959. *Fundamentals of Ecology*. (2nd ed.), Saunders Co., Philadelphia, London, pp. 546.

ÖKLAND, F. 1956. Tiergeographie—Ökologie. Biol. Zbl., 75: 83-85.

SCHWERDTFEGER, F. 1963-1971. *Ökologie der Tiere*. Vol. I: *Autökologie*, 1963, pp. 461. Vol. II: *Synökologie*, 1971, pp. 480. Vol. III: *Demökologie*, 1968, pp. 448. P. Parey Verl., Hamburg, Berlin.

SHELFORD, V. E. 1913. Animal Communities in Temperate America. Bull. Geogr. Soc., Chicago, 5: 1-368.

SHEPARD, P. 1971. Ecology and Man—A Viewpoint. In: *It's Not Too Late*. Eds.: Carvell, F.; Tadlock, M.: 210-222. Glenco Press, Beverly Hills, pp. 232.

Chapter 8. FROM THE ARMCHAIR

CLAUS, G. 1959. Studien über die Algenvegetation der Thermalquelle Bükkszék. Arch. Hydrobiol., 55: 1-29.
DRURY, W. H. 1970. Worldly Problems. Review of Ehrenfeld's *Biological Conservation*. Science, 168: 1333.
EHRLICH, P. R. 1971. Playboy Interview: Dr. Paul Ehrlich. In: *Project Survival*. Editors of Playboy: 65-111. Playboy Press, Chicago, pp. 255.
GRAHAM, F., Jr. 1970. *Since Silent Spring*. Fawcett World Library, New York, pp. 288.
HURD, L. E.; MELLINGER, M. V.; WOLF, L. L.; McNAUGHTON, S. J. 1971. Stability and Diversity at Three Trophic Levels in Terrestrial Successional Ecosystems. Science, 173: 1134-1136.
JORDAN, C. F. 1971. A World Pattern in Plant Energetics. Am. Scientist, 59: 425-433.
KORMONDY, E. J. 1969. *Concepts of Ecology*. Prentice Hall Inc., Englewood Cliffs, pp. xiii + 209.
MARGALEF, D. R. 1957. La Teoría de la Información en Ecología. Mems. R. Acad. Cienc. Art., Barcelona, 32: 373-499.
McALLISTER, C. D.; Le BRASSEUR, R. J.; PARSONS, T. R. 1972. Stability of Enriched Aquatic Ecosystems. Science, 175: 562-564.
ODUM, E. P. 1969. The Strategy of Ecosystem Development. Science, 164: 262-270.
PARK, O. 1963. Ecology. Encycl. Brit. 7: 912-922. Encyclopedia Britannica Inc., Chicago, London, Toronto.
SOÓ, R. 1953. *Növényföldrajz* [Geobotany]. Tankönyvkiadó, Budapest, pp. 67.
WOODWELL, G. M. 1970. The Energy Cycle of the Biosphere. Scient. Amer., 223 (3): 64-74.

Chapter 9. CLEANLINESS IS NEXT TO GODLINESS

ANONYMOUS. 1971a. Detergents—Man's Derived Disaster. Amer. Oceanogr. (Newsletter), March: 7.
ANONYMOUS. 1971b. Water Pollution. SIPI Report, 1: 9.
BURLEW, J.S., Ed. 1953. Algal Culture, from Laboratory to Pilot Plant. Carnegie Inst. Wash. Publ. (600): 1-357.
COMMONER, B. 1971. *The Closing Circle*. Alfred A. Knopf, New York, pp. 326 + x.
DUBOS, R. 1971. Toxic Factors in Enzymes Used in Laundry Products. Science, 173: 259-260.
EPSTEIN, S. S. 1970. Control of Chemical Pollutants. Nature, 228: 816-819.
JANCOVIĆ, V. M.; MANN, H. 1969. Studies of the Acute Toxicity of Nitrilotriacetic Acid (NTA). Arch. Fisch-Wiss., 20: 178-192.
KUENTZEL, L. E. 1969. Bacteria, Carbon Dioxide and Algal Blooms. J. Water Poll. Contr. Fed., 41 (10): 1737-1747.
McCLOSKEY, P. N. 1970. Congress and Environmental Quality: Now or Never. In: *Agenda for Survival*. Ed.: Helfrich, H. W.: 85-96. Yale University Press, New Haven, pp. 234.
The Merck Index. An Encyclopedia of Chemicals and Drugs. 1968. Merck and Co. Inc., Rahway, pp. 1714.
MILLS, S. 1971. Action Imperatives for Population Control: A Woman's View. In: *Agenda for Survival*. Ed.: Helfrich, H. W.: 119-134. Yale University Press, New Haven, pp. 234.
RYTHER, J. H.; DUNSTAN, W. M. 1971. Nitrogen, Phosphorus and Eutrophication in the Coastal Marine Environment. Science, 171: 1008-1013.
U.S. SENATE COMMITTEE ON PUBLIC WORKS. 1970. Hearings on the Use of Nitrilotriacetic Acid as a Detergent Builder. Toxicological and Environmental Implications. U.S. Govt. Printing Office, Washington, D.C.

Chapter 10. FOOD ON EARTH

AMERICAN PUBLIC HEALTH ASSOCIATION. 1965. *Standard Methods for the Examination of Water and Wastewater Including Bottom Sediments and Sludges.* (12th ed.) APHA, Boston, pp. 769.

BROWN, H. 1954. *The Challenge of Man's Future.* The Viking Press (18th printing, March, 1970), New York, pp. 290.

CHOCHRAN, W. W. 1969. *The World Food Problem. A Guardedly Optimistic View.* Thomas Y. Crowell Co., Inc., London, pp. 331.

CHOLNOKY, B.; CLAUS, G. 1961. Beiträge zur Kenntniss der Algenflora und der Ökolgie der Diatomeen in dem Stausee Wemmershoek-Dam nahe Kapstadt. Öster. Bot. Z., *108:* 325-350.

CLAUS, G. 1961. Monthly Ecological Studies on the Flora of the Danube River at Vienna in 1957-1958. Verhandl. Internatl. Ver. theor. angew. Limnol., *14:* 459-465.

————;REIMER, C. 1961. Potomac River Phytoplankton Studies. Acad. Natur. Sci., Philadelphia: Report, pp. 128.

COMMONER, B. 1971. *The Closing Circle.* Alfred A. Knopf, New York, pp. 326 + x.

DELWICHE, C. C. 1970. The Nitrogen Cycle. Scient. Amer., *223:* 137-146.

EHRLICH, P. R. 1971. Playboy Interview: Dr. Paul Ehrlich. In: *Project Survival.* Editors of Playboy: 65-111. Playboy Press, Chicago, pp. 255.

JAPANESE MINISTRY OF FOREIGN AFFAIRS. 1971. *Japan Today.* Japanese Govt. Printers, Tokyo, pp. 118.

KOHL, D. H.; SHEARER, G. B.; COMMONER, B. 1971. Fertilizer Nitrogen: Contribution of Nitrate in Surface Water in a Corn Belt Watershed. Science, *174:* 1331-1334.

KOLKWITZ, R. 1950. Ökologie der Saprobien. Über die Beziehungen der Wasserorganismen zur Umwelt. Schr.-r. Ver. Wasser-Boden-Lufthyg., Berlin-Dahlem, *4:* 1-64.

LANDSBERG, H. H. 1970. The U.S. Resource Outlook: Quantity and Quality. In: *America's Changing Environment.* Eds.: Revelle, R.; Landsberg, H. H.: 108-120. Houghton Mifflin Co., Boston, pp. 314.

LIEBMANN, H. 1960-1962. *Handbuch der Frischwasser- und Abwasserbiologie.* Vol. I, pp. 588, Vol. II, pp. 1149. Oldenburg Verl:, München, Wien.

McKEE, J.E.; WOLF, H. W. 1963. *Water Quality Criteria.* (2nd ed.), State Water Quality Control Board Pub. 3. Water Resources Agency of California, Sacramento, pp. 548.

MacKENTHUN, K. M. 1965. *Nitrogen and Phosphorus in Water. An Annotated Selected Bibliography of their Biological Effect.* U.S. Dept. H.E.W., P.H.S. Div. Water Suppl. Pol Contr., Washington, D.C., pp. 99.

MADDOX, J. 1972. *The Doomsday Syndrome.* Macmillan London Ltd., London, pp. 248.

MAYER, J. 1969. Toward a Non-Malthusian Population Policy. Columbia Forum, *12* (2): 5-13.

MEDVEDEV, ZH. A. 1969. *The Rise and Fall of T.D. Lysenko.* Columbia University Press, New York, pp. 284.

ROSENFIELD, A. B.; HUSTON, R. 1950. Infant Methemoglobinemia in Minnesota Due to Nitrates in Well Water. Minn. Med., *33:* 787-796.

SCHMITT, W. R. 1965. The Planetary Food Potential. Ann. N.Y. Acad. Sci., *118* (7): 645-718.

SEARS, P. B. 1969. *Lands Beyond the Forests.* Prentice Hall, Inc., Englewood Cliffs, pp. 206.

WARING, F. H. 1949. Significance of Nitrates in Water Supply. J. Am. Water Works Asso., *41:* 147-150.

WEINBERGER, L. W.; STEPHAN, D. G.; MIDDLETON, F.M. 1966. Solving Our Water Problems —Water Renovation and Water Reuse. Ann. N.Y. Acad. Sci., *136* (5): 131-154.

WEISS, C. M.; OKUN, D. A. 1967. Water Quality Technology: Present Capabilities and Future Prospects. Internatl. Conf. Water for Peace, May 23-31, Washington, D.C., *1:* 195-207.

Chapter 11. THE TOCSIN OVER TOXINS

COMMONER, B. 1963. *Science and Survival*. The Viking Press, Inc. (7th printing, March 1970), New York, pp. 150.

DINMAN, B. D. 1972. "Non-Concept" of "No-Threshold": Chemicals in the Environment. Science, *175:* 495-497.

EHRLICH, P. R.; HOLDREN, J. P. 1971. Impact of Population Growth. Science, *171:* 1212-1217.

GABLIKS, J.; FRIEDMAN, L. 1969. Effects of Insecticides on Mammalian Cells and Virus Infections. Ann. N.Y. Acad. Sci., *160:* 254-271.

GARRETT, R. M. 1947. Toxicity of DDT for Man. Alabama State Med. Asso. J., *17:* 74-76.

HAYES, W. J. 1964. Occurrence of Poisoning by Pesticides. Arch. Envir. Health, *9:* 621-625.

————.1967. Toxicity of Pesticides to Man; Risks from Present Levels. Proc. Roy. Soc., Ser. B., *167:* 101-127.

————; DURHAM, W. F.; CUETO, C. 1956. The Effect of Known Repeated Oral Doses of Chlorophenothene (DDT) in Man. J.A.M.A., *162:* 890-897.

HUTCHINSON, G. E. 1964. The Influence of the Environment. Proc. Natl. Acad. Sci., U.S., *51:* 930-934.

INNES, J. R. M.; ULLAND, B. M.; VALERIO, G. M.; PETRUCELLI, L.; FISHBEIN, L.; HART, E. R.; PALLOTTA, A. J.; BATES, R. R.; FALK, H. H.; GART, J. J.; KLEIN, M.; MITCHELL, I.; PETERS, J. 1969. Bioassay of Pesticides and Industrial Chemicals for Tumorigenicity in Mice: A Preliminary Note. J. Natl. Cancer Inst., *42:* 1101-1114.

KÜHNELT, W. 1970. *Grundriss der Ökologie, mit besonderer Berücksichtigung der Tierwelt*. (2nd ed.), VEB G. Fischer Verl., Jena, pp. 443.

LAN, H. An Der. 1962. Histopathologische Auswirkungen von Insekticiden (DDT und Sevin) bei Wirbellosen und ihre cancerogene Beurteilung. Mikroskopie, *17:* 85-112.

PARACELSUS, P. A. T. BOMBASTUS Von HOHENHEIM. 1562. *De gradibus, de compositionibus et dosibus receptorum ac naturalium libri septem*. (Ed.: Bodenstein, A. von). P. Fabricius, Myloecium, pp. 67.

————. 1574. *Labyrinthus vnd Irrgang der vermeinten Artzet. Item, Siben Defensiones, oder Schirmreden. Item, von vrsprung vnd vrsachen, vnd steins, so sich im menschen befinden, kurzer begriff*. (Ed.: Bodenstein, A. von). S. Apiarium, P. Perna, Basel, pp. 171.

Report of the Secretary's Commission on Pesticides and Their Relation to Environmental Health. 1969. (Mrak, E., chairman); Part I: i-xvii, Part II: 1-677. U.S. Dept. H.E.W., Washington, D.C.

WEISSKOPF, V. E. 1963. Interview. In: *The Way of the Scientist*. Editors of International Science and Technology: 87-99. Simon and Schuster, New York, pp. 382.

WIRT, W.; HECHT, G.; GLOXHUBER, CH. 1971. *Toxikologie Fibel*. (2nd ed.), Georg Thieme Verl., Stuttgart, pp. 469.

Chapter 12. PANDORA'S BOX

ABELSON, P. H. 1970. Pollution by Organic Chemicals. Science, *170:* 496.

————.1971. The Editing of Science. Science, *171:* 1101.

ALEXANDER, P. 1960. Radiation Imitating Chemicals. Scient. Amer., *202* (1): 99-108.

ANONYMOUS. 1970. 2,4,5-T Cancellations, Suspensions Proposed by PRD. Food Chem. News, *12* (4): 7.

ANONYMOUS. 1971. Wie "naturrein" ist die Natur? Der Pflanzenarzt, Sept. 10: 197.

BATEMAN, A. J. 1966. Testing Chemicals for Mutagenicity in a Mammal. Nature, *210:* 205-206.

BERGSTRÖM, R.M.; ERILÄ, T.; PIRSKANEN, R. 1967. Teratogenic Effects of the Amino Acid Leucine in the Chicken. Experientia, *23:* 767-768.

BOFFEY, P. M. 1971. Herbicides in Vietnam: AAAS Study Finds Widespread Devastation. Science, *171:* 43-47.

BORZELLECA, J. F.; DRILL, V. A.; DUBOIS, K. P.; FRAWLEY, J. P.; GOLBERG, L.; HAYES, W. J.; McCOLLISTER, D. D.; ROUDABUSH, R. L.; SCALA, R. A. 1971. Letter to the Editor: Use of 2,4,5-T. Science, *174:* 545-546.

BROWN, H. 1954. *The Challenge of Man's Future.* The Viking Press (18th printing, March 1970), New York, pp. 290.

CARR, D. H. 1965. Chromosome Studies in Spontaneous Abortions. Obstetr. Gynec., *26:* 308-310.

COLLINS, T. F. X.; WILLIAMS, C. H. 1971. Teratogenic Studies with 2,4,5-T and 2,4-D. Bull. Envir. Contam. Toxicol., *6:* 559-567.

COURTNEY, K. D.; GAYLOR, D. W.; HOGAN, M. D.; FALK, H. L.; BATES, R. R.; MITCHELL, I. 1970. Teratogenic Evaluation of 2,4,5-T. Science, *168:* 864-868.

CROSBY, D. G.;WONG, A. S. 1970. Abstract. 160th Meeting Am. Chem. Soc., Chicago, Sept. 17.

———; ———; PLIMMER, J. R.; WOOLSON, E. A. 1971. Photodecomposition of Chlorinated Dibenzo-*p*-Dioxins. Science, *173:* 748-749.

DEAN, B. J.; THORPE, E. 1972. Studies with Dichlorvos Vapour in Dominant Lethal Mutation Tests on Mice. Arch. Toxicol., *30:* 51-59.

DEMETER, O. 1956. Über Modifikationen bei Cyanophyceen. Arch. Mikrobiol., *24:* 105-133.

DESBARATS, P. 1970. Enough! Pollute Me No More Pollution. Saturday Night, *85* (10):16-17.

DINMAN, B. D. 1972. "Non-Concept" of "No-Threshold": Chemicals in the Environment. Science, *175:* 495-497.

DOBROVOLSKAIA-ZAVADSKAIA, N. 1935. Peut-on Influencer la Localization de l'Adenocarcinome de la Mammelle chez la Souris? C. R. Séances Soc. Biol., *119:* 83-87.

EMERSON, J. L.; THOMPSON, D. J.; GERBIG, C. G.; ROBINSON, V. B. 1970. Teratogenic Study of 2,4,5-Trichlorophenoxyacetic Acid in the Rat. Toxicol. Appl. Pharmac., *17:* 317-318.

EPSTEIN, S. S. 1970. Control of Chemical Pollutants. Nature, *228:* 816-819.

——— 1972. Statement. Official Transcripts. Consolidated DDT Hearings. E.P.A., Washington, D.C.

———; BASS, W.; ARNOLD, E.; BISHOP, Y. 1970a. Mutagenicity of Trimethylphosphate in Mice. Science, *168:* 584-586.

———; JOSHI, S. R.; ARNOLD, E.; PAGE, E. C.; BISHOP, Y. 1970b. Abnormal Zygote Development in Mice after Paternal Exposure to a Chemical Mutagen. Nature, *225:* 1260-1261.

———; SHAFNER, H. 1968. Chemical Mutagens in the Human Environment. Nature, *219:* 385-387.

ERCEGOVICH, G. 1969. Comments During Panel Discussion. Ann. N. Y. Acad. Sci., *160* (1): 407-408, 409-410.

FAHMY, O.G. 1969. Comments During Panel Discussion. Ann. N. Y. Acad. Sci., *160* (1): 406-410.

———; FAHMY, M. J. 1969. The Genetic Effects of the Biological Alkylating Agents with Reference to Pesticides. Ann. N. Y. Acad. Sci., *160* (1): 228-243.

GOFMAN, J. W.; TAMPLIN, A. R. 1969. Testimony. Subcommittee on Air and Water Pollution, Committee on Public Works, U.S. Senate, 91st Congress, Nov. 18. U. S. Govt. Printing Office, Washington, D.C.

GOLBERG, L. 1971. Trace Chemical Contaminants in Food: Potential for Harm. Fd. Cosmet. Toxicol., *9:* 65-80.

GOLDWATER, L. J. 1971. Mercury in the Environment. Scient. Amer., *224:* 15-21.

GRÜNEBERG, H. 1964. Genetical Research in an Area of High Natural Radioactivity in South India. Nature, *204:* 222-224.

HASEMAN, J. K.; HOGAN, M. D. 1970. *Further Statistical Analyses of 2,4,5-T and Dioxin Studies.* Biometry Branch, N.I.E.H.S., H.E.W., Research Triangle Park, June 29, pp. 14.

HAMMOND, A. L. 1971. Mercury in the Environment: Natural and Human Factors. Science, *171:* 788-789.

INNES, J. R. M.; ULLAND, B. M.; VALERIO, G. M.; PETRUCELLI, L.; FISHBEIN, L.; HART, E. R.; PALLOTTA, A. J.; BATES, R. R.; FALK, H. H.; GART, J. J.; KLEIN, M.; MITCHELL, I.; PETERS, J. 1969. Bioassay of Pesticides and Industrial Chemicals for Tumorigenicity in Mice: A Preliminary Note. J. Natl. Cancer Inst., *42:* 1101-1114.

JACKSON, H.; JONES, A. R. 1968. Antifertility Action and Metabolism of Trimethylphosphate in Rodents. Nature, *220:* 591-592.

KALTER, H.; WARKANY, J. 1959. Experimental Production of Congenital Malformations in Mammals by Metabolic Procedure. Physiol. Rev., *39:* 69-72.

KEARNEY, P. C.; TSCHIRLEY, F. H. 1970. Risk and Responsibilities in the Use of Herbicides. Paper presented at the Northeastern Weed Control Conference. Jan. 7, New York, pp. 9.

KLEIN, M. 1963. Susceptibility of Strain B6AF^{1}J Hybrid Infant Mice to Tumorigenesis with 1,2-benzathracene, Desoxycholic Acid and 3-methylcholantrene. Cancer Res., *23:* 1701-1703.

KOESTLER, A. 1967. *The Ghost in the Machine.* Pan Books Ltd. (1970), London, pp. 421.

———. 1969. Discussion of MacLean's Paper. In: *The Alpbach Symposium 1968. Beyond Reductionism.* Eds.: Koestler, A.; Smythies, J. R.: 276. Hutchinson and Co., Ltd., London, pp. 438.

———; SMYTHIES, J. R., 1969. *The Alpbach Symposium 1968. Beyond Reductionism.* Hutchinson and Co., Ltd., London, pp. 438.

KRAYBILL, H. F. 1969. Comments During Panel Discussion. Ann. N.Y. Acad. Sci., *160* (1): 412-413.

MacLEAN, P. D. 1969. The Paranoid Streak in Man. In: *The Alpbach Symposium 1968. Beyond Reductionism.* Eds.: Koestler, A.; Smythies, J. R.: 258-278. Hutchinson and Co., Ltd., London, pp. 438.

The Merck Manual of Diagnosis and Therapy. 1966. (11th ed.), Merck and Co., Inc., Rahway, pp. 1850.

MIDING, J. 1969. Comments During Panel Discussion. Ann. N.Y. Acad. Sci., *160* (1): 412.

MORGAN, K. Z. 1969. Tainted Radiation. Sci. Technol., (90): 46-50.

———. 1971. Adequacy of Present Standards of Radiation Exposure. Envir. Affairs, *1:* 91-139.

NISHIMURA, H.; MIYAMOTO, S. 1969. Teratogenic Effects of Sodium Chloride in Mice. Acta Anat., *74:* 121-124.

PETERS, S. U.; STRASSBURG, M. 1969. Stress als teratogener Faktor. Arzneimittel-Forsch., *19:* 1106-1109.

PLIMMER, J. R.; KLINGEBIEL, U. I. 1971. Riboflavin Photosensitized Oxidation of 2,4-Dichlorophenol: Assessment of Possible Chlorinated Dioxin Formation. Science, *174:* 407-408.

Report of the Secretary's Commission on Pesticides and Their Relation to Environmental Health. 1969. (Mrak, E., chairman); Part I: i-xvii, Part II: 1-677. U.S. Dept. H.E.W., Washington, D.C.

ROSENZWEIG, S.; BLAUSTEIN. F. M. 1970. Two Techniques for Studying Stress as a Cause of Cleft Palate in Mice. 10th Annual Meet. Teratol. Soc., Abstr.: 209.

ROSSI, H.: KELLERER, A. M. 1972. Radiation Carcinogenesis of Low Doses. Science, *175:* 200-202.

RUSSELL, W. L. 1963. *Repair from Genetic Radiation.* Pergamon Press, Oxford, pp. 205.

SANDERS, H. J. 1969. Chemical Mutagens. Chem. Eng. News, *47* (21): 50.

SJÖSTRÖM, H.; NILSSON, R. 1972. *Thalidomide and the Power of the Drug Companies.* Penguin Books, Ltd., Harmondsworth, pp. 281.

SPARSCHU, G. L.; DUNN, F. L.; ROWE, V. K. 1970. Teratogenic Study of 2,3,7,8-Tetrachlorodibenzo-p-dioxin in the Rat. Toxicol. Appl. Pharmac., *17:* 317-318.

STEINER, P. E.; STEEL, R.; KOCH, F. C. 1942. The Possible Carcinogenicity of Overcooked Meats, Heated Cholesterol, Acrolein, and Heated Sesame Oil. Cancer Res., 2: 100-105.

STERLING, T. D. 1971. Difficulty of Evaluating the Toxicity and Teratogenicity of 2,4,5-T from Existing Animal Experiments. Science, 174: 1358-1359.

STOKINGER, H. E. 1971. Sanity in Research and Evaluation of Environmental Health. Science, 174: 662-665.

TUCHMANN-DUPLESSIS, H.; MERCIER-PAROT, L. 1956. Influence d'un Corps de Chélation, l'Acid Ethylènediaminetetraacétique sur la Gestation et le Développement Foetal du Rat. C.R. Acad. Sci., Paris, 243: 1064-1067.

TURNEY, W. G. 1971. Mercury Pollution: Michigan's Action Program. J. Water Poll. Contr. Fed., 43: 1427-1438.

VERRETT, M. J. 1969. Comments During Panel Discussion. Ann. N.Y. Acad. Sci., 160 (1): 412-413.

————; MUTCHLER, M. K.; SCOTT, W. F.; REYNALDO, E. F.; McLAUGHLIN, J. 1969. Teratogenic Effects of Captan and Related Compounds in the Developing Chicken Embryo. Ann. N.Y. Acad. Sci., 160 (1): 334-343.

VINOGRADOV, A. P. [English Translation]. 1953. The Elementary Chemical Composition of Marine Organisms. Sears Found., New Haven, pp. 183.

WADE, N. 1971. Decision on 2,4,5-T: Leaked Reports Compel Regulatory Responsibility. Science, 173: 610-615.

————. 1972a. DES: A Case Study of Regulatory Abdication. Science, 177: 335-337.

————. 1972b. Delaney Anti-Cancer Clause: Scientists Debate on Article of Faith. Science, 177: 588-591.

WEISS, C. M.; OKUN, D. A. 1967. Water Quality Technology and Future Prospects. Internatl. Conf. Water for Peace, May 23-31, Washington, D.C., 1: 195-207.

Part III. THE PESTICIDE BUGABOO

GALLEY, R. A. E. 1971. The Contribution of Pesticides Used in Public Health Programmes to the Pollution of the Environment. I. General and DDT. WHO/VBC (7). 326, Geneva, pp. 29.

HEINRICH, B. 1972. Temperature Regulation in the Bumblebee Bombus vagans: A Field Study. Science, 175: 185-187.

LING, L.; WHITTEMORE, F. W.; TURTLE, E. E. 1972. Persistent Insecticides in Relation to the Environment and their Unintended Effects. FAO, AGPP: MISC/4, Rome, pp. 46.

Chapter 13. A COMPOUND WITH A HISTORY

ADVISORY COMMITTEE ON DDT. 1971. Report. E.P.A., Washington, D.C., pp. 43.

ANONYMOUS. 1972. Bald Eagles Bring Nationwide Publicity. Hungry Horse News. Hungry Horse, Montana, Nov. 17: 2.

BENSON, P. B.; McDERMOTT, W., Eds. 1971. Cecil-Loeb Textbook of Medicine. (13th ed.), Saunders Co., Philadelphia, London, Toronto, pp. 1923.

BISKIND, M. S. 1953. Public Health Aspects of the New Insecticides. Am. J. Dig. Dis., 20: 331-341.

BORLAUG, N. 1971. Quoted in: Starvation Called the Peril; An Argument for DDT. San Francisco Chronicle, Nov. 9.

BRUCE-CHWATT, L. J. 1971. Malaria. In: Cecil-Loeb Textbook of Medicine. Eds.: Benson, P. B.; McDermott, W. (13th ed.): 700-713. Saunders Co., Philadelphia, London, Toronto, pp. 1923.

CANDAU, M. 1969. DDT Defended and Praised. J.A.M.A., 209 (7): 1096.

SIMMONS, S. W. 1959. In: *DDT: The Insecticide Dichlorodiphenyltrichloroethane and its Significance*. Vol. II. *Human and Veterinary Medicine*. Ed.: Müller, P.: 251-502. Birkhauser Verl., Basel, pp. 502.

STEINFELD, J. 1971. Statement. Official Transcripts. Consolidated DDT Hearings. E.P.A., Washington, D.C.

TARJÁN, R.; KEMÉNY, T. 1969. Multigeneration Studies on DDT in Mice. Fd. Cosmet. Toxicol., 7: 215-222.

U.S. DEPARTMENT OF THE INTERIOR. 1967. Pollution Caused Fish Kills—1967. (8): 1-16. F.W.P.C.A., Washington, D.C.

WHITTEMORE, F. W. 1970. Cited in: Wall Street Journal, February 16.

WURSTER, C. F. 1969. DDT: Danger to the Environment. University Rev. (S.U.N.Y.), 2 (3): 20-25.

————. 1970. DDT and the Environment. In: *Agenda for Survival*. Ed.: Helfrich, H.W.: 37-54. Yale University Press, New Haven, pp. 234.

————; VAN DEN BOSCH, R. 1972. Dr. Borlaug and DDT. Washington Star, Jan. 2: 6.

Chapter 14. OF MEN AND MICE

ALLISON, D.; KALLMAN, B. J.; COPE, O. B.; VAN VALIN, C. C. 1964. Some Chronic Effects of DDT on Cutthroat Trout. U.S. Bur. Sport Fish. Wildlife Res. Rept., (64): 1-30.

BALL, J. K.; FIELD, W. E. H.; ROE, F. J. C.; WALTERS, R. 1964. The Carcinogenic Effects of Paraffin Wax Pellets and Glass Beads in the Mouse Bladder. Brit. J. Urol., 36: 225-237.

BIRKS, R. E. 1960. A Clinical Survey of a Cross Section of an Industrial Worker Group. Arch. Envir. Health, 1: 291-296.

BITMAN, J.; CECIL, H. C. 1970. Estrogenic Activity of DDT Analogs and Polychlorinated Biphenyls. J. Agr. Food Chem., 18: 1108-1112.

————; ————; FRIES, G. F. 1971. Non Conversion of o,p'-DDT to p,p'-DDT in Rats, Sheep, Chickens and Quail. Science, 174: 64-66.

————; ————; HARRIS, S. J.; FRIES, G. F. 1968. Estrogenic Activity of o,p'-DDT in the Mammalian Uterus and Avian Oviduct. Science, 162: 371-372.

BRYAN, G. T.; SPRINGBERG, P. D. 1966. Role of the Vehicle in the Genesis of Bladder Carcinomas in Mice by the Pellet Implantation Technique. Cancer Res., 26: 105-109.

BURLINGTON, A.; LINDEMAN, V. F. 1950. Effect of DDT on Testes and Secondary Sex Characteristics of White Leghorn Cockerels. Proc. Soc. Exper. Biol. Med., 74: 48-50.

BUTLER, W. H. 1970. Pathology in Liver Cancer in Experimental Animals. IARC Sci. Publ., Lyons, (1): 30-41.

————. 1972. Statement. Official Transcripts. Consolidated DDT Hearings. E.P.A., Washington, D.C.

CAMERON, G. R.; BURGESS, F. 1945. Toxicity of 2,2-bis (p-chlorophenyl) 1,1,1-trichloroethane (D.D.T.). Brit. Med. J., 1: 865-871.

————; CHENG, K. K. 1951. Failure of Oral D.D.T. to Induce Toxic Changes in Rat. Brit. Med. J., 2: 819-821.

CARSON, R. 1962. *Silent Spring*. Fawcett World Library (11th printing, April, 1970), New York, pp. 304.

CECIL, H. C.; BITMAN, J.; HARRIS, S. J. 1971. Estrogenicity of o,p'-DDT in Rats. J. Agr. Food Chem., 19: 61-65.

COLORADO EXTENSION SERVICE (FORT COLLINS). 1970. Pesticides, Foods and Balance of Nature. Bull., October (45):1-8.

CROSBY, D. G. 1966. *Toxicants Occuring Naturally in Foods*. Natl. Acad. Sci., Natl. Res. Counc., Washington, D.C., pp. 112.

BIBLIOGRAPHY

CARSON, R. 1962. *Silent Spring*. Fawcett World Library (11th printing, April, 1970), N York, pp. 304.

COLE, L. C. 1962. Rachel Carson's Indictment of the Wide Use of Pesticides. Scient. Am 207 (6): 173-180.

CRAMER, V. 1971. Fragen der Umweltbelastung aus dem Blickwinkel der Pflanzenschutz telindustrie. Paper presented at May 12th Meeting Industrieverb. Pflanzenschu Schädlingsbekämpfungsmittel, pp. 13.

DEVLIN, J. 1972. Pesticide Spokesmen Accused of "Lying" on Higher Bird Count. New Y Times, Aug. 14.

DE WITT, J. B. 1965. Effects of Chlorinated Hydrocarbon Insecticides upon Quail and Ph ants. J. Agr. Food Chem., 3: 672-673.

EXECUTIVE BOARD OF THE WORLD HEALTH ORGANIZATION. 1971. The Place of DDT in Op tions against Malaria and Other Vector-Borne Diseases. Off. Rec. W.H.O., (190): 176-1

FISHER, G. 1964. Introduction of Dr. Paul Müller. In: *Nobel Lectures: Physiology or Medic 1942-1962*. Vol. III, p. 226. Elsevier Publ. Co., Amsterdam, London, New York, pp. 61

GOODMAN, L. S.; GILMAN, A., Eds. 1970.*The Pharmacological Basis of Therapeutics*. (4th e Macmillan Co., New York, pp. 1794.

GRAHAM. F.. Jr. 1970. *Since Silent Spring*. Fawcett World Library, New York, pp. 288

HARRISON, H. L.; LOUCKS, O. L.; MITCHELL, J. W.; PARKHURST, D. F.; TRACY, C. R.: WATTS, D YANNACONE, V. J. 1970. Systems Studies of DDT Transport. Science, 170: 503-508.

HEADLY, J. C. 1968. Estimating the Productivity of Agricultural Pesticides. Am. J. Agr. Ec 50 (1): 13-23.

HOFFER, E. 1951. *The True Believer*. Mentor Books (July, 1959), New York, pp. 160.

HUFFAKER, C. B. 1971. Biological Control and a Remodeled Pest Control Technology. Te nol. Rev., June: 31-37.

INGERSOLL, B. 1969. DDT on Trial in Wisconsin—Part II. BioScience, 19: 735-736.

INNES, J. R. M.; ULLAND, B. M.; VALERIO, G. M.; PETRUCELLI, L.; FISHBEIN, L.; HART, E PALLOTTA, A. J.; BATES, R. R.; FALK, H. H.; GART, J. J.; KLEIN, M.; MITCHELL, I.; PETERS, J. 19 Bioassay of Pesticides and Industrial Chemicals for Tumorigenicity in Mice: A Prelimin Report. J. Natl. Cancer Inst., 42: 1101-1114.

IRVING, G. W. 1970. Agricultural Pest Control and the Environment. Science, 168: 1419-14

MARSDEN, P. D. 1971. Protozoan Diseases, General Considerations. In: *Cecil-Loeb Textb of Medicine*. Eds: Benson, P. B.; McDermott, W. (13th ed.): 700. Saunders Co., Philac phia, London, Toronto, pp. 1923.

McCLOSKEY, M. 1971. Cited by Leighty, J. In: Sierra Club Urges Total Ban of DDT. Press. Riverside, California, Feb. 25: C-3.

MILLER, S. KNAPP, C. 1971. Pesticide Regulations Tighten but Choices Are in the Offi Interview with Dr. E. F. Knipling, Agriculture Dept.'s Science Advisor. Envir. Techn., 5 (5): 398-403.

NATIONAL COMMUNICABLE DISEASE CENTER. 1969.*DDT in Malaria Control and Eradicati* U.S. Dept. H. E.W., Atlanta, July 25, pp. 9.

PAL, R. 1962. Contributions of Insecticides to Public Health in India. World Rev. Pest Con 1: 6-14.

PANEL ON MONITORING PERSISTENT PESTICIDES IN THE MARINE ENVIRONMENT (NASCO). 19 *Chlorinated Hydrocarbons in the Marine Environment*. Natl. Acad. Sci., Washingt D.C., pp. 42.

RISEBROUGH, R. 1969. Statement. Transcript of Hearings on DDT Before the Dept. of Nat Resources: 713-715. Madison, Wisconsin.

————; MENZEL, D. B.; MARTIN, J. D.; OLCOTT, H. S. 1972. DDT Residues in Pacific Mar Fish. Paper submitted for publication to Pestic. Monit. J., Aug., pp. 42.

DAVIGNON, L. F.; ST. PIERRE, J.; CHAREST, G.; TOURANGEAU, F. J. 1965. A Study of the Chronic Effects of Insecticides in Man. J. Can. Med. Asso., 92: 597-602.

DAVIS, K. J. 1969. In-House Memorandum to W. Hansen. U.S. Dept. H.E.W., F.D.A. Incorporated in Materials of the Consolidated DDT Hearings. E.P.A., Washington, D.C., p. 1.

DURHAM, W. F.; ORTEGA, P.: HAYES, W. J. 1963. The Effect of Various Dietary Levels of DDT on Liver Function, Cell Morphology and DDT Storage in the Rhesus Monkey. Arch. Internatl. Pharmacodyn., 141: 114-129.

EDITORIAL. 1971. The Mouse: Is it Wrong for the Right Reasons? BIBRA Bull., 10: 115-116.

EPSTEIN, S. S. 1970. Control of Chemical Pollutants. Nature, 228: 816-819.

———. 1972a. Point of View: DDT and the Limits of Toxicology. Science, 175: 610.

———. 1972b. Statement. Official Transcripts. Consolidated DDT Hearings, E.P.A., Washington, D.C.

———; ANDREA, J.; JAFFE, H.; JOSHI, S.; FALK, H.; MANTEL, N. 1967. Carcinogenicity of the Herbicide Maleic Hydrazide. Nature, 215: 1388-1390.

———; JOSHI, S.; ANDREA, J.: CLAPP, P.; FALK, H.; MANTEL, N. 1967. Synergistic Toxicity and Carcinogenicity of Freons and Piperonyl Butoxide. Nature, 214: 526-528.

FALK, H. L.; KOTIN, P. 1969. Pesticide Synergists and Their Metabolites: Potential Hazards. Ann. N.Y. Acad. Sci., 160 (1): 299-313.

FENNAH, R. G. 1945. Preliminary Tests with DDT Against Insects of Food Crops in the Lesser Antilles. Trop. Agr., 22: 222-226.

FISCHER, A. L.; KEASLING, H. H.; SCHUELER, F. W. 1952. Estrogenic Action of Some DDT Analogues. Proc. Soc. Exper. Biol. Med., 81: 439-441.

FITZHUGH, O. G.; NELSON, A. A. 1947. The Chronic Oral Toxicity of DDT (p-Chlorophenyl-1,1,1,-Trichloroethane). J. Pharmacol., 89: 18-30.

FRENCH, M. C.; JEFFERIES, D. J. 1969. Degradation and Disappearance of ortho, para Isomer of Technical DDT in Living and Dead Avian Tissues. Science, 165: 914-916.

GOLBERG, L. 1971. Trace Chemical Contaminants in Food: Potential for Harm. Fd. Cosmet. Toxicol., 10: 418-426.

GRASSO, P.; CRAMPTON, R. T. 1972. The Value of the Mouse in Carcinogenicity Testing. Fd. Cosmet. Toxicol., 9: 65-80

———; GOLBERG, L. 1966. Early Changes at the Site of Repeated Subcutaneous Injection of Food Colourings. Fd. Cosmet. Toxicol., 4: 269-272.

GROSS, M. A. 1969. In-House Memorandum to O. G. Fitzhugh. U.S. Dept. H.E.W., F.D.A. Incorporated in Materials of the Consolidated DDT Hearings. E.P.A., Washington, D.C., pp. 33.

HALVER, J.E. 1967. Crystalline Aflatoxin and Other Vectors for Trout Hepatoma. Trout Hepatoma Res. Conf. Papers. U.S. Dept. H.E.W., N.C.I., U.S. Bur. Sport Fish. Wildlife Res. Rept. (70): 78-102.

HANSON, W.; DAVIS, K. J.; FITZHUGH, O. G.; GROSS, M.A. 1969. Chronic Toxicity of Chlorinated Hydrocarbon Pesticides. (In-House Memoranda). U.S. Dept. H.E.W., F.D.A. Incorporated in Materials of the Consolidated DDT Hearings. E.P.A., Washington, D.C., pp. 38.

HAYES, W. J. 1964. Epidemiology of Pesticides. In: Proceedings of the Short Course on the Occupational Health Aspects of Pesticides. Eds.: Link, E.; Whitaker, R. J.: 109-130. University Oklahoma, Norman.

———. 1969a. Pesticides and Human Toxicity. Ann. N.Y. Acad. Sci., 160 (1): 40-54.

———. 1969b. Statement Communicated to DDT Hearing Coordinator, Washington State Dept. of Agriculture, Oct. 10-11, Olympia, pp. 36.

———; DALE, W.E.; PIRKLE, C.I. 1961. Effects of Known Repeated Oral Doses of DDT. WHO Expert Committee on Insecticides (Toxic Hazards to Man). Oct.11, Zurich, Working Paper, (6): 1-12.

————; ————; ———— 1971. Evidence of Safety in Long-Term High Oral Doses of DDT for Man. Arch. Envir. Health, *22:* 119-131.

————; DURHAM, W. F.; CUETO, C. 1956. The Effect of Known Repeated Oral Doses of Chlorophenothane (DDT) in Man. J.A.M.A., *162:* 890-897.

HEINRICHS, W. L.; GELLERT, R. J.; BAKKE, J. L.; LAWRENCE, N. L. 1971. DDT Administered to Neonatal Rats Induces Persistent Estrus Syndrome. Science, *173:* 642-643.

HOLDEN, A. V. 1965. Contamination of Fresh Water by Persistent Insecticides and Their Effects on Fish. Ann. Appl. Biol., *55:* 332-335.

————. 1966. Organochlorine Insecticide Residues in Salmonid Fish. J. Appl. Ecol., *3* (Suppl.): 45-53.

INNES, J. R. M.; ULLAND, B. M.; VALERIO, M. G.; PETRUCELLI, L.; FISHBEIN, L.; HART, E. R.; PALLOTTA, A. J.; BATES, R. R.; FALK, H. H.; GART, J. J.; KLEIN, M.; MITCHELL, I.; PETERS, J. 1969. Bioassay of Pesticides and Industrial Chemicals for Tumorigenicity in Mice: A Preliminary Note. J. Natl. Cancer Inst., *42:* 1101-1114.

KAPLAN, H. S. 1967. On the Natural History of the Murine Leukemias. Cancer Res., *27:* 1325-1340.

LAUG, E. P.; NELSON, A. A.; FITZHUGH, O. G.; KUNZE, F. M. 1950. Liver Cell Alteration and DDT Storage in the Fat of the Rat Induced by Dietary Levels of 1 to 50 p.p.m. DDT. J. Pharmacol., *98:* 268-273.

LAWS, E. R.; CURLEY, A.; BIROS, F. J. 1967. Men with Intensive Occupational Exposure to DDT. A Clinical and Chemical Study. Arch. Envir. Health, *15:* 766-775.

LEHMAN, A. 1951. Chemicals in Food: A Report to   Association of Food and Drug Officials on Current Development. Part II: Pesticides, Section III: Subacute and Chronic Toxicity. Section V: Pathology. Assoc. Food Drug Officials U.S. Quart. Bull., *15:* 47-60, 126-132.

————. 1965. *Summaries of Pesticide Toxicity.* Association of Food and Drug Officials of the United States. P.O. Box 1494, Topeka.

LILLIE, R. D.; SMITH, M. I. 1944. Pathology of Experimental Poisoning in Cats, Rabbits and Rats with DDT. U.S. Publ. Health Rept., *59:* 979-983.

MACEK, K. J. 1968. Reproduction in Brook Trout *(Salvelinus fontinalis)* Fed Sublethal Concentrations of DDT. J. Fish. Res. Bd. Can., *25* (9): 1787-1796.

NARAT, J. K. 1925. Experimental Production of Malignant Growths by Simple Chemicals. J. Cancer Res., *9:* 135-147.

NEAL, P.A.; VON OETTINGEN, W. F.; SMITH, W. W.; MALMO, R. B.; DUNN, R. C.; MORAN, H.E.; SWEENEY, T. R.; ARMSTRONG, D. W.; WHITE, W. C. 1944. Toxicity and Potential Dangers of Aerosols, Mists, and Dusting Powders Containing DDT. U.S. Publ. Health Rept. (Suppl.), (177): 1-32.

ORTELEE, M. F. 1958. Study of Men with Prolonged Intensive Occupational Exposure to DDT. Arch. Industr. Health, *18:* 433-440.

OTTOBONI, A. 1972. DDT and Reproduction in the Aged Female Rat. Paper submitted for publication, Toxicol. Appl. Pharmacol., April, pp. 38.

Report of the Secretary's Commission on Pesticides and Their Relation to Environmental Health. 1969. (Mrak, E., chairman); Part I: i-xvii, Part II: 1-677. U.S. Dept. H.E.W., Washington, D.C.

ROE, F. J. C.; GRANT, G. A. 1971. Inhibition by Germ-Free Status of Development of Liver and Lung Tumors in Mice Exposed Neonatally to 7,12-dimethylbenz(A)anthracene: Implications in Relation to Tests for Carcinogenicity. Internatl. J. Cancer, *6:* 133-144.

SMITH, M. I; STOHLMAN, E. F. 1944. Experimental Poisoning in Cats, Rabbits and Rats with DDT. U.S. Publ. Health Rept., *59:* 984-1009.

TARJÁN, R.; KEMÉNY, T. 1969. Multigeneration Studies on DDT in Mice. Fd. Cosmet. Toxicol., *7:* 215-222.

THOMPSON, R. P. H.; PILCHER, C. W. T.; ROBINSON, J.; STATHERS, G. M.; McLEAN, A. E. M.; WILLIAMS, R. 1969. Treatment of Unconjugated Jaundice with Dicophane. Lancet, *1969–II:* 4-6.

VAN ESCH, G. J. 1958. The Production of Skin Tumours in Mice by Oral Treatment with Urethane-isopropyl-N-phenyl Carbamate or Isopropyl-N-chlorophenyl Carbamate in Combination with Skin Painting with Croton Oil and Tween 60. Brit. J. Cancer, *12:* 355-362.

VAN RAALTE, H. G. S. 1970. Grundfragen der Pflanzenschutzmittel Toxikologie. Report of January 20th Meeting: Arbeitsgemeinschaft für Pflanzenschutz. Der Pflanzenarzt: 65-68.

WEIL, C. S. 1969. Dissenting Opinion. In: *Report of the Secretary's Commission on Pesticides and Their Relationship to Environmental Health.* (Mrak, E., chairman): 483-488. Part I: i-xvii, Part II: 1-677. U.S. Dept. H.E.W., Washington, D.C.

———. 1970. Selection of the Valid Number of Sampling Units and a Consideration of Their Combination in Toxicological Studies Involving Reproduction, Teratogenesis or Carcinogenesis. Fd. Cosmet. Toxicol., *8:* 177.

———; McCOLLISTER, D. D. 1963. Relationship between Short and Long Term Feeding Studies in Designing an Effective Toxicity Test. J. Agr. Food Chem., *11:* 486.

WEINBERG, A. 1971. Letter to the Editor. Science, *174:* 547.

WELCH, R. M.; LEVIN, W.; CONNEY, A. H. 1969. Estrogenic Action of DDT and Its Analogs. Toxicol. Appl. Pharmacol., *14:* 358-367.

———; ———; KUNTZMAN, R.; JACOBSON, M.; CONNEY, A. H. 1971. Effect of Halogenated Insecticides on the Metabolism and Uterotropic Action of Estrogens in Rats and Mice. Toxicol. Appl. Pharmacol., *19:* 234-246.

WITSCHI, E. 1956. In: *Biology Data Book.* Eds.: Altman, T. L.; Dittmer, D.S. (1964 ed.), Fed. Am. Soc. Exper. Biol., Washington, D.C., pp. 615.

WOLFE, H. R. 1969. Statement to DDT Hearing Officer, Washington State Dept. of Agriculture, Oct.16, Seattle, pp. 7.

———; WALKER, K. D.; ELLIOTT, J. E.; DURHAM, W. F. 1959. Evaluation of the Health Hazards Involved in House-Spraying with DDT. Bull. W.H.O., (20): 1-14.

Chapter 15. WURSTER'S SENSATIONAL SCIENCE STORY!

ALLISON, D.; KALLMAN, B. J.; COPE, O. B.; VAN VALIN, C. C. 1964. Some Chronic Effects of DDT on Cutthroat Trout. U.S. Bur. Sport Fish. Wildlife Res. Rept., (64): 1-30.

ANDREWS, A. K.; VAN VALIN, C. C.; COPE, O. B. 1966. Some Effects of Heptachlor on Bluegills *(Lepomis macrochirus).* Trans. Am. Fish. Soc., *95:* 297-309.

BITMAN, J.; CECIL, H. C.; HARRIS, S. J.; FRIES, G. J. 1969. DDT Induces a Decrease in Eggshell Calcium. Nature, *224:* 44-46.

BLUS, L. G.; GISH, C. D.; BELISLE, A. A.; PROUTY, R. M. 1972. Logarithmic Relationship of DDE Residues to Eggshell Thinning. Nature, *235:* 376-377.

———; HEATH, R. G.; GISH, C. D.; BELISLE, A. A.; PROUTY, R. M. 1971. Eggshell Thinning in the Brown Pelican; Implication of DDE. BioScience, *21:* 1213-1215.

BROWN, R. M., Jr. 1969. Observations on the Relationship of the Golgi Apparatus to Wall Formation in the Marine Chrysophycean Alga, *Pleurochrisis scherffelii* Pringsheim. J. Cell Biol., *41:* 109-123.

———; FRANKE, W. W.; KLEINIG, H.; FALK, H.; SITTE, P. 1970. Scale Formation in Chrysophycean Algae. 1. Cellulosic and Noncellulosic Wall Components Made by the Golgi Apparatus. J. Cell Biol., *45:* 246-271.

BUTLER, P. A. 1969. Monitoring Pesticide Pollution. BioScience, *19:* 889-891.

BURDICK, G. E.; HARRIS, E. J.; DEAN, H. J.; WALKER, T. M.; SKEA, J.; COLBY, D. 1964. The Accumulation of DDT in Lake Trout and the Effect on Reproduction. Trans. Am. Fish. Soc., *93:* 127-136.

CADE, T. J.; LINCER, J. L.; WHITE, C. M.; ROSENAU, D. G.; SCHWARTZ, L. G. 1971. DDE Residues and Eggshell Changes in Alaskan Falcons and Hawks. Science, *172*: 955-957.

COX, J. L. 1970a. Accumulation of DDT Residues in *Triphoturus mexicanus* from the Gulf of California. Nature, *227*: 192-193.

————. 1970b. DDT Residues in Marine Phytoplankton: Increase from 1955-1969. Science, *170*: 71-72.

ENDERSON, J. H.; BURGER, D. D. 1968. Chlorinated Hydrocarbons, Residues in Peregrines and Their Prey Species from Northern Canada. The Condor, *70:* 149-153.

GRAHAM, F., Jr. 1970. *Since Silent Spring.* Fawcett World Library, New York, pp. 288.

GROSCH, D. S. 1967. Poisoning with DDT: Effect on Reproductive Performance of *Artemia.* Science, *155:* 592-593.

————. 1970. Poisoning with DDT: Second and Third Year Reproductive Performance of *Artemia.* BioScience, *20* (16): 913-914.

HEATH, R. G.; SPANN, J. W.; KREITZER, J. F. 1969. Marked DDE Impairment of Mallard Reproduction in Controlled Studies. Nature, *224:* 47-48.

HICKEY, J. J.; ANDERSON, D. W. 1968. Chlorinated Hydrocarbons and Eggshell Changes in Raptorial and Fish-Eating Birds. Science, *162:* 271-273.

HUANG, J. C. 1971. Effect of Selected Factors on Sorption and Desorption in the Aquatic System. J. Water Poll. Contr. Fed., *43* (8): 1739-1748.

LEWIN, V. 1970. A Simple Device for Measuring Eggshell Thickness. Can. Field-Natural., *84* (3): 305.

MACEK, K. J. 1968. Reproduction in Brook Trout *(Salvelinus fontinalis)* Fed Sublethal Concentrations of DDT. J. Fish. Res. Bd. Can., *25* (9): 1787-1796.

MENZEL, D. W.; ANDERSON, J.; RANDTKE, A. 1970a. Unpublished data. Cited by SCEP Panel, p. 128.

————; ————; ———— 1970b. Marine Phytoplankton Vary in Their Response to Chlorinated Hydrocarbons. Science, *167:* 1724-1726.

MOSSER, G. H.; FISCHER, N. S.; TANG, T. C.; WURSTER, C. F. 1972. Polychlorinated Biphenyls: Toxicity to Certain Phytoplankters. Science. *175:* 191-192.

MOUNT, D. L. 1962. Chronic Effects of Endrin on Bluntnose Minnows and Guppies. U.S. Bur. Sport Fish. Wildlife Res. Rept., (58): 1-38.

NIMMO, D. R.; WILSON, A. J., Jr.; BLACKMAN, R. R. 1970. Unpublished data. Cited by SCEP Panel, p. 129.

PANEL ON MONITORING PERSISTENT PESTICIDES IN THE MARINE ENVIRONMENT (NASCO). 1971. *Chlorinated Hydrocarbons in the Marine Environment.* Natl. Acad. Sci., Washington, D.C., pp. 42.

PETERLE, T. J. 1966. The Use of Isotopes to Study Pesticide Translocation in Natural Environments. J. Appl. Ecol., *3* (Suppl.): 181-191.

PORTER, R.D.; WIEMEYER, S. N. 1969. Dieldrin and DDT: Effects on Sparrow Hawk Eggshells and Reproduction. Science, *165:* 199-200.

RATCLIFFE, D. A. 1967. Decrease in Eggshell Weight in Certain Birds of Prey. Nature, *215:* 208-210.

RISEBROUGH, R. W.; HUGGETT, R. J.; GRIFFIN, J. J.; GOLDBERG, E. D. 1968a. Pesticides: Transatlantic Movement in the Northeast Trades. Science, *159:* 1233-1236.

————; MENZEL, D. B.; MARTIN, J. D., Jr.; OLCOTT, H.S. 1972. DDT Residues in Pacific Marine Fish. Paper submitted for publication, Pestic. Monit. J., Aug., pp. 42.

————; REICHE, P.; PEAKALL, D. B.; HERMAN, S.; KIRVEN, M. 1968b. Polychlorinated Biphenyls in the Global Ecosystem. Nature, *220:* 1098-1102.

ROGIN, G. 1968. There Are Problems When Man Plays God. Sports Illustrated, *29* (19): 78-80, 84, 87-90.

SÖDERGREN, A. 1968. Uptake and Accumulation of C^{14} DDT by *Chlorella* sp. (Chlorophyceae). Oikos, *19* (1): 126-138.

SPANN, I. W.; HEATH, R. G.; KREITZER, J. F.; LOCKE, L. N. 1972. Ethyl Mercury *p*-Toluene Sulfonalide; Lethal and Reproductive Effects on Pheasants. Science, *175:* 328-330.

STARRETT CO., LTD. 1955. How to Read, Use, Care for Micrometers and Vernier Gauges. Bull. (805J) Issue 2: 1-20. The L. S. Starrett Co., Ltd., Jedburgh.

TUCKER, R. K.; HAEGLE, H. A. 1970. Eggshell Thinning as Influenced by Method of DDT Exposure. Bull. Envir. Contam. Toxicol., *5*(3): 191-194.

VANCE, B. D.; DRUMMOND, W. 1969. Biological Concentration of Pesticides by Algae. J. Am. Water Works Assoc., *61* (7): 360-362.

WOODWELL, G. M. 1972. Statement. Official Transcripts. Consolidated DDT Hearing. E.P.A., Washington, D.C.

————; CRAIG, P. P.; JOHNSON, H. A. 1971. DDT in the Biosphere; Where does it Go? Science, *174:* 1101-1107.

————; WURSTER, C. F.; ISAACSON, A. 1967. DDT Residues in an East Coast Estuary. A Case of Biological Concentration of a Persistent Insecticide. Science, *156:* 821-824.

WORK GROUP ON ECOLOGICAL EFFECTS. 1970. In: *Man's Impact on the Global Environment:* 113-166. Report of the Study of Critical Environmental Problems (SCEP), MIT Press, Cambridge, pp. 319.

WURSTER, C. F. 1968. DDT Reduces Photosynthesis by Marine Phytoplankton. Science, *159:* 1474-1475.

————. 1969. DDT: Danger to the Environment. University Rev. (S.U.N.Y.), *2* (3): 20-25.

————. 1970. DDT and the Environment. In: *Agenda for Survival.* Ed.: Helfrich, H.W.; 37-54. Yale University Press, New Haven, pp. 234.

————. 1972. DDT in the Environment. Seminar Lecture Given at the University of California at Berkeley, Feb. 11.

————; WINGATE, D. 1968. DDT Residues and Declining Reproduction in the Bermuda Petrel. Science, *159:* 979-981.

Chapter 16. EXPERTS

ADELMAN, M. R.; BORISY, G. G.; SHELANSKI, M. L.; WEISENBERG, R. C.; TAYLOR, E. W. 1968. Cytoplasmic Filaments and Tubules. Fed. Proc., *27:* 1186-1193.

ANDERSON, D. W.; HICKEY, J. J.; RISEBROUGH, R. W.; HUGHES, D. F.; CHRISTENSEN, R. E. 1969. Significance of Chlorinated Hydrocarbon Residues to Breeding Pelicans and Cormorants. Can. Field-Natural., *83:* 92-112.

ANONYMOUS. 1970. What Happened to Our Crabs? Pollution! San Francisco Examiner, Nov. 14: 11.

BITMAN, J. 1972. Statement. Official Transcripts. Consolidated DDT Hearings. E.P.A., Washington, D.C.

————; CECIL, H. C.; FRIES, G. J. 1970. DDT Induced Inhibition of Avian Shell Gland Carbonic Anhydrase: A Mechanism for Thin Eggshells. Science, *168:* 594-595.

————; ————; HARRIS, S. J.; FRIES, G. J. 1969. DDT Induces a Decrease in Eggshell Calcium. Nature, *224:* 44-46.

BLUS, L. G.; HEATH, R. G.; GISH, C. D.; BELISLE, A. A.; PROUTY, R. M. 1971. Eggshell Thinning in the Brown Pelican; Implication of DDE. BioScience, *21:* 1213-1215.

BOWMAN, M. C.; ACREE, F., Jr.; CORBETT, M. K. 1960. Solubility of Carbon-14 DDT in Water. J. Agr. Food Chem., *8:* 406-408.

BUTLER, P. A. 1966. Pesticides in the Marine Environment. J. Appl. Ecol., *3* (Suppl.): 253-259.

————. 1971. Statement. Official Transcripts. Consolidated DDT Hearings. E.P.A., Washington, D.C.

CONNEY, A. H. 1967. Pharmacological Implications of Microsomal Enzyme Induction. Pharmacol. Rev., 19: 317-366.

DVORCHIK, B. H.; ISTIN, M.; MAREN, T. H. 1971. Does DDT Inhibit Carbonic Anhydrase? Science, 172: 728-729.

GIBBONS, B. H.; GIBBONS, I. R. 1972. Flagellar Movement and Adenosine Triphosphatase Activity in Sea Urchin Sperm Extracted with Triton X-100. J. Cell Biol., 54: 75-79.

GIELEN, J. E.; NEBERT, D. W. 1971. Microsomal Hydroxylase Induction in Liver Cell Culture by Phenobarbital, Polycyclic Hydrocarbons, and p,p'-DDT. Science, 172: 167-169.

GOODMAN, L. S.; GILMAN, A., Eds. 1970. The Pharmacological Basis of Therapeutics. (4th ed.), The Macmillan Co., New York, pp. 1794.

GRAY, R.; BOYLE, I.; DELUCA, H. F. 1971. Vitamin D Metabolism: The Role of Kidney Tissue. Science, 172: 1232-1233.

HEATH, R. G.; SPANN, J. W.; KREITZER, J.F. 1969. Marked DDE Impairment of Mallard Reproduction in Controlled Studies. Nature, 224: 47-48.

HICKEY, J. J.; ANDERSON, D. W. 1968. Chlorinated Hydrocarbons and Eggshell Changes in Raptorial and Fish-Eating Birds. Science, 162: 271-273.

JEFFRIES, D. J. 1969. Induction of Apparent Hyperthyroidism in Birds Fed DDT. Nature, 222: 578-579.

————; FRENCH, M.C. 1969. Avian Thyroid: Effect of p,p'-DDT on Size and Activity. Science, 166: 1278-1280.

————; PRESTT, I. 1966. Post-mortems of Peregrines and Lanners with Particular Reference to Organochlorine Residues. Brit. Birds, 59: 49-64.

KELLER, H. 1952. Die Bestimmung kleinster Mengen DDT auf enzymanalitischem Wege. Naturwissenschaften, 39: 109.

LOWE, J. I.; WILSON, P. D.; RICK, A. J.; WILSON, A. J. 1971. Chronic Exposure of Oysters to DDT, Toxaphene and Parathion. Proc. Natl. Shellfisheries Asso., 61: 71-79.

MANIGOLD, D. B.; SCHULZE, J. A. 1969. Pesticides in Selected Western Streams—A Progress Report. Pestic. Monit. J., 3: 124-135.

MATSUMURA, F. 1970. DDT Action and Adenosine Triphosphate Related Systems. Science, 169: 1343.

————; PATIL, K. C. 1969. Adenosine Triphosphatase Sensitive to DDT in Synapses of Rat Brain. Science, 166: 121-122.

MEADOWS, D. H.; MEADOWS, D. L.; RANDERS, J.; BEHRENS, W. W. 1972. The Limits to Growth. Universe Books, Washington, D.C., pp. 205.

MENZEL, D. W.; ANDERSON, J.; RANDTKE, A. 1970. Marine Phytoplankton Vary in Their Response to Chlorinated Hydrocarbons. Science, 167: 1724-1726.

MOUNT, D. L.; PUTNICKI, G. J. 1966. Summary Report of the 1963 Mississippi Fish Kill. Trans. 31st North Am. Wildlife Natl. Resources Conf.: 177-184.

NIMMO, D. R.; WILSON, A. J., Jr.; BLACKMAN, R. R. 1970. Unpublished data. Cited by SCEP Panel, p. 129.

PANEL ON MONITORING PERSISTENT PESTICIDES IN THE MARINE ENVIRONMENT (NASCO). 1971. Chlorinated Hydrocarbons in the Marine Environment. Natl. Acad. Sci., Washington, D.C., pp. 42.

PEAKALL, D. B. 1967. Pesticide-induced Enzyme Breakdown of Steroids in Birds. Nature, 216: 505-506.

————. 1970a. p,p'-DDT: Effect on Calcium Metabolism and Concentration of Estradiol in the Blood. Science, 168: 592-594.

————. 1970b. Pesticides and the Reproduction of Birds. Scient. Amer., 222 (12): 72-78.

POCKER, Y.; BEUG, W. M.; AINARDI, V. R. 1971. Carbonic Anhydrase; Interaction with DDT, DDE, and Dieldrin. Science, *174:* 1336-1339.

PORTER, R. D.; WIEMEYER, S. N. 1969. Dieldrin and DDT: Effects on Sparrow Hawk Eggshells and Reproduction. Science, *165:* 199-200.

Report of the Secretary's Commission on Pesticides and Their Relation to Environmental Health. 1969. (Mrak, E., chairman); Part I: i-xvii, Part II: 1-677. U.S. Dept. H.E.W., Washington, D.C.

RISEBROUGH, R. W. 1972. Statement. Official Transcripts. Consolidated DDT Hearings. E.P.A., Washington, D.C.

————; DAVIS, J.; ANDERSON, D. W. 1970. Effects of Various Chlorinated Hydrocarbons. Oregon State Univ. Envir. Health Sci. Ser., (1): 40-53.

————; HUGGETT, R. J.; GRIFFIN, J. J.; GOLDBERG, E. D. 1968b. Pesticides; Transatlantic Movement in the Northeast Trades. Science, *159:* 1233-1236.

————; REICHE, P.; PEAKALL, D. B.; HERMAN, S. G.; KIRVEN, M. N. 1968a. Polychlorinated Biphenyls in the Global Ecosystem. Nature, *220:* 1098-1102.

ROBINSON, J. 1967. Dynamics of Organochlorine Insecticides in Vertebrates and Ecosystems. Nature, *215* (5096): 33-35.

————; RICHARDSON, A.; CRABTREE, A. N.; COULSON, J. C.; POTTS, G. R. 1967. Organochlorine Residues in Marine Organisms. Nature, *214* (5095): 1307-1311.

SCHWARTZ, H.L.; KOZYREFF, V.; SURKS, M. I.; OPPENHEIMER, J. H. 1969. Increased Deiodination of L-thyroxine and L-triiodothyronine by Liver Microsomes from Rats, Treated with Phenobarbital. Nature, *222:* 1262-1264.

SKOU, J. C. 1965. Enzymatic Basis for Active Transport of Na^+ and K^+ Across Cell Membrane. Physiol. Rev., *45:* 596-617.

SNOW, C. P. 1934. *The Search.* (1958 ed.), Charles Scribner's Sons, New York, pp. 343.

WILSON, A. J., Jr.; FORESTER, J.; KNIGHT, J. 1970. *Chemical Assays.* U.S. Dept. Interior, Circular 335. Progress Rept. FY 1969, Gulf Breeze Lab, Florida, pp. 38.

WILSON, H. J. 1969. Arms and Bridges on Microtubules in the Mitotic Apparatus. J. Cell Biol., *40:* 854-859.

WORK GROUP ON ECOLOGICAL EFFECTS. 1970. In: *Man's Impact on the Global Environment* 113-166. Report of the Study of Critical Environmental Problems (SCEP). MIT Press, Cambridge, pp. 319.

WURSTER, C.F. 1968. DDT Reduces Photosynthesis by Marine Phytoplankton. Science, *159:* 1474-1475.

Chapter 17. VANISHING RESIDUES

ACREE, F., BEROZA, M.; BOWMAN, M. C. 1963. Codistillation of DDT with Water. J. Agr. Food Chem., *11:* 278-280.

ANDERSON, L. D.; GUNTHER, F. A.; SHORY, H. H. 1963. *Fate of Pesticide Residues in the Soil.* Mimeographed Copy Submitted to California Senate Fact Finding Committee on Agriculture. Oct. 27, pp. 9.

ANDO, K.; KATO, A.; SUZUKI, S. 1970. Isolation of 2,4-dichlorophenol from a Soil Fungus and its Biological Significance. Biochem. Biophys. Res. Comm., *39:* 1104-1107.

BREIDENBACH, A. W.; GUNNERSON, G. G.; KAWAHARA, F. K.; LICHTENBERG, J. J.; GREEN, R. S. 1967. Chlorinated Hydrocarbon Pesticides in Major Rivers, 1957-1965. U.S. Publ. Health Rept., *82:* 139-156.

BROWER, D. 1970. The Search for an Environmental Perspective. In: *Agenda for Survival.* Ed.: Helfrich, H. W.: 55-70. Yale University Press, New Haven, pp. 234.

BUTLER, P. A. 1969. Monitoring Pesticide Pollution. BioScience, *19:* 889-891.

————. 1972. Statement. Official Transcripts. Consolidated DDT Hearings. E.P.A., Washington, D.C.

CARSON, R. 1962. *Silent Spring*. Fawcett World Library (11th printing, April, 1970), New York, pp. 304.

COMMONER, B. 1971. *The Closing Circle*. Alfred A. Knopf, New York, pp. 326 + x.

CROSBY, D. G. 1969. Summation of the Session on Occurrence and Distribution of Pesticide Residues. Ann. N.Y. Acad. Sci., *160* (1): 201-203.

FOCHT, D. D.; ALEXANDER, M. 1970. DDT Metabolites and Analogues: Ring Fission by *Hydrogenomonas*. Science, *170:* 91-92.

FRAZIER, B. E.; CHESTERS, G.; LEE, G. B. 1970. "Apparent" Organochlorine Insecticide Contents of Soils Sampled in 1910. Pestic. Monit. J., *4* (2): 67-70.

GEORGE, J. L.; FREAR, D. E. H. 1966. Pesticides in the Antarctic. J. Appl. Ecol., *3* (Suppl.): 155-167.

GRAHAM, F., Jr. 1970. *Since Silent Spring*. Fawcett World Library, New York, pp. 288.

GUENZI, W. D.; BEARD, W. E. 1967. Anaerobic Biodegradation of DDT to DDD in Soils. Science, *156:* 1116-1117.

GUNTHER, F. A. 1969. Current Status of Pesticide Residue Methodology. Ann. N.Y. Acad. Sci., *160* (1): 72-81.

GUSTAFSON, C. G. 1970. PCB's—Prevalent and Persistent. Intensified Search is Needed to Minimize their Dangers. Envir. Sci. Technol., *4* (10): 814-819.

HARRIS,C. R.; LICHTENSTEIN, E. P. 1961. Factors Affecting the Volatilization of Insecticides from Soils. J. Econ. Entom., *54:* 1038-1045.

HARRISON, H. L.; LOUCKS, O. L.; MITCHELL, J. W.; PARKHURST, D. F.; TRACY, C. R.; WATTS, D. G.; YANNACONE, V. J. 1970. Systems Studies of DDT Transport. Science, *170:* 503-508.

HOLDEN, A. V. 1970. Source of Polychlorinated Biphenyl Contamination in the Marine Environment. Nature, *228:* 1220-1221.

HUTZINGER, O.; NASH, D. M.; SAFE, S.; DeFREITAS, A. S. W.; NORSTROM, R. J.; WILDISH, D. J.; ZITKO, V. 1972. Polychlorinated Biphenyls: Metabolic Behavior of Pure Isomers in Pigeons, Rats, and Brook Trout. Science, *178:* 312-313.

HYLIN, J. W.; SPENGER, R. E.; GUNTHER, F. A. 1969. Potential Interferences in Certain Pesticide Residue Analyses from Organochlorine Compounds Occurring Naturally in Plants. Residue Rev., *26:* 127-133.

JAEGER, R. J.; RUBIN, R. J. 1970. Plasticizers from Plastic Devices: Extraction, Metabolism, and Accumulation by Biological Systems. Science, *170:* 460-462.

JENSEN, S. 1966. Report of a New Chemical Hazard. New Scientist, *32:* 612.

————; JOHNELS, A. G.; OLSSON, M.; OTTERLIND, G. 1969. DDT and PCB in Marine Animals from Swedish Waters. Nature, *224:* 247-250.

KALLE, K. 1937. Meereskundliche chemische Untersuchungen mit Hilfe des Zeis'schen Pulfrich Photometers. Ann. Hydrogr., *65:* 276-282.

LEDERBERG, J. 1971. Letter to the Editor. Am. Scientist, *59:* 399.

McLEAN, L. A. 1967. Pesticides and the Environment. BioScience, *17:* 613-617.

MENZIE, C. M. 1966. Metabolism of Pesticides. U.S. Fish Wildlife Serv. Spec. Sci. Rept. Wildlife, (96): 1-274.

NASH, R. G.; BEALL, M. L., Jr. 1970. Chlorinated Hydrocarbon Insecticides: Root Uptake Versus Vapor Contamination of Soybean Foliage. Science, *168:* 1109-1111.

NICHOLSON, H. P. 1967. Pesticide Pollution Control. Science, *158:* 871-876.

PANEL ON MONITORING PERSISTENT PESTICIDES IN THE MARINE ENVIRONMENT (NASCO). 1971. *Chlorinated Hydrocarbons in the Marine Environment*. Natl. Acad. Sci., Washington, D.C., pp. 42.

PATIL, K. C.; MATSUMURA, F.; BOUSH, G. M. 1972. Metabolic Transformation of DDT, Dieldrin,

Aldrin, and Endrin by Marine Microorganisms. Envir. Sci. Technol., *6* (7): 629-632.

PETERLE, T. J. 1969. DDT in Antarctic Snow. Nature, *224:* 620.

PICHIRALLO, J. 1971. PCB's: Leaks of Toxic Substances Raises Issue of Effects, Regulation. Science, *173:* 899-902.

REYNOLDS, L. M. 1969. Polychlorobiphenyls (PCB's) and Their Interference with Pesticide Residue Analysis. Bull. Envir. Contam. Toxicol., *4:* 128-133.

RISEBROUGH, R. W.; HUGGETT, R. J.; GRIFFIN, J. J.; GOLDBERG, E. D. 1968. Pesticides; Transatlantic Movement in the Northeast Trades. Science, *159:* 1233-1236.

————; REICHE, P.; PEAKALL, D. B.; HERMAN, S. G.; KIRVEN, M. N. 1968. Polychlorinated Biphenyls in the Global Ecosystem. Nature, *220:* 1098-1102.

SCHECHTER, M. S. 1969. Summation of the Session on Pesticide Residue Analysis and on Metabolism of Pesticides. Ann. N.Y. Acad. Sci., *160* (1): 140-142.

STANLEY, C. W.; BARNEY, J. E.; HELTON, M. R.; YOBS, A. R. 1971. Measurement of Atmospheric Levels of Pesticides. Envir. Sci. Technol., 5 (5): 430-435.

SUTHERLAND, D. J.; SIERWIERSKI, M.; MAREI, H. H.; HELRICK, K. 1970. The Effects on Mosquitoes of Sublethal Exposure to Insecticides. II—DDT Metabolism. Mosquito News, *30* (1): 8-11.

SVERDRUP, H. V.; JOHNSON, M. W.; FLEMING, R. H. 1942. *The Oceans.* Prentice Hall, Inc., New York, pp. 1087.

TARRANT, K. B.; TATTON, J. O'G. 1968. Organochlorine Pesticides in Rainwater in the British Isles. Nature, *219:* 725-727.

VIOLA, P. L. 1970. Cancerogenic Effect of Vinyl Chloride. 10th Internatl. Cancer Congr., Houston, Abstr.: 20.

WEAVER, L.; GUNNERSON, C. G.; BREIDENBACH, A. W.; LICHTENBERG, J. J. 1965. Chlorinated Hydrocarbon Pesticides in Major U.S. River Basins. U.S. Publ. Health Rept., *80:* 481-493.

WHEATLEY, G. A.; HARDMAN, J. A. 1965. Indications of the Presence of Organochlorine Insecticides in Rainwater in Central England. Nature, *207:* 486-487.

WILLIAMS, C. M. 1967. Third-generation Pesticides. Scient. Amer., *217:* 13-17.

WILSON, A. J. Jr.; FORESTER, J.; KNIGHT, J. 1970. *Chemical Assays.* U.S. Dept. Interior, Circular 335. Progress Rept. FY 1969, Gulf Breeze Lab., Florida, pp. 38.

WIRTH, W.; HECHT, G.; GLOXHUBER, CH. 1971. *Toxikologie Fibel.* (2nd ed.), Georg Thieme Verl., Stuttgart, pp. 469.

WOODWELL, G. M. 1968. Radioactivity and Fallout: The Model Pollution. BioScience, *19:* 884-887.

————; CRAIG, P. P.; JOHNSON, H. A. 1971. DDT in the Biosphere: Where does it Go? Science, *174:* 1101-1107.

————; MARTIN, F. T. 1964. Persistence of DDT in Soils of Heavily Sprayed Forest Stands. Science, *145:* 481-483.

————; WURSTER, C. F.; ISAACSON, P. A. 1967. DDT Residues in an East Coast Estuary. Science, *156:* 821-824.

WORK GROUP ON ECOLOGICAL EFFECTS. 1970. In: *Man's Impact on the Global Environment* 113-166. Report of the Study of Critical Environmental Problems (SCEP). MIT Press, Cambridge, pp. 319.

YATES, M. L.; HOLSWADE, W.; HIGER, A. L. 1970. Pesticide Residues in Hydrobiological Environments. 159th ACS Natl. Meeting, Houston, Abstr. Water-032.

Chapter 18. DEUS EX MACHINA

BURNSIDE, O. C.; FURRER, J. D.; ROSELLE, R. E. 1970. *Pesticide Use and the Impact of Their Elimination.* Mimeographed manuscript. Extension Service, University of Nebraska, Lincoln, pp. 21.

CAMERON, R. 1971. Op Ed Page. New York Times, Aug. 18.

ECONOMIC RESEARCH SERVICE. 1972. *Cotton Situation*. U.S. Dept. Agr., Publ. CS-255, April, Washington, D.C., pp. 44.

EXECUTIVE BOARD OF THE WORLD HEALTH ORGANIZATION. 1971. The Place of DDT in Operations against Malaria and other Vector-Borne Diseases. Off. Rec. WHO, (190): 176-182.

GILLETTE, R. 1971. DDT: In Field and Courtroom—A Persistent Pesticide Lives On. Science, *174*: 1108-1110.

HOFFER, E. 1951. *The True Believer*. Mentor Books (July, 1958), New York, pp. 160.

———— 1964. *The Temper of Our Time*. Harper and Row, New York, Evanston, London, pp. 111.

LEIGHTY, J. 1971. Sierra Club Urges Total Ban of DDT. The Press, Riverside, California, Feb. 25: C-3.

NELSON, G. 1971. S. 232. A Bill to Prohibit the Sale or Shipment for Use in the United States of the Chemical Compounds Known as Aldrin, Chlordane, DDD/TDE, Dieldrin, Endrin, Heptachlor, Lindane, Toxaphene. 92nd. Congress, 1st Session, Jan. 26. Govt. Printing Office, Washington, D.C., pp.2.

RAPPOLT, R. T., Sr. 1969. Statement to DDT Hearing Officer, Washington State Dept. of Agriculture, Oct. 16. Seattle, pp. 4.

RUCKELSHAUS, W. D. 1972. *Opinion of the Administrator*. Consolidated DDT Hearings. Order dated: 2 June, E.P.A., Washington, D.C., pp. 40.

SWEENEY, E. M. 1972. *Hearing Examiner's Recommended Findings, Conclusions, and Orders*. Consolidated DDT Hearings. Issued: April 25, (40 CFR 164.32). E.P.A., Washington, D.C., pp. 113.

SWIFT, J. 1711. The Art of Political Lying. The Examiner, (14). In: *Collected Works:* Vol. V: 22-28 (1738); Vols. I-XX (1735-1772), Faulkner Press, Dublin.

U.S. HOUSE OF REPRESENTATIVES. 1972. Department of Agriculture–Environmental and Consumer Protection Appropriation Bill, 1973. Committee Report No. 92-1175, June 26. U.S. Govt. Printing Office, Washington, D.C.

WILLIAMS, J. M. 1971. Breast Cancer Induced by Overdose of Water. J. Irrepr. Results, *18*: 85-86.

WURSTER, C. F. 1969. DDT Goes to Trial in Madison. BioScience, *19*: 809-813.

———— 1971. Letter to the Committee on Agriculture. In: U.S. House of Representatives. Hearings Before the Committee on Agriculture; 92-A, 58-542, p. 268. U.S. Govt. Printing Office, Washington, D.C.

YANNACONE, V. J. 1971. Remarks at Paper Industry PR Luncheon Group, Union League Club, New York, N.Y., May 20, 1970. In: U.S. House of Representatives. Hearings Before the Committee on Agriculture; 92-A, 58-542, p. 267; and a Copy of Mr. Yannacone's Filed Speech. U. S. Govt. Printing Office, Washington, D.C.

INDEX

573